UYLENBURGH & SON

Art and commerce
from Rembrandt to De Lairesse

1625-1675

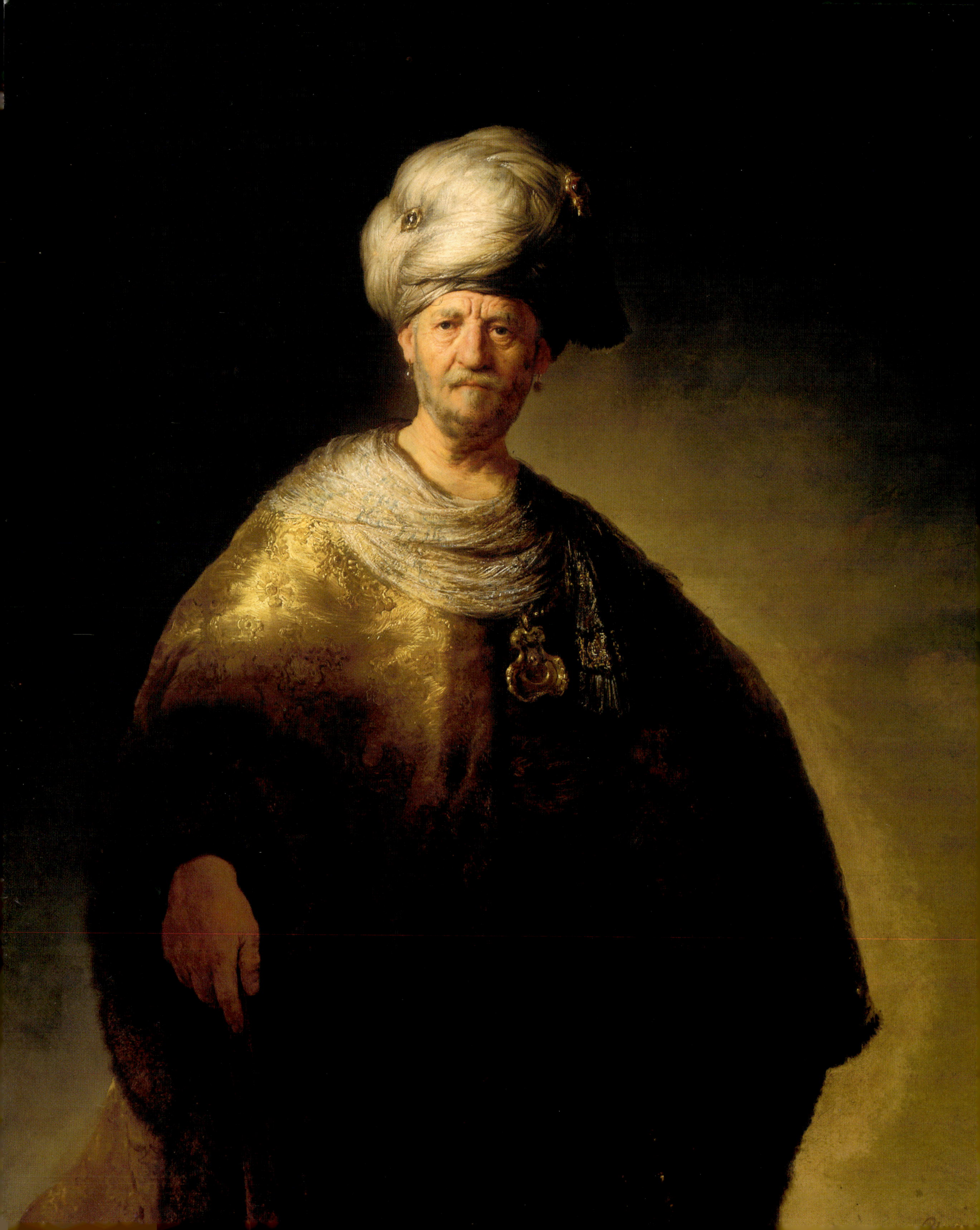

UYLENBURGH & SON
Art and commerce
from Rembrandt to De Lairesse
1625-1675

FRISO LAMMERTSE | JAAP VAN DER VEEN

Waanders Publishers, Zwolle

The Rembrandthouse Museum, Amsterdam

Published on the occasion of the exhibition
Rembrandt & Co: Dealing in Masterpieces,
Dulwich Picture Gallery, London,
7 June – 3 September 2006 and
Rembrandt en Uylenburgh, handel in meesterwerken,
The Rembrandt House Museum, Amsterdam,
16 September – 10 December 2006.

PUBLISHER
Waanders Publishers, Zwolle
The Rembrandt House Museum, Amsterdam

AUTHORS
Friso Lammertse
Jaap van der Veen

TRANSLATION
Yvette Rosenberg (Chapter 1 and 2)
Murray Pearson (Chapter 3)
Lynne Richards (Chapter 4)

FINAL EDITING
Dorine Duyster

IMAGE ADMINISTRATION
Mechtild Beckers

PRODUCTION MANAGEMENT
Mariska Vonk

DESIGN
Marjo Starink, Amsterdam

PRINTING
Waanders Printers, Zwolle

Information about Waanders Publishers can be found on
www.waanders.nl
Information about the Rembrandt House Museum can be found on www.rembrandthuis.nl
Information about Dulwich Picture Gallery can be found on
www.dulwichpicturegallery.org.uk

ISBN 90 400 8164 6 [hardback]
ISBN 90 400 8252 9 [paperback]
EAN 9789040081644
NUR 646

For the exhibition and publication the Rembrandt House Museum received financial support from:

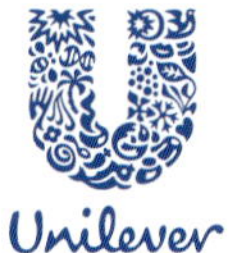
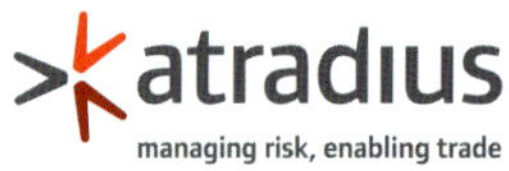
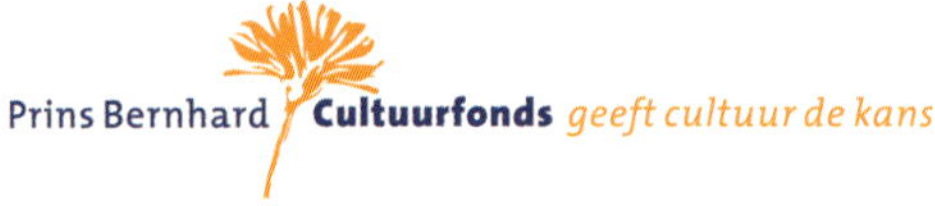
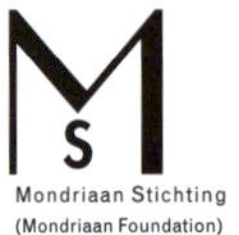
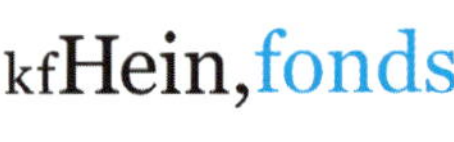
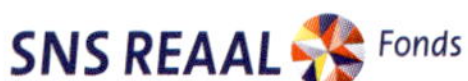
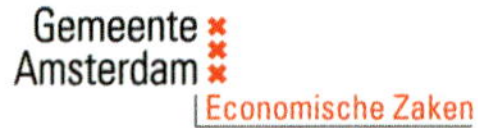
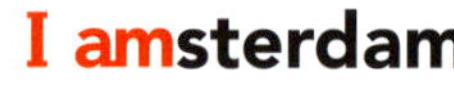
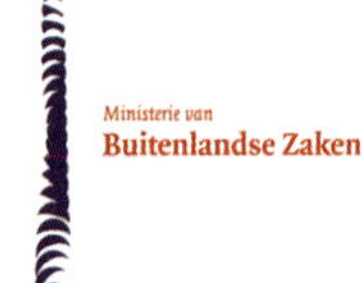
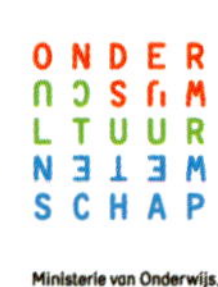
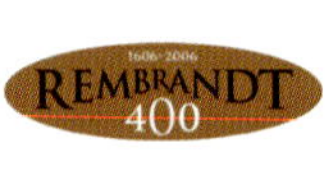

For the exhibition and publication the Dulwich Picture Gallery received financial support from:

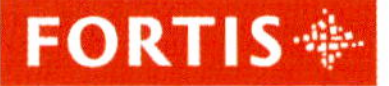

FRONT COVER ILLUSTRATION
Rembrandt van Rijn, Portrait of Agatha Bas, signed and dated 'Rembrandt f. 1641' and the inscription 'AE 29', canvas, 105.2 x 83.9 cm, London, The Royal Collection, Her Majesty Queen Elizabeth II, Buckingham Palace (fig. 141)

ILLUSTRATIE FRONTISPIES
Rembrandt van Rijn, Man in oriental dress, known as 'The Noble Slav', signed and dated 'RHL van Rijn 1632', canvas, 152.7 x 111.1 cm, New York, N.Y., The Metropolitan Museum of Art (fig. 73)

CONTENTS

Foreword

Between 1625 and 1675 Hendrick Uylenburgh and his son Gerrit were art dealers who ran an important artists' workshop. The firm of Uylenburgh dealt in valuable works of art by Dutch, Flemish and Italian masters and played a key role in the artistic life of the Golden Age. Their name is an indelible one in art historical literature because when Rembrandt settled in Amsterdam around 1631, he spent four years working in Hendrick Uylenburgh's studio. During this period the style and subjects of Rembrandt's etchings changed dramatically, and he started to paint portraits for the first time. Launched by Uylenburgh, Rembrandt rapidly became the most eminent and best paid portrait painter in Holland. The wealthy Amsterdam merchants who had their portraits painted by Rembrandt generally moved in the same Mennonite circles as Hendrick Uylenburgh. Several of them lent Uylenburgh money, which he used to finance his purchases. Uylenburgh did business far beyond the Dutch border. He bought paintings for the Polish King, maintained contacts with Jacob Jordaens and – as a recently discovered document reveals – had in stock work by a number of Flemish masters, among them Frans Floris, Abraham Janssen and Geerart van den Bossche. He also dealt in paintings by his brother Rombout Uylenburgh, who worked in Cracow, Warsaw and Danzig.

From the mid sixteen-fifties onwards, the business was gradually taken over by Gerrit Uylenburgh, whose operations were even more international than his father's had been. As well as dealing in Flemish, Dutch and Italian paintings, he also bought and sold antique statuary. He maintained business relations with agents and customers in Paris, Genoa, Gottorf and Berlin.

Gerrit Uylenburgh had a 'branch manager' in London in the person of the court painter Sir Peter Lely. In 1677 Gerrit settled in London, where he continued to work as an art dealer and landscape painter until his death in 1679. Never before has an exhibition been devoted to these important art dealers and their significance in Rembrandt's development.

We are greatly indebted to Jaap van der Veen, research associate at the Rembrandt House Museum, and Friso Lammertse, curator of Museum Boijmans Van Beuningen, who undertook in-depth research into the fortunes of Hendrick and Gerrit Uylenburgh's art dealership in preparation for the exhibition and were responsible for compiling the exhibition and the accompanying publication. Thanks to their detective work, we now have a clear picture of the way Gerrit and Hendrick Uylenburgh's firm operated, of its importance and of the works they dealt in. Friso Lammertse's involvement was only possible thanks to his employer's willingness to release him for the Uylenburgh project and The Mondriaan Foundation made a grant available to make this possible.

Like any exhibition, this one could not have come about without the generosity of the lenders. We are most grateful to them for their willingness to make their valuable works available to us for the duration of the show.

Our thanks also go to the institutions, companies and private individuals who have provided financial support for the project at both venues.

At Dulwich Picture Gallery lead sponsorship was provided by Fortis and we are deeply grateful for their crucial support. Essential funding also came from the Friends of Dulwich Picture Gallery, Edith Callam Memorial Trust, Timothy Franey Charitable Foundation, The Lillian Jean Kaplan Foundation, Julie & Lawrence Salander – New York, Basil Samuel Charitable Trust and The Stanley Scott Bequest as well as from another anonymous charitable organization and two private individuals. We also received substantial contributions from a consortium of fine art dealers in recognition of the great master and his relationship with his own dealer. This was made up of Bernheimer Fine Old Masters, Munich; P. & D. Colnaghi & Co. Ltd., London; Johnny van Haeften Ltd, London; Bob P. Haboldt; Robert Holden Ltd.; Jack Kilgore; Otto Naumann, Ltd and Noortman Master Paintings.

The list of those giving grants and sponsorship for the exhibition at the Rembrandt House Museum is no less impressive. First and foremost we thank the two lead sponsors, Unilever and Atradius, for their friendly and vital support. We also received a substantial contribution out of the HGIS culture fund from the Ministry of Foreign Affairs and the Ministry of Education, Culture and Science. The VSB-Fonds and the SNS-Reaalfonds made grants available for the educational projects that the museum is organizing as part of the Rembrandt Year. Contributions also came from the Prins Bernhard Cultuurfonds, the City of Amsterdam, kfHeinfonds, Delta Lloyd Groep NV, Stadsdeel Amsterdam Centrum, Amsterdam Chamber of Commerce, Kattendijke-Drucker Stichting and the Directie der Oostersche Handel and Reederijen.

Both museums owe a special debt of gratitude to the Minister of Finance and the Minister of Education, Culture and Science in the Netherlands for providing Dutch indemnity and HM Government (DCMS) and the Museums, Libraries & Archives Council for UK indemnity cover for their respective venues.

Our thanks also go to all those who were involved in the production of the accompanying publication, which was written by Jaap van der Veen and Friso Lammertse. Their contributions were meticulously edited and prepared for the press by Dorine Duyster. The picture editor was Mechtild Beckers, who also, with Mariska Vonk, coordinated the publication process. Lynne Richards, Yvette Rosenberg and Murray Pearson were responsible for the excellent English translations, and the superb design is the work of Marjo Starink. The book was printed by Waanders Uitgevers of Zwolle. Our thanks to Wim Waanders and his staff for the dedication with which they have overseen the production of the book.

The exhibition was organized by Jaap van der Veen and Victoria Norton, assisted by Mechtild Beckers, Eloise Stewart and Mella Shaw. Our thanks also go to Desmond Shawe-Taylor, who in his then capacity as director of Dulwich Picture Gallery helped lay the foundations for the rewarding collaboration between our institutions.

Lastly, we should like to express our sincere gratitude to the Ambassador of the Kingdom of the Netherlands, His Excellency Count Jan de Marchant et d'Ansembourg, who kindly agreed to act as honorary patron of the exhibition in London. His support and enthusiasm has been invaluable and is testimony to the importance of this exhibition.

Ian AC Dejardin
Director of Dulwich Picture Gallery

Ed de Heer
Director of the Rembrandt House Museum

Acknowledgements

The authors wish to express their gratitude to the following people for their help:

Stijn Alsteens
Dr. Joost Vander Auwera
Kenneth Awebro
Ronni Baer
Prof. Dr. Arnout Balis
Dr. Gerd Bartoschek
Mechtild Beckers
Mevr. Th. J. M. Becking
Mària van Berge-Gerbaud
Dien Bos
Dr. Pieter Biesboer
Martin Bijl
Marcin Birenat
Peter Black
Piero Boccardo
Dr. Marten Jan Bok
Bob van den Boogert
Peter van den Brink
Dr. Ben Broos
Edwin Buijsen
Quintin Buvelot
Görel Cavalli-Bjorkman
Dr. J. A. Chroscicki
Daan de Clercq
Peter van der Coelen
Baukje Coenen
Ian Dejardin
Dr. Diana Dethloff

Jan Diepraam
Blaise Ducos
S. A. C. Dudok van Heel
Frits Duparc
Dorine Duyster
C. P. van Eeghen
Prof. dr Rudi Ekkart
Sjarel Ex
Prof. dr C. W. Fock
Michiel Franken
Lucia Frattarelli Fischer
Dr. Ivan Gaskell
Dr. Jeroen Giltaij
Eymert Jan Goossens
Dr. Emile Gordenker
Lia Gorter
Sepp-Gustav Gröschel
Stefaan Hautekeete
Dr. W. J. op 't Hof
Rob Huijbrecht
Dr. K. J. A. Jonckheere
Dr. Erik de Jong
Prof. dr Edmund Kizik
Rita Klauschenz
Dr. Eloy Koldeweij
Dr. Paula Koning
Michal Kurzej
Suzanne Laemers
Mr. Alastair Laing
Ruud Lambour
Arthur Lammertse
Dr. G. Th. M. Lemmens
Dr. Clé Lesger

Walter Liedtke
Prof. Dr. Bernd W. Lindemann
Ger Luijten
Dr. Michael Maek-Gérard
Dr. Bernd Mayer
Prof. dr Bert W. Meijer
Dr. Bas de Melker
Sir Oliver Millar
Peter Mitchell
Otto Naumann
Dr. Mirjam Neumeister
Lawrence W. Nichols
Rob Noortman
Vicky Norton
Leonoor van Oosterzee
Murray Pearson
Adriaan Plak
Dr. Nora De Poorter
Dr. Beata Purc-Stêpniak
Mme. Christine Raimbault
Tom Rassieur
Tony Reeve
Nils Reinaerts
Dr. Konrad Renger
Lynne Richards
Yvette Rosenberg
Johannes Rosenplänter
Dr. Martin Royalton-Kisch
Jaco Rutgers
Dick Schakel
Peter Schatborn
Eddy Schavemaker
Robert Schillemans

Prof. Dr. Andreas Scholl
Frits Scholten
Dr. Gero Seelig
Dr. Christian Tico Seifert
Desmond Shawe-Taylor
Dr. Martina Sitt
Prof. dr Eric Jan Sluijter
Dr. Nicolette Sluijter-Seijffert
Gert Jan van der Sman
Malgorzata Sobczak
Timothy Standring
Eloise Stewart
Mevr. A. Stoesser-Johnston
Dr. Christian Theuerkauff
Dr. Milja van Tielhof
Dr. J. Tylicki
Tonko Ufkes
Ruud en Casper van der Veen
Prof. dr Henk van Veen
Bernard Vermet
Dr. Gerdien Verschoor
Prof. dr Piet Visser
Jørgen Wadum
Adriaan Waiboer
Sophie Walkinshaw
Dr. Arie Wallert
John Walsh
Prof. Dr. Gregor Weber
Prof. dr Ernst van de Wetering
Arthur K. Wheelock
Betsy Wieseman
Dr. David de Witt
Dr. Antoni Ziemba

Lenders

Amsterdam, Collectie Six
Amsterdam, Gemeentearchief
Amsterdam, Museum Het Rembrandthuis
Amsterdam, Rijksmuseum
Amsterdam, Rijksprentenkabinet
Amsterdam, Universiteitsbibliotheek van de Universiteit van
    Amsterdam
Amsterdam, Verenigde Doopsgezinde Gemeente
Berlin, Staatliche Museen zu Berlin, Antikensammlung
Berlin, Staatliche Museen zu Berlin, Gemäldegalerie
Boston, Museum of Fine Arts, on loan from a private collection
Brussels, Koninklijke Musea voor Schone Kunsten
Braunschweig, Herzog Anton Ulrich-Museum, Kunstmuseum
    des Landes Niedersachsen
Chicago, private collection
The Hague, Koninklijke Bibliotheek
The Hague, Koninklijk Kabinet van Schilderijen, Mauritshuis
Dresden, Staatliche Kunstsammlungen Dresden, Gemäldegalerie
    Alte Meister
Frankfurt am Main, Städelsches Kunstinstitut
Glasgow, Hunterian Museum and Art Gallery, University of
    Glasgow
Great-Brittain, private collection
Hamburg, Hamburger Kunsthalle
Heino / Wijhe, Museum de Fundatie
Karlsruhe, Staatliche Kunsthalle
Kassel, Staatliche Museen Kassel, Gemäldegalerie Alte Meister
Cologne, Wallraf-Richartz-Museum – Fondation Corboud
Kingston, Agnes Etherington Art Centre, Queen's University
Copenhagen, Statens Museum for Kunst
Le Havre, Musée des Beaux-Arts André Malraux
Leeuwarden, Fries Museum
Leiden, Rijksmuseum van Oudheden

London, The British Museum
London, Daily Mail and General Trust plc
London, Dulwich Picture Gallery
London, National Portrait Gallery
London, The Royal Collection, Her Majesty Queen Elizabeth II
Londen, Victoria and Albert Museum
Louisville, The Speed Art Museum
Maastricht, Noortman Master Paintings
Milwaukee, Dr. Alfred en Isabella Bader
New York, The Metropolitan Museum of Art
Oxford, Ashmolean Museum, on loan from Sir Denis Mahon,
    C.H., C.B.E., F.B.A.,
Paris, Fondation Custodia (coll. F. Lugt), Institut Néerlandais
Paris, Musée du Louvre
Rotterdam, Museum Boijmans Van Beuningen
Schwerin, Staatliches Museum Schwerin
Stockholm, Nationalmuseum
Utrecht, Museum Catharijneconvent, bruikleen van Instituut
    Collectie Nederland
United States, private collection
United States, private collection
United States, private collection
United States, private collection
United States, private collection
Wolfegg, Kunstsammlungen der Fürsten zu Waldburg-Wolfegg

The authors of this book and curators of the exhibition
Rembrandt & Co: Dealing in Masterpieces are deeply indebted
to all those who lent works.

In this book all the paintings and other objects on show in the
exhibitions in London and Amsterdam are illustrated in colour,
while all the secondary illustrations are in black and white.

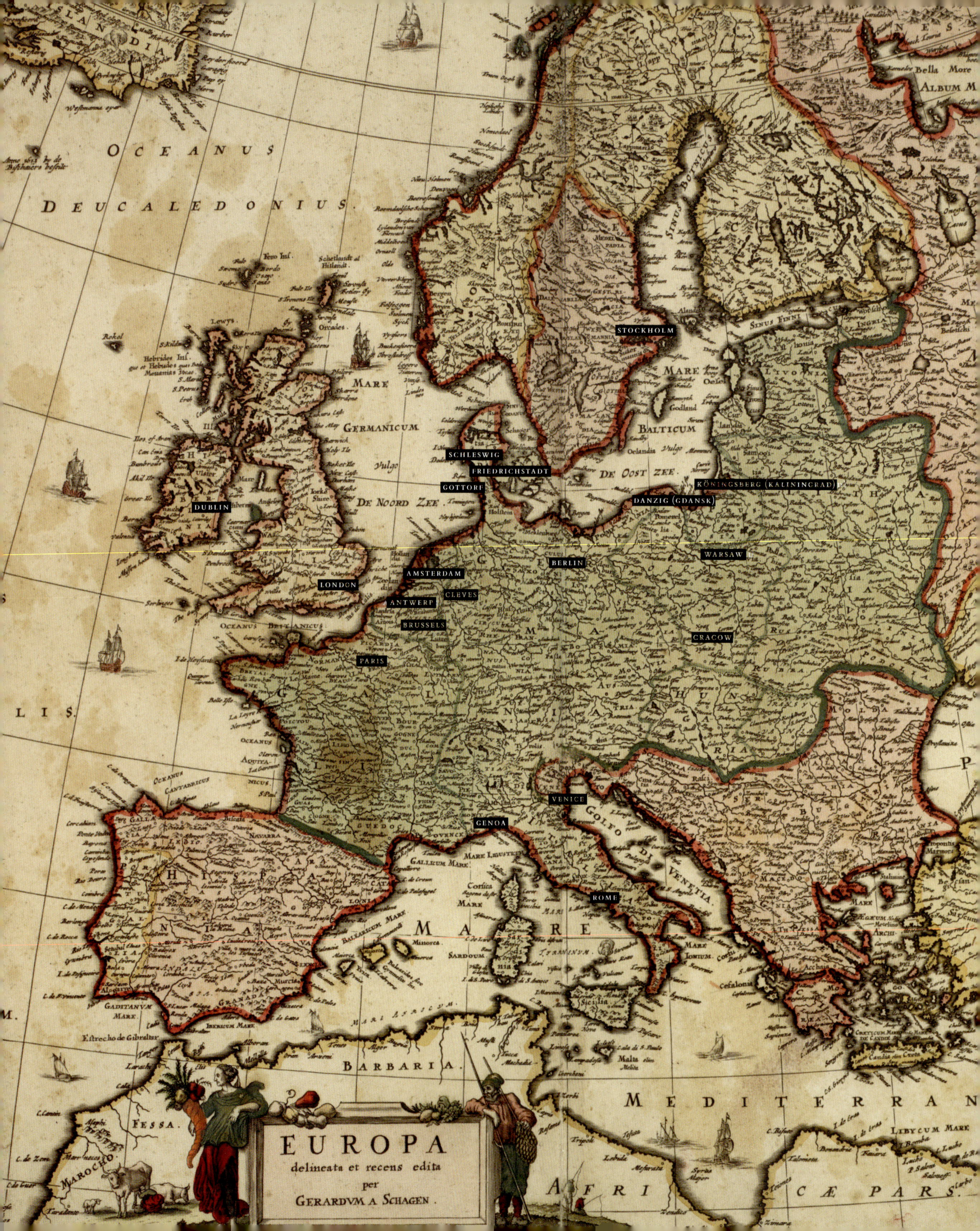

OCEANUS
DEUCALEDONIUS.
MARE GERMANICUM
De Noord Zee
De Oost Zee
MARE BALTICUM
SINUS BOTNICUS
SINUS FINN.
OCEANUS BRITANNICUS
OCEANUS CANTABRICUS
BARBARIA.
MEDITERRAN
MARE
LIBYCUM MARE
AFRICÆ PARS
STOCKHOLM
SCHLESWIG
FRIEDRICHSTADT
GOTTORF
DUBLIN
KÖNINGSBERG (KALININGRAD)
DANZIG (GDANSK)
WARSAW
BERLIN
LONDON
AMSTERDAM
ANTWERP
CLEVES
BRUSSELS
PARIS
CRACOW
GENOA
VENICE
ROME
FESSA.
MAROCCO
EUROPA
delineata et recens edita
per
GERARDVM A SCHAGEN.

1   Hendrick Uylenburgh, agent of the king of Poland and art dealer in Amsterdam

JAAP VAN DER VEEN

The Uylenburgh family

The biographer's task is never an easy one, but sketching the lives of people who lived in the seventeenth century is a formidable challenge. It is all the more daunting when so little is known about them. Only a few fragments of information are available regarding the two protagonists of our study, Hendrick Uylenburgh and his son Gerrit, both of whom were painters and art dealers in Amsterdam in the second and third quarters of the seventeenth century. The few facts we have managed to extricate from records and documents reveal little of consequence about their lives or those of their immediate families. Gerard Uylenburgh, the father of Hendrick and his older brother Rombout, was born in Leeuwarden in the province of Friesland and moved to Cracow in the latter half of the sixteenth century. Though he held a high position at the court of the king of Poland, the archives have yielded few documents concerning his life or work. Uylenburgh's children, a daughter and two sons, spent their youth in Poland. Nothing is known about their education other than that the sons, Rombout and Hendrick, trained as painters and worked for the king of Poland. Rombout Uylenburgh moved to Danzig around 1612. Hendrick served at the court for some time longer and is believed to have lived in Warsaw as well. He may have joined his brother in Danzig at a later stage.

A little more is known about the lives of the Uylenburgh brothers and their families after 1612. New documents have been found concerning Rombout's work as a painter in Danzig and his relationship with his family in the Dutch Republic. They add a few more pieces to the puzzle and, together with the work attributed to him, give an impression of his career as an artist. They also contain interesting information about his brother Hendrick. After his departure from Poland around 1620 and his subsequent travels in the Spanish Netherlands, Hendrick settled in Amsterdam in 1625 or perhaps a year or two earlier. He started off as an art dealer and established a business which gradually developed into a highly successful enterprise. He engaged talented and prolific artists to assist in the studio, while he himself worked as a painter and managed the firm, which must have had an eclectic assortment of art on offer. His son Gerrit gradually took over the reins in the 1650s. The business, which thrived for approximately half a century, is discussed at length in the following chapters.

Though there are more documents concerning the Uylenburghs from after 1625, the details of their lives remain sketchy. With so little information available, one is inclined to extract as much as possible from even the most trivial details and perhaps read more into them than one should. We must also remember that our information is drawn from just a few random documents that have fortuitously survived, and that a number of basic facts are simply not known. For example, we do not know when or where Hendrick Uylenburgh was born or the place and date of his marriage to Maria van Eyck. There are huge gaps in the biographies of both Hendrick and Gerrit Uylenburgh, and years of their lives are wholly undocumented. Hendrick left no letters or personal documents whatsoever, and although considerably more information is available concerning his son, it reveals little about his private life.

Even so, by piecing together these few arbitrary facts, we can form at least some impression of their family background, the circles they moved in, and the general pattern of their professional lives and personal fortunes. But we can only guess at the factors that motivated them to shape their lives as they did. No portraits exist of either Hendrick or Gerrit, nor are any mentioned in contemporary sources, so in this respect too, the two men remain shadowy and elusive figures.

Little is known about Hendrick Uylenburgh's business activities in the second half of the 1620s, shortly after his arrival in Amsterdam, or for most of the 1640s. No correspondence or account books have emerged that might have shed light on his art firm. His activities in the 1630s and early 1640s, on the other hand, are comparatively well documented, so that we have some idea of the way Uylenburgh ran his business and managed his finances. We learn about his investors and clients and the painters who worked in his studio, among them Rembrandt and Govert Flinck.

Like many seventeenth-century entrepreneurs, Hendrick Uylenburgh must have had several of his children working for him, but nothing is known about their contribution to the firm, except in the case of Gerrit. We know roughly how large the family was, but there are no records of the children's baptisms, as Uylenburgh and his wife Maria van Eyck were Mennonites and, as such, opposed to infant baptism. The Uylenburghs' religious background will be discussed in greater detail below and in the chapter concerning their art business for, as we shall see, a significant number of Hendrick's financiers, patrons and other business associates adhered to the same faith. This changed as time went by. Hendrick's son Gerrit, who started taking control of the business in the 1650s, was no less dependent on investors than his father had been, but few, if any, of them were Mennonites. Gerrit's marriage to a Dutch Reformed woman and the fact that his children were baptised in her church have prompted speculation that he

abandoned his faith. However, a recent study reveals that he remained a member of the Mennonite church.

We will also discover that Gerrit had business contacts in several countries and travelled abroad to purchase works of art. For lack of evidence it is impossible to say whether his father had done so as well, although around 1620, while still in the service of the King of Poland, Hendrick Uylenburgh had been active in the Antwerp art market and may have kept in touch with the painters and art dealers he knew there. Be that as it may, Gerrit Uylenburgh continued to run the business in the same way his father had done, producing as well as dealing in art.

The father and son also appear to have moved in different social circles. Hendrick Uylenburgh was a respected member of the community and a successful art dealer, with investors and patrons from the higher echelons of society. He was, of course, a newcomer to the Dutch Republic and needed time to adapt, but it may also have been a question of temperament or his attitude to life, which would most likely have been strongly inspired by his faith. As a Mennonite, he did not occupy any public functions, but it is impossible to say whether he would have aspired to do so in the first place. As far as we know, he did not play a prominent role in the Mennonite community, and though he was a member of the artists' guild, he was never involved in its management. His son Gerrit moved further up the social ladder, notwithstanding his financial difficulties in the early 1670s. We will return to this episode later. But it is thanks to his insolvency that we have an inventory of his moveable assets. This and other documents drawn up at the time give an excellent idea of the stock in his gallery at the time. A few years later Gerrit decided to move to London, where he obtained a good position at court. He lived in London for just under two years and died there in 1679, shortly before or after his wife. Their deaths mark the end of our study, which spans the half century from 1625 to 1675, the Dutch Golden Age, in which so many celebrated artists lived and worked. The most outstanding of the artists to work for the Uylenburghs was Rembrandt. His masterly portrait

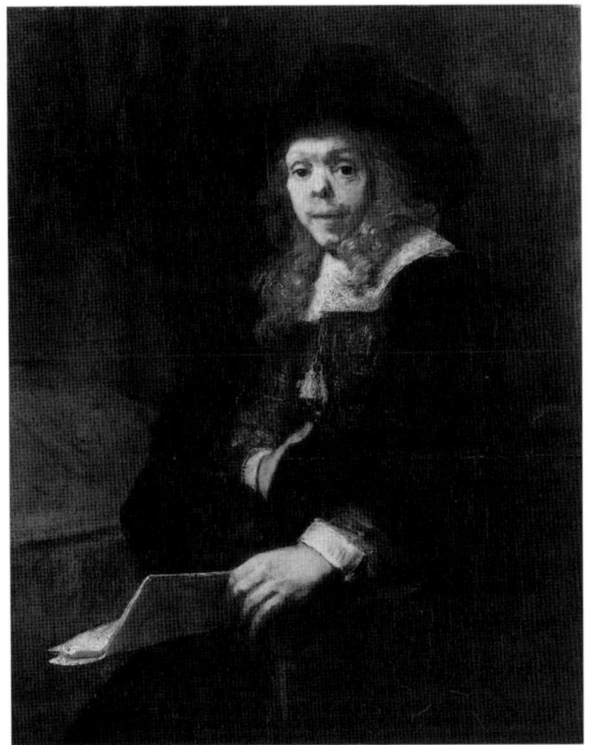

of the talented young Gerard de Lairesse, who joined the studio more than thirty years later, illustrates in striking fashion the high level of the work maintained by painters employed in Hendrick and Gerrit Uylenburgh's workshop (fig. 2).

THE ORIGINS OF THE UYLENBURGH FAMILY

Hendrick Uylenburgh was believed to be a descendant of the 'Ulenburch' family who lived in Leeuwarden in the sixteenth century.[1] That assumption has now been confirmed by a power of attorney drawn up in 1636, which refers to him as 'the honourable Hendrick Gerritssen Uijlenburch' residing 'in the said city', namely Amsterdam.[2] The signature at the end of the document is unmistakeably that of the Amsterdam art dealer (fig. 3a). The patronymic used in the deed leaves very little doubt that he was the son of Gerard, or Gerrit, Uylenburgh. It is not by chance that precisely this document mentions

a patronymic: it concerned an inheritance and it was therefore important to specify the subject's ancestry.[3] On the basis of this document we can conclude with a reasonable degree of certainty that Hendrick Uylenburgh was a descendant of the Uylenburghs from Friesland.

The surname is spelt differently in various documents, most commonly as Ulenburch, Uijlenburch, Wlenburch, Oldenborg, Ulenbork, Uylenburgh or Vuijlenborch. The name Vuijlenborch was first recorded in Leeuwarden in 1571 and derived from lands belonging to members of the family. At some point it acquired the prefix 'van', the Dutch word meaning 'of'. Hendrick Uylenburgh originally signed his name with the prefix but later abandoned it (figs. 3b and 3c). To avoid confusion we have opted here for the consistent use of 'Uylenburgh', arbitrary though it may be. The name occurs frequently in seventeenth-century documents from Amsterdam, the majority of Uylenburghs, or 'Uylenberchs', being descendants of the textile merchant Pieter Rommertsz The Uylenburghs who were not demonstrably related to the Frisian-Amsterdam family are not discussed in this study.[4]

The history of the Uylenburgh family can be traced fairly well from the sixteenth century onwards. Rommert Pietersz may be regarded as the progenitor. An inhabitant of Leeuwarden, he married towards the end of the first half of the sixteenth century and fathered at least five children (Genealogy 1, p. 291), four of whom are relevant here. His eldest son was Pieter Rommertsz Uylenburgh, a textile merchant and councillor in Leeuwarden. Of his six children, one daughter married a Reformed minister, another a burgomaster of Franeker, and a third, Aeltje Pietersdr Uylenburgh, married the

1 See the following publications and the articles Van der Meer 1971 and Kutsch Lojenga 1982.

2 GAA, not. S. Cornelisz, NA 642, fol. 79, 20 March 1636; the deed was first published in Lammertse 2002, p. 143 and note 27.

3 Hendrick Uylenburgh claimed the sum of one thousand guilders owing to him from the estate of his father's sister Sas Rommertsdr Uylenburgh, whose will provided for her nieces and nephews. Saskia was one of them. In 1640 Rembrandt authorised a lawyer on her behalf to claim her share of the inheritance, Doc. 1640/7.

4 Persons whom we have not been able to identify satisfactorily are not discussed here, although they may have been members of the Uylenburgh family.

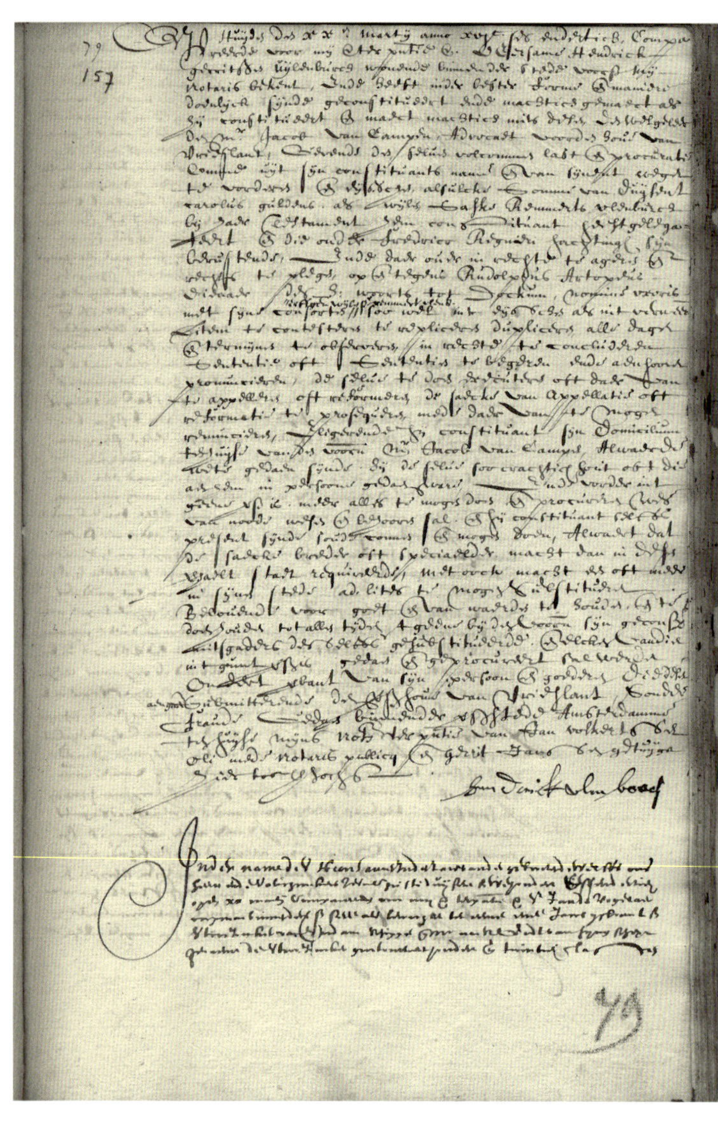

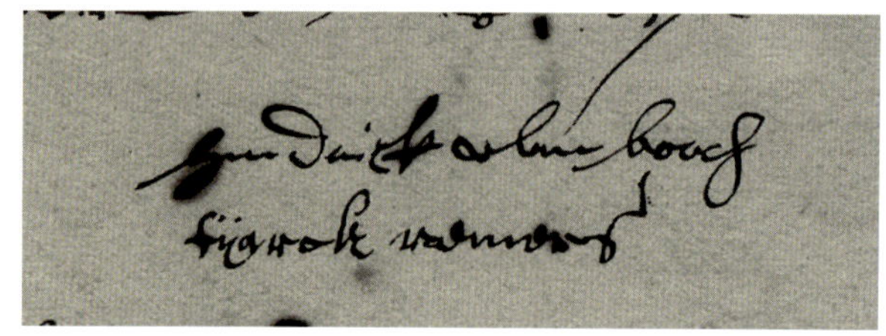

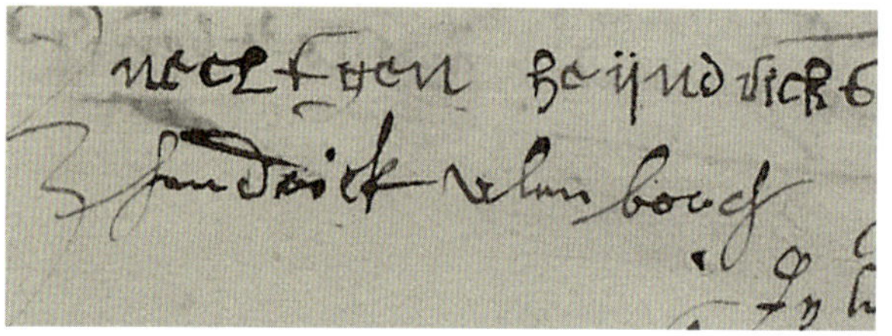

3a Power of attorney of Hendrick Uylenburgh of 20 March 1636, Amsterdam, Gemeentearchief

3b Hendrick Uylenburgh's signature in 1631 (detail of fig. 68)

3c Hendrick Uylenburgh's signature in 1638 (detail of fig. 138)

Reformed minister Johannes Cornelisz Sylvius. Further on we will return to the latter couple, who moved to Amsterdam in the early years of the seventeenth century. One of Pieter's younger brothers was Gerard Rommertsz Uylenburgh, a cabinetmaker and the father of Rombout and Hendrick Uylenburgh. Gerard Rommertsz and his two sons are discussed in more detail below. The next child was Sas Rommertsdr who, late in life and as the widow of a cloth merchant, married a member of the States of Friesland.[5] The youngest son Rombertus Uylenburgh made a great success of his life and pursued a dazzling career: a qualified lawyer and barely thirty years old, he became burgomaster of Leeuwarden and went on to hold a variety of influential posts.[6] Rombertus Uylenburgh and his wife Sjoukje Wlkesdr had a family of eight children. Their daughter Saskia married Rembrandt in 1634. In other words, Saskia was Hendrick Uylenburgh's niece.

'GIERARD RUMBOLTH ULEMBERG', CABINETMAKER IN CRACOW

From the above we know that Gerard Uylenburgh belonged to a prosperous family of merchants and skilled craftsmen from Leeuwarden. A couple of them held high public office, like

5 See note 3.

6 N N B W vol. 10, col. 1069.

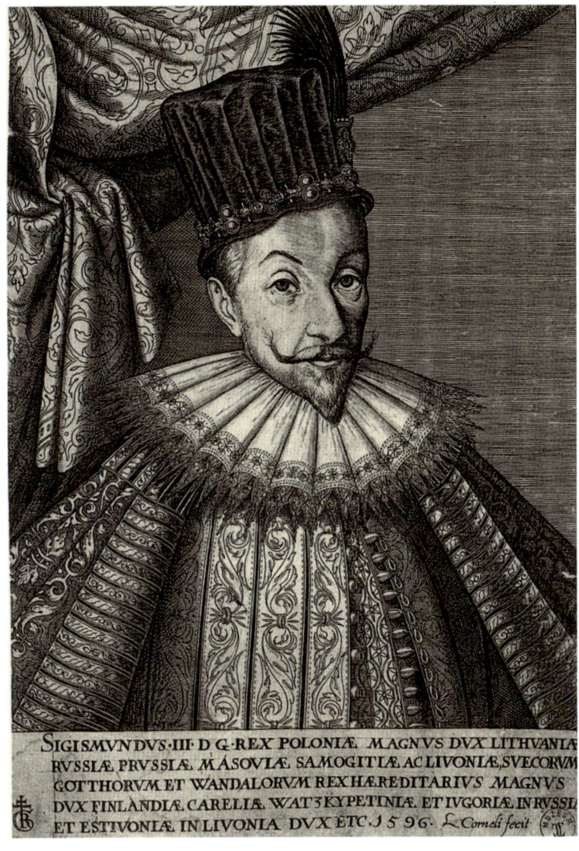

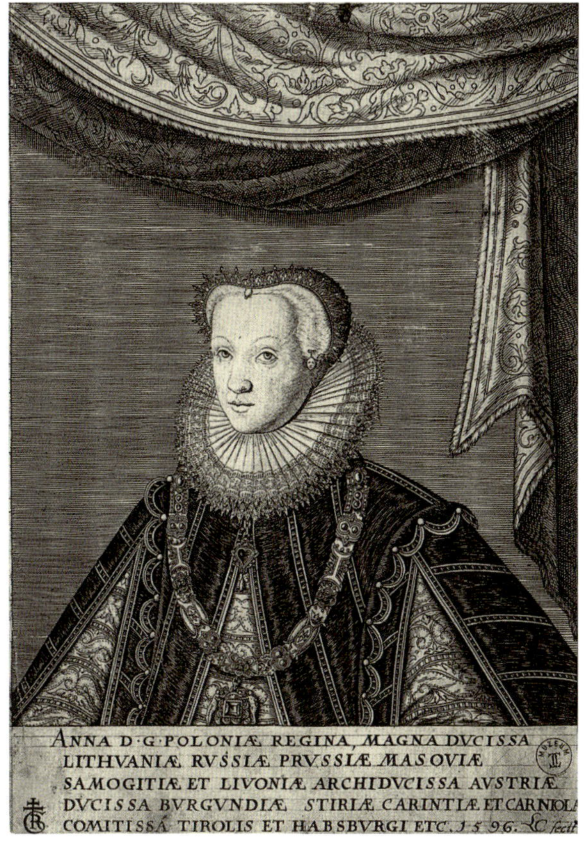

his brother Rombertus Uylenburgh. Although an artisan would normally occupy a fairly humble position in the social hierarchy, Gerard Uylenburgh gained prestige as cabinetmaker to the court of the Polish king Sigismund III in Cracow (figs. 4a and 4b).[7] We do not know why or in what year Uylenburgh moved to Poland. Was it because of his skill as a craftsman or did he flee, as has been suggested, for religious reasons? The latter scenario is unlikely. All his close relatives were Dutch Reformed, while the King of Poland and his entourage were Catholic. It is possible that his two sons who were Mennonites, as we shall see, converted to that faith later in life.

The royal court was in Cracow, for centuries the capital of Poland, which had formed an alliance with Lithuania. The university of Cracow, established in 1364, attracted students from far and wide. Cracow was also an important trade centre. In the sixteenth century it had a population of 30,000, which included a significant number of foreigners from Germany, England, Scotland, France and Italy.[8] The majority of Italians in Cracow were either independent merchants who traded with Italian, German or Austrian cities, or representatives of large concerns. And in view of the ties of marriage between Polish rulers and Italian princesses, many of them were engaged as painters, architects, musicians and sculptors during the reign of Sigismund III. It is uncertain whether Dutch artists were likewise favoured by the court, but if so, that would help to explain Gerard Uylenburgh's presence there. He may also have been invited by agents of the Polish king who visited the Netherlands.[9] Many Poles studied at the university of Franeker in Friesland from the time it was founded in 1585. King Stefan Batory of Poland, who died in 1586, was succeeded a year later by Sigismund, the son of the Johan III of Sweden and the daughter of Sigismund I of Poland. The new king, Sigismund III Vasa, who was married in Cracow in 1592, was a passionate music lover

7 The following is based on the biography in Tomkowicz 1912, pp. 232-234. Thanks to Gerdien Verschoor for translating the Polish text.
8 See Quirini-Poplawska 1977.
9 In 1583 two Polish noblemen came to the Netherlands and visited Haarlem and other cities. One was the cousin of King Stefan Batory of Poland (1533-1586), Thijssen 1992, pp. 96-97 and 176.

and a more generous patron of the arts than his predecessor. It may well have been he who appointed Gerard Uylenburgh, in which case Uylenburgh would only have moved, possibly from Leeuwarden, to Cracow in 1587 or later.

Gerard Uylenburgh married twice (Genealogy 1, p. 291). His first wife is known only as Sara. In 1610 an attestant stated that he was well acquainted with Gerard Rombolt and his wife Sara and that they were the parents of Rombout.[10] An earlier statement, drawn up in Cracow in 1602, reveals that Sara was the mother of Anna, Rombout and Hendrick Uylenburgh.[11] The children's father, Gerard Uylenburgh, whose name appears in Polish documents as 'Gierard Rombolth', occasionally with the surname 'Ulemberg', subsequently married Marina van de Brandt. This second marriage, which was almost certainly solemnised in Cracow, may have taken place in 1598, as on 8 January of that year Uylenburgh signed an agreement with his children, presumably in connection with his marriage. A short time later, Marina van de Brandt was described as his widow. If Gerard Uylenburgh indeed moved to Poland in or after 1587, his children could not have been born there. The couple's daughter Anna married Henricus Fondermil (Hendrick von der Mil or Van der Mullen), who is described in Polish documents as a gardener (*hortulanus*) at the castle in Lobzow, near Cracow.

In 1602 Gerard Uylenburgh's widow had an inventory made of her late husband's estate.[12] The first few items relate to moveable property in one of the downstairs rooms. Among them were three paintings stored on shelves, three more small paintings, a carpenter's chest containing pieces of cloth, a carpenter's bench made of oak, and a large wardrobe painted yellow and filled with clothing, some of which had belonged to Gerard's first wife. There was also a box in the room containing what the inventory describes as a portrait of Her Majesty the Queen, beautifully carved from wood and covered with gold. It had been made for her funeral and was accompanied by woodcarvings, candlesticks and a coffin trimmed with silver. This brilliantly executed and costly portrait was displayed at the castle in Cracow on the occasion of the queen's interment. Uylenburgh valued it at 300 Polish zloty. The young queen in question was the Anna of Austria (fig. 4b), the first wife of Sigismund III, who died in 1598, six years after her marriage.

In an adjoining room, described as the hall, were fourteen large, beautifully executed paintings, a round canvas painting with a view of the city of Cracow, eight small 'coloured' unframed paintings of good quality – possibly painted or coloured prints – and a larger one, likewise unframed, eight copperplates in white frames, and a painted clock with chimes. A large 'instrument' belonging to the deceased was presumably a musical instrument, as this item is followed by a clavichord which was also Uylenburgh's personal property. Also in this room was a small, unfinished chest intended for a Polish nobleman. There was a bookcase, painted green, containing some twenty Dutch books, two more in folio and a large number of letters, registers, official documents and contracts in Dutch. A small chest contained numerous small, unframed paintings and other unspecified works of art. There were even more Dutch books, and a cabinet holding vast quantities of paperwork, mostly in Dutch. The last items on the list were two carpenter's benches.

Opposite the hall, in another large room, was a workshop containing the tools of a cabinetmaker or woodcarver's trade: planes in all shapes and sizes, iron hammers, saws, chisels, pliers, vices and drills. Among the manufactured objects were eleven finished items, four large woodcarvings and twenty-one elaborate wooden carvings for church pews, and two long ebony rods belonging to a Polish sheriff, who had probably brought them in to be carved. An attic, surprisingly, contained a large quantity of glass articles and other equipment used for alchemy.[13] And in front of the attic were more than fifty chests ready to be carved by the journeymen.

Though there were liabilities, the inventory attests to a certain degree of prosperity. The household was adequately furnished and equipped, and to judge by the large number

10 Cracow, Archiwum Państwowe (AP), Acta Consularia Cracoviensis inscriptionum, inv. no. 457/100, 102, p. 721, 1610; the statement was made by Jacob van Boven (a Dutchman?) at the request of Rombout Uylenburgh, who acquired burghership of Cracow that year and was required to submit evidence of his origins. Documents from the archives in Cracow, cited here, were transcribed and translated for us by Marcin Birenat and Michal Kurzej. We also wish to thank Dr Antoni Ziemba of the Muzeum Narodowe w Warszawie for arranging this.
11 Cracow, AP, Acta officii advocatialis Cracoviensis, inv. no. 226, p. 1128, 1602.
12 Cracow, AP, Acta officii advocatialis Cracoviensis, inv. no. 226, pp. 1502, 1602; the introduction to this document is in Latin, the specification of property in Polish.
13 The entry reads: 'Szklienic rozmaitych do Alchemiey należących malych, y wielkich niemalo, których trudno belo zliczić'.

5 Deed signed by Rombout and Hendrick Uylenburgh with their mark and signature, Cracow, Archiwum Państwowe

of tools and carvings on the premises, the workshop was apparently quite sizable. Most of the books and papers in the estate were in Dutch. The paintings and other works of art are not described, nor are their makers identified, but, as we shall see, they were fairly valuable. A few musical instruments were found in the house, while the attic served as a laboratory. It is in any event clear that the brothers Rombout and Hendrick Uylenburgh grew up in a reasonably well-to-do family at the court of the king of Poland. The many books and papers in their home suggest that their parents were erudite and undoubtedly devout, but above all they were keenly interested in science, culture, art and music.

The inventory also sheds light on the nature of Gerard Uylenburgh's work. He was engaged as a cabinetmaker to the court, but was predominantly occupied as a woodcarver, producing sculptures, reliefs and decorative objects. The wooden carvings found in his workshop, which are now in the Church of St Mary in Cracow, were presumably commissioned shortly before his death.[14] Gerard also appears to have had private clients who commissioned woodcarvings of all kinds.

Documents drawn up some years later contain more information about the estate. A document of 1609 concerns the condition of the possessions he left at his death.[15] His property had been valued and his widow was requesting the return of her dowry. As no cash was available, creditors were paid out in goods from the workshop. The owner of the house in which the Uylenburghs had lived received paintings in lieu of outstanding rent. The works in question must therefore

have had a certain monetary value. The same document confirms that Uylenburgh had accepted the commission to carve pews for the cathedral of Cracow and that he had been paid for the work either in part or in full. His son-in-law and his widow assumed responsibility for the order, which was presumably completed by assistants in the workshop. In 1603 the brothers 'Rombertus' and 'Henricus Ulemberg', as well as their sister Anna and their stepmother had reached an agreement on the disposal of the assets. Anna's husband was appointed guardian of the brothers, who must therefore have still been minors. In 1609 the terms of the agreement were implemented.[16] The property was shared out and the brothers undertook to redeem all outstanding debts. Both signed the deed and affixed their marks (fig. 5). The papers drawn up for the division of the estate stipulate that Rombout was a painter in Cracow. Now we shall see that he was not to remain there for long.

ROMBOUT UYLENBURGH, PAINTER IN CRACOW AND DANZIG

Rombout, the eldest son of Sara and Gerard Uylenburgh, must have been born between 1580 and 1585. Little is known about his schooling other than that he was apprenticed to a painter. He was clearly an educated man, as can be seen from the fluent signature on the deed of transfer of his father's estate, which his brother Hendrick signed as well (see fig. 5). It is not known where he studied painting or who taught him. To judge by a work attributed to him and discussed below, one might assume that he received his

14 Tomkowicz 1912, fig. 28 is a photograph taken at the beginning of the twentieth century of the pews, which are still in place, that may have been made by Gerard Uylenburgh.
15 Cracow, A P, Acta Controversiarum advocatialis Cracoviensis officii, inv. no. 231, pp. 1441, 1609.
16 Cracow, A P, Acta Consularia Cracoviensis inscriptionum, inv. no. 457, p. 507-508, 1609. It might be possible to deduce Hendrick Uylenburgh's date of birth from this document. In 1603 he was still a minor and was assigned a guardian, in 1609 he acted on his own behalf. Had he (recently?) attained majority? If so, he must have been born in or around 1584.

19

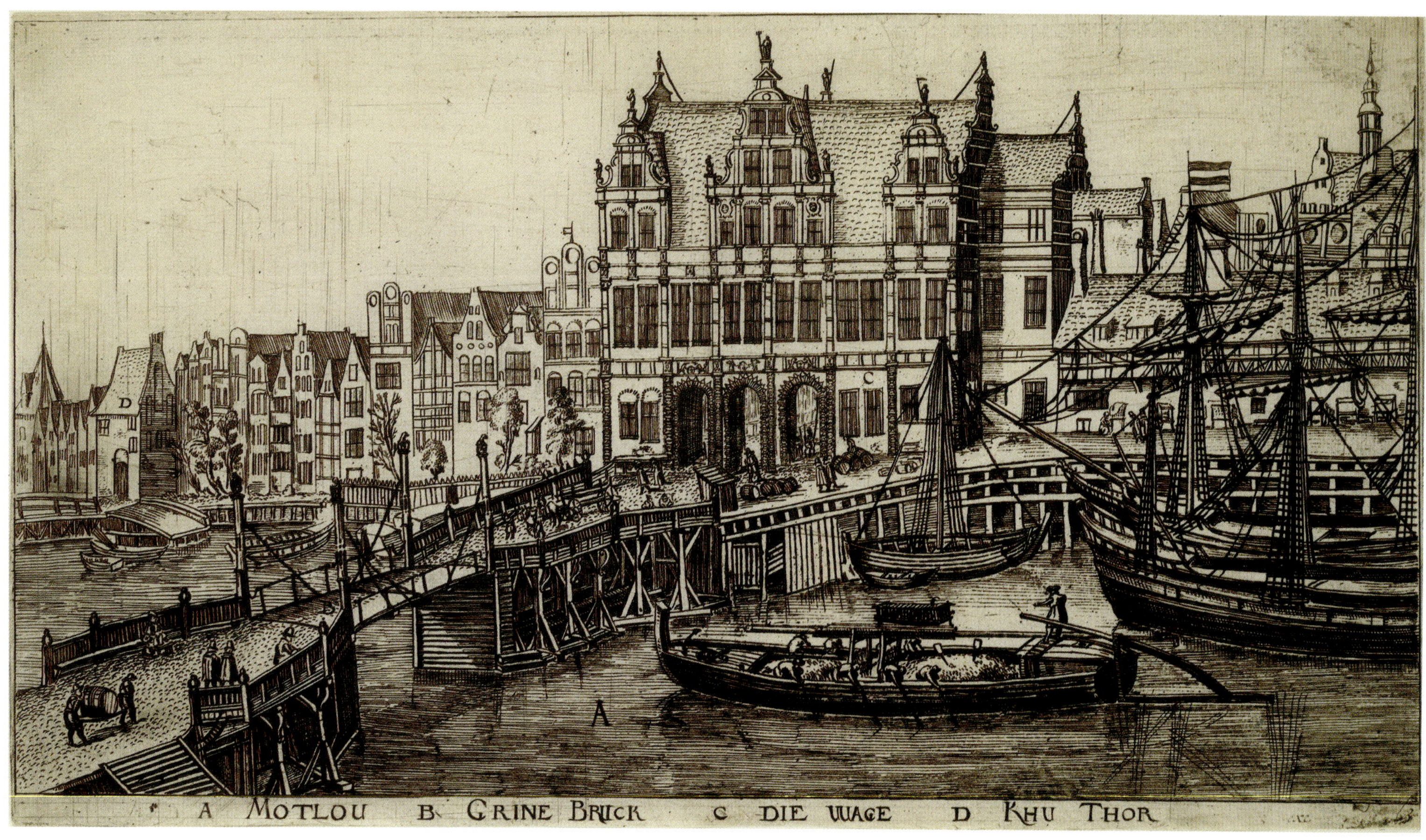

training in the Netherlands or under a master with a 'Dutch' background. He may also have studied closer to home for, as we have seen, the Polish court in Cracow was highly cosmopolitan. From the second half of the sixteenth century onwards, the court engaged architects, sculptors, goldsmiths and silversmiths, artisans and artists from all parts of western and southern Europe.[17] It is also possible that Rombout studied in the Polish city of Danzig which, from the mid-sixteenth century to the mid-seventeenth century, was home to a succession of Dutch and Flemish artists, who exercised a strong influence on the artistic life of the city.[18] One of the painters living there around 1600 was Hans Vredeman de Vries of Leeuwarden. Whatever the case, Rombout Uylenburgh completed his training successfully. His talent did not go unnoticed, as he was appointed painter to the Polish king.

In 1610 Rombout Uylenburgh was still living in Cracow. In that year 'Rombertus Vlemberk Pictor' was granted burghership of the city.[19] He promised to present a painting to the city council of Cracow, in return for which he was probably exempted from various obligations or perhaps obtained his burghership free of charge. He is referred to as 'Robert' (Rombout) the painter and son of the late Gerard Rombolt, cabinetmaker to His Highness the King. A short time later, around 1612, Rombout Uylenburgh cancelled his membership of the local artists' guild.[20] Had he fallen out with his colleagues? Or, as a court painter, was he unwilling to submit to the rules of the guild? It may have been in connection with the fact that the gradual move of the court from Cracow to Warsaw, which began in 1596, was completed in 1609. In any event, there was a dispute and, as a document reveals, Rombout was expecting the king to intervene. Rombout Uylenburgh remained in Cracow until about 1612. In 1613 he is docu-

6 Johann Dickmann, View of Danzig with the Green Gate and activity in the harbour, etching, 17.5 x 31.2 cm, Amsterdam, Rijksprentenkabinet

17 For an overview, see Tomkowicz 1912; the cosmopolitan nature of the Polish court is described in a review of this book in *Bulletin de la Société Polonaise pour l'avancement des sciences* 1912, pp. 31-36.
18 Kandt 2003 with bibliography.
19 Cracow, A P, Liber Iuris Civilis, inv. no. 1423, pp. 718, 1610.
20 Cracow, A P, Consularia Cracoviensia Controversiae, inv. no. 509, p. 485, 1613.

mented as having left for Danzig a short time before. He may have been unhappy with the king's decision in the dispute, or perhaps unwilling to move to Warsaw. Or did he simply believe that his prospects in Danzig were better?

In the last decades of the sixteenth century the Baltic countries were the Netherlands' principal trading partners. The Netherlands was dependent on the region for grain and other agricultural produce.[21] Ships from the Baltics also brought wood and a variety of raw materials, returning with textiles, wine and luxury goods. Danzig was the hub of that constantly expanding trade. At least half the vessels plying the Baltic Sea called in on the Polish-German port, and more than half of those were Dutch. It stands to reasons that many Dutch merchants made their homes in Danzig, if only on a temporary basis. In the first half of the seventeenth century the Dutch population burgeoned in this city, whose harbour, warehouses and step-gabled mansions resembled those back home (fig. 6). Some of the newcomers became burghers of Danzig and remained there for the rest of their lives. The majority were traders in either goods or currency, while others earned their livelihood as entrepreneurs, artists or artisans. Rombout Uylenburgh belonged to the latter category. He established himself as a painter in Danzig and later sold some of his work through his brother Hendrick in Amsterdam.

Rombout Uylenburgh's presence in Danzig is documented in the *Mahlerbuch,* a manuscript register of painters belonging to the artists' guild, which was founded in 1612. It ranks 'the youngest confrères' and includes a short biography of 'Rumboldt von Flenbarck'. The author was unable to give the date of Uylenburgh's death, but noted that he had been widely acclaimed. He had read about Uylenburgh's

21 Van Tielhof 2002.

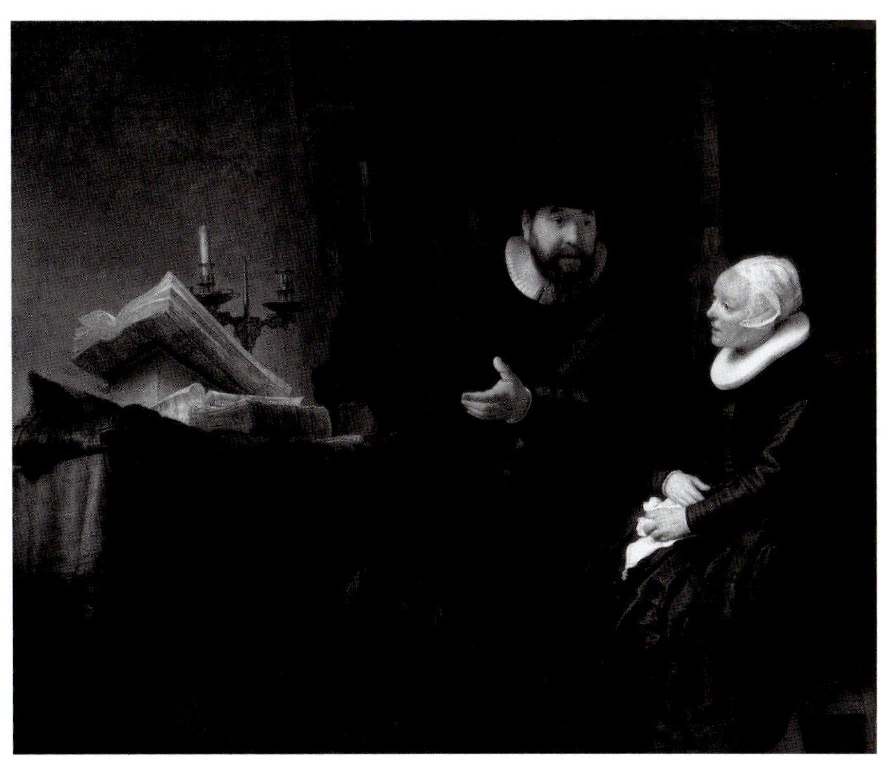

7 Rembrandt van Rijn, Double portrait of the Mennonite preacher Cornelis Claesz Anslo and his wife Aeltje Gerritsdr Schouten, signed and dated 'Rembrandt f. 1641', canvas, 176 x 210 cm (upper corners rounded), Berlin, Staatliche Museen zu Berlin, Gemäldegalerie (Br. 409; Corpus III A 143)

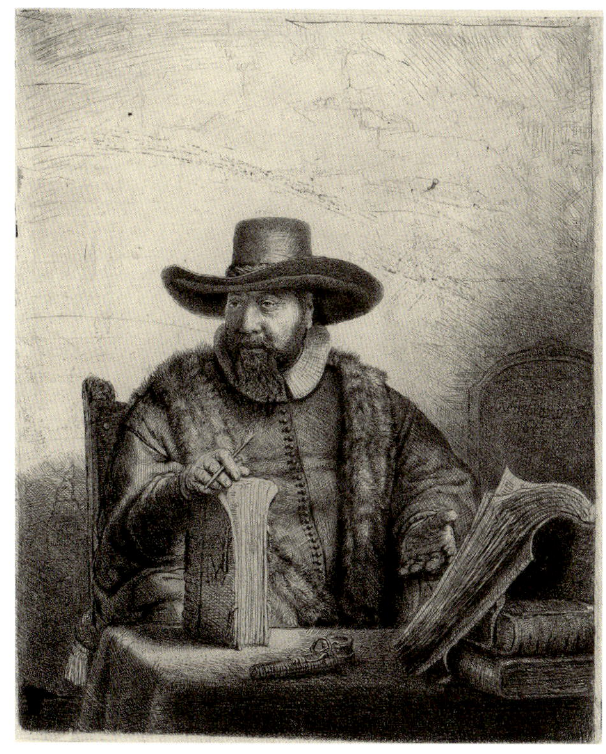

8 Rembrandt van Rijn, Portrait of Cornelis Claesz Anslo, signed and dated 'Rembrandt. f. 1641', etching and drypoint, 10.8 x 15.8 cm, Amsterdam, The Rembrandt House Museum (B. 271 II, 2)

reputation as a distinguished portraitist and was astonished that he had not been an 'overman' (or one of the founding fathers?) of the guild, all of whom had been proficient artists.[22] Was he perhaps not eligible for a management position in the guild on account of his religion?

In 1612 Rombout Uylenburgh would have been about thirty years old. Around this time, most probably between 1612 and 1620, he married Ibeltje Haye Fries. The marriage took place in Danzig, as we can infer from the following facts. Ibeltje had a sister and two brothers, one of whom was married in Leiden in 1616, on which occasion he stated that he came from Danzig.[23] But the other brother, Sijbrant Haye Fries, lived there as well. Up to now, this Sijbrant has escaped the notice of Uylenburgh scholars. Research on Sijbrant Fries – Rombout Uylenburgh's brother-in-law – has helped to clarify many relationships. It transpires that Sijbrant Fries was married to Marretje Cornelisdr Schouten. Genealogy 1 shows the relationships between the Schouten family and Rombout and Hendrick Uylenburgh. Pieter Gerritsz Hooft, for instance, one of Hendrick Uylenburgh's financiers in 1640, belonged to this family, as did Aeltje Gerritsdr Schouten and her husband Cornelis Claesz Anslo, a prominent minister of the Waterland Mennonite congregation in Amsterdam and for this reason, undoubtedly, a close acquaintance of Hendrick Uylenburgh. In 1640/1 Anslo had his portrait painted by Rembrandt (figs. 7 and 8). As we shall see, Hendrick Uylenburgh acted on behalf of Swaentje Cornelisdr Schouten; and Sijbrant Fries, finally, settled in Leiden and from there ordered paintings from his brother-in-law Rombout Uylenburgh in Danzig.

Sijbrant Haye Fries was born around 1571/2. He lived in Danzig from about 1598 to 1613. He was a brewer in Weesp, near Amsterdam, and was probably married there. He occasionally visited Amsterdam during those years and subsequently moved to Leiden, where he was declared insolvent in 1628. Fries returned to Weesp in 1638 and remained there until his death in 1648.[24] His wife Marretje belonged to the affluent and politically influential Schouten family of Weesp, some of whose members were civic dignitaries.[25] Fries's brother-in-law Lambert Cornelisz Schouten occupied a high-ranking position in Weesp for many years and served seventeen terms as burgomaster in Weesp between 1612 and 1644. His brother Laurens Cornelisz Schouten, a prodigiously wealthy brewer, was an officer of the Weesp orphanage from 1619 to 1622 and a regent there from 1623 until his death in 1642. His sister Niesgen served as a visiting officer of the same institution on many occasions from 1611 on. Laurens Schouten was a deacon of the Waterland Mennonite church in Amsterdam. He had a house built on the Keizersgracht in Amsterdam in 1616 and was one of the first members of the Amsterdam élite to acquire a country manor on the banks of the River Gein.[26] It is a mark of his distinction that Stadholder Frederick Hendrick stayed at his home when passing through Weesp en route from Den Bosch to The Hague and later remarked that he had been deeply impressed.[27]

What we discover here is that the Schoutens held senior posts in civic government, despite the fact that they were Mennonites and would not normally have been eligible for such positions. Even so, exceptions were made in smaller communities. Burgomaster Lambert Schouten

22 'Rumboldt von Flenbarck [Ulenborch] zu welcher Zeit er entschlafen habe nicht finden können, sonsten hat er die Ehre und den Ruhm daß man sich nicht gescheurt ihm in einer Berichtschrift als ein guten und vortrefflicher Conterfäyer an zu führen seiner Zeit und ist nicht wenig zu bewundren daß er nicht unter die Zahl deren damahligen ältesten mit einverleibet weil man solch großes Ruhmen von ihm had gemacht müssen also die dazumahligen ältesten keinen unerfahrene Männer gewesen sein', Gdańsk, Archiwum Państwowe, inv. no. 300 C, no. 613, fol. 182; the author of this manuscript, possibly dating from the eighteenth century, consulted archive documents which are now probably lost.

23 RAL, DTB 3, fol. 51v, 20 May 1616, betrothal of 'Gerbrant Hayes Fries' van 'Danswijck' and Geertgen Laurens van Valkenburg.

24 In 1617 Sijbrant Fries testified that he had been in the brewery trade for about fifteen consecutive years and subsequently moved to Leiden, RAL, not. J. van Kuyck, NA 119, deed 47, 16 April 1617. In 1605 he represented a widow in Weesp and signed 'Sibrant Haies Fries', NHA, ORA, inv. no. 2933, fol. 67, 7 August 1605. In the entry of his registration as a burgher of Leiden in 1613 his name is followed by the words 'brewer in Weesp', RAL, Register of Burghers F 53, 7 January 1613. He was probably born elsewhere (in Danzig?). It took more than ten years to settle his bankrupt estate.

25 Brood 1977a and Brood 1977b.

26 De Clercq 1998(b).

27 Van Tricht 1976-1979, vol. 2, p. 75.

made no secret of his faith. When a new town council was being formed in Weesp in 1622 a list was drawn up naming twenty-one people who were to be invited to take the oath. Three of the candidates – one of whom was Lambert Schouten – declined to do so on religious grounds, but instead undertook on their 'word of honour' to fulfil their obligations.[28] This would have been consistent with Mennonite doctrine, which prohibits the taking of oaths. Further evidence of Schouten's religious affiliation emerges from the will he drew up in 1642, bequeathing the preacher of the Waterland congregation in Weesp an annual stipend of twenty-give guilders for a period of twenty years.[29]

Documents from the archives in Leiden confirm that Sijbrant Fries was a Mennonite as well. In 1625 he declined to make a statement under oath 'on religious grounds', but instead gave 'his word of honour as a man'.[30] Sijbrant Fries was a member of the Frisian Mennonites in Leiden and played an active part in the community. From a list of his creditors, drawn up at the time of his insolvency, it transpires that he was to distribute a sum of seventy-eight guilders among 'impecunious Frisians' in Leiden 'should the need arise'.[31] In other words, he was responsible for dispensing alms on behalf of the Mennonite community.

Rombout Uylenburgh's wife Ibeltje came from a wealthy family. Her aunt Geertgen Sijbrantsdr was married to Saeff Hendricxz, burgomaster of Harlingen.[32] In 1621 the widowed Geertgen was living in Leiden, most probably in the home of Sijbrant Fries.[33] She moved out of the house, possibly because of Sijbrant Fries's bankruptcy. Whatever the case, at the time of her death in 1629, she was living on the Houtmarkt in Leiden. According to an inventory of her possessions compiled shortly after her death,[34] more than twenty paintings, mostly biblical scenes, were hanging in two rooms of her home. Among them were a large painting depicting a 'Moor' (presumably the Baptism of the Eunuch), a Tower of Babel, a 'Paradise' (Adam and Eve), a scene from the narrative of the young Tobit, and a 'Three Kings' (Adoration of the Magi). Above the linen closet in the downstairs room was a painting 'with shutters that open', but the subject of this triptych is not mentioned.

Geertgen Sijbrantsdr's securities and paperwork included a batch of letters addressed to her. One was from Stijntje Haye Fries, the wife of Dirck Willemsz Druijst and Rombout Uylenburgh's sister-in-law, but we are not told where she was living. Another of these letters to Geertgen, dated 29 May 1629, is signed 'from Ibel Haijs *Yr.l. niece*'. Rombout Uylenburgh's widow may have written to her aunt regarding the claim to Sijbrant Fries's estate, which, as we shall see, included paintings by her late husband. Finally, we can infer from the inclusion in the inventory of a silver crucifix, a small statue of the Virgin with the Child on her lap, an icon of Christ and a book of 'Catholic prayers' that Geertgen Sijbrantsdr was Catholic. As the artists who painted the pictures in her home are not named in the inventory, it is impossible to say whether she possessed paintings by Rombout Uylenburgh. However, the biblical scenes may well have been his work.

We can conclude from the above that Rombout and Hendrick Uylenburgh belonged to an extensive network of Mennonite families in Danzig, Amsterdam, Weesp, Leiden and, as we will discover, Leeuwarden. Their relatives by blood and marriage occupied high-ranking positions. Their uncle Rombertus Uylenburgh was burgomaster of Leeuwarden, an aunt of Rombout Uylenburgh's wife was married to a burgomaster of Harlingen, and one of Rombout's brothers-in-law was burgomaster of Weesp. Many of them were comfortably off. In those circles the brothers found clients for art from their atelier and gallery. Sijbrant Fries, for instance, was apparently one of their business associates. After Rombout Uylenburgh's death in Danzig in late 1627 or early 1628, his widow claimed payment from her brother-in-law Sijbrant Fries for art that her husband had sold him. The documents concerning this claim shed light on Rombout Uylenburgh's output.

28 Brood 1977a, p. 2 and Van Tricht 1976-1979, vol. I, pp. 435-436.

29 NHA, ONA (access no. 185), Weesp, not. J. Cornelisz Verlaen, NA 5179, 27 April 1642.

30 RAL, ORA (access no. 508), inv. no. 79P, fol. 1, undated [1625]; the deed was not passed.

31 RAL, ORA (access no. 508), inv. no. 52N, fol. 240-264, 20 July – 27 August 1638, notably 263. The list of Sijbrant Fries's creditors mentions the same amount for 'Frisian indigents of this city', ibid., inv. no. 50J, fol. 146-147v and 161-166, 20 July 1638, notably 164.

32 In 1628 she describes herself as the widow of Saeff Hendricxz, former burgomaster of Harlingen, '73 years old [..] and aunt of Ibel Haye Fries', RAL, not. L. Vergeyl, NA 331, deed 12, 2 March 1628.

33 A power of attorney in the name of Geertgen Sijbrantsdr was drawn up 'at the home of her counsel on Oude Chingel in the new estate of this city', RAL, not. J. van Kuyck, NA 120, deed 66, 20 April 1621. This was the location of Sijbrant Fries's home and brewery 'The Double Key'. A power of attorney in his name was drawn up at the same time and place, ibid., deed 67, 20 April 1621. In 1628 Fries transferred bonds and book debts to his aunt by marriage, RAL, not. L. Vergeyl, NA 331, deed 6, 6 February 1628.

34 RAL, not. P. den Oosterlingh, NA 365, deed 62, 20 and 22 October 1629; Professor C.W. Fock kindly brought this document to my attention.

In 1613 Sijbrant Fries took charge of the brewery 'The Double Key' in Leiden and is known to have had an interest in other commercial ventures in Weesp. In 1627 he found himself in debt and tried, in vain, to salvage the business. One of his many creditors was the Geertgen Sijbrantsdr, referred to above.[35] Rombout Uylenburgh's widow and children also entered a claim. Fries's possessions were confiscated and a warrant was issued for his arrest. He managed to abscond, however, 'without anyone being able to discover his whereabouts'.[36] On 8 March 1628 'the honourable Henrick van Ulenburch, merchant in Amsterdam' appeared before a notary in Leiden as the uncle and guardian of the children of the late 'Rombout van Ulenburch, painter in Danzig'. He was also representing the widow Ibel Haye Fries, the 'trustee of the estate and joint guardian of the children born of her marriage' to Rombout Uylenburgh. Hendrick Uylenburgh instructed a solicitor at the Court of Holland and another at the district court in Leiden to file objections to the envisaged sale of certain paintings. The works in question are listed in a notarial deed: a Judgment, a Beheading of Saint John the Baptist, a Moses striking water from the rock, a Polish game market, a Lithuanian game market, a Vegetable market and a Flower pot with two naked children.[37] These paintings, which according to the document belonged to the widow and children of Rombout, were in the home of Sijbrant Fries. The names of the artists are not mentioned, but later documents reveal that some were by

Rombout Uylenburgh, and we can assume that others, if not all, were from his hand as well.

The documents describe the course of events in detail. On 10 March the administrator of Sijbrant Fries's insolvent estate submitted an application for assignment to the Supreme Court in The Hague.[38] He explained that Fries had incurred 'substantial debts and was unable to pay his creditors' and that his property was to be sold under a writ of execution. The debts amounted to 80,000 guilders or more. One of the creditors requested a court bailiff to seize the goods and, as a result, four people were engaged to ensure that nothing was removed from the house.[39] On 7 April 1628, two witnesses were called to testify at the administrator's request. One reported that *a few years previously* he had been given lodgings in a small room at the back of Sijbrant Fries's brewery in Leiden, where he had found a letter signed by a person called Uylenburgh. Unable to restrain himself, he had proceeded to read it. Uylenburgh had written to inform Fries that the paintings he had ordered from him were not yet ready. Fries had apparently stipulated that they should be executed with 'exceptional care', and he therefore wanted more money for the extra work involved. Furthermore, Fries had told the witness on several occasions that the paintings in his home and those that Uylenburgh had sent him actually belonged to him. Fries had also told him how much they had cost, but the witness was unable to recall the exact amount. A woman subsequently testified that either Fries or his wife Marretje had told her that the *Judgment* had been made for them. Marretje's brother, Lambert

liciteren, deselve te hoven pronunchieren, t'acquiesceren off daervan te mogen provoceren, bij appèl, refermatie off anderssins, sulcx de gelegentheyt den saecke vereysschen ende haeren goeden raet gedraegen sal', R A L, not. L. Vergeyl, N A 331, deed 15, 8 March 1628 and Bredius 1915-1922, vol. 5, p. 1685(a); the authorised representatives were Robbrecht van der Burch, solicitor for the Court of Holland and Johan van Kuijck, solicitor for the Tribunal of the city of Leiden. On Agniesgen Willemsdr, who was owed money by Sijbrant Fries, see notes 39 and 40.
38 The Hague, National Archives, Supreme Court of Holland and Zeeland (3.03.02), inv. no. 32, 10 March 1628.
39 This creditor was Agniesgen Willemsdr van Voorburch, widow of Claes Jansz van der Vorst, residing in Delft, see notes 37 and 40.

---

35 R A L, not. L. Vergeyl, N A 331, deed 6, 6 February 1628, Sijbrant Fries transfers bonds and book debts to Geertgen Sijbrantsdr; ibid., deed 9, 27 February 1628, security for Geertgen Sijbrantsdr 'and the guardians of Swaentgen Cornelisdr to the value of the [deleted: seized] goods [..] for the account of Sybrant Fries'. The inventory of Geertgen Sijbrantsdr (see note 34) notes that Fries and his wife Marretje

Cornelisdr Schouten had received 6,000 guilders from her in 1615.
36 R A L, Leiden Municipal Archives II (access no. 501A), inv. no. 6508, fol. 98, undated; Sijbrant Fries must have been in Amsterdam, as the court there gave him leave to request assignment from the Supreme Court in The Hague. Leiden filed a protest on the grounds that Fries was a burgher of that city.

37 'Om 'te opposeren tegens d'executie ende vercopinge bij Agniesgen Willemsdr van der Vorst door Jan van Geesdorp, deurwaerder 's Hooffs van Hollt. begost, ofte bij allen anderen te beginnen, op de schilderijen, het eene genaempt het Oordeel, het [deleted: twede] derde Johannes onthooffdinge, het [deleted: derde] twede [deleted: genaempt] daer Moysis 't water [deleted: in de] uyt

de steen slaet, het vierde [deleted: een] ende vijffde een Poolsche ende Letousche wiltmarct, het seste een groenmarct ende het sevende een blompoth met 2 naecte kinderkens, alle toebehorende de voorsz wede. ende kinderen van Rombout van Ulenburch ende berustende ten huyse van Sybrandt Fries, geëxe[cuteer]de, tot dieneynde alle termijnen van rechten te observeren, sententie te sol-

Cornelisz Schouten, the burgomaster of Weesp, had complained to the first witness about the great loss Schouten's relatives had suffered as a result of the bankruptcy, adding that his sister Swaentje had lost about 18,000 guilders, for which they had stood security. In reply to a question by the first witness, Schouten confirmed that Fries was Swaentje's joint guardian, but stated that there was no written evidence to that effect.[40]

In 1629 Hendrick Uylenburgh filed an application with the Supreme Court in The Hague, as uncle, blood relative and guardian of the minor children of his late brother Rombout and Rombout's widow, and on behalf of the guardians of Swaentje Cornelisdr Schouten. The widow, her children and Swaentje claimed entitlement to 'certain paintings of great significance' and household goods in the home of Sijbrant Haye Fries. They had previously submitted a claim to the Court of Holland, but their application had failed.[41]

It emerges from the above that Rombout Uylenburgh had painted the *Last Judgment* and other pictures for his brother-in-law Sijbrant Fries. This is confirmed by a document of 1634 referring to 'the Judgment believed to have been made by Mr Rombout van Uylenburch'. Representations of the Last Judgment, depicting the second coming of Christ and, according to

Christian doctrine, the resurrection of the dead, incorporate several episodes with numerous figures, and as a result, they tend to be sizable works. Rombout Uylenburgh's version was evidently 'exceptionally large'. He illustrated this subject on more than one occasion: in 1627 he had sent his brother Hendrick several grisailles of biblical scenes, one of which was 'a Judgment'.[42] The document of 1634 also states that The *beheading of Saint John the Baptist* was the work of the same master. The *Polish game market* and the *Lithuanian game market* are unusual subjects and were most likely painted by Rombout Uylenburgh. The *Vegetable market* belongs to the same genre and was therefore presumably from his hand too. The *Moses striking water from the rock* can probably be attributed to him as well, given that Hendrick Uylenburgh had several of his brother's biblical scenes in stock in 1627. The flower still life with two naked children was presumably likewise by Rombout.

The paintings were sold at auction in Leiden. One of the buyers, an Amsterdam art dealer, failed to pay the full amount for the two he had bought.[43] He had bid 542 guilders and ten *stuyvers*, but by December 1633 he had paid only 150 guilders.[44] As the paintings were still hanging in Fries's brewery, the administrators of Fries's estate put them up for auction again and

40 The first witness stated as follows: 'eenige jaren geleden, sonder behael van den juysten tijt' he 'in de brouwerije van de Double Sleutel alhier in seecker achtersaeltgen alwaer hij gelogeert ende door Sijbrant Fries gewesen was den nacht te rusten, heeft gevonden seeckere missive onderteyckent Uijlenburch, waerbij denselve Uijlenburch aen den voorn. Sijbrant Fries onder andere schreef, dat de schilderijen daerom hij (de Fries) aen hem (Uylenburch) heftel[ijk] hadde geschreven, sodrae niet gedaen en costen werden, dat hij deselve so curieus begeerde te hebben ende daerinne geheel veel werc most zijn, dat oic daeraen veel gelts hing, sulcx dat hij wel begeerde dat Sijbrant Fries hem meerd[er] gelts soude senden dan hij tot die tijt toe gedaen hadde'. He added that he 'de voorsz. Sybrant Fries verscheyden malen heeft horen seggen, dat de schilderijen die t'sijnen huyse hingen ende onder anderen mede de stucken die hem door de voorn. Uijlenburch waren gesonden, ende hij deposant weet alsnoch in de brouwerije die Double Sleutel te hangen, hem eygentlic toebehoorde, van gelijcken dat hij denselven de Fries hem dicmaelen heeft verclaert hoeveel hem deselve schilderijen costen, edoch dat hem de precise somme is vergeten'. The second person stated that: 'een geruymen tijt geleden de voorn. Sybrant Fries of desselfs huysvrouwe jegens haer deposante ten huyse van deselve Fries verclaert hebben, dat haer swager de schilderije,

daerop zij deposante stont ende sach, wesende namentlic het Oordeel, 't welc noch jegenwoordich hangt in de brouwerije van den Doublen Sleutel, voor henluyden hadde gemaect [deleted: ende hen overgesonden hadde]'. The first witness also stated: 'dat op huyden morgen Lambrecht Cornelis Schouten, burgermeester der stadt Weesp, jegens hem deposant heeft geclaecht van 't groot verlies dat de vrunden van Sijbrant Fries aen denselve quamen te lijden, expresselic verclarende dat sij souden verliesen eerst de thienduysent guldens daermede sij op te brouwerije specialicken waren gehipotheyceert ende noch de achtienduysent guldens die

Swaentgen Cornelis, innocente dochter, waren competerende ende waervooren zijluyden borgen waren. Dat voorts hij deposant daerop den voorn. Lambrecht Cornelisz afvraechde of niet Sijbrant Fries en was medevoocht over deselve Swaentgen Cornelisdr ende of sij mitsdien niet and hadden legael hypotheec op desselfs, Sybrants, goederen, maer dat deselve Lambrecht Schouten hem deposant alsdan antwoorde, dat Sybrant Fries wel was medevoocht over den voorsz Swaentgen edoch dat [deleted: sijluyden daeraf geen bewijs and hadden] daeraf geen schrift and was [deleted: sulx dat zij aen de schaden souden moeten], wijders niet',

RAL, not. J. van Sandwech, NA 352, deed 41, 7 April 1628. Of interest here is the fact that both Cornelis Evertszoon van der Pol, corn factor, aged approximately 65 and residing in Delft, and the 58-year-old Agniesge Willemsdr van Voorburch, widow of Claes Jansz van der Vorst, likewise of Delft, testified 'on [their] conscience and divine soul instead of under oath'. Were they Mennonites? The abridged version of this deed in Bredius 1915-1922, vol. 5, p. 1686(b) is incorrect, as it states that someone in Leiden had ordered paintings 'from Hendrick Uylenburch in Amsterdam'.
41 The Hague, National Archives, Supreme Court

of Holland and Zeeland (access no. 3.03.02), inv. no. 33, (endorsed on) 18 December 1629. This petition was published in Bredius 1915-1922, vol. 5, p. 1686(c), but the passage concerning Swaentje Schouten was not included.
42 See p. 30.
43 As Johannes Nicasius la Toir (Letoir), summonsed regarding his 'two seized paintings', failed to appear, the magistrates declared 'the seizure of the paintings accordingly enforceable', RAL, ORA (access no. 508), inv. no. 45LL, fol. 243v, 26 August-2 December 1633.
44 RAL, ORA (access no. 508), inv. no. 45LL, fol. 264-265, 2 December 1633.

sold them once more. The works offered for sale in 1634 were described as 'an exceptionally large and outstanding painting of the Judgment, made (to the best of our knowledge) by the late master Rombout van Ulenburch, painter to the King of Poland' and 'and a large painting of the beheading of Saint John, made, to the best of our knowledge, by the said master Rombout van Ulenburch'. The *Last Judgment*, which went to auction at a starting price of 300 guilders, fetched the respectable sum of 156 guilders, while the *Beheading of Saint John the Baptist,* starting at 100 guilders, went for 58 guilders.[45]

Is it possible that Sijbrant Fries managed to retain some of his paintings? Several years went by before his affairs were settled.[46] The destitute Sijbrant Fries and his family moved to Weesp without any means of support. In 1636 Lambert, Laurens and Niesgen Schouten agreed to give their sister and brother-in-law and 'some of their children' the sum of 700 guilders a year to ensure that they were 'provided for in their hour of need'.[47] They continued to support Fries, who was by then in his sixties, for several years. He and his wife died shortly after one another in late 1647 or early 1648. No inventory of their possessions has been found,[48] and it is therefore impossible to ascertain whether they still possessed paintings by Rombout Uylenburgh after the sale of the estate in Leiden. Their children may have acquired some of their assets.[49] One of their daughters, Christina Fries, married Jan Hennebo in 1625, a few years before her father's insolvency.[50] The Mennonite Hennebo family were acquainted with Hendrick Uylenburgh. In 1651 Uylenburgh appraised paintings belonging

to Jan le Pla and Peroontgen Hennebo in connection with the widower's marriage in 1650 to Maria Rutgers, the widow of Ameldonck Leeuw. The ties between Leeuw and Hendrick Uylenburgh are discussed in chapter 3. It should be noted, however, that at his death in 1647, Leeuw possessed 'a large kitchen piece by Ulenborch', which went to one of his sons in 1653.[51] This was undoubtedly a painting by Rombout Uylenburgh.

Rombout Uylenburgh remained active as an artist in Danzig up to the time of his death in Danzig in or shortly before 1628. He worked for the Polish court and sold to clients in Poland as well as the Dutch Republic, as can be seen from an inventory of 1617 listing the assets of a married couple in Cracow, which includes seven new framed paintings 'by the painter Rombert Ulemberg'.[52] He may have continued to work for the Polish court even after moving to Danzig, as he is described posthumously as painter to the king of Poland. In any event, he was not forgotten in Cracow. In 1628 a Polish painter working there was accused of borrowing a new, beautifully executed painting with a view to copying it.[53] The work in question, a representation of *Christ in Gethsemane*, was by the 'celebrated' painter 'Rombolt Uylenbergh' and measured six by three el (approximately 180 x 90 cm). The Polish painter had promised to make a second copy as well and would return the original to the owner in pristine condition as soon as possible. But, according to the document, he failed to do either. He had allegedly used the work for his own purposes and ruined it into the bargain, rendering it all but worthless.

45 RAL, ORA (access no. 508), inv. no. 50K, fol. 162v, 15 July 1634; the *Last Judgment* was bought by Adriaen van Leeuwen and the other work by Jan de Smet. In 1641 Adriaen van Leeuwen was documented as the owner of a painting of the five senses by Jan Lievens, Orlers 1641, p. 376. There can be no doubt that he was the person who bought the painting by Rombout Uylenburgh.

46 A list of Sijbrant Fries's creditors was compiled as early as 1638, RAL, ORA (access no. 508), inv. no. 50J, fol. 146-147v and 161-166, 20 July 1638; neither the widow of Rombout Uylenburgh nor her children appear on the still alarmingly long list.

47 NHA, ORA (access no. 184), inv. no. 2871, fol. 198-199, 14 January 1636.

48 In view of the magnitude of the bankruptcy, an inventory must have been drawn up in Leiden, but no such document has been found; the earliest inventories in the Bankruptcy Chamber date from 1652. I searched through the archives of notaries in Leiden and Weesp for a will drawn up by the Fries-Schouten couple, but unfortunately found nothing.

49 A daughter of this marriage was Lysbeth, who married Dirck Casteleijn in Amsterdam in 1640, GAA, DTB 675, p. 290, 29 October 1640. In 1692 the couple left a substantial estate, which refers only to the numbers of paintings in the rooms. Among them was 'a large *old-fashioned* painting' and 'an *old* painting', GAA, not. J. de Winter, NA 2415, fol. 277-283v, 5 and 8 November 1692-17 January 1693. No further details are available at present.

50 RAL, DTB 3, fol. 169v, 15 April 1625. In 1641 this Jan Hennebo, son of Robert Hennebo, signed the marriage contract of his brother Abraham Hennebo and Elisabeth Anslo (GAA, not. L. Lamberti, NA 582, 6 January 1641), the daughter of Cornelis Claesz Anslo and Aeltje Gerritsdr Schouten (see fig. 7 and 8 and Genealogy 2, p. 292).

51 See p. 175.

52 Tomkowicz 1912, pp. 170 and 152.

53 Cracow, AP, Acta Controversiarum, inv. no. 514, p. 1143, 1628; the copier in question was Laurens Cieszyński.

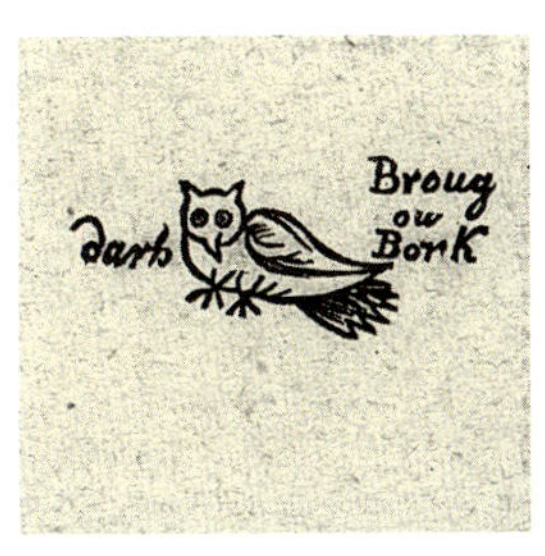

9 F. Brulliot, Dictionnaire des monogrammes, marques figurées, lettres initiales, noms abrégés.., vol. 3 (1834), p. 184, Amsterdam, Universiteitsbibliotheek

54 The 100 thaler referred to was probably the price paid for the original painting.
55 Füssli/Füssli 1779-1821, vol. 1, p. 695.
56 Von Winckelman 1796, p. 218.
57 As 'hoch 1 Schuh 10 Zoll breit 3 Schuh', Ketelsen/von Stockhausen 2002, p. 1689.
58 Brulliot 1832-1834, vol. 3, p. 184.
59 Siret 1883, p. 338 used the words 'manière d'A. Cuyp', but was probably referring to Benjamin Cuyp.
60 Leonard Bramer was another artist who used these colours for biblical scenes.
61 Nagler 1835-1852, vol. 19 (1849), p. 217.
62 Th./B vol. 34, p. 17; this painting can no longer be traced.
63 Van der Veen 2001, pp. 46-47 and note 8.

The applicant was demanding one hundred *thaler* in compensation as well as the promised copy.[54] What emerges from this incident is that Rombout Uylenburgh's work was in demand and his contemporaries were willing to pay handsomely for it. The Polish artist again undertook to make a painting for his client and to execute it to the best of his ability. But this time, too, he appears to have broken his word.

The document containing this information also reveals that the applicant was demanding the return of various goods he had supplied, including twenty dozen small paintbrushes sent by Rombout Uylenburgh 'from the Netherlands'. Unfortunately, the original Polish text is ambiguous. On the face of it, it would seem that the brushes were sent from the Republic. But it is also possible that 'from the Netherlands' refers to Rombout himself, in which case Rombout would either have sent them from Danzig or instructed someone to dispatch them from the Netherlands. In the latter case, the consignment might have come from Hendrick Uylenburgh. There is no evidence that Rombout ever visited the Republic, but it is very well possible that he went there to see his family.

Sought after during his lifetime, Rombout Uylenburgh was not entirely forgotten after his death. His name appears in a lexicon of artists dating from the closing decades of the eighteenth century. A reference book published in 1779 recalls that he was active in Danzig around 1615 and painted excellent portraits and kitchen pieces.[55] Another notes that his kitchen pieces were superior to his other work.[56] His paintings frequently appeared in auctions in both Danzig and other parts of Germany. Two that can be singled out were 'Kitchen pieces. By Ulenbork', both on canvas and both the same size, which were auctioned in Germany in 1799.[57] The fact Uylenburgh's name would no longer have been widely known raises the question of whether the paintings were signed. Of interest in this connection is a hitherto unremarked passage in a three-volume publication on monograms and other marks on paintings.[58] The third volume, dating from 1834, contains a description of a painting which was then in a private collection in Augsburg. It was a representation of a brawl between blind peasants or beggars, executed in a style that put the author of the entry in mind of 'Cuyp', which we may safely assume to have been Benjamin Gerritsz Cuyp.[59] The artist's technique was described as 'très hardie et très spirituelle' and as 'peu coloré et peint de façon, qu'on remarque dans toutes les demi-teintes le fond du bois sur lequel la peinture est pour ainsi dire ébauchée'. The author discovered a rebus on the painting which he took to be an owl (in Dutch, 'uyl', fig. 9), and as a result suggested that the work might be by 'le peintre Rombolt van Ulenbrok'. His theory is quite plausible as the mark is followed by 'Broug' or, rather, 'Bork', and before it is an illegible word, possibly 'durch', meaning 'by'. It is interesting to note that he associated the style with work by Benjamin Cuyp, whose biblical scenes, peasant groups and cavalry battles are rendered in mat greens and muted shades of greyish and yellowish brown, bordering on grisaille.[60] The author stops short of attributing the painting on the grounds that no other work was known by Rombout Uylenburgh which could be used for the purpose of comparison. A lexicon of artists published fifteen years later was less circumspect.[61]

Although numerous documents in the archives of Cracow, Danzig, Leiden and Amsterdam refer to paintings by Rombout Uylenburgh, an actual work by him was discovered only recently. At the beginning of the twentieth century a kitchen piece at the Museum of Danzig was believed to be either by, or a copy after Uylenburgh, but the work in question has since been lost.[62] However, two drawings and a painting by him, which is discussed in detail below, have since come to light. A sheet depicting *The Flight to Egypt* in the Rijksmuseum Print Room in Amsterdam (fig. 10a) was long attributed to Hendrick Uylenburgh.[63] The word 'Vylenburch' appears beneath the drawing, but it is unclear whether it is a signature or an annotation. The name 'roelant uijlenburch' is inscribed on the reverse in a seventeenth-century hand (fig. 10b), but none of the Uylenburghs were called Roelant. It was assumed that

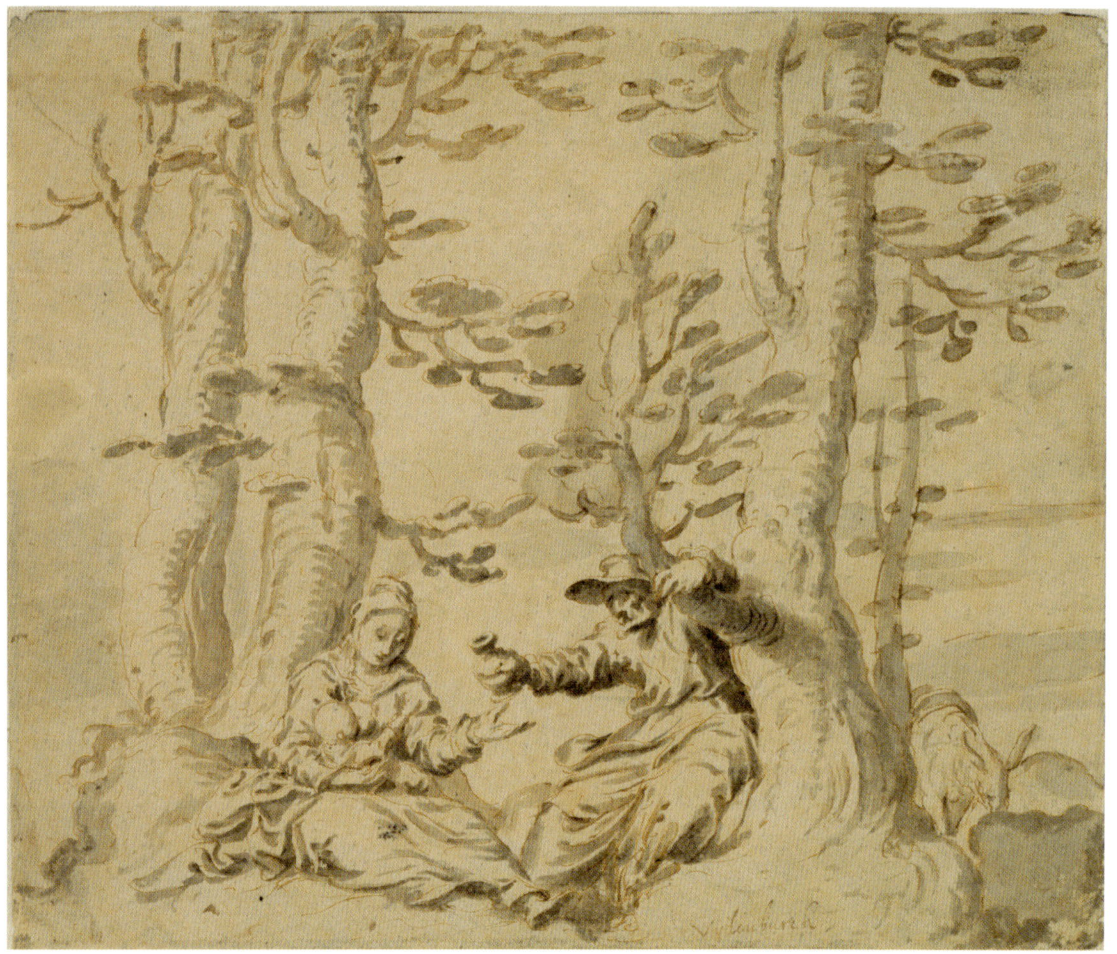

10a Rombout Uylenburgh, attributed to, The rest on the flight to Egypt, with the inscription 'Vylenburch', pen and brown ink, brush in grey, 17.5 x 21.2 cm, Amsterdam, Rijksprentenkabinet

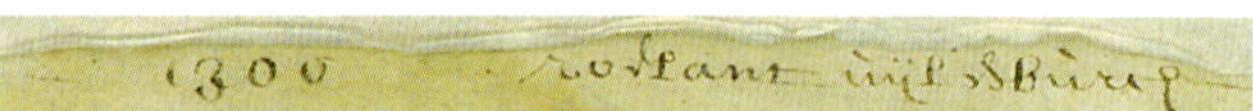

10b Inscription on the back of fig. 10a: 'roelant uijlenburch'

the person who inscribed the name, if it was not the draughtsman himself, may have meant Rombout Uylenburgh. The style of the drawing has been compared to that of Abraham Bloemaert and recalls work from the 1620s.

A second drawing, a *Diana and Actaeon* in Waldburg-Wolfegg (fig. 11), bears a close resemblance to the Amsterdam drawing.[64] Inscribed beneath it in black ink are the words 'Rombolt von Vllenburg in Danzig', followed by a cross, which might indicate that the presumed author was no longer alive when the inscription was added. Once again, it is uncertain whether this should be regarded as a signature. If this is not the case, it was not simply conjecture by an astute contemporary – the artist was too obscure – but an attribution by someone with first-hand information. In this connection the qualification 'in Danzig' is especially significant. If the two sheets are examined side by side, it is clear that the rendering of the trees is identical. However, the drawing in Wolfegg is sketchier than the Amsterdam sheet, and as a result it is difficult to compare the figures. Both sheets are the same size and both are pen drawings in brown ink with a pale grey wash. The composition of the Wolfegg drawing recalls some of Abraham Bloemaert's work, while the execution hints at Southern Netherlandish or even Italian influences.

From the documents Rombout Uylenburgh emerges as a versatile artist who employed a

64 Tylicki 2005, p. 245 (with ill.) and 286. Dr Jacek Tylicki kindly allowed us to study the as yet unpublished text of a lecture given in Danzig in 2003 in which he examines the *Diana and Actaeon* in relation to the drawing at the Rijksmuseum Print Room in Amsterdam.

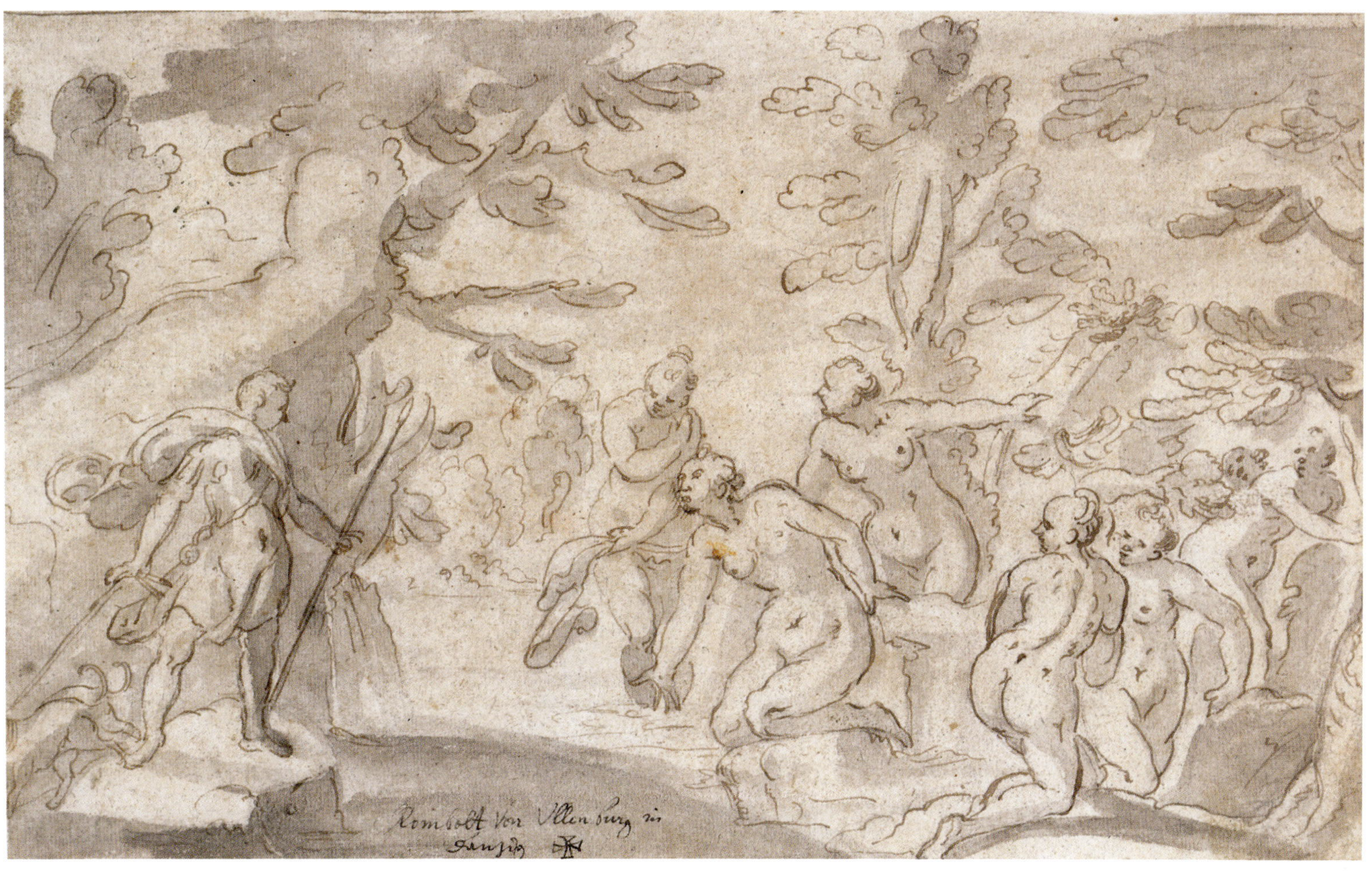

11 Rombout Uylenburgh, attributed to, Diana and Acteon, with the inscription 'Rombolt Von Vllenburg in Danzig', pen and brown ink, washed in grey, 16.8 x 27.6 cm, Wolfegg, Fürstlich von Waldburg-Wolfegg'sche Kunstsammlungen

range of techniques and painted biblical subjects, kitchen pieces and market scenes as well as the occasional portrait. A print after a portrait of the Mennonite teacher Jan Gerritsz van Emden bears the inscription 'Uijlenburch pinxit' and notes that the painting was made in 1616 (fig. 12). From 1607 to 1617 Van Emden was a preacher in Danzig, where Rombout Uylenburgh was active from 1612 on. It is safe to assume that the portraitist was Uylenburgh. The print appeared in a compilation of sermons by Jan Gerritsz, published in Amsterdam in 1650.[65] It was made by

Cornelis van Dalen and based on a drawing by 'J. Casteleyn' after the painted portrait by Uylenburgh. Casteleyn worked in Haarlem and the original may have been in the home of Jan Gerritsz's eldest son, who was living in Haarlem at the time of his father's death in Danzig in 1617.

A contemporary reference to work by Rombout Uylenburgh occurs in an auction catalogue of 1684, announcing the sale of 'a grisaille History of Athalia by Rombout Uylenburgh for f 7:6:-' and 'the Death of Athalia, by the same artist, for f 15'.[66] A catalogue of 1997 advertising

65 Two different editions are known, both published in Amsterdam. The preface notes that that the first edition, published by Adriaen Roman in Haarlem in 1617, had been sold out for some time. I have not managed to trace a copy of that edition to ascertain whether it included a portrait of Jan Gerritsz.

66 'Catalogus van schilderyen, van den graaf van Arondel, verkocht den 26. September 1684. in Amsterdam', in Hoet 1752, vol. 1, pp. 1-4, notably p. 3, nos. 33 and 34. The auction of 1684 concerned the art holdings of Thomas Howard, the son of the famous English collector of the same name.

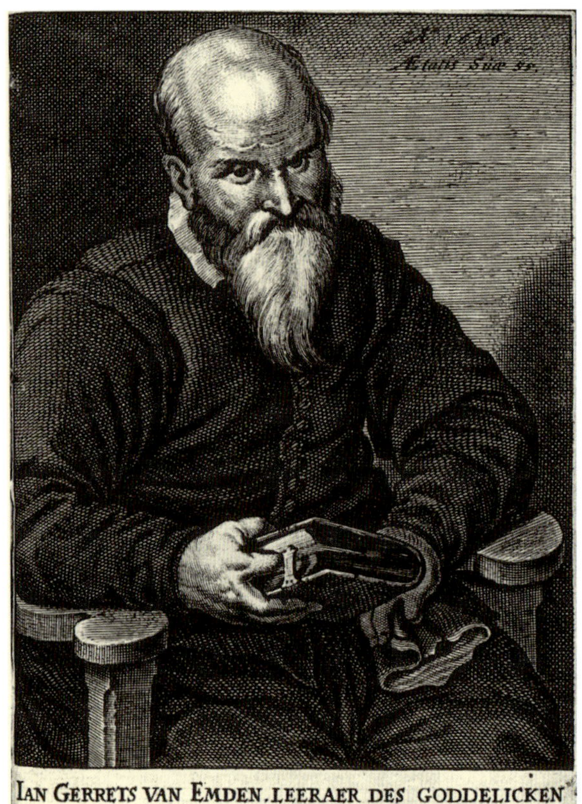

12 Cornelis van Dalen after J. Casteleijn after (Rombout?) Uylenburgh, Portrait of Jan Gerritsz van Emden, signed 'Uijlenburgh pinxit J. Casteleijn delineavit C. v. Dalen sculp:', with the date and inscription 'A° 1616 Aetatis Suae 55', engraving, 11.8 x 9.1 cm, Amsterdam, Universiteitsbibliotheek, Mennonietenzaal

the sale of a painting in New York linked the work in question to the first of the two mentioned above.[67] The astute attribution to Rombout Uylenburgh was by Willem van de Watering, who observed that this scene from the Book of Kings had rarely, if ever, been depicted in Dutch art. The painting in New York was acquired for the Rembrandthuis (fig. 13).[68]

The work is unusual for a number of reasons. The biblical subject was scarcely ever represented in seventeenth-century painting, the grisaille technique in itself is uncommon and, most importantly, it is the only identified painting by Rombout Uylenburgh. It is significant that the Athalia referred to in 1684 was a grisaille. It transpires from a document published after 1997 that Rombout Uylenburgh produced a large number of grisailles. In 1627 his brother Hendrick Uylenburgh possessed the following sixteen works: 'four grey paintings by Romtelt

van Uylenborch', 'two more grisailles ditto by the same Uylenborch, slightly smaller, all six of them biblical scenes', 'another two grisailles ditto by the said Uijlenborch, one depicting Tobit and the other a Judgment' and 'eight more grisailles ditto, half the size, including several scenes from the bible'.[69] The painting acquired by the Rembrandthuis may have been one of these works. As we have seen, the Athalia auctioned in 1684 was accompanied by a counterpart, and from the document of 1627 we know that Rombout Uylenburgh produced biblical scenes in series.

A grisaille is a painting executed in different tones of a single colour, most commonly white, grey, black or brown. In seventeenth-century Holland such works were called 'graeuwtjes' (deriving from the Dutch word for 'grey') or 'black and whites'.[70] Light and shadow are used to suggest depth, and the effect can be emphasised by the application of white heightening. The object is to create an illusionistic bas-relief. In the eighteenth century Gerard de Lairesse was acclaimed for his paintings of 'recesses with white marble bas-reliefs that embellish entrance halls along the Keizersgracht and Herengracht in Amsterdam, so lifelike that they could be taken for sculpted marble'.[71] Grisailles were also made on paper, as design sketches for engravings. Before selling them, the artist would sometimes transfer the image on to canvas or panel and perhaps produce an enlarged version. Rembrandt's *Sermon of Saint John the Baptist* is a good example of this kind of work, which was always in demand (see fig. 109).

Grisailles were also made for the market, as works of art in their own right. Biblical scenes were particularly sought after and it may be

67 Sale catalogue Sotheby's New York, 30 January 1997, no. 144. Robert Schillemans, curator of Museum Amstelkring in Amsterdam, drew our attention to the publication of the painting in this catalogue.

68 With financial support from the Titus Circle of the Rembrandt Association and a generous contribution from the Friends of the Rembrandthuis Museum.

69 Van der Veen 2001, pp. 49-51 and below pp. 121-124.

70 De Pauw-de Veen 1969, pp. 113-116, and the entry 'grisaille' in *The Dictionary of Art* vol. 13(1996), pp. 672-677.

71 Houbraken 1718-1721, vol. 3, pp. 117-118.

that Mennonites were the principal clients. The Rembrandthuis painting illustrates a passage from the Book of Kings (2 Kings 11, 13-15), an episode of special significance to Mennonites. It shows the story of Queen Athalia, a worshipper of Baal, whom the priest Joiada imprisoned in the temple after she had proclaimed her seven-year-old nephew and his own protégé, Joas, king. The scene was occasionally illustrated in prints in the sixteenth century, but no other painted version of it is known from the first half of the seventeenth century. These facts taken together leave no doubt that the attribution to Rombout Uylenburgh is correct: firstly, we have a seventeenth-century reference to a grisaille *Athalia* by Uylenburgh, and secondly, there is no record of any other painting of this subject.

In terms of style, Rombout Uylenburgh's *Athalia* can be placed in the context of early seventeenth-century Dutch painting. Adriaen van de Venne painted numerous grisailles, but

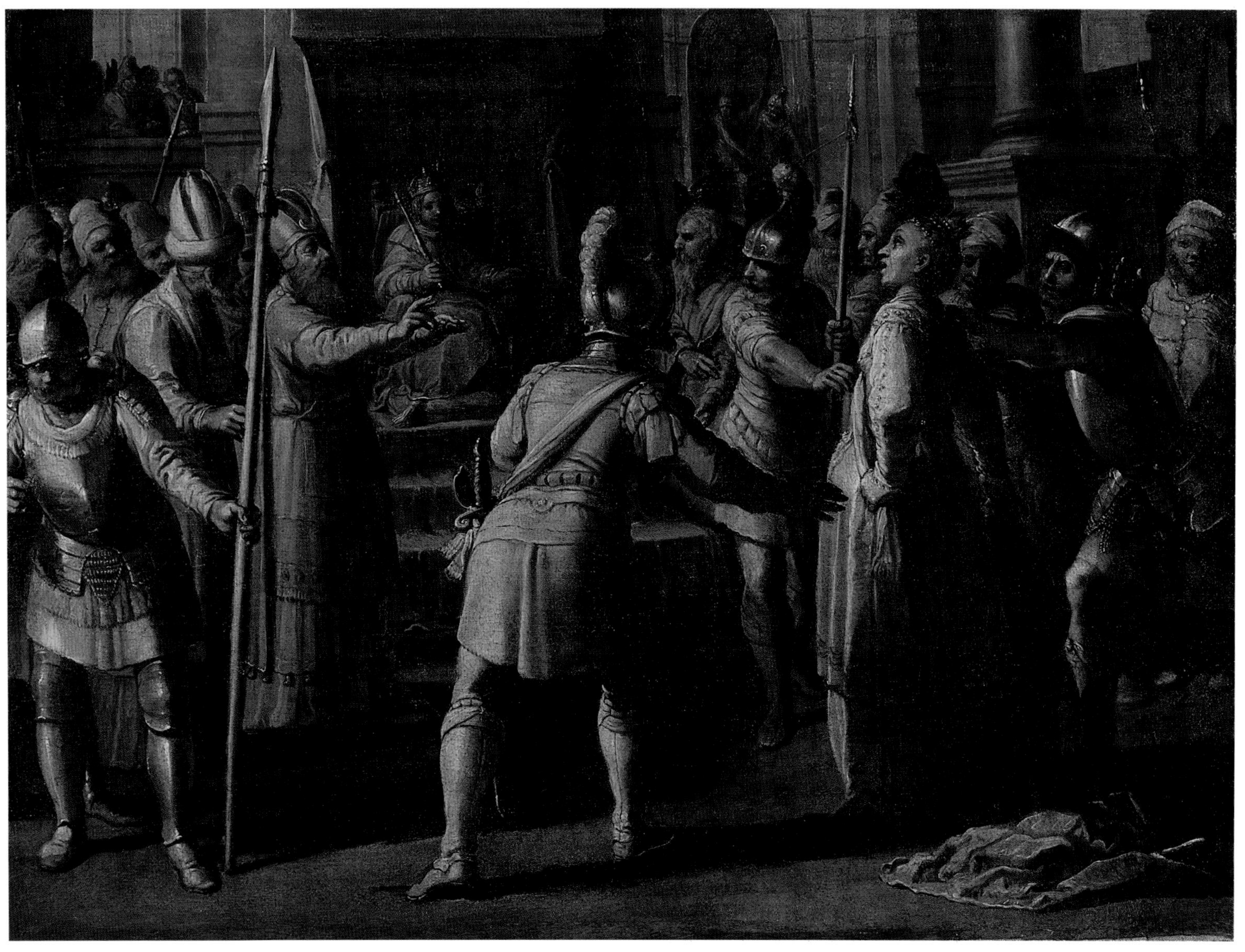

13 Rombout Uylenburgh, Athaliah driven from the temple, canvas, 39.7 x 54.3 cm, Amsterdam, The Rembrandt House Museum

opted for allegorical or moralistic subjects. In any event, it would appear that Uylenburgh's grisailles predated those by Van de Venne.[72] Uylenburgh's work is a fine piece of art and can be tentatively dated to c. 1620.

Hendrick Uylenburgh and Maria van Eyck

HENDRICK UYLENBURGH, AGENT OF THE KING OF POLAND

Although Hendrick Uylenburgh's date of birth is unknown, it is almost certain that he was the youngest child of Gerard Uylenburgh and his first wife Sara. The existing documents contradict one another regarding his age. In December 1649 Hendrick Uylenburgh signed a document stating that he was approximately sixty years old, in which case he would have been born around 1589.[73] A deed of 16 September 1653, gives his age as sixty-six, which puts his date of birth at around 1587.[74] Towards the end of 1654 he made a statement before a notary, giving his age as seventy,[75] which implies that he was born 1584. To avoid any error we shall assume that he was born between 1584 and 1589.[76] His place of birth is unknown. Hendrick is described as a 'painter' in archive documents in Amsterdam, so he presumably studied painting, like his brother Rombout. Though it is doubtful that he actually practised, his training would have been indispensable for his work as an art dealer later in life. What we do know for certain is that he served as an agent and trade emissary to the king of Poland in the early 1620s. On 19 March 1620 the States-General in The Hague gave Hendrick Uylenburgh permission to transport a large number of paintings to the king of Poland, 'exempt from convoy tariff'. He was to produce evidence within four months that the consignment had been delivered. According to the decrees of the States, the shipment consisted of 'sixteen religious paintings, sixteen poetic works, eighteen landscapes, six paintings of fruit, four battle scenes, eight pictures of ships, twelve apostles, twelve emperors and twenty double-barrelled rifles, both long and short'.[77] In other words, Hendrick was exporting not only ninety-two paintings, but also a consignment of firearms. A year later, on 23 April 1621, Archduke Albert and the Infanta Isabella in Brussels granted Uylenburgh clearance from the port of Antwerp for paintings, precious objects and other works of art, once again to be delivered to the king of Poland.[78]

The Dutch document notes that he was conducting business 'at the king's behest', while the clearance from Brussels states that he had acquired the paintings and other art works in Antwerp 'in the service and at the command of His Majesty of Poland'.[79] The fact that Uylenburgh obtained a permit from The Hague on the first occasion and from Brussels a year later was probably connected with the ending of the Twelve Year Truce (1609-1621). The ceasefire between Spain and the Republic had facilitated the movement of persons and goods between the Northern and Southern Netherlands, which became more difficult after the resumption of hostilities. Uylenburgh received clearance from the Archduke and the Infanta on 23 April 1621, thirteen days after the truce had expired. It would therefore have been easier and safer for him to dispatch the goods directly from Antwerp.

72 The earliest dated monochrome paintings by Adriaen van de Venne are from 1621 (Amsterdam, Rijksmuseum, inv. no. C 606 and 607), the large portrait of the Winter King and his wife and retinue (Rijksmuseum, inv. no. A 958) in grisaille dates from 1628. The grisailles, many of which carry an allegorical inscription, date from the second half of the 1620s and the 1630s. His monochrome *Adoration,* at the Nationalmuseum in Stockholm, is dated 1644.
73 GAA, not. G. Coren, NA 1000, 21 December 1649.
74 GAA, not. J. van der Hoeven, NA 1649, pp. 1239-1240, 16 September 1653; see below p. 201.
75 GAA, not. L. Lamberti, NA 604, p. 622, 23 December 1654; Bredius 1915-1922, vol. 5, p. 1689 (o).
76 The fact that the division of his father's estate in Cracow took place only in 1609, about eight years after his death in 1601, may have been because his sons were minors. If Hendrick attained the age of majority in 1609, his year of birth might have been 1584. The age of majority was 25.
77 The Hague, National Archives, Archives of the States-General, no. 45, 1620, fol. 87. The section on the export of arts works by Uylenburgh in 1620 and 1621 is an abridgment of Lammertse 2002.
78 First published by Pinchart 1859. The document was recovered and published again in Szmydki 2002, pp. 152-153.
79 'Leurs Altesses Séréniesimes [..] ont [...] ordonné et ordonnent par ceste aux officiers des licences en Anvers, de laisser passer librement et franchement par la rivière de l'Escault, les peintures, raretez et aultres œuvres artificielz que le suppliant [Henry Ulenborch] at achapté pardeça pour le service et par ordre de Sa Majesté de Poloigne'.

Unfortunately, little is known about the objects in question. The document in The Hague gives a brief description of the subjects of the paintings, but says nothing about the artists. From various other documents, however, it can be inferred that the 'twelve apostles' were probably by Anthony van Dyck. The documents in question were drawn up in 1660 and 1661 in connection with a dispute over the authenticity of a series of paintings.[80] The Antwerp art connoisseur Canon François Hillewerve had purchased a series of twelve apostles in 1660 on the understanding that they were 'genuine originals' by Van Dyck. Shortly afterwards he concluded that he had been duped. As a result, he instituted legal proceedings in which virtually every painter in Antwerp was called in to testify.

The controversy centred on paintings dating from forty years earlier, so few were able to give first-hand evidence. Van Dyck had died in 1641, but two of his erstwhile assistants, Herman Servaes and Justus van Egmont, asserted that they were employed at the studio when the master was in the process of painting the series. They identified one or two of the paintings as copies that they themselves had made after Van Dyck's originals. But Van Dyck, they insisted, had added the finishing touches.[81]

The statement given by Jacob Jordaens is of particular relevance here. On 11 July 1661 this celebrated Antwerp painter stated that Hillewerve's series consisted of copies, and testified to 'having seen the originals in 1622 or thereabouts, unintelligible, which at the time were bought by a certain Henricus Vuylenborch, whom the attestant knew personally and with whom he had conducted various transactions. Three days before Whitsun this year, he, the attestant, had seen the foresaid originals by Antonio van Dyck in Utrecht, where they were presumably still located'.[82] Even earlier, in October 1660, the painter Abraham Snellinck stated that he had seen the originals in Antwerp. By his account, they had been 'bought by a person called … Bontemuts, who had taken them out of the country thirty-six years ago, at a guess, if not before'.[83] There can be no doubt that 'Bontemuts' (literally: fur hat) referred to Uylenburgh. Fur hats were commonly worn in Poland and Hendrick Uylenburgh, an emissary of the King of Poland, would surely have possessed one.[84] Dressed in Polish costume, he would have been a conspicuous figure in Antwerp and an obvious target for a nickname.

As we see from the above testimonies, the witnesses were unable to say exactly when Uylenburgh had taken the paintings. The dates they gave in other affidavits in the case range from 1615/16 to 1624. In February 1618 Van Dyck was appointed master of the Antwerp artists' guild; in October 1620 he left for a short visit to England, and in the intervening years he had a workshop in Antwerp known as the Cologne Cathedral (Dom van Ceulen). The apostle series – both the original and other versions – were most probably made during this period.[85]

Hence, Uylenburgh may have acquired the twelve apostles from Van Dyck in Antwerp shortly before obtaining permission to export them in March 1620. Unfortunately, the authors of the other paintings that Uylenburgh took to Poland are unknown, but at least some of these works were probably produced in Antwerp. The second batch he exported in 1621 are explicitly said to have been purchased in Antwerp.

None of Van Dyck's apostle series have survived intact. A German art dealer possessed a complete series from 1914 to 1920, but sold the pieces individually. These paintings came from Genoa and are first documented at the auction of Palazzo Brignole in 1748. Five apostles once belonging to a complete series were, until recently, at Althorp House. The series was first recorded in the collection of Robert Spencer, who had probably bought them in London 1693 at the auction of Prosper Henry Lankrink, where a complete series was offered for sale (see fig. 14).[86] Five pieces of a third series are in Dresden (figs. 15-17). They first appear in the inventory of the electors of Saxony in 1722-1728 and were acquired for the collection during the reign of Augustus II, Elector of Saxony and King of Poland.[87]

All three series are described in recent publications as original works by Van Dyck. In any

80 The documents is the case were published in Galesloot 1868. See Lammertse 2002 and the incorporated bibliography.
81 Statement of 11 November 1660, Galesloot 1868, pp. 598-599.
82 Statement of 11 July 1661, Galesloot 1868, p. 602.
83 Statement of 29 October 1660, Galesloot 1868, pp. 603-604.
84 On conventional Polish dress, see Zygulski 1965.
85 For theories on the dating of the various apostle series, see Lammertse 2002 and Barnes/De Poorter/Millar/Vey 2004, pp. 67-80.
86 The painting from Museum Boijmans Van Beuningen in Rotterdam which is reproduced here was in the collection of the Duke of Devonshire in the eighteenth century, Barnes/De Poorter/Millar/Vey 2004, pp. 67-80.
87 See Barnes/De Poorter/Millar/Vey 2004, pp. 67-80.

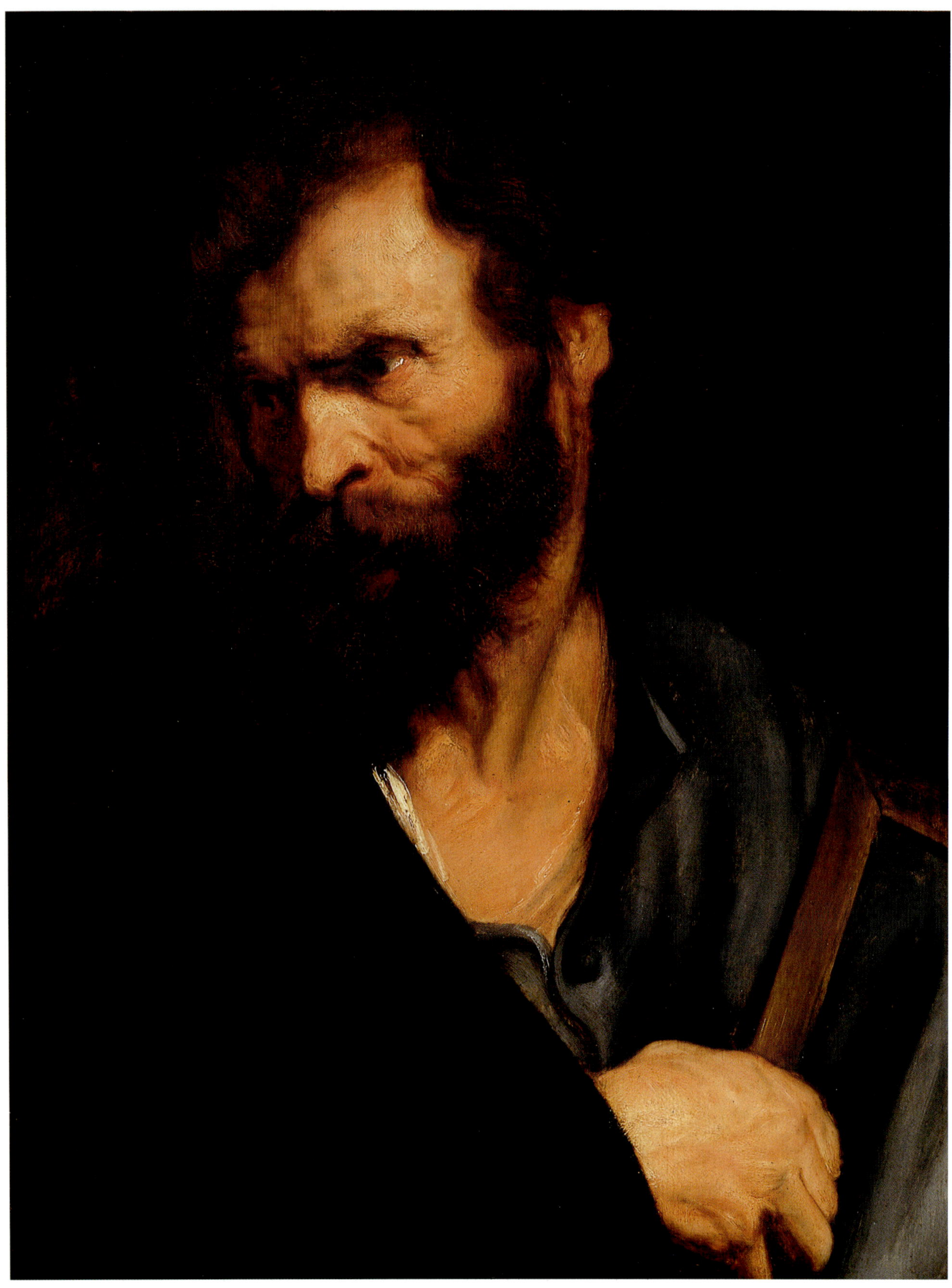

14 Anthony van Dyck, The apostle Judas Thaddeus, panel, 63.5 x 48.3 cm, Rotterdam, Boijmans Van Beuningen Museum

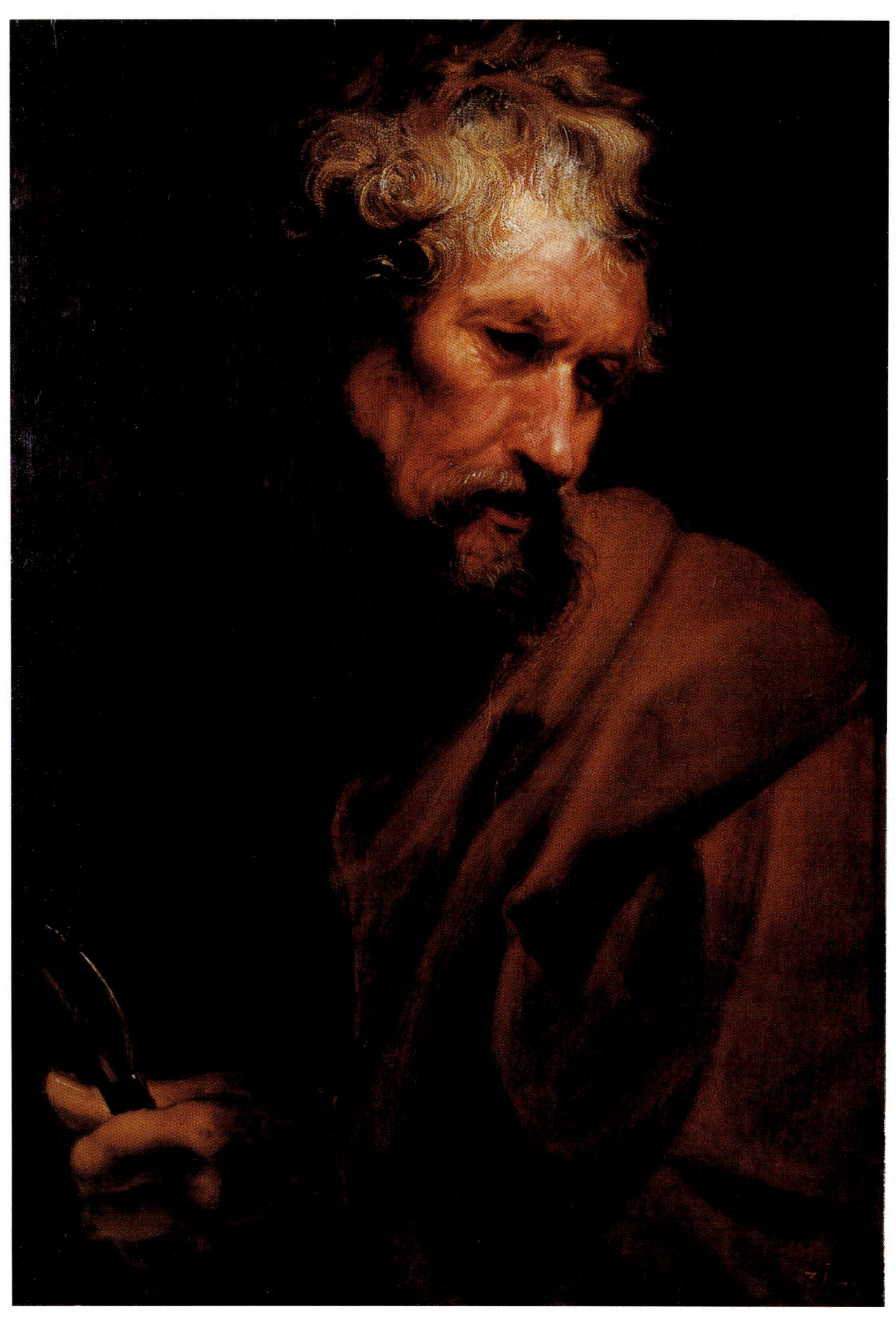

15 Anthony van Dyck, The apostle Bartholomew, panel, 62.5 x 46.5 cm, Dresden, Staatliche Kunstsammlungen Dresden, Gemäldegalerie Alte Meister

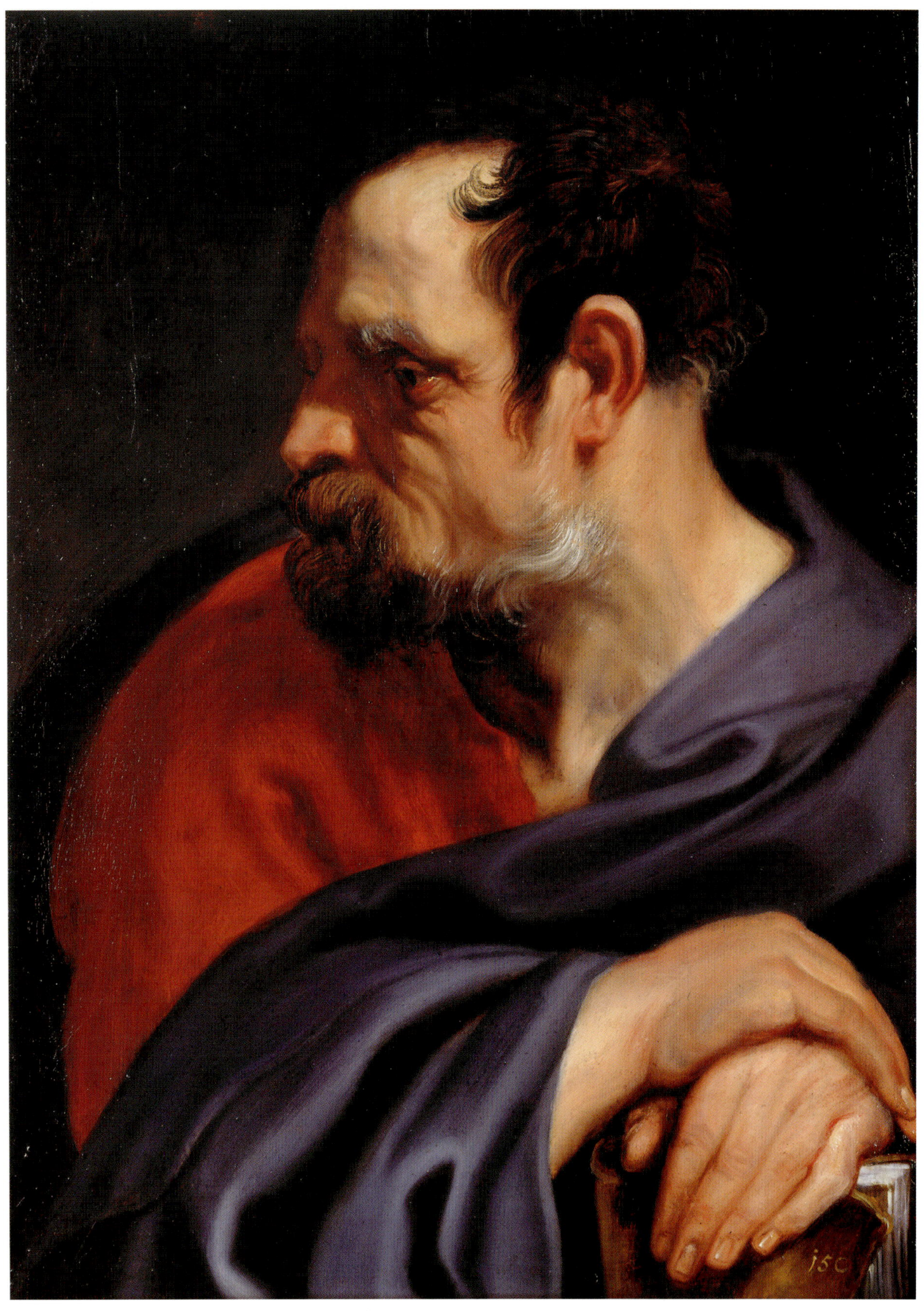

16 Anthony van Dyck, the apostle Matthew, panel, 63 x 46.5 cm, Dresden, Staatliche Kunstsammlungen Dresden, Gemäldegalerie Alte Meister

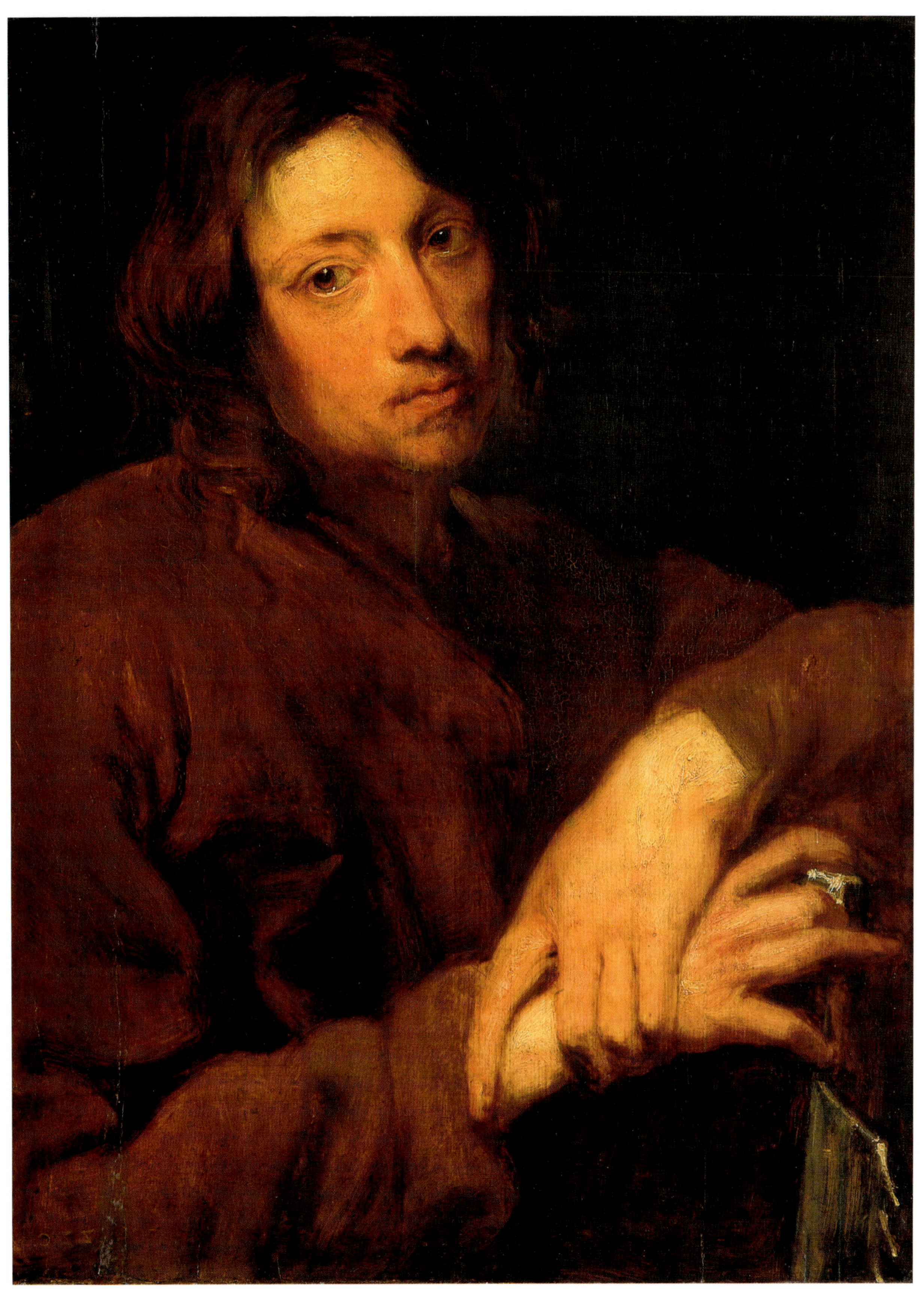

17 Anthony van Dyck, The apostle Simon, panel, 63 x 48 cm, Dresden, Staatliche Kunstsammlungen Dresden, Gemäldegalerie Alte Meister

event they come from his workshop. In all three cases the paintings vary in quality,[88] and it is very much the question whether Van Dyck himself ever painted a complete series. Right from the start these series may have comprised both originals and retouched copies. None of them has a provenance dating back to the beginning of the seventeenth century, and none is so exceptional in terms of quality that it could be taken for the original. It is therefore difficult to ascertain which series Uylenburgh acquired for the king of Poland, but considering the close historical ties between Poland and Saxony, it is most likely to have been the series in Dresden.[89]

MARIA VAN EYCK:
ORIGINALLY FROM WEESP
AND RESIDING IN DANZIG?

There is reason to believe that Hendrick Uylenburgh met his future wife in Danzig, where his brother Rombout had settled in 1612. He was married by the time he moved to Amsterdam, in or shortly before 1625. Until recently almost nothing was known about Maria van Eyck. Not long after her death in Amsterdam in 1638, her cousin by marriage, Bartelt Jansz, gave Hendrick Uylenburgh permission to remain in the house he had lived in with Maria. The document to this effect has yielded vital information about the family of Uylenburgh's wife.[90]

On 11 January 1614, the 26-year-old Bartelt Jansz published the banns of his marriage to Aeltje Marcus in Amsterdam.[91] Originally from Leens in Groningen, he had been living in Amsterdam for several years and gave his occupation as needlemaker. Aeltje Marcus, aged 27, came from Weesp and was still living there at the time. The betrothal contract notes that her father 'Marcus van Eycken' gave his consent to the marriage at the secretary's office. Her father's

surname was the key new material: Maria van Eyck had a cousin living in Amsterdam by the name of Aeltje Marcusdr van Eyck. On the basis of this information, it was possible to carry out further research in Amsterdam and Weesp (see Genealogy 2, p. 292). Within a short space of time the aforementioned Bartelt Jansz was a prosperous iron merchant in Amsterdam. He bought a house there in 1615. He and his wife were prominent members of the Flemish Mennonite church, where Bartelt Jansz served as deacon from approximately 1628 to 1658.

The founder of the Van Eyck family in Weesp, Dirck van Eyck, must have had at least three children who survived to adulthood. One of his sons was a bricklayer in Weesp and the latter's two children, both sons, later settled in Amsterdam. The second son, Marcus Dircksz van Eyck was a burgher of Weesp and the owner of a home there. He was married twice and fathered seven children. Aeltje Marcus was born of his first marriage. If she was indeed a first cousin of Maria van Eyck, then Maria must have been the child of Dirck van Eyck's third son, who was most probably Isaack van Eyck. Information about him is sparse. His wife's name, for instance, is unknown, but we do know that he was living in Danzig at the same time as the brothers Rombout and Hendrick Uylenburgh. In 1618 two Amsterdam merchants in their capacity as the guardians of a girl authorised a third guardian, Isaack van Eyck of Danzig, and one other party to wind up the girl's parents' estate.[92] Both of those Amsterdam merchants were Mennonites. The names Maria gave her children corroborate the hypothesis that Isaack van Eyck was her father. It was customary at the time to name the firstborn son after his paternal grandfather and the second son after his maternal grandfather. The eldest son of Hendrick Uylenburgh and Maria van Eyck was called Gerrit, after Gerard Rommertsz, the second son

<hr>

88 Ibid.

89 However, this undermines Jordaens's statement of 1661 to the effect that he had seen the painting Uylenburgh bought in the 1620s a short time earlier in Utrecht. Considering that the two series are very similar, it is feasible that, forty years later, he mistook one for the other. On the other hand, he may have been correct, in which case the paintings must have left the Polish Royal Collection and found their way to Dresden by some other route.

90 Ruud Lambour's assistance in identifying this person is greatly appreciated.

91 GAA, DTB 667, p. 108, 11 January 1614; they were married in the Mennonite church on 26 January of that year; the magistrates were subsequently notified to that effect, GAA, DTB 1008, p. 9, undated.

92 GAA, not. J. Franssen Bruijningh, NA 151, fol. 148v-149, 9 March 1618 and fol. 198-199, 29 March 1618.

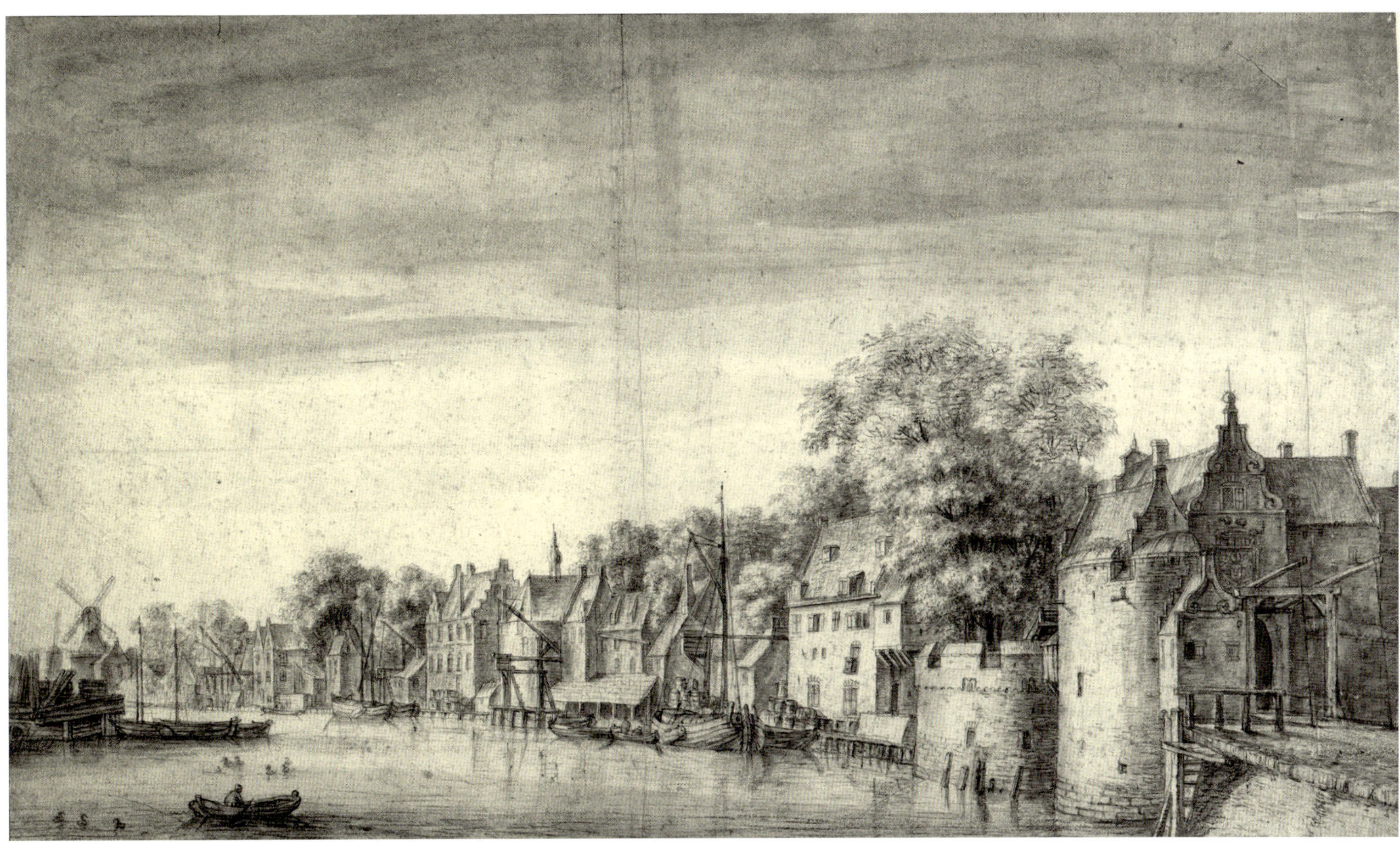

Isaack, most probably after Isaack van Eyck. The third son Rombertus was named after a relative on his father's side, and Marcus presumably after his great-uncle Marcus van Eyck in Weesp.

The Van Eycks were established and well-connected members of the Weesp community. One of Marcus Dircksz van Eyck's brothers-in-law served several terms as a magistrate between 1612 and 1623,[93] and Marcus himself was comfortably off. In 1608, after the death of his first wife, he undertook to support his four daughters – one being Aeltje – and to endow each with 350 guilders. He guaranteed this pledge by mortgaging a house and land.[94] One of his sons was appointed magistrate of Weesp in 1639 and on several subsequent occasions, another was a tax functionary. Weesp was a thriving community in the early seventeenth century. In 1616 Pieter

93 Lasman Willemsz the brother of Haesje Willemsdr, who was married to Marcus Dircksz van Eyck.
94 NHA, Weesp, ORA (access no. 184), inv. no. 2933, fol. 109r-v, 9 February 1608; his children were allowed to retain the household effects that their grandfather had promised them. This document was signed by Marcus Dircksz van Eyck and his brother-in-law Lasman Willemsz. A note in the margin records that Bartelt Jansz received the said sum of money from his father-in-law on 7 June 1614. In 1621 Marcus van Eyck represented the child of one of his daughters, who had died; he owed that child two hundred guilders and ten guilders a year in interest, ibid., fol. 225, 7 August 1621 and ibid., fol. 225v. In 1652 the brother Dirck and Isaack van Eyck agreed to share an as yet undivided portion of a house and land in Weesp; the house was 'inherited through the death of her late parents and sister'. The house was appraised at no less than 2,775 guilders and was transferred to Dirck van Eyck, a magistrate of Weesp at the time, NHA, Weesp, not. S. Jansz Verlaen, NA 5184, 20 January 1652. The name of the deceased sister is not mentioned. Four years later the widow of Dirck Marcusz van Eyck passed on to the children of his first marriage the portion of the inheritance to which his children were lawfully entitled, which included silverwork, two gold rings, clothing and more than eighty guilders, being the proceeds of clothing sold, NHA, ORA Weesp, inv. no. 2934, fol. 219v, 25 November 1656; ibid., fol. 220, 23 January 1649, fol. 220v, 20 May 1660, fol. 221, 25 March and 6 May 1662 and fol. 221v, 19 June 1670. Dirck Marcusz van Eyck was related to Gijsbert Jansz Sybilla (ca. 1597-1655), painter and burgomaster of Weesp. In 1652 Sybilla painted a portrait of the judicial authorities of Weesp, which shows not only burgomaster Cornelis Schouten and the magistrates Jacob Leeuw, but also Dirck Marcusz van Eyck.

Cornelisz Hooft reported that the town had for some time been 'munificently blessed with prosperity and a burgeoning population'.[95] Hooft was in a position to know. He was bailiff of Gooiland, drost of Muiden, high bailiff and dike reeve of Weesp and Weesperkarspel. And in any event, he had family living there.

The population of Weesp was approximately 2,300 in 1620 (fig. 18).[96] Its beer industry, the mainstay of the local economy, flourished in the first quarter of the century. The town had about a dozen breweries, the largest of which belonged to the Schouten family. Clean water was readily available from the Vecht, the Smal Weesp and the Gein rivers, which were also ideal waterways for transport. Amsterdam was within easy reach by water, and a ferry plied daily between the two towns. Weesp was strongly oriented towards Amsterdam and its wealthiest families, like that of Laurens Cornelisz Schouten, possessed homes in both towns. The Uylenburghs maintained close ties with Weesp: the family of Rombout Uylenburgh's wife lived in Weesp, Hendrick Uylenburgh's wife came from there, in 1629 Hendrick himself represented the guardians of Swaentje Cornelisdr Schouten, his financier Pieter Gerritsz Hooft lived there, as did Rombout Uylenburgh's brother-in-law Sijbrant Haye Fries as well as various members of the Anslo and Leeuw families and, as we shall see in chapter 3, those of the Van Tongerlo and Haesbaert families, both of which were closely associated with the Uylenburgh firm. What is more, most, if not all, of them were Mennonites.

There was nothing unusual in the fact that one of Dirck van Eyck's sons was living in Danzig. By the beginning of the seventeenth century Danzig had emerged as the most important seaport in the Baltic. It attracted large numbers of people from the Dutch Republic, many of whom settled there permanently. Others lived there for varying lengths of time, often as agents or representatives of trading companies. They were sent abroad on the basis of trust, and those who commissioned them felt safer engaging members of their families. This was particularly true in the case of Mennonite families. One of these agents was the merchant Reijer Claesz of

Enkhuizen,[97] who worked in Danzig for several years before moving to Amsterdam, where he died in 1638. An inventory of his possessions was taken in December of that year.[98] The list of his household goods is followed by an itemised schedule of his ledgers, debit books, account books, registers and journals, from which it emerges that he lived in Danzig from 1608, or possibly earlier, until the spring of 1618. One of these ledgers covers the years 1609 and 1610 in 'Dantsich'. At the back of another, covering the whole of 1608, is an inscription which says 'trading in currency etc. in Dansic in partnership with Herman Wolff and Isaac van Eyck from 7 December 1612 to 2 May 1614'.

Deeds from Danzig confirm that Isaack van Eyck was an associate of Herman Wolff and Reijer Claesz from 1612 to 1614. He had formed a partnership with one of his compatriots and a local merchant-banker to export 'rijksdaalders' to the Netherlands which they exchanged there for coins with a low silver content, and these they brought back to Danzig. The people of Danzig objected to this form of speculation on the grounds that it depleted their reserves of valuable coins, and managed to have Van Eyck arrested.[99] We do not know how the affair ended, whether Isaack van Eyck remained in Danzig or whether, like his partner Reijer Claesz, he subsequently returned to the Republic. An important point in this episode of currency speculation is that it was Dutch Mennonite families in and around Danzig who entrusted vast sums of money to 'Isaak van Eicken and his sons'.[100] Perhaps he was a fellow-believer as well as a compatriot. In theory, the money was going to Koningsbergen, which at the time belonged to Poland, but from there it was forwarded to Holland. More information is needed to ascertain whether it was sent predominantly to Amsterdam.[101]

Reijer Claesz was a close associate of Isaack van Eyck, but he must also have been in touch with the Uylenburghs. Once again, his religion played a role. In 1620 Reijer Claesz was elected deacon of the Waterland church in Amsterdam. According to the list of candidates, he had 'come here from Dantzick'.[102] The Van Eycks were

95 Van Tricht 1976-1979, vol. I, p. 284.
96 Unless otherwise mentioned, the information on Weesp is based on Zondergeld-Hamer 1990.
97 Bogucka 1990, p. 24.
98 GAA, not. J. Cornelisz Hoogeboom, NA 840, 10 and 11 December 1638.
99 Bogucka 1990, p. 30, which refers to Jacob Jacobson van Emden as a partner.
100 Bogucka 1971, p. 68.
101 More people in Danzig were involved in money speculation 'die übrigens nicht nur mit Amsterdam Beziehungen unterhielten', Bogucka 1971, p. 68. This could imply that Isaack van Eyck also conducted transactions with Amsterdam.

Mennonites as well, but the two families had far more in common. In 1624 Reijer Claesz's son Hans Reijers married Stijntje Gerritsdr Niesen, the sister of Lysbeth Gerritsdr Niesen, who married Joris Sijen a couple of years later. The relationship between Uylenburgh and the Mennonite Pieter Sijen is discussed in Chapter 3. Hans Reijers also had business dealings with the brothers Jan and Pieter Hooft, who were related by marriage to Rombout Uylenburgh and investors in his brother Hendrick's business. From a hitherto unpublished document of 1631 we learn that Reijers possessed a large collection of paintings, including one by Rombout Uylenburgh.

In 1631 Hans Reijers, who owed 6,600 guilders to Jan and Pieter Gerritsz Hooft, drew up a list of possessions that would serve as security. It includes a large number of paintings, among them the following panels: three by 'Jacques Foeckeer' (and another by him on copper), three by Joos de Momper (the Younger?), two by Esaias van de Velde, and one each by Frans Francken (the Younger?), 'Pieter Kuijper' (Hendrick Cuyper?), Hans Jordaens (the Elder?), Pieter Quast, Jan van Goyen, Roelant Saverij, Pieter (de) Molijn and (Cornelis or Herman) Saftleven. Reijers also owned canvases by Jan Lievens and Alexander Keirincx, one by 'a master in Italy' and one by the aforementioned Hans Jordaens. The last painting on the list was a panel 'done by Romboet Ulenburch'.[103] This document is a testament to the artistic sensibility of Amsterdam's Mennonite business community. Hans Reijers appears to have bought work by the Leiden painter Jan Lievens from the artist himself. In any event, in 1632 he owed him three hundred guilders as 'the final instalment for the purchase and delivery of a painting'.[104] He may well have bought the painting by Rombout Uylenburgh from Hendrick Uylenburgh who, as we have seen, had family and other ties with the Sijen and Reijers families. In that event, other works

on the list – some of them by Antwerp painters – may also have come from Uylenburgh, who just at that time, in the 1620s, was predominantly interested in the Southern Netherlandish art market. But it is also possible that Reijers acquired the work directly from Rombout Uylenburgh in Danzig, as Reijers's father lived there for many years.

An inventory of the contents of the late Reijer Claesz's home in Amsterdam includes five paintings in the front room and eleven in the room behind it, valued by two sworn appraisers at prices ranging from one to fifty guilders. The most expensive was a painting of 'nudes' by Cornelis Cornelisz van Haarlem (fifty guilders), followed by an anonymous *Incredulity of Saint Thomas* (thirty guilders). Reijer Claesz lived in Danzig until 1618 and may well have bought the painting by Rombout Uylenburgh there. If so, he must have taken it with him when he returned to Amsterdam, after which it ended up in the home of his son. The family may have possessed other works by Rombout, who was living in Danzig at the time, but there is no evidence to this effect, as the inventory of Reijer Claezs's paintings does not name the artists. Intriguingly, however, it refers to five 'grisaille paintings in ebony frames' and a 'vegetable market', and as we now know, Rombout Uylenburgh produced both grisailles and market pieces.[105]

The preceding paragraphs have established that Hendrick Uylenburgh's wife, Maria van Eyck, was born in Weesp as the daughter of Isaack van Eyck, a merchant who spent the first two decades of the seventeenth century in Danzig and from there traded with clients in the Netherlands. It may be assumed that Uylenburgh met Maria in Danzig, converted to the Mennonite faith, and married her in the early 1620s. However, the details of their marriage are unknown.[106] As neither they nor Rombout

102 Visser 1988, vol. 2, p. 18, note 109; at that point Jan Gerritsz Hooft resigned from his post as deacon.
103 GAA, not. J. Cornelisz Hoogeboom, NA 842, 5 December 1631.
104 RAL, not. P. den Oosterlingh, NA 366, deed 84, 6 February 1632 and Bredius 1915-1922, vol. 1, pp. 195-196(m).
105 Noted beside the 'Vegetable Market' are the words 'for half of 18', which presumably means that someone else was the joint owner, perhaps Reijers's (third) wife, whom he married in 1629 on the basis of an antenuptial agreement and whose property was explicitly excluded from his inventory.
106 We examined the surviving betrothal registers in the archives in Danzig but were unable to find any record of this marriage. However, the records from that time are far from complete and in any event the marriage may have taken place elsewhere, possibly in the suburb of Schottland where many Mennonites were living, Bogucka 1980, p. 159.

Uylenburgh were baptised in Amsterdam, they were presumably admitted to the Waterland church in Danzig as adults.[107] Of interest in this connection is the portrait of Jan Gerritsz van Emden painted by (presumably Rombout) Uylenburgh in 1616. Jan Gerritsz, a prominent Mennonite minister in Danzig from 1607 to 1617 (see fig. 12), may have baptised the brothers Rombout and Hendrick in, or shortly after 1612.[108] As we have seen, a significant number of the families discussed so far had ties with the Mennonite movement. There were the Uylenburghs in Danzig and Amsterdam, the Schoutens in Weesp and their brother-in-law Sijbrant Fries in Leiden, Maria van Eyck and her family in Weesp, her cousin by marriage Bartelt Jansz in Amsterdam, and the brothers Hooft and Reijer Claesz in Danzig and Amsterdam. Moreover, in the following chapter we shall see that Hendrick Uylenburgh's principal investors and a number of his clients were Mennonites as well. Hence, a few words about this movement are in order.[109]

THE MENNONITE MOVEMENT

The Mennonite faith has its roots in Anabaptist theology, which gained a foothold in northern Europe in the early sixteenth century, when a debate on ethical issues caused a rift in the Catholic Church. Dissenters rejected the established doctrine, and though they recognised the authority of the bible, they disagreed with the Church – and among themselves – on the interpretation of certain biblical texts. A violent confrontation in Munster in 1534 brought the entire Anabaptist movement into discredit. The movement nevertheless continued to spread, and from about 1545 the majority of its followers in the northern Netherlands, under the leadership of

Menno Simons, came to be known as Mennonites.

Their fundamental tenet is spiritual regeneration achieved through adult baptism and manifest through ascetic piety and strict ethical values. Anabaptist doctrine opposes infant baptism on the grounds that people are not punishable for sin until they are capable of exercising free will. Though there are exceptions, its followers abstain from the swearing of oaths, from holding public office or carrying arms which, in seventeenth-century Holland, excluded them from membership of the civic guards.

Their unorthodox views on religion and society led to frequent clashes with both the church and the state. In the Netherlands the movement was persecuted up to about 1580 and grudgingly tolerated after that time, gaining acceptance only in the early seventeenth century. In those circumstances its adherents closed ranks by encouraging marriage within the faith and fostering their own identity. Even so, they played an undiminished role in the social and economic life of the wider community and, contrary to popular myth, were both patrons and producers of art.[110]

The Mennonite movement in the Netherlands in the seventeenth century comprised a number of distinct groups with different views on points of doctrine and ethics. The two largest factions in Amsterdam were the Waterland and the Flemish Mennonites. The Waterlanders, the more liberal of the two, held services in 'de Toren'; the Flemish Mennonites worshipped in 'het Lam'. The two merged in 1668. Though the Waterland Mennonites, the faction to which Uylenburgh and his wife belonged, was comparatively tolerant, it was nevertheless opposed to marriage out of faith. Even so, mixed marriages were not as uncommon as was once believed.[111] In business, Mennonites tended to form partner-

107 The Waterland minister Reynier Wybrants registered all baptisms and marriage that took place in his church in his 'Memorandum', G A A, archive no. 1120, inv. no. 117. His records are complete and cover the period 1612-1641. The names of Hendrick Uylenburgh and his wife do not appear in them.
108 Wijnman 1959, p. 7 considered this possibility.
109 The following section is based on Zijlstra 2000, the most recent synthesising study of the Mennonite movement in the Netherlands. I wish to thank Adriaan Plak, keeper of the Mennonitica Collection of Amsterdam University Library, and Ruud Lambour and Daan de Clercq, who offered willing assistance with my endless questions about Mennonite life in the seventeenth century.
110 Zijlstra 2000, pp. 26-29, notably 27, note 44 (on the concept of 'world') in Mennonite teachings and note 45 (on the concept of 'identity').
111 Lambour 2001 cites Gerrit Uylenburgh and his Reformed wife, among others, as examples, see pp. 113-114. Another good example is the Amsterdam burgomaster Cornelis Pietersz Hooft, who asked his wife to attend the Reformed Church with him. She consented, but preferred to worship in the Mennonite church, which she found more inspiring, Enno van Gelder 1918, p. 6.

ships and deal with members of their own community,[112] and in this respect Hendrick Uylenburgh was no exception.

In the early seventeenth century the various Mennonite factions in Amsterdam formed approximately seven percent of the population. Few though they were – and their numbers declined sharply in the course of the century – this religious minority comprised many affluent merchants and artisans and exercised a disproportionately strong influence on the city's economic life. Many Mennonite merchants traded in the Baltic, if only because ships sailing to that region did not need to carry arms. Interestingly enough, their religious leaders wrote little about economic matters, but evidently had no objection to their followers earning money.

In Amsterdam

THE UYLENBURGH FAMILY

Hendrick Uylenburgh and his wife Maria van Eyck settled in Amsterdam in or shortly before 1625, when they are said to have made a 'sudden appearance' in the city.[113] Amsterdam's economy was booming, the arts were flourishing and the prospects for newcomers were favourable. In the early 1620s Uylenburgh was in Antwerp, where he may have associated with Amsterdam merchants who encouraged him to take this step. He may have had personal reasons as well, perhaps a disagreement with his Polish patron, although no evidence to this effect has emerged. In any event, there were probably a number of reasons for the move, not least of which is the fact that both Uylenburgh and his wife had relatives living in Amsterdam, Leiden and Weesp.

The Uylenburghs formed part of a wave of migrants who arrived in the Republic between 1575 and 1625 (fig. 19).[114] The thousands of Brabanders and Flemings who decided to settle in the country were followed by Germans, Scandinavians and Portuguese Jews. Uylenburgh, however, stood out from the crowd. He was born to Frisian parents, probably in Leeuwarden, had worked for the Polish court in Cracow and Warsaw, and held a prestigious position as agent of the king of Poland. Moreover, he was approaching forty and was no longer young. From documents concerning Maria van Eyck which are published here it would appear that Maria was born in Weesp and, as a child, moved to Danzig with her parents. She is believed to have met her future husband in Danzig, perhaps through her parents' acquaintances, some of whom are likely to have been Dutch merchant families. In other words, Hendrick and Maria had their roots in the Netherlands and both must have spoken Dutch. It would therefore have been comparatively easy for them to adapt to their new environment in Amsterdam.

At some point in the period between 1628 and 1631 Uylenburgh wound up the estate of his brother Rombout. He was also in touch with his wife's family in Weesp. In 1629 he represented the guardians of Swaentje Cornelisdr Schouten,[115] one of whom was Sijbrant Fries. The others are not named, but they were probably Swaentje's brothers Laurens and Lambert Cornelisz Schouten.[116] They must have authorised Uylenburgh to act on their behalf some time in 1629. What we learn from this is that Swaentje's guardians were closely acquainted with Uylenburgh.

112 Examples are Goris de Weert (see note 138 and Chapter 3, note 15) who was in business with Laurens Cornelisz Schouten (see p. 22) and the business partners Jasper van Tongerlo and Jacob Haesbaert (see Chapter 3, p. 193 and note 255).
113 Schwartz 1984, p. 369, chapter 20, note c; Uylenburgh's sudden appearance in the Amsterdam art world around 1625 is linked to 'the king of Poland's visit to the Republic in September 1624'. This probably refers to the visit of the king's eldest son, Prince Ladislas, to the Spanish Netherlands. There is no evidence that Uylenburgh was involved in any way, see Antwerp 1997.
114 Kuijpers 2005.
115 In the petition of 1629 to the Supreme Court (see note

41) Hendrick Uylenburgh represented Ibel Haye Fries, the mother and guardian of the children born of her marriage to Rombout Uylenburgh, and 'the guardians of the minor daughter of Swaentgen Corns Schouten'. This passage should be read without the words 'daughter of' before Swaentje's name: she herself was the person in question. A letter from Leiden city council to the Supreme Court in The Hague referring to the case 'against the guardians of the children of Rombout van Ulenborch and the minor Swaentgen Isbrants' [sic] states that Johan van Kuijck and Johan van Leeuwen stood surety for Geertgen Sijbrantsdr 'and the guardians of Swaentgen Cornelisdr', and that Geertgen Sijbrantsdr nominated a representative to act on behalf of 'herself and the minor Swaent[j]e Cornelis Schouten', RAL, Leiden Municipal Archive 11 (access no. 501A), inv. no. 304 (Correspondence Book G), fol. 67v-68, 16 January 1631 respectively RAL, not. L. Vergeyl, NA 331, deed 9, 27 February 1628 and ibid., deed 11, 2 March 1628.
116 Their brother Gerrit Schouten had died in 1625. On the guardianship of Sijbrant Fries, see note 40.

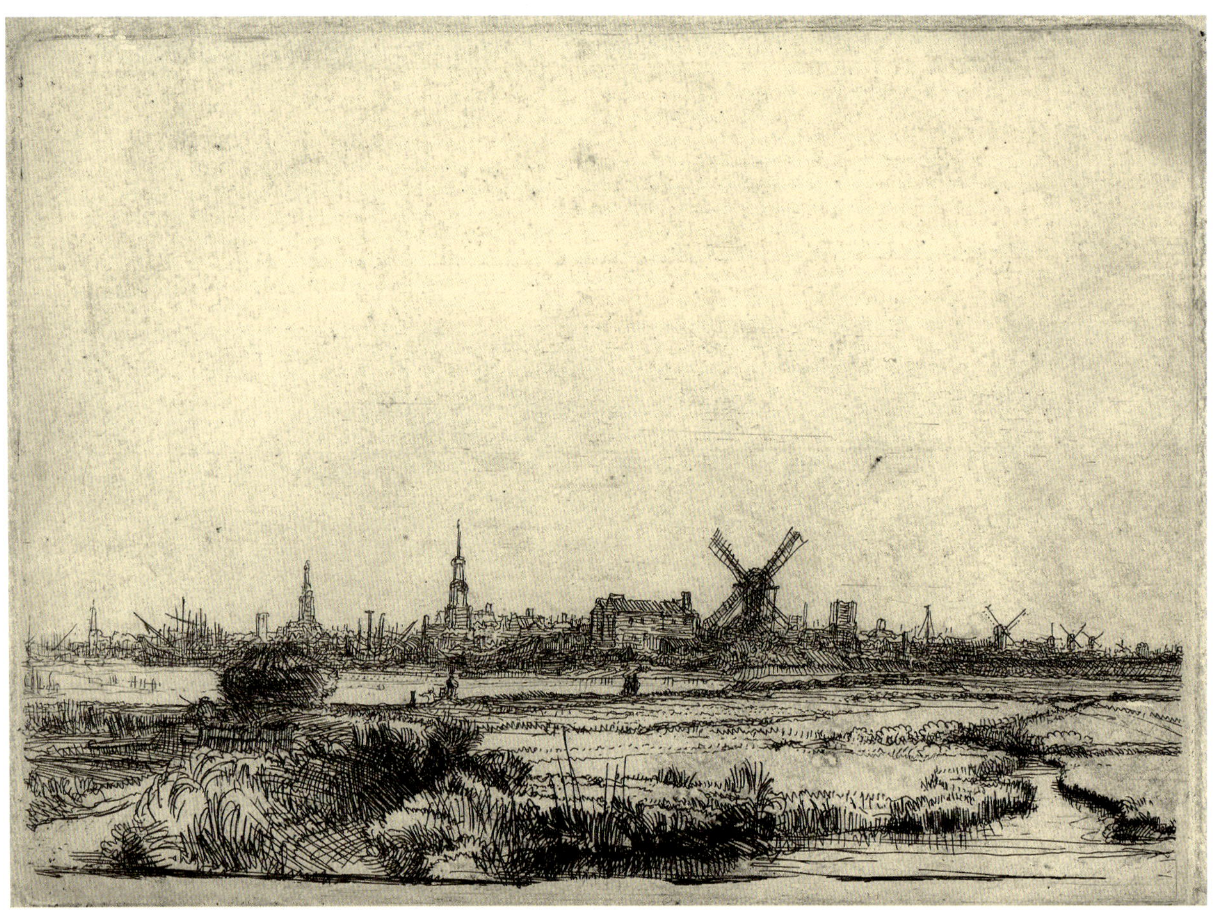

The structure of Hendrick and Maria's family was known by and large, but a hitherto unremarked entry in the burial registers of the Orphans' Chamber pertaining to Maria's interment in the Zuiderkerk on 15 July 1638 brings a few new facts to light.[117] The entry states that Maria had lived in a house called Cronenburch in Sint-Anthoniesbreestraat, that the widower Hendrick Uylenburgh had submitted the couple's joint will for examination on 10 September of that year, and that, under the provisions of the will, the Orphans' Chamber had no authority over the minor children.[118] Two more of these registers have come down to us, one of which contains an entry which is of particular interest here. It conveys essentially the same information, but adds that Maria van Eyck had ten surviving minor children and that on 15 September 1638 Hendrick Uylenburgh had submitted the couple's will, under the terms of which he was enti-tled to retain the couple's communal property and was not required to give account for that portion of the inheritance to which the children possessed a statutory right. Bartelt Jansz, Maria's cousin by marriage, had given his consent to that effect.[119] Hence we know that the couple had ten children at the time of Maria van Eyck's funeral in 1638, and that Maria had relatives living in Amsterdam.

As far as the couple's family is concerned (see Genealogy 2, p. 292), we know that by the time Hendrick and Maria settled in Amsterdam, around 1625, they were already married and probably had at least one child. Little is known about their children. They were not baptised as infants and, as a result, there are no records of their birth. Moreover, their son Gerrit was the only one of their offspring to marry. The others died young or presumably remained celibate or else settled abroad. On 15 July 1634, Hendrick

117 'Maeiken van Yck, small stone, 8 guilders', GAA, DTB 1090, fol. 68, 15 July 1638. Another source gives the date as 14 July 1638, see notes 118 and 174.
118 'Marritien van Eijck, in the house Cronenburch in Breestraet' and the annotation that on '10 September Hendrick Uijlenburch, widower of Maritien van Eyck, presented the will of his deceased wife, which discharged the Orphans' Chamber of responsibility, stating that he acquiesced, hence no evidence produced', GAA, Burials Register Wk no. 4, fol. 57v, 15 July 1638; first published by Dudok van Heel 1982, p. 89, note 40.
119 'Maritgen van Eyck, in the house Croonenberch in Breestraet do. [14 July 1638] – 10 ß' with a reference to the will of 15 July 1634 signed in the presence of not. Sybrant Cornelisz. On 15 September Hendrick Uylenburgh presented the document, which stated that he was not required to produce evidence, having obtained 'the consent of Bartelt Jansz, the deceased's cousin by marriage', GAA, Burials Register Wk no. 20, 14 July 1638. The date in the deed is different from that in the other two burials registers, see notes 117 and 118.

and Maria drew up their will, which is discussed in detail below. They had six children at the time: Gerrit, Isaack, Sara, Anna, Susanna and Lyntgen, listed in the conventional manner, with the boys' names first, and in order of seniority. Their eldest son, Gerrit, one of the two principal subjects of this study, was named after his paternal grandfather and must have been born in Amsterdam in about 1625. He was baptised in Amsterdam in 1645, at which time he would have been approximately twenty years old. It is unclear whether he was the couple's first-born, as a child of Hendrick Uylenburgh was buried in the Zuiderkerk on 27 July 1626,[120] and that child may have been born before Gerrit. Sara must have been born directly after Gerrit. She was baptised in the Mennonite church in 1661 and in 1668 signed a power of attorney. A deed of 1632 refers to a 'certain daughter', presumably Sara, who was living in Uylenburgh's home. Sara died in Amsterdam in 1696 and appears to have remained single.[121] Another child of Hendrick Uylenburgh was buried in the Zuiderkerk on 17 April 1634.[122] Two daughters, Anna and Susanna, were baptised in 1661, at the same time as their sister Sara. Anna Uylenburgh died in 1681 and was also presumably unmarried.[123] The second eldest son Isaack was born in or shortly before 1634. Susanna is documented around 1697 as an almoner for the Mennonite poor relief board. She must have died in the early eighteenth century, to all appearances without having married.[124] The youngest child named in the will of 1634 was Lyntgen, who was buried, under the name Magdalena Uylenburgh, in 1661.[125] She remained single and at the time of her death was living with her father, who passed away a few days after her. The Uylenburgh's had four more children between 1634 and 1638. At the time the couple drew up their will Maria may have been expecting a child, possibly twins – she may also have had twins previously. Rombertus was born

in or shortly after 1634, and baptised in 1661. He was followed by Marcus and subsequently Abraham, who died in Dublin in 1668. In 1659 Hendrick Uylenburgh testified as an expert in a case concerning a portrait by Rembrandt; he was accompanied by his sons Marcus and Abraham who signed the deed as witnesses.[126] The eldest witness was usually named first. The name of the tenth child is unknown.[127]

From the above we see that almost the entire family were Mennonites. According to the register of members of the Waterland church in Amsterdam, five of Hendrick Uylenburgh's children were baptised in 1661: on 26 September of that year the brothers Isaack and Rombertus, both 'bachelors', and on 11 December their sisters Sara, Anna and Susanna, all 'young daughters', which is to say, unmarried. The baptisms were registered by their brother Gerrit Uylenburgh, who was described as 'our member'. He himself had been baptised in 1645. Their recently deceased father is referred to as 'our brother', meaning that he, too, had been a member of the church.[128] The register states that the baptism of Isaack and Rombertus took place with special consent from the church officers 'because they [were] intending to travel abroad'. What we should note here is that the children were baptised relatively late in life. The youngest must have been born in or shortly before 1638 and would therefore have been approximately twenty-three in 1661, while his siblings were obviously older.

The family was large even by seventeenth-century standards. Ten children were alive at the time of Maria van Eyck's death in 1638. She had borne fourteen in all, which was not uncommon in itself, but it was unusual for so many to survive to adulthood. Surprisingly little is known about their lives, but one reason at least is that several sons left the country and presumably settled abroad.[129]

120 Buried in the Zuiderkerk 'a child [of] Hijndrick Wullenburch, 27 July, small stone, 4 guilders', GAA, DTB 1090, p. 4, 27 July 1626; Dudok van Heel 1976, p. 28, note 2.
121 Buried in the Leidsekerkhof 'Sara Uijlenburg in Elantsstraat, past the side-street', GAA, DTB 1230, p. 101, 18 May 1696.
122 Buried in the Zuiderkerk 'a child [of] Hyndrick Uillenburch', GAA, DTB 1090, 17 April 1634.
123 Buried in the Leidsekerkhof 'Anna Uijlenburgh, in Elantsstraat in 't Hofje van Venetia', GAA, DTB 1228, p. 84, 22 January 1681.
124 Not to be confused with her namesake Susanna Uylenburgh of Baangracht, who was buried in 1676, GAA, DTB 1161, p. 233, 24 November 1676.

125 Buried in the Westerkerk 'Magdalena Uijlenborgh', GAA, DTB 1100(B), p. 178, 11 March 1661.
126 The witnesses are not named in Doc. 1659/21;

their names appear in the first publication of that document, see Bredius/De Roever 1885, p. 93 and Urk. no. 208. On this matter, see also p. 201 and note 290.

127 He may have been the Tobias Uylenburgh who became a broker in Amsterdam around 1670, but this is purely speculative.
128 GAA, archive no. 1120

(Archive of the Mennonite Church), Register of Members, vol. 4, fol. 7v, 1661; first published in Wijnman 1930, p. 168 and note 2.
129 See also p. 71.

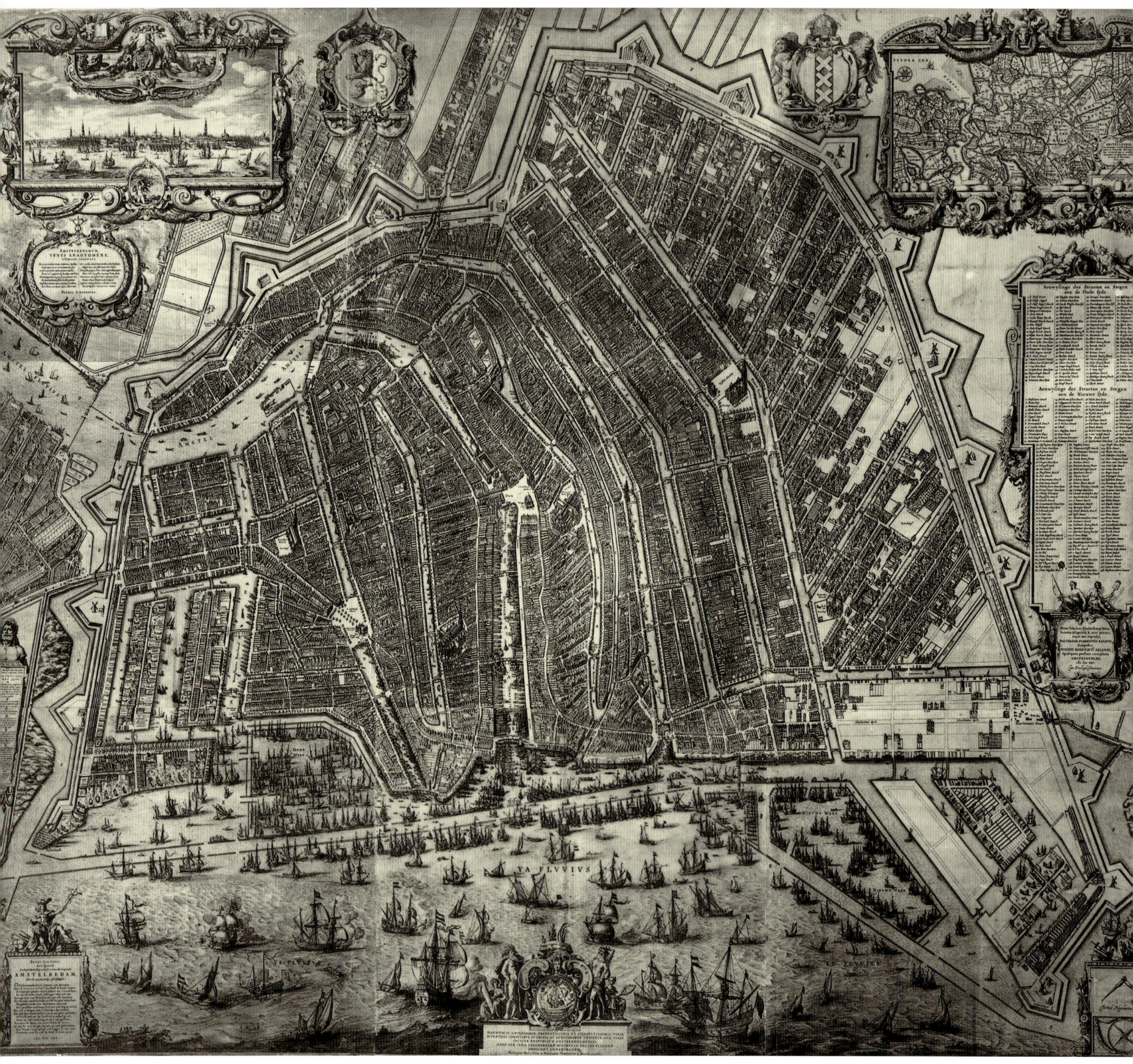

20 Balthasar Florisz van Berckenrode, Amstelredamum emporium Hollandiae primaria totius Europae celeberrimum, engraving with burin and etching needle, 140 x 160 cm (in nine sheets with title strip), Amsterdam 1625 (first state), Amsterdam, Gemeentearchief

Hendrick Uylenburgh is known to have been living in Amsterdam in 1626, as the name of one of his children appears in the burials register of that year. Further evidence exists in the form of the marriage banns of his son Gerrit, published in 1666, on which occasion Gerrit gave his age as forty and stated that had been born in Amsterdam.[130] It is thus clear that Hendrick Uylenburgh and his wife Maria van Eyck settled in Amsterdam around 1625. A document concerning Uylenburgh in 1625 has recently come to light. The records of the Amsterdam exchange bank confirm that he had an account with the bank in that year. In fact, a full four pages of the ledger are devoted to his account, which suggests that he had already been living in the city for some time or had perhaps been doing business with Amsterdam merchants. This matter is discussed further in Chapter 3.

We have thus established that Uylenburgh and his wife moved to Amsterdam in or shortly before 1625, but the question is, where did they live? (fig. 20) A few years after their arrival they occupied a house on the corner of Sint-Anthoniesbreestraat and Zwanenburgwal (fig. 21), but it is uncertain whether that was their home from the start. Around 1606 the weaver Hans van der Voort bought three adjacent plots in Breestraat and built two houses on the terrain. The house on the corner of Zwanenburgwal was narrower than the building next door, which contained two separate dwellings. This is the property that Rembrandt bought in 1639. In 1608 Van der Voort sold it to Pieter Belten. Van der Voort also built and subsequently sold a third house, set at a right angle to the other two, with the entrance on Zwanenburgwal. He himself occupied the house on the corner,[131] and sold it to Nicolaes Pauw in 1620. We shall return to Nicolaes Pauw below.[132] It would appear that Hans van der Voort rented the house and continued to live there with his younger brother, the celebrated and sought-after portraitist Cornelis van der Voort, who established his workshop on the premises. The brothers passed away shortly after one another, Cornelis at the end of October 1624 and Hans a few weeks later.[133] Cornelis van der Voort's widow, the mother of seven minor children, did not vacate the house right away. An inventory of the family's possessions was drawn up only on 7 June 1625, and two weeks later the widow was requested to allow experts to value her late husband's paintings.[134] On 30 August 1625 Cornelis van der Voort's moveable property was sold from the premises 'on the corner of Breestraet'.[135] His widow must have remained in the house until September 1625, before moving to Leiden.

As Cornelis van der Voort's widow lived in the corner house until late 1625 and rental agreements normally entered into effect on 1 May of each year, in theory Hendrick Uylenburgh would have been able to occupy the house as from May 1626. If this was the case, he must have found temporary accommodation elsewhere at the time of his arrival in Amsterdam. He may have stayed with relatives, such as Aeltje Marcusdr van Eyck and her husband Bartelt Jansz, his wife's cousin and cousin by marriage.

The fact that Uylenburgh's child was buried in the Zuiderkerk is further evidence that the family was living in Breestraat or its environs in 1626.[136] The church was in the neighbourhood and people were usually laid to rest in a church near their home. The address is confirmed by

---

130 See pp. 72-74.
131 Hans van der Voort and his wife drew up their will in 1609 in the house 'on the corner across St Anthonissluys', GAA, not. J. Gijsbertsz, NA 27, pp. 653-654, 11 January 1609.
132 GAA, Kw. 27, fol. 145r-v, 5 March 1620; the purchase price is not stated.

133 Buried in the Zuiderkerk 'Corn. van (der) Voort, painter, on the corner of St Thonissluys', GAA, Burials Register Wk. no. 20, 2 November 1624. A Hans van der Voort was buried in the Zuiderkerk, GAA, DTB 1089(A), p. 46, 25 November 1624; he was presumably

Cornelis's brother; the name occurs more often.
134 GAA, not. W. Cluijt, NA 369(A), fol. 225-228v, 7 June 1625; the household effects are not listed room by room, which makes it difficult to reconstruct the layout of the house. By deed of 20 June 1625, the widow was

requested to have 'all the portraits left by [her] late husband appraised by independent experts', Bredius 1915-1922, vol. 7, p. 265.
135 GAA, archive no. 5073, inv. no. 952, 13 May and 30 August 1625; Bredius 1915-1922, vol. 4, pp. 1180-1182.
136 See note 120.

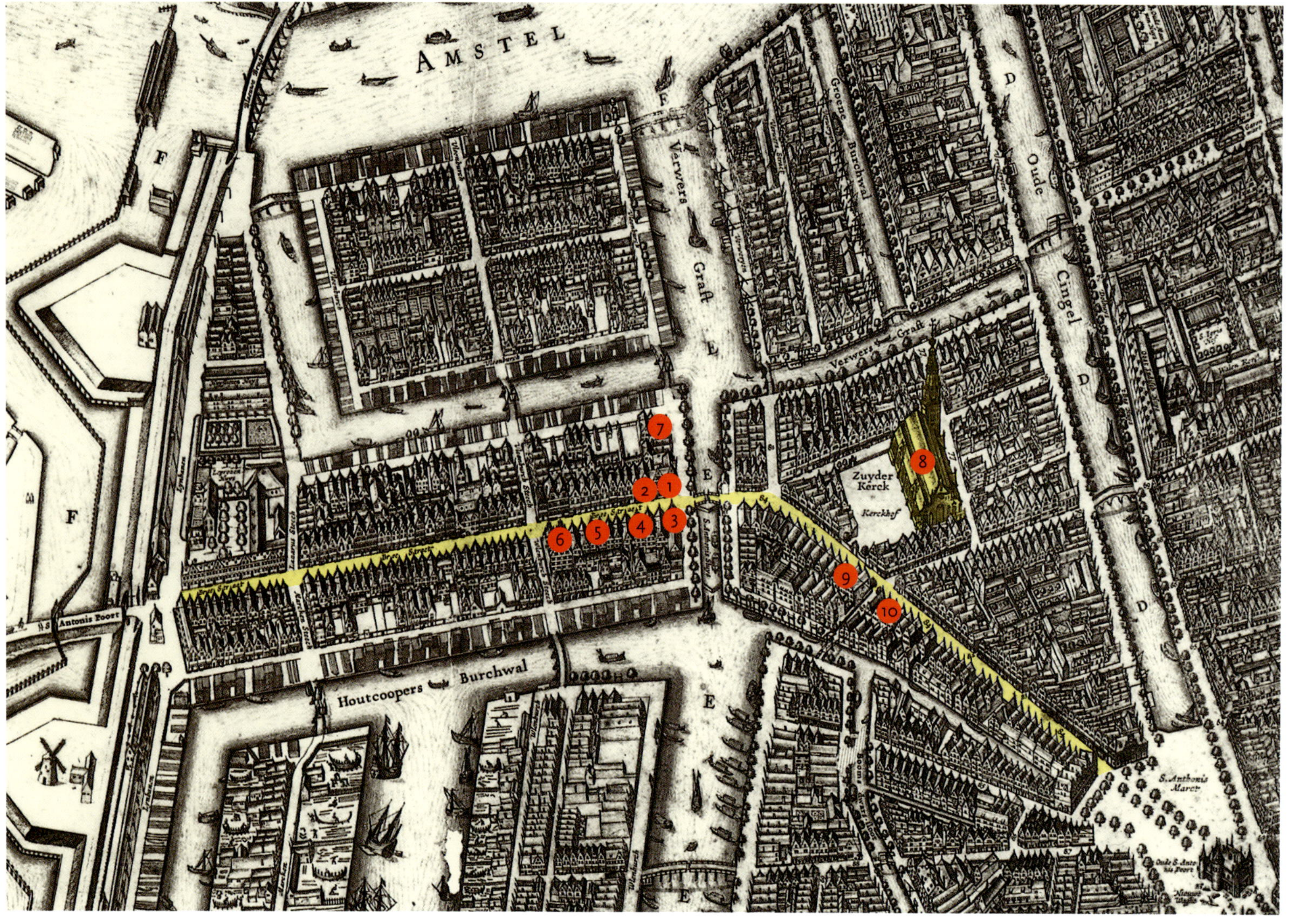

21 Detail of fig. 20

[1] The house on the corner of the Zwanenburgwal where Hendrick Uylenburgh lived. [2] The house Rembrandt bought in 1639 and in which he continued to work until 1658 (now the Rembrandt House Museum). [3] Pieter Isaacksz [4] Adriaen van Nieulandt. [5] Govert Spruijt. [6] Nicolaes van Bambeeck and Agatha Bas. [7] Possible address of Heere Jansz [8] De Zuiderkerk. [9] Pieter Lastman. [10] 'Cronenburch', the house where Hendrick Uylenburgh lived

a deed of 1632, which is discussed below. Moreover, it is documented again in the official report of a sale of porcelain on 16 October 1626, on which occasion Hendrick Uylenburgh, described as a painter at the Sint-Anthoniessluis (in the vicinity of Breestraat), purchased three double butter dishes for nine guilders and eighteen stuyvers.[137] A few of the bidders were merchants, but others were private buyers. Like them, Uylenburgh probably acquired porcelain for his personal use.

Sint-Anthoniesbreestraat was located in a new quarter of the city that was constructed at the beginning of the seventeenth century. Amsterdam's population burgeoned in the last decades of the sixteenth century, resulting in unprecedented urban expansion. Land on the east side of the city was sold and rapidly developed from 1605 on. Wealthy merchants built their homes in Breestraat, one of the main thoroughfares in the district. Uylenburgh rented his house there, undoubtedly at considerable

137 '3 ditto [double butter dishes] at 66 stuyvers. Hendrick van Ulenburch, painter at St Theunissluys f9:18:-', GAA, archive no. 5073, inv. no. 952, 16 and 17 October 1626; this public sale of porcelain held at the request of Anthonie Nijs raised more than 800 guilders. Montias 2002, p. 122 and note 353 erroneously gives the date as 11 October 1627; his note 187 gives the correct date but an incorrect source.

expense. The exact amount of his annual rent is unknown, but it would presumably have been proportionate to that paid by other tenants in the area. Goris de Weert, for instance, bought a house called 'het Vergulde Weseltje' in Breestraat for 14,000 guilders in 1639, and in 1640 rented it out for 650 guilders a year.[138] The corner house in Breestraat was sold for 9,000 guilders in 1645, after Uylenburgh had moved out. We can thus deduce that Uylenburgh would have paid four to five hundred guilders in rent for the house unless, as has been suggested, he occupied only part of it.[139] The other part is said to have been occupied by the merchant Balthasar de Visscher and his family. Although it was common practice in Amsterdam to divide buildings into more than one dwelling, this was predominantly the case in low-rental neighbourhoods. Breestraat, where splendid mansions sold for upwards of 10,000 guilders in the first decades of the seventeenth century, did not fall into this category. In 1639 Rembrandt paid 13,000 guilders for the property immediately adjacent to the house that Uylenburgh had occupied for over a decade, and Goris de Weert paid even more for his home.[140] It goes without saying that rent in that area was high.

The proposition that Hendrick Uylenburgh shared the house with the De Visscher and his family remained unchallenged for decades.[141] The names of both men appear on the tax assessment form for 1631. However, De Visscher was a prosperous merchant with taxable assets of at least 10,000 guilders, and it is unlikely that he would have rented only part of a house. In any event, a document stating the address of the house in which his wife Sara Cobbaut passed away overturns the hypothesis that the family lived in the corner house. At her death in 1638 Sara Cobbaut was living on the other side of the lock – viewed from the city centre – in the second house in Breestraat.[142] In other words, the De Visschers lived in the house that Rembrandt bought in 1639. It is not known when they moved there. When Balthasar married Sara Cobbaut in 1626, he was living on the Singel and the bride in her parents' home. They had not moved to Breestraat by December of that year.[143] The

house was renovated in 1627, and they may have taken occupation of it in that year.

Hence, we can assume that the Uylenburghs were the sole occupants of the house in Breestraat and that Hendrick established his home and business there in May 1626. Considering that the house was in an expensive neighbourhood where the rent would have been high, we can also infer that his business was doing well. His success is hardly surprising, for up to that time he had been an agent of the king of Poland. In the deed of 8 March 1628 he is referred to as 'the Honourable' Hendrick Uylenburgh, and in some instances he is addressed as 'Sr.', the abbreviation for seigneur, a title reserved for the prosperous middle class.

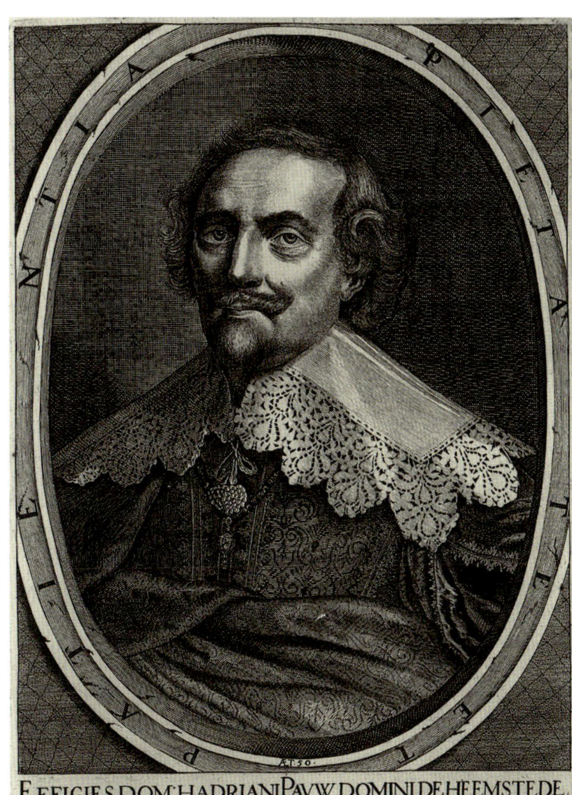

22 Michiel van Lochom after Pieter van Mol, Portrait of Adriaen Pauw, signed and dated 'Michael de Lochom fecit. Lutetiae Parisiorum Anno Dom. MDCXXXV' with the inscription 'aet. 50', engraving, 30.5 x 19.8 cm, Amsterdam, Rijksprentenkabinet

138 The rent is stated in the inventory of the house, GAA, not. J. Cornelisz Hogeboom, NA 840, 1 March 1641.
139 Meischke 1956, pp. 5-6 and Wijnman 1956, p. 97. Did these authors work independently of one another? In any event, neither refers to the other. Wijnman incorporated Meischke's information a few years later, when preparing his article for publication in a volume of collected works, Wijnman 1959, p. 6, note 2.
140 Doc. 1639/1 respectively GAA, Kw. 37, fol. 139r-v, 4 May 1639.
141 Wijnman 1956, p. 97.
142 Buried 'Sara Cobbauts of Breestraet, the second house across St Tonissluys', GAA, Burials Register Wk no. 2, 19 January 1638; Kam 1969, p. 160 refers to this entry; the passage describing the location of the house appears not to have been cited by other authors, although the article is frequently included in bibliographies.
143 Balthasar de Visscher and Sara Cobbaut made their will and submitted it, sealed, to a notary, who drew up a deed to that effect. This took place in the home of Sara's mother on Singel, GAA, not. F. van Banchem, NA 317, fol. 60-61, 13 December 1626; no address is given in the will of that date (ibid., fol. 58-60).

49

The person named as the owner of the house in the deed of sale of 1620 was Nicolaes Pauw, but since Nicolaes was barely thirteen years old at the time, his father Adriaen Pauw must have bought the property in his name.[144] Nothing is known about Uylenburgh's association with Pauw. Adriaen Pauw moved away from Amsterdam in 1627, but visited the city quite frequently after that time. He was an art connoisseur and apparently possessed a large collection (fig. 22).[145] When Joachim von Sandrart left Amsterdam in about 1642, Pauw bought a landscape by Claude Lorrain from him for five hundred guilders.[146] He decorated the interior and grounds of his castle in Heemstede with classical sculptures which his son Nicolaes had acquired in Italy (in 1630?). Given that Uylenburgh did business with his landlords on other occasions, as we shall see, Adriaen Pauw and his son Nicolaes, who are known to have spent substantial sums of money on art, may likewise have belonged to his clientele.

Hendrick Uylenburgh must have acquired burghership soon after his arrival in Amsterdam, as a document of 26 March 1627 describes him as a 'merchant and burgher of this city'.[147] Burghership entailed legal, social and economic rights and obligations.[148] It was also one of the requirements for admission to a guild. As a newcomer to the city, Uylenburgh had to buy this status, which was not an entitlement but a privilege enjoyed by relatively few. No more than an estimated twenty-five per cent of the population were burghers, although in Amsterdam, unlike other cities in the Republic, religion was not a criterion for eligibility. In 1624, a few years before Uylenburgh was granted his status, the fee was fourteen guilders and therefore not beyond the means of a merchant of his stature.

The cost increased significantly in the following years, rising to fifty guilders in 1650. It was a hereditary right and therefore often acquired shortly before marriage to secure the children's status.

Merchants did not belong to a guild, but Uylenburgh was an art dealer and painter and was required to join the Guild of St Luke in order to ply his trade.[149] As the registers of members of the Amsterdam branch of St Luke's have been lost, it is impossible to ascertain whether he joined the guild immediately upon his arrival in the city, or whether he initially earned his livelihood in some other field of commerce. Be that as it may, documents of 26 March 1627, 8 March 1628 and December 1629 consistently describe him as a 'merchant (in Amsterdam)'. The document of 1629 is of particular interest, as it was an application from Uylenburgh addressed to the Supreme Court in The Hague in which Uylenburgh himself gave his occupation as 'merchant'. A document of 26 July 1632 refers to 'Mr. Heyndrick Ulenburch, painter'. The designation 'Master' (abbreviated as 'Mr') indicates that he had become a member of the guild. A few years later, he was appraising paintings in an official capacity, a task for which he would not otherwise have been eligible.

Uylenburgh's acquisition of burghership had far-reaching implications. Anyone living within the city limits was classified as either a burgher, a citizen or a foreigner. Those belonging to the first two categories were registered as residents of the city, but citizens enjoyed fewer civic rights. Those classified as foreigners were admitted on a temporary basis only. Hence, the fact that Uylenburgh applied for burghership suggests that he probably intended to settle in Amsterdam permanently. Burgership would also

144 See note 132. Nicolaes inherited 60,000 guilders from his mother in 1607 and 80,000 guilders from his grandmother in 1619, both of which sums his father administered, Elias 1903-1905, vol. I, p. 201, note j. His father must have bought the house in Breestraat for him in 1620 (as well as two other plots).

145 Much has been published about Pauw's library and about the many portraits made of him. However, his collection has not been comprehensively researched, for the time being see Krol 1985, pp. 21 and 71-91.

146 Sandrart 1675/Peltzer 1925, p. 210; Sandrart mentioned paintings that 'the connoisseur Renier Pau, Herr von Hemstätten' had bought from him, among them a Titian and a work attributed to Paolo Veronese, ibid., pp. 272-273. No one called Reynier Pauw is known to have been Lord of Heemstede.

147 See pp. 121-124. Register D, which lists the names of persons who acquired burghership between 1620 and 1636, has been lost.

148 On the following, see Prak 2001 and Kuijpers/Prak 2002.

149 The first article of the Amsterdam ordinance of 1579 states that 'no person engaging in the arts or any activity within the scope of the Guild of St Luke [...] shall practise their métier or be admitted to the guild *without being citizens and burghers of this city*', quoted from Hoogewerff 1947, p. 143 (present author's italics). In 1617 the civic authorities ruled that only burghers were permitted to own 'freely accessible shops' selling paintings, and that they were to be members of the guild; this provision was tightened up four years later: ibid., pp. 155-156.

have enabled him to play an active role in the community.[150] Apart from what it meant to the Uylenburghs from a personal point of view, their status as fully-fledged members of the community would have boosted their self-esteem and enhanced their social standing. We see, for instance, that in 1627 a notary made a point of mentioning that Uylenburgh was a 'burgher'.

Another document of interest is the tax register of 1631, pertaining to a wealth tax of one half per cent which was levied on assets in excess of 1,000 guilders. A demand for fifteen guilders was issued to an 'Abraham van Ulemburch' residing in Breestraat,[151] whose taxable assets must have amounted to 3,000 guilders. It is possible that the wrong name was inscribed due to a clerical error, and that the person in question was Hendrick Uylenburgh,[152] or alternatively that 'Abraham' was Hendrick's son from a previous marriage.[153] One might argue that if Hendrick was married in the first half of the 1620s, he would have been almost forty years old at the time, whereas Mennonites tended to marry relatively young. However, there were of course exceptions. Uylenburgh's eldest son Gerrit, for example, was over forty by the time he married. The estimate of 3,000 guilders on which Uylenburgh's wealth tax was based would appear to be on the low side. That said, it was not based on income or total assets, but only on immoveable property and securities. Neither incoming payments nor moveable property, such as household effects or merchandise and stock, were included in the calculation.[154] As we shall see, Hendrick Uylenburgh had few liquid assets. He invested his capital in the business, and borrowed money whenever he needed ready cash to purchase art or enlarge his workshop.

The earliest document linking Hendrick Uylenburgh's name with Rembrandt's dates from 1631, when Uylenburgh lent the artist one thousand guilders.[155] We can assume that the loan did not come out of the blue and that the two men were already acquainted. They may have met in Leiden in 1628, when Uylenburgh visited the city to wind up his brother Rombout's estate, as Rembrandt happened to be working there at the time, or they may have been in contact even earlier. Around the time that Uylenburgh moved to Amsterdam, in 1625 or shortly before, Rembrandt was working with Pieter Lastman,[156] whose studio was in Sint-Anthoniesbreestraat, near the lock.[157]

A document of 1632 contains valuable information. On 26 July of that year, at the request of a burgher of Leiden, an Amsterdam notary, accompanied by two witnesses, visited the home of 'Mr. Heyndrick Ulenburch, painter, near St Anthonissluys in Brestraet in this city'. The notary asked 'a certain daughter who came to the door' whether 'Mr Rembrant Harmensz van Rijn, painter (lodging at this address), was at home and disposed to receive visitors'. The girl called for Rembrandt, who spoke to the notary in 'the front room' and confirmed that he was indeed the painter Rembrant Harmensz van Rijn. The notary remarked that he appeared to be 'hale and hearty and faring well', to which Rembrandt replied that he was 'of sound constitution, the Lord be praised'.[158] The report of this encounter is illuminating. Uylenburgh was addressed as 'master' in acknowledgement of his status as a painter and member of the guild. His address was narrowed down to 'Brestraet, near St Anthonissluys'. The girl who opened the

---

150 This aspect of burghership is emphasised in Frijhoff/Spies 1999, pp. 182-184.

151 Kohier 1631, p. 36, fol. 157, no. 93.

152 Wijnman 1956, p. 97 suggests that 'Abraham' may have been a clerical error and that the name should have been 'Hendrick'. He expresses the same view later with more conviction, Wijnman 1959, p. 6. The names in the assessment register are indeed not always correct. For example, Pieter Belten is entered as 'Bittes'.

153 Montias 2002, p. 122 and note 358.

154 This was especially difficult to ascertain in the case of merchants. As one contemporary wrote, 'one cannot judge how wealthy merchants are, because all their assets are tied up in securities for debts', Kohier 1631, p. iv. These tax assessments were estimates and must often have been on the low side, since they were based on information furnished by the taxpayer. See Kernkamp 1906, pp. 17-24 and passim, a review still well worth reading by Elias 1903-1905.

155 See pp. 126-127.

156 Broos 2000 maintains that Rembrandt studied under Lastman in 1625.

157 The present no. 59.

158 GAA, not. J. van Zwieten, NA 861, fol. 244v-245, 26 July 1632 and Doc. 1632/2 (the commentary on this document is incorrect); first published in Bredius 1899, pp. 1-2.

door must have been one of Uylenburgh and
Maria van Eyck's older children. The notary was
invited to take a seat in the front room. The incident confirms that Rembrandt had lodgings in
Uylenburgh's home. He was called from his
work to meet with the notary and witnesses,
who spoke to him in person and remarked that
he was in visibly good health.

Rembrandt lived in Uylenburgh's home for
several years until May 1635. At the time of his
betrothal to Saskia Uylenburgh on 10 June 1634,
he stated that he was 'residing in Brestraet'.[159]
About a week later, presumably at the same
time, Uylenburgh and Rembrandt received a
visit from the German scholar Burchard Grossmann, who travelled to various parts of the
Dutch Republic between May and July of that
year. Rembrandt wrote the following inscription in Grossmann's album amicorum: 'the
righteous value honour above gold' (een vroom
gemoet / acht eer voor goet) which he signed,
adding the place and date, 'Amsterdam. 1634'
(fig. 23a).[160] He also made an ink sketch of an
elderly man with a beard (fig. 23b). Hendrick
Uylenburgh contributed the following maxim:
'moderation sustains', (midelmaet hout staet)
which he signed as 'Hendrick Ulenborch, art
dealer in Amsterdam, 18 June 1634' (fig. 23c). We
shall examine this inscription in some detail, as
it is one of very few extant documents that tell
us anything about Uylenburgh personally.

It has been observed that Uylenburgh's epigram also appears in *Banket-werk van goede ge-
dachten*, an anthology published by the poet
Johan de Brune in 1657.[161] It was concluded at
the time that both De Brune and Uylenburgh
had quoted the text from the same, hitherto
unidentified, source. Or had it perhaps appeared
in an earlier publication by De Brune? It now
transpires that this was indeed the case.[162] It was
printed beside an emblem in his *Emblemata of
sinnewerck,* published in Amsterdam in 1624.[163]
Its meaning is clear from the accompanying
print, which shows a horse that has been flogged
unseating its rider. The epigram to a second
emblem with the motto 'Self-love blinds the
soul and the intellect' (Eyghen-min blint ziel
en zin) is entirely unequivocal. It ends with the

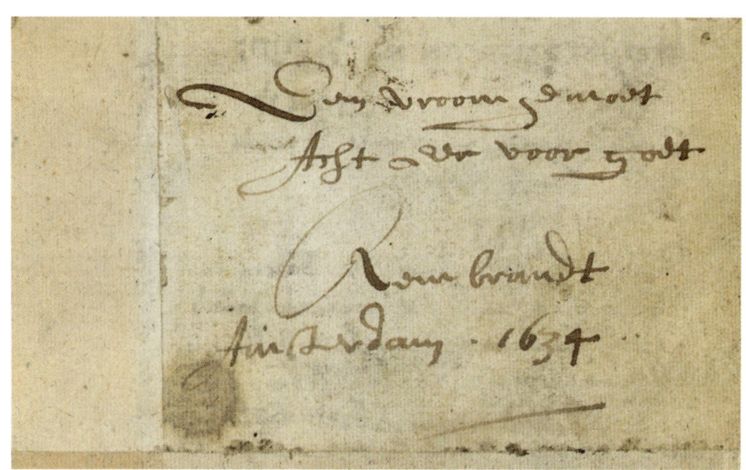

23a Inscription by Rembrandt van Rijn in the album of Burchard Grossmann,
The Hague, Koninklijke Bibliotheek

verse, 'Moderation sustains, Enough and no
more' (De middel-maet hout staet, Genough,
niet al te veel) (fig. 24).[164] It is impossible to draw
a direct link between Hendrick Uylenburgh's
inscription, which may have been his personal
credo, and Johan de Brune's text, but there can
be little doubt that Uylenburgh had read De
Brune's book. One might argue that the Cal-
vinistic De Brune was an orthodox counter-
Remonstrant. Little is known about Uylenburgh's religious convictions other than that
he was a member of the Waterland Mennonites,
who were far more liberal than the Flemings.
For all we know, Uylenburgh may have held
similar views to De Brune, who also had Pietist
sympathies.[165] The Waterland faction were more
susceptible to the influence of Pietism than
other Mennonite groups. The fundamental aim
of Pietists and Mennonites, and of Calvinists
inspired by their teachings, was to place the
spirit of Christianity above doctrinal beliefs.[166]

However, we may be complicating the matter
more than necessary. De Brune's *Emblemata*
expressed an essentially Christian ethic with a
moralistic slant. The title page announced that
the aim of the book was to 'right some of the
wrongs of our age'. Both here and in other writings De Brune denounced the pernicious extra-

159 Doc. 1634/2.
160 Doc. 1634/6.
161 Observed by Michael
Hoyle and published in a
footnote in Broos 1981-1982,
p. 254, note 46.
162 Paula Koning kindly
revealed her source and furnished additional information.
163 De Brune 1624, p. 134,
emblem 16.
164 Ibid., p. 173, emblem 24.
165 Op 't Hof 1990; for De
Brune's emblems, see also
Koning 2001.
166 Op 't Hof 1994.

52

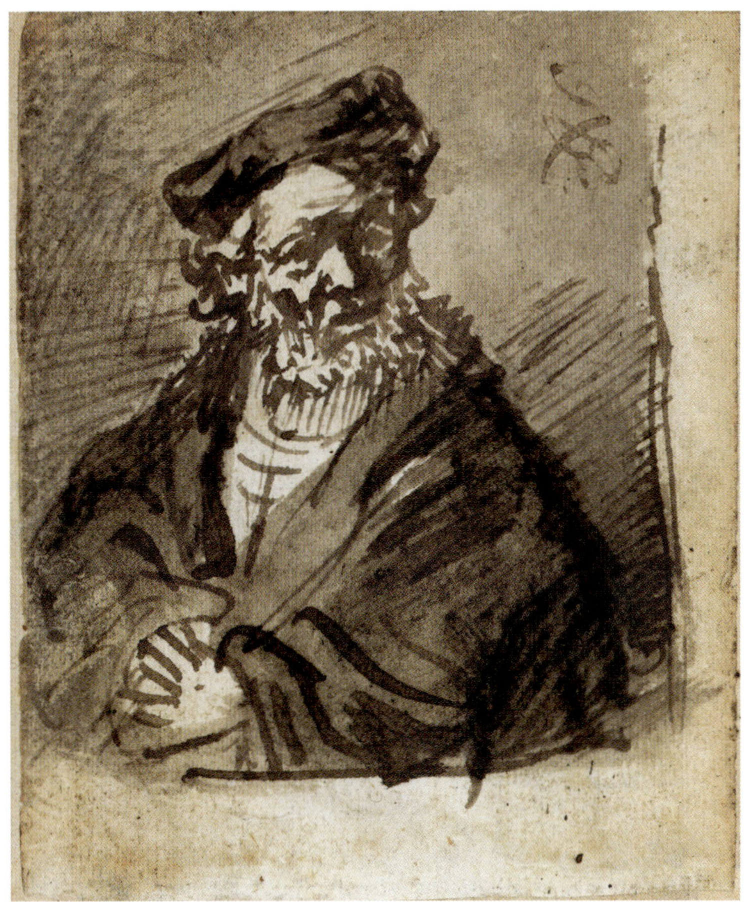

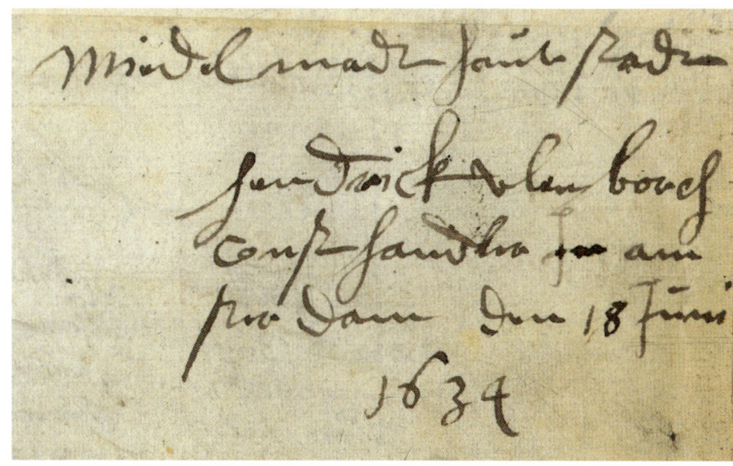

23b Rembrandt van Rijn, *Old man with beard*, pen and brush and brown ink, 8.9 x 7.1 cm, The Hague, Koninklijke Bibliotheek (Ben. 257)

23c Inscription by Hendrick Uylenburgh in the album of Burchard Grossmann, The Hague, Koninklijke Bibliotheek

vagance and excesses of his contemporaries. Were these the moral precepts that Uylenburgh chose to live by? This would not be an unreasonable assumption, as De Brune's moralistic and edifying critique was not inconsistent with conservative Mennonite dogma. Be that as it may, the fact that Hendrick Uylenburgh was familiar with writings of this kind gives us an idea of his cultural affinities and interests. It is also interesting to note that he stated his occupation in German, presumably mindful of the fact that the intended recipient of the album was German. The inscription, however, was in Dutch, even though a man with Uylenburgh's background would have been reasonably fluent in both languages. That said, he misspelt one of the words. Was he overhasty and careless, or was his Dutch perhaps not quite impeccable?

Finally, the value of publications like De Brune's emblem book lay predominantly in their illustrations, and Uylenburgh may have kept works of this kind in stock. The *Emblemata of sinnewerck* contains more than fifty prints after work by Adriaen van de Venne, executed by various engravers, and it was probably just the kind of material that Uylenburgh had on offer.

Another personal document is the will drawn up by Hendrick Uylenburgh and Maria van Eyck in 1634.[167] Uylenburgh's name is preceded by the title 'The Honourable', while Maria is designated 'his lawful wife'. The couple were said to be living in Amsterdam and known to the notary. Uylenburgh was in good health and Maria 'indisposed', but of sound mind and therefore able to make a will. More likely than not, she was expecting a child. The couple revoked their earlier, but otherwise unspecified, wills and testaments and nominated as the heirs to their entire estate, in equal share, their six children 'begotten by the grace of God', namely,

167 GAA, not. S. Cornelisz, NA 641, pp. 79-80, 15 July 1634; Bredius 1915-1922, vol. 5, p. 1687(e).

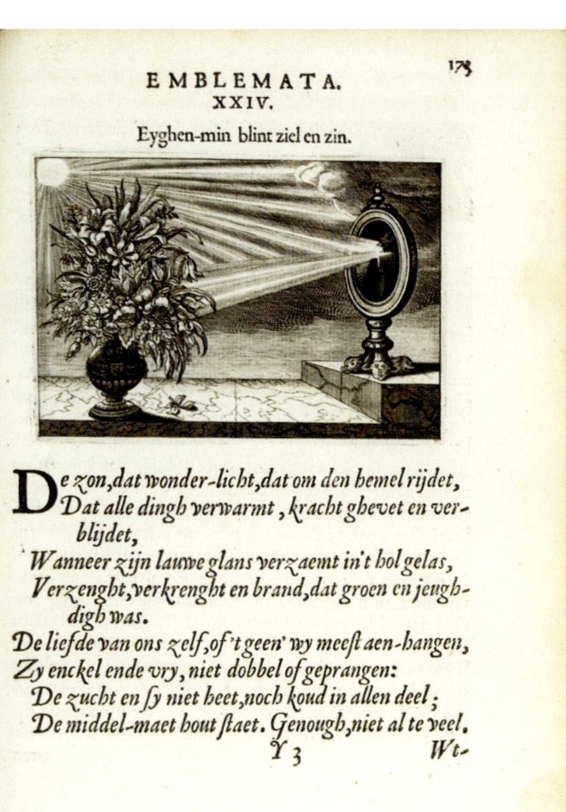

24 J. de Brune, Emblemata of zinnewerk (Amsterdam 1624), Amsterdam, Universiteitsbibliotheek

'Gerrit', 'Isack', 'Sara', 'Anna', 'Susanna' and 'Lyntgen', as well as any children yet to come. The surviving partner was to be granted custody of the children for life, and was entitled to retain the communal property until such time as he or she remarried, without being accountable to relatives or the Orphans' Chamber. The testators expressed their confidence that the surviving partner would not disadvantage any of the children, but would care for them and provide for their 'sustenance, clothing, schooling and other physical needs'. They were to 'teach them God's ways and raise them in fear of the Lord'. The surviving partner was also authorised to administer the children's share in the estate until such time as they married or attained the age of majority (twenty-five). In this they were accountable to the children's guardians but the Orphans Chamber was not to intervene. If the surviving partner remarried, each child was to receive a hundred guilders, representing one sixth of their statu-

tory share of the inheritance, 'or such amount as the surviving partner deems appropriate, having regard to the value of the estate at that time'. The money was to be transferred in the presence of two or three members of the deceased's family. The will was drawn up and signed by both parties in the couple's home, but their address is not stated (fig. 25). No provision was made for household effects, paintings or the business, nor were any bequests made to individuals or, for example, to assist destitute members of the Mennonite community. Both husband and wife had complete confidence in their partner's ability to manage the household and care for the family. Although they subsequently had several more children, the will was not superseded. It was executed four years later, after the death of Maria van Eyck.

One of the two witnesses to the will was the Mennonite Govert Spruijt, who lived in the house diagonally opposite the Uylenburghs' in Breestraat (see fig. 21).[168] Spruijt was a brazier and acquainted with the artists living in Breestraat.[169] He was married to the widow of the painter Jacques Saverij. His sister married the painter and art dealer Mattheus van Hoven in 1612.

FROM THE MID-1630S UP TO HENDRICK UYLENBURGH'S DEATH IN 1661

Some time between 1635 and 1638 Hendrick Uylenburgh and his family moved to a house called 'Cronenburch', further up the road in Breestraat (fig. 21).[170] The following facts suggest that the move may have taken place on 1 May 1638. On 16 January 1636 the merchant Jan Arentsz van Naerden purchased 'Cronenburch' for more than 7,800 guilders and occupied it himself.[171] In early 1637 he drew up his will in

168 The other was Jan Volckertsz Oli, a Catholic notary, whose protocol begins in 1638.
169 Braziers were categorised as artist-craftsmen. This is illustrated by the marriage banns of Govert Spruijt, who was described as a 'copper-smith'. However, the words were deleted and replaced by 'brazier', GAA, DTB 763, p. 25, 11 January 1614.
171 In the vicinity of the present Sint-Anthoniesbreestraat 53. Dudok van Heel (1982, p. 89, note 40) initially argued that Uylenburgh moved to the home of the painter Pieter Isaacksz, diagonally opposite the corner house on Zwanenburgwal (see fig. 21), but rectified this statement in later publications.

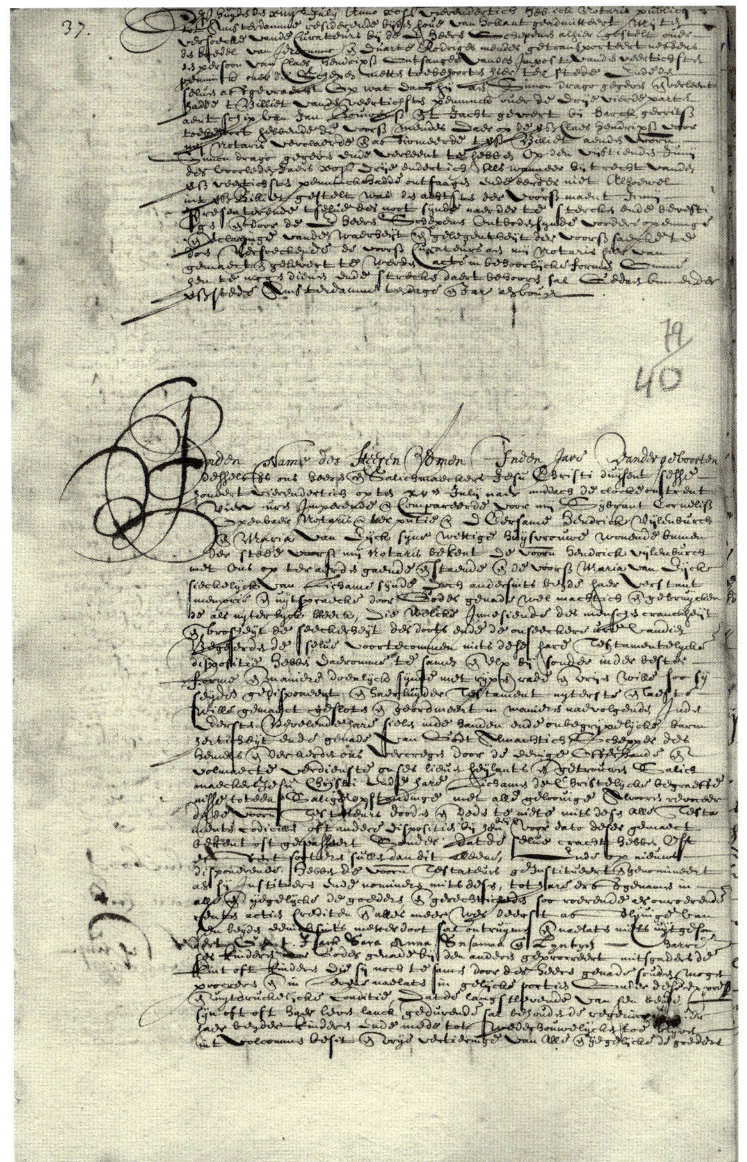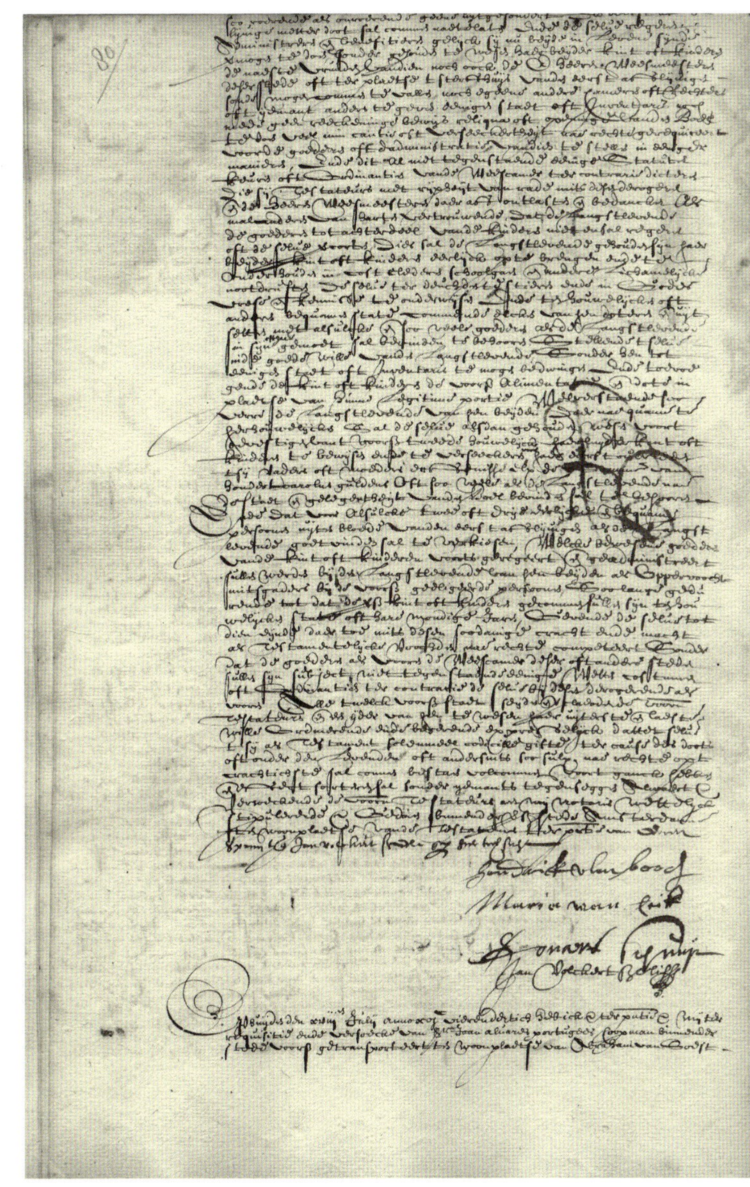

25 Will of Hendrick Uylenburgh and Maria van Eyck of 15 July 1634, Amsterdam, Gemeentearchief

172 GAA, archive no. 5061, inv. no. 2167, fol. 164v, 16 January 1636.

173 GAA, not. L. Lamberti, NA 580, fol. 934, 31 January 1637.

174 GAA, not. L. Lamberti, NA 569, pp. 310-322, 11 December 1637; Bredius 1915-1922, vol. 4, pp. 1230-1232.

175 GAA, Burials Register WK no. 20, 14 July 1638. Other sources give the date as 15 July 1638, see notes 117 and 118.

the house 'in Breestraat, opposite Hoogstraat'.[172] Van Naerden died within the year and an inventory of his possessions was made on 11 December.[173] Lucas Luce and Hendrick Uylenburgh appraised his collection of art. Jan Arentsz van Naerden's brother, Claes Arentsz van Naerden, inherited the house and rented it to Hendrick Uylenburgh and his family. As rental agreements normally entered into effect on 1 May, Uylenburgh presumably acquired tenancy on 1 May 1638. The family is first documented at this address on 14 or 15 July 1638, the date of Maria van Eyck's burial. According to the burials register, she had passed away 'in the house Croonenberch in Breestraet'.[174] If the family indeed moved there on 1 May 1638, Uylenburgh must have rented his previous home from the celebrated portraitist Claes Eliasz, who, in the spring of 1637, was the registered owner of that property.[175] Uylenburgh was apparently closely acquainted with Claes van Naerden, who invested money in his business in 1640. Two years later Van Naerden sold the house to Adriaen van der Heeden,[176] who continued to rent 'Cronenburgh' to Uylenburgh. Uylenburgh appraised art for these families as well.

A number of documents dating from the second half of the 1630s shed light on Hendrick Uylenburgh's business. They are discussed at length in chapter 3. The majority refer to appraisals of art for private individuals, the earliest of these being from 1637. Others pertain to arbitration assignments. In 1642, for instance, Uylenburgh was called upon to mediate in a dispute between Rembrandt and one of his clients concerning remuneration for a portrait. Some of the documents refer to auctions held in 1635, 1637 and 1638, when Uylenburgh bought paintings for his shop, while others concern transactions with painters and art dealers in various parts of the country. Lambert Jacobsz managed Uylenburgh's affairs in Leeuwarden up to the time of his death in 1636. A recent discovery is that Uylenburgh had business connections with the painter and art dealer Pieter de Neyn in Leiden. He visited the painter's home in December 1638, when De Neyn signed his will, 'in the presence of and witnessed by Seigneur Heynrick Ulemburgh, merchant of Amsterdam' (see fig. 138).[177] Around 1640 Uylenburgh borrowed money on at least three occasions to finance acquisitions for the firm. In 1639 he obtained a loan from two Mennonite merchants, in 1640 he received a large sum of money from a consortium of eighteen financiers, and in 1641 1,000 guilders from the Waterland Mennonites. He emerged as one of the leading art dealers in the Dutch Republic. The German painter Joachim von Sandrart, who lived in Amsterdam from 1637 to 1642, described him as 'the famous art dealer Ulenburg'.

Little is known about the private lives of Hendrick Uylenburgh or his family. Uylenburgh remained a widower after the death of his wife. His unmarried daughters presumably managed the household and probably lent a hand with the business. To the best of our knowledge, he did not draw up a will after 1638. Rembrandt's wife Saskia died in 1642.[178] Uylenburgh represented her family and in that capacity authorised Rembrandt to continue to administer her entire estate. Uylenburgh lived in Breestraat for about twenty-two years, and in 1647 moved to a house called 'De Bril' in Dam Square (fig. 26).[179] De Bril, which belonged to the municipality, had previously been rented by the little-known painter Barent Jansz Veris, who may have run an art business on the premises. The rent was substantial, at 700 guilders a year, plus an additional 250 guilders for the use of the basement. Up to 18 August 1649 the tenant was also liable for the annual property tax, which, after that time, was paid from the municipal coffers. For use as an art gallery, the house was conveniently located near the town hall and close to shops selling luxury goods. There were also several print shops at the top end of Kalverstraat, just off Dam Square, and in the nearby Damrak a large bookshop belonging to Jacob Aertsz Colom. One of the few surviving documents from those years is a statement of 21 December 1649 concerning a person who had sailed to the East Indies. Hendrick Uylenburgh's name appears in the deed and on that occasion he gave his age as approximately sixty.[180]

Uylenburgh continued to run his shop in Dam Square until 1653. In that year the city fathers decided to demolish a number of houses in and around the square to make way for a new town hall. As a result, Uylenburgh was forced to move. At that stage he owed two years' rent, which he promised to pay on 18 January 1658. In the preceding years he or his assistants had restored and revarnished paintings belonging to the city of Amsterdam that were to be hung in the new town hall. Perhaps he was given the assignment to compensate for the eviction.

On 23 December 1654 Uylenburgh and a fellow citizen made a statement concerning a public disturbance.[181] They had witnessed a man hurling abuse at someone in the street, and two days later submitted a report at the victim's request. The assault was outrageous, they declared, on a man 'who frequents the stock exchange'. In other words, the victim was a person of some social standing. As Mennonites, the witnesses declined to take the oath, but testified

170 The remissions from that period have been lost.
176 Claes van Naerden sold him two houses, one being 'Cronenburch, in Breestraet, which house was transferred to Jan Arentsz van Naerden in 1636', GAA, not. L. Lamberti, NA 609, 12 June 1642.
177 RAL, not. J. Jansz Verwey, NA 112, deed 5, 15 December 1638.
178 Buried 'Sasgen van Uijlenburch of Breestraet across St Tonissluys, the second house, 19 June do.'. The entry refers to the will of Rembrandt and Saskia as well, and notes that Rembrandt retained the undivided estate and was exempted from giving account, 'with the consent of Hendrick Uylenburch', GAA, Burials Register Wk no. 6 (Oude Kerk), 19 June 1642 and Doc. 1642/9.
179 GAA, archive no. 5044, inv. no. 272 (Property Tax Register 1647-1649), fol. 6, first noted in Breen 1909, p. 162; Wijnman 1959, p. 16, and Dudok van Heel 1982, pp. 78 and 89 and note 41.
180 GAA, not. G. Coren, NA 1000, 21 December 1649; Bredius 1915-1922, vol. 5, p. 1689(l).
181 GAA, not. L. Lamberti, NA 604, p. 622, 23 December 1654; Bredius 1915-1922, vol. 5, p. 1689(o).

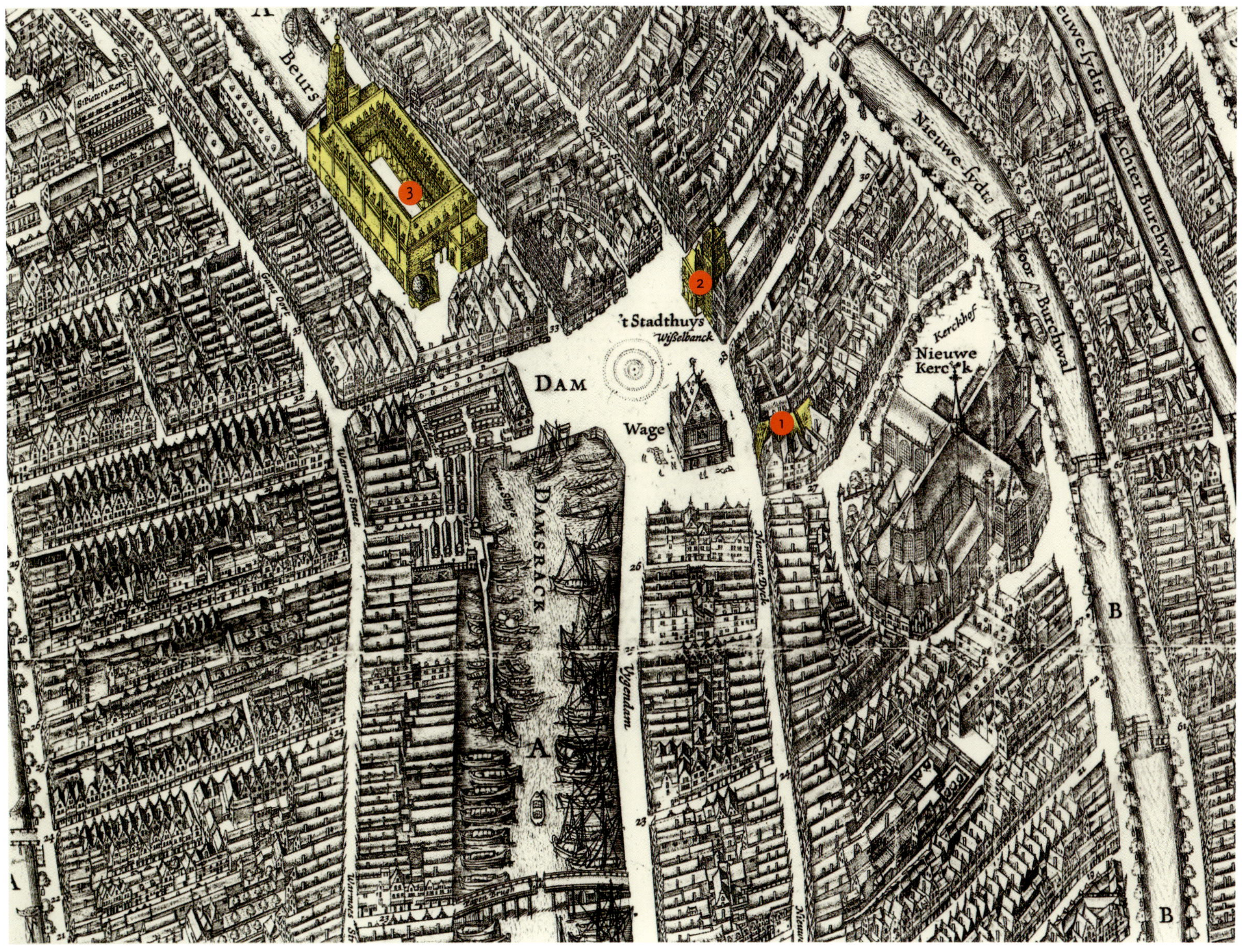

26 Detail of fig. 20

[1] 'De Bril' the house on the Dam where Hendrick Uylenburgh lived. Immediately next door was the Town Hall [2], with the Stock Exchange [3] a little further along.
Jacob Aertsz Colom lived in Damrak (the Vijgendam), just off the map

182 G A A, archive no. 5044, inv. no. 281, fol. 95 and inv. no. 284, fol. 232v.

183 The house at Prinsengracht no. 283, Wijnman 1959, p. 16.

184 Jacob Colom had bought the house on Damrak (now no. 45), which he called 'de Vurighe Colom', for 11,500 guilders in 1627.

'on their word of honour instead'. Nothing more is known about the second witness. He may have been an acquaintance of Uylenburgh's or simply a chance passer-by.

It is uncertain where Uylenburgh moved to in 1653. It may have been the Leliegracht, as he paid the annual property tax on a house there on two occasions.[182] In any event, he did not remain there for long, as in 1658 he moved to rented premises on the corner of Prinsengracht and Westermarkt (fig. 27).[183] The owner of the property was the bookseller and publisher Jacob Aertsz Colom, whom we have encountered above (fig. 28). Colom published numerous works by Mennonites, Remonstrants and free-thinkers, but was best known for his maps and nautical charts. His shop was close to the house 'De Bril', Uylenburgh's home from 1647 to 1653.[184] Like Uylenburgh, Colom was a member of the Waterland Mennonite Church, where

57

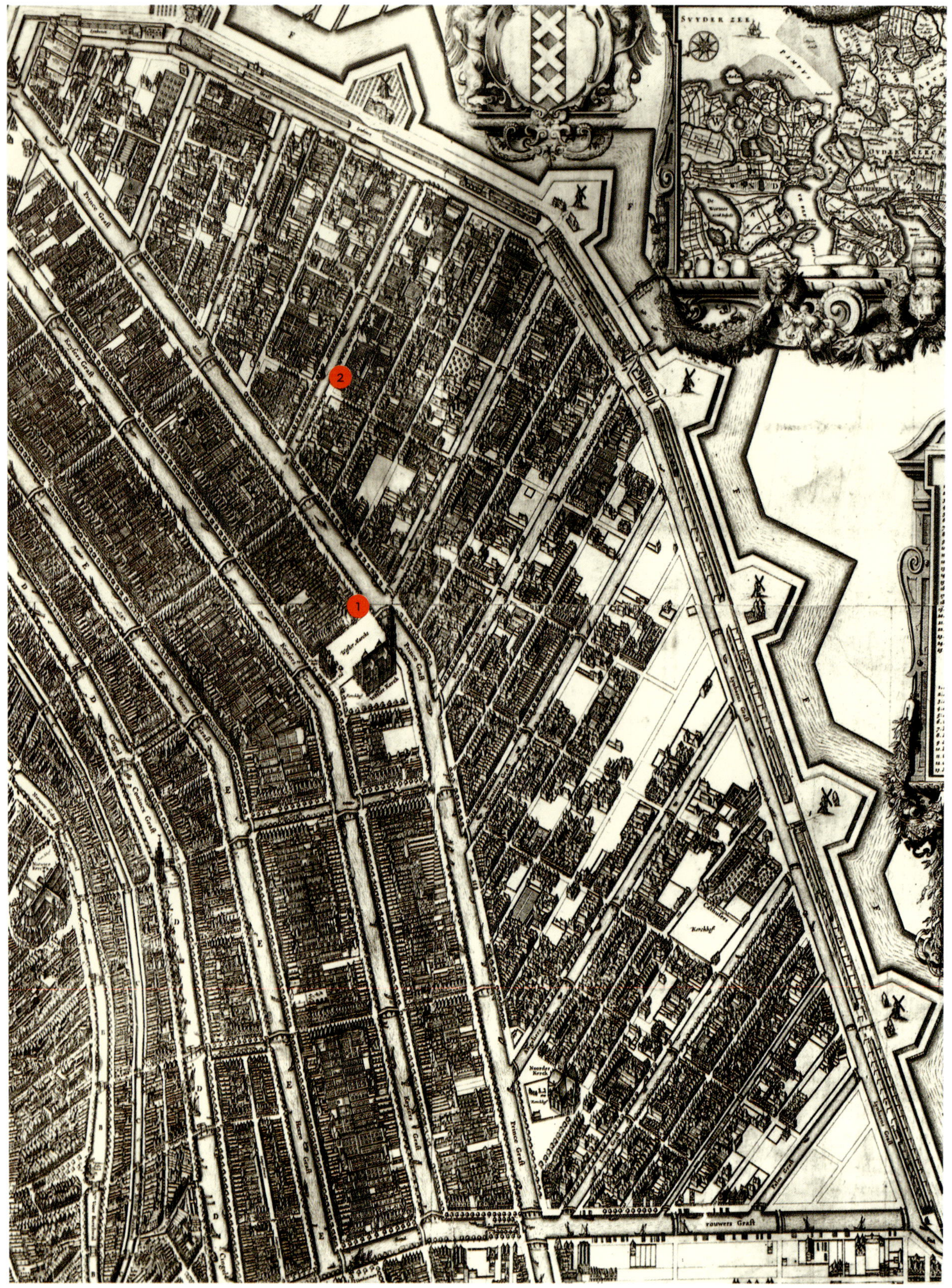

27 Detail of fig. 20
The house where Hendrick Uylenburgh lived [1] was in the Westermarkt, by the Westerkerk, close to the old centre of Amsterdam.
He then moved to the Lauriergracht [2] into the house in which the painter Govert Flinck had worked, and where Gerrit Uylenburgh's business was located

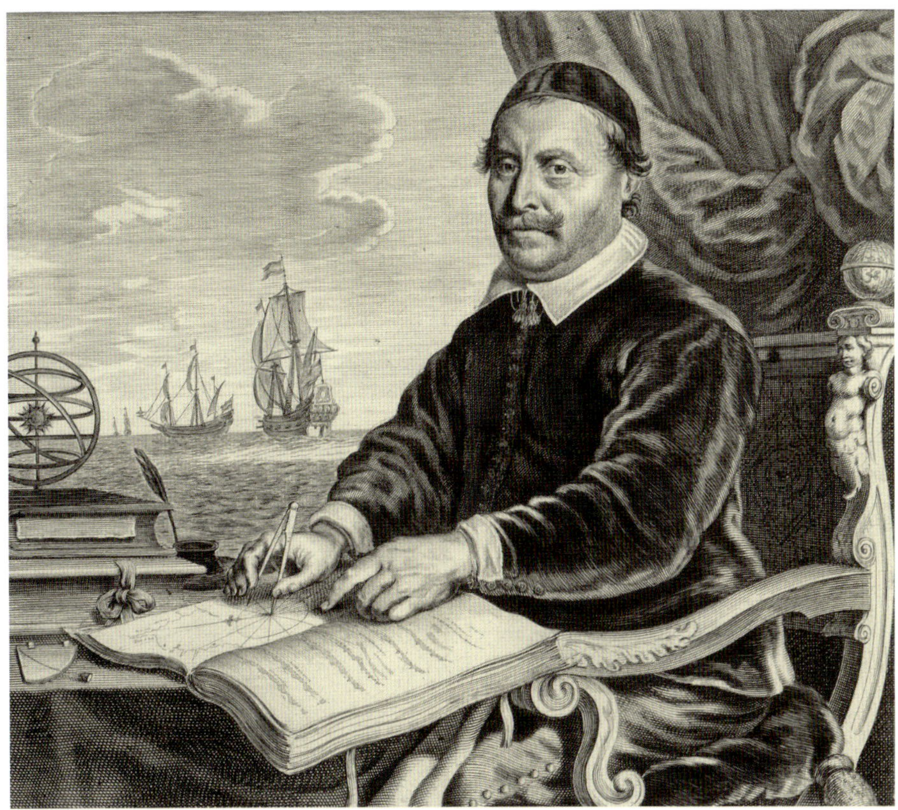

185 See NNBW vol. 9, col.
156-160, and Visser 1978.
186 GAA, not. H. Westfrisius,
NA 2805, pp. 105-106, 7 February 1662, and the preceding
deed of the same date, ibid.,
p. 105; Bredius 1915-1922,
vol. 5, p. 1690(s).
187 Buried in the Westerkerk
'Hendrick Uijlenborgh, Lauriergracht', GAA, DTB 1100(B),
p. 178, 22 March 1661.

he was baptised in 1622.[185] The two men must therefore have known each other quite well. Uylenburgh rented the premises on Prinsengracht for a period of two years, after which time his son Gerrit took over the lease and sublet the house. This information emerges from a statement Gerrit made two years later, at Colom's request.[186] Uylenburgh, and presumably the children still living at home, moved to a house on the Lauriergracht that was previously occupied by Govert Flinck, who had died at the beginning of February 1660.

In 1660 the elderly Hendrick Uylenburgh still played an active role in the business and received commissions to appraise works of art. But he lived in the house on Lauriergracht only briefly. He passed away there in 1661 and was buried in the nearby Westerkerk on 22 March of that year.[187] No documents have come to light concerning his estate. His eldest son had essentially taken over the business, but all the children were entitled to a statutory share of the inheritance. Those who were still living in Amsterdam may have remained active in the business, but it was Gerrit who took the helm.

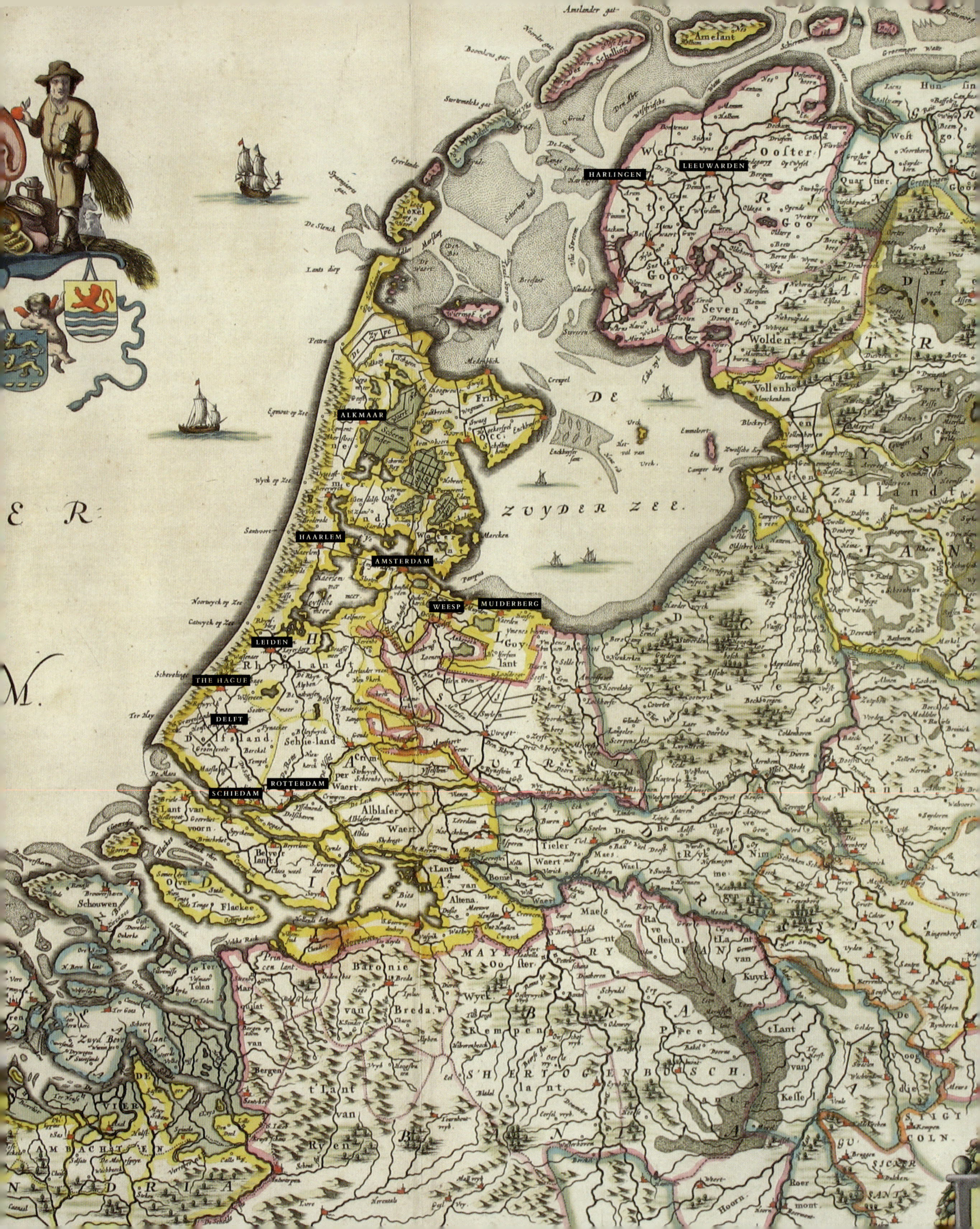

HARLINGEN
LEEUWARDEN
ALKMAAR
HAARLEM
AMSTERDAM
WEESP
MUIDERBERG
LEIDEN
THE HAGUE
DELFT
SCHIEDAM
ROTTERDAM
ZUYDER ZEE
Texel
Amelant
Ooster
WEST
FRIESLANT
Seven Wolden
Gooyland
De Veluwe
Schouwen
Breda
Kempen
'S HERTOGENBOSCH
't Lant van Breda
Baronie van Breda
Rynen
Alblaser Waert

Gerrit Uylenburgh, art dealer and painter in Amsterdam and London

FRISO LAMMERTSE

Early years, 1625-1659

Gerrit Uylenburgh, the eldest son of Hendrick Uylenburgh and Maria van Eyck, continued to build up the art business his father had founded,[1] transforming it into an international enterprise with contacts in several European cities. Almost nothing is known about Gerrit's youth. At his betrothal on 6 April 1666 he stated that he was 40 years old, and a notarial deed of 27 May 1667 gives his age as 42. We can therefore conclude that he was probably born between 6 April and 27 May 1625,[2] at which time his parents were living in the vicinity of the Zuiderkerk. He lost his mother when he was about thirteen, and his father never remarried. As the eldest child, Gerrit must have shouldered much of the responsibility for his siblings. As we have seen, the family were staunch members of the Waterland Mennonite church. On 17 December 1645, when he was about 20 years old, Gerrit and 24 other congregants were baptised in 'het Lam'.[3]

TRAINING AS A PAINTER

Gerrit Uylenburgh's teacher has never been identified. Even Houbraken, writing in 1719, was unable to shed light on the matter. However, as a youngster, Gerrit must have been closely acquainted with the artists who worked for his father, and one or more of them, possibly Rembrandt and later Govert Flinck, may have helped him along when he first starting learning to draw.[4] In terms of style, the paintings that may be tentatively attributed to Gerrit Uylenburgh offer no indication as to who might have taught him.

Most of Uylenburgh's paintings listed in seventeenth-century inventories are landscapes. He evidently specialised in this genre and indeed Houbraken writes that 'he took to painting landscapes'.[6] Even so, he must have produced figure pieces and portraits as well. The earliest reference to a painting by him dates from 1653, when 'a work by Uylenburgh's son, with my portrait painted by Ovens' was said to be in the possession of Jacob Leeuw.[7] Uylenburgh presumably painted the landscape, and Jürgen Ovens the portrait of Jacob Leeuw.[8] Leeuw and his family were Mennonites and well acquainted with the Uylenburghs, while Ovens was associated with the Uylenburghs' firm in the 1640s. Ovens returned to Schleswig-Holstein in about 1651 and must therefore have painted the portrait before that date, when Jacob Leeuw (b. 1636) was still a youngster. Records of Gerrit's work in a number of inventories reveal that he was active as a painter by at least the early 1650s.

In 1653 Joan Dullaert published a poem inspired by a painting by Gerrit. His 'Reflections

1 Gerrit Uylenburgh generally signed his name as Uylenborch. However, in most documents his name appears as 'Uylenburgh'.
2 GAA, DTB 488, fol. 350 (betrothal); see fig. 38; not. J. Hellerus, NA 2078, fol. 265, 27 May 1667.
3 GAA, archive no. 565, fol. 16v and 17r. On 1 December 1645 'Gerrit Uilenburg, the son of Hendrick Uilenburg' applied to be baptised. The baptism took place on 17 December during a service conducted by Dionys Verschuer.
4 Houbraken 1718-1721, vol. 2, p. 293
5 See p. 207.
6 Houbraken 1718-1721, vol. 2, pp. 293-294.

7 GAA, archive no. 88, inv. no. 809, 7-14 February 1653. See p. 174. See Van Eeghen 1953, pp. 170-174. On Ovens, see Schmidt 1922 and Drees 1997, and pp. 212-214, 258-263.
8 Paintings by an Uylenburgh are mentioned before 1653, but the artist's first name is not given. They may have been works by Gerrit, but this seems unlikely. One document concerns the sale on 8 April 1647 of 'an original by Uylenburgh', which the pensionary Boreel bought in The Hague for 24 guilders, Bredius 1915-1922, vol. 2, p. 467. Also on record is that on 10 November 1650 in the home of Anna Kerckrinck 'a painting by Uylenburgh was hanging in the main hall, of her esteemed brother'. See Bredius 1915-1922, vol. 5, p. 1689. Both may have been paintings by Rombout. See also p. 124, note 34.

Van Velt - en Watergoôn kunt trekken.
De dieren luiſtren na uw ſpel.
Gy zult voor Orfeus ons verſtrekken;
Want ghy godt Pluto in de hel
Kunt door uw' brave zwier bewegen.
Den Garamant, zoo ver' gelegen
By Kaukazus in 't koude Noordt,
Schut zijn' beſneeude kruin, vol boomen,
Van vreugde als hy u ſpelen hoordt.
Hoe zouden wy ons kunnen toomen?
Maatrijke MAAS, die deur de klank
Van uwen Veel verdooft mijn Zangk,
Speel eeuwig op uw ſchelle ſnaren,
De Goôn en Nimfjens aan den dans.
Ghy zult hier na ten Hemel varen,
Met Fébus goude Zonnekrans.

Op 't afbeeltzel van de ſchoone Herderinne

ANNA.

O UYLENBORCH, uw levensverven,
Als zy deze ANNA zien, beſterven.
Want zulk een proefſtuk van natuur,
Blaakt gloeyender als Hemelvuur.
Als ghy hare oogjens recht zout malen,
Moſt ge uw penzeel aan Zonneſtralen
Ontvonken, en met leventgit
Deurmengen; maar om 't rechte wit

Van

Van 't purpre montje wel te treffen,
Moſt ge uw vernuft noch hoger heffen.
Neem Roozen van de Roozekrans
Die Venus draagt, mengt die met glans
Van heldre Starren, uitgekozen;
Dat zal dan als heur lipjens blozen.
Maar wiſt ghy raat heur zoete taal,
Daar door zy harten meenigmaal
Ten ooren uitrukt, ons te toonen,
Dan mogt ghy wel by Goden woonen.
Natuur u deze kunſt verbiet,
En al uw arbeidt is om niet,
O UYLENBORCH, dies is 't van nooden
Dat ge, als Pigmalion, de Goden
Aanbidt met nederig gekniel;
Op dat ze in ANNAAS beelt een ziel
En leven ſtorten uit heur zalen.
En anders kuntg'er geeſt niet malen.

J. DULLAART.

'Amſterdam, Ter Drukkerye van TYMON HOUTHAAK,
in de Pottebakkersſtraat, over de Nieuwezijds Kolk.

on the portrayal of the lovely shepherdess Anna' muses over Uylenburgh's inability to capture Anna in all her beauty (fig. 30). The picture must have been a portrait of a woman in the guise of a shepherdess, but without knowing her family name it is impossible to establish her identity. Was she perhaps Gerrit's sister Anna? The poem was first published as a supplement to *Alexander de Medicis of 't Bedrooge betrouwen,* Dullaert's adaptation of a Spanish play, which was produced in the municipal theatre in Amsterdam in the same year as another drama by Dullaert, about the life of Charles I of England.[9]

The son of a Rotterdam physician, Joan Dul-laert lived in Amsterdam in the 1640s and early 1650s.[10] He may have met Gerrit Uylenburgh through his cousin Heymen Dullaert. In 1652-1655, around the time that Joan was starting to gain a reputation in Amsterdam's theatre world, the Rotterdam-born Heymen was apprenticed to Rembrandt.[11] Heymen was a painter, a poet and, according to his biographer, an outstanding musician 'blessed with a beautiful voice'.[12] The two cousins, Heymen and Joan, both of them poets, translators and music lovers, were close companions throughout the 1650s.[13] Joan Dullaert's interest in the arts is expressed in a poem he wrote in 1658 to mark the anniversary of the Rotterdam

wijck. The couple lived in Rotterdam, Dordrecht and Werkendam. In the 1660s Joan returned to Amsterdam, where he earned his livelihood as a merchant. On Joan Dullaert, see De Jong 1976/77, Van Putte 1978a, p. 46, note 43, p. 57, note 98 and Van Putte 1978b. Joan's father, Willem Dullaert, was an older brother of the father of Heymen Cornelis.

11 A short biography accompanying the publication of Heymen's collected poems notes that Heymen was apprenticed to Rembrandt (see note 12). In 1653 Joan was named as the witness to a deed signed by Rembrandt, see Doc. 1653/14.

12 See the 'Kort berecht wegens het Leven van Heiman Dullaert' in *H. Dullaerts gedichten,* Amsterdam 1719.

13 See Van Putte 1978a.

---

9 *Alexander de Medicis, of 't Bedrooge betrouwen* was an adaptation of Jacobus Baroces's prose translation of the Spanish *Los Medicis de Florencia,* by Diego Ximenez de Enciso. It was published by Gerrit van Goedesberg in Amsterdam and printed by Tymon Houthaak. The play was first produced in Amsterdam's municipal theatre on 16 June 1653. Dullaert's *Karel Stuart of Rampzalige Majesteit* (Charles Stuart, or Disastrous Majesty), was published by the same publishing house in 1652. On the productions of these plays, see Jong 1976/77.

10 Joan drew up his will in Amsterdam at the age of fourteen. His father had died in 1631, and Joan nominated his mother, the Amsterdam-born Hester Pels, as the sole heir to his estate (GAA, NA 507, not. J. Westfrisius, fol. 107v-108v, 30 May 1645). The introduction to *Karel Stuart of Rampzalige Majesteit* (Charles Stuart, or Disastrous Majesty) is dated 'Amsterdam, 1649, den 12 van Lentenmaant'. The dedication to Joan Hulft in *Alexander de Medicis* is dated 'Amsterdam, 1653 den 2. van Bloeimaant'. In 1654 Joan married Anna van Beverwijck, the daughter of the prominent Dordrecht physician Johan van Bever-

branch of the Guild of St Luke.[14] From his verse on Uylenburgh's painting of the shepherdess Anna it transpires that by the 1650s Uylenburgh was associating with Amsterdam's literati. Later, too, his circle of friends included several writers.

The German artist Jürgen Ovens studied painting in Amsterdam in the 1640s. Born in 1623, he was Gerrit Uylenburgh's contemporary and came from the North Sea port of Tönning at the mouth of the Eider River. His father Ove Broders was a wealthy merchant and shipowner. In 1652 Ovens married a woman from his hometown, Maria Martens, whose father, like his own, was a prosperous shipowner and art collector.[15] The couple made their home in nearby Friedrichstadt, which had been founded by Friedrich III, Duke of Schleswig-Holstein-Gottorf in 1621. The town's population was predominantly Dutch, and regular shipping services between Friedrichstadt and the Dutch Republic enabled Ovens to keep in touch with his acquaintances in Amsterdam. Friedrichstadt also had a large Mennonite community to whom the duke had granted religious freedom and other privileges. The community maintained close ties with their coreligionists in Amsterdam.[16]

Ovens's acquaintance with Duke Friedrich III dates back to at least 1650. In 1652 he was granted ducal privileges which exempted him from civic taxation and placed him under the patronage of the court. Though not officially a court painter, probably in view of his financial independence, he was nevertheless engaged for every important commission for the duke. Friedrich III ruled as an absolute monarch, manoeuvring deftly between the neighbouring superpowers, Sweden and Denmark. At Gottorf Castle, near Schleswig, he assembled a collection of paintings and established an outstanding art chamber and library.[17]

Gerrit was invited to the court in Gottorf in 1655, undoubtedly through the intercession of Jürgen Ovens. On 13 June of that year he received 250 rijksdaalders for paintings.[18] Two weeks later, on 26 June, according to the account books of Friedrich III's wife, 'a Dutch painter by the name of Davidt Uhlenburg' received 74 rijksdaalders in payment for engravings and 'carvings'. The inscription of the name David was probably an error, and the recipient would most likely have been Gerrit or one of his brothers.[19] In 1665, Gerrit's name occurs again in the ledgers of the dukes of Schleswig. On 5 January of that year Ovens received 71 rijksdaalders for Gerrit Uylenburgh for 'rare books' and engravings for the library.[20] He had apparently acted as an intermediary in the transaction. Ovens's pursuits as a collector and art dealer are discussed in more detail below.

The journey to Schleswig is one of the first indications that Gerrit was becoming more involved in the art trade. In the second half of the 1650s he appears to have assumed more and more responsibility for his father's affairs. Hendrick Uylenburgh was already in his late 60s, turning 70, and it was only to be expected that his eldest son would gradually start taking over the business. In any event Gerrit must have been helping out before that time. In 1649 he and Lucas Luce had valued paintings.[21] Although his father would normally have carried out such assignments in those years, on this occasion, for unknown rea-

---

14 *Bloemkrans van verscheiden gedichten, door eenige liefhebbers der Poëzij bij een verzamelt*, Amsterdam, Louwijs Spillebout 1659, pp. 573-577, 'Aan de broeders van Sant Lukas Gilde te Rotterdam'. Few have commented on the poem, in which Dullaert addresses himself to Sorgh, Ludolph de Jongh and Saftleven.
15 On Ovens, see the outstanding book by Schmidt 1922.
16 Claussen 1997.

17 The custodian of this collection, the German scholar Adam Olearius, was also the court mathematician and librarian. He visited Enkhuizen in the Dutch Republic in 1650 to buy the famous collection of curiosities belonging to the physician Berent ten Broecke, better known as Paludanus, from the heirs to Ten Broecke's estate (see Van Gelder 1992, pp. 263-266). The library's expenditure rose sharply under Olearius. It was renowned for its manuscripts and was visited by the Dutch philologist Isaac Vossius on the recommendation of Nicolaas Heinsius and others (see Lohmeier 1997a and b).
18 Schmidt 1922, p. 93. See also p. 263 of this book.
19 Schmidt 1922, p. 93, and p. 260 of this book. The names of all but the youngest of the ten children born to Hendrick Uylenburgh and Maria van Eyck are known.

If the name David was not a clerical error, the person in question may have been this youngest child. He must have been born around 1637 and would have been about eighteen in 1655.
20 Schmidt 1922, p. 93, and p. 263 of this book.
21 See p. 293.

sons, the responsibility fell to Gerrit. Gerrit's next commission of this kind came only in 1657.

In November 1655 Gerrit and his father jointly undertook to repay a sum of money that Hendrick owed Nicolaes van Bambeeck. They arranged to remit 2251:15:8 guilders in instalments from that date up to 1660.[22] The fact that Gerrit co-signed the document gave Van Bambeeck the assurance that, in the event of Hendrick's death, he would still be able to claim any outstanding amount.

Another document concerning Gerrit was drawn up a few months later, on 7 February 1656. The art collector Jan Six, who is best remembered as an acquaintance of Rembrandt's, had asked Uylenburgh to underwrite the transfer of the full and unencumbered ownership of a house in Tuinstraat.[23] Jan's brother Pieter Six was the second signatory. The property was sold for 1,465 guilders. By signing the document, Gerrit accepted liability for any debts that might later come to light, although considering Jan Six's prodigious wealth, the chances were remote. Uylenburgh was not really at risk, but the fact that he was asked to underwrite the transaction implies that he was a man of some means and on at least cordial terms with Jan Six. Their relationship must have lasted at least until Gerrit left the Dutch Republic permanently in 1677. Uylenburgh was also closely acquainted with Pieter Six, who in 1671 was a witness to the baptism of one of his children.[24] He was moreover a client of Uylenburgh's, as we shall see in chapter 4. The sale of the house was effected in the presence of the magistrates Gerrit Hasselaer and Simon van Hoorn. A few years later Van Hoorn awarded Uylenburgh the prestigious assignment to select paintings for the king of England.

In 1657 Gerrit paid 500 guilders in final settlement of a 1,000-guilder loan that his father had obtained from the Waterland church in 1641.[25] Up to 1656 Hendrick had paid interest but not redeemed any of the capital. In that year he paid off 500 guilders and in the following year his son paid the balance. Gerrit's name occurs again in 1657, in connection with money he owed to the Mennonite cloth merchant Cornelis van Tongerloo, the son of Jasper, an investor in Hendrick Uylenburgh's business. The debt of a little over 66 guilders may have been the cost of a consignment of linen to be used for paintings. The debtors named in the document included a number of artists, among them Simon Luttichuys and Elias Vonck.[26]

All in all, little is known about Gerrit's life in the 1650s. As head of the family and director of the business, Hendrick Uylenburgh's name appears in several documents in connection with various transactions. However, this is not to say that he managed his affairs single-handed. In 1657, for instance, the city of Amsterdam paid him for the restoration of paintings, but he is unlikely to have completed the assignment on his own. We may reasonably assume that he delegated at least some of the work to Gerrit and possibly other members of the family.[27]

No documents pertaining to Gerrit are known from the years 1658 or 1659. He may have gone abroad during this period, perhaps to Italy. In any event, by 1660 he had apparently acquired a reputation as a connoisseur of Italian art, as he was invited to select paintings for the 'Dutch Gift' to Charles II. He may of course have gained this knowledge in the Netherlands without actually visiting Italy.

The Dutch Gift, 1660

In May 1660 the British parliament invited Charles II to return to England to take the throne. After the execution of his father Charles I in 1649, the crown prince had fled to Europe and

---

22 See p. 196.
23 GAA, Kwijtscheldingen (Discharges), C2, fol. 122v, 7 February 1656; Bredius 1886, p. 45. See also p. 276.
24 See p. 76.
25 GAA, archive no. 565, Kasboek Waterlandse gemeente (Waterland Church ledger), 336, V, fol. 45.
26 GAA, not. B. Coornhart, NA 2858, fol. 307-331verso, 17/24 August 1657, especially fol. 329v ('Gerret Uillenburgh f 66:10:-'). 'Two octagonal paintings by Uijlenburgh' were hanging in Cornelis van Tongerloo's home at the time of his death (fol. 313). See also NA 2861, deed 27, 22 August 1658; Van der Veen 2001, p. 55, note 26. On Van Tongerloo, see also p. 192-193.
27 See p. 56.

remained there in exile. Charles II received the good news in Breda, where his court had landed on 14 April 1660 and remained ever since. Both the States General and the States of Holland and West Friesland immediately dispatched envoys to Breda to congratulate the future king and pave the way for a close alliance.[28]

On 24 May Charles II and his entourage left Breda for The Hague, where they remained for a few days before embarking on their voyage to London.[29] On Saturday 29 May, before Charles II left for England, the executive committee of the States of Holland and West Friesland met to consider what they would need to spend on a gift to curry the king's favour. They agreed on the exorbitant sum of 600,000 guilders. Part of this amount was to cover the costs of the Dutch envoys' journey to Breda, part for a banquet to be held in the Mauritshuis the following day, and the remainder was to be spent on 'suitable gifts and presents'.[30] At the farewell dinner held on the eve of Charles II's departure, Amelis van Bouchorst, Lord of Wimmenum, delivered a speech on behalf of the States of Holland. He announced that the States had decided to present the king with 'a number of rare objects' as a token of their esteem. To which Charles II graciously replied that the honour they were bestowing on him there and then was more than he could wish for. That same evening Van Bouchorst called on the king's two brothers, the Dukes of York and Gloucester. After explaining that there had been no opportunity for the States to obtain an appropriate gift, he presented them with a cheque of 60,000 guilders 'from the States' coffers'.[31]

On 2 June crowds gathered to cheer as Charles II embarked in Scheveningen for the passage to London. A day later the States General decided to dispatch a delegation of 'ambassadors extraordinary' to London to strengthen the ties between the two parties and endeavour to enter into a 'treaty of alliance, friendship and commerce' with the new king. The importance they attached to the mission is evident from the number of servants assigned to the delegation. Each of the four ambassadors was attended by eight servants in livery, instead of the customary four.[32] But it was not until November that the party actually set foot on English soil.[33]

Both the States General and the States of Holland were anxious to maintain cordial relations with England, their most formidable mercantile rival. It was therefore of the greatest importance for the States of Holland to select an appropriate gift for the king. Three weeks after his departure, on 21 June, they agreed that he would in any event be presented with an 'exquisitely embroidered' bed. What they had in mind was a bed belonging to Mary Stuart, the widow of the Stadholder William II and the sister of Charles II. Van Bouchorst was entrusted with the task of 'prevailing upon' the widow to part with the bed, for which the States were willing to pay 100,000 guilders.[34] An account of Charles II's sojourn in the Republic describes the bed as 'indisputably the grandest and most splendid ever made in Paris'. It included a 'canopy, chairs, a fire screen, tapestries and all the accoutrements of a suite'. For good measure, it was to be accompanied by 'a magnificent tapestry wall hanging, wrought with silver and gold, specially ordered' for the occasion.[35] The meeting was also called upon to suggest other 'precious and suitable rarities' to present to the king, and to expedite the proposed acquisitions when it transpired that the gift could

28 See Wickevoort 1660, pp. 10, 21. The States of Holland sent Louis van Nassau, Lord of Leck and Beverweerd. He had stood by Charles II during his exile and his daughter was married to Thomas, Earl of Ossory and son of the Duke of Ormonde, one of the most influential noblemen at the English court. On the dukes of Ormonde, see Barnard/Fenlon 2000 and p. 76-77 of this book.

29 During his stay in The Hague the king had his portrait painted by Jürgen Ovens. The work was made for Prince Johan Maurits. See Schmidt 1922, p. 278. Its whereabouts are unknown, but Vondel wrote a poem about it which notes that the king was 'ready for the journey' to London. Ovens possessed a copy of the work, which is listed in the inventory of his widow's estate. See Schmidt 1914, p. 42.

30 Wickevoort 1660, pp. 78-79, seems to suggest that the executive committee resolved at their meeting on 29 May to present the king with a bed, tapestries and paintings. According to the minutes of the States of Holland, however, they only decided on the nature of the gift in the course of the following months. Wickevoort presumably compressed the information in order to keep his account as simple as possible. See The Hague, National Archives, States of Holland, 3.01.04.01, no. 2403, fol. 183r, 29 May 1660 (the quotation was taken from this source). The document mentions an allocation of 700,000 guilders for a gift for the king. However, a note in the margin gives the figure as 600,000 guilders, the amount consistently referred to thereafter. The reference to 700,000 was probably a clerical error.

31 Wickevoort 1660, p. 117.

The Hague, National Archives, States of Holland, 3.01.04.01, no. 2403, fol. 199v, refers to 75,000 guilders for the two brothers.

32 The Hague, National Archives, States of Holland, 3.01.04.01, no. 2403, fol. 321r-v. They were also to be accompanied by a treasurer, three clerks and three chamberlains.

33 The Hague, National Archives, States of Holland, 3.01.04.01, no. 2403, fol. 207r (3 June 1660, it was decided to send a delegation), 221r, 228v, 333r.

34 The Hague, National Archives, States of Holland and West Friesland 1572-1795, 3.01.05, no. 3010. Published by Leupe 1876, p. 184. See also Logan 1979, p. 77, note 83.

35 Wickevoort 1660, p. 79.

be sent along with the four ambassadors who were preparing to leave for England.[36]

It was common practice in the seventeenth century to bestow extravagant gifts on heads of states who were influential in the Republic's trade relations. The States General had already presented gifts to England on two previous occasions. In 1610 Henry, Prince of Wales, had received a number of paintings, including one by Hendrick Vroom,[37] in gratitude for England's assistance in negotiating the Twelve Year Truce and in the hope of persuading the government to rescind its prohibition on fishing off the coasts of England, Scotland and Ireland. In 1636, the States General presented Charles I with porcelain, embroidery, damask and horses, as well as two famous paintings by Geertgen tot Sint Jans and works that were attributed at the time to Jan Gossaert and Lucas van Leyden.[38]

Hence, there was a precedent for the decision taken by the executive committee of the States of Holland and West Friesland to present paintings to Charles II in addition to the bed and all its accessories. On 2 September they wrote to Cornelis de Vlaming van Oudtshoorn, a former committee member and former burgomaster of Amsterdam, asking him to call in on the widow of Gerard Reynst and persuade her to sell some of her late husband's paintings at a reasonable price. They were especially interested in the collection, having been reliably informed that the king was 'not partial to paintings by modern artists, but preferred antique pieces and Italian masters'.[39] Charles I had been one of the greatest collectors of Italian art of his day, with a passion for sixteenth-century artists like Raphael and Titian. The collection was sold after his death in 1649, and in 1660 his son probably intimated that he

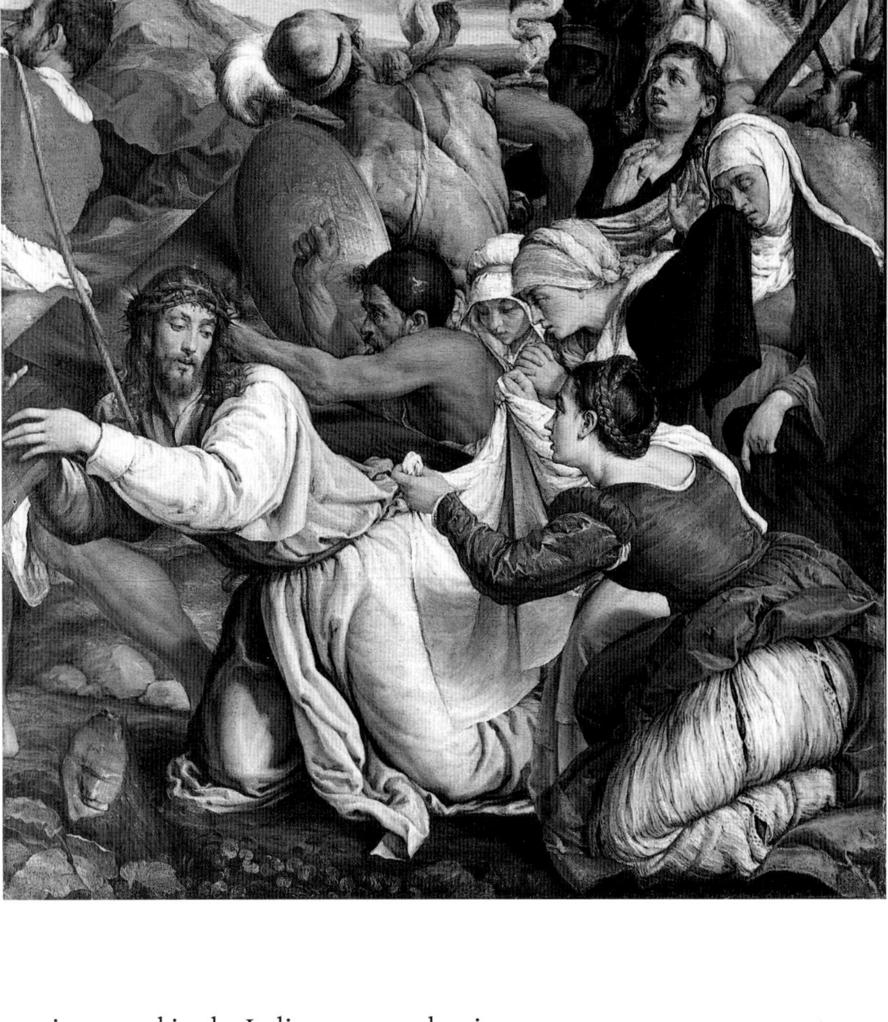

31 Jacopo Bassano, The Way to Calvary, canvas, 145 x 133 cm, London, The National Gallery

was interested in the Italian masters, hoping, perhaps, to reinstate this part of the royal collection.[40]

The collection of Italian paintings and classical sculpture belonging to Gerard Reynst, who died in 1658, was the largest of its kind in the Republic. It had been assembled by Gerard with the help of his brother Jan, who is known to have been living in Venice since at least 1625. After his death there

36 The Hague, National Archives, States of Holland, 3.01.04.01, no. 2403, fol. 255, 256, Friday 23 July 1660 resolution of the States of Holland and West Friesland.
37 Van Gelder 1963, pp. 541-544.
38 Bruyn/Millar 1962, pp. 291-294. The States General were anxious to strengthen their ties with Charles I out of concern about his pro-Spain stance and his navigation policy. The two paintings by Geertgen tot Sint Jans were *The Lamentation* and *The Legend of the Relics of Saint John the Baptist*, now at the Kunsthistorisches Museum in Vienna. The Gossaert may have been the large panel depicting Adam and Eve, which has remained in the British Royal Collection. The *Saint Jerome,* then attributed to Lucas van Leyden, may have been the painting, or one very similar to it, which is now at the Rijksmuseum, Amsterdam, and attributed to Aertgen van Leyden or an anonymous painter of the Leiden School (inv. no. A 3903).
39 The Hague, National Archives, 3.01.04.01, no. 1396, States of Holland and West Friesland 1621-1795, register van minuten van uitgaande missieven van de Staten en Gecommitteerde Raden van Holland (register of minutes of outgoing missives from the States and the Executive Committee of Holland). Published by Leupe 1876; see also Logan 1979, p. 77, note 84. In the same letter De Vlaming van Oudtshoorn was asked to call on the widow of the gentleman-dealer Michel le Blon to see whether she possessed any suitable paintings.
40 On Charles I's zeal as a collector, along with some of his courtiers, and on the dispersal of this collection, see Brown 1995.

in 1646 he left part, if not the entire collection to Gerard, a merchant and member of the city council in Amsterdam. The brothers are believed to have bought the complete collection owned by the Venetian nobleman Andrea Vendramin shortly after Vendramin's death in 1629, thereby acquiring numerous sixteenth-century Venetian paintings, classical sculptures and Egyptian antiquities, all of which were shipped to Amsterdam. With the Vendramin acquisition as a basis, the Reynst brothers gradually assembled a formidable collection of art.[41] Years later, in 1663, the widow Reynst's house was described as one of the 'most celebrated homes in Amsterdam for its collection of fine paintings and exotic treasures from distant climes'.[42] Some of those paintings and sculptures are known today from engravings.[43]

The letter to De Vlaming van Oudtshoorn suggested that if need be he might call on the burgomasters of Amsterdam for assistance in wresting paintings from the widow Reynst. And indeed he appears to have done so, as it was not he, but burgomaster Simon van Hoorn who went to visit her. Van Hoorn was De Vlaming van Oudtshoorn's successor on the executive committee of the States of Holland and one of the ambassadors appointed for the mission to England. He was also a close friend of the Reynst family and had been a pallbearer at Gerard Reynst's funeral.[44] On 17 September a report of Van Hoorn's visit was presented to the executive committee of the States of Holland. He had selected twenty-four paintings and twelve sculptures worth a total of 80,000 guilders, 'all of them of the highest calibre and the most painstakingly executed, in the opinion of connoisseurs of the art of painting and all it entails', Van Hoorn had not relied solely on his own judgment, but 'in appraising the foresaid paintings and sculptures [had] sought guidance and advice from Gerrit Uijlenburch and Culinus'. The Culinus in question was the Antwerp sculptor Artus Quellinus, who was working on the

41 Logan 1979.
42 Fokkens 1663, p. 71.
43 On the Vendramin/Reynst collection, see also pp. 92-99.
44 See Logan 1979, pp. 26-27.

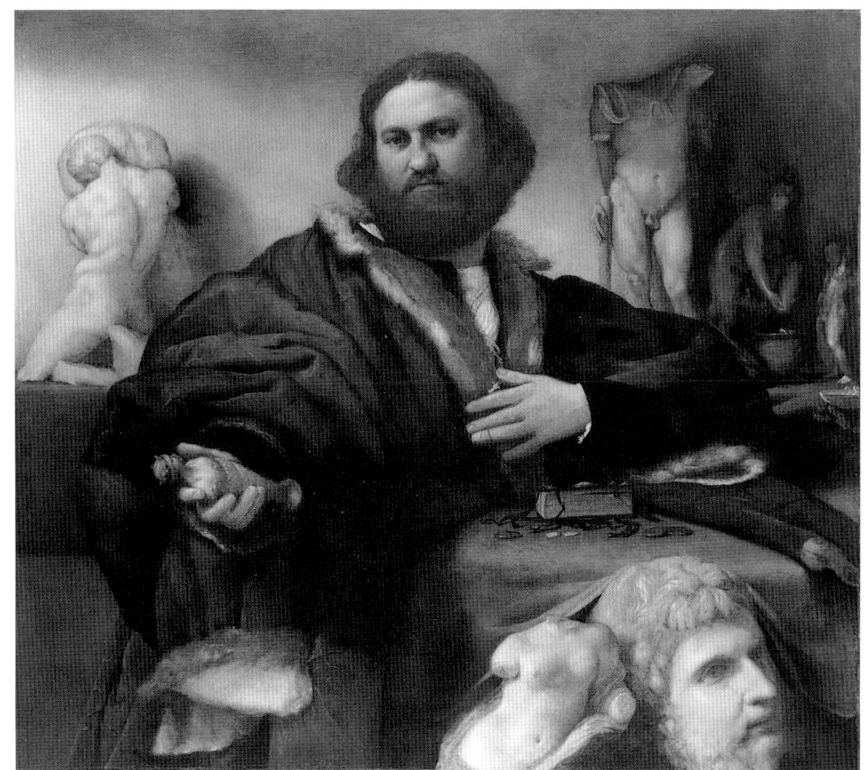

32 Lorenzo Lotto, Portrait of Andrea Odoni, signed and dated 'Lavrentivs lotvs 1527', canvas, 102 x 115 cm, London, Hampton Court, collection of Her Majesty Queen Elizabeth II

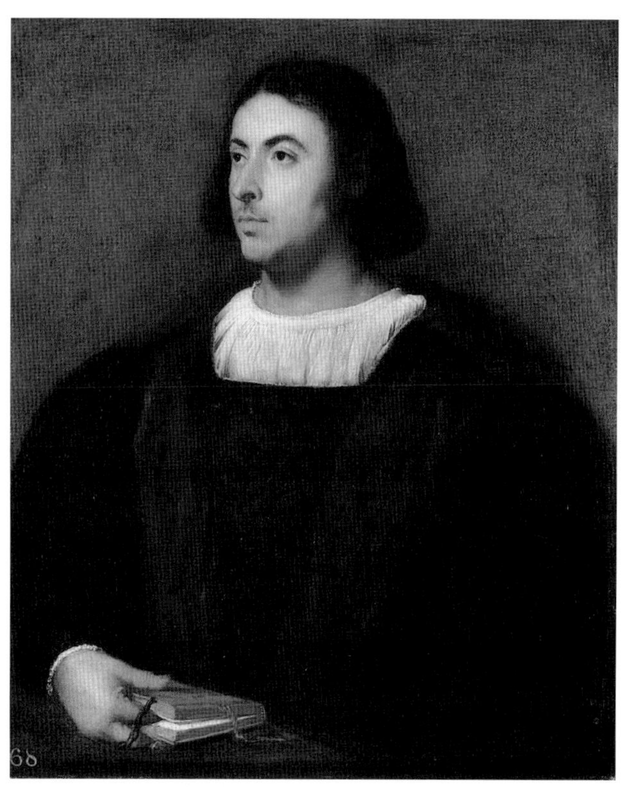

33 Titian, Portrait of a man, the so-called 'Jacopo Sannazaro', canvas, 84 x 71 cm, London, Hampton Court, collection of Her Majesty Queen Elizabeth II

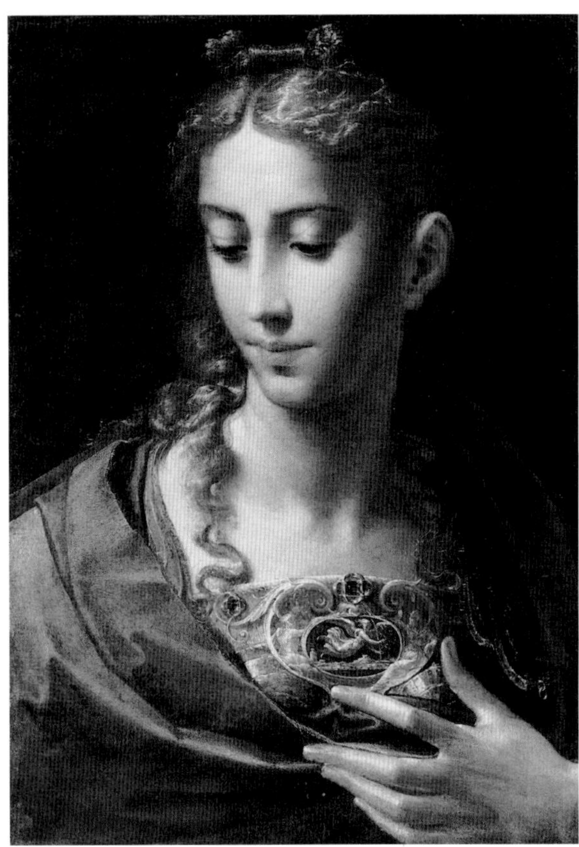

34 Parmigianino, Minerva, canvas 63.8 x 45.1 cm, London, Hampton Court, collection of Her Majesty Queen Elizabeth II

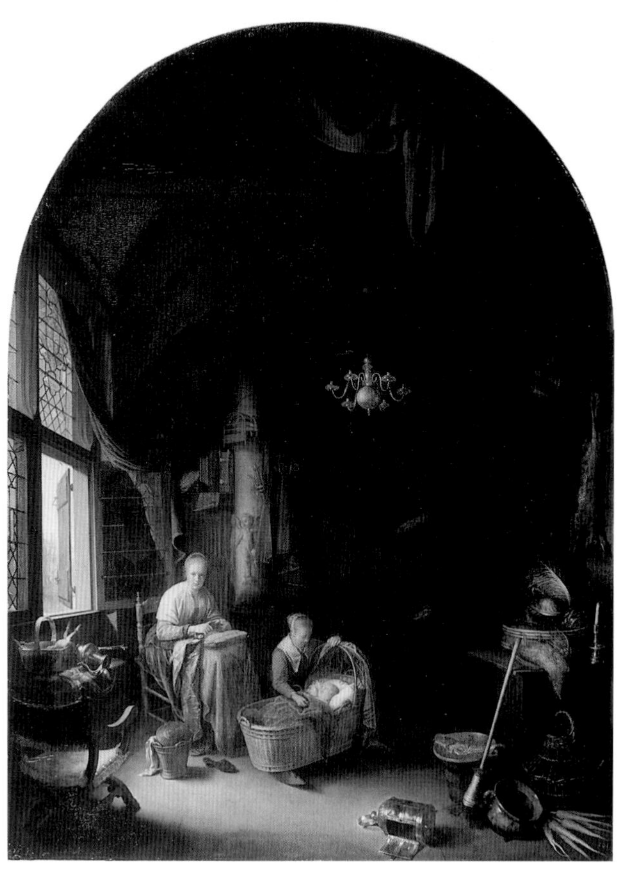

35 Gerrit Dou, The young mother, signed and dated 'G DOV 1658', panel, 73.5 x 55.5 cm, The Hague, Royal Cabinet of Paintings, Mauritshuis

decoration of Amsterdam's new town hall. He had visited Italy and was presumably consulted on this occasion as an authority on classical sculpture. Not only was the proposal accepted, but Gerrit Uylenburgh was also asked to pack the paintings and sculptures and accompany the consignment on the voyage to London ' to protect them from damage as well as possible'. For this he was to receive a 'reasonable remuneration'.[45]

The twenty-four paintings Uylenburgh selected included a number of superlative works, such as *The Way to Calvary* by Jacopo Bassano, Lorenzo

Lotto's *Portrait of Andrea Odoni,* Titian's *Portrait of Jacopo Sannazaro* (figs. 31, 32 and 33) and paintings by Schiavone, Tintoretto, Veronese, Giulio Romano and Parmigianino (fig. 34). All were sixteenth-century works except the *Allegory of Painting*, then attributed to Guido Reni, and Guercino's *Semiramis.*[46] The classical sculptures, by anonymous Roman masters, consisted of a figure of a woman, a man in a toga, the god Aesculapius, a Cupid, and eight portrait busts. Many of the paintings have remained in the British Royal Collection, but very few of the sculptures have survived.[47]

not mentioned by name in the documents. It is listed in the inventory of Charles II's estate, which notes that it was part of the Dutch Gift. See Mahon 1950 and Logan 1979. It is possible that the painting did not come from Andries de Graeff, but was the third, unknown painting from Dou's collection. However, an entry in Evelyn's journal of 6 December 1660 notes that 'two rare pieces of Drolerie, or rather a Dutch kitchin, painted by Douce' were included in the gift presented to Charles II. It thus seems that the gift included two genre scenes (*droleries*), from which one might assume that two genre pieces were bought from Dou. See Beer 1955, p. 262.

45 The Hague, National Archives, States of Holland and West Friesland 1572-1795, 3.01.05, no. 3010. Published by Leupe 1876; see also Logan 1979, pp. 77-78, note 85.

46 For details on the objects comprising the Dutch Gift, see Mahon 1949, Mahon 1950 and Logan 1979. The painting attributed to Reni in the seventeenth century has since

been given to Francesco Gezzi, see Logan 1991.
47 Logan 1979.
48 '[...] peerden, schilderien, linden, 't stuck mit de naelde gemaect etc. waren vruchten

and wercken van ons landt'. Quoted from Bruyn/Millar 1962, p. 292, note 9.
49 The painting is now in the National Gallery of Scotland, Edinburgh. The Saenredam is

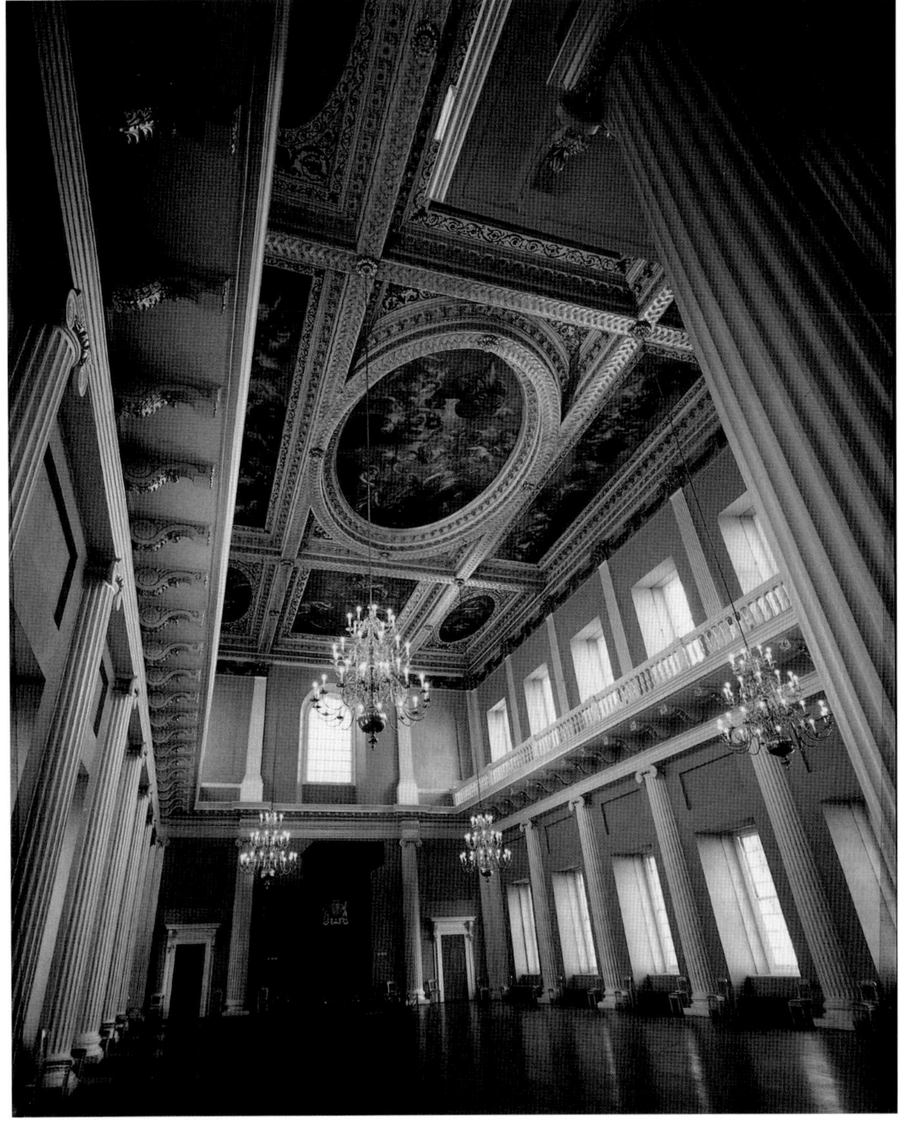

that the 'horses, the paintings, the linen, the piece of embroidery etc. were the fruits and works of our nation'.[48] This was not the case in 1660, when a gift was chosen to indulge Charles II's love of Italian art. Even so, the States made a point of including a few Dutch paintings. They bought the *View of St Bavo's Church in Haarlem* by Pieter Saenredam[49] from the collection of the Amsterdam burgomaster Andries de Graeff, which had been valued beforehand by the Rotterdam collector Reinier van der Wolff and the Leiden painter Gerrit Dou.[50] Dou also contribute three paintings from his personal collection: his own painting of the *Young mother* (fig. 35), a version of Adam Elsheimer's *The Mocking of Ceres*, and another, unidentified work.[51]

On 18 October the executive committee of the States wrote to ask Dou to pack the three paintings and transport them to Rotterdam. On the same day Dou replied that he would be unable to accompany them in person. The committee's response came a day later. They suggested that he send the consignment with the messenger who had delivered the letter – the messenger being none other than Gerrit Uylenburgh.[52] The question of whether Uylenburgh himself had a hand in choosing the Saenredam and the works from Dou's collection has yet to be answered.

In any event, Uylenburgh must have taken the three paintings directly to a ship waiting for him in Rotterdam. From there he sailed to Den Briel to join the vessel conveying the ambassadors.[53]

For the two earlier gifts to the British royal house, those of 1610 and 1636, the States General appear to have made a point of selecting work by Dutch artists. In any event, the report from the ambassador who presented the gift in 1636 notes

50 The Hague, National Archives, 3.01.04.01, no. 1396, States of Holland and West Friesland 1621-1795, register van minuten van uitgaande missieven van de Staten en Gecimmitteerde Raden van Holland (register of minutes of outgoing missives from the States and Executive Committee of Holland). Copy of a letter to Reinier van der Wolff,

asking him to appear in The Hague at ten o'clock on 29 September to value the paintings. It emerges from a note in the margin that an identical letter was sent to Dou: 'Aen Reijnier van Wolff oudt schepen der stadt Rotterdam ende mutatis mutandis aen Ger. Douw tot Leyden'. Published by Leupe 1876; see also Logan 1979, pp. 78-79, note 88.

51 Logan 1979, pp. 79-83. Elsheimer's *Mocking of Ceres* is probably the painting now in the Bader Collection, see Klessman 1997.
52 The Hague, National Archives, 3.01.04.01, no. 1396, States of Holland and West Friesland 1621-1795, register van minuten van uitgaande missieven van de Staten en Gecommitteerde Raden van

Holland (register of minutes of outgoing missives from the States and Executive Committee of Holland); published by Leupe 1876; see also Logan 1979, p. 81, note 91. Dou's reply has not survived, but the purport of his letter can be inferred from the States' reply, which was written a day later.
53 Joost van den Vondel wrote a poem about the gift entitled

'De Kunstkroon voor den Koningk van Groot Britanje &c', expressing his confidence that Charles II would greatly appreciate the paintings. The poem was dedicated to Van Hoorn, 'ready and waiting to sail for England with his fellow envoys'. An illustration of a folio edition of the poem can be seen in Logan 1979, p. 24.

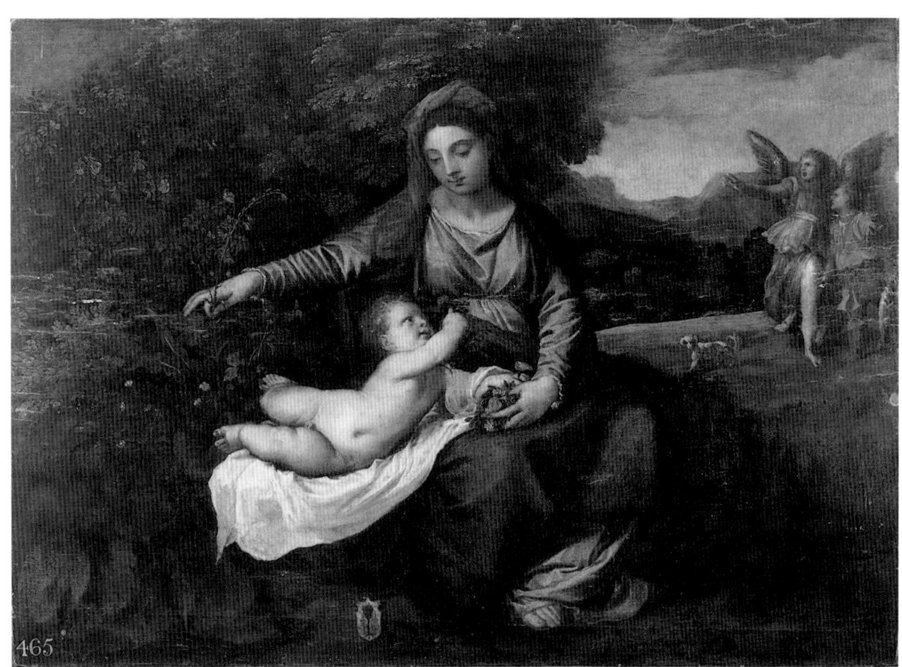

37 Titian, school of, *Virgin and child with Tobias and the angel*, panel, 81.2 x 143 cm, London, Hampton Court, collection of Her Majesty Queen Elizabeth II

Unfortunately, the wind was unfavourable and the mission was delayed for several days. On 25 October two members of the delegation wrote that they had been 'ready to depart along with the fully laden vessel chartered from Rotterdam (which is now here)'. But, with the wind coming from the wrong direction, they were obliged to set course for 'Rotterdam on the vessel laden with horses to allow the cargo to be discharged there'. They would wait for the weather to improve before embarking again. Uylenburgh and his paintings were probably on the same ship. The party finally set sail on 29 October and arrived in England on 2 November.[54]

In a letter sent from London on 26 November (16 November in Britain, where the Gregorian calendar was not yet in use) two of the ambassadors reported on their audience with the king. On 21 November they had requested leave to present the king with 'paintings and other fine objects' on behalf of the States of Holland and West Friesland. The king replied that he would be delighted to receive them. The presentation was to take place the following day in the Banqueting House at Whitehall Palace, the venue normally used for receiving foreign ambassadors (fig. 36). In the words of the two envoys, the gifts were 'removed from their crates and put in order, the bed by the concierge Boer and the paintings and sculptures by the painter Uylenborgh, both experts in their respective fields'.[55] Twenty-five years earlier Peter Paul Rubens had painted his apotheosis of King James I for the ceiling of the Banqueting House, and while the treasures were being unpacked Uylenburgh must have gazed up to admire the large allegories.

The gifts were well received and all agreed that this was 'one of the best presents ever bestowed on a prince'.[56] The king expressed his satisfaction at a private audience held for the delegation the following day. He was overjoyed with Titian's *Virgin and Child* (fig. 37) and the paintings by Dou and Elsheimer, although, as the Dutch ambassadors observed in their report, 'it was plain to see that the king thought highly of them all'.[57]

During his stay in London Uylenburgh must have met up with the successful portraitist Peter Lely, who was appointed Charles II's official court painter a short time later. Lely (originally Pieter Faes) was born in Soest, Westphalia, and studied under Frans de Grebber in Haarlem.[58] It is uncertain whether Uylenburgh knew him from that time or whether they first met in England. Whatever the case, they clearly formed a close attachment. In 1668 Lely was described as a 'well beloved friend' of the Uylenburgh family.[59] He was an avid collector of drawings and paintings and, as we shall see, he conducted several transactions with Gerrit.

Uylenburgh's involvement in the preparation and presentation of the Dutch Gift must have boosted his reputation. Many years later, in 1674, when Pieter Blaeu introduced him to Leopoldo de' Medici, he made a point of mentioning that Uylenburgh had been a member of the delegation appointed to present the gift to Charles II.[60]

54 The Hague, National Archives, States of Holland, 3.01.04.01, no. 2403, fol. 413r, 416v, 419.
55 The Hague, National Archives, 3.01.17, no. 2810; see also 3.01.04.01, no. 2403, fol. 437; published by Leupe 1876; see also Logan 1979, pp. 83-84, note 96.
56 Idem.
57 Idem.
58 On Lely, see especially Millar 1978. Lely moved to London in 1641, if not earlier. In October 1661 Charles II awarded him an annual 'pension' of 200 pounds. On Lely, see also p. 263-270 of this book.
59 GAA, NA 3658, not. J. Price, p. 741, 3 February 1668. Bredius 1884, pp. 219-220. See also p. 76-77 of this book.
60 See Mirto/Van Veen 1993, p. 291; see also p. 103 of this book.

THE HOUSE ON LAURIERGRACHT

After presenting the 'Dutch Gift' Uylenburgh must have returned to Amsterdam. The year 1661 began inauspiciously. On 17 March Gerrit's unmarried sister Magdalena was buried in the Westerkerk. According to the burial registers the family was living on Lauriergracht at the time. Five days later, Hendrick was also laid to rest.[61] Gerrit, the eldest son, was now head of the family as well as the business, in which some of his siblings were involved. Unlike his father, Gerrit had emerged as a painter of some note, while two of his brothers were painters as well. Hendrick's second son, Isaack, joined the Guild of St Luke in Alkmaar in 1658,[62] and Abraham, who was witness to a document in 1659, also trained as a painter and was later to leave the country.[63] Almost nothing is known about Hendrick's sons Marcus and Rombertus, whose names appear in only one archive document.[64] All his daughters remained single and would probably have worked for the firm, but no further information has come to light.

In 1661 five of Hendrick's children were baptised in the Waterland church. On 26 September Gerrit submitted a request for the baptism of his three sisters, Sara, Anna and Susanna, and his brothers Isaack and Rombertus. The two brothers were baptised that same day, after obtaining special permission from the Mennonite ministry. They were given priority in view of their plans 'to travel abroad'. This is the last known record of Isaack and Rombertus.[65] The three sisters were baptised during the service held on 11 December.

Shortly before the death of Hendrick Uylen-burgh in March 1661 the family must have moved from the Prinsengracht to the Lauriergracht.[66] They occupied one or perhaps both of the houses that had belonged to Govert Flinck (the site of the present nos. 76 and 78).[67] In 1644 Flinck had bought two adjacent properties on the Lauriergracht in the Jordaan in Amsterdam.[68] In one of them, according to Arnold Houbraken, soon after his marriage in 1645 Flinck had 'built a large painting studio with high windows surmounted by busts of the emperors'.[69] After Flinck's death on 2 February 1660 the properties had passed to his only, under-age son Nicolaes Anthonie Flinck, whose guardians leased them to Uylenburgh.

For the first few years the premises must have been occupied not only by the Uylenburgh family, but also by the German artist Jürgen Ovens, who had left Amsterdam for his homeland around 1651, but returned to Amsterdam in 1657.[70] He is believed to have lived on the Lauriergracht from 1661, before settling in Schleswig-Holstein once and for all in May 1663.[71] A survey of Amsterdam published in 1664 notes that Ovens had lived 'in the famous painter's house' on the Lauriergracht 'for two years'.[72] It is unclear whether Uylenburgh and Ovens had rented both houses and each occupied one of them. In any event, as we shall see, Uylenburgh spent much of 1663 abroad.

TO ITALY

On 10 September 1663, a few months after Ovens had left Amsterdam to settle permanently in his native land, two sisters, one of whom was presumably a servant living in Gerrit Uylenburgh's home, drew up their will in the house on the

61 GAA, DTB 1100, p. 178.
62 Alkmaar Regional Archives, Collectie Aanwinsten (Acquisitions Collection) 13, p. 1351, registered with the Alkmaar guild 1658: 'Ysak Uilenburg'; Bruinvis 1909, p. 123.
63 GAA, not. Nicolaes Listingh, NA 2613 fol. 429; Bredius 1915-1922, vol. 5, p. 1690. On Abraham, see p. 76-77.
64 Marcus Uylenburgh, as well as Abraham, acted as a witness in the case concerning Rembrandt's portrait of Andries de Graeff. See p. 45. On Rombertus, see below.
65 GAA, Archive of the Mennonite Church, Baptism Applications, 1657-1673, fol. 7v; Wijnman 1959.
66 They had previously lived on the corner of Prinsengracht and Westermarkt, see p. 57-59. In 1658 Hendrick had rented that house for two years. He must have moved to the Lauriergracht when the contract expired, some time in 1660.
67 For further details, see Dudok van Heel 1982.
68 GAA, Kwijtscheldingen (Discharges), v, fol. 102, 26 May 1644; Dudok van Heel 1982, p. 70.
69 Houbraken 1718-1721, vol. 2, pp. 21-22.
70 Schmidt 1922, pp. 27-28. According to a statement by their heirs in 1694, the Ovens family returned to Amsterdam following Sweden's invasion of Schleswig-Holstein. They give the date of their departure as 25 August 1657.
71 In a deed of 23 April 1661 Miss Dingma Boelens, who was a tenant in Ovens's home, complained that the storage cellar, which was not covered by the rental agreement, was being used as a 'beer cellar, as it is a place for public entertainment'. Unfortunately, the address is not given. It is reasonable to assume that Ovens had rented the house to Dingma Boelens because he was about to move to the Lauriergracht. See GAA, NA 1137, not. J. van de Ven, 23 April 1661. The approximate date of Ovens's departure emerges from a letter of 2 May 1663 from Pieter de Graeff to Johan de Witt, noting that Ovens was intending to 'move to Friedrichstad with his whole family shortly after Whitsun', and a letter of 7 May 1663 from Johan de Witt to Pieter de Graeff, saying that Ovens was 'ready to depart for Friedrichstad', see Fruin 1922, pp. 489-490. On 15 June 1663 Ovens received payment in Friedrichstadt, Schmidt 1922, p. 37.
72 Von Zesen 1664, p. 209.

Lauriergracht. The document explicitly describes the house as the residence of 'the late Mr Flinck'. The interesting point here is that the document was signed in Uylenburgh's home, but there is no further reference to Uylenburgh himself, nor did he witness the signing.[73] The person who did so was the painter Nicolaes Rosendael, who was therefore presumably employed by Uylenburgh at the time.

Gerrit Uylenburgh is not mentioned because he was in Italy at the time, as we discover from a letter Contantijn Huygens the Younger sent to his brother Christiaan, who was in London during that period. After a few complimentary words about a pastel of a 'beauté Angloise' that his brother had sent him, he writes that Gerrit Uylenburgh had returned from Italy with beautiful paintings by Palma Vecchio and other masters. The letter was written on 12 October 1663 and from the tone it would seem that Uylenburgh had just arrived home.[74]

Uylenburgh must have spent at least eight months in Italy. On 23 February 1663 he signed an agreement with Jan Houwaert in Genoa.[75] After completing his apprenticeship in Antwerp in 1635, Houwaert had left for Genoa, where he worked in the studio of Cornelis de Wael before establishing himself as an independent master. Uylenburgh entrusted him with 200 scudi d'oro which, as we know from Houwaert's will of 16 December 1663, was to be spent on paintings.[76] However, nothing came of this commission. Houwaert passed away in 1665 and in November 1667 Uylenburgh authorised Hendrick van Weert, who was later appointed the Dutch consul in Genoa, to try and recover his money from Houwaert's heirs.[77] The document stipulates that he expected the full amount. Some time later, Van Weert received 855 guilders and six stuyvers from the Orphans' Chamber in Genoa, and that amount was finally returned to Uylenburgh in December 1669

through the intercession of the merchant Isaac Jan Nijs.[78]

We do not know what other cities Uylenburgh visited in Italy, but an Amsterdam inventory dating from 1704 lists a painting entitled 'Rome' by Gerrit Uylenburgh,[79] which suggests that Rome was probably on his itinerary. It is also unknown whether he entered into other agreements such as that with Houwaert, or who managed the business in Amsterdam during his absence. His brother Abraham would in any event have been in a position to do so.

After his return to Amsterdam Uylenburgh's name occurs again, in 1663, in the correspondence of the Huygens brothers. On 6 December of that year Constantijn urged his brother Christiaan, who was in Paris at the time, to view the collection of Everhard Jabach. He had a special reason for this request, as he wanted Christiaan to examine a drawing of bathers by Annibale Carracci (see fig. 198). Rembrandt possessed a similar sheet and Constantijn wanted to know which was the original. According to the letter, Gerrit Uylenburgh had informed him about the drawing in Jabach's possession.[80]

Uylenburgh must therefore have been familiar with Jabach's collection and had presumably been to Paris to see it himself, but when such a visit might have taken place is unknown. He may have stopped in Paris on his way to or from Italy. In any event, as we shall see, Jabach and Uylenburgh were close business associates.

MARRIAGE AND CHILDREN

The records are even sparser concerning Uylenburgh's activities in the following years. A document from early 1664 in the Amsterdam archives reveals that he possessed a garden on the Weespad, outside St Anthony's Gate.[81] In 1665 he paid 2,000

73 GAA, NA 2071, not. J. Hellerus, fol. 105, 10 September 1663; Dudok van Heel 1982, p. 78.
74 See Huygens 1888-1950, vol. 4, p. 413.
75 The date of the agreement appears in the power of attorney that Gerrit gave Hendrick van Weert in 1667 to enable him to recover the money. See GAA, NA 3677, not. J. Tixerandet, pp. 484-485, 7 November 1667; deed referred to in Bredius 1915-1922, vol. 5, p. 1675.

76 Archivio di Stato, Genoa, ASG, Notai antichi 8457. Giacomo Bollino. Testamenti, fil. 33, 16 December 1663. '[...] e piu doppie cento sera Italia e stampe quali doppie cento spettano a Ghirardi Uulemborch, lasciatele e consignatele per impiegare in compra de quadri e de quali gliene ha fatto ricevuta privata [...]'. The will is referred to in Belloni 1988, pp. 118-119. With thanks to Alison Stoesser, who kindly sent us her information on Houwaert.

77 See note 75.
78 GAA, NA 2331, not. A. Lock, p. 1212, 19 December 1669.
79 See p. 277.
80 Huygens 1888-1950, vol. 4, p. 456. See also p. 257.
81 GAA, NA 2738, not. J.H. Leuven, p. 65, 14 January 1664; Bredius 1915-1922, vol. 5, p. 1674.

38 Notice of the publication of the banns of Gerrit Uylenburgh and Elisabeth Juyst of 6 April 1666, Amsterdam, Gemeentearchief

39 Pieter Verhoek, Ter bruilofte van den konstschilder Gerrit Ulenborg en jongkvrouwe Elisabeth Juste. Vereenigt den 5den mei 1666. Gedicht van Pieter Verhoek, in: Pieter Verhoek, Poëzy. Nevens zyn Treurspel van Karel den Stouten, Hertogh van Bourgondie (Amsterdam 1726), Amsterdam, Universiteitsbibliotheek

82 GAA, NA 2872, not.
H. Westfrisius, p. 48, 27 January 1665 and pp. 49-50, 9 February 1665. The house belonged to Cornelis Dolleman, sheriff of Muiderberg.
83 GAA, DTB 488, fol. 350 (church marriages), betrothal on 6 April. In Verhoek's poem the date of the wedding is said to be 5 May. The marriage contract has not been traced.
84 GAA, DTB 1100, p. 201, Anna van Eyck, buried 17 November 1663 in the Westerkerk, from the Lauriergracht.

guilders for a plot of land with a house and garden in Muiderberg, on the Zuyder Zee. The sale was cancelled thirteen days later, but the reason is not disclosed.[82]

Even though the deal fell through, Uylenburgh appears to have been comfortably off. He rented a house on the Lauriergracht and was in a position to purchase a country retreat, modest though it may have been. In this he was apparently aspiring to the lifestyle of Amsterdam's wealthy merchants and regents, who, almost without exception, possessed second homes outside the city.

On 4 May 1666 Gerrit Uylenburgh married Elisabeth Juyst, the daughter of a well-to-do merchant.[83] At her betrothal at the town hall, the 30-year-old Elisabeth was attended by her father Hendrick (fig. 38). Her mother, Anna van Eyck, had died three years earlier.[84] The Juyst family was Dutch Reformed and the marriage was solemnised in the Nieuwe Kerk. As we shall see, even after his marriage Uylenburgh remained a member of the Waterland church. All his children, however, were baptised as infants. Pieter Verhoek wrote a commemorative poem entitled 'On the marriage of the painter Gerrit Ulenborg and Elisabeth Juste. Joined in matrimony on 5 May 1666' (fig. 39).[85]

Verhoek was a painter as well as a poet. He had studied in Gorinchem under Jacob van der Ulft, and subsequently moved to Amsterdam where, according to his biographer, his art was 'nurtured through diligent study [and] the erudite company of the most distinguished poets and the best painters of his day'[86] He later joined Nil volentibus arduum, an association committed to the promotion of classicism in literature and painting. The group met at the home of one of its members, Gerard de Lairesse. Verhoek enjoyed a 'brotherly friendship' with the Mennonite poet Joannes Antonides van der Goes, who introduced him to Joost van den Vondel. Some years later Van der Goes also dedicated a poem to Uylenburgh.[87]

Verhoek may have worked for Uylenburgh or perhaps received commissions through his mediation. Houbraken writes that he specialised as a marble painter in Amsterdam,[88] and it is possible that he and Uylenburgh collaborated on the decoration of some of the city's canalside mansions.[89] As a poet, he was apparently sought after by artists who wanted their special occasions commemorated in verse.[90]

However, not a word of the poem he dedicated to Uylenburgh alludes to his activities as an art dealer. Verhoek portrays him solely as a painter of landscapes. The poem itself is about the rivalry between love and art. The Goddess of Art reproaches Venus for distracting Uylenburgh from his work, but in the end Venus wins her over with the promise of talented progeny:

'Behold, even now I espy
A succession of babes issuing from this
matrimonial bed,
Brandishing the charcoal, the red chalk
and the brush,
Your gift, oh Goddess of Art, shall advance
from the stem to the shoots.'

Gerrit and Elisabeth must have known each other for many years before their marriage in 1666. They were quite likely related to one another and both of them lived on the Lauriergracht in the 1660s.[91] Elisabeth's father Hendrick Juyst was the son of a prominent merchant family from Schiedam. He was born in Schiedam on 25 November 1597,[92] but appears to have moved away at an early age.[93] In the 1630s he was in Königsberg, the present-day Kaliningrad, which was an important trading port on the Baltic Sea. It is not known where or when he married Anna van Eyck, but most, if not all his children were born in Königsberg. Anna van Eyck had previously been married to Pieter Philipsz (Maijer), with whom she had two sons, Philip and Pieter Maijer.

Hendrick Juyst settled in Amsterdam, probably in the 1640s or early 1650s. He conducted various business with his stepsons, who had likewise made their home in Amsterdam.[94] Interestingly enough, Hendrick Uylenburgh also had contact with Philip Pietersz Maijer as early as 1649,[95]

85 Verhoek 1726, pp. 74-76. The poems were compiled by Pieter Verhoek's nephew Johannes Verhoek, who wrote the short biography at the beginning of the book.
86 Verhoek 1726, p. 11.
87 See p. 91.
88 Houbraken 1718-1721, vol. 3, p. 188. He was described as a 'marble painter' at his funeral in Amsterdam on 3 October 1702.
89 Verhoek and Uylenburgh may have met through Van der Ulft. On Van der Ulft, see Jellema/Plomp 1992, pp. 16-17; Tissink/De Wit 1987, pp. 38-43. Van der Ulft must have had good connections in Amsterdam. In 1667 he executed a *View of the Town Hall of Amsterdam*, which hung in the burgomasters' chamber. He would also have known Jan de Bisschop and Constantijn and Christiaan Huygens, all of whom were acquainted with Uylenburgh. In 1672 Christiaan Huygens tried to sell Van der Ulft's work to a French clientele.
90 Verhoek 1726. A poem on pp. 171-172, 'Ziekte en herstellinge van jongkvrouwe Elizabeth' (The illness and recovery of Lady Elizabeth), may have been about Elisabeth Juyst, but the woman's surname is not mentioned. Houbraken notes that Verhoek was an 'exceptionally good friend' of the painter Adam Pijnacker. His brother Gijsbert Verhoek was apprenticed to Pijnacker. Pieter Verhoek also wrote poems about work by Pijnacker and De Lairesse, and poems to commemorate the marriages of Willem Goeree, Michiel van Musscher and Steven Vennecool.
91 GAA, DTB 1101, p. 42, 27 September 1666. At his funeral it was said that Elisabeth's father had come from the Lauriergracht. The same was said at her mother's funeral in 1663 (DTB 1100, p. 201). At the time of the marriage of his daughter Abigael in 1659, Hendrick Juyst was still living in the Rapenburg.
92 His parents were Hendrick Juyst and Anna Bartholomeusdr Vis. This Hendrick Willemsz Juyst was a regent of the elderly women's residence in Schiedam. He is described in notarised deeds as a merchant. The fact that he was wealthy emerges from the will he and his wife drew up, which provides that at the death of either the considerable sum of 10,000 guilders was to be held in trust for the children. See Schiedam Municipal Archives, Notaries' Archive, ONA 741, p. 298 (3 August 1620, will), p. 323; ONA 747, p. 118 (15 August 1627, will). On the Juyst family, see also Van Laer 1925.
93 In any event, there is no reference to him in the Notaries' Archives in Schiedam.
94 GAA, NA 2136, deed no. 98, 10 May 1651, Hendrick Juyst gives Pieter Philipsz Meijer power of attorney.
95 GAA, NA 1000, not. G. Coren, 21 December 1649. Reference to Philips Pr Meijer. Philips Meijer went bankrupt in 1658, GAA, DBK, 5072, no. 587, fol. 70-78 (inventory), 11-21 May 1658 (among other things a 'cabinet' belonging to a certain Schimmelpenningh 'of Konincxbergh'. He further possessed '3 bales of Koninxberg wool' and 'approximately 17 packages of conincxberg rye'. See also 28 November 1659, fol. 251-257 (another inventory).

having met him, most likely, through his wife, Maria van Eyck. It would not be unreasonable to assume that Maria was related to Anna van Eyck, the wife of Hendrick Juyst, but no evidence to this effect has been found. When Hendrick Juyst and Anna van Eyck drew up their will in Amsterdam in 1652, they had seven children: Hendrick, Abigael, Maria, Willem,[96] Elisabeth, Johannes and Margarita (see Genealogy 2, p. 292).[97]

Hendrick Juyst was a merchant with a large network of associates in the Baltic. He had clients not only in Königsberg, but also Sweden, for example. A document describes him as 'engaged in commerce in various regions beyond the confines of these provinces'.[98] The inventory drawn up after his death in 1666 includes an abundance of silver, porcelain and household effects. On the other hand, he possessed only a small collection of paintings, and those were of little value. The costliest was a painting of 'children', valued at a mere ten guilders. The only paintings with attributions were two 'history pieces by Pinas', worth six guilders apiece. Juyst's entire estate was valued at a little over 3,400 guilders.[99]

Of all Hendrick Juyst's children, Gerrit and Elisabeth appear to have had the most contact with Abigael and her London-born husband Pieter Deldeijm, a chest maker who lived in Warmoesstraat.[100] The two couples apparently maintained close ties, as they were witnesses to the baptisms of each other's children.[101] A younger brother of Abigael and Elisabeth, Johannes Juyst, is documented as a burgher of Amsterdam on 20 November 1659. On that occasion he stated that he was originally from

Königsberg, but he had apparently been living in Amsterdam for some time. In 1657 Adam Samuel Hartmann had visited his home on the Keizersgracht and remarked on the splendid room in which Juyst had received him. 'Polished to a shine (the floor was made of marble or tiles)', as he noted in his journal.[102] From a document we know that Johannes Juyst was acquainted with the painter Emanuel de Witte.[103] His possessions, which were inventoried in 1659 and 1661, comprised a substantial number of paintings, including a large work by De Witte.[104] It is unknown whether Gerrit Uylenburgh was in touch with the art connoisseur Juyst.[105]

Gerrit must have felt that he had made a good match by marrying the daughter of a wealthy merchant with an extensive network of associates abroad. Hendrick Juyst died that same year and was buried in the Westerkerk on 27 September 1666, a little more than four months after the marriage. To the family's dismay, it transpired that he was heavily in debt. On 16 November Gerrit Uylenburgh and Pieter Deldeijm wrote to Abraham and Jacob Momma in Stockholm, informing their 'very dear cousin' of their predicament: '[...] we have huge debts to pay, the largest being a loan of 3,000 guilders, which our late father took on interest; there are various other debts that we are now aware of and others that have not yet come to light'. They had found two letters in Juyst's office in which the Mommas acknowledged that they owed Hendrick between ten and eleven thousand guiders. Uylenburgh and his brother-in-law appealed to their 'cousin' to look into and settle the matter as quickly as possible. The brothers Abraham and Jacob Momma were

96 Willem married Geertruijda Bruijn in Curaçao on 19 September 1662. See Van Laer 1925. For their will, see G A A, not. J. Backer, N A 4532, pp. 62-64, 10 January 1680. On 14 October 1678 their sons Mathias, who was already two years old, and Balthasar were baptised in Amsterdam. Apart from Abigael Juyst, the witnesses were Adam Oortmans and Petronella de la Court.
97 G A A, N A 1596, not. Willem Hasen, fol. 13, 9 April 1652. Margarita, or Margaretha, died a few months after making her will. She was buried on 22 November 1652 (D T B 1130, p. 152).
98 The Hague, National Archives, 3.03.02, inv. no. 70. Requesten Hoge Raad van Holland en Zeeland (Applications, Supreme Court of Holland and Zeeland), 30 November 1666; Bredius 1915-1922, vol. 5, p. 1674.
99 G A A, N A 2852, not. D. Danckerts, pp. 641-647, 2 and 9 December 1666.
100 Abigael and Pieter Deldeijm, or Deldijn, were married on 30 November 1659. Deldeijm was 29 years old at the time, Abigael was 26 (D T B 479, p. 369). See also Kam 1968, Warmoesstraat 75.
101 On Pieter Deldeijm and Abigael Juyst's presence at the baptisms of the children of Gerrit and Elisabeth, see below. Moreover, Elisabeth

was a witness to the baptisms of two of her sister's children. In 1662 she attended the baptism of her namesake Elisabeth, and in 1672 the baptism of Henrij. On 6 February 1667 Gerrit was a witness to the baptism of his nephew Pierre, the son of Pieter Deldeijm and Abigael Juyst. G A A, D T B 131, p. 405 (baptism Elisabeth); D T B 132, p. 51 (baptism Henrij); D T B 131, p. 457 (baptism Pierre).

102 Hartmann 1657-1659/ Prümers 1899-1900. The visit took place on 30 June 1657.
103 G A A, not. Vincent Swanenburgh, N A 2714, pp. 456-457, 22 September 1659; Bredius 1915-1922, vol. 5, p. 1833. Another document that suggests he was acquainted with painters is N A 2488, not. Jac. Hellerus, pp. 30, 33-34, 7 January 1661, in which Abraham Spithoff states that goods were removed from his house

and taken to the home of Johan Juste (Juyst). The items were lent 'because they had a painter at home who was painting for them and making new paintings'.
104 G A A, 5072, D B K, no. 365, fol. 254v– 258, 28 November 1659; no. 368, fol. 83v– 86v, 7 January 1661. Johannes Juyst appears to have moved to Sweden shortly after 1661.
105 Several authors have suggested that Isaac Juyst

may have been related to Hendrick Juyst. This Isaac Juyst was involved in transporting Rembrandt's *Alexander* to Antonio Ruffo in Sicily. However, the person in question is referred to as both Isaac Just and Isaac Cuijsten. 'Just' must therefore also have been a clerical error, the person in question being Isaac Cuijsten, an Amsterdam merchant. For the documents, see Giltaij 1999, pp. 164-165.

originally from Aachen, and after spending some time in Amsterdam in the 1640s they had moved to Stockholm. Elisabeth's sister Maria was married to Lars Buirens and lived in Sweden. From the letter it transpires that Buirens had already notified the Mommas of Hendrick Juyst's death.[106]

On 30 November 1666 Hendrick Juyst's heirs filed a joint application with the Supreme Court of Holland and Zeeland, from which it transpires that only Pieter Deldeijm and his wife Abigael Juyst and Gerrit Uylenburgh and his wife Elisabeth Juyst were in the country at the time. Maria, Willem and Johannes Juyst were all living abroad. They were concerned about accepting an inheritance 'burdened with debts', and accordingly requested benefit of inventory.[107] The inventory of Hendrick Juyst's possessions referred to above was made on 2 and 9 December 1666 in response to this petition. It is uncertain how the matter was finally settled. But the generous inheritance that Uylenburgh may have been anticipating undoubtedly failed to materialise.

The children born to Gerrit Uylenburgh and Elisabeth Juyst were all baptised in infancy. In other words, on this count Elisabeth's faith prevailed over Gerrit's Mennonite convictions. Their first child was baptised in the Westerkerk on 18 March 1667 and was named Anna Maria after her two grandmothers. The witnesses to the ceremony were Clara Ruttens and the child's uncle Pieter Deldeijm. The second child, named Abigael after Elisabeth's sister, was baptised in the Westerkerk on 13 May 1668. As one would expect, her aunt Abigael appeared as a witness, together with the art collector Hendrick Scholten, who was an important client of Uylenburgh's. Sara was baptised in the Nieuwezijds Chapel on 9 April 1670, from which we can infer that the Uylenburgh family had left their home on the Lauriergracht. Their new address is unfortunately unknown. One of the two witnesses to the baptism was

Margaretha Tulp, the wife of the prominent art collector Jan Six.[108]

Maria's baptism in the Amstelkerk on 7 June 1671 was witnessed by Pieter Six who, like his brother Jan, possessed a collection of art, and Maria Munter, the wife of the collector Isaac Jan Nijs. This was the Nijs who, as we have seen, had helped Gerrit recover money from Jan Houwaert's heirs in Italy in 1669. The last child to be baptised was Magdalena, on 3 January 1674. Once again, the ceremony took place in the Amstelkerk, the church nearest the house on the Keizersgracht to which the Uylenburghs had moved in 1672. On this occasion the witnesses were the painter Theodoor Ferreris and the appraiser Barbara Elsevier, who married the auctioneer Jacob Haringh in 1682.

Uylenburgh appears to have chosen the witnesses to his daughters' baptisms with something of an eye for business. On the first two occasions he adhered to the convention of inviting members of his family, but the witnesses he chose subsequently were friends or associates of his in the art business. Even Sara's baptism was not witnessed by his sister, the aunt for whom she was named. The people he chose on all these occasions would obviously have been close friends of his, but there were clearly also business interests at stake.

In 1667 Gerrit Uylenburgh and Elisabeth Juyst drew up a will, nominating each other their sole heirs in affirmation of their 'shared conjugal love'. The longest surviving partner was to provide for the children and raise them 'in awe of God and teach them to write and ensure that they learnt an art, trade, vocation or craft'.[109]

ABRAHAM UYLENBURGH

On 3 February 1668 Gerrit Uylenburgh and his sisters Sara, Anna and Susanna consulted an English-speaking notary, as their brother Abraham had passed away in Dublin. According to a docu-

106 Stockholm, Riksarkivet, Momma-Reenstiernas Samling, E 2526. In letters to Hendrick Juyst Jacob Momma addressed him as 'uncle'.

Jacob Momma was married to Elisabeth Crönstrom, whose mother's name was Elisabeth van Eyck. She was presumably the sister of Anna

van Eyck, Hendrick Juyst's wife. Thanks to Kenneth Awebro, who researched the correspondence between the Juyst and Momma families in the

national archives in Stockholm.
107 See note 98. The other children named in the will of Hendrick Juyst and Anna

van Eyck in 1652 were no longer alive.
108 The second witness was the otherwise unknown Jacobus van Oosterwijck.
109 GAA, NA 2133, not. N. van Born, p. 124-127, 7 October 1667; Bredius 1915-1922, vol. 5, p. 1675.

ment drawn up on that occasion, Abraham had been painter to 'Her Highnesse the Dutchesse of Ormond'. The Uylenburghs now nominated their 'trusty and well beloved friend mr. Peter Lely' to represent their interests abroad, and authorised him to claim from the duchess or any other party any money or possessions belonging to Abraham. The document was signed by the Uylenburghs and by Theodoor Ferreris.[110]

The Ormondes were the most prominent aristocratic family in Ireland. James Butler, the first Duke of Ormonde, served as viceroy of Ireland and was a close personal friend of Charles II of England. He had accompanied the sovereign into exile on the continent and played a leading role in restoring the monarchy in 1660. His wife, Elizabeth Preston, was the duchess for whom Abraham Uylenburgh had worked.[111]

After Charles II's return to England the Duke and Duchess of Ormonde commissioned extensive renovations to their country estates in Ireland and England. They embarked on an ambitious building and decoration programme for their principal residence, Kilkenny Castle in Ireland, envisaging a home that would rival Charles II's castle at Windsor.[112] The family possessed the largest art collection in the country, which included more than 500 paintings. Disappointingly, however, only a few artists are named in their inventories. The majority appear to have been Dutch, but they also owned a few works by Italian masters, including copies after Titian and Jacopo Bassano. Among the Dutch paintings was a 'large painting of Melchisdeck and other figures' by Gerbrandt van den Eeckhout, which was valued at 20 pounds.[113]

The duchess was closely involved in the decoration work. Abraham Uylenburgh is not mentioned in any of her correspondence,[114] nor are there any paintings that can be firmly attributed to him, but he nevertheless appears to have worked for her. He may have been engaged to execute decorative paintings, such as landscapes, or perhaps a number of portraits. He would probably have met the Ormondes through Peter Lely who, in the 1660s, was the foremost painter and portraitist at the English court. The duchess would certainly have sought Lely's advice before commissioning a painter and we can assume that Lely would have introduced her to Abraham Uylenburgh, who may have been employed in his studio. It is thus uncertain whether Abraham was employed by the duchess and, if so, how long he remained in her service. The only document in the archives in Ireland that refers to him at all is one that concerns his shroud.[115]

110 GAA, NA 3658, not. J. Price, p. 741, 3 February 1668; Bredius 1884.
111 On the Ormondes, see especially Barnard 2000.
112 Barnard 2000, p. 6.
113 On the Ormondes's art holdings, see Fenlon 2000
114 In a letter sent from London in February 1668 the duchess wrote about accommodation for the Dutchman whom she was expecting to accompanying her. She may have been referring to Abraham, Fenlon 2000, p. 156, note 121.
115 Idem.
116 GAA, not. A. v.d. Ven, NA 3610, fol. 289; Bredius 1886, p. 44; Dudok van Heel 1982, p. 82 and note 51; see also Breen 1909, pp. 75-80.
117 Van Eeghen 1962. The house in which Van Gheel lived is the present Herengracht 468.
118 GAA, Backer family archive, 172, no. 731.

A NEW HOME

On 12 December 1670 Gerrit Uylenburgh signed a contract with Daniel van Gheel, Lord of Spanbroeck, regarding the construction of two houses that Uylenburgh was intending to rent.[116] The document describes the buildings in detail. They were to stand on the Keizersgracht (no. 567 today, between Spiegelstraat and Vijzelstraat) on a plot directly behind Van Gheel's home on the Herengracht, which was completed in 1669.[117]

The two houses on the Keizersgracht were to be 38 foot wide and 48 to 49 foot deep (almost 11 x 14 metres). Each was to have an entrance hall, a side room and a back room. The kitchen was located under the back room, with a cellar in front of it. One of the buildings had a front room and a back room on the first floor, with a door leading from one of those rooms into the house next door. A large hall was built on the first floor of the second house. It extended over the roof of Van Gheel's coach house, which created enough space for a room measuring 8.5 x 14 metres. The contract stipulated that this room was to be used 'for hanging paintings and, at Uylenburgh's discretion, for painting'.

Van Gheel and his neighbour on the Herengracht, Anna Boom, who also wanted two houses behind her home (the present no. 468), engaged an architect to draft the plans. As a result, four almost identical houses were built on the Keizersgracht, flanked by coach houses for Van Gheel and Boom. As three and a half inches of the doorstep would encroach on municipal land, Van Gheel and Boom applied for a permit from the burgomasters before starting to build. They also submitted the plans (fig. 40).[118] A permit was

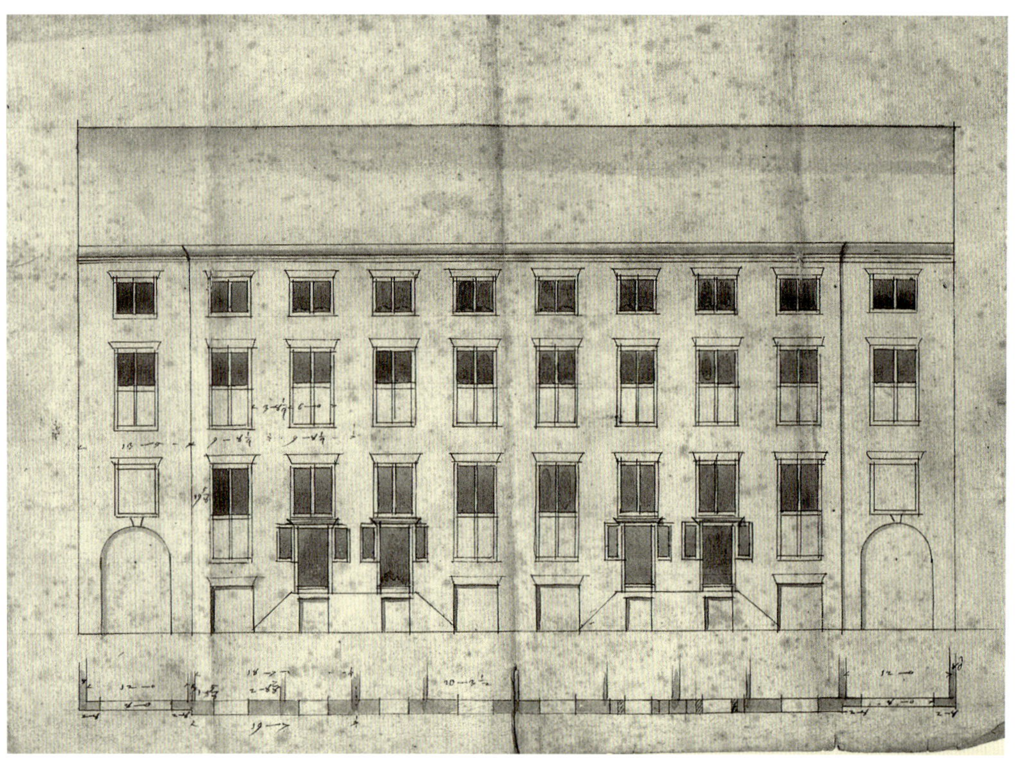

40 Anonymous, Four houses on the Keizersgracht, 1671, graphite, pen and brown ink, brush and grey ink, washed, 24.8 x 34.5 cm, Amsterdam, Gemeentearchief

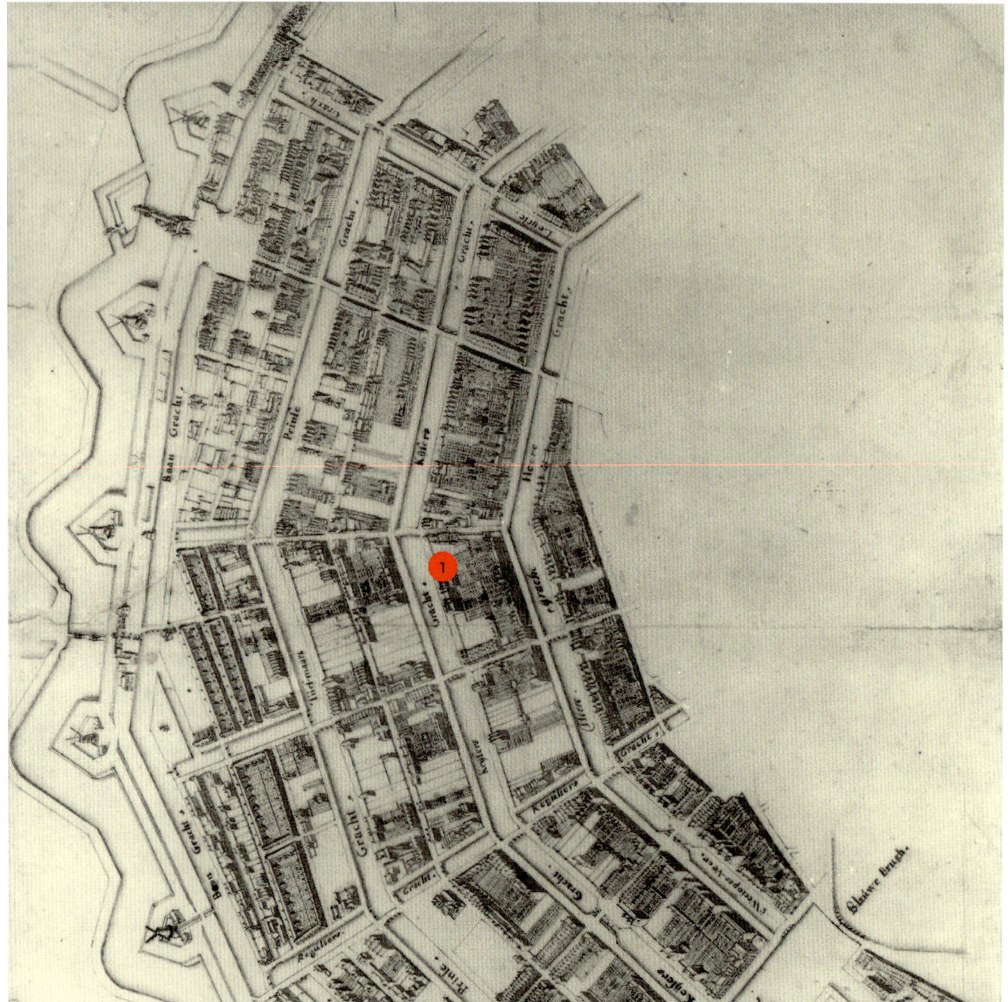

41 Jacob Bosch, Map of a section of the Amsterdam ring of canals, pen and brown ink, brush in blue-green, 45 x 85.5 cm (in two sheets), Amsterdam, Gemeentearchief
[1] is Uylenburgh's house on Keizersgracht

issued on 9 April 1671, allowing the work to proceed. Uylenburgh signed a contract to rent the two houses for a period of eight years as of 1 May 1672. The rent of 975 guilders a year was payable in two annual instalments and the landlord was liable for municipal taxes. The two houses were later converted into a single dwelling.

ART DEALER AND PAINTER

Gerrit Uylenburgh's art business must have flourished in the 1660s and early 1670s. Though sparsely documented, it was clearly an international enterprise, and the place to go for not only for Dutch and Flemish art, but also for paintings, drawings and prints from Italy, Spain and France. The firm is discussed in more detail in chapter 4.

The correspondence between Constantijn Huygens the Younger and Christiaan Huygens has yielded a wealth of information. We discover, for instance, that in the early 1660s Constantijn Huygens was trying to sell an album of etchings by Jacques Callot and enlisted Uylenburgh's assistance in doing so. There is also a letter of 1663, in which Huygens reported on his visit to Peter Lely in London. Lely had told him that the core of his collection of drawings consisted of the cream of the collection belonging to Walter van de Voort, a Flemish merchant who had lived in Venice. According to Lely's account, he and Uylenburgh had acquired the entire collection. This was presumably around 1657. Then in 1666 Christiaan Huygens asked Uylenburgh whether he knew of any coins for sale for a prominent Parisian numismatist.

One of the Huygens brothers' closest friends was Jan de Bisschop who, in the late 1660s, published *Icones* and *Paradigmata*, three beautiful books of his etchings after classical sculptures and Italian drawings. The second volume of *Icones*, which appeared in 1669, contained etchings of four sculptures, which were said to belong to Uylenburgh. Apart from four sculptures belonging to the Amsterdam collector Hendrick Scholten, these were the only sculptures in Dutch collections that were included in the book. From this we learn that Uylenburgh sold classical sculp-

ture as well as paintings, drawings and etchings. And, if need be, he was evidently able to obtain coins as well. Moreover, we have already seen that in 1665, through his contact with Jürgen Ovens, he had sold rare books and engravings to the court in Gottorf in Schleswig-Holstein.[119]

A great many artists must have worked for Uylenburgh in the 1660s, although the only source of information about them in this connection is the *Groote Schouburgh* by Arnold Houbraken.[120] Apart from Jürgen Ovens and Nicolaes Rosendael, Gerard de Lairesse was employed by Uylenburgh for a few months, probably in 1665, and Anthonie de Grebber and Jan van Pee were in his service around the same time. Johannes Lingelbach and Theodoor Ferreris are also believed to have worked for the firm. See below for a more detailed account of these artists' activities.

Uylenburgh was not only an employer, but also active as a painter. Houbraken's *Groote Schouburgh* notes that at the beginning of the eighteenth century there was 'a large hall with paintings by him in the home of the Lord of Kerkwyk in Amsterdam'.[121] The Lord of Kerkwyk was Justus Ranst Kemp, whose father Joost Kemp had a double residence built on the Herengracht (the present no. 554) in 1665. Uylenburgh was probably commissioned to paint the hall not long after the building was completed.[122] As his name occurs frequently in inventories dating from that period, his work must have been much sought after. However, no works bearing his signature have come to light.[123]

Transaction with the Great Elector, 1671-1672

FRIEDRICH WILHELM, ELECTOR OF BRANDENBURG

On 1 August 1671 Gerrit Uylenburgh received a visit from high-ranking guests. Friedrich Wilhelm, the Elector of Brandenburg, had dispatched a delegation led by Alexander Freiherr von Spaen to purchase works of art.[124] But before discussing

119 See p. 63.
120 Houbraken 1718-1721, vol. 3, p. 109.
121 Houbraken 1718-1721, vol. 2, p. 294.
122 See, p. 208-209.
123 For possible attributions, see p. 209-210.
124 Much has been written about this transaction with the elector. The first author to discuss it was Houbraken 1718-1721, vol. 2, pp. 294-297, who mentioned it in his biography of Uylenburgh. In the modern era, Dohme, 1883, was the first to return to this subject, followed by Bredius 1886; Seidel 1890, p. 123; Galland 1893; Bredius 1916; Jacobs 1925; Logan 1979; Meijer 1999. However, the documents in the Berlin archive have never before been examined alongside those in the Dutch archives. Moreover, the documents in Berlin had not been consulted since 1925 and the inventory number was unknown. We are deeply grateful to Rita Klauschenz of the Geheimes Staatsarchiv, Preussischer Kulturbesitz, Berlin, who traced the package of documents concerning the transaction (I. HA Rep. 76 alt III, no. 167). As the package contains all the documents pertaining to the sale, the German archive documents are consistently identified by that inventory number. For the Dutch archive documents, some previously unpublished, reference is made to the relevant notarial deed.

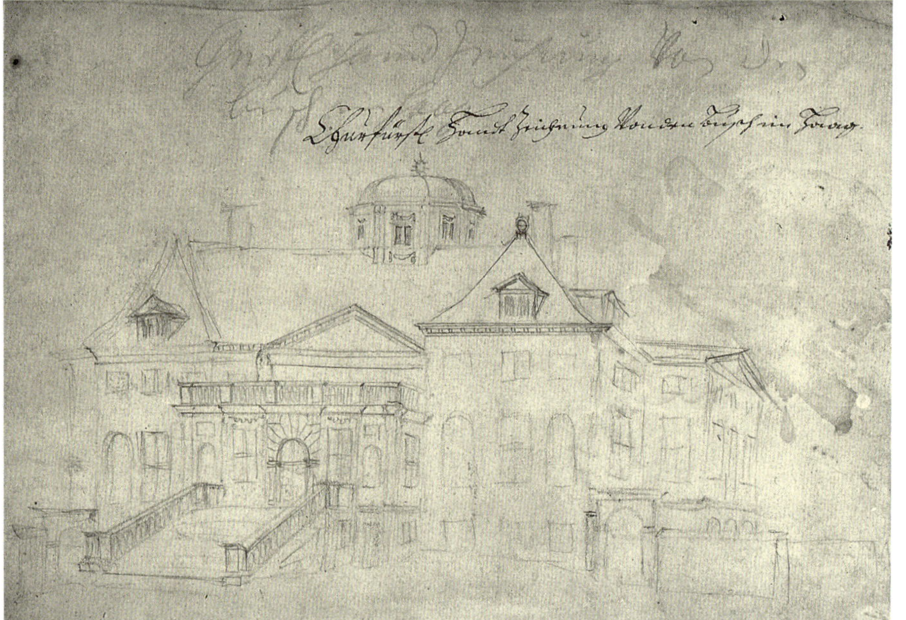

42 Friedrich Wilhelm, Elector of Brandenburg, Huis ten Bosch in The Hague, pen, 20.5 x 29.1 cm, Berlin, Geheimes Staatsarchiv, Preussischer Kulturbesitz

this transaction and its disastrous conclusion, a few words must be said about the elector.

In the realms of both politics and culture, Friedrich Wilhelm, known as the Great Elector, was strongly influenced by events in the Dutch Republic. He had studied in Leiden and established close ties with the court in The Hague through his marriage in 1646 to Louise Henriette, the eldest daughter of the Stadholder Frederik Hendrik. He returned to visit the country on several occasions. Friedrich Wilhelm became elector of Brandenburg in 1640 and ruled over territories not only in Prussia, but also near Cleves, right on the border of the Republic. Many of his courtiers were of Dutch origin.[125]

He had studied painting and drawing as a youngster, and continued to draw later in life.[126] A few of his sketches of architecture have come down to us, including one of Huis ten Bosch in The Hague (fig. 42).[127] Art remained a passion all his life. A number of artists, nearly all of them Dutch, worked for him in Berlin and Potsdam. He employed history and portrait painters, such as Willem van Honthorst, Nicolaes Willingh and Jacques Vaillant, as well as still-life painters, among them Willem Frederiksz van Royen, Ottomar Elliger the Elder and Hendrick Fromantiou. In 1661, the talented German painter Hans Georg Wolfgrübel studied under various masters in the Netherlands at the elector's expense.[128]

Over the years, the elector acquired a collection of paintings, sculpture, coins and rarities, mostly purchased in the Dutch Republic. He engaged

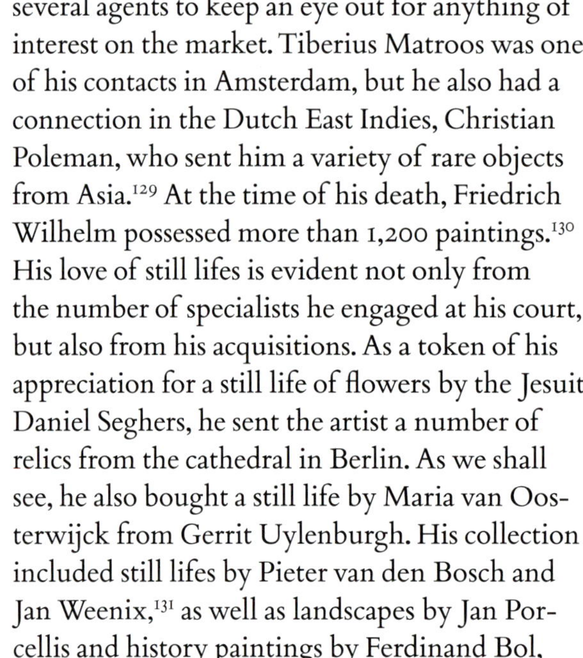

several agents to keep an eye out for anything of interest on the market. Tiberius Matroos was one of his contacts in Amsterdam, but he also had a connection in the Dutch East Indies, Christian Poleman, who sent him a variety of rare objects from Asia.[129] At the time of his death, Friedrich Wilhelm possessed more than 1,200 paintings.[130] His love of still lifes is evident not only from the number of specialists he engaged at his court, but also from his acquisitions. As a token of his appreciation for a still life of flowers by the Jesuit Daniel Seghers, he sent the artist a number of relics from the cathedral in Berlin. As we shall see, he also bought a still life by Maria van Oosterwijck from Gerrit Uylenburgh. His collection included still lifes by Pieter van den Bosch and Jan Weenix,[131] as well as landscapes by Jan Porcellis and history paintings by Ferdinand Bol, Govert Flinck and Salomon Koninck.

125 Bahl 2001.
126 Seidel 1890, p. 120. In 1628 the eight-year-old prince was said to be extremely fond of paintings.
127 Berlin, Geheimes Staatsarchiv, Preussischer Kulturbesitz, Rep. 94, IV, HA, no. 6, portfolio of drawings by the Great Elector.
128 On the elector's collection and the painters who worked for him, see Seidel 1890; Galland 1893; Kühn 1965; and especially Giersberg 1988.
129 Reidemeister 1932. Berlin, Geheimes Staatsarchiv, Preussischer Kulturbesitz, I HA Rep. 36 (letters from Matroos); I HA Geheimer Rat, Rep. 9, Allgemeine Verwaltung, D2, Fasz. 1 and 2 (letters from agent Mathias Doege, Poleman from Batavia, and Matroos from Amsterdam, mentioning, among other things, a painting by Wouwerman for 240 rijksdaalders (letter of 13 October 1681).
130 Giersberg 1988, p. 135. The estate of his second wife Dorothea included more than 1,200 paintings worth a total of 31,174 Taler and 28 Groschen, according to the painters Jacques Vaillant and Hendrick Fromantiou in 1689/1690.
131 On the Pieter van den Bosch, see below. On Weenix, see Huygens the Younger 1888, vol. 3, p. 36.

But no respectable seventeenth-century collection was considered complete without Italian paintings, ideally by Raphael, Titian or other great masters of the sixteenth century. Notwithstanding his explicit preference for Dutch art, the elector must have taken pride in his Italian paintings as well. Around 1680 Johann Gottfried Bartsch produced engravings of twenty-five paintings from Friedrich Wilhelm's collection.[132] We can reasonably assume that the series represented the most important works in his collection and the majority of them – fifteen in all – were prints after Titian, Guercino, Guido Reni and other Italian masters. They were presumably made in emulation of similar series of famous paintings in the collections of Leopold Wilhelm, for instance, or of Louis XIV of France.[133]

However, connoisseurs were evidently aware that the engravings as well as the paintings they were taken from compared rather unfavourably with the examples referred to above. Constantijn Huygens the Younger, who visited Berlin in 1680, was unimpressed by the elector's collection. 'Between 25 and 30 good pieces', he concluded in his journal, adding that 'a great many of them were worthless'. He spoke highly of a *Descent from the Cross* by Van Dyck, a *Hercules and the Nemean lion* by Rubens, and a *Saint Sebastian* by Guido Reni, but he was sceptical about some of the other attributions, which he described as follows: 'a man with a red beard, half-length figure, which they list as a Correggio, one or two portraits by Tintoretto and another of a wizened, emaciated man by Titian, or at least Uylenberg attributes it to him; the beheading of John the Baptist, by Titian, Uylenberg claims, but without his pleasing palette; a small head of Saint Catherine, taken to be a Parmigianino, a man asleep in a landscape by Giorgione [...]'. Huygens was even more dis-

paraging about the elector's collection of drawings and prints. After leafing through one or two large albums, he concluded that there were 'only ugly sheets consisting of copies and a few inferior originals'.[134] By Huygens's account, years after the transaction with Uylenburgh in 1671, Friedrich Wilhelm's collection was nothing to write home about. Sovereigns and other wealthy collectors of the day were parting with huge sums of money for a painting by Raphael or Titian,[135] but Friedrich Wilhelm was not in a position to do so. He nevertheless coveted the famous Italians, and it was this ambition that Gerrit Uylenburgh turned to his advantage. It is uncertain how the two men came into contact with one another but they must have met before the visit of the elector's delegation in August 1671. Gerrit Uylenburgh was the leading art dealer in Amsterdam at the time, with a variety of Italian paintings in stock. The elector may have heard about him from one of his agents in the Republic or from his court painters or other acquaintances. Or perhaps Uylenburgh took the initiative and wrote to Friedrich Wilhelm or one of his agents. Johannes de Renialme, for instance, had done so before; he had written to the elector in 1650 and sent him a list of his entire stock.[136] Be that as it may, on 1 August 1671 Friedrich Wilhelm's envoys turned up on Uylenburgh's doorstep.[137]

SALE OF ITALIAN PAINTINGS
AND CLASSICAL SCULPTURES

Besides Von Spaen, who at the time was in charge of government affairs in Cleves, the delegation consisted of Quartermaster General Philipp de Chieze, Master of the Horse Justus David Coulombel, and Chamberlain Simon van de Water.

132 Giersberg 1988, pp. 143-146.
133 On this series of prints, see Van der Waals 1988, pp. 103-109.
134 Huygens the Younger 1876-1888, vol. 3, pp. 35–38. Huygens viewed the collection on 19 and 21 October 1680, escorted by Hendrick Fromantiou. 'Je vis encore trois chambres ou sont la plus part des tableaux de Mr l'Electeur et ou parmy peut-estre 25 ou 30 bonnes pièces il y en avoit une grande quantité qui ne valoyent rien. Parmy ceux-là il y avoit une descente de la croix de van Dijck très-excellente, un Hercule estranglant le lion de Nemée de Rubbens, un St. Sebastien à demy corps de Guide, un tableau avec trois ou quatre figures en detrempe, tant que l'on pouvoit juger de loin de Giulio Romano; un homme avec une barbe rouge à demye corps qui passoit là pour estre de Correggio, un portrait ou deux de Tintoretto et un autre d'un homme sec et maigre de Titien ou donné pour tel par Uylenberg; la decollation de St Jean de Titien au dire d'Uylenberg, mais non pas de son bon colory; une petite teste de Ste Catherine, tenue du Parmesan; un homme couché dans un paysage de Giorgione, à ce qu'il sembloit, en petit; un bon portrait de femme du maistre qui a fait les deux figures auprès d'une table, qu'a Mr. van Ommeren; un tableau ou il y a des noix et autres choses. De là nous fusmes dans la chambre ou sont gardés ses livres d'estampes et de desseins, dont j'en feuilletay un ou deux forts grands, ou il n'y avoit que des mauvaises pièces, force copies et quelques méschants originaux'.
135 Brown 1995.
136 Seidel 1890 refers to this letter, but without quoting the inventory number. We are greatly indebted to Rita Klauschenz of the Geheimes Staatsarchiv, Preussischer Kulturbesitz, who managed to recover the letter. Berlin, Geheimes Staatsarchiv, Preussischer Kulturbesitz I HA, Rep. 76, alt 111, no. 167. See p. 256.
137 According to the deed of 20 June 1672, Von Spaen's visit took place on 1 August (GAA, not. A. Lock, NA 2239, pp. 505-507). Moreover, in a letter to the elector, sent from Cleves on 12 August 1671, Von Spaen says that the visit took place twelve days previously ('vor ein zwölff Tagen in Amsterdam gewesen'), Berlin, Geheimes Staatsarchiv, I HA Rep 76, Alt 111, no. 167.

It is telling that the last three were all from the Netherlands. De Chieze was born in Amersfoort in 1629 and had spent his youth in the Netherlands. His father had been captain of the horse to Stadholder Maurits. De Chieze entered into the elector's service in 1660 and emerged as the most influential of the many Dutch attendants at the court in Berlin.[138] Before taking up posts at the court of Friedrich Wilhelm, Coulombel and Van de Water had been chamberlains to Louise Henriette, whom they accompanied to Berlin at the time of her marriage to the elector in 1646.[139] De Chieze and Von Spaen must have been the heads of the delegation. It seems that De Chieze, the elector's confidant who perhaps possessed some knowledge of art, was sent to Amsterdam especially for this mission.[140]

Von Spaen reported back to the elector twelve days after the visit.[141] He enclosed with his letter a detailed specification, which has unfortunately been lost, of the paintings and sculptures he had acquired. The works had been purchased on the explicit understanding that they could be returned if the elector so wished. The specification, Von Spaen wrote, not without a hint of pride, revealed how successfully he had managed to reduce Uylenburgh's price. Uylenburgh, he continues, had already sent the paintings and sculptures to Otto von Guericke, the elector's representative in Hamburg, with a letter requesting him to forward the consignment to Berlin as quickly as possible, while ensuring that it came to no harm. Von Spaen advised the elector to send a similar letter to Von Guericke to drive the point home.

At the beginning of September the elector notified Von Spaen that the art had arrived safely and that 'We are entirely satisfied with it'. The letter intimates that the elector had also acquired art from Uylenburgh some time earlier. He instructed Von Spaen to pay for it the following year, so that those works could be dispatched as well. The order must have been fairly substantial, as the elector spoke of a 'consignment known as the large consignment'.[142] In view of the subsequent course of events in the transaction described here, it is unlikely that these objects were ever actually paid for or sent on to Berlin.

On 21 September the elector approved the payment of 2,721 rijksdaalders to Uylenburgh for the paintings and sculptures Von Spaen had ordered. Uylenburgh also received an additional 126 rijksdaalders for a still life of flowers by Maria van Oosterwijck.[143]

A month later, on 23 October, the elector sent a letter informing Von Spaen that Uylenburgh had swindled him with the paintings. He instructed him not to pay the amount he still owed, but to demand a refund of the 2,000 rijksdaalders he had already remitted.[144] A few weeks later Von Spaen replied that he would heed the elector's wishes, but urged him not to return the paintings until the money had been recovered. Von Spaen ended the letter by insisting that he himself was beyond reproach: he had merely carried out the elector's instructions by sending the art to Berlin and paying a deposit in Amsterdam (in the presence of De Chieze and Van de Water).[145]

From the sequel to this episode we discover why the elector's initial satisfaction with the art works subsequently turned into bitter disillusionment. In the meantime, the Dutch still-life painter Hendrick Fromantiou had convinced him that the paintings were copies and not originals (fig. 43). Fromantiou had worked in Amsterdam in the 1660s before being appointed court painter to Friedrich Wilhelm in 1670. According to Houbraken, who apparently knew the ins and outs

---

138 Mielke 1965; Bahl 2001, pp. 164, 452-453.
139 Bahl 2001, pp. 164, 456, 612.
140 He is in any event the only person, as far as we know, who received the royal allowance of more than 75 rijksdaalders in accordance with the elector's instructions of 21 September 1671 (Berlin, Geheimes Staatsarchiv, I HA Rep 76, Alt 111, no. 167) On Chieze, see also Mielke 1965.
141 See note 142.
142 Berlin, Geheimes Staatsarchiv, I HA Rep 76, Alt 111, no. 167. Draft of a letter of 5/15 September 1671 from the elector to Von Spaen, Potsdam.

143 Berlin, Geheimes Staatsarchiv, I HA Rep 76, Alt 111, no. 167. On the elector's instructions, Potsdam 21 September 1671. The painting by Maria van Oosterwijck was probably *Flowers in a vase decorated with reliefs of episodes from the life of the Virgin.* This painting was in the exhibition held in Berlin in 1890, *Niederländische Kunstwerke des 17. Jahrhunderts aus Berliner Privatbesitz,* no. 203. It was presented to the Von Hohenzollern family in 1926. Its present whereabouts are unknown. We are grateful to Gerd Bartoschek, who kindly furnished this information.

144 This letter has been lost, but the date and its purport can be inferred from the letter of 11 November 1671 from Von Spaen to the elector, see below.
145 Berlin, Geheimes Staatsarchiv, I HA Rep 76, Alt 111, no. 167. Letter of 11 November 1671 sent from Cleves.

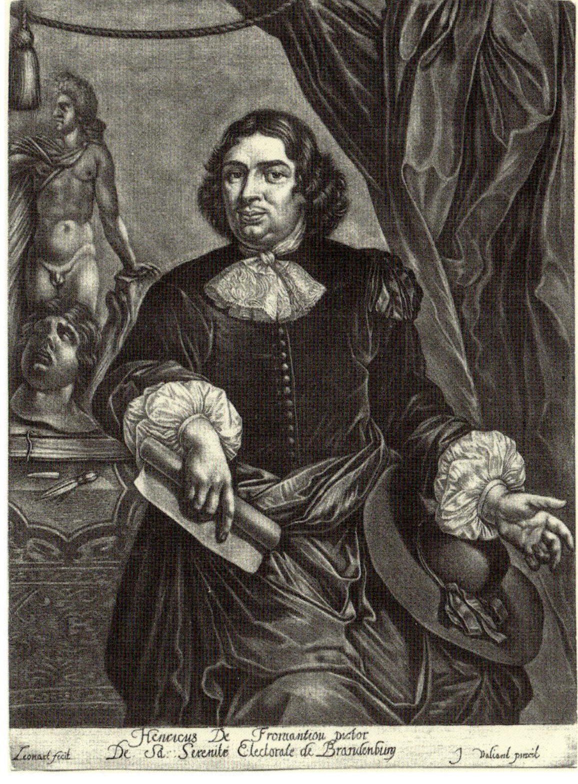

Uijlenburgh, we hereby attest to Your Excellency the Elector that we have availed ourselves of his services in several important transactions involving art and paintings and found him always to be honest, trustworthy, sincere and of absolute integrity, a reputation he also enjoys among all decent people here, such that we can state without reservation that, should he have the honour to serve Your Excellency the Elector in similar matters, he will acquit himself to complete satisfaction'.[147]

Uylenburgh must have spoken to the elector some time around 6 January 1672 and perhaps delivered the burgomasters' letter to him in person. At first, his efforts to remedy the situation appeared to be bearing fruit. On 12 January the elector wrote a letter to his 'dear faithful' Fromantiou and enclosed Uylenburgh's indignant objection to Fromantiou's allegation that the paintings were copies and not originals. 'As we recall', the elector wrote, 'that you persisted in your views, it is only reasonable that you also prove them to be true. You should therefore go to Amsterdam on a certain date [...] and confirm before masters with experience in the art of painting that the works Uylenburgh sold are not authentic originals, but merely later copies'.[148]

Fromantiou took his time. On 25 January the elector ordered him to notify Uylenburgh within three days of the date of his arrival in Amsterdam, so that Uylenburgh would be able to return.[149] Hence, it would appear that Uylenburgh had remained in Berlin. A week later the elector instructed Fromantiou to travel to Amsterdam with the paintings, packed and sealed, as soon as the ice had melted and the waters were again open for shipping.[150]

To show that he was taking the matter seri-

of the transaction, Fromantiou had been 'on the galley (the expression commonly used in Italy for those who paint for cutthroats) and had himself painted for Uilenburg'. He therefore 'knew how that fox did business, and designated them copies'.[146]

As soon as Uylenburgh heard the elector's reason for cancelling the purchase, he travelled to Berlin to protest his innocence. Before leaving Amsterdam, he asked the burgomasters, who were on cordial terms with the elector, to vouch for his good character. The burgomasters agreed and wrote as follows: 'At the request of Gerrit

146 Houbraken 1718-1721, vol. 2, pp. 294-295.
147 Berlin, Geheimes Staatsarchiv, I HA Rep 76, Alt III, no. 167. The letter from the burgomasters to the elector was not dated, but the date 6 January 1672 was inscribed in a different hand, that probably being the date on which the elector received it. The municipal secretary Hendrick Spiegel signed on behalf of the four incumbent burgomasters. The burgomasters' remark about having engaged Uylenburgh to conduct various important affairs might allude to his work in connection with the 'Dutch Gift'.
148 Berlin, Geheimes Staatsarchiv, I HA Rep 76, Alt III, no. 167, the elector's instructions to Fromantiou, Cölln a.d. Spree, 12 January 1672: 'Lieber getreuer, Du wirst aus/ beijligender Supplication ersehen, wie höchlich/ Gerit Uylenborch, Schilder und Kaufmann/ in Schildereijen Zu Amsterdam sich/ über dich beschweret, dass du vorgeben/ dörfte, dass die Schildereijen, die er/ Uns vor originalien verkaufft, nur/ Copien seijn solten. Weil wir/ Uns nun erinnern, dass du solches/ beständig asseriret hast, so ist nicht/ mehr dan billig, dass du solches/ beweisest. dahero nötig seijn wird,/ dass du auf einen gewissen tag,/ welchen du bestimmen dem Supplicanten benennen wirst, dich/ nacher Amsterdam begebest, und/ aldar Vor einige in der Mahler-/kunst erfahren Meistern Klärlich/ darthust und beweisest, dass die/ Uns Von dem Supplicanten verkaufften/ stück keine wahre Originalien/ sondern nur nachgemachte Copien/ seijn [...].'
149 Berlin, Geheimes Staatsarchiv, I HA Rep 76, Alt III, no. 167, the elector's instructions to Fromantiou, Cölln a.d. Spree, 25 January 1672.
150 Berlin, Geheimes Staatsarchiv, I HA Rep 76, Alt III, no. 167, the elector's edict to Fromantiou of 31 January 1671.

ously, on 17 February the elector officially rescinded the order given to Von Spaen on 21 September 1671 to pay the money to Uylenburgh, and made this decision known to Uylenburgh.[151] In response, Uylenburgh wrote to the elector on 22 March, thanking him for instructing Fromantiou to substantiate his allegations in Amsterdam in five weeks' time, but also expressing his disappointment at the elector's refusal to pay the amount they had agreed upon. He suggested that the elector might have the paintings appraised by Nicolaes Willingh, whom he recommended as one of the best painters and connoisseurs.[152] Willingh, or Wielingh, was a Dutch history painter who, like Fromantiou, had been appointed to the court in Berlin, where he enjoyed a good reputation. Uylenburgh may have met Willingh during his visit to Berlin and heard that he saw the paintings in a more favourable light than Fromantiou. It is also possible that they met while Willingh was still working in the Republic. Willingh had provided drawings of classical Roman sculptures for Jan de Bisschop's *Icones*.[153]

More than a month went by. With Fromantiou's arrival in Amsterdam at the beginning of May the dispute over the authenticity of the paintings finally erupted.

CONNOISSEURS IN AMSTERDAM

From the moment Fromantiou arrived in Amsterdam, Uylenburgh fretted that the court painter from Berlin might solicit the opinions of like-minded painters, without inviting him to be present. On 7 May he sent the notary Lock to Fromantiou to propose that they submit a joint petition to the district court requesting the magistrates 'to authorise and instruct a few impartial masters, painters and other connoisseurs of painting to examine the paintings in question and decide whether they were predominantly later copies or old antique works'.[154] Uylenburgh also made it known that he would instantly object if Fromantiou asked other artists to judge the paintings behind his back. Fromantiou's curt reply was that he had 'no business with the magistrates'.

Two days later the notary paid another visit to Fromantiou to inform him that, in view of his unwillingness to cooperate, Uylenburgh had himself submitted a petition to the magistrates, and that they had 'nominated fifteen of the best experts and connoisseurs in the city, for the most part painters themselves' to appraise the works. Uylenburgh asked Fromantiou to appoint a time and place for them to examine the paintings. Once again Fromantiou refused to have any dealings with the magistrates, adding that he took instructions only from the elector. If the court ordered him to do so, he would be prepared to produce those instructions for inspection.[155]

From a deed drawn up on 12 May it transpires that Fromantiou had objected to the experts nominated by the magistrates, and submitted an alternative list of candidates. Of those, the magistrates chose the chief officers of the Guild of St Luke and the artists Adam Pijnacker, 'Van Oort', presumably meaning Joan van Noordt, Gerbrandt van den Eeckhout, Abraham van den Tempel, Daniel Wolfraet, Jan Blom, Anthonie de Grebber, Ferdinand Bol, Adriaen Backer, Philips Koninck, Jacob de Wet, Johannes Lingelbach, Wallerant Vaillant and Gerard de Lairesse. In response to Uylenburgh's request for an appointment, Fromantiou replied that he was welcome to visit him the following day, 13 May, accompanied by whomever he wished.[156]

On the same day, 12 May – the day before the visit – Fromantiou invited a number of artists to examine the paintings and record their findings in a notarial deed.[156] Three of the artists appointed by the magistrates were present: Adam Pijnacker, Daniel Wolfraet and Gerard de Lairesse. In addition, there were also Willem van Aelst, Jan Andre Lievens, Willem Kalf, Otto Marseus van Schrieck, Mattheus van Pellecum, Jan Wijnants, Melchior de Hondecoeter, Bartolomeus Appelman, Hendrick van Someren, Barend Graat, Roeland Roghman, Jacob Vennecool, Lambert Doomer and Jean Wils. Fromantiou must have been confident that they were sympathetic to his cause. The paintings were displayed in the Keijserskroon inn in Kalverstraat. The notary's deed lists the paintings with Uylenburgh's attributions. Each entry is followed by two prices in Dutch

151 Berlin, Geheimes Staatsarchiv, I HA Rep 76, Alt III, no. 167, the elector's edict to Von Spaen, 17 February 1672, Cölln a.d. Spree.
152 GAA, NA 2857, not. D. Danckerts, pp. 771-772, 22 March 1672.
153 On Willingh, see Buijsen 1998, p. 360. Willingh was married to the daughter of the Hague painter Andries de Haen. In 1667 he left The Hague for Berlin. The fact that one of his works was included in the series of prints by Bartsch attests to the high regard in which he was held at the elector's court (see above). Moreover, his work was among the most valuable of the 1,200 paintings appraised in 1689/90 in the inventory of the elector's widow. See Giersberg 1988, pp. 139, 145, and Bartoschek 2001, p. 36 and note 28. On De Bisschop and Willingh, see Van Gelder/Jost 1985, p. 36.
154 GAA, not. A. Lock, NA 2239, pp. 80-81.
155 GAA, not. A. Lock, NA 2239, pp. 82-83
156 GAA, not. A. Lock, NA 2239, pp. 130-131. The incumbent chief officers of the Guild of St Luke are unknown. 'Van Oort' may have been the little-known painter W. van Oort; see Dirkse 2001.

rijksdaalders, which are said to be estimated values. It may be that the first amount was Uylenburgh's asking price and the second the price that Von Spaen had ultimately paid. The list is as follows:

	Rijksdaalders Dutch currency
A Venus and Cupid, figures larger than life by Michiel Angelo Bonaroti	350 : 320
A portrait of Giorsion Del Castel francko by Titiaen, painted from life	250 : 240
A shepherd and shepherdess by Titiaen	160 : 150
A counterpart of the same size by Titiaen	120 : 110
Naked children dancing, lifesize, by Jacomo Palma	250 : 240
A Venetian lady by Paris Pordinon	160 : 150
A portrait of a prelate by Hans Holbeen	120 : 110
A Ceres with cornucopia and a multitude of naked children by Giorgion del Castel Francko	120 : 110
A portrait of an old man by Raphael Urbin	150 : 140
A St Paul, half figure, lifesize, by Jacomo Palma the Elder	80 : 70
A beautiful Venetian woman by Titiaen	200 : 185
A landscape by Titiaen with a satyr caressing the nymph	240 : 23

In the opinion of the artists Fromantiou had summoned, the works were 'not only not [...] outstanding Italian paintings, but, on the contrary, rubbish and poor work, each and every one worth far less than a tenth of the price paid, and they, the attestants, had no regard for such paintings '. The document adds that 'they, the attestants are at all times willing to confirm their statement, if necessary under oath'. A copy of the original document and a German translation of it were hastily dispatched to the elector, possibly on the following day.[158] On 12 or 13 May Jan Lievens also went to view the paintings; as we have seen, Fromantiou had already invited his son Jan André to do so. On 14 May Lievens signed an identical deed, with verbatim descriptions of the paintings. Fromantiou and his notary must have drafted a standard document in which only the names of the attestants needed to be inserted. As Lievens was the only person who signed his copy, all references in the plural were deleted.[159]

Uylenburgh did not leave it at that. As arranged, he arrived at Kalverstraat on 13 May, with a troop of artists in tow. The official report for the magistrates no longer exists, but from a notarial deed drawn up at Uylenburgh's request we can deduce which of the painters appointed by the magistrates expressed a favourable opinion. Dirck Santvoort, one of the chief officers of the guild, pronounced that the paintings would not be out of place 'in a good cabinet of Italian art'. Jan Blom was more reserved, but believed he had seen comparable paintings in Holland and Italy. Wallerant Vaillant considered many of them good, some mediocre, but on the whole, they were 'competently executed'. Anthonie de Grebber found the majority 'reasonable' and endorsed Santvoort's view that they were worthy of a place in an 'Italian cabinet of art'. Gerbrandt van den Eeckhout and Abraham van den Tempel agreed that most were fine pieces, but there were also a few that fell short. Adriaen Backer's verdict was that they were good, by and large, though some were 'slightly battered here and there'. Johannes Lingelbach considered some of them 'outstanding'. Philips Koninck presented the most comprehensive and favourable report. He said the paintings were 'good and competently painted' and 'worthy of the masters under whose names they were sold', adding that 'impartial painters and connoisseurs of Italian art could not but regard and accept them as such'.[160] Hence we know the findings of all the experts appointed by the magistrates except those of Van Noordt, Ferdinand Bol and Jacob de Wet. Apparently neither side stood to benefit from their opinions. Considering that Uylenburgh recorded even Blom's totally noncommittal remarks, they most probably declined to pass judgment. But Uylenburgh had more strings to his bow. The painters Philips de Momper, Willem Strijcker and Theodoor Ferreris prefaced their statements by announcing that they had all three been to Italy and seen a great deal of art. The paintings were excellent, De Momper declared, and quite as good as anything he had seen in the collections of the cardinals in Rome. Strijcker described them as 'admirable' and 'painted by commendable masters'. In Ferreris's view they were 'fine Italian paintings'. None, he believed, were copies. Pieter Pietersz Niedeck, Lodewijck van Ludick, Abraham Begeyn, Harmanus Collenius, Pieter Codde, Christiaan Striep and David Eversdijck signed a unanimous state-

157 G A A, not. Dirck van der Groe, N A 4074, fol. 367r-v. Copy and German translation in Berlin, Geheimes Staatsarchiv, I H A Rep. 76, Alt III, no. 167.

158 Idem. The copy and the German translation in Berlin included a note by the three Amsterdam notaries Outgers, Padthuijsen and Tixerandet, stating that Van der Groe was a notary in Amsterdam and that the deed in question had been drawn up correctly. The note is dated 13 May 1672.

159 G A A, not. Dirck van der Groe, N A 4074, fol. 377r-v.

160 G A A, not. A. Lock, N A 2239, 17 May 1672, pp. 178-180. Copy and German translation in Berlin, Geheimes Staatsarchiv, I H A Rep. 76, Alt III, no. 167. With a postscript signed by Hendrick Spiegel on behalf of the burgomasters of Amsterdam, attesting to the trustworthiness of not. A. Lock, dated 21 May 1672.

ment to the effect that 'the majority [were] good and accomplished Italian paintings'.[161] Uylenburgh had both reports translated into German, and sent them to the elector, with a copy of the Dutch, some time around 21 May.

Leaving no stone unturned, Fromantiou sought the opinions of Karel Dujardin and Willem Dodijns, the last two artists he consulted in Amsterdam. Dodijns was living in The Hague at the time and either made a special trip to Amsterdam at Fromantiou's request, or perhaps happened to be there on some other business. Fromantiou may have met these two artists in the 1650s, when he himself was stationed in The Hague. The deed drawn up on this occasion was not the standard form, but a detailed report of Dujardin and Dodijns's appraisal of each individual painting.[162] We shall return to this subject later.

Around 21 May, after all the Amsterdam painters had been heard, Uylenburgh sent a lengthy letter to inform the elector of the events of the preceding weeks. Once more, he fulminated against Fromantiou's 'preposterous accusations and outpourings'. Uylenburgh was aware that Fromantiou had been instructed to satisfy accomplished masters that the paintings were not 'authentic originals, but merely later copies'. However, in his opinion, Fromantiou had not even attempted to find independent arbiters. Instead, he had 'surreptitiously prevailed upon some of his acquaintances who were envious of the petitioner [Uylenburgh] to testify to that effect'. This, Uylenburgh continued, could never have been the elector's intention. He was angered, moreover, by Fromantiou's quibbling over the experts the magistrates had nominated. And then, Uylenburgh added, none of the new experts 'had the presumption to say, let alone the means to prove that [the paintings were] copies, not

originals'. In short, he wanted Fromantiou to admit that he had failed to accomplish his mission and that he had wished only to 'denigrate' Uylenburgh. His malicious slander had sullied Uylenburgh's 'good name and reputation'. Indeed, people might even believe that he would 'deliberately deceive people by passing off copies as originals'. The letter ends with a request to the elector to send a testimonial stating t hat he had been 'wrongfully accused and maligned' by Fromantiou'.[163]

However, the letter arrived too late to make any difference. On 22 May, probably immediately on receipt of the first deed that Fromantiou had sent from Amsterdam, the elector ordered his court painter to give the paintings to Uylenburgh and return to the court as soon as possible.[164] The statements made by the painters that Uylenburgh had summoned were copied in Amsterdam only on 21 May. In other words, the elector would not have seen them when he took his decision a day later. Fromantiou, however, was unaware that the tide had turned in his favour, and had set off for The Hague with the paintings.

CONNOISSEURS IN THE HAGUE, ANTWERP AND ROTTERDAM

On Saturday 21 May, Fromantiou displayed the paintings in the 'confrères' room' frequented by the Hague painters. Before moving to Berlin, he had lived in The Hague as well as Amsterdam and must have been acquainted with artists there, too. Willem Dodijns, one of the leading members of the Hague painters' association, had already appraised the works in Amsterdam. It is reasonable to assume that he would have urged Fromantiou to take his case to The Hague, where he could expect to find the association and its direc-

161 GAA, not. A. Lock, NA 2239, pp. 178-180. Two copies in Berlin, Geheimes Staatsarchiv, I HA Rep. 76, Alt III, no. 167. With a postscript signed by Hendrick Spiegel on behalf of the burgomasters of Amsterdam, attesting to the trustworthiness of not.

A. Lock, dated 21 May 1672. 162 GAA, not. F. Tixerandet, NA 680, 16 May 1672, pp. 214-217, damaged by fire. On Dodijns, see Buijsen (1998), pp. 300-301; on Dujardin, Kilian 2005. The earliest record of the Amsterdam-born Dujardin dates from 1656,

when he was in The Hague. He remained there until at least June 1658. He is known to have been back in Amsterdam in May 1659. Dodijns served eleven terms as dean and four as headman of the Hague fraternity of painters. Fromantiou is known to have visited The

Hague, as he witnessed two deeds there on 15 March 1658 (The Hague Municipal Archives, not. A. Croll, NA 476). He could therefore have met both Dodijns and Dujardin there.
163 The letter is undated but we can infer from the contents

that it was written around 21 May 1672. Berlin, Geheimes Staatsarchiv, I HA Rep. 76, Alt III, no. 167.
164 Berlin, Geheimes Staatsarchiv, I HA Rep. 76, Alt III, no. 167. Notes for a letter dated 22 May 1672, 'Befehl an Fermento den Mahler dass er die Schildereien an Eulenburg geben undt sich so fort wiederum anhero und nacher Potsdam verfügen soll'.

tors on his side. Johan de Baen, the dean of the association, and the two headmen Johan le Ducq and Jeronimus van Diest, prepared a statement for Fromantiou,[165] using the list of paintings that had been compiled in Amsterdam. Their conclusions were less harsh and none employed the word 'rubbish'. Nevertheless, the paintings were not worthy of attribution 'to any great master, let alone such outstanding masters as those to whom they were ascribed'.[166] Fromantiou also managed to persuade Johannes Jordaens and Johannes Vermeer to come from Delft to The Hague, and once again the word 'rubbish' fell.[167] Their statement was witnessed by Vermeer's patron, Pieter van Ruyven, Lord of Spalant, who may have accompanied Vermeer to The Hague to view the paintings.[168] Van Ruyven probably acquired many of his paintings directly from Vermeer.

Uylenburgh made the same journey as his adversary and he too apparently knew many artists in The Hague. On 23 May he had two deeds drawn up, recording their views. The first contains the opinions of Theodoor van der Schuer and Jacques Vaillant, who stated that they had seen the paintings on 21 May. There were 'many good Italian masters among them as well as some whose attribution was uncertain because of their age and the repairs they had undergone but which were nevertheless good, anonymous Italian paintings'. In any event, none could be dismissed as 'rubbish'. On the contrary. 'If the most outstanding works were undamaged and executed by those masters, they would be worth not hundreds but thousands'.[169]

The second deed reflects the views of Johanna van Aerssen van Wernhout, Caspar Netscher,

Pieter Moninckx, Dirck Dalens, Johan von Sandrart, Johan Moninckx, Johan van Haensbergen, Martinus Mijtens, François van Santwijck and Daniel Haringh, 'all of them artist-painters'. They agreed that there were definitely no copies among them. 'On the whole', they were 'good Italian paintings [...] worthy of a place in a cabinet of superlative Italian art'. Flaunting their credentials, they made it known that Pieter Moninckx, Dirck Dalens and Johan von Sandrart had all visited Italy.[170]

Not only painters but many other interested observers made their way to the 'confrères' room' on Saturday 21 May. One was Constantijn Huygens. He reported on the proceedings in a letter to Georg Bernhard von Poellnitz, one of the most influential members of the elector's court and the husband of Stadholder Maurits's daughter. Huygens attended the hearing with a group of friends whom he described as connoisseurs of Italian painting. He himself had few kind words to say about Fromantiou who, to his way of thinking, had 'left no stone unturned ' in his efforts to persuade his acquaintances to testify that the paintings were copies. In company, Huygens continued, he was unpleasant and rude, and intent on ruining Uylenburgh's reputation. Huygens took exception to Fromantiou's attitude to Uylenburgh because, the two men had been close friends for many years and Uylenburgh deserved better. Huygens and his companions considered some of the paintings superior to others, but none, they insisted, were copies. Moreover, Huygens pointed out that they had all been accepted as originals when they were in the famous collection of Gerard Reynst.[171] In 1660 Uylenburgh had

165 It transpires from an inventory of 1740 listing the possessions of the widow of Daniel Vicentius, who had previously been married to the daughter of Jan de Baen, that the latter executed a portrait of Fromantiou, see Bredius 1915-1922, vol. I, p. 281. However, it is uncertain when he did so. Fromantiou and De Baen could also have met after 1672, considering the cordial nature of De Baen's relationship with the Berlin elector. On De Baen, see Ekkart in Buijsen 1998, pp. 82-85.
166 The Hague Municipal Archives, not. P. van Swieten, NA 392, fol. 295 recto and verso.
167 The Hague Municipal Archives, not. P. van Swieten, NA 392, fol. 299.
168 Van Ruyven's presence has hitherto passed without remark. This would appear to support Montias's hypothesis that Van Ruyven was Vermeer's benefactor and that he bought numerous paintings from him. It is possible that Van Ruyven was living in The Hague in March 1672 and would therefore not have accompanied Vermeer from Delft, but met him in The Hague. In 1674, in any event, Van Ruyven was said to be living in The Hague. See Montias 1989, especially pp. 247-254.
169 The Hague Municipal Archives, not. M. Beeckman, NA 284, deed 122; Bredius 1886.
170 The Hague Municipal Archives, not. M. Beeckman, NA 284, deed 122. Some of the

Hague artists that Uylenburgh summoned must have known each other well. Johanna van Aerssen was a witness to the baptism of Caspar Netscher's twins. Daniel Haringh was a witness to the will drawn up by Netscher and his wife. Like Haensbergen, he was a faithful follower of Netscher, and both painters probably worked in his studio. After Netscher's death, Haensbergen was one of the guardians of his children.

See Wieseman 2002, pp. 118, 129, 131, 132, 140, 187.
171 Worp 1917, vol. 6, pp. 303-304, Logan 1979, pp. 93-95. The letter is in the Koninklijke Bibliotheek in The Hague. From the letter it transpires that it was Von Poellnitz who sought Huygens's opinion. On Von Poellnitz, see Bahl 2001, pp. 556-557. '[...] Je l'ay trouvé si rudement persecuté par le peintre Fermenteau, qui remue icy toute pierre pour amasser

des voix qui veuillent decrier pour copies une douzaine des pieces qui ledit Uylenburgh a vendues à Son Alte Electorale [...]et puis vous declarer, Monsieur, qu'apres avoir visité le tout par le menu, nous avons bien trouvé que d'aucunes de ces pieces en surmontent d'autres en valeur, mais non pas qu'aucune du nombre puisse estre reprochée pour copie, comme en effect toutes ont esté avouées orginales, par

longues années, dans le fameux cabinet de feu le Sieur Reinst à Amsterdam. Nous avons donc bien jugé par la verité du faict, et mesme par des discours aigres et effrontez du persecuteur, que toute sa visée ne tend qu' à ruiner la reputation du persecuté, qu'on dit n'avoir pas merité ceste recompense pour des effects de sincere et ancienne amitié. [...] Het doet mij genoegen, dat gij u in deze zaak op mij hebt beroepen.'

selected paintings from the Reynst Collection for the Dutch Gift to Charles II. The collection must nevertheless have remained reasonably intact, as a letter from Constantijn Huygens the Younger reveals that his widow sold it at an auction in May 1670, which Jan de Bisschop attended.[172] Uylenburgh must have bought numerous paintings and sculptures on that occasion, although he may have acquired some even earlier.[173]

From The Hague Fromantiou proceeded to Antwerp. On 27 May the twelve paintings were shown at the local Guild of St Luke, where they were examined by Ambrosius Brueghel, Peter van Halen, Peter Verbruggen, Jan Brueghel, Jan Galle, Matthijs Musson, Gaspar Huijbregts and Martinus Huijbregts, all deans or former deans of the guild. They unanimously pronounced the paintings 'extremely poor' and 'unsuitable for sale as works by masters of that calibre'. Like some of their Dutch counterparts, they remarked on the poor condition of what they described as 'spoilt' works.[174] Not only they, but also the painters Johannes Paulus Gillemans, Philippo Augustino Immenraet, Hendrick Minderhout and Cornelio Martens were invited to examine the works. The views they expressed were literally identical.[175] Fromantiou is not documented as having had any previous association with Antwerp, yet there must have been painters there whom he knew could trust to take his side. In any event, he is unlikely to have gone there on the off chance that he might find support.[176]

Fromantiou's subsequent movements are unknown. But three weeks later, on 16 June, he showed the twelve paintings to Jacob Lois and Albert Verschuer in Rotterdam. They dismissed them as 'shoddy merchandise and not originals'.

The notarial deed drawn up on that occasion mentions that they had seen several other works by the masters in question and even possessed paintings by some of them, which 'as works of art' surpassed anything that Uylenburgh had to offer.[177] Lois was a merchant and magistrate who painted in his free time and possessed a beautiful collection, which included work by Titian and Holbein. He also dealt in paintings from time to time. Fromantiou had a brother and sister living in Rotterdam and he may have met the collectors through them.[178]

REACHING A SETTLEMENT
IN AMSTERDAM

Fromantiou must have grown weary. On Saturday 18 June he sent notary Dirck van der Groe to ask Uylenburgh whether he was prepared to accept the twelve paintings. If so, Fromantiou would deliver them that afternoon. Uylenburgh replied that he would take them in for safekeeping on Monday 'until further notice', but only if others were present to examine their condition.[179]

That Monday, 20 June, Uylenburgh asked his notary, A. Lock, to serve a lengthy warrant addressed to Fromantiou. Once again, Uylenburgh set out his side of the story, relating that Von Spaen had called on 1 August 1671 and handed him a promissory note of 2,771 Dutch rijksdaalders for paintings and sculptures, and that the elector had expressed his satisfaction and made it known that he intended to buy more work from him.[180] In his view, the transaction with Von Spaen was 'cut and dried'. He demanded payment in full, with interest, and would not

172 Huygens 1888-1950, vol. 7, no. 1808, letter of 29 May 1670 from Constantijn Huygens the Younger to his brother Lodewijk. '[...] nostre Bisschop [...] est à Amsterdam ou se vend presentement le Cabinet tant renommé de Reinst.'
173 The fact that he acquired paintings from the Reynst Collection is also evidenced by a letter Pieter Blaeu wrote in 1674, when he was looking for a self-portrait by Palma Vecchio for Leopoldo de' Medici. Blaeu first went to the Reynst family, but discovered that it was no longer in their possession. He then went to Gerrit Uylenburgh who had indeed possessed the portrait in 1671-1672. See p. 103.
174 Antwerp, Academy Archive, inv. no. 81 (13), fol. 16v.
175 Antwerp Municipal Archives, not. J.B. Claus, NA 502, fol 83r-v.
176 The only hint that Fromantiou may have had some connection with Antwerp exists in the form of a garland he painted in the typical Antwerp style. The work, which is monogrammed and dated 1668, is at the Koninklijk Museum voor Schone Kunsten in Brussels. The garland surrounds a grisaille painted and signed by C. Lambrechts. This is probably the Christiaan Lambrechts referred to in the Antwerp Liggeren (Register of master painters and pupils) between 1636 and 1660.
177 Rotterdam Municipal Archives, not. J. Verschueren, NA 1076, pp. 162-163 (old fol. 2632-v). On Loys, see Van der Veen 1992, pp. 129-130.
178 Fromantiou's mother Antonetta Pels and his brother and sister, Johannes and Anna Fromantiou, lived in Rotterdam. Johannes was a tailor. See Rotterdam Municipal Archives, not. Nicolaes van Cleeff, NA 992, p. 108, deed 54, 22 April 1670 and DTB. See also GAA, not. A. van Santen, NA 3815, p. 309, 7 December 1683.
179 GAA, not. D. van der Groe, NA 4074, fol. 465r-v, 18 June 1672.
180 GAA, not. A. Lock, NA 2239, pp. 505-507, 20 June 1672.

contemplate taking the paintings back. If Fromantiou were to entrust them to someone else, it would be at his own risk: they were no longer Uylenburgh's property. Once again, Uylenburgh was enraged at Fromantiou's attitude. He had 'wrongly and maliciously' cast doubt on the paintings' authenticity. To prove that they were 'nothing more than copies of the originals, and inferior to boot', he had 'incited and prevailed upon painters to attest to that effect'. However, none had declared them to be copies, and that was the proof the elector had insisted upon. Uylenburgh threatened to sue Fromantiou personally for the 771 rijksdaalders still owing to him. Here, for the first time, the deed hints at the anguish that gripped the nation in 1672, a year of political and economic disaster. Uylenburgh speaks of 'these troubled and dangerous times'. On 6 April 1672 Louis XIV had declared war on the Republic. His armies advanced rapidly and had crossed the IJssel River by the beginning of June. By the end of the month Amersfoort, Utrecht, Naarden and other cities had fallen to the French, who were preparing to advance on Amsterdam.[181] The entire country was overwrought, and Uylenburgh was understandably despondent.

On the same day, 20 June, Fromantiou sent his notary, Van der Groe, to inform Uylenburgh that he could collect the paintings from Jean Wils on the Nieuwe Waalseiland.[182] He also summoned Carel Dujardin, Willem van Aelst, Bartolomeus Appelman and Jan André Lievens to judge the condition of the paintings.[183] All these painters, who had been present at the appraisal in the Keijserskroon on 12 May, confirmed that they were still in the same condition, except that some had lost a few 'small flakes' of paint. They singled out the works by Holbein (because 'the wood had warped'), Michelangelo, Palma Vecchio and Raphael. However, the damage was 'negligible' and really not worth mentioning at all.

It had become increasingly evident that Fromantiou was anxious to leave Amsterdam. On 21 June Van der Groe called on Uylenburgh to complain that he had failed to collect the paintings from Wils the previous day. Fromantiou had been kept waiting all day long. He said that the paintings would now remain in Wils's care – at Uylenburgh's risk and expense.[184] Fromantiou appears to have left for Berlin around this time, but a few months later he was back in Amsterdam. On 2 September 1672 he published the banns for his marriage to 28-year-old Luduwina Wouwermans, whose father, the late Philip Wouwermans, had been a prominent painter.[185] Uylenburgh must have got wind of Fromantiou's return. A week after the betrothal notary Lock turned up on Fromantiou's doorstep. He had been sent to inform him that Uylenburgh had obtained an official copy of the elector's instructions of 12 January, which categorically required Fromantiou to produce evidence that the paintings were copies. Uylenburgh was triumphant. Fromantiou had consistently denied that this was the purpose of his mission, and Uylenburgh was now in a position to prove that he had been 'economical with the truth and anxious to conceal it'. He challenged him once again to prove that the paintings were copies. Fromantiou replied that he wanted no further dealings with Uylenburgh and that the affair was 'over and done with'. He must have returned to Germany fairly soon afterwards.[186]

But the affair was not 'over and done with' at all. On 3 January 1673 notary Lock called on Jean Wils. Uylenburgh's fury had not subsided and in Fromantiou's absence he vented his spleen on Wils.[187] Fromantiou's allegations were 'muck raked up and promulgated to slander him and tarnish his good name and reputation and, if possible, destroy both him and his business'. Uylenburgh instituted proceedings for defama-

181 On this period of Dutch history, see, for example, Roorda 1971. The Brandenburg elector took the side of the Republic. A treaty with Brandenburg was signed in May and the elector dispatched troops. Münster was hostile to the Republic. Its southern and eastern borders were contiguous with territories belonging to the elector. In June 1672 Johan Maurits, the elector's stadholder in Cleves, was stationed in Muiden, where he was in command of the Republic's troops.

182 GAA, not. D. van der Groe, NA 4074, fol. 478, 21 June 1672. In this deed Fromantiou states that his notary had informed Uylenburgh the day before, which is to say 20 June, that he could collect the paintings.

183 GAA, not. D. van der Groe, NA 4074, fol. 466r-v, 20 June 1672.

184 GAA, not. D. van der Groe, NA 4074, fol. 478, 21 June 1672.

185 According to Houbraken, Luduwina received a dowry of 20,000 guilders. See Houbraken 1718-1721, vol. 2, p. 71.

186 GAA, not. A. Lock, NA 2240, pp. 71-72, 9 September 1672.

187 GAA, not. A. Lock, NA 2241a, pp. 11-14, 3 January 1673.

tion of character, but the case was suspended when it transpired that Fromantiou had left the country. Once again, Uylenburgh defended his honour, insisting that he had been upright in his dealings and could not be obliged to take the paintings back. Even more to the point, 'prices have plummeted, especially those of paintings and other rare objects, because of these worrying times and the wretched state of affairs in the country'. He nevertheless agreed to take the twelve paintings and place his trust in the elector's discretion to compensate him for any loss or damage. But he insisted on having the works within twenty-four hours, as he had an opportunity to sell them at a decent price 'under the present circumstances'. He concluded by saying that he had no intention of withdrawing his charges against Fromantiou but, on the contrary, would pursue the matter 'with the full force of the law'. Wils gave no response. Lock sent his clerks round to visit him on several occasions, but they were told that Wils was not home. On 7 January Lock himself called on Wils. Wils was not available, but his wife said that her husband would not deliver the paintings without permission from Fromantiou, to whom he had written for further instructions.[188] On 20 January Lock returned to Wils's home and again spoke to his wife. He informed her that Uylenburgh still wanted the twelve paintings back and produced Uylenburgh's guarantee in a court decision from the magistrates.[189] If Wils refused to return the paintings, he would petition the magistrates again. Wils's wife invited the notary to return at nine o'clock the following day, when her husband would be at home. Uylenburgh and the notary called at the appointed time on the following day. Wils informed them that he would first send an application to the magistrates to avoid any misunderstanding regarding the delivery of the paintings.

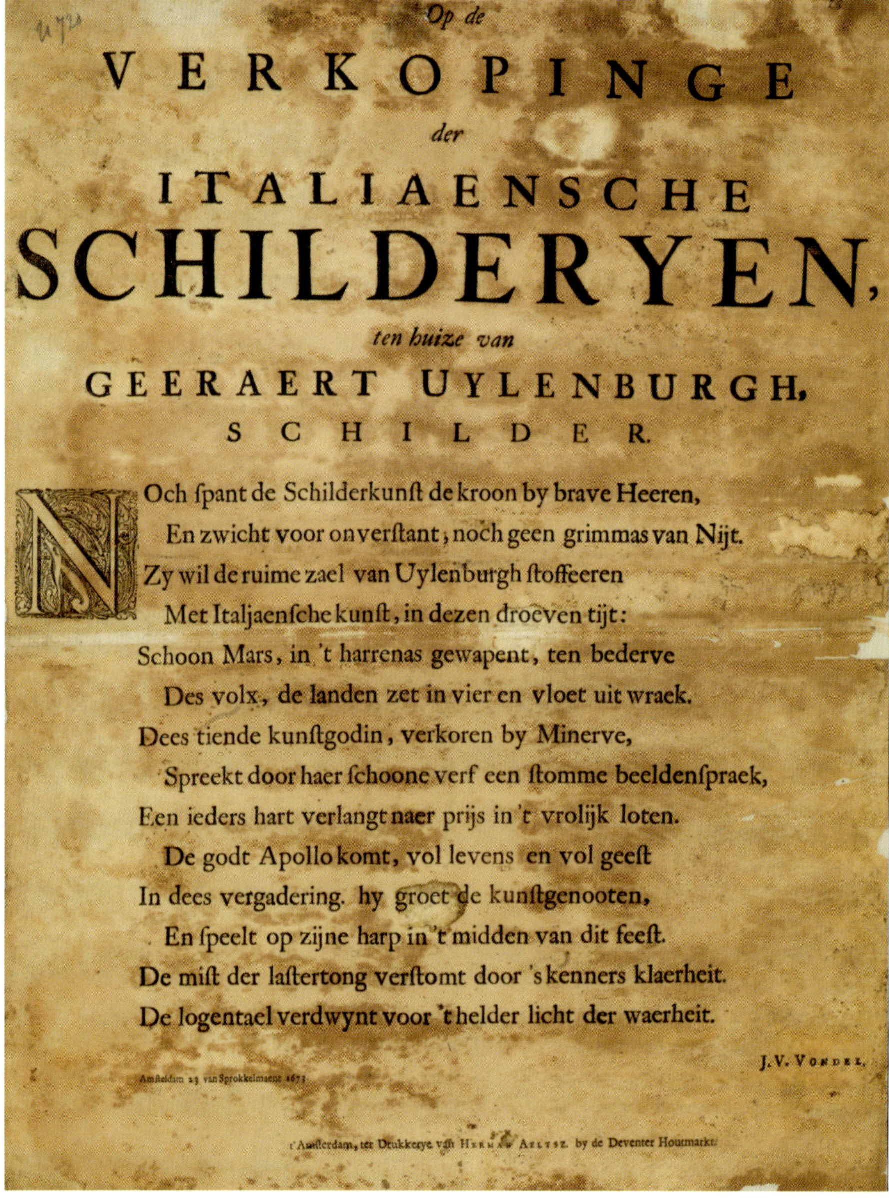

44 Joost van den Vondel, On the sale of the Italian paintings, at the house of Geeraert Uylenburgh, painter, dated 23 Sprokkelmaent (February) 1673, paper, 42.4 x 32.2 cm, Amsterdam, Universiteitsbibliotheek

On 8 February 1673, more than eighteen months after Von Spaen's visit to the shop, Uylenburgh confirmed receipt of the twelve paintings from Wils. The document meticulously records that the two largest works, the Michelangelo and the *Dancing children* by Palma Giovane, had been removed from their frames, and that the portrait by Holbein and Giorgione's *Ceres* had suffered more damage since the time they were shown at the Keijserskroon inn.[190]

From a poem by Vondel it would appear that Uylenburgh disposed of the paintings in a lottery held two weeks later, on 23 February (fig. 44).

188 See note 187.
189 GAA, not. A. Lock, NA 2241a, p. 145, 20 January 1673.
190 GAA, not. A. Lock, NA 2241a, p. 328, 8 February 1673.

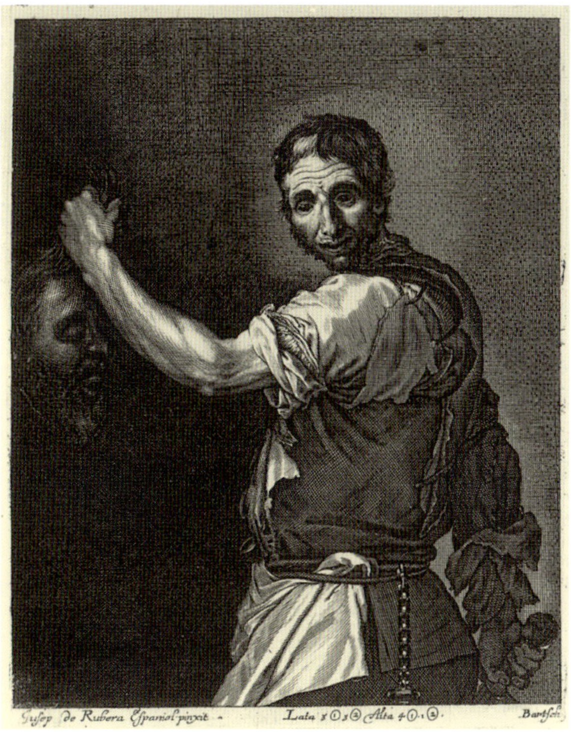

45 Johann Gottfriet Bartsch after Jusepe de Ribera, The executioner with the head of John the Baptist, signed 'Bartsch' with the inscription 'Jusep de Rubera Espaniol. pinxit', engraving, 21.8 x 16.6 cm, Berlin, Staatliche Museen zu Berlin, Kupferstichkabinett

This, Houbraken believed, was a direct result of the whole affair. The closing lines of Vondel's poem allude to Fromantiou's smear campaign. 'The fog of libel is dispelled by the clarity of cognoscenti/ Lies vanish before the searing light of truth'.[191] Antonides van der Goes also dedicated a poem to Uylenburgh, but said nothing about the transaction. Instead, he wrote about Art's victory in banishing the misery attending the war against France and other disasters of the year 1672.[192]

Uylenburgh obtained a permit to hold the lottery from the city authorities and it would be logical to assume that he did so some time earlier. In any event, this might explain his sudden haste to have the paintings returned. On 3 January 1673, when he mentioned the possibility of selling them at a reasonable price, he may have had a particular buyer in mind, but it is also possible that he was planning to hold the lottery. The more time he had to sell tickets, the more lucrative it would be. Had he waited until the paintings were returned, he would have had little more than a fortnight to make the necessary arrangements. Nothing is known about the outcome of the lottery other than that Uylenburgh was unable to sell all twelve of the paintings. As we shall see, some of them were still in his possession when he fell on hard times in 1675.[193]

In the meantime, the elector was still waiting for Uylenburgh to refund his deposit of 2,000 rijksdaalders. On 5 May 1674 he instructed his vice-chancellor in Cleves to enquire whether Uylenburgh was still intending to repay the money.[194] We learn from the letter that one of the paintings from the original transaction, an *Executioner with the head of Saint John the Baptist* by Jusepe de Ribera, had remained in Berlin and that the elector was willing to pay the 180 rijksdaalders he still owed for it. All told, the vice-chancellor was to secure a reimbursement of 1,820 rijksdaalders. It is uncertain whether or not

he succeeded. Uylenburgh may have kept the money. According to Houbraken, the elector lost his 4,000-guilder deposit.[195] Although the amount Houbraken cites is incorrect, there may nevertheless be some truth to his account.

The painting by Ribera has unfortunately been lost, but we know what it looked like from an engraving made by Gottfried Bartsch for a series of the best paintings in the elector's collection (fig. 45).

THE PAINTINGS AND CLASSICAL SCULPTURES

In his first letter to the elector, dated 12 August 1671, Von Spaen mentions that he had bought 'statues' as well as paintings. They arrived in Berlin in September, and on 21 September the elector approved a payment of 2,771 rijksdaalders for all the sculptures and paintings. There are no subsequent records of the sculptures. No information is available as to what they looked like, how many there were, or the price for which Uylenburgh sold them. If we tot up the prices for the

191 The poem was published in Houbraken 1718-1721, vol. 2, pp. 295-296. The date may have been that on which the poem was written rather than the date of the lottery. In that event, the lottery may have been held some time later in 1673.

192 Likewise published in Houbraken 1718-1721, vol. 2, pp. 296-297. See also Antonides van der Goes 1685, pp. 248-250.

193 The lottery may have been cancelled. In 1675 Jean Gericot demanded the return of two paintings he had given Uylenburgh for a lottery which was ultimately called off because too few tickets had been sold. Gericot referred to a lottery held a year earlier, in 1674, but it is plausible that he was mistaken and meant 1673. See note 260, p. 108.

194 Berlin, Geheimes Staatsarchiv, I HA Rep. 76, Alt III, no. 167.

195 Houbraken 1718-1721, vol. 2, p. 295. The incumbent vice-chancellor in Cleves was Von Rombswinkel.

paintings in the second column of Fromantiou's list, we arrive at a total of 2,055 rijksdaalders. Add to that the 180 rijksdaalders for the Ribera which remained in Berlin, and we can conclude that the paintings fetched a total of 2,235 rijksdaalders. That being the case, the sculptures would have cost 536 rijksdaalders. The puzzling thing is that, after returning the paintings, the elector demanded a refund of the total amount he had remitted. As there is nothing to suggest that the sculptures were also sent back, one would expect the price he paid for them to have been deducted from the total. Was he so angry that it slipped his mind? Or were the sculptures paid for separately? The latter seems more likely, since Uylenburgh never raised the subject of payment for the sculptures and he would certainly have complained had there been reason for doing so.

Despite the scarcity of information about these works, we nevertheless have a few leads to go on. Like the paintings, the majority of the sculptures Uylenburgh sold must have come from the Reynst Collection. Gerard Reynst possessed a large collection of classical sculptures – probably around 300 or more – most of which he had acquired, along with the paintings, from the Venetian collector Vendramin.[196] He commissioned prints of 110 of his best sculptures, which he published under the title *Signorum veterum icones*. In the light of our understanding of classical sculpture today, the collection was mediocre and much of it had been restored, but in the seventeenth century it was in any event the largest of its kind in Holland.

Ten of the elector's sculptures which are known to have come from the Reynst/Vendramin collection are in museums in Berlin and Dresden. We can reasonably assume that these were the works that Uylenburgh sold to the elector. They comprised a sculpture of Trajan (catalogued as 'The Gladiator' in the Reynst and Vendramin collections, fig. 46), a bust of an elderly woman ('Agrippina Major' in the Reynst Collection), a bust of a young woman ('Calphurnia' in the Reynst Collection), a head of a youth ('Aristea' in the Reynst Collection, fig. 47), a bust of a young woman ('Flavia' in the Reynst Collection, fig. 48), a small figure of a youth ('Bacchus' in the Vendramin Collection, fig. 49), a bust of Gordian III (ditto in the Reynst Collection), a herm of Priapus (ditto in the Reynst Collection), a bust of a man wearing a priest's crown, and a herm of a bearded god.[197] This is not to say that these were all the sculptures Uylenburgh sold. The first inventory of the elector's holdings of classical sculptures, which was made in 1672, lists twenty-two pieces. It is quite feasible that they originated from the Reynst Collection and were bought and sold by Uylenburgh.[198] He may have sold them in batches on different occasions, and not all at

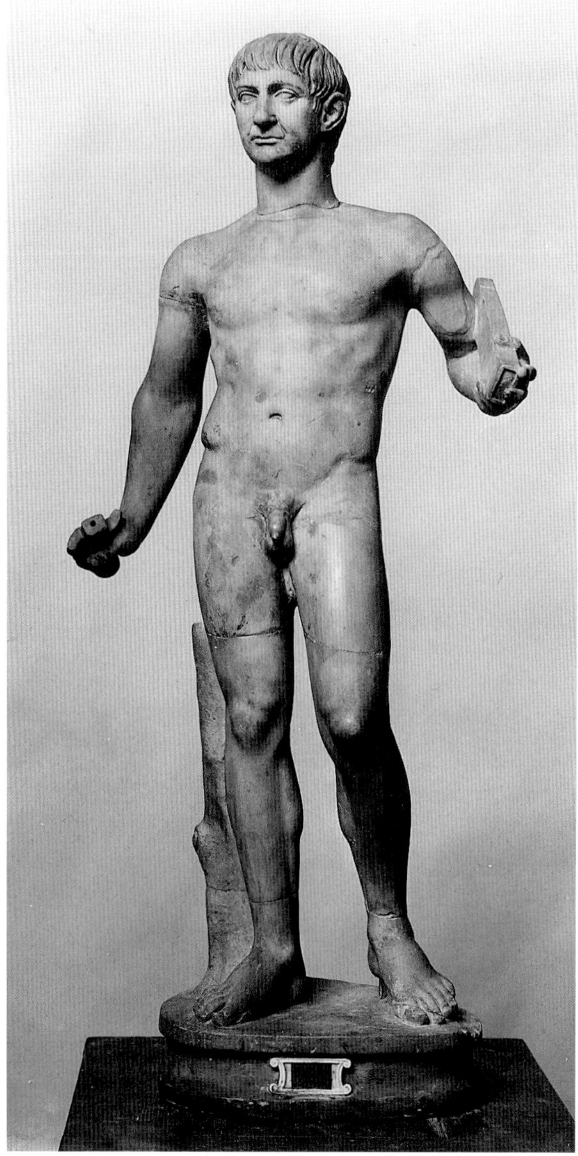

46 Roman, Trajan period (AD 98-117) Emperor Trajan, white marble, height 81.5 cm, Berlin, Staatliche Museen zu Berlin, Antikensammlung
The head and the body did not originally belong together; they were joined at some time unknown. The head is a portrait of the emperor Trajan

196 See Logan 1979 and Jacobs 1925.
197 The last four sculptures are in Dresden, Staatliche Museen, Skulpturensammlung, inv. nos. Hermann 409, 1810, no. 439, Hermann 411, Hermann, no. 69 respectively. The others are all in the Antikensammlung in Berlin.
198 On the Reynst Collection and the sculptures, see in particular Logan 1979. For the list of 1672, p. 49, note 28. See also Heres 1977.

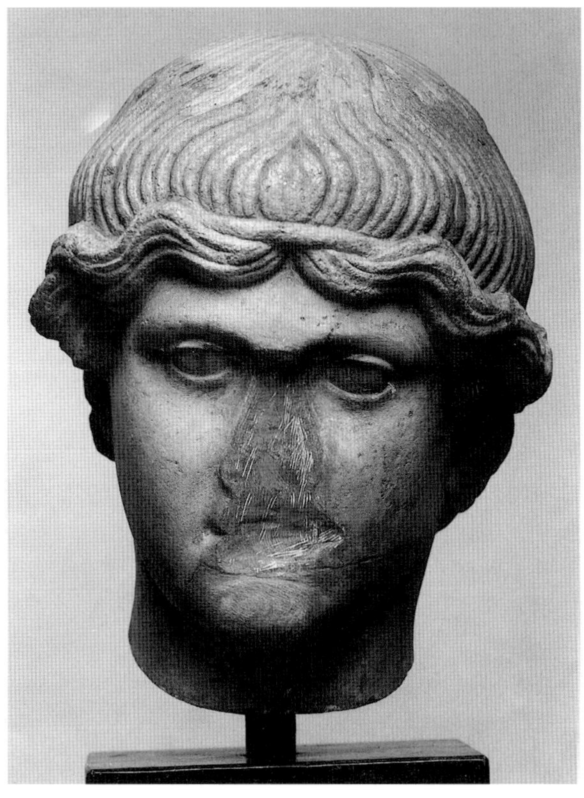

47 Roman, copy after a
Greek original of *c.* 460 BC,
Head of a youth, white marble,
height 23.5 cm, Berlin,
Staatliche Museen zu Berlin,
Antikensammlung

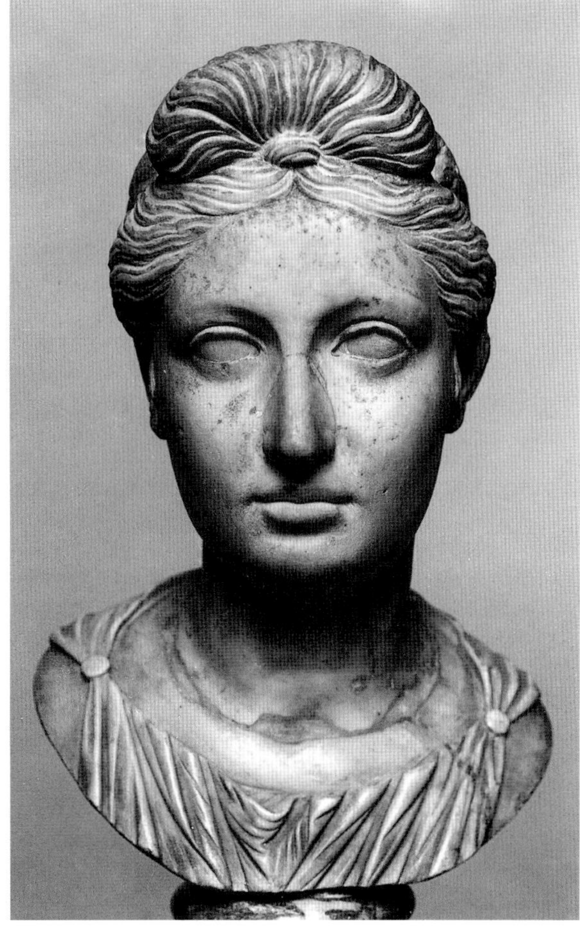

48 Roman, period of Hadrian
(117-138 A.D.), Bust of a
young woman, white marble,
height 37 cm, Berlin,
Staatliche Museen zu Berlin,
Antikensammlung

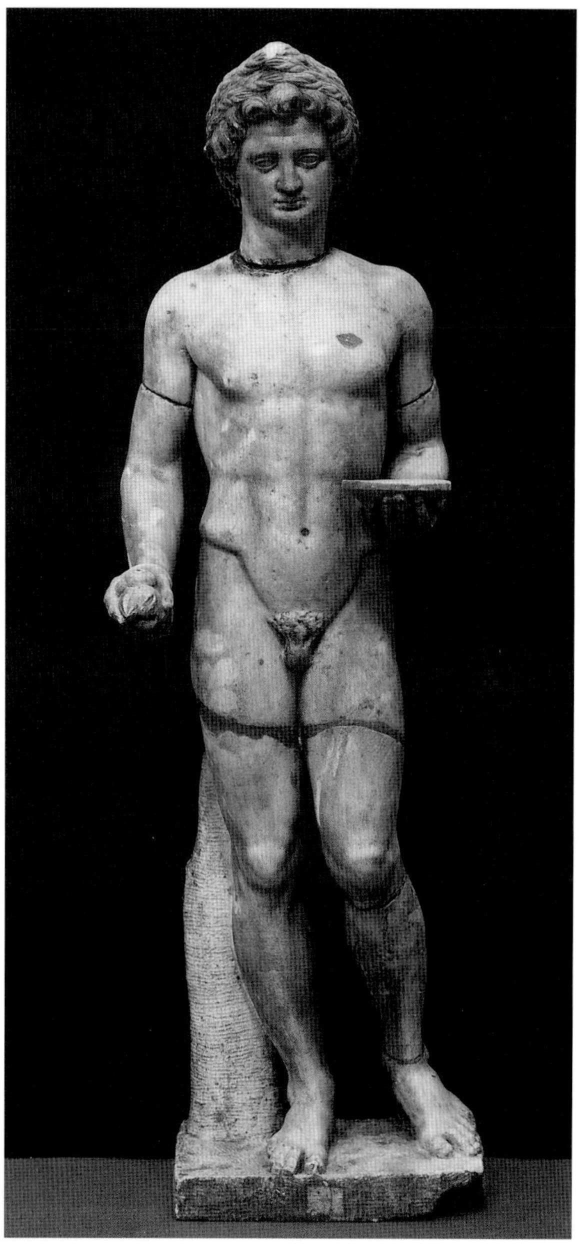

49 Roman with sixteenth-century additions, Statue of a youth,
white marble, height 91 cm, Berlin, Staatliche Museen zu Berlin,
Antikensammlung
The torso is antique. The head, arms, hands and attributes are
later additions, probably for the most part from the sixteenth
century

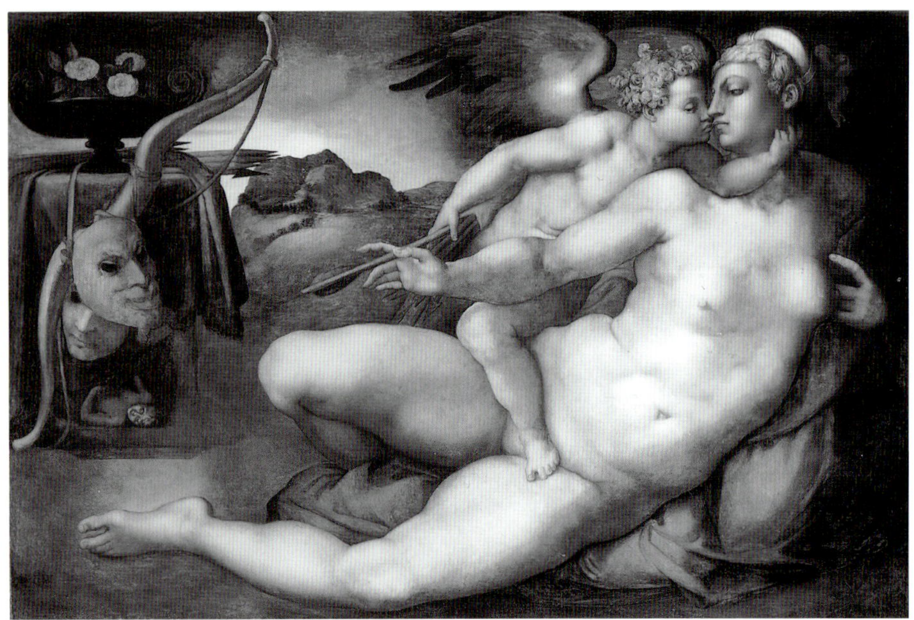

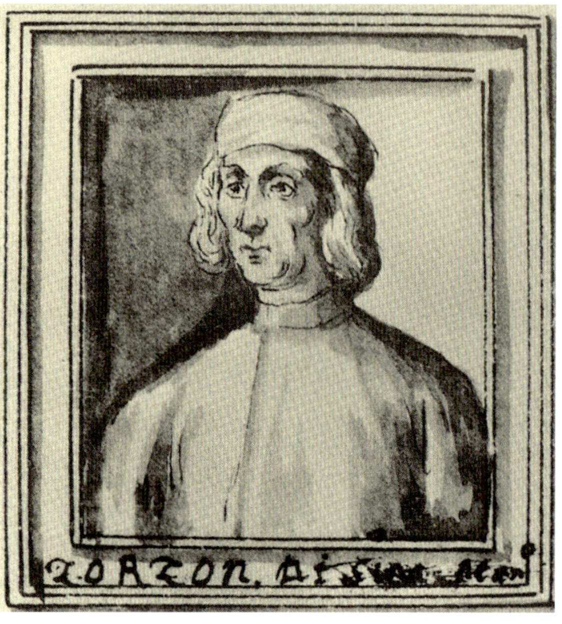

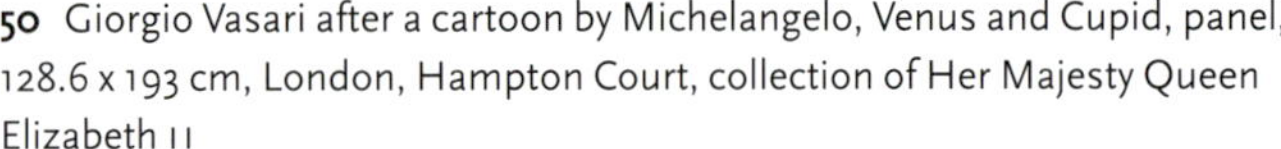

50 Giorgio Vasari after a cartoon by Michelangelo, Venus and Cupid, panel, 128.6 x 193 cm, London, Hampton Court, collection of Her Majesty Queen Elizabeth II

51 Anonymous, after Giorgione or Titian, Portrait of Giorgione, pen and brush, in: the *De Picturis* manuscript catalogue of the collection of Andrea Vendramin, Sloane 4004, fol. 52, London, British Library

once. This would imply that he had dealt with the elector before the transaction of 1671, but there is no evidence to confirm this.

By Huygens's account, the twelve paintings originated from the Reynst Collection. The most important paintings and sculptures in the collection are known from two series of prints, but without an inventory it is impossible to establish precisely what the collection comprised. After the death of the Venetian Andrea Vendramin the Reynst brothers acquired most, if not all of his collection.[199] Catalogues still exist which contain drawings of Vendramin's paintings, sculptures and other holdings.[200] The collection included about 300 paintings, mainly by Venetian artists, such as Giorgione (13 pieces), Giovanni Bellini (11), Titian (5), Palma Vecchio (7) and Andrea Schiavone (8). Some of the catalogue drawings clearly correspond to the descriptions of the paintings that Uylenburgh was hoping to sell to the elector. It is therefore tempting to assume that Uylenburgh acquired them from the Vendramin,

subsequently Reynst, collection. Regrettably, not a single one of those paintings can be traced. Only one of the twelve can be identified as an extant work. The painting Fromantiou described as 'Naked children dancing, lifesize, by Jacomo Palma' is now in the Six Collection in Amsterdam (see below). The painting does not appear in the Vendramin catalogues, nor was a print made for Reynst.

The following paragraphs examine the twelve paintings one by one, on the basis of Fromantiou's list and Dujardin and Dodijns's comments.[201]

1. 'A Venus and Cupid, figures larger than life by Michelangelo Buonarroti'
Willem Dodijns and Carel Dujardin felt that 'in terms of draughtsmanship and elegance' the painting did 'not stand up to comparison with even the weakest Michelangelo' and concluded that it was 'not by, but after Michelangelo'. It was probably one of the many versions made after a cartoon by Michelangelo, which the artist himself never worked up into a painting. However, count-

199 See Logan 1979 and Jacobs 1925.

200 The manuscript catalogue of the paintings is in the British Library, *De Picturis*, Ms Sloane 4004. The two-volume catalogue of the sculptures was formerly in the library of the Staatliche Museen Berlin, but has been missing since the Second World War. The most detailed description can be found in Jacobs 1925, p. 21, note 3.

201 This section is based largely on Meijer 1999. The document drawn up by Dodijns and Dujardin (see note 162) has been badly damaged by fire. From Bredius's transcription of 1886 it appears that the document was reasonably legible in his day.

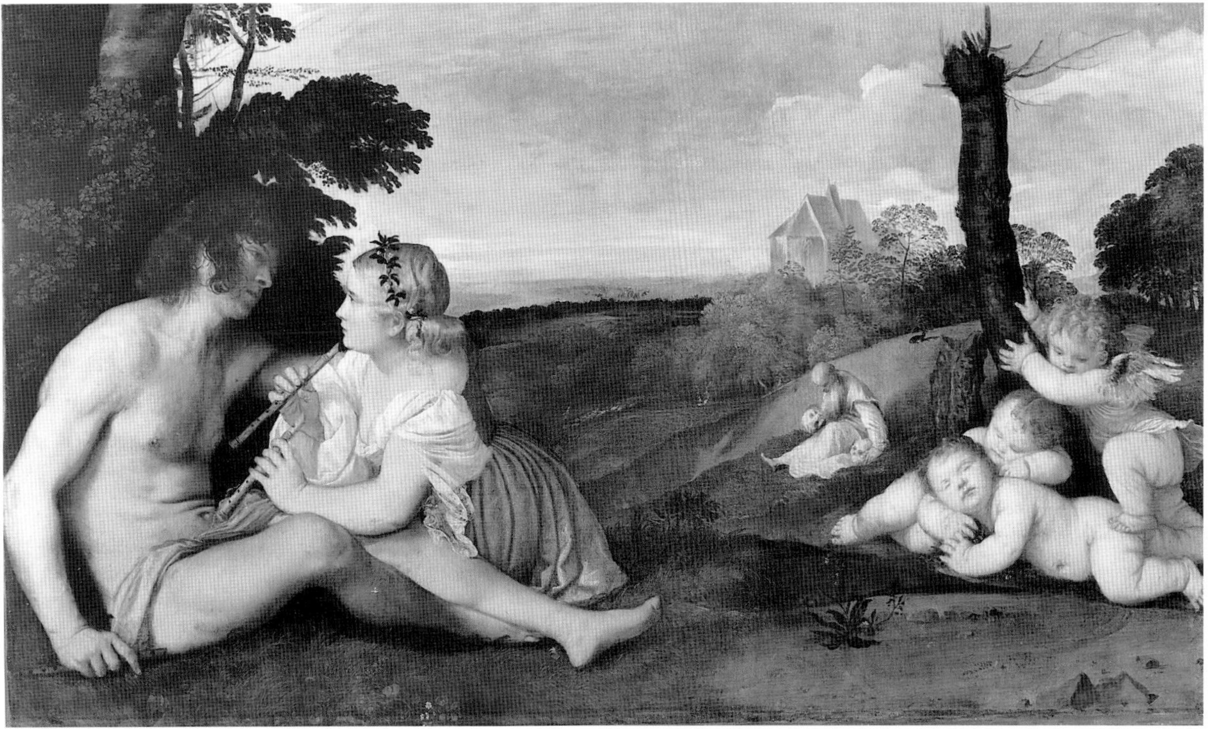

less other painters used the cartoon as a model for their paintings. A good example is the panel by Vasari at Hampton Court (fig. 50).[202]

2. 'A portrait of Giorgione del Castelfranco by Titian, painted from life'
After some deliberation, Dodijns and Dujardin agreed that the 'palette and brushwork [were] consistent with Titian's finest', but felt that 'the draughtsmanship fell short'. The painting in question may have been the one listed in the Vendramin Collection as a self-portrait by Giorgione (fig. 51).[203]

3. 'A shepherd and shepherdess by Titian'

4. 'A counterpart of the same size by Titian'
Dodijns and Dujardin took a fairly favourable view of the 'shepherd and shepherdess'. They detected 'some of Titian's quality [...] for instance in the harmonious light and colours', but it was not 'as exceptional as one is led to believe'. They were less impressed by the pendant of' 'children with a hermit in the background', which was of

an entirely different calibre and 'neither strong nor colourful'. The two paintings must have been inspired by Titian's famous canvas of the Three Ages of Man (fig. 52), with the left half serving as a model for the 'shepherd and shepherdess' and the right half for its counterpart. Considering Dodijns and Dujardin's good opinion of the first work, the two pieces were presumably executed in the sixteenth century, possibly in Titian's workshop. Jan de Bisschop's drawing of 1667 after the 'shepherd and shepherdess' and Wallerant Vaillant's subsequent mezzotint of the picture give an impression of what the original must have looked like (figs. 53 and 54). De Bisschop produced a number of drawings after work in Uylenburgh's possession; he also attended the Reynst sale in 1670. Vaillant was one of the artists who supported Uylenburgh in the dispute, and Uylenburgh had several of his paintings for sale.[204]

5. 'Naked children dancing, lifesize, by Jacomo Palma'
Dujardin and Dodijns's comments are scathing. The painting 'left much to be desired' and

202 Shearman 1983, pp. 277-278. The Countess of Arundel, who died in 1655, also possessed a version of this painting, hers being attributed to Sebastiano del Piombo ('Una Venere con cupido piu grande dal naturale di man de Fra: Sebastiano. Inventione di Michelangelo'). See Cox 1911, p. 282.
203 Suggested by Meijer 1999. It is fol. 52 in the Vendramin manuscript catalogue (Borenius 1923, pl. 40).
204 See p. 108. From the date 1667 on the drawing we might deduce that De Bisschop copied the painting when it was still in the possession of the Reynst family, i.e. before it went to Uylenburgh.

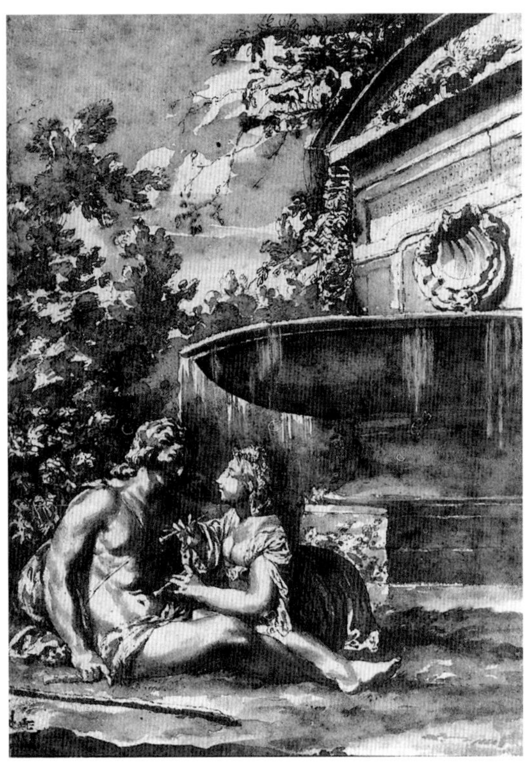

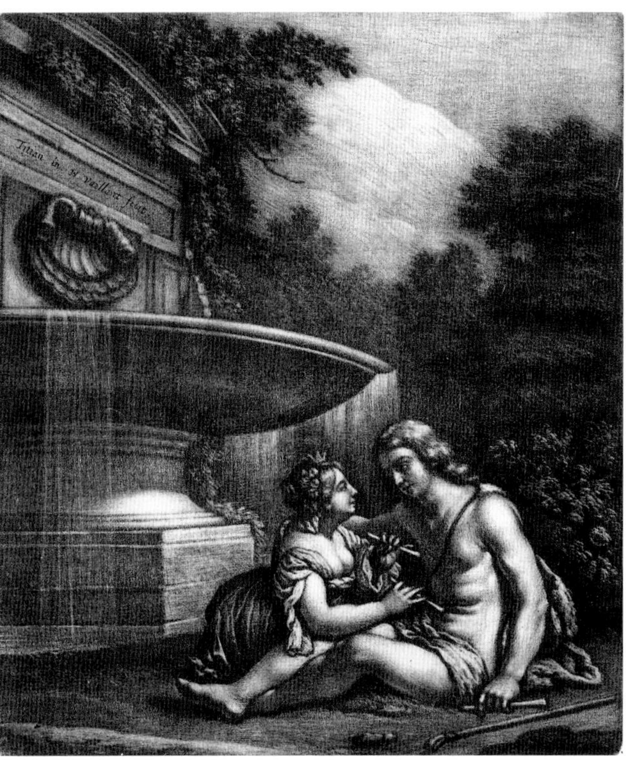

53 Jan de Bisschop (after Titian?), Shepherd and shepherdess, dated on the back '19. marti 1667', pen, brush, brown wash, 18.3 x 13 cm, Amsterdam, Rijksprentenkabinet

54 Wallerant Vaillant (after Titian?), Shepherd and shepherdess, with the inscription 'Titian in W. Vaillant fecit', mezzotint, 16.3 x 14 cm. Braunschweig, Herzog Anton-Ulrich Museum

revealed 'no trace of the qualities possessed by the artist to whom it is attributed, in terms of colour, draughtsmanship, vitality, composition and light'. It was entirely 'unworthy of attribution to that excellent master'. This is the only one of the twelve paintings that can be firmly identified. It may originally have been in the Reynst Collection and must have been in the Netherlands even earlier, but it did not come from the Vendramin Collection (fig. 55).[205] Uylenburgh's close acquaintance Jan Six presumably acquired it after the abortive transaction, possibly in the lottery of 1673. It was one of the two largest paintings that Uylenburgh offered the elector. Dodijns and Dujardin may have been under the misapprehension that it was attributed to Palma Vecchio and were perhaps more critical in their judgment as a result.[206] Fromantiou, however, knew that it was by Palma Giovane, as it is attributed to him in the Rotterdam statement of 16 June.[207]

6. 'A Venetian lady by Paris Pordinon'
Dodijns and Dujardin felt that the work 'pos-sessed a certain elegance, but [was] not outstand-ing and not worth the price'. It may have been Paris Bordone's painting of a woman nude to the waist from the Vendramin Collection, but this assumption is purely speculative (fig. 56).[208]

7. 'A portrait of a prelate by Hans Holbein'
Dodijns and Dujardin considered the work 'inconsistent with Holbein's brush in every respect' and 'vastly inferior to an original by Holbein'. Lois and Verschuer dismissed it as a 'fat red face attributed to Holbein'. The panel has not been identified. It was still in Uylenburgh's possession in 1675, at which time he valued it at no more than 100 guilders.

8. 'A Ceres with cornucopia and a throng of naked children by Giorgione del Castelfranco'
In the words of Dodijns and Dujardin, this small painting was 'too flat and [...] pasted onto a black background', whereas 'the master's colours were outstanding'. On those grounds they considered it 'entirely unlike a true original by Giorgione'. It must have been a work that was in the Vendramin

205 The possessions left by Samuel Godin, who died in 1633, included, in the main hall, a 'Judgment of Midas by mr. Palma' and a 'Children's dance, idem', valued by the painters Lucas Luce and David Colijn(s) at 150 and 180 guilders respec-tively. G A A, not. J. Warnaertz, N A 694(B), 29 November 1633.
206 Meijer 1999. The canvas is generally accepted today as an original work by Palma Gio-vane; only Weber 2003, p. 131, expresses reservations.
207 Rotterdam Municipal Archives, not. J. Verschueren, N A 1076, pp 162-163, '[...] a life-size children's dance by Palma Giovane'.
208 Fol. 60 in Vendramin's manuscript catalogue (Bore-nius 1923, pl. 48).

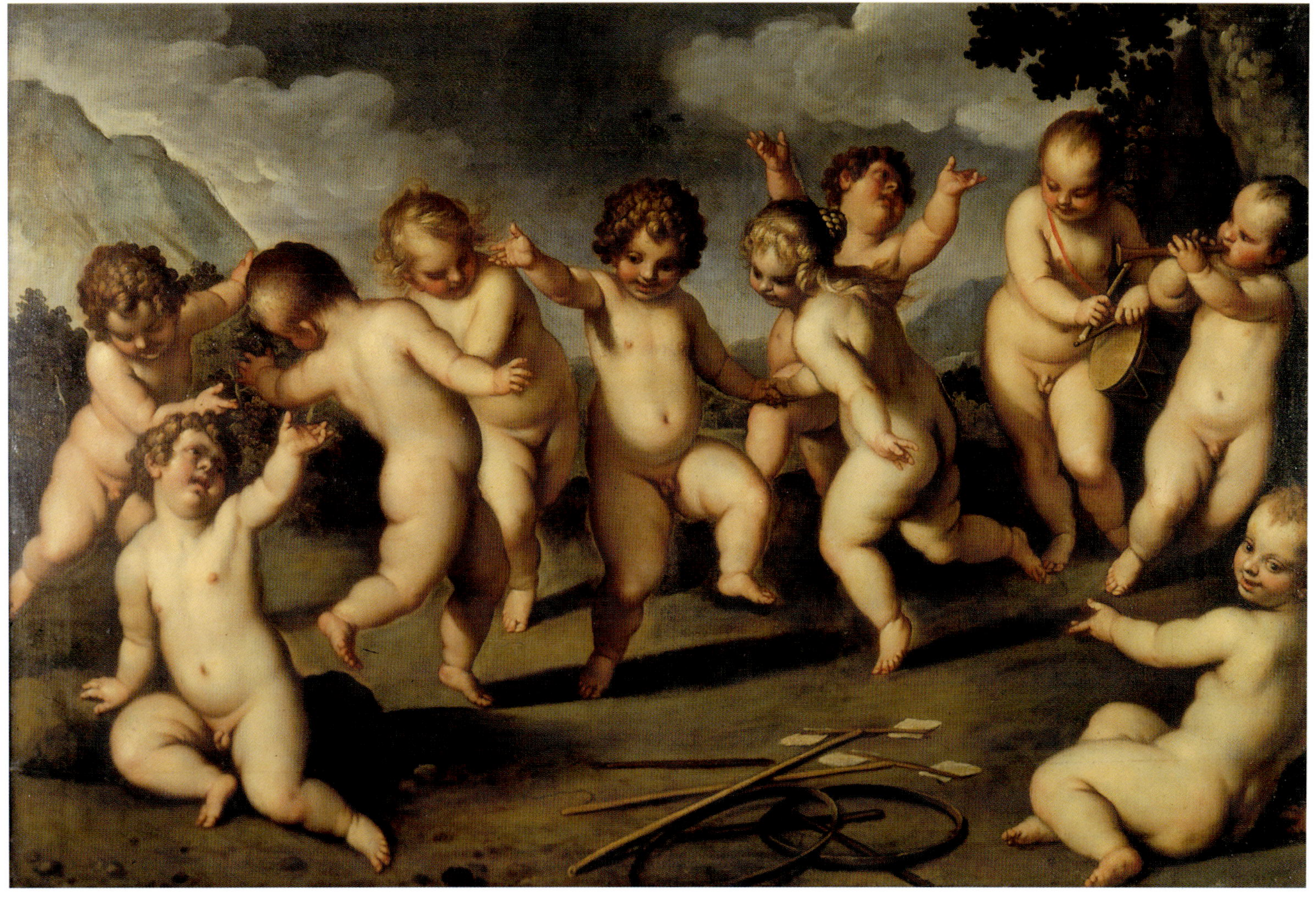

55 Jacopo Negretti, called Palma Giovane, Naked children dancing, signed 'Jacobus Palma', canvas, 133 x 200 cm, Amsterdam, Six Collection

Collection (fig. 58).[209] The painting was still in Uylenburgh's possession in 1675 and, by his estimate, worth 160 guilders.

9. 'A portrait of an old man by Raphael Urbin' Dodijns and Dujardin felt that one could not 'jeopardise the reputation of such a fine master by encumbering him with this inferior painting'. The descriptions of the work are too vague for it to be identified with an extant painting.

10. 'A Saint Paul, half figure, lifesize, by Jacomo Palma the Elder'
'Poorly drawn, especially the hand, which would be unable to clasp the sword, nor is the rest any

better'. Dodijns and Dujardin were unimpressed. This is most probably the Saint Paul from the Vendramin Collection (fig. 57).[210]

11. 'A beautiful Venetian woman by Titian' Dodijns and Dujardin described this painting as 'a beautiful Venetian lady with her hand in her hair, one of the best in this collection [...] but not one of Titian's great masterpieces'. A mezzotint was made after the work, probably by Wallerant Vaillant (fig. 59). A similar painting was in the possession of Archduke Leopold Wilhelm; an engraving of it was made for a series of prints of work from his collection.[211]

209 Fol. 23 in Vendramin's manuscript catalogue (Borenius 1923, p. 11).
210 See Rylands 1988, p. 305. It is the only *Saint Paul* by Palma Vecchio of which an illustration exists. Fol. 45 in Vendramin's manuscript catalogue (Borenius 1923, pl. 33).
211 See Meijer 1999.

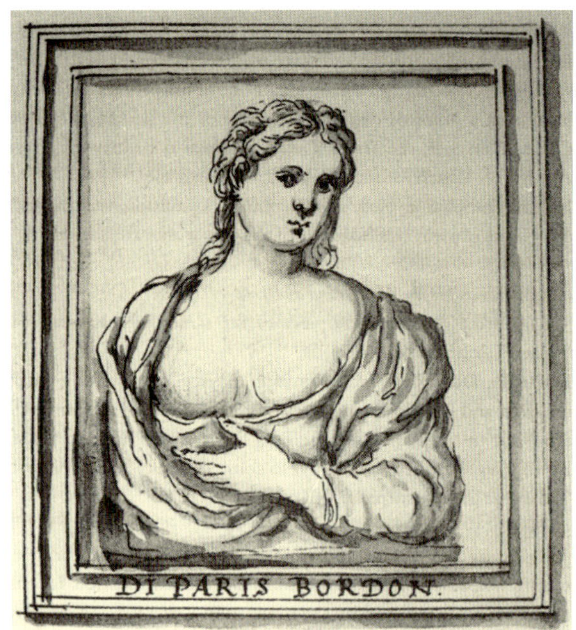

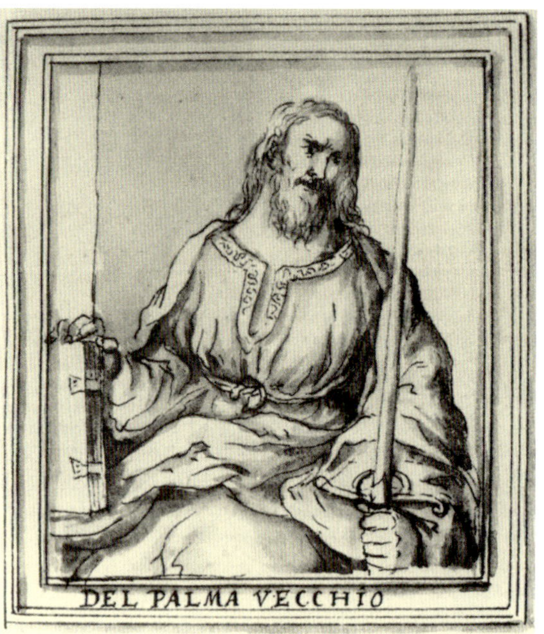

56 Anonymous, after Paris Bordone, Woman stripped to the waist, pen and brush, in: the *De Picturis* manuscript catalogue of the collection of Andrea Vendramin, Sloane 4004, fol. 60, London, British Library

57 Anonymous, after Palma Vecchio, St Paul, pen and brush, in: the *De Picturis* manuscript catalogue of the collection of Andrea Vendramin, Sloane 4004, fol. 45, London, British Library

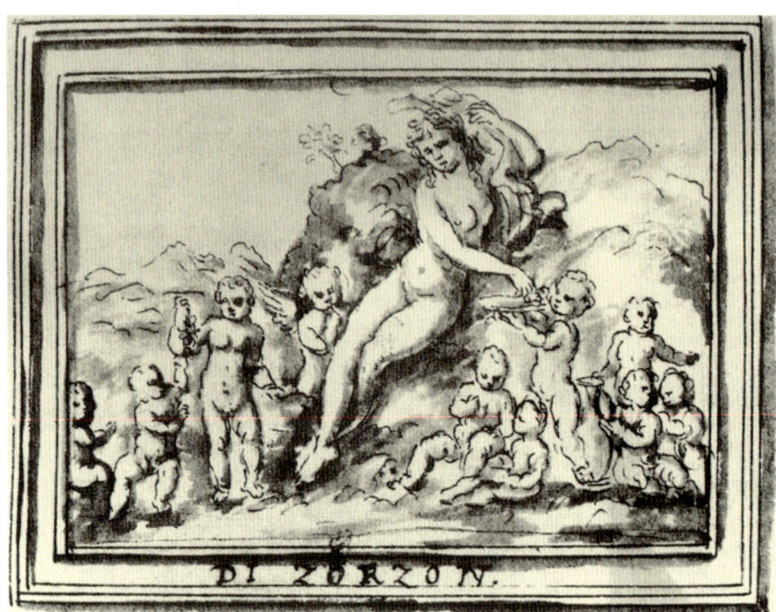

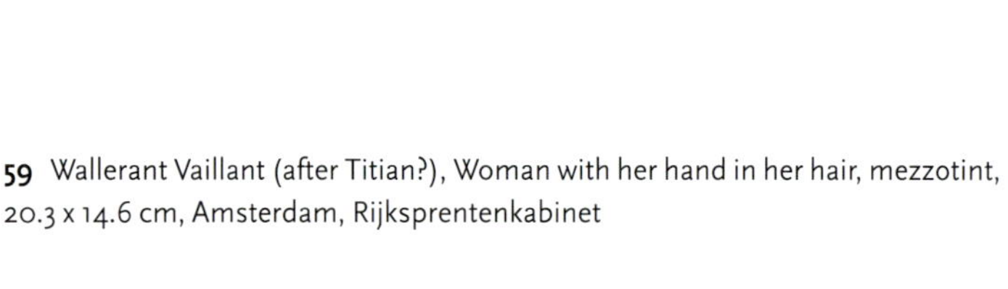

58 Anonymous, after Giorgone, Ceres with children, pen and brush, in: the *De Picturis* manuscript catalogue of the collection of Andrea Vendramin, Sloane 4004, fol. 23, London, British Library

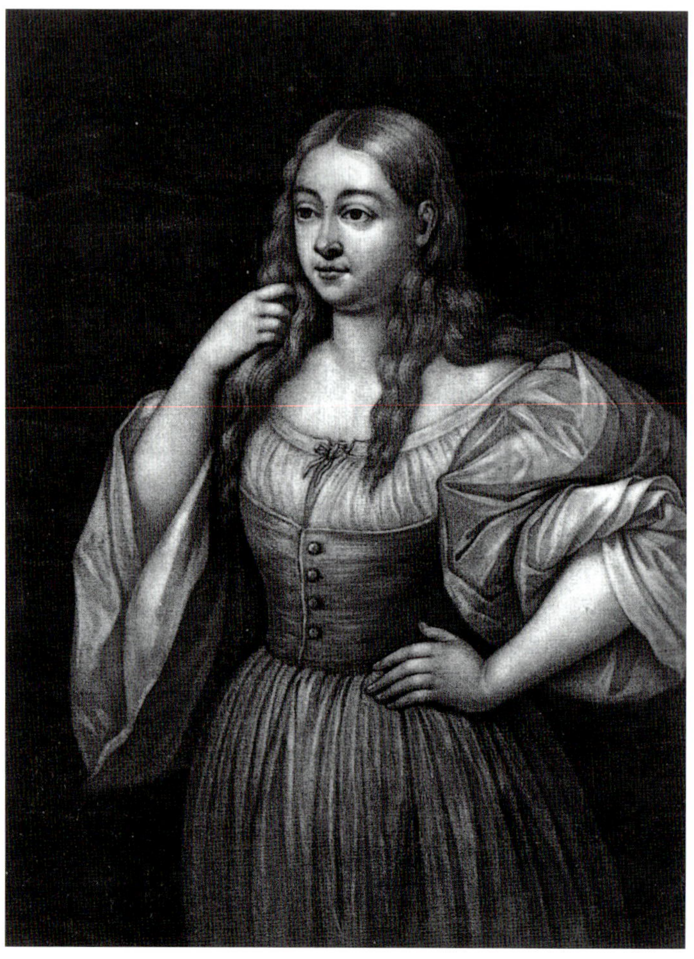

59 Wallerant Vaillant (after Titian?), Woman with her hand in her hair, mezzotint, 20.3 x 14.6 cm, Amsterdam, Rijksprentenkabinet

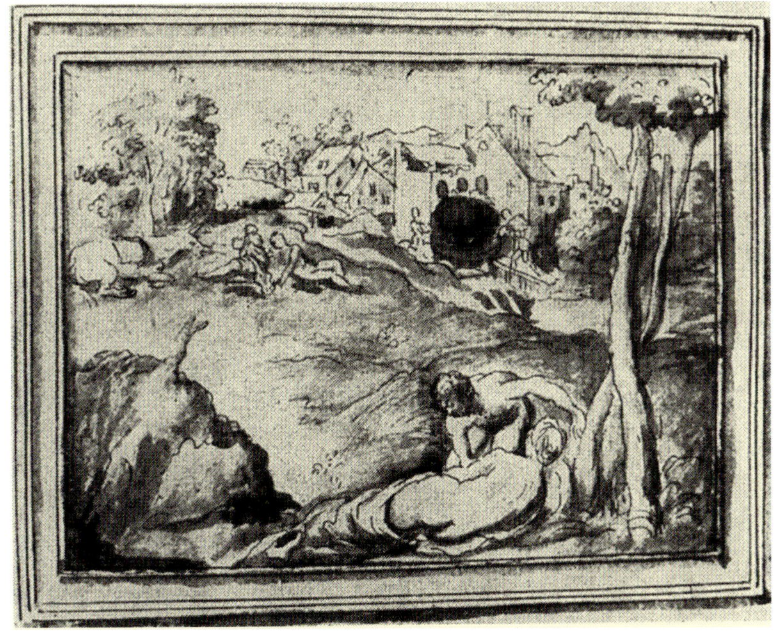

60 Anonymous, after a sixteenth-century Venetian master, Nymph and satyr in a landscape, pen and brush, in: the *De Picturis* manuscript catalogue of the collection of Andrea Vendramin, Sloane 4004, fol. 41, London, British Library

12. 'A landscape by Titian with a satyr caressing the nymph'
To Dodijns and Dujardin the work 'recalled Andreas Schiavoni rather than Titian, but time and circumstance had taken their toll, and over-painting in several places had obscured its merits'. It may have been one of the paintings in Vendramin's collection (fig. 60).[212]

More than six of the paintings are believed to have come from the Vendramin Collection in Venice and must have found their way to Uylenburgh through the collection belonging to the Reynst brothers. There is no doubt that those paintings are sixteenth-century works, but the attributions cannot be verified. Two of the works that cannot be traced back to Vendramin – the *Shepherd and shepherdess* and the *Venetian lady arranging her hair* – were well thought of even by Fromantiou's specialists, Dodijns and Dujardin, who left the attribution to Titian open. In other words, most of the paintings were probably sixteenth-century works. However,

to judge by the views expressed by many of the artists, they were evidently not masterpieces and at least some of the attributions were incorrect. In any event, Reynst's best works had been sold for the Dutch Gift in 1660.[213] The paintings acquired for the elector must have been of a far lower standard.

ORIGINALS, COPIES OR OLD ANTIQUE WORKS

No less interesting than the question of how we would regard the twelve paintings today, is what the two adversaries really thought of them at the time. To find the answer we need to examine their accusations against one another. One of the key issues was the elector's instructions to Fromantiou of 12 January – which Uylenburgh knew about and alluded to on several occasions. Fromantiou had been sent to Amsterdam to establish in the presence of accomplished masters that the paintings sold by Uylenburgh were 'not authentic originals, but merely later copies'.[214]

Shortly after Fromantiou's arrival in Amsterdam on 7 May, Uylenburgh invited him through the notary Lock to submit a joint petition requesting the magistrates to appoint a group of 'impartial' connoisseurs. The notarial deed explains that their assignment would be to judge whether the paintings were 'originals or predominantly copies painted later, and not old antique works'. However, the word 'originals' was subsequently struck through. Further on, a few more words were amended in the sentence requesting the magistrates to nominate experts to 'examine the paintings in question and judge whether they [were] predominantly later copies or old antique works'. The word 'predominantly' was clearly added later and here, too, the word 'originals' was deleted and replaced by 'old antique works'.[215] These changes must have been introduced at Uylenburgh's instigation. The fact that he deleted the word 'original' – which is normally used to designate a fully autograph work – may be taken to mean that he himself had misgivings about the authenticity of some of the paintings, while his insertion of the word 'predominantly' suggests

212 Fol. 41 in Vendramin's manuscript catalogue (the group of figures is repeated in fol. 70) (Borenius 1923, pl. 29; the repetition, pl. 58). The painter is not named in the manuscript catalogue.
213 A letter from the States of Holland and West-Friesland notes that they had selected the cream of the collection. See p. 67.
214 See note 148.
215 See note 154.

that he in fact suspected that a couple of them might be copies.

According to the eighteenth-century biographer Houbraken, after denouncing the paintings as copies, Fromantiou assured the elector 'that he could find and acquire the real ones in Holland and other parts of the world'.[216] Houbraken's biography of Uylenburgh tends to embroider on the facts, and one wonders whether Fromantiou actually made such a statement. In any event, the surviving documents contain nothing to that effect. A 'copy' can be understood to mean either a work produced during the master's lifetime or one made later after the example of an existing painting. Houbraken's words seem to imply the latter. But we can infer from a remark that Uylenburgh made in response to Fromantiou's outburst that the paintings were 'not originals but later copies and rubbish painted by youngsters and pupils for their masters' that Fromantiou likewise took them to be old paintings from the studios of the artists to whom they were ascribed.[217]

Interestingly enough, none of the painters that Fromantiou called on actually used the word 'copy', although some of them did say that they were not 'originals'. Dodijns and Dujardin even went a step further, suggesting that the painting attributed to Michelangelo was more likely to have been made after an example by the master. Fromantiou's appraisers focused mainly on the quality of the paintings or, more accurately, their lack of quality. In their view, the paintings were 'bad' and 'rubbish', and some of them challenged the attributions. The Antwerp contingent stated categorically that they were not up to the standard of the masters to whom they were attributed.[218]

The artists on Uylenburgh's side described the works as 'commendable', 'painted by respectable masters' and 'on the whole, good and competent Italian paintings'. Philips Koninck was the only one to discuss attributions and he agreed with Uylenburgh. In The Hague, some of the connoisseurs called by Uylenburgh qualified the works as 'good unknown Italian paintings'.[219]

The artists in both camps were either complimentary or disparaging about the quality of the paintings, and a number of them, from both sides,

remarked on their poor condition. However, Uylenburgh's allies Theodoor van der Schuer and Jacques Vaillant added that in good condition they would have been worth thousands of guilders instead of hundreds. Fromantiou's cohorts, on the other hand, considered Uylenburgh's valuation excessive.

Both Fromantiou and Uylenburgh tried to steer the course of events to suit their own ends. The amendments that Uylenburgh instructed his notary to make expose his own misgivings about the merits of some of the paintings. The fact that almost no one on his side raised the question of attribution suggests that Uylenburgh and his connoisseurs knew that they were not all Titians, Giorgiones or Raphaels. The most likely scenario is that Uylenburgh simply maintained the old attributions from the Reynst/Vendramin collection. His position was weak, however, because they were just too good to be true and some of the paintings were in poor condition. He must have been convinced that Fromantiou would never be able to find painters who could prove that the works were copies in the sense of works painted by a later hand. That was the essence of Fromantiou's allegation and what the elector had expressly instructed him to do, which is why Uylenburgh held him to the literal terms of his mandate.

But Fromantiou played his hand well, in the first place by rejecting Uylenburgh's proposal to put the case before the magistrates. He was probably concerned that the magistrates would be prejudiced in Uylenburgh's favour, for it was no secret that they were well disposed towards him. Above all, it would appear that Fromantiou was unwilling to carry out his instructions to the letter and prove that the works were copies. Were this not the case, it would be difficult to explain why he was so secretive about his mandate and why it was only under pressure that he divulged its precise nature. In fact, the elector had never mentioned the magistrates. In the directive of 31 January 1671, when he dispatched Fromantiou to Amsterdam as quickly as possible to gather evidence, he scored out the words 'before the committee of art connoisseurs', which had originally appeared in the sentence instructing Fromantiou

216 Houbraken 1718-1721, vol. 2, p. 295.
217 See note 187.
218 See p. 88.
219 See p. 87.

to have the paintings appraised by third parties.[220] The word 'committee' seems to imply an official body. The elector apparently did not require this and left Fromantiou at liberty to select his own appraisers.

Secondly, Fromantiou made certain that the painters he consulted did not pronounce on whether or not the pictures were copies. He simply wanted them to be derogatory. Even though Fromantiou failed to furnish the evidence that the elector had insisted upon, the documents he sent him made it perfectly clear that the paintings were not top of the range and, needless to say, the discredited works no longer seemed quite so desirable.

Uylenburgh accused Fromantiou of calling as appraisers not impartial connoisseurs, but cronies who were envious of Uylenburgh's success.[221] Fromantiou must surely have thought the same of Uylenburgh. Too little is known about Fromantiou's circle of acquaintances to ascertain whether there was any truth to Uylenburgh's allegations. Some of the experts Uylenburgh summoned are known from various sources to have been people he knew and had worked with. Theodoor Ferreris, for instance, must have been a very close friend; others, like Johannes Lingelbach and Anthonie de Grebber, must have worked for the firm, while Adriaen Backer, Caspar Netscher, Wallerant and Jacques Vaillant were artists whose paintings he sold. Still, there were others, like Gerard de Lairesse, who had worked for Uylenburgh yet took Fromantiou's side.

The big question is why Fromantiou conducted such a virulent campaign against his former art dealer. It is almost impossible not to suspect that there was something more at play than Fromantiou's desire to shield his principal from inferior paintings. Huygens wrote that Fromantiou had once been an old and trusted friend of Uylenburgh's, while Uylenburgh insinuated that Fromantiou was bent on tarnishing his reputation and even destroying his business.[222] Huygens, too, believed that Fromantiou was intent on discrediting Uylenburgh. Houbraken suspends judgment on Fromantiou's motives: 'I set aside the question of whether *Fromentjou's* criticism of the works was justified, or whether he begrudged Uilenburg his advantage or harboured some grievance against him'.[223]

The court painter from Berlin evidently had a propensity for causing offence. Later, in May 1680, he fell out with his brother-in-law, Pieter Wouwerman, over a painting the elector had commissioned in 1677. Wouwerman complained because Fromantiou had neither fetched nor paid for the huge canvas (15 feet wide by 20 feet long) of the *Battle of Fehrbellin*, which he had completed eighteen months earlier. His protest elicited a vitriolic response. It was a pack of lies 'from beginning to end', Fromantiou retaliated, and he was astonished 'that a man of your age would make such a spectacle of himself and not be ashamed to expose his dishonesty and gutted conscience for all the world to see'.[224]

Besides the personal grudge he appears to have held against Uylenburgh for reasons we will probably never know, Fromantiou may have resented him for business reasons as well. He, too, was in the art trade and purchased work on the elector's behalf. According to an eighteenth-century account, Fromantiou once made it known that he had sought out art worth 100,000 rijksdaalders, and that the elector had spent no more than 6,000 rijksdaalders.[225] As Uylenburgh had apparently not consulted Fromantiou about this transaction, it would be feasible to suppose that Fromantiou wanted to exact retribution. He had the advantage, moreover, of being on extremely cordial terms with his principal. As the same author observes, the elector appreciated Fromantiou's 'shrewdness, exuberance and bright ideas'.[226]

Last years in Amsterdam, 1671-1677

A SELF-PORTRAIT OF PALMA VECCHIO

The Great Elector was not the only foreign dignitary to take an interest in Gerrit Uylenburgh's stock. Around 1672 Cardinal Leopoldo de' Medici of Florence, who was assembling a collection of

220 Berlin, Geheimes Staatsarchiv, I HA Rep 76, Alt III, no. 167.

221 See p. 86.

222 See p. 89.

223 Houbraken 1718-1721, vol. 2, p. 296.

224 GAA, not. S. Fraes, NA 4460, p. 227, 6 May 1680; not. C. van Poelenburg, NA 3441, 23 May 1680. The painting by Pieter Wouwerman has been lost. Thanks to G. Bartoschek.

225 Nicolai 1786, p. 46. 'Er trieb überhaupt einen starken Handel mit Malereyen. Er rühmte sich, daß er an 100.000 Rth Malereyen zusammen gebracht, wovon der Kurfürst nur für 6000 Rth gekauft hätte'. At the time of his death, Nicolaes Rosendael, who may have met Fromantiou during his stay with Uylenburgh, had entrusted two paintings 'for sale' to Fromantiou in Berlin. Bredius 1915-1922, vol. 2, p. 545. See also p. 216.

226 Nicolai 1786, p. 46. 'Er hatte sowohl wegen seiner Geschicklichkeit als auch wegen seiner Munterkeit und vieler lustigen Einfälle, einen freyen Zugang zum Kurf. Friedrich Wilhelm'.

self-portraits, heard that Uylenburgh possessed a self-portrait of Palma Vecchio. Francesco Ferroni, a Florentine merchant living in Amsterdam and a confidant of the cardinal, was requested to contact him. Ferroni traded with Africa, the West Indies and East Asia, and sent oriental porcelain and other precious objects to the cardinal. While on a visit to Amsterdam, Leopoldo's cousin Cosimo III de' Medici stayed in Ferroni's home. During the period that he was in touch with Uylenburgh,

Ferroni commissioned a painting from Frans van Mieris on Cosimo's behalf.[227]

Ferroni's negotiations with Uylenburgh were unsuccessful, firstly because Ferroni disputed the authenticity of the work. Once, during a visit to Amsterdam, Lorenzo Panciatichi, the cardinal's librarian, had examined the painting at Uylenburgh's in the company of a 'Sig. Doyma', and neither was convinced that it was by Palma. Moreover, the price of 100 ducats was considered excessive.[228] Ferroni wrote that he himself lacked the knowledge ('scienza') to judge the authenticity of the work and that no one in all Amsterdam was competent to do so, except 'Doyma'. He suggested that Doyma be asked to look at it again, but whether or not he did is uncertain. The negotiations appear to have been broken off, but were resumed in November 1674. Ferroni had returned to Italy in the intervening years, and Leopoldo now contacted Pieter Blaeu, the son of the celebrated publisher Joan Blaeu. Pieter had been to Italy on business and from 1660 on had maintained a regular correspondence with the Florentine bibliophile Antonio Magliabecchi. It was he who introduced Blaeu to Leopoldo de' Medici.[229] The cardinal appears not to have informed Blaeu correctly, as Blaeu then tried to track down the work. He wrote to tell Leopoldo that he had called on a member of the Reynst family, a close friend of his, whom he believed to be the owner of the painting. The person in question was probably Gerard Reynst's son Joan. However, it appeared that he had been mistaken. From there he had gone to Uylenburgh's shop and examined all the paintings in stock. As he was unable to find what he was looking for, he discussed the matter with Uylenburgh, who told him that the painting had indeed been in his possession, but that he

had entered it in a lottery at the beginning of that year, 1674. It had gone to a connoisseur ('un virtuoso'), who subsequently exchanged it with Uylenburgh for a more harmonious ('più piacevole') painting. After that the work was acquired by Stadholder William III, along with paintings by Raphael and other sixteenth-century masters. Uylenburgh did not believe it was a self-portrait of Palma, but nevertheless a work from his hand. It was, he said, one of the best and most beautiful paintings he had ever seen. Blaeu ended his letter with regrets for not having been able to be of service to the cardina l in this matter. It was out of the question, he believed, that the stadholder, 'a gentleman and a lover of rare objects', could be persuaded to part with the painting.[230] Unfortunately, the painting in question has never been identified.

BUSINESS AS USUAL

The fiasco with Elector Friedrich Wilhelm must have dealt Uylenburgh a severe blow, though for a while it was business as usual. From 1671 to 1676 he received numerous commissions to appraise paintings in Amsterdam.[231] His reputation as an expert was apparently still intact. This is confirmed by the fact that in 1673 the magistrates invited him to arbitrate in a dispute between Pieter de la Tombe and his brother Isaac, both of whom were booksellers, art dealers and collectors.[232]

Constantijn Huygens the Younger, with whom Uylenburgh had had frequent dealings in the 1660s, was now secretary to Stadholder William III. We know from his journal that he wrote to Uylenburgh on several occasions in 1673.[233] The

227 Prinz 1971, pp. 95 and 131.
228 See Prinz 1971, pp. 95-96. Florence, Archivo di Stato, Med. Princ. f. 5537, c. 171-173, 180, 185; letters of 4, 10, and 24 December 1671, and 19 January 1672. I am grateful to Gert Jan van der Sman and Henk Th. van Veen for help in obtaining the reproductions of the documents and for help in transcribing them.

229 See Mirto/Van Veen 1993.
230 Mirto/Van Veen 1993, p. 291. '[...] però fui necessitato di farne un discorso, egli mi disse che haveva havuto quel quadro del Palma, e che fra altri quadri nel principio die quest' anno l'haveva posto in una lotteria e che un virtuoso l'hebbe per sua sorte il quale poi con esso Uijlenburg fece un baratto contra un altro quadro più

piacevole, che doppo il Sig.re Principe d'Oranges lo comprò da lui con alcuni altri quadri di Rafaele d'Urbino e d'altri pittori di quel Secolo: che del resto lui non dubitava che non fusse il ritratto del Palma, e di più fatto del Palma medesimo, al che lui soggionse ch'era un de' più insigni e più eccelenti quadri che habbia mai visti [...] ella vede che hora

è in mani d'un Signore et amatore di cose rare, donde non si portà cavare [...] 12 novembre 1674'.
231 A further nine appraisals by Uylenburgh are known from the period 1671-1676; see p. 294.
232 See p. 254.
233 Huygens the Younger 1876-1888, vol. 4, 1881, pp. 21-23 (16 and 20 November 1673).

letters have not survived, but they probably concerned purchases for the stadholder's collection. On Monday 20 November 1673 Huygens noted that he had written to both secretary De Wilde and Uylenburgh regarding sculptures that William III was hoping to acquire.[234] From the aforementioned letter from Pieter Blaeu to Cardinal Leopoldo, it emerges that the stadholder purchased a number of costly paintings from Uylenburgh, once again probably through Huygens's intercession. In 1674 Uylenburgh obtained a loan of 1, 710 guilders from the art collector Herman Becker.[235] In April of that year he borrowed another 118 guilders and 14 stuyvers from the merchant Christian Meschman, promising to settle the debt on 1 June. The document was witnessed by the painter Horatius Paulijn.[236] But why did Uylenburgh need to borrow money. Did he have debts to pay off or did he perhaps need money to purchase art?

In 1674 the authorities estimated his taxable assets at 7,000 guilders.[237] Most of his capital must have been invested in paintings and sculptures. At the beginning of t he following year, as we shall see, he himself valued his holdings at almost double the amount for which he was taxed.

THE INTERIOR OF THE HOUSE ON THE KEIZERSGRACHT

Just at the time that he was embroiled in the affair with the elector, Uylenburgh moved to the new house on the Keizersgracht, for which he had signed a contract in 1670.[238] The contract entered into effect on 1 May 1672. Two and a half years later, when Uylenburgh found himself in financial difficulty, all his possessions were catalogued in an inventory, from which we can form an impression of what the interior of his home must have looked like (see Appendices).[239]

A flight of stone steps led up to the front door, which opened onto the entrance hall. Three small plaster figures were displayed here. This area gave on to the side room, which was decorated predominantly in green. The room contained four chairs upholstered in green velours, with an armchair and bedcover in green as well. There were ash-grey cushions on the chairs, a small oak table covered with a green cloth, and an 'East Indies' blanket on the bed. A Lutheran bible and two psalm books were kept in this room. Beyond the entrance hall and the side room was the best room of the house. In it were twelve chairs with yellow velours seats and yellow say cloths. There was an oak table covered with a black camlet cloth. The room was decorated with small plaster cupids and other figures. A large nutwood commode afforded storage space, mainly for items of clothing.

The kitchen was located under this room. It contained the usual household commodities: twenty pewter dishes, forty-four plates, a copper fish-kettle, six pewter salt cellars, a tin bucket to take to market, six earthenware jars with pewter lids, seventeen pewter spoons, and a few odds and ends such as gridirons, tongs and a skewer for the hearth. There was also a bed and three chairs with rush seats. The kitchen led onto a small courtyard, where there were a few pots and pans, a plaster head and a plaster statue on a base. A room in the front section of the house was furnished with a pine table and a few more rush-seat chairs. Here, the family kept their linen. There were pillow cases, fourteen tablecloths, table napkins, aprons, blue and white mantelpiece covers, handkerchiefs and nightgowns. There were also ten books in the room, among them two psalm books, a bible in folio and another in octavo.

On the first floor was a front room and a back room, as well as a large painting room which extended over the main floor of the house next door and the adjacent coach house. The back room contained six turned wooden chairs with green velours seats and ash-grey cushions, and a plaster statue on a pedestal. There was also an oak chest containing table napkins, tablecloths, yellow curtains and no fewer than eighteen silk curtains to cover paintings. There were also four sets of linen underwear and three packages containing children's clothing and napkins. Most of the family probably slept in the front room, which was furnished with a painted bedstead with striped dornick hangings as well as another five beds. There was a mirror in a gilt frame and eight chairs with tapestry upholstery and red covers.

The sparsely furnished painting room con-

234 Idem, pp. 22-23. 'J'escrivis à madame la douairière a ma femme, à Uijlenburg et au Secretaire de Wilde, aux derniers touchant des statues que S.A. vouloit faire achepter'.
235 See p. 275.
236 GAA, NA 2243, not. A. Lock, pp. 321-322, 5 June 1674. At Meschman's request, not. Lock approached Uylenburgh on that date to ask him to settle the debt. The substance of the original bill and the date 17 April 1674 are stated here; Bredius 1915-1922, vol. 5, p. 1675.
237 GAA, archive no. 662. Kohier (Tax Register), the amount due was 1/200th of his taxable assets, 1674.

tained an armchair and two rush-seat chairs, a painter's easel, a few plaster figures and, of course, all the paintings and marble and terracotta sculptures listed in the last section of the inventory.

The contents of the attic included a pinewood table and bench, two easels and a chest filled with clothing and linen.

The inventory gives an overall impression of modest luxury, although interestingly enough, there were no really valuable articles like silverware, jewellery or porcelain. To judge by the contents and furnishing of the house, Uylenburgh must surely have possessed items of that kind. The most obvious conclusion is that his reduced circumstances had compelled him to deposit them with a pawnbroker.[240]

FINANCIAL ADVERSITY

During the dispute over the sale of art to the elector of Brandenburg, Gerrit Uylenburgh accused Hendrick Fromantiou of trying to 'ruin his business as well as himself'.[241] These bitter words seemed prophetic in 1675, when Uylenburgh's fortunes de clined.[242] His transaction with the elector probably brought in 2,000 rijksdaalders.[243] All things considered, it was probably the aftermath rather than the failure of the transaction as such that precipitated his downfall. His reputation as one of the leading and most respectable art dealers must have suffered a severe blow. Even so, for some time after the affair he continued to enjoy the patronage of a distinguished clientele. The economic downturn in the Republic after 1672 was probably the ultimate cause of his financial collapse. The demand for luxury goods such as paintings and sculpture dwindled. At the beginning of 1673 Uylenburgh himself complained that 'prices have plummeted, especially when it comes to paintings and other rare objects, as a result of these worrying times and the wretched state of affairs in our country'.[244] A contemporary of his drove the point home: 'Before the war, in the days of flourishing commerce and trade, there were people in Holland who scarcely knew what to do with their money or how best to indulge their whims; they would spend 500, 600 or even 1,000 guilders on a painting or 200 to 300 guilders on a single tulip bulb or any plant with unusual flowers. But from 1672 to 1694, throughout that terrible war, they stopped buying paintings and planting flowers. Many earned less in a year than they would hitherto have squandered in an hour'.[245]

The seed of Uylenburgh's discomfiture was sown by his landlord Gerrit Hooft (fig. 61). As from 1 May 1672 Uylenburgh had rented two houses for a period of eight years from Hooft's father-in-law Daniel van Gheel. Half the annual rent of 975 guilders was payable at six-monthly intervals. On 30 November 1674 he asked Hooft, who had taken over the houses from Van Gheel, to release him from his contract for the remaining five and a half years.[246] He explained that he was obliged to go to Italy on business, but the truth

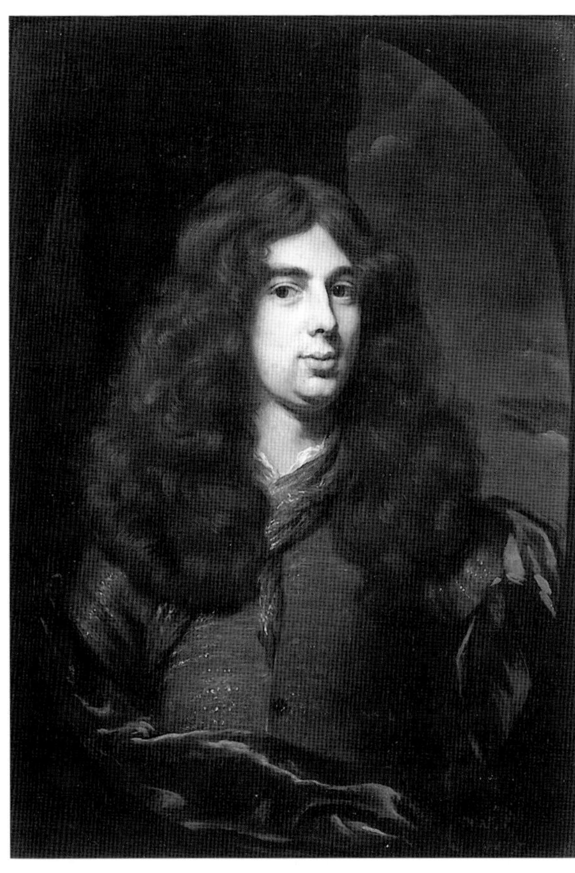

61 Nicolaes Maes, Portrait of Gerrit Hooft, signed and dated 'NMaes 1675', panel, 44 x 31 cm, private collection

238 See p. 77.
239 G A A, 5072 D B K, no. 603, fol. 70-77v and 84-87v, 27-28 March and 26-27 April.
240 By no means all the documents pertaining to Uylenburgh's financial problems have come down to us. For example, the statement of incomings and outgoings is missing.
241 See note 187.
242 The decline of Uylenburgh's fortunes has been comprehensively analysed by Dudok van Heel (1982), who first published the assessment of 1675 (see Appendices p. 301-305). However, several sources of information on Uylenburgh's firm, notably the Bankruptcy Chamber's Preferential Creditors' Roll, have never been consulted before. Our findings are incorporated in this study.
243 See p. 91.
244 See note 187.
245 Quoted from L. van der Saan, Aantekeningen L. van der Saan, B P L 1325. Universiteitsbibliotheek Leiden, see Van der Sman 1996, p. 137. In 1676, for instance, Johannes Vermeer's widow complained that her husband had earned next to nothing since 1672 and that he had lost money on the paintings he had bough for resale. On Vermeer, see Montias 1989, pp. 344-345. On the decline of the art trade in and after 1672, see also Bok 1994, pp. 121-124.
246 G A A, not. J. Matham, N A 4491, pp. 174-175, 30 November 1674, '[...] he is obliged to travel to Italy business [...]'. De Vries 1886, p. 143 (date incorrect); Bredius 1915-1922, vol. 5, p. 1676 (notary incorrect).

is that he was probably unable to pay the rent. By that time he was already sub-letting one of the houses. If Hooft withheld his consent, Uylenburgh wrote, he would have no alternative but to let the second house as well. In the event, Hooft refused to cancel the contract, but he did give Uylenburgh permission to sublet the premises. As a result, Uylenburgh was bound by this commitment for years to come.

From a brief inscription in a notebook belonging to the Amsterdammer Pieter van Brederode we know that Uylenburgh held an auction in January 1675.[247] He appears to have organised an annual auction or lottery of some kind for several consecutive years. There is in any event reason to believe that he did so in 1673, 1674 and again in 1675. Lotteries of this kind were unusual and whoever held them was required to obtain a permit from the city council. The burgomasters may have been accommodating in consideration of Uylenburgh's reduced circumstances.

It may be that Uylenburgh organised the sale at the beginning of 1675 to raise enough cash to keep his landlord and possibly other creditors at bay. But it was not the success he had probably hoped for. A month later he defaulted on his rent payment of 487 guilders and ten stuyvers for the preceding six months, from May to November 1674. Hooft had reached the end of his tether. On 26 February 1675 he applied to Amsterdam's magistrates for a sequestration order in respect of Uylenburgh's property to enable him to recover the money owing to him. In addition, he demanded sufficient security, for rental until the contract expired.[248] Two weeks later, on 12 March 1675, the art collector Herman Becker also filed for a court order constraining Uylenburgh to settle a debt. The amount was not specified at the time,[249] but it later emerged that Uylenburgh owed him 1,195 guilders.

After hearing the two creditors, the magistrates referred the case to the Bankruptcy Chamber, an institution headed by five commissioners who were appointed for a term of one year.[250] They were responsible for restoring order in the affairs of debtors and winding up insolvent estates. One of their main tasks was to make an inventory of the debtor's possessions and inspect his account books to assess his assets and liabilities. Their office was on the main floor of the town hall, the present Royal Palace in Dam Square. Above the entrance to the office is a relief of the *Fall of Icarus* (fig. 62), alluding to the hero of Greek mythology who escaped from imprisonment on wings of feathers and wax. According to the legend, Icarus flew too close to the sun, which melted the wax, causing him to plummet into the sea. The parable served as a warning to anyone visiting the town hall that recklessness could result in insolvency. A contemporary poet conveyed the message in verse: 'Daedalus rose to a moderate height, Icarus came to grief [...] Those who rise too high forfeit property and fortune'. The relief is surmounted by a festoon of empty coffers, letters and papers, where, in the words of the poet, 'rats creep in, eat and gnaw'.[251] The decorations were the work of Artus Quellinus, an acquaintance of Uylenburgh's and the sculptor with whom he had selected art for the Dutch Gift in 1660. Uylenburgh also possessed some of the terracotta models Quellinus had made for other sculptures in the town hall. The significance of the relief above the door of the Bankruptcy Chamber must have hit home every time he entered the room.

The commissioners' first task was to appoint a curator to administer and wind up the bankrupt estate. On 26 March Matthijs Crayers was assigned to Uylenburgh's case.[252] A day later he started to draw up an inventory of the possessions in the house on Keizersgracht.[253] His lengthy report gives an impression of the interior of the house and includes a detailed list of Uylenburgh's paintings.[254] Harmen Zuyr, a 'common workman' employed by the Bankruptcy Chamber, was sent to guard the house and make sure that nothing went missing.[255]

On the day that Crayers started making his inventory, Jan Six went to the town hall to submit an application for preferential status.[256] On 28 March he received permission to remove from the house three paintings he had loaned to Uylenburgh. They were a 'Vulcan' by Giovanni Benedetto Castiglione, a 'Bear hunt' by Frans Snyders and a 'Flower pot' by 'Bruegel', presumably Jan Brueghel the Elder or the Younger. If they turned out to be worth more than the

247 The Hague, Hoge Raad van Adel (Supreme Council of Nobility), Van Slingelandt family archive.
248 GAA, 5061, no. 1348 Vierschaarboek (Tribunal Register), fol. 182v, 26 February 1675.
249 GAA, 5061, no. 1348 Vierschaarboek(Tribunal Register), fol. 190v, 12 March 1675.
250 See Wagenaar 1760-1802, vol. 3, pp. 461-465. In 1675 the commissioners were Cornelis Kloeck, Rombout Hudde, Albertus Geelvinck, Nicolaes Haringcarspel and Jonas Witsen. Witsen died on 20 September of that year and was succeeded by Dirck Boelensz.
251 Fokkens 1663, p. 136.
252 GAA, 5072, no. 476 Register van Curatelen (Register of Guardians), p. 149.
253 GAA, 5072, no. 603, fol. 70-77v, 27/28 March and 26/27 April 1675. Previously published by Bredius 1915-1922, vol. 5, pp. 1662-1673.
254 See Appendices.
255 GAA, 5072, 253 (Ledgers), p. 183. On 10 May Zuyr received 52 guilders and 10 stuyvers for 'guarding the house' on 30 August he received an additional 2 guilders in wages. See also 5072, no. 213 (Balances), p. 185 ('Harman Zuyr ordinaris arbyder van de camer') and p. 208; and 5072, no. 164 (account book), fol. 80r and fol. 112r. The same procedures applied in the bankruptcy of Sijbrant Fries, see p. 23-26.
256 GAA, 5072, no. 1018, fol. 133v, 27 March 1675.
257 GAA, 5072, no. 22, fol. 29v, Thursday 28 March 1675; previously published in Bredius 1915-1922, vol. 5, p. 1676.
258 Idem.
259 GAA, archive no. 5072, inv. no. 1018 (Preferential Creditors' Roll), fol. 134 v., Thursday 4 April 1675: Bardewits appeared for the first time,

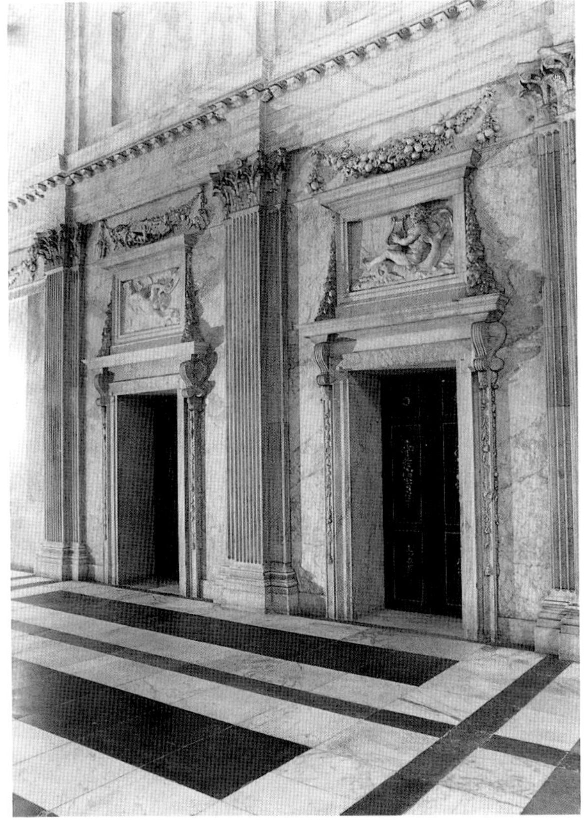
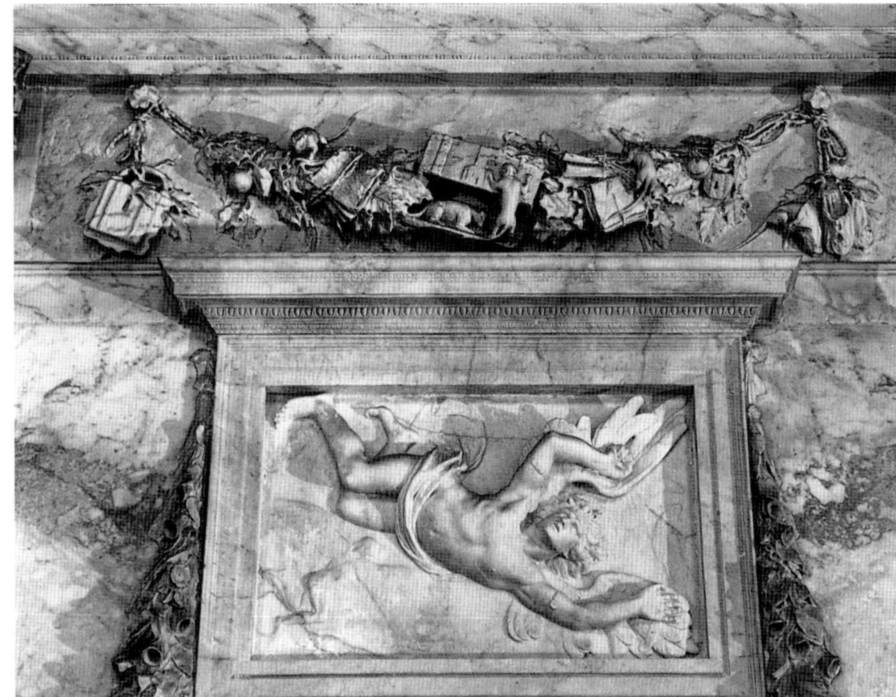

62 The entrances to the Bankruptcy Chamber (left) and the Insurance Chamber in Amsterdam Town Hall, now the Royal Palace, with a detail of the relief above the left door by Artus Quellinus

but what he claimed on that occasion is not documented. On Tuesday 9 April he appeared again (fol. 136r) but once more no reason is given. On 23 April Daniel Vermout appeared with power of attorney from Bardewits to collect the following paintings: '[...] painting of Noah in the Ark by Nicolaes Poesijn, an Emmaus by Bassan, one of David and Goliath by Paulo Veronees, a landscape by Paulus Bril, a tooth puller, a tronie by Carvasio, tronie of a youth by Gorgion and a Minerva by Parmasaen'. The Bankruptcy Chamber's books mention not only Bardewits's name, as they normally would, but added that he was married to the widow of Jan van Weert,

amount, with interest, for which they had been loaned, the balance was to be deposited into the account of Uylenburgh's estate. If they were worth less, Six would be entitled to claim the difference.[257] The descriptions of the three paintings are too vague to enable us to identify them with extant works.

At the same meeting, on 28 March, the commissioners approved Uylenburgh's application to the burgomasters of Amsterdam for leave to petition the Court of Holland and West Friesland for

'seurete de corps' for a period of six months. This meant that he could not be committed for failure to comply with a judicial order during that time. As part of the procedure Uylenburgh submitted a list of his creditors, some of whom were interviewed by the commissioners.[258]

In the following months several people came to collect works they had consigned to Uylenburgh for sale. The first to put in an appearance was Jan Bardewits, on 4 April.[259] Among those who followed were the Hague painter Jean Gericot,[260]

probably because the paintings he was claiming had once been the property of this Van Weert. Bardewits also claimed 853 guilders. On the paintings listed above, see also p. 239-241 and on Bardewits and Van Weert, p. 276.
260 On 16 April Jean Gericot instructed the Hague notary Johan van den Plas to issue a power of attorney authorising a person whose name was not

inserted, 'residing in Amsterdam', to recover the 'two paintings, one being a landscape on copperplate in a gilded frame, made by de Mole, and the other likewise a landscape on copperplate, unframed, by Augustijn Carraccio'. In addition, 129 guilders was to be claimed 'being the balance for two paintings supplied to the foresaid [Uylenburgh]'. On the same day, Theodoor van der

Schuer and Caspar Netscher stated that 'approximately a year ago' Gericot had given Uylenburgh the two paintings 'to sell in a lottery he was planning, which paintings were not entered in the said lottery as not enough lots were sold'. (The Hague Municipal Archives NA 367, p. 175; see also Bredius 1915-1922, vol. 5, p. 1679). In the end, Gericot collected the two paintings

himself on 24 April (GAA, archive no. 5072, inv. no. 1018 (Preferential Creditors' Roll), fol. 139r). The money had been claimed on Gericot's behalf a few days earlier, on 19 April, by the art collector Abraham Peronneau. The amount in question was 120 guilders, not the 129 guilders referred to in the deed from The Hague; on Peronneau, see Bredius 1915-1922, vol. 3, pp. 849-851 (inventory).

Wallerant Vaillant[261] and the Delft painter Pieter Jansz van Ruyven.[262] The person with the most works in consignation was the well-known Parisian collector Everhard Jabach, who had appointed Gideon Cruydenier to represent him. Cruydenier reported to the Bankruptcy Chamber on 26 April, the same day that Wallerant Vaillant filed a claim for the return of his paintings. He handed over a document signed by Jabach which incorporated a list of the paintings and drawings that belonged to him.[263] The document has unfortunately been lost, so that it is impossible to identify the works in question. However, the fact that a separate list was drawn up suggests that his holdings must have been fairly substantial. Jabach also claimed an amount of 5,142 guilders, representing by far the largest claim against Uylenburgh.

In the meantime, Uylenburgh managed to reach a settlement with his creditors. According to the rules of the Bankruptcy Chamber, insolvents were given a period of six weeks to negotiate an agreement with their creditors, in the presence of a delegation of commissioners. From the surviving deeds drawn up in this connection, it transpires that Uylenburgh's twenty-seven creditors were claiming amounts ranging from 5,142 guilders (Jabach) to 34 guilders (Jacob de la Tour). Among them were prominent art collectors and members of the city council, including Pieter Schaep and Jan Six, painters like Willem Schellincks and Adriaen Backer, and others such as the frame maker and supplier of painting equipment Pieter Heeremans.

On 19 April they agreed to Uylenburgh's proposal to write off the total debt in exchange for upwards of 120 paintings and a group of sculptures (see Appendices).[264] The art was to be sold and the proceeds distributed pro rata among the creditors, who would thereby forfeit their right to institute legal proceedings to recover any shortfall. Nor would they be entitled to lay claim to Uylenburgh's furniture, household effects or outstanding debts. Uylenburgh, however, undertook to repay them according to 'his means' should he ever return 'to prosperity'. The total amount owing was 12,422 guilders. Interestingly enough, the creditors accepted Uylenburgh's valuation of the works – apparently most of them still had confidence in his judgment and integrity. He compiled a fairly detailed list of the items, mentioning for instance the prices he had paid for fifteen of them. The first painting on the list was a still life by Francesco Maltese, which he had bought for more than 600 guilders, and which he now valued at 500 guilders. But not all the paintings were worth less than he had paid. He believed that Adriaen Brouwer's 'Farmer with the big shoe', for example, which had cost him 280 guilders, would now fetch 300 guilders, and Netscher's 'Young woman with a parrot', for which he had paid 140 guilders in 1674, was still worth about the same. However, on the whole, he expected his stock to fetch less than he had paid for it. This is due mainly to the last entry, which is his estimate for all the sculptures together. He had paid over 1,800 guilders for them, but considered them now worth no more than 1,000 guilders. At the end he mentioned seven paintings which at the time were in London with Peter Lely, who apparently acted as his agent. Uylenburgh's creditors – among them artists and collectors who would have known the value of art – appear to have been satisfied with the appraisal. Even so, the proceeds of the sale were significantly lower than they had estimated. Uylenburgh had expected to

261 GAA, archive no. 5072, inv. no. 1018 (Preferential Creditors' Roll), fol. 140r, dated 26 April 1675. Vaillant collected the following paintings: 'a large landscape by Jan Looten, a Venus and Cupid by Carel Lorijn, a music piece by Walrant Valiant, and Apollo with a Satyr, a Bacchanal by Jacomo Valliant, and a Narcissus by the said Valiant'.

262 Delft Municipal Archives, NA 2778, not. Willem van Ruyven, 12 April 1675, deed 36, fol. 119. Noted by Montias 1982, p. 216. That day, the painter Pieter van Ruyven gave Gerard Klinck power of attorney to collect two paintings 'executed by him, the person appearing [Van Ruyven]', namely, 'one representing the sacrifice of Cain and Abel, and the other, a Ceres by candlelight'. On Tuesday 7 May 'Gerardo Klinck' appeared before the Bankruptcy Chamber in Amsterdam and obtained permission to take the paintings with him. GAA, archive no. 5072, inv. no. 1018 (Preferential Creditors' Roll), fol. 141r. The painter Gerard Claesz Klinck, of whom little is known, married Geertruijt van Pollinckhoven in Pijnacker on 8 November 1671. On 10 December 1671 he was referred to as 'master painter' residing in Delft (see Delft Municipal Archives, NA 2255, not. Roeland van Edenburgh, deed 173, dated 10 December 1671).

263 GAA, 5072, no. 1018 (Preferential Creditors' Roll), fol. 140r.

264 GAA, Bankruptcy Chamber, 5072, no. 1573, document 340. This document incorporates the contract and the terms agreed between Uylenburgh and his creditors, the list of paintings and sculptures with their estimated values, and the list of creditors plus the amounts they were claiming. The contract is dated 19 April 1675. Dudok van Heel 1982 erroneously cites 16 October 1675 as the date on which the works were appraised. In fact, this is the date on which Uylenburgh received a copy of the contract, after the matter had been settled.

raise a total of 13,276 guilders, a good 800 guilders more than he owed. In the event, the work raised a mere 5,321 guilders. On top of this, the city authorities levied one percent tax, leaving no more than 5,267 guilders and 16 stuyvers to be divided among the creditors.[265] The market for art was apparently even worse than they had anticipated.

The records do not show the precise date of the sale. A document of 10 May notes that Hooft would receive his outstanding rent from the proceeds of the goods 'to be sold'.[266] The Bankruptcy Chamber's minutes of 26 June state that Hendrick van Heijst, the auctioneer from the Orphans' Chamber, which had organised the sale, was not to disburse any proceeds before Hooft had been paid out.[267] The auction must therefore have taken place some time between those dates. In passing it should be said that Gerrit Hooft was not one of the official creditors who had signed the covenant with Uylenburgh. He apparently had no further claims. Having collected the rent every six months, he was the least disadvantaged of all the creditors. On two occasions he had received rent arrears, paid in full, through the intervention of the Bankruptcy Chamber.[268] Apart from the remittance to Hooft, a number of relatively small amounts were paid out to preferential creditors. One was Uylenburgh's serving woman Margareta Cornelis, who received 40 guilders from the commissioners for six months' employment.[269]

Besides creditors, Uylenburgh also had money owing to him, but there are unfortunately no records to show where it came from. On 2 May he received the considerable sum of 1,000 guilders from Louis de Labistraat, but it is unclear what

this was for. Pieter Noordijck paid him 125 guilders for six months' rent. He was presumably the tenant to whom Uylenburgh was subletting the adjacent house on the Keizersgracht.

On 11 October the commissioners of the Bankruptcy Chamber met to discuss the settlement of Uylenburgh's affairs. Five creditors still needed to sign the covenant of 19 April. Daniel van Gheel, the first owner of the houses on the Keizersgracht (45 guilders outstanding), Herman Becker (1,195 guilders outstanding), Jan van Wickevoort (585 guilders outstanding), Anna Becx (153 guilders outstanding) and Jacob van Anstenraet (154 guilders outstanding) had not yet signed the agreement and were still entitled to lodge an objection. The commissioners gave them four days to do so. Becker and Van Anstenraet responded to the summons and appeared before the commissioners. Apparently they failed to reach an agreement on that occasion. Becker finally signed the covenant almost two years later. The remaining three failed to appear at first, but Van Wickevoort signed on 15 October and Anna Becx only in August 1677. It appears that neither Van Anstenraet nor Van Gheel consented to the arrangements, as neither signed at all.[270]

On 15 October 1675, not quite seven months after the Bankruptcy Chamber took on the case, Uylenburgh was rehabilitated, even though some of his creditors had not signed the agreement. The Bankruptcy Chamber required the consent of only three quarters of the claimants; the rest had no option but to accept the terms.[271] Once this condition was satisfied Uylenburgh was 'discharged from the [commissioners'] chamber and was once more at liberty to trade and conduct business, receive and disburse money just as he

---

265 The proceeds of the sale and the municipal tax of one percent were inscribed in small letters on the list of creditors, see GAA, 5072, no. 1573, document 340.
266 GAA, 5072, no. 1018 (Preferential Creditors' Roll), fol. 141r.
The reference to furniture and household effects was incorrect. Only paintings and sculptures were sold at the auction.

267 GAA, 5072, no. 22, fol. 141v, 142r, 26 June 1675.
268 The outstanding rent for the six-month period from 1 May to 1 November 1674, which heralded Uylenburgh's financial decline, is not documented in the Bankruptcy Chamber's registers. The rent for the following two six-month periods was paid to Hooft on 10 May and 21 November 1675 (GAA, 5072,

no. 253 (ledger), p. 183; 5072, no. 164 (account book), fol. 81r, 135r; 5072, no. 213 (balances), pp. 184, 221; 5072, 1018 (Preferential Creditors' Roll), fol. 141r).
269 GAA, 5072, no. 253 (ledger), p. 183; 5072, no. 164 (account book), fol. 89r; 5072, no. 213 (balances), p. 189; 5072, 1018 (Preferential Creditors' Roll), fol. 142v.
270 For unknown reasons, the

names of Cornelis Meijer and Willem van Siepesteijn do not appear in the minutes among those of the creditors who had not signed the contract and therefore still had to be heard. Meijer did not sign as he was probably in Rome by that time (see p. 283) and Van Siepesteijn's heirs signed only on 23 April 1676.
271 Wagenaer 1760-1802, vol. 3, pp. 461-464.

had done before his insolvency'.[272] A day later he received a copy of the covenant with his creditors. On 18 October he even received 55 guilders and nine stuyvers from the Bankruptcy Chamber because he was 'unencumbered by debt'.

Uylenburgh must have tried to resuscitate his all but insolvent business, but it could not have been easy. He had lost almost his entire stock. He had also been in debt to some of his principal clients, who may not have been happy with the way the case was resolved. All of them had lost money in the process. Uylenburgh was aware that if he were to start accumulating capital again, some would leap at the chance to recover their money. He probably left the houses on the Keizersgracht, even though the contract had not expired. Hooft would have realised that there was little chance of him ever being in a position to pay the high rent, but we do not know where the Uylenburghs moved to from there.

Uylenburgh had remained in touch with Constantijn Huygens the Younger, who wrote to him on 24 June 1676. The contents of the letter are unknown. Uylenburgh was still receiving orders from the same circle of clients. Prince Johan Maurits of Nassau-Siegen – none other than the Great Elector's stadholder in Cleves – had commissioned him to restore a number of paintings.[273] But the support he received from these quarters was presumably not enough. On 5 April 1677 Uylenburgh asked his trusted notary Lock to draw up a power of attorney for his old acquaintance Jan Six, his brother-in-law Pieter Deldeijm and his friend, the painter Theodoor Ferreris, who were to manage his affairs during his stay in England.[274]

In fact, he had probably been to England some time earlier. In December 1676 he was described as the 'Purveyor & Keeper' of the British Royal Collection.[275] Perhaps he was uncertain as to how the venture would work out and had not settled all his affairs before his departure earlier that year. Once he was confident that he could build a new life for himself in London, he returned to Amsterdam on a brief visit to straighten matters out.

Huygens wrote to him again on 4 and 15 September 1677 and presumably sent these letters to Uylenburgh's new address in London. By 6 October 1677 Uylenburgh had left Amsterdam for good. On that date Prince Johan Maurits requested Jacob Cohen, his agent in Amsterdam, to make alternative arrangements for paintings he had wanted Uylenburgh to restore.[276]

To England

Uylenburgh was not the only Dutch artist to migrate to England in the 1670s. The troubles of 1672 precipitated a small exodus of painters, the most prominent among them being the two Willem van de Veldes, but also lesser luminaries such as Adriaen van Diest, Adriaen Hennin, Abraham Begeyn, Adam de Colonia, Jan Griffier, Jan van der Vaart and many more left the Dutch Republic to seek their fortunes in Britain.[277] Other painters, such as Jan Looten, Hendrick Danckerts, Pieter van Roestraten, Thomas Wijck and Abraham Hondius, had settled in London even earlier.[278] Uylenburgh would undoubtedly have had acquaintances in these circles.

As the seat of government and home of the royal court, London had always been the political centre of England (fig. 63). It was also the largest port in the country. From the 1660s on, its mercantile interests flourished not only in Asia, Africa and America, but also in Europe. London became an increasingly formidable rival of Amsterdam. Towards the end of the seventeenth century the city emerged as the commercial and financial centre of Europe. Around 1660 its population was between 400,000 and 500,000, with 8,000 new immigrants arriving each year. Most moved to the capital from other parts of Britain, but a substantial number also came from the continent.[279]

In 1666, a decade before Uylenburgh's arrival in London, much of the city was destroyed in the Great Fire. The massive reconstruction programme launched in the aftermath created an unprecedented demand not only for contractors and builders, but also for skilled professionals to add the finishing touches to the interiors. The demand for paintings in Britain in the first half of the seventeenth century had come almost exclu-

272 GAA, 5072, no. 22, fol. 69.
273 See note 276.
274 GAA, not. A. Lock, NA 2251, 5 April 1677.
275 See p. 111.
276 The Hague, Royal Archives, IV 1463, fol. 15. See also Lemmens 1979, p. 273. The paintings were restored by Jacobus de Lange and probably Paulus de Milly. See also p. 253.
277 See Gerson 1942, pp. 365-431; Ormrod 2001; Kollmann 2000; Sluijter 2003.
278 Idem.
279 See Earle 2001.

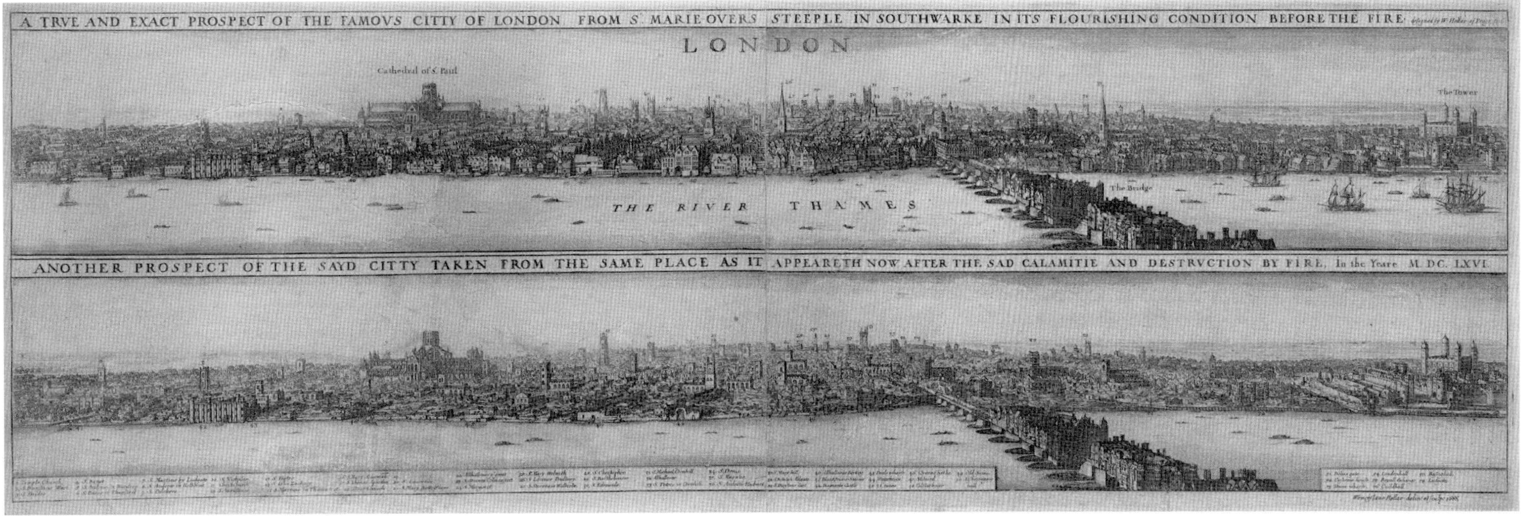

63 Wenzel Hollar, View of London before and after the fire ('A True and Exact Prospect of the Famous Citty of London'), signed and dated 'Wenceslaus Hollar delin: et sculp: 1666', etching, 21.7 x 33.6 and 23 x 34.3 (left section) and 21.7 x 33.8 and 23 x 34.7 (right section), London, Museum of London

sively from the court and the aristocracy, but from the 1660s on, the middle classes took a growing interest in art.[280] Moreover, London had a large aristocracy with extravagant tastes and a great deal of money to spend.[281] For a painter and art dealer like Uylenburgh, it must have seemed the perfect place to build a new life. He had the advantage of being on close personal terms with the celebrated court painter, Peter Lely, and may also have had relatives by marriage living there. Pieter Deldeijm, for instance, who was married to the sister of Gerrit's wife, was himself originally from London.

According to Houbraken's biography, Uylenburgh left for England after his failed transaction with the elector and 'every once in a while' painted 'the costumes and landscapes in [Peter Lely's] portraits'.[282] There is no reason to doubt the truth of this report, but Houbraken's account of the decline of one of the Republic's greatest art dealers to the status of a mere workshop assistant should be taken with a pinch of salt. Lely offered him more than just an opportunity to lend a hand in the studio. This 'well beloved friend' secured him a job as curator of the royal collection. Around Christmas of 1676, Gerrit became keeper of Charles II's collection, for which he received an annual stipend of 100 pounds. According to the letter of appointment, he was engaged as 'Purveyor & Keeper [...] for the better preservation of Our pictures'. His duties were 'to cleanse, mend and take care of them from time to time'.[283]

What the position entailed emerges from a description of Uylenburgh's successor, the still-life painter Parry Walton.[284] In 1706 it was said that Charles II appreciated Walton in particular

280 Earle 2001; Ormrod 2001.
281 Earle 2001. London's growth between 1660 and 1730 is attributed predominantly to the burgeoning overseas trade and the extravagant consumerism of the aristocracy.
282 Houbraken 1718-1722, vol. 2, p. 297.
283 Millar 1977, p. 81. Calendar of State Papers. Domestic Series 1913, pp. 119-120; Calendar of State Papers. Treasury Books 1911, p. 1154. London, Public Record Office, National Archives, SP44, 344, p. 480. Sir Oliver Millar kindly passed on to us the archive reference he had received from Lady Gibson. Sophie Walkinshaw examined the document for us in London. 'Whereas We thought fit for the better preservation of Our pictures from decay to appoint & constitute in December 1676 Gerrit Wylenburch to be Purveyor & Keeper of Our pictures to cleanse, mend and take care of them from time to time, and whereas he hath accordingly since been employed by us in that service to Our satisfaction & particularly in removing & fitting severall of Our pictures for the furnishing of our new buildings at Windsor and that we think fitting to give him an allowance of one hundred pounds per annum [...] April 17 1678'. This and other allusions to Uylenburgh's service to the English court were recorded after his death. It would appear that everything was committed to paper only once he had passed away.
284 His only known extant painting, at the Dulwich Picture Gallery, is based entirely on seventeenth-century Dutch examples.

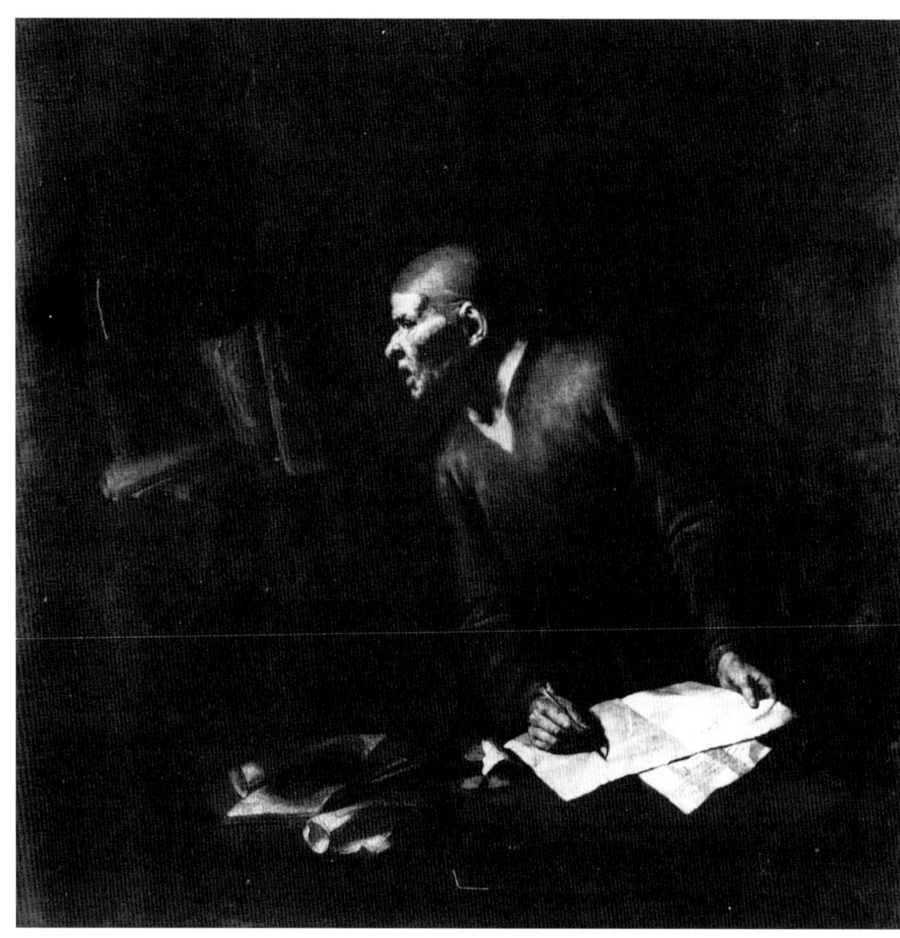

64 Jusepe de Ribera, also attributed to the master of The angel appearing to the shepherds, A philosopher writing, canvas, 169.5 x 163 cm (original measurements 123 x 94 cm), London, Hampton Court, collection of Her Majesty Queen Elizabeth II

for his 'knowing and discovering of Hands. He was well vers'd in *Italian* Pictures and was also remarkable for mending the Works of many of the great Masters, that had suffered either by age or ill Usage [...]'.[285] Walton was not only the keeper but also the 'Menderer & Repairer' of the royal collection.[286] As far as we know, Uylenburgh was assigned the same tasks. When Lely introduced him to the king, he would have recommended him for his role in the Dutch Gift.

Uylenburgh entered the king's service just when work was in progress on the renovation of Windsor Castle, Charles II's most ambitious architectural enterprise. The new apartments built for the king and queen were decorated in 1677 and 1678.[287] The architect, Hugh May, was a close friend of Lely's. In 1650 he had lodgings in Lely's home and in 1656 the two men had visited the Republic together. Around 1675 Lely painted a double portrait of himself with his old companion May, who was also one of the executors of his will.[288]

A large team of artists were employed to execute the decorations for Windsor Castle. Uylenburgh was also involved in the project, apparently to the king's satisfaction. The king gave him a bonus of 50 pounds as a token of gratitude for his 'Extraordinary Care and Paines in Enlargeing Painting, fitting and placeing of severall of his Mat.ties Pictures sett over all the Chimneys and

doores in the Kinges & Queenes Lodgings in Windsor Castle and for severall Journeys to some of his Ma.ties Howses to make Choice of such Pictures as were most fitt to be sett in the sever.ll places aforesaid'.[289] Uylenburgh had thus been instrumental in selecting the paintings that were to form an integral part of the decoration of Windsor Castle. They were restored and in some cases enlarged or reduced to fit into the panelling on the walls. Some were set in simple frames, others in elaborate creations, all made by Grinling

sion, he worked on paintings by 'great masters', modifying and enlarging them to fit in the panelling of Windsor Castle. Charles II was evidently immensely impressed by his retouching of a *Sleeping Amor,* which involved painting the legs from scratch because that section had been so badly damaged. The painting in question was a work by Giovanni Battista Caracciolo, which has remained in the British Royal Collection to this day. See Levey 1991, pp. 51-52.

285 Quoted from Millar 1977, p. 85. The passage from the *Essay towards an English-School* was added to Roger de Piles, *The Art of Painting*, 1706, p. 476.
286 Millar 1977, p. 85.
287 John Hope 1913.
288 Millar 1978, pp. 14, 67. The painting is now in a private collection in Britain.

289 John Hope 1913, p. 317. See also London, Public Records Office, T 54/8, p. 288, 'To Gerrard Hijlenburgh for his care & paines fitting repeiring all ye pictures in ye privye lodgings ye sume of 50 p by his ma.ties verball comands'. This payment along with several others was dated 13 January 1680 (we

are indebted for this note to Sir Oliver Millar, who received it from Lady Gibson. Sophie Walkinshaw examined the reference in the archive). In 1676-1677 Nicolas Largillierre and Philip Dolesam received a little over nineteen pounds in remuneration for comparable assignments (see idem, p. 315).

Incidentally, Largillierre had worked for Lely for a brief period. On Largillierre, see the highly reliable biography by Dezaillier d'Argenville 1745-1752, vol. 3, p. 247, who reports that Largillierre left for England at the age of eighteen and remained there for four years. Under Hugh May's supervi-

Gibbons and Henry Phillips. A good example is a painting of a philosopher writing, attributed to Jusepe de Ribera, which was enlarged on all sides (fig. 64). It can still be seen today in its original – simple – frame. The preparation and restoration of this work may well have been assigned to Uylenburgh.[290]

In England, too, Uylenburgh must have been highly regarded for his knowledge of paintings and their value. On 14 June 1677 Charles Beale, the husband of the painter Mary Beale, noted in his journal that he had visited Lely, who told him that Uylenburgh had valued his, Lely's, collection at 10,000 pounds.[291] Besides assisting Lely, Uylenburgh must also have worked independently. However, even less is known about his output in England than that from his career in the Netherlands.[292]

In 1678 Lely brought Uylenburgh's friend Theodoor Ferreris to England, perhaps on Uylenburgh's recommendation. Ferreris agreed to the move, evidently believing that he would receive commissions for Windsor Castle. However, in this respect he was disappointed. All the large ceiling paintings he had probably set his sights on had already been completed or were promised to the Italian Antonio Verrio. According to George Vertue's journal, Ferreris had nothing to do and subsequently returned to Holland.[293] However, that was not entirely correct. Ferreris was commissioned by John Cecil, the fifth Earl of Exeter, to produce paintings for Burghley House, near Stamford in Lincolnshire. Cecil inherited the house in 1678 and immediately organised a major renovation programme. Ferreris was taken on to decorate a rather insignificant 'dressing room'.[294]

Once again, Verrio was engaged to execute the large ceiling paintings in the principal rooms. Perhaps to compensate for the assignments he had missed, Lely commissioned Ferreris to paint a *Venus and Cupid* as an overmantel in the best room in his home. The painting was based on a drawing from Lely's collection.[295]

Ferreris remained in England for two years at most. By April 1680 he was back in Holland, where he was responsible for executing a will.[296] He probably decided to return to the Republic soon after Uylenburgh's death.

The exact date of Gerrit Uylenburgh's death is unknown. His wife Elisabeth Juyst is believed to have predeceased him in England, but no firm evidence to that effect has been found.[297] In April 1679 Parry Walton succeeded Uylenburgh as keeper of the royal collection.[298] Uylenburgh had presumably died a short time earlier.

On 10 August 1679 two merchants, Willem Bruyn and Antoni Rooleeuw, presented themselves at the council meeting of the Flemish and Waterland Mennonites.[299] These two Mennonite movements had united in 1668 and now called themselves after their former respective churches, 'the Lamb and the Tower'.

The visitors reported that Gerrit Uylenburgh had passed away in England, leaving behind three daughters. The family had agreed that the girls were to be committed to an orphanage run by an independent religious association, which was willing to accept them in return for an advance fee of 600 guilders. In addition, the orphanage would be entitled to one third of Uylenburgh's 'incoming debts' up to a maxi-

290 Other candidates are Largillierre and Dolesam. See preceding note.
291 See p. 264.
292 Five landscapes by Uylenburgh are listed in English sale catalogues dating from 1660 to 1700. See Ogden & Ogden 1955, p. 123.
293 Vertue, notebooks I, p. 71: '1678 Mr Frerres a history painter came over into England (by encouragement from Sr. P. Lilly) who had been some years in Italy [...] expecting to have painted for the King those works at Windsor which Verrio had already, or before hand got orders to go about this Frerres having wherewith to live on without Painting return'd again to Holland soon after'.
294 Croft-Murray 1962, pp. 247-248, and for commissions to Verrio, pp. 236-237.
295 According to a note written by Roger North, Lely's friend and the executor of his will, British Library, Add Ms 32, 507, fols. 36-37. See Dethloff 1996, p. 49, note 82.
296 See Theunisz 1927, p. 87. not. Ouckama, 28 April 1680, executor of the will of Thys Claesz van Bassen. Ferreris acted as executor for the same person before his departure for England (notary Ouckama, 16 February 1676).
297 Elisabeth Juyst's name does not appear in Amsterdam's burial registers, which suggests that she died in England. As noted below, in August 1679 Gerrit and Elisabeth's three daughters were described as orphans.
298 Millar 1977, p. 82.
299 GAA, archive no. 1120, no. 174 (minutes), p. 166 and no. 179 (draft minutes), unpaginated. First published in Lambour 2001, pp. 186-188.

mum of 300 guilders. Bruyn and Rooleeuw had now come to inquire whether their orphanage would accept the children on the same terms. The ministers were furious with their lapsed congregants Bruyn and Rooleeuw. They berated them for having 'wronged by entering into an agreement of that nature concerning children who belong to our chamber and orphanage', and told them to stop interfering in the matter. The Mennonite ministers would 'try to speak to the friends [meaning relatives] of these orphans' and make arrangements as they saw fit.[300] Two members of the board were dispatched to pursue the matter. A week later they reported to the council meeting. They had spoken to the uncles of the three girls and arranged for them to be admitted to the orphanage on Prinsengracht under the same conditions as had been agreed with the board of the independent religious association. The records do not show which members of the family they spoke to, but one was probably Uylenburgh's brother-in-law Pieter Deldeijm who, as it happens, was Dutch Reformed.

It transpires from this episode that the Waterland community regarded Gerrit Uylenburgh as one of their own. Even though he had married in the Dutch Reformed church and had his children baptised there, the children, too, were considered members of their community. In 1672 and 1676, when the church organised a fundraising cam-

paign in aid of the Mennonite orphanage, Uylenburgh's name appeared on the list of members who would be asked to donate. He did not contribute on either occasion,[301] but he never formally renounced his faith.

Uylenburgh's marriage to a member of the Reformed Church had disqualified his children from automatic entitlement to a place in the Mennonite orphanage. Instead, they were admitted 'subject to' payment of the sums of money that Bruyn and Rooleeuw had proposed. On 23 August 1679 the three girls were registered in the 'Orphans Book': Anna Maria Uylenburgh aged 12, Abigael Uylenburgh aged 11, and Sara Uylenburgh aged 9. Over the next few years detailed records were kept of the clothing they received and the cost of providing it.[302] The sisters were later taken into the homes of devout Mennonite families in Amsterdam. Anna Maria entered into the service of Perijntje Vorsterman, Abigael was employed by the orphanage house matron Niesje Bosch, and Sara found a home with Barend Eppenhof.[303] Not surprisingly, all three were baptised for the second time upon reaching adulthood.[304] In spite of their Reformed background, after returning from London the three orphaned children were embraced by the Mennonite community in Amsterdam – the community that had played such an important role in the development of their grandfather Hendrick Uylenburgh's art business.

300 See preceding note. The draft minutes refer to an uncle of the three orphans. The official minutes refer to more than one uncle. No names are given in either case. In the Resolutions Book of the Mennonite orphanage (GAA, 812, no. 3, 23 August 1679) two spaces were left vacant following the word 'uncles', but neither was filled in.

301 On the fundraising campaign of 1672, see GAA, 812, no. 2 and 1120, no. 217, district 1, no. D. The entry relating to the campaign is dated 6 March 1672. The aim was to collect money for the rebuilding and maintenance of the orphanage. According to the rules, 'all members' would be asked to contribute except those receiving financial assistance. On the campaign of

1676, see GAA, archive no. 1120, no. 631. The collection was held among 'the brothers and sisters of our community and all well-wishers' with a view to raising extra funds to support the growing orphanage population. 'Gerrit Uijlenburg and sisters' were classified under district 1. The campaign appears to have started in June 1676 and continued into 1677. Antonides

van der Goes wrote a poem about the action: Antonides van der Goes 1685, p. 213. 302 GAA, 812, no. 37, nos. 75, 76 and 77. See also 812, no. 43 for the names of the children living in the orphanage. 303 Idem. 304 Anna Maria was baptised for the second time on 24 November 1686, Abigael on 12 February 1690 and Sara on 14 February 1694.

▶ Detail of fig. 55

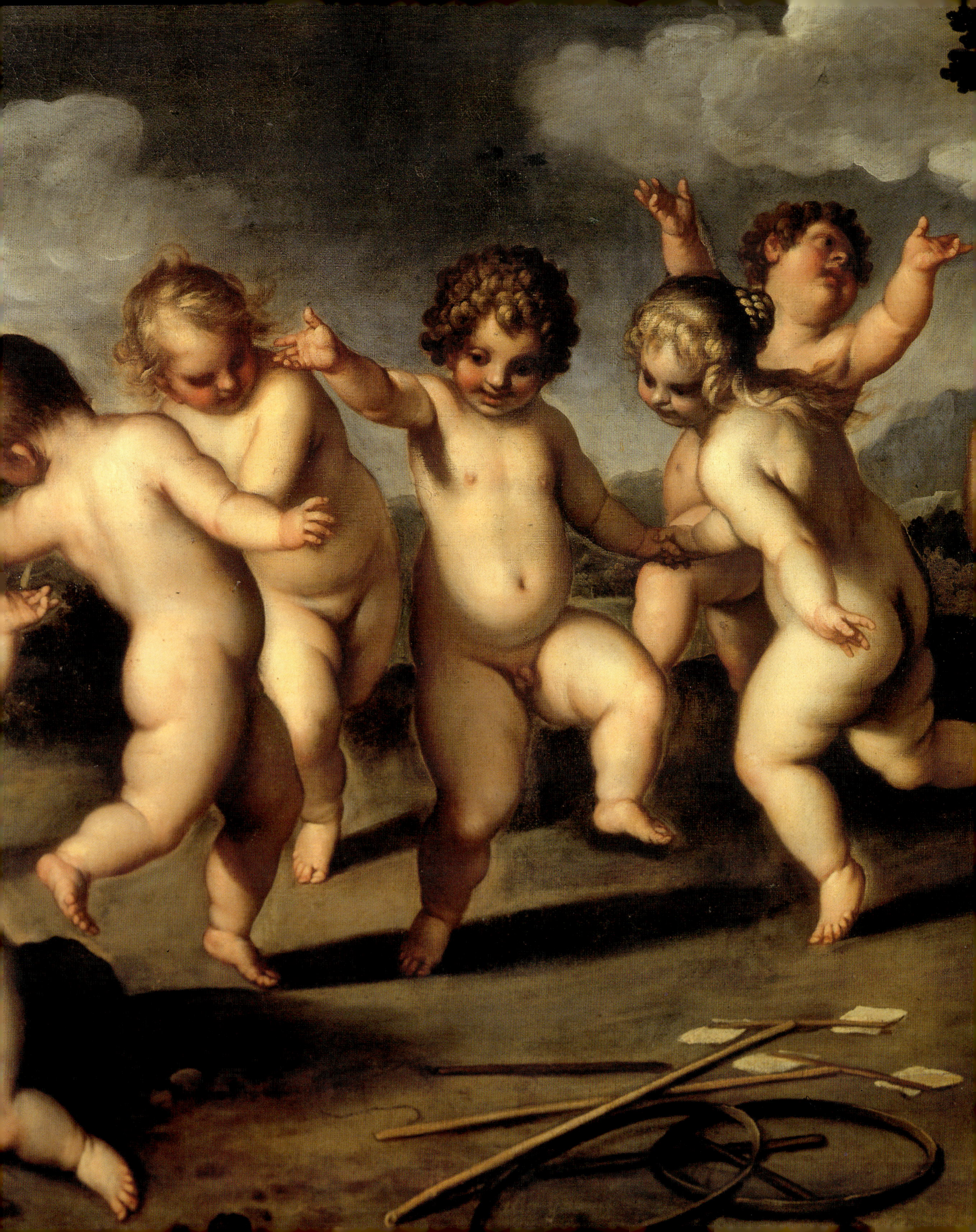

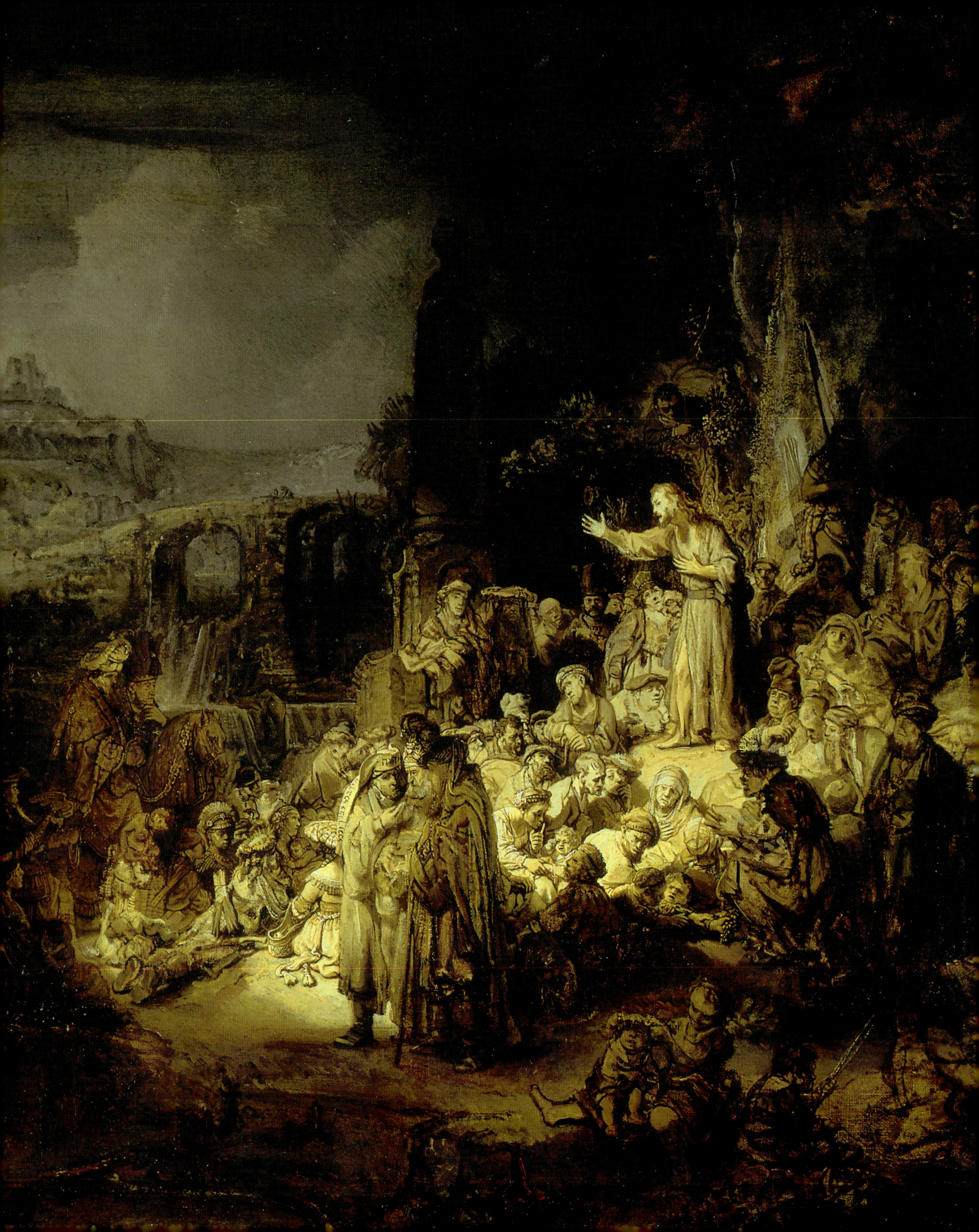

3 Hendrick Uylenburgh's art business. Production and trade between 1625 and 1655

JAAP VAN DER VEEN

To date, the publications dealing with Hendrick Uylenburgh have almost exclusively been concerned with the art dealer's significance in relation to Rembrandt's career. In these texts, he is portrayed as a shrewd entrepreneur, a man of commercial insight who also had excellent contacts with potential patrons. Indeed he must have had an eye for talent, for he was able to interest Rembrandt in his enterprise and establish a working relationship that lasted for four consecutive years, during which they came to dominate the Amsterdam art market. Exactly what transpired in Uylenburgh's workshop remains unknown, but it is generally accepted that he himself had control of the business side of the enterprise and that Rembrandt was responsible for production. What this meant was that Uylenburgh took care of the workplace, the necessary finance and commissions and the sale of the produced and purchased art works, while Rembrandt painted history pieces, portraits and 'tronies', made prints and supervised pupils and assistants. There can be little doubt that Rembrandt's stay in Uylenburgh's workshop, roughly between the end of 1631 and 1635 or perhaps even a little longer, was of major significance for him in more than one respect. Not only did his production increase during those years, it also changed in character. From the time of his arrival in Amsterdam Rembrandt executed countless commissions for portraits, while his etching underwent a radical change both in style and subject. The influence extended into Rembrandt's personal life too, for he must have met his future wife Saskia, Uylenburgh's niece, in the art dealer's house.

The fact that Hendrick Uylenburgh was an important figure in Rembrandt's life and work was early recognized. Attention was first paid to the Uylenburgh family in the mid-nineteenth century,[1] followed by the publication of a number of important documents concerning Hendrick and Gerrit Uylenburgh.[2] In the 1920s, the art historian Jan Six drew attention to a contemporary text by Filippo Baldinucci, published in the eighteenth century, in which 'la famosa Accademia di Eeulenborg' was mentioned.[3] From that moment, Uylenburgh's business has always been associated with the idea of an 'academy'. Wijnman applied this term to Uylenburgh's art business, and although others have since followed him without demur[4] one cannot help wondering whether it is justified. In any case, we owe it to Wijnman that he was the first to record the prehistory of the Uylenburghs in Leeuwarden and in Poland, an account of which is given in the first chapter here. Moreover, Wijnman brought to light valuable information on the Mennonite milieu to which the Uylenburghs belonged. In the foregoing chapters, his findings were supplemented with new information.

It would be impossible to imagine the Rembrandt literature without the name of Uylenburgh, but whenever the subject of the art business is raised as such it is always in the context of the first half of the 1630s, while the literature gives no indication that the character of the business might have altered over time. From its inception in 1625 the enterprise had an unbroken existence of more than fifty years, but surely that does not mean it underwent no change at all. What was Hendrick Uylenburgh doing immediately after his arrival in Amsterdam in or shortly before 1625? Did he set up an artists' workshop at the very outset, as has been suggested? Were there many young

1 Scheltema 1853; Eekhoff 1862.
2 Contributions from Bredius alone can be cited from 1884, 1886, 1889, 1891, 1915-1922, and 1916.
3 Six 1925-1926.
4 Wijnman 1956 and Wijnman 1959.

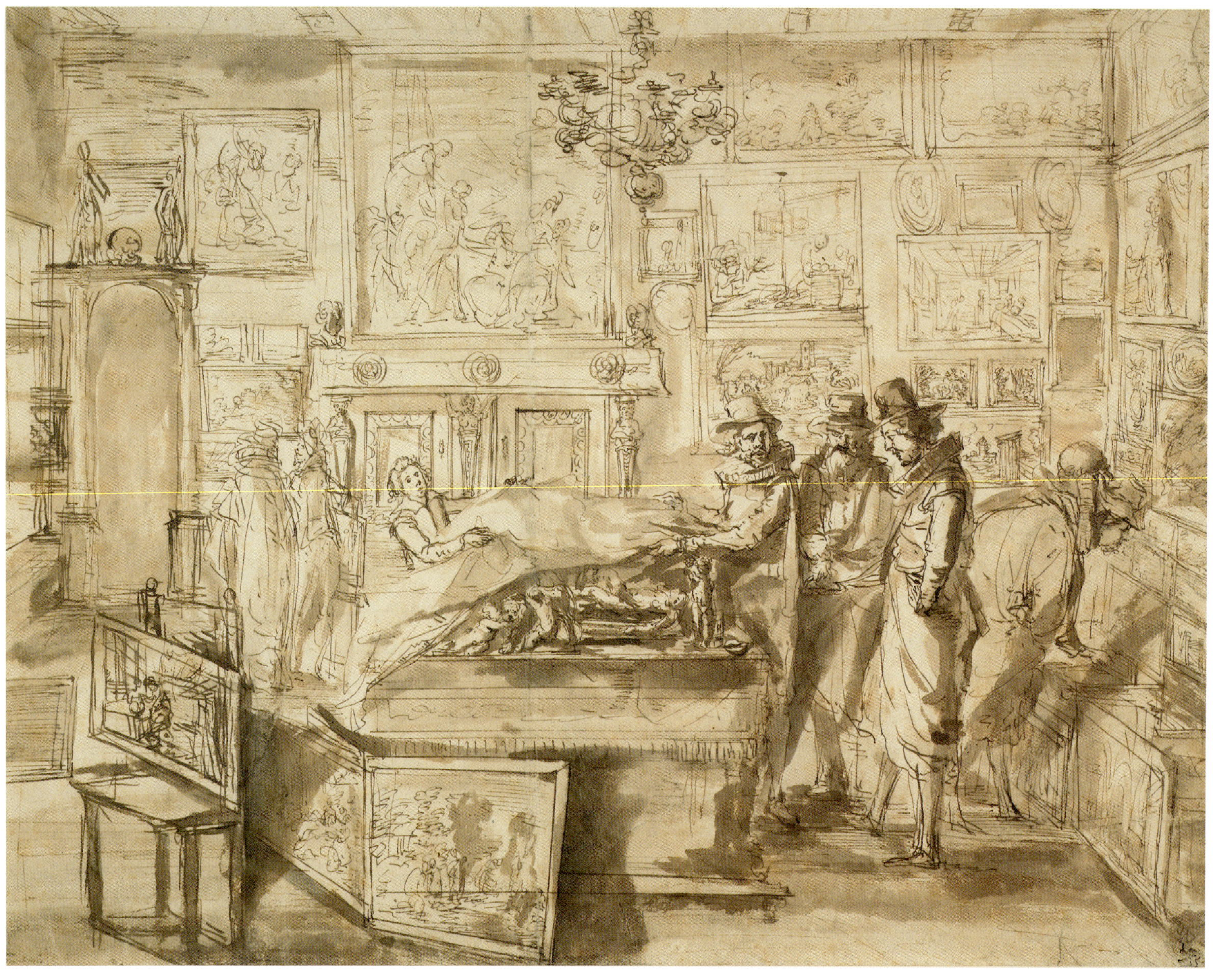

65 Anonymous, Interior of an art dealer's shop, washed pen and ink drawing, 31.1 x 45.4 cm, London, British Museum

painters around the workshop in the mid-thirties, or was the number of assistants strictly limited? What happened to the workshop after first Rembrandt and then Govert Flinck worked there? Can one really speak of an 'academy'? And to what extent did his activities in the art trade develop over the course of time? These are questions that will be addressed in this chapter.

On the basis of the changes that seem to have taken place within the Uylenburgh enterprise – both in the trade and the production of art – three different phases can be distinguished. The first phase covers the years 1625-1631, during which, I shall argue, it is likely that Uylenburgh was active as a merchant and art dealer, while at the same time there is no indication that he headed an artists' workshop. A second phase began with Rembrandt's arrival in 1631. Their collaboration lasted almost four years, after which Rembrandt left to work independently

and was succeeded in Uylenburgh's workshop
by Flinck, who remained until roughly 1638.
The emphasis during the 1630s was on the production of high quality art works and copies of
such works, and on their sale. There were business contacts with art dealers and painters in
Leeuwarden and in Leiden and possibly also in
Haarlem. The third phase that I believe one can
discern in the development of the enterprise ran
from 1639 to the mid-fifties, after which the business continued until 1675 under the management
of Gerrit Uylenburgh. The workshop remained
in existence, but to the best of our knowledge
there were by then no more pre-eminent artists
working there. One cannot exclude the possibility that there were still painters of repute working for the firm, but any such documentation
is lacking. It is fairly certain that Jürgen Ovens
painted for the Uylenburghs between 1661 and
1663, and there were other painters who applied
themselves to copying art works present in the
'shop'. Baldinucci, already mentioned above,
records that Uylenburgh had assembled a considerable collection of paintings by the most important masters in Europe and had in his employ
a number of young painters who copied these
paintings for him. His informant was the painter
Eberhard Keil, who worked for Uylenburgh
between 1644 and 1647. In those years the firm
must have functioned as a family concern, with
most of the children of the Uylenburgh-van
Eyck couple actively engaged in the business.
Did the trade in art become more important than
original productions in the workshop? Around
1640 Uylenburgh took out three loans that were
intended for the purchase of new acquisitions for
the shop. These loans involved considerable sums.
In the mid-fifties, with the involvement of his
eldest son Gerrit, Uylenburgh was able to pay
off most of these debts. Gerrit Uylenburgh, who
followed in the footsteps of his father as the new
head of the firm, continued to run the business
along more or less the same lines, but became –
at least, according to the source material available
– far more involved with the international market than had previously been the case. The period
from the mid-fifties onward is the subject of the
following chapter.

5 Dudok van Heel 2001, p. 13
and Dudok van Heel 2002,
p. 52 and p. 51, figs. 62a-b and
63a-b; Wybrand de Geest
married Hendrickje Fransdr
Uylenburgh (1600-after 1665)
in 1622. She was a cousin of
Saskia (not a sister, as has been
asserted).

The early years as a merchant in Amsterdam, 1625-1631

In 1626 Hendrick Uylenburgh was living in
Sint-Anthoniesbreestraat, on the corner with the
Zwanenburgwal (see p. 47-50 and fig. 21), in the
house where, shortly before, the painter Cornelis
van der Voort had established his workshop. The
latter had made his name mainly with portraits of
prominent Amsterdammers, including several full
length, life-size portraits. The historian Dudok
van Heel has suggested that, after his death in
1624, Van der Voort's art practice was continued
by Uylenburgh, who had, in his words, 'a well-
organized workshop with many assistants'; and
that although Uylenburgh was a painter, 'he no
longer, or hardly ever practised the craft himself'.
According to Dudok van Heel, Uylenburgh must
have employed painters to execute portrait commissions, including the life-size, full length pieces
similar to those that Van der Voort or his assistants had produced. He drew attention to two
pendant pairs of portraits of this type, painted
by an unknown artist around 1630-1631, suggesting that these could very well have originated in
Uylenburgh's workshop. Was there a connection,
he wondered, with the work of Frisian painters?
Wybrand de Geest, for example, who painted
large, standing portraits in 1628 and in 1632 in
Leeuwarden, had a family connection with
Uylenburgh.[5]

The hypothesis that Uylenburgh carried on
the workshop in the corner house is an extremely
attractive idea, but so far unsupported by any concrete evidence. In fact, there are documents from
the years 1625-1631 which cast strong doubt on
this hypothesis but lead rather to the opposite
conclusion that, during this period, Uylenburgh
did not yet have a workshop of his own. The evidence leading to this conclusion are dealt with
below. First of all, there is the history of occupation of the house and the auction of Cornelis van
der Voort's workshop possessions. Then there
should be mentioned the way that Uylenburgh
is referred to in relation to his profession. One
document from 1628 that was continually, albeit
always briefly, referred to in the literature was
generally taken to imply that paintings could be

ordered from Hendrick Uylenburgh in advance; but a closer reading of this archive document shows that this inference is incorrect. A recent discovery, Hendrick Uylenburgh's appearance as an account holder with the Amsterdam Bank of Exchange in the years 1625 and 1627, would seem to indicate that he was involved in merchant trading. Finally, a document from 1628 is discussed in which more than twenty paintings in Uylenburgh's possession are mentioned, not one of them originating from his (alleged) workshop.

In the discussion of the history of occupation of the house in the Breestraat it became clear that Cornelis van der Voort's widow and her children must have still been living in the house in the autumn of 1625 and only moved out subsequently.[6] At the earliest, one has to assume, Uylenburgh therefore could not have moved into the house before early 1626. The fact that Uylenburgh went to live in what had previously been the house of Van der Voort has raised the question of whether he carried on the latter's workshop. In the light of the above, we know that in any case this could not have happened immediately, since between the death of Van der Voort and Uylenburgh taking over his house there was an intervening period of around eighteen months. In addition to which, Van der Voort's effects relating to his workshop were auctioned on 30 August 1625 at a public sale in front of the house of the deceased.[7] Among the items sold were frames for stretching canvases, picture frames, unpainted panels, various 'tronies' of men and women (presumably models that could be useful in a painter's work), wooden mannequins, four painter's easels, palettes, various grinding stones and pestles for fine-grinding pigments, fragments of paintings, some plasterwork, and four chairs and three stools the painter and his assistants must have used to sit on whilst working. This must represent the entirety of his workshop effects. A few other effects belonging to Pieter van der Voort, the son of Cornelis who also died in 1624, were auctioned separately. Only in the case of four items is there no entry for the buyer, merely the sign for 'sold' – indicating that they had been paid for on the spot. All other entries give the names of buyers, among whom we find well known artists such as Pieter Lastman (who bought unpainted canvases on stretchers among other items), Dirck Pietersz Bontepaert, Nicolaes Eliasz and a former servant of Van der Voort. As already said, Uylenburgh was not one of these buyers.[8]

How was Hendrick Uylenburgh referred to in documents from his early years in Amsterdam? Whenever there is a need to refer to his occupation in legal documents from the years 1627, 1628 and 1629, he is consistently called a 'koopman' – a merchant. Subsequently, in June 1631, he is called a 'cunsthandelaer' – an art dealer (see fig. 68). The references to his profession, which must have come either from Uylenburgh's own mouth or from his own written statement, deserve special attention. In the petition that Uylenburgh submitted to the Supreme Court in The Hague in late 1629, he referred to himself as a 'merchant of Amsterdam'. In 1634 he recorded his profession in the album of Burchard Grossman as 'art dealer in Amsterdam' (see fig. 23c), while in the summer of 1632 he is for the first time in any document called a 'painter'.[9] In archival material from subsequent years this description is found more often, but he was also referred to – in 1638, for example – as a merchant, and in 1653 among other occasions as an art dealer. A striking description of his profession is found after his name in 1640: 'merchant of paintings and art works'.[10]

A merchant occupies himself with commerce, the buying and selling on of goods. If he has a quantity of wares in stock and is not selling them on fast enough, there is the question of stockpiling. He can store his wares in a warehouse or in his own home, but in doing so he does not become a retailer. In seventeenth-century Amsterdam there was no separate merchants' guild, but merchants who specialized in a specific product had to join the relevant guild: a merchant of paintings thus came under the St Lucas Guild. The profession of merchant was an almost natural development from Uylenburgh's activities in the period immediately before he settled in Amsterdam, during which he had been an agent for the Polish King. In all probability, once in Amsterdam he would have maintained trade contacts with Danzig. One thinks, of course, of his brother Rombout, who supplied him with paintings from

6 See p. 47.
7 'Sijn vercocht dese navolgende goederen achtergelaten bij Cornelis van der Voort, *op 't hoeckgen van de Breestraet'*, GAA, arch. no. 5073, inv. no. 952, 30 August 1625, and Bredius 1915-1922, vol. 4, pp. 1180-1182. The many paintings among the effects were all sold on 13 May 1625, see De Roever 1885, pp. 187-207.
8 Dudok van Heel 2001, p. 21 writes: 'Uylenburgh seems to have taken over and continued this workshop, possibly complete with the inventory'.
9 For the document of 1627 see note 17 below, for the documents of 1628 and 1629 Chapter 1, notes 37 and 40, for the document of 1631 notes 37 and 38 below, and for the documents of 1634 and 1632 Chapter 1, pp. 51-53.
10 The legal document of 1638 is cited below (see note 195), that of 1653 in Chapter 1, note 74, and below note 290; the legal document of 1640 below in note 212.

11 Van Straten 2005, p. 74.
12 See p. 24.
13 G A A, arch. no. 5077 (Exchange Bank Archive), Index of names for the ledger of 1625 (no inventory number). The names of account holders' debtors and creditors were entered in the Exchange Bank's ledgers; the indices contained only the names of account holders. The indices for the ledgers of the years 1621-1624 have not been preserved. Hendrick Uylenburgh's name does not appear in the index for 1620.
14 References to pages 501, 699, 1136, and 1622.
15 Jasper van Tongerlo and company had two pages, as did Pieter Gerritsz Hooft, while the latter's brother Jan Gerritsz Hooft was given three pages, likewise Goris de Weert and company. For an analysis of the indices from this period see Lesger 2001.
16 G A A, arch. no. 5077 (Exchange Bank Archive), Index for the ledger of 1627. For purposes of comparison: Hans Reijers and Balthasar de Visscher each had a single page, Marten van den Heuvel had two (with several crossings-out).
17 G A A, not. J. Warnaertz., N A 661, fols. 131v-132, 26 March 1627; first published in Van der Veen 2001, pp. 49-51.

his own hand, but surely Uylenburgh would also have been in contact with Isaack van Eyck, who is thought to have been his father-in-law. It was shown in the first chapter that this merchant from Danzig was probably operating on the Dutch market with the help of his sons. In theory, Uylenburgh as a merchant could also have run a workshop, but the nature of his activities between 1625 and 1630 certainly does not suggest this.

It is significant that Uylenburgh was first called a 'painter' for the first time in 1632, and not earlier. In subsequent legal documents this occurred more frequently, mainly when he had paintings valued, but this need not necessarily mean that he himself sat behind the easel. We know of no paintings from his hand and, much more importantly, we know no contemporary documents in which any work by him is mentioned. In the past it was assumed that, where the name 'Uylenburgh' was entered with paintings in household inventories, this related to Hendrick Uylenburgh. In most such cases, however, this must have been the work of his brother Rombout, while painted landscapes would have been done by his son Gerrit. The assumption that Uylenburgh was early involved in the making of works of art was crucially based on a document composed in Leiden in 1628, in which it was read that some years previously someone had ordered paintings from Uylenburgh that had to be 'curieus' (exceptional).[11] It is now certain that this order concerned Rombout, not Hendrick Uylenburgh.[12]

The earliest dated, previously unpublished document that witnesses to the presence of Hendrick Uylenburgh in Amsterdam comes from 1625. The name 'Hendricq van Uijlenbch.' appears in the register of names in the archive of the Amsterdam Bank of Exchange for that year.[13] This means that Hendrick Uylenburgh held an account with the exchange bank, and whoever wanted to open an account with this bank could only do so after first depositing a sum of at least 300 guilders. Because the ledger itself for 1625 has not been preserved, we have no precise data regarding the magnitude or nature of the transactions; but the information that Uylenburgh in this particular year had an account with the Amsterdam Bank of Exchange is highly significant,

for the bank took care of transactions on behalf of its account holders and made international payments possible. The international transfer of money largely passed through exchange bills. Merchants bought a bill of exchange (a kind of cheque) from a banking or trading firm that they put in the name of their foreign trading partner and subsequently sent to him. The bank then passed on to their own financial intermediary, in the place of residence of the trading partner, the order to pay the sum on production of the bill of exchange. The City Governors of Amsterdam had ruled shortly after the founding of the Bank of Exchange (in 1609) that all exchanges of 600 guilders or more must be conducted via the bank. Any merchant of significance could therefore hardly remain outside it. The fact that Uylenburgh had a bank account in 1625 indicates that he was trading on a considerable scale, all the more so since there are references to four pages after his name.[14] This is an indication of just how active a merchant he was, for of the approximately 1300 account holders in 1625 the vast majority could only muster one or two pages.[15]

The register of the ledger for 1626 has not been preserved, but we do have the register for 1627, when Hendrick Uylenburgh was again an account holder. This time, however, he warrants only a single page,[16] indicating a marked decline in the number of his transactions. Although the indices give no clue as to the nature of the transactions, we are able to get some insight thanks to a document from 1627. On March 26th of that year, Uylenburgh, who is referred to as a 'merchant and citizen of this city', had a notary record that the Amsterdam merchant Jan van de Wouwer had at his own request stood surety for him (Uylenburgh) on behalf of the merchant Marten van den Heuvel 'for the payment of five hundred Frankfurt florins in change'.[17] This is a highly interesting document, firstly because it provides information on Uylenburgh in his early years in Amsterdam and secondly because it contains a list of the paintings that he gave as collateral on this occasion. Uylenburgh transferred to Van de Wouwer – 'for his act of friendship' – his household effects, clothing and valuables and 21 paintings, all specified. That list gives an idea of what

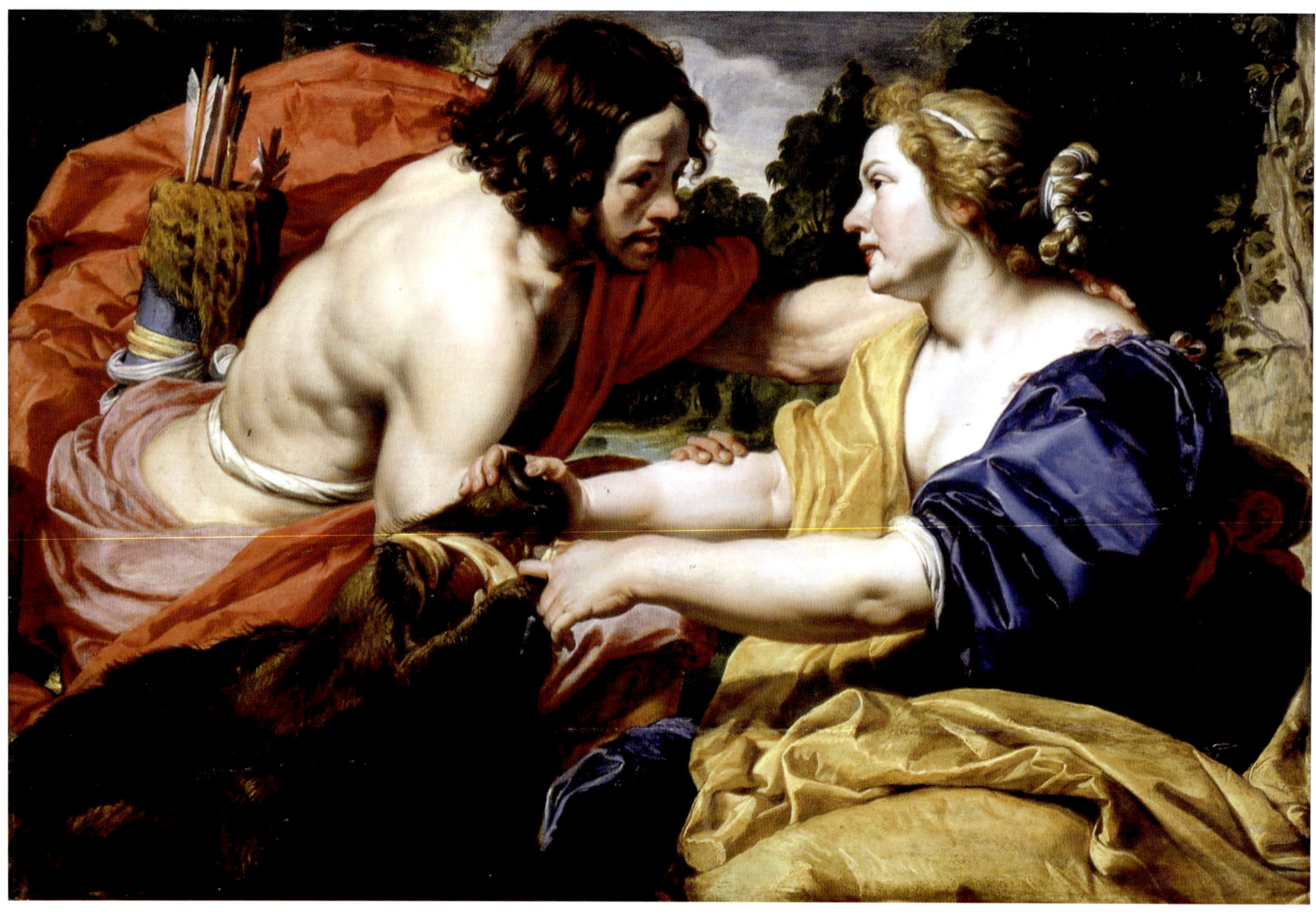

66 Abraham Janssen, Meleager and Atalanta, panel, 71 x 133 cm, Le Havre, Musée des Beaux-Arts André Malraux

Uylenburg had at that moment in stock. The most remarkable piece is 'an original painting, being an Attalante, done by Abraham Janssen'. To the best of our knowledge, Abraham Janssen, one of the leading history painters of Antwerp, twice depicted this mythological subject. The earliest version, perhaps painted around 1614, was lost in 1945. Janssen's other *Meleager and Atalanta* (fig. 66) is dated to around 1620.[18] One cannot say for certain whether Uylenburg had one of these versions in his possession, or if so, which one; but if he did have the later work, he must have been one of its first owners. Whatever the case, there was at that moment a work by Janssen circulating in the Amsterdam art trade.

Another painting on the list was 'an original painting' depicting wild deer, by 'Gerrart de Bos' – evidently the still-life and animal painter Geerart van den Bossche, who became a master of the Antwerp St Lucas Guild in 1623.[19] That year is significant. It is highly unlikely that Hendrick Uylenburgh had a painting from his hand from his apprentice years, which means that Uylenburgh had a painting by Van den Bossche that must have been done between 1623 and 1627. This further confirms the active contacts that Uylenburgh must have maintained with Antwerp art dealers and painters in the 1620s. We saw that around 1620 he was in Antwerp buying paintings for the Polish King.[20] One can only conclude

18 Larsen 1995.
19 Information about this painter can be found in Sauer, *Allgemeines Künstler-Lexikon*, vol. 13, p. 159, where there are references to a still life in the style of Frans Snyders and Paul de Vos.
20 See p. 32-38.

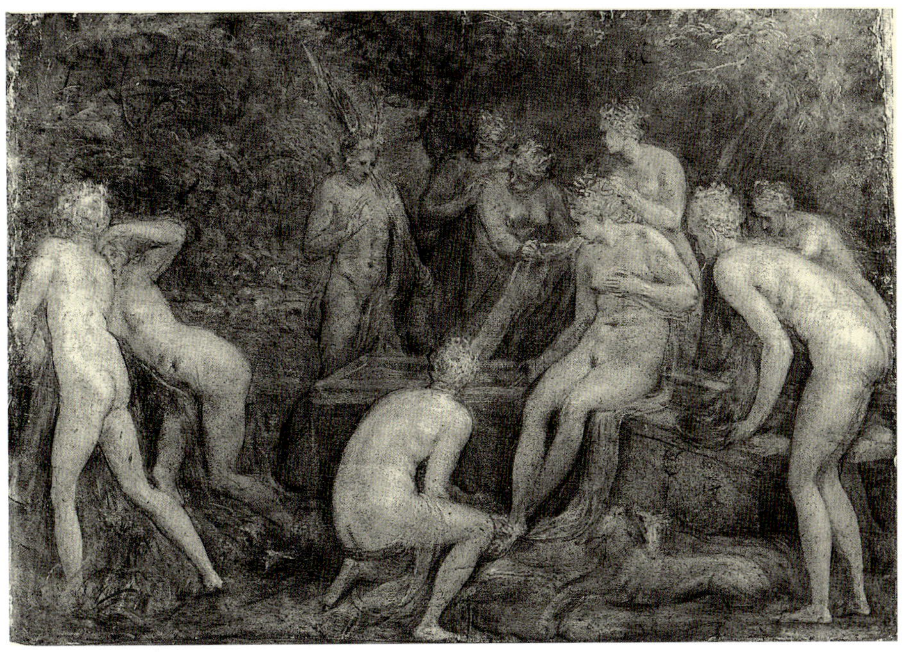

67 Frans Floris, Diana and Acteon, brown monochrome, heightened with white, on parchment mounted on wood, 41.5 x 58.5 cm, Oxford, Christ Church Picture Gallery

21 Van de Velde 1975, vol. 1, pp. 99-103.

22 Canvas, 194 x 247 cm, Brunswick, Herzog Anton Ulrich-Museum. In 1622, in an Amsterdam evaluation of household effects, 'een koecken van Nieulant' was valued at 72 guilders.

23 Van Eeghen 1986.

24 Doc. 1637/3 and 1656/12, resp. nos. 44 and 107.

25 A second candidate is the 'zijdereder' Marten van den Heuvel, who together with his wife made a will in Amsterdam in 1629. He must have been a son of the gold-leather manufacturer.

from the appearance of a painting by Geerart van den Bossche in Uylenburgh's possession that he must either have returned to Antwerp after 1623 or have obtained art from an Antwerp dealer. The close connecetions with Antwerp and the clear evidence that he was buying in new work leads one to suppose that the painting by Abraham Janssen in his possession was the *Meleager and Atalanta* painted around 1620 and not the version dating from around 1614.

Hendrick Uylenburgh did not only have works by contemporary masters in stock. The 1627 list also includes 'a grisaille by Frans Florissen, original' – again a painting produced in Antwerp. The term 'principael' here could either refer to an original work, i.e. a painters own invention, or to the autograph execution. In the case of Frans Floris, the latter meaning would certainly be of interest, because his assistants were responsible for a large proportion of his workshop output.[21] In the seventeenth century, his autograph works were sought after. The subject of this work is not given, but grisailles are rather exceptional in his œuvre (fig. 67). Yet another painting listed in the document, 'an original painting by Adriaen in the Three Rings', depicts a kitchen. We cannot be sure who the author of this painting was; the name 'the Three Rings' is probably the name of the house where he lived. Adri-

aen van Nieulandt is a likely candidate: there exists a large kitchen piece from his hand, signed and dated 'Adriaen Van Nieulant Fecit in Amsterledam Anno 1616'.[22] In 1614 Van Nieulandt bought a house in the Breestraat, across the street from Uylenburgh, which he himself lived in (see fig. 21). His mother declared in 1623 that she lived with him in his house in the Breestraat. She died there in 1627. When Adriaen van Nieulandt's wife died in 1645, the record of her burial gives the house of her decease as 'on the Breestraat over the lock, across Rembrant the painter'.[23] Unfortunately no house name or signboard is given in any of these documents.

The 1627 list also has a landscape painting without further description by Govert Jansz called Mijnheer. His work was highly regarded in the seventeenth century. Rembrandt paid thirty guilders in 1637 for a landscape painted by him and in 1656 had 'a small landscape' and 'a village scene' by him.[24] The other sixteen paintings were all works from the hand of Rombout Uylenburgh. These works have already been discussed in the first chapter.

Uylenburgh did not leave the debt to Van den Heuvel standing for long. In the margin of the legal document there is a note to the effect that the matter was settled on 20 August 1628, which meant that Uylenburgh once more had possession over the paintings listed in the document and was able to sell them. One can give a rough estimate of the sum of money involved. The Frankfurt florin or German gold guilder was worth 28 stuyvers; it was therefore worth more than the Dutch (carolus) guilder, worth 20 stuyvers. The sum owed must have amounted to approximately 700 guilders. The document offers no clue as to what the actual business transaction was about, although Marten van den Heuvel can be tentatively identified with the merchant of that name who was demonstrably in Amsterdam from c. 1610 and who made his name as the manufacturer of gold leather.[25] However, one cannot be certain that a delivery of this luxury product was the object of this particular transaction, for Marten van den Heuvel was dealing in various goods by the 1620s and also dealt in shipping insurance. As a merchant he operated on a grand scale with customers both in the Netherlands and abroad. He was evidently unfazed by financial risks and eventually, in 1640, came a cropper,[26] but in 1627 there was still no hint of financial dangers ahead. There are, however, no indications that Marten van den Heuvel dealt in art.[27] It is very well possible that he was a Mennonite.[28]

We don't know for certain who the Jan van de Wouwer was who had shown Hendrick Uylenburgh (on the latter's admission) so many favours, because there were two Jan van de Wouwers: both father and son bore the same name. Van de Wouwer senior must have been born around 1560, his son probably shortly before 1600, and although the facts known about them are few, they were unquestionably Mennonites and would have belonged to the Waterland community. Firstly, Jan van de Wouwer the Elder was related to Mennonite families by marriage. One of his daughters married a son of the Mennonite teacher of the Waterland Mennonite community in Workum (Friesland), the father coming over to Amsterdam from Friesland for the wedding.[29] Another daughter married Goris de Weert, a wealthy Mennonite merchant. An inventory of De Weert's estate was drawn up in 1641 in the

presence of Laurens Cornelisz Schouten, in partnership with whom he had done business and who was the brother-in-law of Sijbrant Haye Fries.[30] This inventory also shows the extent of De Weert's art possessions. There were some 45 paintings hanging in his house in Amsterdam, almost half of which were landscapes, while he had another twenty or so paintings in his house outside the city.[31]

Jan van de Wouwer the Younger was married to Anneke Uytenhove, offspring of another Mennonite family.[32] Together with other members of the Van de Wouwer family, this married couple must have moved to Hamburg,[33] where in 1636 a French traveller interested in art seems to have come across them: he mentions two individuals in whose homes there were good paintings to be seen,[34] one of them a Dutchman called 'Jan van de Wonner', by which he must surely have been referring to Jan van de Wouwer. In view of the presumed date of birth of Jan van de Wouwer the Elder, this would have been his son. The ornamented signature under the 1627 document could similarly point to the same conclusion. Precisely what paintings Jan van de Wouwer possessed, we don't know: the Frenchman apparently had

married Joost van den Vondel, who was a member of the Waterland community until 1620.

33 I suspect that this occurred around 1630/31: another child of Jan van de Wouwer was buried in Amsterdam in 1630, but the tax register of 1631 does not give his name.

34 Ogier 1636/Schottmüller 1910, p. 252; the other individual who possessed good paintings was Matthijs Bode, who also came from Amsterdam. An indirect contact between the Bode family and Uylenburgh can be demonstrated. In 1650, Anna Kerckrinck (1626-1689), who married Matthijs Bode (1612-1670) two years later, bequeathed a painting 'van Uylenburgh gemaeckt, hangende in 't voorhuys van haer voorn. broeder' (made by Uylenburgh, hanging in the forehouse of her forementioned brother) – i.e. Willem Kerckrinck (1616-1668), G A A, not. J. van de Ven, N A 1095, fols. 294-295, 7 November 1650. This could have been a landscape by Gerrit Uylenburgh, though more probably a work by Rombout Uylenburgh. The same bequest is named in the will of Anna's sister Maria Kerckrinck, G A A, not. J. van de Ven, N A 1095, fols. 228-229, 7th November 1650. The sisters thus owned the painting by Uylenburgh jointly, which leads one to suspect that they in turn had inherited it from their parents. According to Schwartz 1984, p. 370, note 141d and p. 371, note 197, it was a portrait of Willem Kerckrinck painted by Hendrick Uylenburgh. Before he married in 1652, Matthijs Bode actually lived in Hamburg, where a brother is also recorded in 1639. Their father, Godert Kerckrinck (1577-1645), had his portrait painted by Govert Flinck.

---

26 In 1640, as a result of Marten van den Heuvel's bankruptcy, his possessions were inventorized. G A A, not. J. Cornelisz Hogeboom, N A 840, 15 August 1640, and Koldeweij 1998, pp. 522-525. Among the effects were listed some 16 paintings, including two small landscapes by 'De Momper' (Joos de Momper the Younger?), a number of prints and a drawing by Hendrick Goltzius. In view of the fact that Marten van den Heuvel had been declared insolvent a few months earlier, it is well possible that in the intervening period various things could have been mortaged or sold. For example, the inventory records the portrait of his father, but not his own portrait. The following year, in 1641, his property, his assets and his debts were inventorized, G A A, not. G. Coren, N A

1004, 12 June 1641, and Koldeweij 1998, pp. 526-528. This and other documents reveal multiple international commercial contacts, including with Danzig, Frankfurt and Poland.

27 This can, however, be shown to be the case for his younger brother Govert van den Heuvel, who was involved in the art trade in Haarlem. In 1637 he tried to do business with the Amsterdam art dealer Johannes de Renialme, Bergvelt/Kistemaker 1992, p. 126 and note 35. Frans Hals probably painted his portrait, Biesboer 2001, p. 239. His heirs sold his paintings – 'desselfs naergelaten Schilderyen, van diversse uytsteeckende Meesters' (by various outstanding masters) – by public auction in Haarlem, *Oprechte Haerlemsche Courant*, 22 March 1670.

28 His parents were members of the Mennonite community of the Dantziger Oude Vlamingen (Old Flemish of Danzig) in Haarlem.

29 In publishing the banns of marriage between Wilhelmina (Meijntje) van de Wouwer and Enoch Ripperts (de Vries) he was assisted by his father Rippert Eenkes, teacher in the Waterland community of Mennonites at Workum; on the latter, see N N B W vol. 8, cols. 457-458. The painted portraits of Eenkes and his wife are recoded in the inventory of the house of decease of Lambert Jacobsz., the Frisian painter whose business relations with Uylenburgh will be discussed in detail below in this chapter: Straat 1925, p. 73, no. 31.

30 See p. 22-23 and Genealogy I on p. 291.

31 G A A, not. J. Cornelisz Hogeboom, N A 840, I, 2, 6 and

8 March, and 5 April 1641 (this document has been damaged by fire and is only incompletely preserved); four paintings bear the names of their presumed authors: a ruin by (Cornelis van) Poelenburch, a small landscape with a beggar by (Abraham?) Bloemaert, a small painting by (Roelant?) Saverij and a figure piece by Cornelis Cornelisz van Haarlem. The children of Goris de Weert were baptized as Remonstrants after his death. The Van de Wouwer family may also have transferred from the Mennonite to the Remonstrant Church.

32 She was a daughter of Joost Uytenhove and Margriete Willemsdr. de Wolff, who lived in Cologne. When the latter lived briefly in Amsterdam in 1614, she was baptized with the Waterland community. In 1610 her sister Maeycken de Wolff

124

no time to visit his house. Is it too far-fetched to think that Jan van de Wouwer had acquired a number of these paintings from Hendrick Uylenburgh, to whom he had earlier extended such 'vruntschappe'?

Hendrick Uylenburgh's name thus appears in the register of the ledgers of the Bank of Exchange for the years 1625 and 1627. The number of pages devoted to him is a good indication of active business contacts that were not necessarily connected to the art trade. In the next preserved register, from 1631, one looks in vain for his name and similarly in the registers for the following years: he never appears again in the Exchange Bank ledgers.[35] Had Uylenburgh transferred his activities elsewhere in the intervening years? It looks as though he was active in commerce and in art dealing during the first years of his residence in Amsterdam and that subsequently he gradually changed his direction. His brother Rombout Uylenburgh had died in late 1627 or early 1628. With no more work to be had from that source, the need for his own 'production' may have become more urgent. One can imagine, furthermore, that his brother had assumed responsibility for business interests in Danzig. But in addition to Rombout's death, there had been major developments on the Amsterdam art market in the 1620s. The demand for art was rapidly growing; there was a bourgeois class that was interested in art and had purchasing power. During the late 1620s and shortly thereafter, there were changes on the supply side: several artists of repute either died during this period or left the city. For example, Cornelis van der Voort died in 1624, Pieter Isaacksz in 1625, Werner van den Valckert died around 1627/28 and Jan Pynas in 1631. The landscape painter Hercules Segers, plagued by financial problems, found it necessary to leave the city in 1631, while the pre-eminent history painter Jan Tengnagel produced no further paintings after he was appointed deputy-sheriff in 1625.

While the documents discussed above from the period 1625-1631 do not conclusively refute the hypothesis that Uylenburgh carried on the painters' workshop of Cornelis van der Voort, when one takes them all together it is, in my view, difficult to maintain this idea. The documents we have at our disposal point in another direction. At the same time, it should be borne in mind that source material from these years concerning Uylenburgh is meagre, that the most significant documents from 1625 en 1627 were only recently found, and that no individual piece of information is decisive. The house where Van der Voort had worked remained occupied by his widow for some time. Uylenburgh probably rented it in May, 1626, a year and a half after Van der Voort's death. The contents of his workshop had already been sold at auction – and we know that Uylenburgh bought nothing at that sale, although, of course, if he had wanted to equip a workshop he could have always got what he needed from shops. Of greater significance is the finding that between 1625 and 1631 Uylenburgh was without exception referred to as a merchant, and only later – for the first time in 1632 – as a painter. Of course, 'merchant' could mean various kinds of activity, including trading in art, and it was perfectly possible to be a merchant and manage a painters' workshop at the same time. However, there is no suggestion of the latter in the available documents up to 1631. The new information that Uylenburgh – as early as 1625 – held an account with the Amsterdam Bank of Exchange, and that the extent of this account covered four pages in the ledger also points clearly to his occupation as a merchant. Two years later, his financial dealings required only a single page, while in 1631 the bank records no further transactions. It is evident that he was dealing in, or at least possessed, a stock of art works during this period: in 1627, he was able to give 21 paintings as collateral, including several paintings produced in Antwerp and sixteen works by his brother Rombout from Danzig. At that time there was no mention in the relevant document of any paintings coming out of a workshop of his own. It seems likely that changes in the Amsterdam art market, both in supply and in demand, led Uylenburgh to go into production as well as trading. As far as we are concerned, this becomes 'visible' when, in 1631, Uylenburgh managed to attract the 25-year old Rembrandt into his enterprise.

35 I have looked at the indices of names for the years 1641, 1644-1649 and 1651-1654. I have also searched in vain the earliest preserved ledger of 1644 for the name Hendrick Uylenburgh.

COLLABORATION WITH REMBRANDT, 1631-1635

On June 20th, 1631, the 'cunsthandelaer' (art-dealer) Hendrick Uylenburgh had a notary draw up a document to certify that he owed Rembrandt – or the bearer of the document – a thousand guilders for a loan. If after a year Rembrandt wished to have the loan repaid, he was to give Uylenburgh three months notice in advance. That, in brief, is the content of this document first published in 1887. It has, of course, been included in subsequent publications on Rembrandt sources,[36] but what has always been overlooked in the process is the fact that the text was taken from a transcript produced by the notary or by a clerk.[37] But besides that transcript, the original rough draft was also preserved, and this – which one might well consider to be the original document – is highly interesting for the various crossings out and marginal additions that it contains (fig. 68).[38] Evidently the original loan was slightly higher: behind the figure of 'ten hundred guilders' an additional 'and fifty guilders' has been crossed out. The passage in which Uylenburgh promised 'to pay back a year after this date' is crossed out and replaced with the text which states that Rembrandt, if he wanted his money back after a year, was obliged to give Uylenburgh three months notice in advance. At the same time, the interest to be paid to Rembrandt annually was set at five percent, while Uylenbugh committed as surety 'all his goods, nothing excepted'. The fact that these alterations were introduced into the rough draft leads one to suspect that the two parties negotiated the conditions under which the loan should be signed. One often encounters this arrangement in the seventeenth century whereby the debtor and not, as one might expect, the money-lender has had the document drawn up.[39]

The loan of 1631 is the earliest documented contact between Hendrick Uylenburgh and Rembrandt. One can safely assume that they already knew each other: Rembrandt would hardly have lent so much money to just any old Amsterdam art dealer. A meeting between the two men could very well have occurred before 1630, either in Amsterdam or in Leiden. Around 1625, Rembrandt spent some six months training with Pieter Lastman in the latter's house in the Breestraat, at a time therefore when Uylenburgh had already settled in the city. Later – and certainly in 1628 – Uylenburgh was active in Leiden where Rembrandt was active as an independent artist. We don't know exactly why Uylenburgh needed the money, the document doesn't say. It has been suggested that Rembrandt bought himself into Uylenburgh's business in this way, but this is not really plausible. Firstly, it is far too large a sum of money; secondly Rembrandt stipulated the normal rate of interest and, if he wished, he could reclaim the entire loan after a year. But whatever the case, the loan marks the collaboration between Uylenburgh and Rembrandt, a collaboration that was to last for four years and saw Rembrandt executing commissions in Uylen-

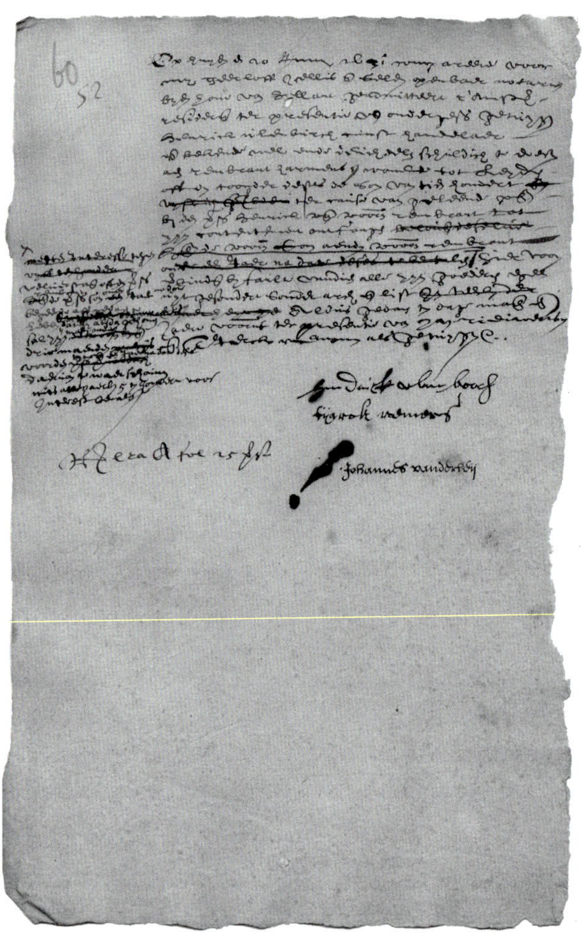

68 Document dating from 1631 in which Hendrick Uylenburgh declares that he has borrowed a thousand guilders from Rembrandt, Amsterdam, Gemeentearchief

36 Bredius/De Roever 1887, p. 213, Urk. no. 20 and Doc. 1631/4; the transcription in the Doc. is more complete because the level of the interest is given there, albeit omitted again from the English summary.
37 GAA, not. G. Jellisz Selden, NA 945, fol. 25v, 20 June 1631.
38 Ibid., NA 946, deed 52, p. 60, 20 June 1631; Bredius and De Roever saw this document, for they included a facsimile print of Hendrick Uylenburgh's signature in their article of 1887.
39 Gehlen 1986, p. 97.

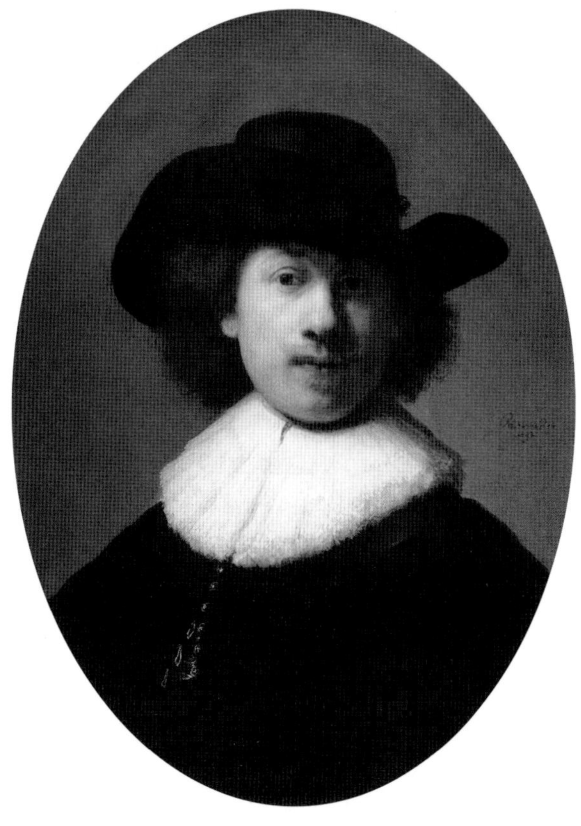

69 Rembrandt van Rijn, Self-portrait, signed and dated 'RHL van Ryn 1632', panel, 64.4 x 47.6 cm, Glasgow, The Burrell Collection (Br. 17; Corpus II A 58)

40 Doc. 1632/2 and 1634/2.
41 Doc. 1632/2.
42 Doc. 1635/1.
43 Van Eeghen 1969b, p. 87.
44 Orlers 1641, p. 375.
45 In this connection, one can point to the Leiden document in which Jan Lievens requested approval for a public sale of paintings at the end of August, 1630, together with three unnamed painters, Doc. 1630/3. Rembrandt could very well have been one of these artists. Lievens must have already conceived the plan to go to England, although he only put it into effect in early 1632. Perhaps Rembrandt had similarly decided at this time to go and work elsewhere.
46 Wijnman 1959, p. 2.

burgh's house. From various documents, we know that between 1631 and 1635 Rembrandt actually had his lodgings with Uylenburgh. The first record is from 1632, followed by the confirmation of his address on the occasion of his betrothal to Saskia Uylenburgh in 1634.[40] In 1632, it was recorded that Rembrandt 'logeerde' (lodged) at the house of the art dealer,[41] i.e. that he was either temporarily staying there, or had taken accommodation there for a longer period. When Rembrandt made a purchase at an art sale in Amsterdam in 1635, against the sum owed for the purchase of the item was written 'Rembrant van Rijn tot Hendrick Uylenburch'.[42] It was usual to record the name of the purchaser if he did not pay cash, because there was then money to be recovered. It has been suggested that the person whose name was written after that of the buyer stood surety for him,[43] but it is much more likely that the 'tot' should be taken as indicating Rembrandt's address.

The reason for Rembrandt's departure to Amsterdam is given by Jan Jansz Orlers in 1641 in the second edition of his account of the city of Leiden: 'Because his art and his work was so highly rated by the burghers and citizens of Amsterdam', wrote Rembrandt's well-informed fellow-citizen, 'and because he was so often requested to paint portraits and other pieces, he found it a good idea to move from Leiden to Amsterdam'. According to Orlers, Rembrandt left Leiden in 1630 and thenceforward resided in Amsterdam.[44] The data supplied here are accurate, as will be shown below, except that Rembrandt's departure from the city of his birth is given too early. The contact with Uylenburgh, however, could well date from this time.

Rembrandt's move to Amsterdam was not undertaken precipitately, but was probably a gradual one. In the latter part of 1631 and early 1632 he may well have kept up his Leiden studio, but it is doubtful whether he often spent time there.[45] The portraits he made during this period were, as far as we know, all commissioned in Amsterdam. It is certainly striking that not a single Leiden document concerning Rembrandt is known from 1631 onward. The previously mentioned statement of 1632 is very telling in this regard: in order to be able to see Rembrandt in the flesh, an Amsterdam notary was instructed from Leiden to visit Uylenburgh's house. Had Rembrandt been regularly returning to Leiden, it would certainly have been easier to await his arrival there. Perhaps his initial stay in Amsterdam was not definitive; we shall see below that he had not yet made a permanent base there, for in 1632 he was executing commissions in The Hague.

It was argued above that Uylenburgh, during his first five years in Amsterdam, was active solely as a merchant-art dealer, and that until 1630 he had no workshop of his own. If this is correct, the workshop was set up at the same time that Rembrandt took up employment with him in 1631. This is not a new proposition. Wijnman wrote that there was possibly a causal link 'between the origin of Uylenburgh's Art academy and Rembrandt's sojourn with the art dealer, for we do not know in what year the academy was founded'.[46] Whatever the case, Uylenburgh had very good contacts with the Mennonite merchants of Amsterdam, a number of whom wanted their portraits painted. Around 1630 there seems to have been an explosion in the demand for painted portraits,[47] and it may well have been this increase in demand that prompted Uylenburgh to look for a painter who could execute portrait commissions in his house. In Rembrandt he certainly found the right man (fig. 69).[48]

As far as we know, Rembrandt had not been given a single portrait commission in Leiden. The one possible exception is the so-called *Leiden History piece* from 1626. The subject of this painting is still disputed, but it is plausible that the figure in the foreground, the man with short hair and moustache and beard, who looks out at the viewer, is a portrait of the patron who commissioned the work.[49] Although Rembrandt may not yet have painted formal portraits during these years, he certainly made a thorough study of the human face. He painted 'tronies' from life and he practised the rendering of emotional expression in several studies and in various self-portraits for which he made a study of his own physiognomy in front of the mirror.[50]

However, it was only in Amsterdam that Rembrandt began painting individual portraits of his fellow-citizens. Toward the end of 1631 he produced three portraits that are remarkable for their high quality and grand scale. It is no accident that two of the three men portrayed belonged to Uylenburgh's Mennonite circle. The first work, dated 1631, is an imposing portrait of the Amsterdam merchant Nicolaes Ruts (fig. 70).[51] In the early modern period, portraits were usually only to be seen in domestic circles, but the portrait of Ruts, showing him in his capacity of dealer in furs, in all probability hung in his shop. Could Ruts perhaps have shown his portrait as testimony to his creditworthiness? The identity of the subject of the second portrait, a man at a writing table, is unknown (fig. 71). It could be said that Rembrandt reveals himself to be a history painter even in his portraits, since portraits like these are exceptional for the vitality with which their subjects are represented. In fact, this is his major innovatory contribution to the tradition of the large-scale individual portrait.

The third portrait on which Rembrandt worked in 1631 was that of Marten Looten (fig. 72).[52] Looten was another Amsterdam merchant who was also one of Uylenburgh's co-religionists,

another significant indication that it was the art dealer who attracted these portrait commissions and then had Rembrandt execute them. The painter dated the work in January, 1632. The production of portraits must have been extremely profitable for both Uylenburgh and Rembrandt:

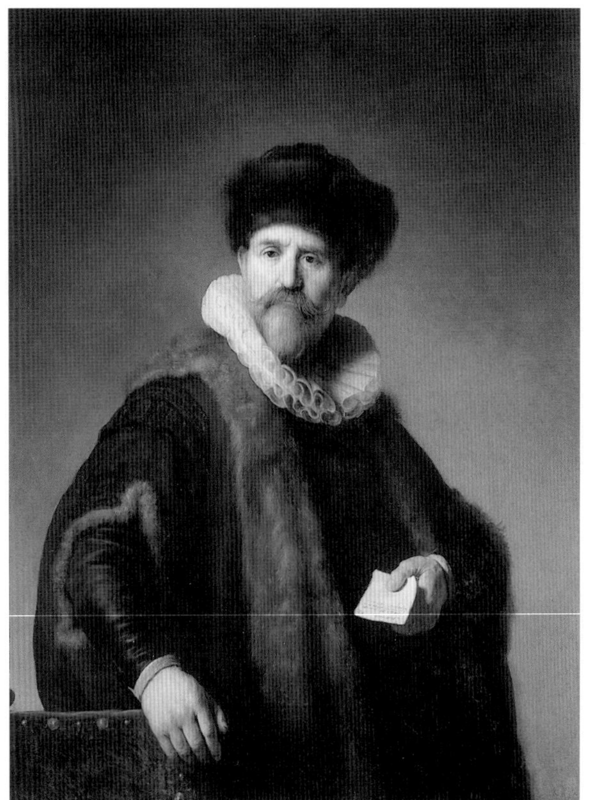

70 Rembrandt van Rijn, Portrait of Nicolaes Ruts, signed and dated 'RL. 1631', panel, 116 x 87 cm, New York, N.Y., The Frick Collection (Br. 145; Corpus II A 43)

71 Rembrandt van Rijn, Portrait of a man at a writing-desk, signed and dated 'RHL 1631', canvas, 104.4 x 91.8 cm, St Petersburg, The Hermitage Museum (Br. 146; Corpus II A 44)

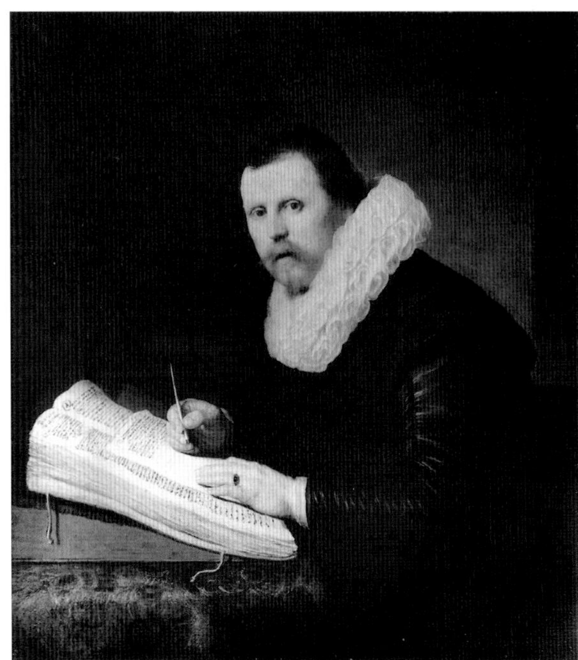

47 Ekkart 2002, p. 32.
48 In the following paragraphs, particularly Rembrandt's paintings from the first half of the 1630s that can be seen at the *Rembrandt & Co* exhibition at the Dulwich Picture Gallery and in the Rembrandthuis Museum will be dealt with in detail.
49 Br. 460 and Corpus I A 6. Van Straten 2005, pp. 47-48 and 301-313, sees in this man the Leiden merchant and art lover Matthijs van Overbeke (1584-1638).
50 For this, see Van de Wetering 2005.
51 Nicolaes Ruts was a Reformed member of a Mennonite family. His brother David Rutgers (Ruts) the Elder (d. 1623), member of the Waterland community in Amsterdam, was the father of Maria Rutgers (c. 1603/4-1652), who in 1628 married Ameldonck Leeuw, see pp. 174-175.
52 Br. 166 and Corpus II A 52.

72 Rembrandt van Rijn,
Portrait of Marten Looten,
signed and dated 'RHL / xj.
Januuary 1632', panel, 92.8 x
74.9 cm, Los Angeles,
California., Los Angeles County
Museum of Art (Br. 166;
Corpus II A 52)

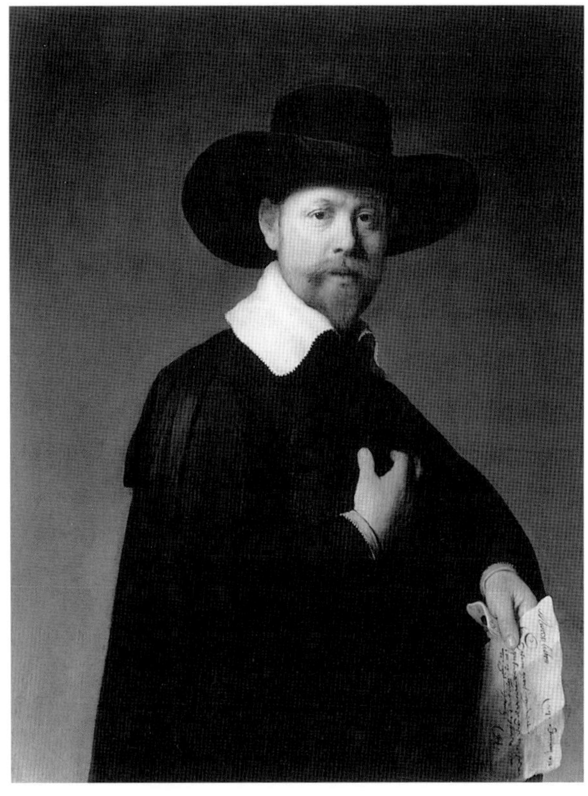

53 Bruyn 1986 gives several
examples.
54 Br. 169 and Corpus II A 48.
55 New York 1995-1996, vol.
2, no. 2 and Copenhagen 2006,
no. 5.
56 In the 1637 inventory of
Lambert Jacobsz is mentioned
'een schone jonge Turcksche
prince *nae* Remb.' (a handsome
young Turkish prince *after*
Rembrandt) (see below pp.
175-182); in 1639 there is mention of 'een Turx tronie *nae*
Rembrant' (a Turkish tronie
after Rembrandt), in 1646 of
'een Turcxe tronie *van* Rembrandt' (a Turkish tronie *by*
Rembrandt) and in 1648 of
'een Turcxe tronie *van* Rembrant' (a Turkish tronie *by*
Rembrandt), valued at 30
guilders.
57 New York 1995-1996, vol.
2, p. 45 and below p. 178, note
175.
58 See p. 184.

not only did they sell for very good money,
patrons not infrequently went on to a further
purchase.[53] Because they usually posed more than
once in the workshop they were able to see what
other works were in stock, which could lead to a
purchase or an order. This is what seems to have
happened in the case of the wealthy Looten, who
was probably the first owner of the *Man in oriental
dress* (fig. 73). At least, this painting which originated in the same year as his portrait, 1632, was
later to be found in the possession of a grandson
of Looten.[54] In this monumental figure piece,
Rembrandt has lighted only the head and upper
part of the body. The interaction of light and
shadow in the painting contributes strongly to
the effect the painter must have intended here.
The work does not seem to have been conceived
as a specific portrait of an oriental man so much
as the image of a figure with a very striking head
and wrapped in an exotic costume.[55] There was a
large market in the Republic for such large-scale
figure pieces and for tronies of people in strange
attire. We know of various reports before 1650 of
similar pieces by and after Rembrandt.[56] Dutch
models normally posed for these pieces; the man
who modelled for Rembrandt's *Man in oriental
dress* was probably the same who posed for Jacob
Backer.[57] We shall see too that Maria van Eyck
was painted by Rembrandt in 'oriental' fashion
in her husband's workshop.[58]

During this period, Rembrandt's work as a
portraitist was to a large degree his main production. If we estimate the total number of his
painted portraits produced between 1625 and
1669, in so far as we can judge from those that
have been preserved and from contemporary
documents, these amount to around a hundred
works. Almost half of these originated during the
years 1631-1635, the one period in Rembrandt's
career when he produced a steady stream of portraits. It was this production which laid the basis
for his financial prosperity and Uylenburgh
played a crucial role in this: it was he who looked
after the commissions and brought Rembrandt
into his house where most of these commissioning patrons would have posed. Little or nothing is
known of how the prestigious commission came
about that led Rembrandt to paint the group of
seven Amsterdam surgeons with their demonstra-
tor Nicolaes Tulp (fig. 74). The *Anatomy lesson of
Nicolaes Tulp* must have been painted in the early
months of 1632, but the commission would have
been agreed earlier. That Rembrandt was chosen
for this group portrait must have been rather sensational since he was still a relative newcomer and
had not yet demonstrated that he could master a
work of such a large size. One can only speculate
on Uylenburgh's part in gaining this commission,
but it is scarcely conceivable that he was not in
some way involved, quite apart from the fact that
it would have been executed in his house.

From the summer of 1631, then, Rembrandt
executed portrait commissions in Amsterdam
for Uylenburgh. They would have made verbal
agreements, no doubt, and in the course of time
their collaboration would have become closer
and Rembrandt must have lived virtually permanently in Uylenburgh's house. The question is
whether Uylenburgh put their collaboration on a
contractual basis at some point. We know nothing
about payment. Presumably Rembrandt would
have been paid for each painting and Uylenburgh
also received a commission. There would have

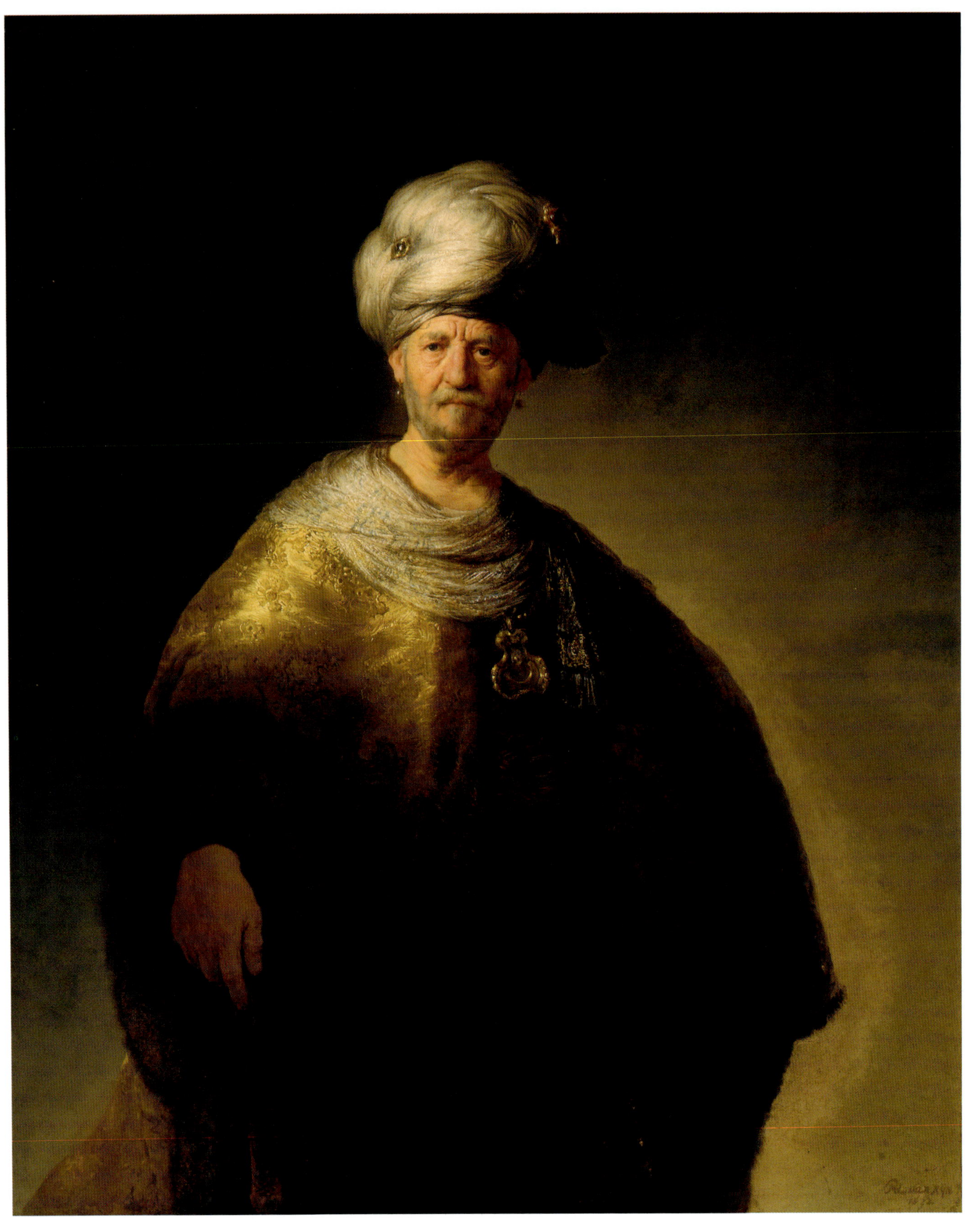

73 Rembrandt van Rijn, Man in oriental dress, known as 'The Noble Slav', signed and dated 'RHL van Rijn 1632', canvas, 152.7 x 111.1 cm, New York, N.Y., The Metropolitan Museum of Art (Br. 169; Corpus II A 48)

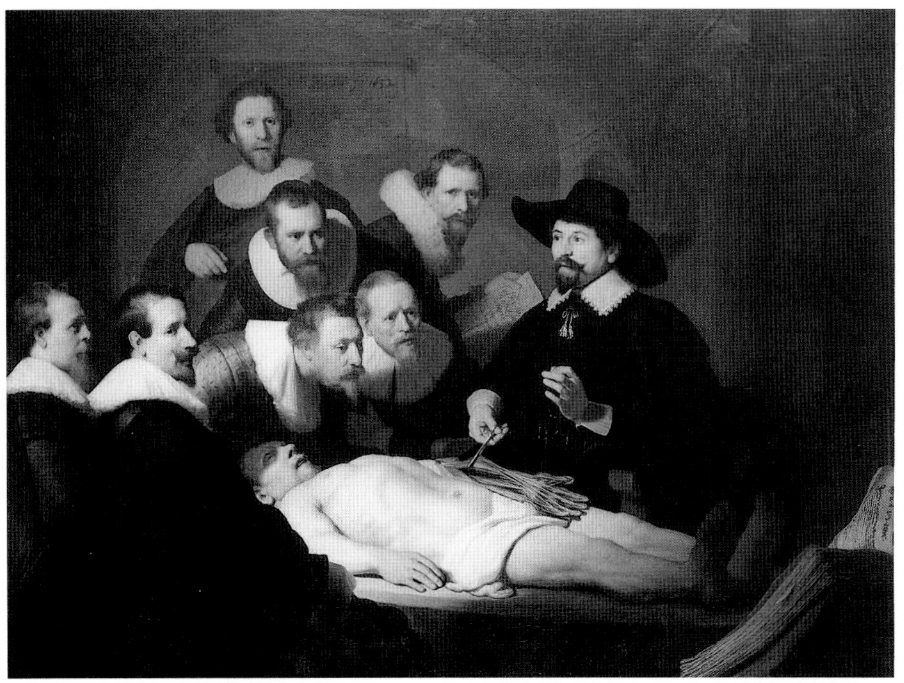

74 Rembrandt van Rijn, The anatomy lesson of Nicolaes Tulp, signed and dated 'Rembrant. f 1632', canvas, 169.5 x 216.5 cm, The Hague, Koninklijk Kabinet van Schilderijen, Mauritshuis (Br. 403; Corpus II A 51)

Christ. The passage just cited from the letter to Huygens refers to this so-called Passion series. Rembrandt's portrait of Amalia van Solms in profile may possibly have served as a pendant to the portrait of Frederik Hendrik by Gerrit van Honthorst, although the pieces did not actually hang beside each other.[61] It is doubtful whether Uylenburgh was responsible for the contacts with the court, however, for Rembrandt had already supplied the court with history pieces, to wit *Samson and Delilah* and *Simeon in the temple*.[62] It is generally accepted that it was Constantijn Huygens, the influential secretary to the Stadholder, who was responsible for these purchases. Huygens, after all, played a huge role in the selection for the art collection of Frederik Hendrik and Amalia and around 1630. In his autobiographical writing, he praised highly the exceptional qualities that, as he saw it, promised so much for Rembrandt's future and the good contacts that held between the Huygens family and the painter are

been some settlement – possibly with written agreements – governing the payment of overheads and the cost of bed and board, while one can only speculate about the practical arrangements for the production. It will be shown below that when Govert Flinck worked with Uylenburgh, he was more or less given the freedom to paint whatever he wished. It could hardly have been different in the case of Rembrandt, except that he had his hands full with portrait commissions – which did not all come from Amsterdam, incidentally. In 1632 Rembrandt worked for a while for the Stadholder's court in The Hague and at that time painted the portrait of Amalia van Solms (fig. 75).[59] In the same period Rembrandt painted the portraits of at least four other persons who lived in The Hague, in all probability producing these pieces there. We can deduce that Rembrandt was actually in The Hague from a passage in a letter he wrote to Constantijn Huygens, in which he reports on the paintings he had been working on for the court and observes that they would be best seen in the gallery 'because there is a strong light there'.[60]

Rembrandt's stay in The Hague can be directly linked with work that he undertook for the court. During the course of the thirties he painted a series of – in total – seven scenes from the life of

59 Br. 99 and Corpus II A 61.
60 Doc. 1636/2.
61 The Hague 1997-1998, pp. 132-141.
62 Br. 489 and Corpus I A 24 ; respectively Br. 543 and Corpus I A 34.

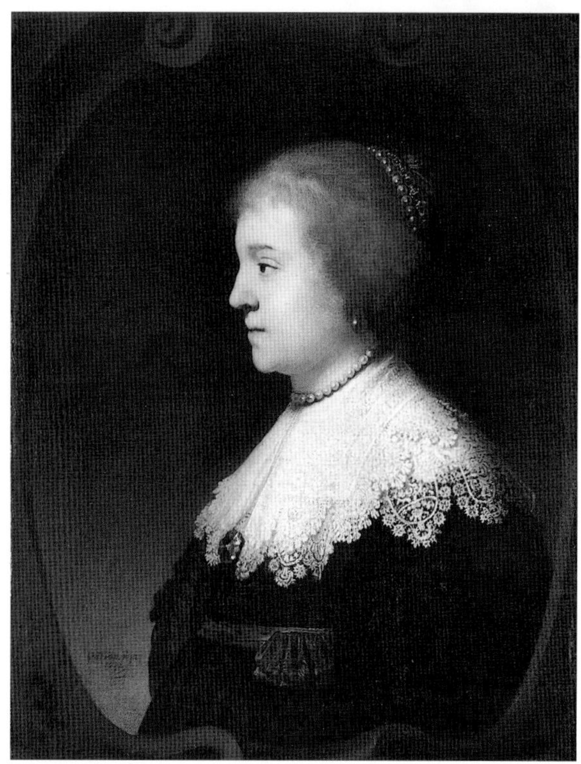

75 Rembrandt van Rijn, Portrait of Amalia van Solms, signed and dated 'RHL van Ryn 1632', canvas, 69.5 x 54.5 cm, Paris, Institut de France, Musée Jacquemart-André (Br. 99; Corpus II A 61)

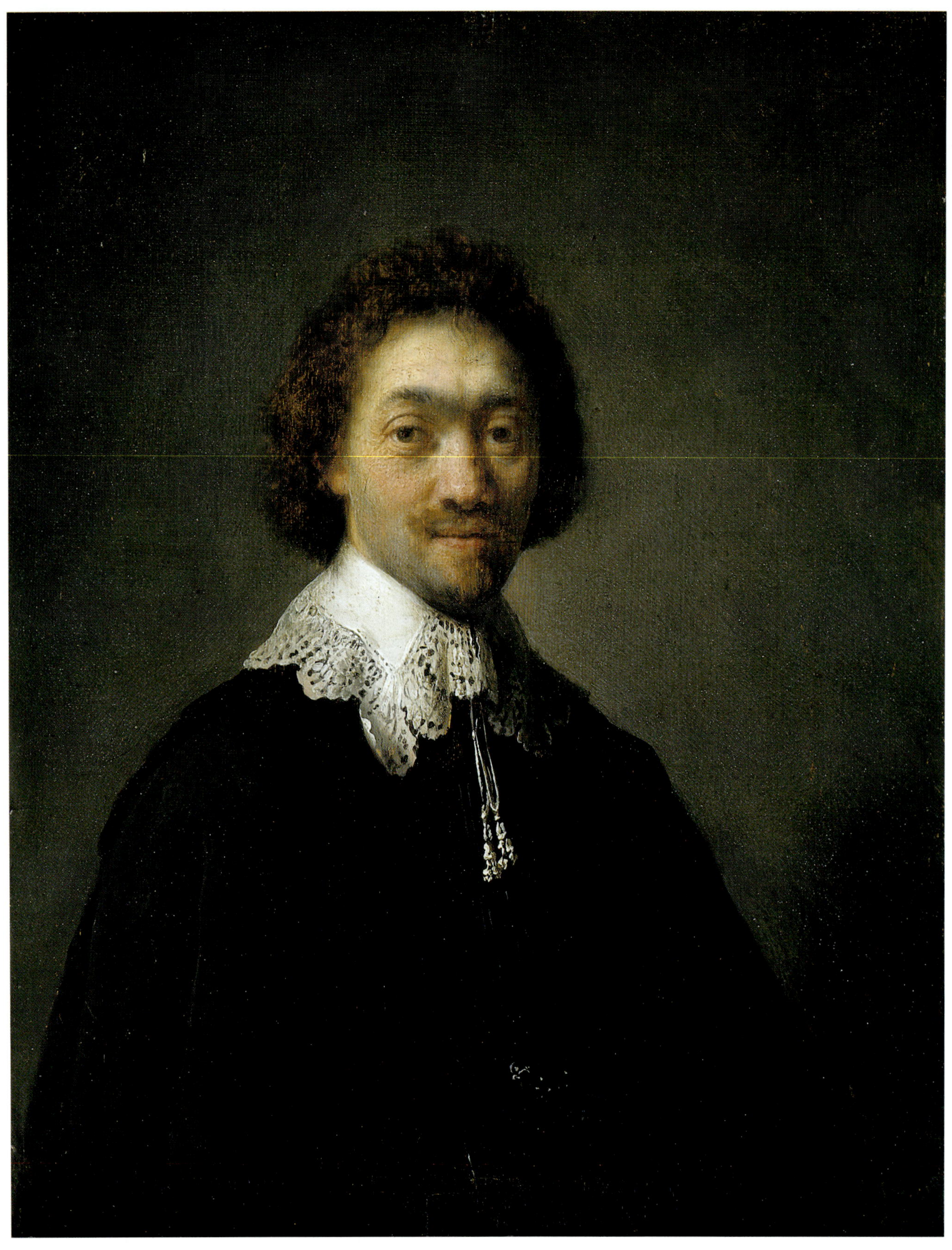

76 Rembrandt van Rijn, Portrait of Maurits Huygens, signed and dated 'RH. van Rij[n] 1632', panel, 31.1 x 24.5 cm, Hamburg, Hamburger Kunsthalle (Br. 161; Corpus II A 57)

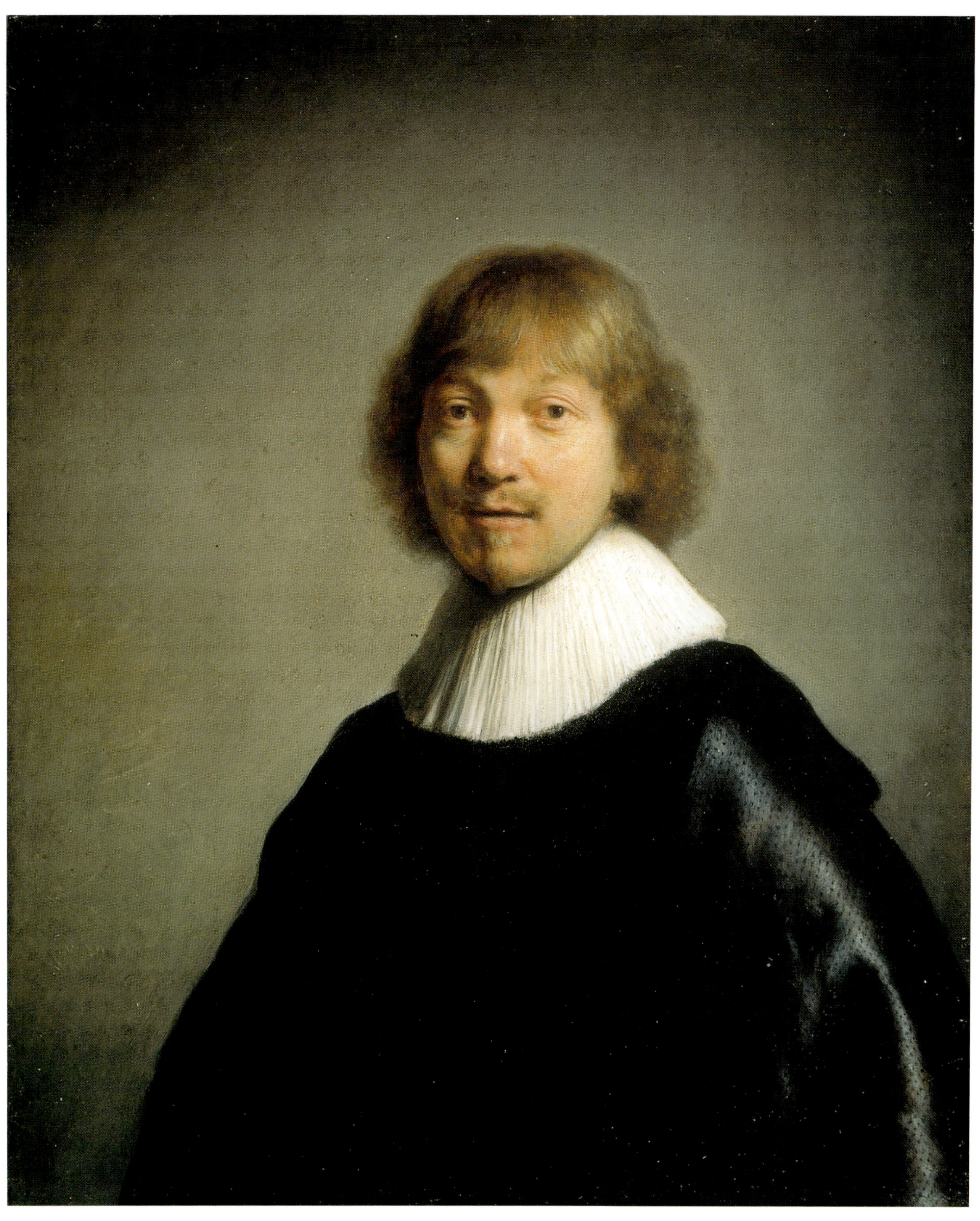

77 Rembrandt van Rijn, Portrait of Jacques de Gheyn, signed and dated 'RH van Ryn 1632', panel, 29.9 x 24.9 cm, London, Dulwich Picture Gallery (Br. 162; Corpus II A 56)

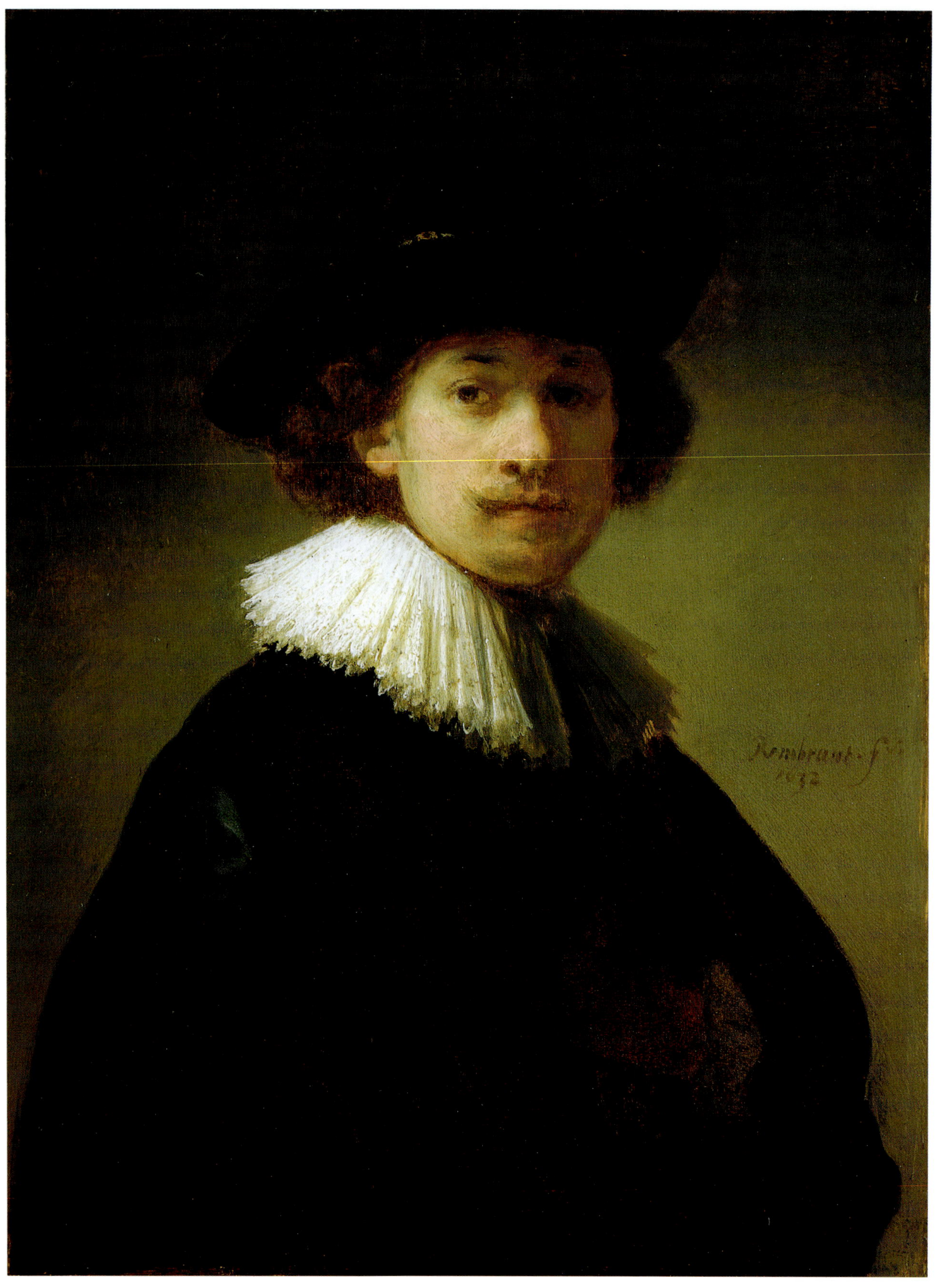

78 Rembrandt van Rijn, Self-portrait, signed and dated 'Rembrant. f 1632', panel, 21.8 x 16.3 cm, private collection United States (Corpus IV Add. 1)

79 Rembrandt van Rijn, Portrait of Joris de Caullery, signed and dated 'RHL van Ryn 1632', canvas stuck on panel, 102.5 x 83.8 cm, San Francisco, California, Fine Arts Museums of San Francisco, Roscoe and Margaret Oakes Collection (Br. 170; Corpus II A 53)

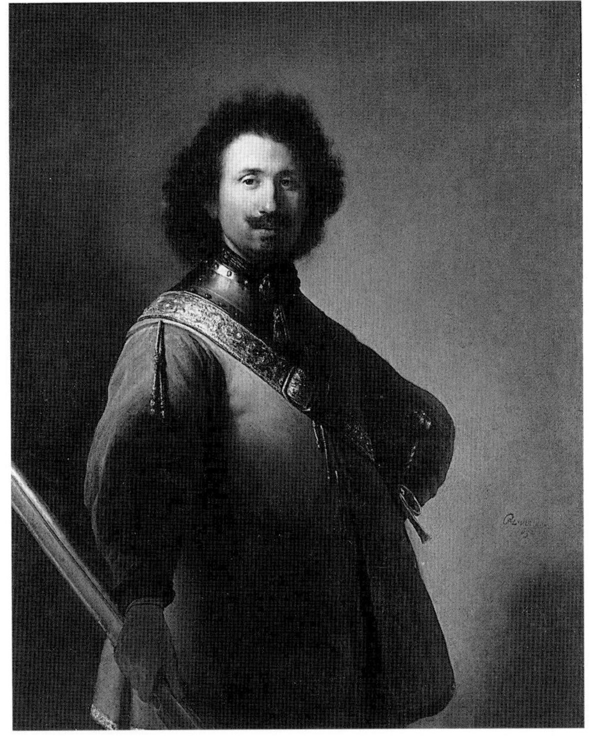

also evident from the portrait that Rembrandt painted in 1632 of Maurits Huygens (fig. 76), an elder brother of Constantijn.[63] The effigy of Maurits' friend Jacques de Gheyn served as a pendant (fig. 77).[64] We know the latter owned a choice art collection that contained several early works by Rembrandt.

Art-lovers in the seventeenth century were particularly interested in self-portraits by artists whom they admired. In this context, one can point to a small portrait of Rembrandt dated 1632 which, after restoration and after thorough investigation by Van de Wetering, can now be accepted as an autograph work. This small self-portrait shows Rembrandt in half-figure, dressed in smart, fashionable attire with a pleated collar and wearing a dark hat (fig. 78).[65] Dendrochronological research has demonstrated that the panel on which this self-portrait is painted was cut from the same wood on which Rembrandt painted the portrait of Maurits Huygens around the same time. The attribution to Rembrandt is based on the artistic qualities of this work and also on the presence of pentimenti rendered visible by X-radiography. These changes have been introduced into the contours of the body and the hat.

Corrections of this kind, carried out during the realization of the image, were hardly likely to have been done by copyists. The signature has been introduced in the wet paint. The reliability of the signature can hardly be doubted, and the form of this signature – 'Rembrant' – is highly significant, for there was only a short period during which Rembrandt used this form of his signature, from late 1632 to early 1633. It is therefore tempting to assume that the small self-portrait was not only painted by Rembrandt in The Hague, but that – in view of its unusually small size – it is associated with the portraits of De Gheyn and Huygens, either purchased by or presented to one of these two patrons. One tends to think first of Maurits Huygens as candidate for the honour, but no inventory of his possessions is known.

The portrait of Joris de Caullery is the last of this group of portraits to be mentioned that were painted in The Hague (fig. 79).[66] There is mention in a legal document from 1654 of portraits of this individual painted by various artists, including Anthony van Dyck and Jan Lievens. The piece reproduced here is described in that deed as 'het conterfeytsel' (the likeness) of himself, the deponent, with a firearm in his hand done by mr. Rembrant'.[67] Nor did it rest there: in 1661 there was mention of the portrait of Joris de Caullery's son Johan, similarly painted by Rembrandt – and I presume at the same time as the father's portrait. That portrait, however, appears not to have survived.[68] Although Joris de Caullery is depicted in his capacity as a lieutenant of the musketeers' militia, he was also during this period the owner of 'de Grote Zwaan', a fashionable hostelry in The Hague. It is therefore by no means inconceivable that Rembrandt could have taken lodgings at this inn during his stay in The Hague, and consequently came to paint the portraits – possibly even as a form of payment – of father and son De Caullery. The same could equally be true in the case of Van Dyck, who also stayed for some time in the court-capital for reasons of work.

The portraits that Rembrandt executed in The Hague are without exception wholly autograph works. In the brief time that he worked there, Rembrandt would have had no assistant at his

63 Br. 161 and Corpus II A 57.
64 Br. 162 and Corpus II A 56.
65 Corpus IV Add. 1; first published in Van de Wetering 1997.
66 Br. 170 and Corpus II A 53.
67 Doc. 1654/9.
68 Doc. 1661/7. The *Portrait of a young man* from 1632 (Br. 155) has been thought incorrectly to be the portrait of Johan de Caullery, see Corpus II A 60.

disposal. But what was the situation in Amsterdam? It is conceivable that he may have taken an assistant with him from Leiden. In his Leiden period he had had Gerrit Dou and Isaac Jouderville as pupils and one cannot exclude the possibility that Jouderville, whose guardian paid Rembrandt for his tuition between 1629 and 1631, may have accompanied his master to Amsterdam. If so, he would have been one of the first assistants in Uylenburgh's workshop. After a while, with the increase in the number of commissions, one or more assistants would have contributed a share to the execution of constantly growing series of portraits. No documents have been recovered concerning any of the painters who worked in Uylenburgh's workshop during these years. Rembrandt would still have worked on his own on the individual, large-scale portraits mentioned above, but it may well be the case that Uylenburgh's workshop gradually developed from 1632 onward into the well-organized business enterprise so often referred to in the literature, with different advanced assistants capable of taking an active part in the work of production.

The portrait of Johannes Wtenbogaert is a case in point where a painting by Rembrandt seems to have benefited from assistance.[69] According to the record in his own diary, this prominent Remonstrant preacher only posed for Rembrandt for part of a single day on April 13th, 1633. Wtenbogaert was simply not in Amsterdam over the following days. Rembrandt would have concentrated particularly on the face and on the composition as a whole and subsequently the painting would have been finished in the workshop. Perhaps Rembrandt sketched the positioning of the preacher's hands during the sitting and left their execution, and perhaps other minor constituent parts of the portrait, to an assistant. In this context, it is important that the portrait had been ordered by an enthusiastic admirer of this influential preacher who first and foremost would have wanted a good likeness and would not have minded if he knew that a particular part of the painting had not been executed by Rembrandt himself. Whether this happened more often in Uylenburgh's workshop is difficult to say; quite possibly it was an accepted practice in large work-

shops with an on-going production of portraits.

Assistance in the execution, as in the case of the Wtenbogaert portrait, raises the question of who that assistant could have been. The Rembrandt Research Project takes the view that in the thirties Rembrandt must have had various pupils and collaborators at his disposal[70] although it is impossible to be certain of the names of young painters who may have worked in Uylenburgh's workshop. In several publications, Liedtke has opposed this idea that there were several painters active in the workplace. In his view, a number of paintings whose attribution to Rembrandt has been doubted were indeed from his hand, while other paintings that have been attributed to Rembrandt's assistants did not originate in the workshop at all.[71] It may be wondered whether Uylenburgh's workshop was essentially differently organized from other seventeenth-century workshops engaged in large-scale production. Probably not, as far as the interior set-up was concerned; but it is certainly possible that there were young painters working in Uylenburgh's workshop who had already had several years' training behind them and were capable of actively contributing to production. Perhaps another exceptional feature of Uylenburgh's enterprise was the combination of a productive workshop with the purchase and retail of art on a large scale.

Given the extent of the production, after a while Rembrandt must have had several collaborators. He probably assumed the role – as Govert Flinck did after him – of the active head of the workshop, whereas Uylenburgh was responsible for running the business. Uylenburgh could also have hired in extra forces whenever there was a particularly heavy load of work to be completed. We don't know, because the documentation is lacking, but there is evidence that Dirck Dircksz Santvoort (b. 1610/11), who lived quite close to Uylenburgh's house in the Breestraat, had connections with the workshop. In such of his works as have survived, he comes across as an accomplished portraitist who was also highly skilled in painting lace collars. Contact with Uylenburgh's workshop is evident from two signed copies of works after Rembrandt: the latter's self-portrait from 1632 (see fig. 69) and the portrait of a young

69 Br. 173 and Corpus II A 80; for the entries in Wtenbogaert's diary see Doc. 1633/2. Rembrandt would make an etched portrait in 1635 (B. 279).
70 Corpus vol. 2 and 3; in the essay by E. van de Wetering in vol. 2, pp. 45-90, considerable attention was paid to the collaboration between Rembrandt and Hendrick Uylenburgh.
71 Liedtke 2004, pp. 65-67 and passim, Liedtke 1989 and Liedtke 1997.

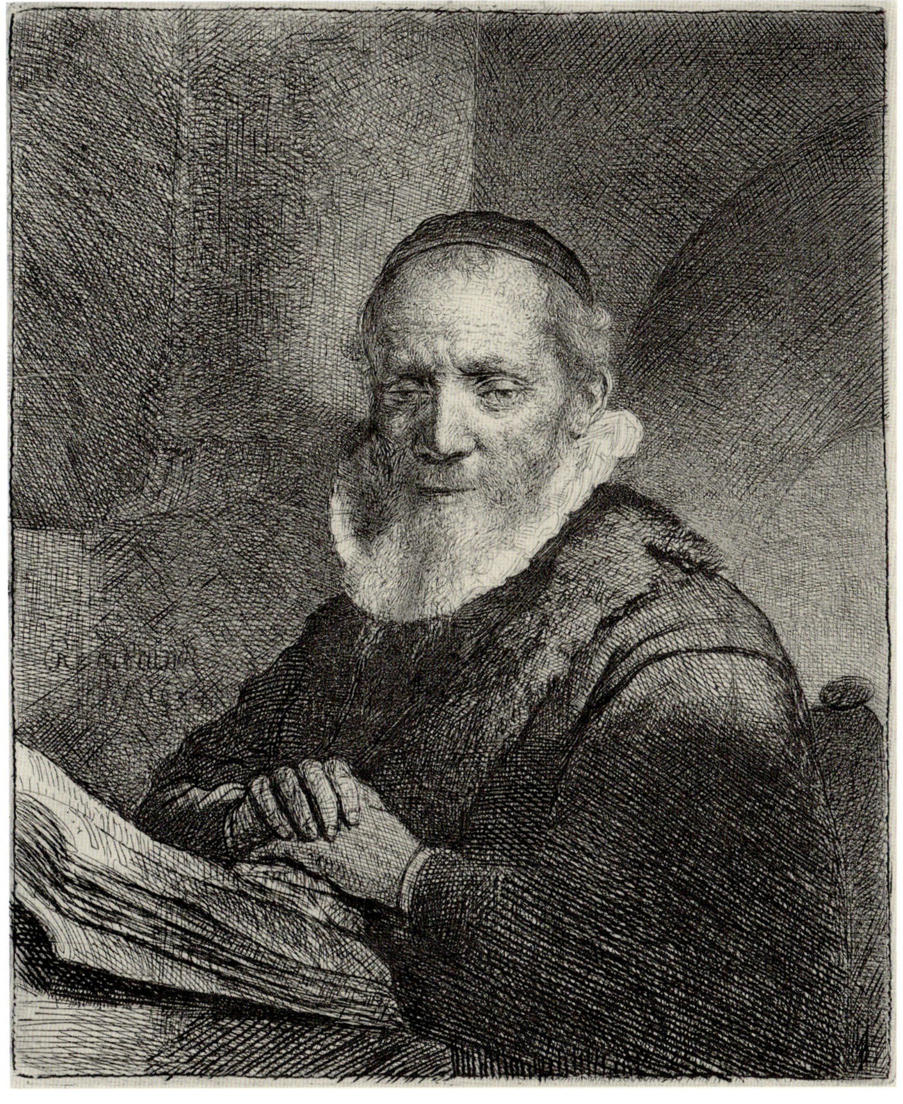

80 Rembrandt van Rijn, Portrait of Johannes Cornelisz Sylvius, signed and dated 'Rembrandt f 1633, etching, 16.6 x 14.1 cm, Amsterdam, The Rembrandt House Museum (B. 266 I, 3)

but only became a member of the Amsterdam St Lucas Guild in 1636.

Of Rembrandt's portraits from the first half of the thirties that have survived, the identity of roughly half the sitters is known with a high degree of certainty. In Amsterdam, the commissions for portraits continued to stream in: from merchants, preachers and scholars, figures of authority of various stripe, and individuals with whom he had either a business or a more personal connection. They needed to possess considerable wealth, for in the seventeenth century a painted portrait was certainly not cheap. Rembrandt in particular asked the highest prices, and as a portraitist he was also highly sought after. We know that various patrons were of the same religious denomination as Uylenburgh, while several members of Uylenburgh's family – or of Rembrandt's family – bought or were presented with a painted portrait. Several examples can be given. The connection with the Amsterdam preacher Johannes Sylvius and his wife Aeltje Uylenburgh has already been alluded to: Rembrandt and Saskia maintained a close relationship with them.[75] Saskia, the daughter of a brother of Aeltje's father, was thus a first, although much younger cousin to Aeltje. Aeltje's husband assumed the role of Saskia's guardian and he accompanied her at the public announcement of her intended marriage to Rembrandt, on several occasions later acting as witness at the christening of her children. Once, in 1638, he himself baptized a daughter of Saskia and Rembrandt. How good the relationship was can be judged from the following hitherto unpublished information: whereas the baptism of the eldest child of a daughter of the Sylvius-Uylenburgh couple was witnessed by the grandparents, it was 'Saskia Ulenburgh van Rijn' who was present at the christening of the youngest child Aeltje in 1637.[76] This is the sole occasion on which Rembrandt's wife is referred to as such in a document.

woman with an embroidered dress.[72] In addition, Santvoort's *Supper at Emmaus* in the Louvre, signed and dated 1632, refers back to Rembrandt's earlier version of the same subject.[73] As a further argument, one can point to an entry in the 1647 inventory of the married couple Jarich Lubberts and Reijncke Gerrits of 'a trony *after* Rembrant *by* Dirck van Santvoort', a work valued at ten guilders by Uylenburgh, who would unquestionably have taken the attribution into account.[74] Santvoort dated his paintings from 1632 onward,

72 Br. 17 and Corpus II A 58, and Br. 87 and Corpus II C 57 (as possibly by Dirck Santvoort), and Schatborn 1981, p. 40 and figs. 25 and 26.

73 Foucart 1988, no. 30, and Br. 539 and Corpus I A 16.

74 See p. 171.

75 See pp. 15-16.

76 GAA, DTB 42, p. 49, 25 October 1637; with thanks to Ruud Lambour. It is worth mentioning that Thomas Thomasz Uylenburgh (c.1614/5-1679), a son of Aeltje Uylenburgh's youngest brother, and his wife Titie Taeckes (d. 1666) had a son in 1654 whom they named Titus. Maria Sylvia, the mother of the Aeltje born in 1637, attended as a witness at his baptism, GAA, DTB 105, p. 23, 13 December 1654. At the time of his marriage in 1680, this Titus Uylenburgh was a mariner by profession.

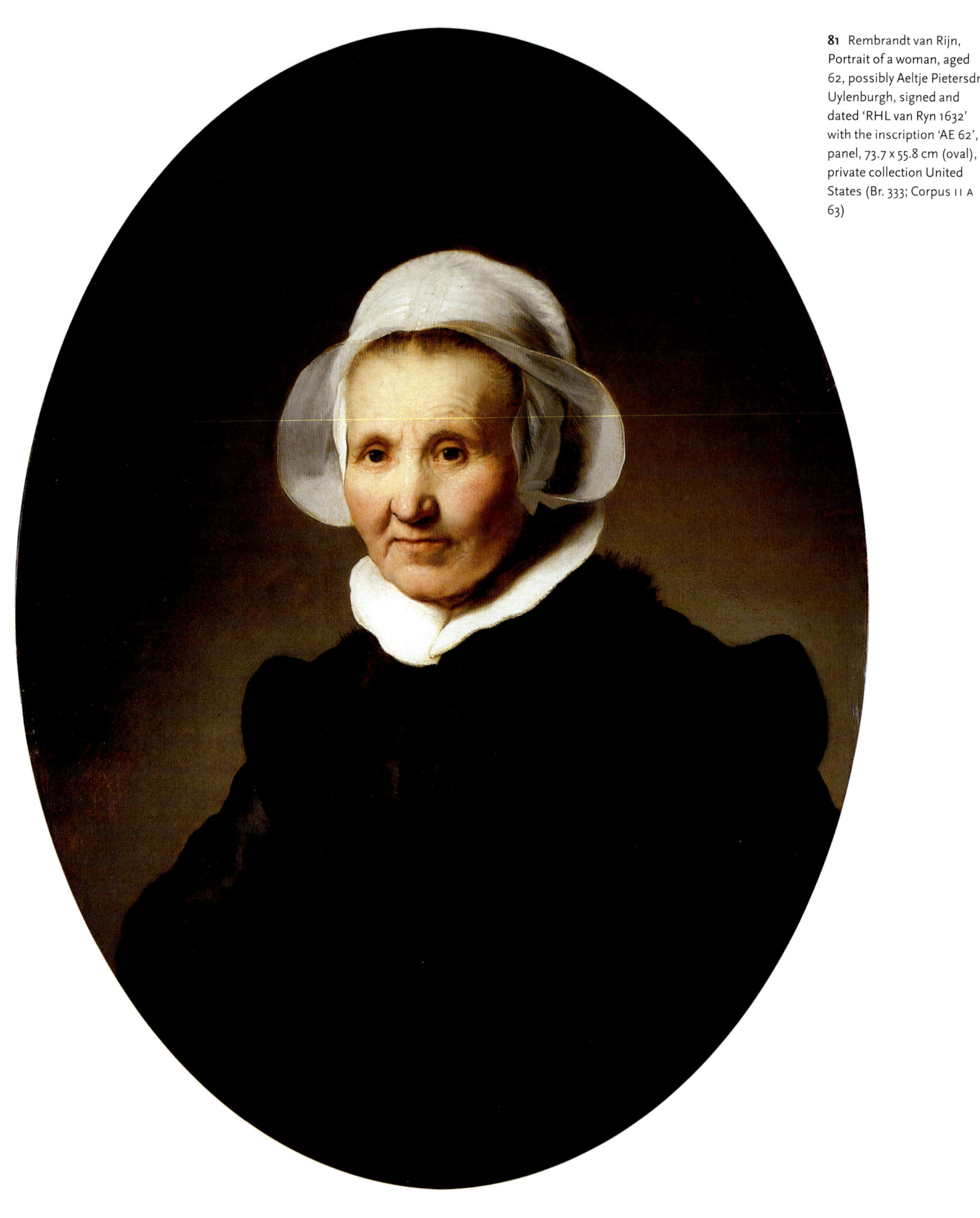

81 Rembrandt van Rijn, Portrait of a woman, aged 62, possibly Aeltje Pietersdr Uylenburgh, signed and dated 'RHL van Ryn 1632' with the inscription 'AE 62', panel, 73.7 x 55.8 cm (oval), private collection United States (Br. 333; Corpus II A 63)

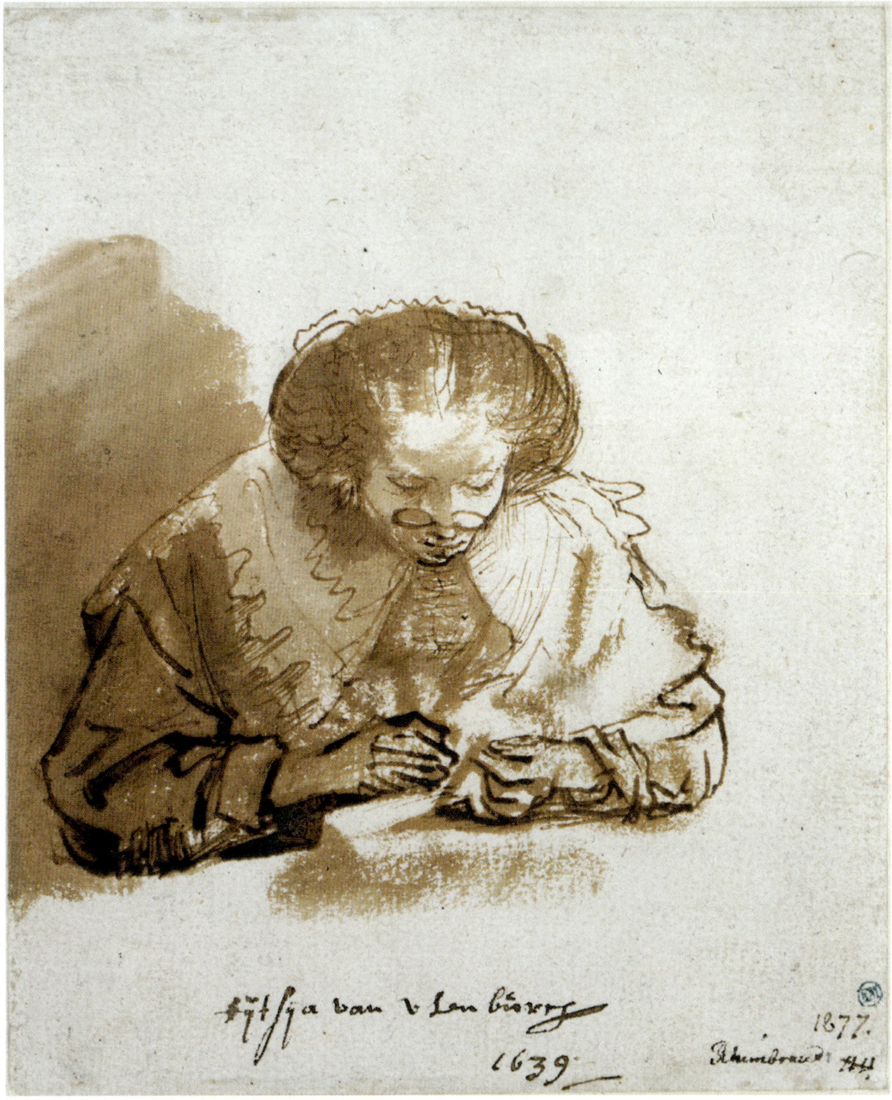

82 Rembrandt van Rijn, Portrait of Titia Uylenburgh, dated '1639', pen and brush, 17.4 x 14.6 cm, Stockholm, Nationalmuseum (Ben. 441)

77 B. 266. A second, posthumously produced portrait etching comes from 1646 (B. 280). Preliminary drawings for this etching are known.

78 B. 268.

79 The passage from the will and the identification were first published by me in Christie's sale catalogue, London, December 13th, 2000, no. 52. Confirmation of Aeltje Uylenburgh's year of birth is to be found in a manuscript genealogy of the family in a States Bible (the Dutch Authorized Version) that belonged to the Sylvius family (in 2005 owned by Antiquariaat Forum).

80 Br. 333 and Corpus II A 63.

81 On the reverse side of a contemporary copy of the portrait of the woman in the Anhaltische Gemäldegalerie in Dessau is written 'H. Roos', that is Johann Heinrich Roos (1631-1685). This German painter moved to Amsterdam with his parents in 1640 and entered into apprenticeship in 1647 with Guilliam du Gardijn (1618-1667). In 1650 or shortly thereafter Roos left for Italy, see Th.-B. vol. 28, p. 579, where it is recorded that Roos also trained in Amsterdam with Cornelis de Bie (c. 1621/2-1664) and Barend Graat (1628-1709), which is not, however, very likely. Given his work as a copyist, one wonders whether Roos could have worked for Uylenburgh?

Given this connection, it is no surprise that Rembrandt portrayed various members of the Sylvius and Uylenburgh families. In 1633 he made a portrait etching of Johannes Sylvius (fig. 80).[77] In 1637 he etched the portrait of a young man who, on the basis of a seventeenth century inscription on a specimen print is identified as Petrus Sylvius, a son of the Sylvius-Uylenburgh couple.[78] There were also painted portraits. In 1681 the eldest son of the Sylvius-Uylenburghs bequeathed 'the two likenesses of the present testator's father and mother painted by Rembrandt van Rijn'.[79] There is a very suitable candidate for one of these portraits, a painting of a woman dressed in a dark costume offset with fur and with a white bonnet on her head (fig. 81).[80] On the basis of the year of her birth, which must have been around 1571, and the possession by the eldest son of a pair of portraits painted by Rembrandt, it is very likely that this painting depicts the 62 year-old Aeltje Pietersdr Uylenburgh. Rembrandt paid careful attention to the execution of this portrait. X-radiographs show that the contours of the body were twice re-worked in order to enhance the three-dimensionality of the portrait. After her death in 1644 the portrait together with its pendant must have been inherited by the eldest son, while conceivably copies could have been made for the other children.[81]

Another married couple with whom Rembrandt and Saskia had close relations was that of Saskia's elder sister Titia Uylenburgh and her hus-

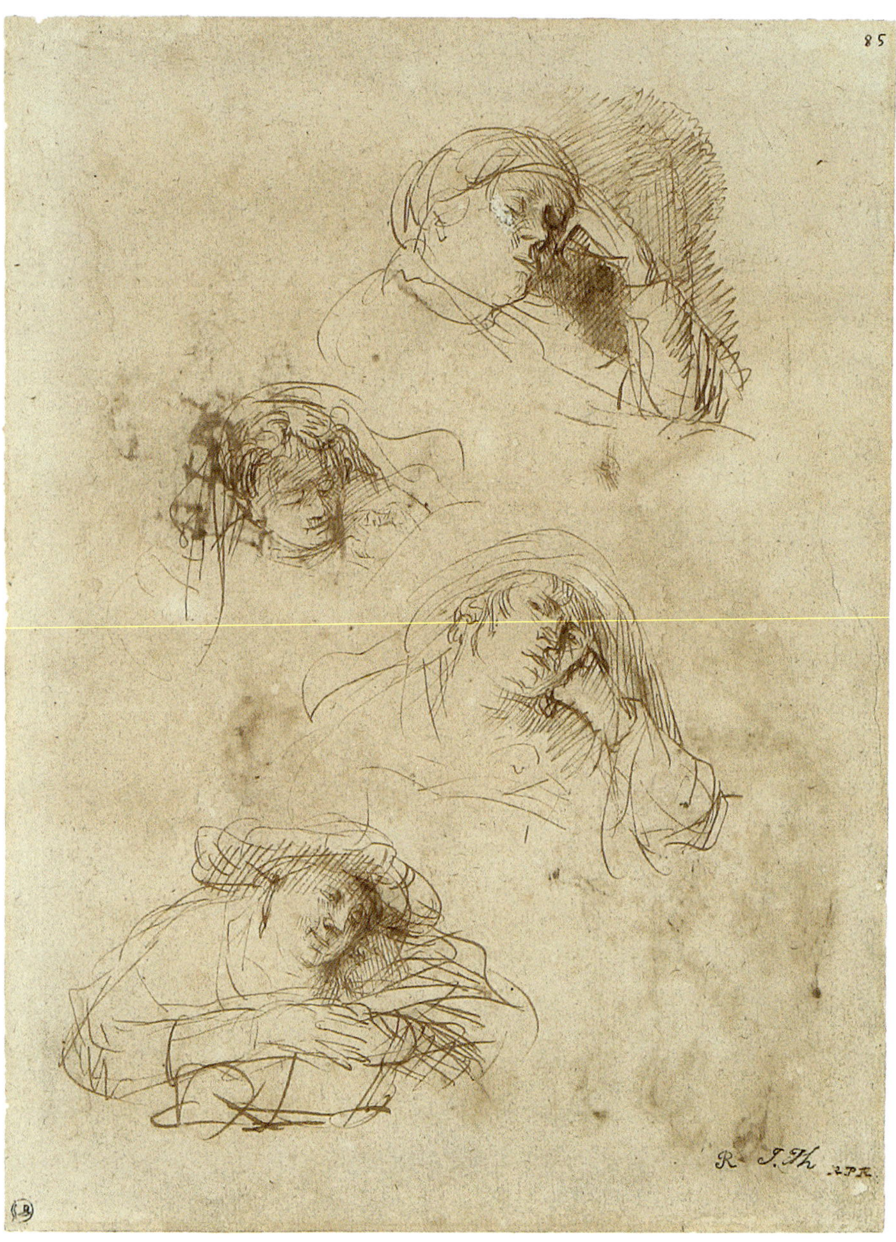

83 Rembrandt van Rijn, Four studies of Saskia, pen and brown ink, washed in grey and corrected in white, 20 x 15 cm, Rotterdam, Boijmans Van Beuningen Museum (Ben. 360)

band François Coopal.[82] Titia was asked to act as a witness at the baptism of several of Saskia and Rembrandt's children. At the baptism of the eldest child, Rumbartus, on December 15th, 1635, the Coopal-Uylenburgh couple were unable to attend but were represented by Johannes Sylvius and Aeltje Uylenburgh.[83] At the christening of Saskia's second child on July 22nd, 1638, Titia was a witness while Sylvius baptized the child.[84] For the third child, baptized on July 29th, 1640, François Coopal and Titia Uylenburgh were asked to be godparents.[85] Titus' baptism on September 22nd, 1641 was witnessed by Gerrit van Loo, who had mar-

ried Saskia's sister Hiskia Uylenburgh, by François Coopal and by Aeltje Uylenburgh.[86] Titus was in all probability named after his aunt Titia, who died in Vlissingen shortly before he was born. Saskia must have been very attached to her sister. In 1639 Rembrandt drew an intimate portrait of his sister-in-law (fig. 82) in which one sees Titia Uylenburgh with pince-nez, immersed in her handiwork.[87] The annotation and dating is in Rembrandt's handwriting: 'tijtsija van Ulenburch 1639'. Rembrandt's drawing is not a direct portrait study so much as a genre-like portrait that could have served the function of a family document. Rem-

82 For members of the Coopal family, see Broos 2005.
83 Doc. 1635/6.
84 Doc. 1638/8.
85 Doc. 1640/5.
86 Doc. 1641/4.
87 Ben. 441.

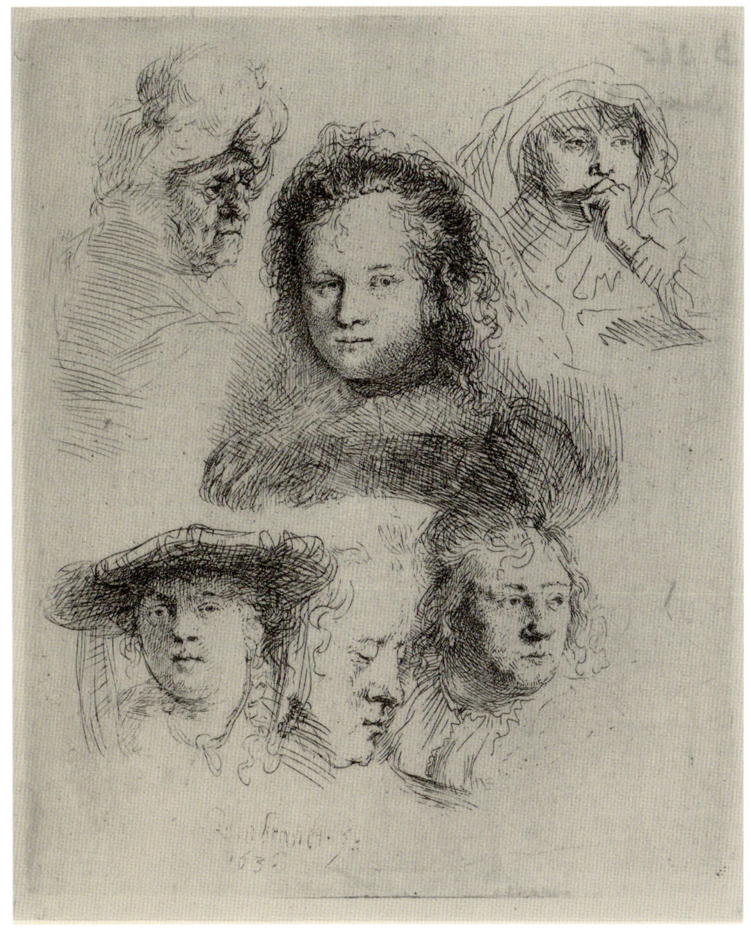

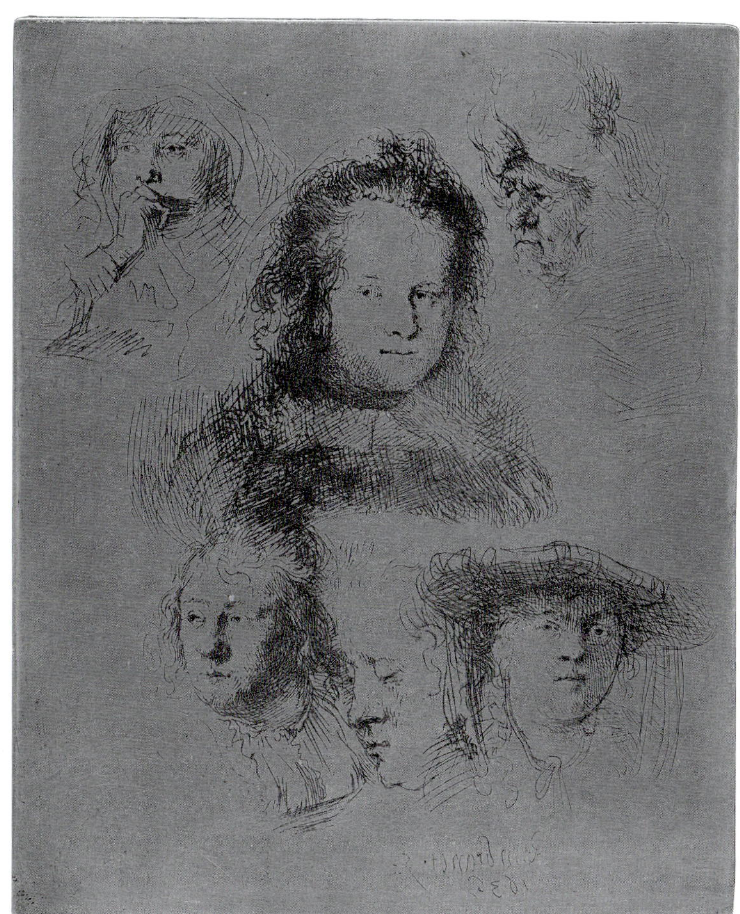

84 Rembrandt van Rijn, Five studies of Saskia and one of an old woman, signed and dated 'Rembrandt. f 1636', etching, 15.1 x 12.6 cm, Amsterdam, The Rembrandt House Museum (B. 365, only state)

85 The original copper plate of B. 365, Amsterdam, The Rembrandt House Museum

brandt would have drawn her, no doubt, on one of her visits to Amsterdam. It is conceivable that Titia visited her sister in the house on the Breestraat that she and Rembrandt had taken possession of sometime during 1639. Rembrandt made other similar informal portraits including several of his own wife. One of these is a sketch sheet with four studies of Saskia, each one representing her in a different position: first sleeping, with an arm supporting her head; below this she is shown looking inquisitively at a child; then one looking straight at the viewer, and in the bottom sketch with both arms round a child (fig. 83).[88] One assumes that this woman is Saskia on the basis of comparisons with other drawings and etchings. Indeed, there is an etching with studies of Saskia that is related to this study sheet (figs. 84 and 85),[89] and in one of these

etched studies she is wearing the same hat with a broad rim as shown in the drawing. The etching is dated 1636 and the drawing would appear to have been made at the same time, in which case the baby could well be Rumbartus.

We don't know whether the married Coopal-Uylenburgh couple got Rembrandt to paint their portraits. One would expect it, given their close relations with Saskia and Rembrandt, just as portraits of the two other significant godparents at the baptism of their children were painted by Rembrandt. Their wills, however, have not been recovered, nor has any trace survived of their estate. There is, however, a surviving portrait of François' brother, Anthonie Coopal, which must have been painted in Uylenburgh's workshop (fig. 86). Although the Rembrandt Research

88 Ben. 360.
89 B. 365.

141

Project does not consider this imposing portrait, made in 1635, to be an autograph work by Rembrandt, others do see his hand in it, although perhaps in collaboration with an assistant.[90] Coopal, the subject of this portrait, was not just anybody: in 1633 he became a councillor of Vlissingen, he was alderman repeatedly from 1638, and from 1666 until his death in 1672 he was the Pensionary of this Zeeland city. In 1626 he studied medicine in Leiden and two years later his brother married Titia Uylenburgh. He himself did not marry until 1637, so that at the time of his portrait of 1635 there was no need for a pendant. Unfortunately, in not a single case of the above-mentioned members of the Sylvius, Uylenburgh and Coopal families do we possess an inventory of their household effects, so we simply don't know whether they had more paintings by Rembrandt from his Uylenburgh period.

The identification of several of the sitters indicates that it was Uylenburgh who provided the initiative for Rembrandt's portrait production. We saw earlier that the earliest known commissions came from members of the Mennonite community to which Uylenburgh belonged. Further investigations serve to confirm and to fill out this picture. Thus, the inventory of effects drawn up in 1703 by the Gouda merchant draper and entrepreneur Pieter Sijen records 'two portraits of forebears painted by Rembrandt'.[91] One wonders, of course, who these forebears were. Were these portraits of the man's grandparents or from an older generation – and were they really from Rembrandt's hand? In general, attributions to famous artists have to be treated with caution, since auctioneers and art dealers prefer for obvious reasons to offer works with resounding names attached to them. There is perhaps less need for scepticism in the case of household inventories, even though those compiling them were not always exactly reticent where attributions were concerned. In most cases, the compilers of inventories would have had a fairly thorough knowledge of the material at hand; but where portraits were involved and where the identity of the sitter and the name of the presumed maker of the portrait were at stake, one assumes that this information would have come from relatives or close associates and would accordingly be fairly reliable. This is the case with the present document, for the inventory was compiled by the person concerned himself.

It is not insignificant that 'voorouder' (forebear) is the term used in connection with the portraits. One encounters the term occasionally employed in seventeenth century inventories but, as far as I am aware, exclusively in relation to portraits and indicating a direct line of descent. When compiling an inventory, if one wanted to refer to one's grandparents, one could avail oneself in Dutch of the terms 'bestevader' and 'bestemoeder'. 'Voorouder' could then refer to an earlier generation. In this case, therefore, although it is possible that the portraits were of Sijen's grandparents, it is more likely that they were portraits of family members of an earlier generation. Indeed, this becomes a stronger probability when one finds that the owner of these portraits, painted by Rembrandt, was the great-grandson of the Amsterdam merchant Pieter Sijen, who in 1639 together with Gilbert de Flines invested money in Hendrick Uylenburgh's business enterprise.[92] Could it be this Pieter Sijen and his wife Marretje Cornelisdr van Grotewal who had their portraits painted by Rembrandt?

In any attempt to identify the subjects of these portraits by Rembrandt and mentioned in 1703, Pieter Sijen and his wife would seem to be the obvious candidates. To see whether there were any other family members who might fit the bill, the genealogy of the Sijen family has been sifted as thoroughly as possible. On the basis of the data relating to five generations of Sijens, there are – apart from Pieter and his wife – three other married couples whose candidacy needs to be considered: two younger brothers of Pieter Sijen and their wives, and an only child of the Sijen-Van Grotewal couple and his wife. The inheritance of the portraits, however, gives no indication; but if one of Pieter Sijen's two brothers and his wife were the subjects portrayed by Rembrandt, the inheritance of the paintings had not run in a direct line. The relevant documents that have been found, including wills and deeds concerning the division of their estate, indicate that no portion of the latter went to the youngest generation

90 Br. 203, Corpus III C 108 (probably made in Rembrandt's workshop), Slatkes 1992, no. 158 (as Rembrandt, with possible contribution from an assistant in the costume), and Liedtke 2004, p. 67 (who agrees with Slatkes).
91 Van der Veen 2003, p. 47. What follows below is based entirely on this article.
92 Below pp. 187-188.

86 Rembrandt van Rijn or workshop, Portrait of Anthonie Coopal, signed and dated 'Rembrandt. ft 1635', panel, 83.7 x 67 cm, Boston, Mass.,
Museum of Fine Arts (Br. 203; Corpus III C 108)

87 Rembrandt van Rijn, *Portrait of a 41-year-old man with beard and broad-brimmed hat, possibly Pieter Sijen*, signed and dated 'Rembrandt. f. 1633' with the inscription 'AET 41.', panel, 69.5 x 54.7 cm, Pasadena, California., Norton Simon Museum of Art (Br. 177; Corpus II A 86)

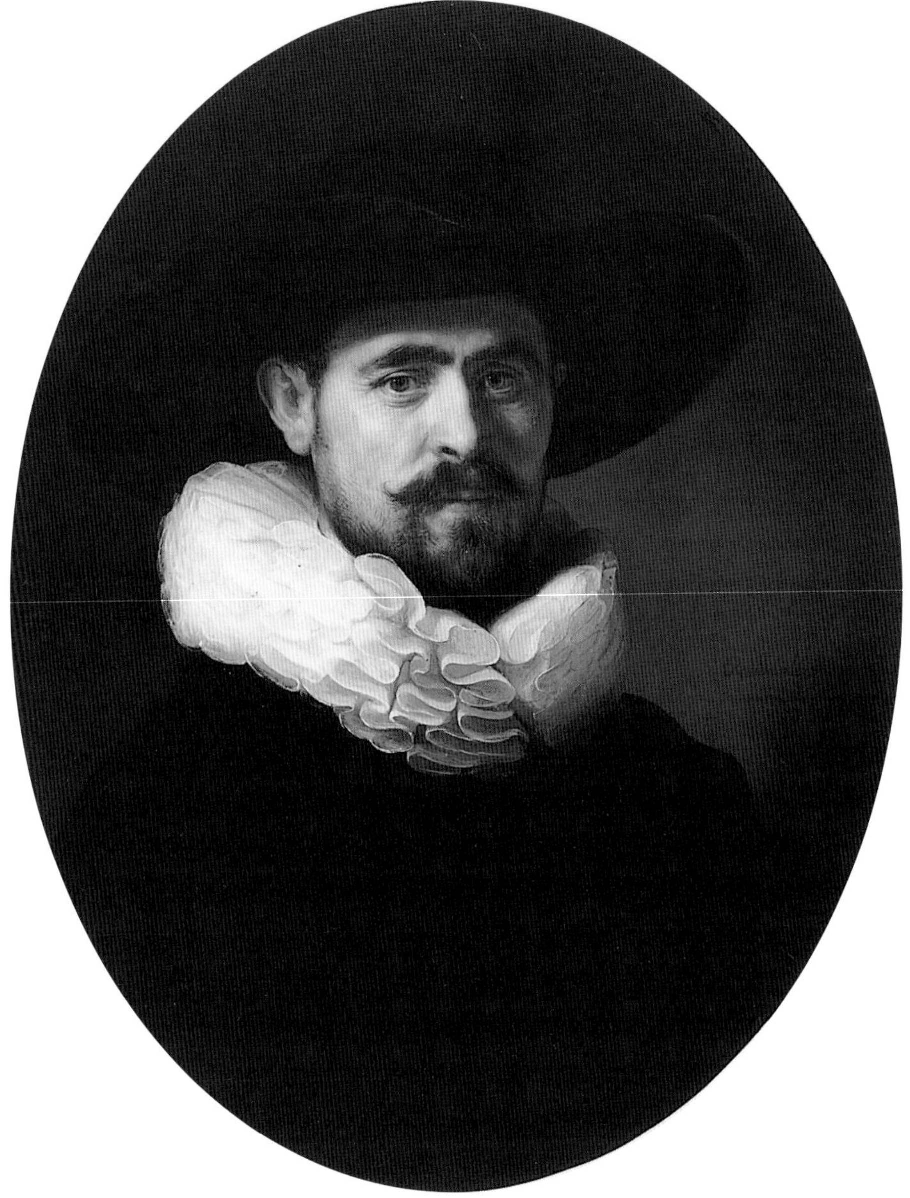

Pieter Sijen or his offspring. The only son of the Sijen-Van Grotewal couple was married in 1636, so that any putative portraits of himself plus his wife could not have originated before that date.

The most likely subjects of the portraits mentioned in 1703, then, are Pieter Sijen and his wife Marretje Cornelisdr van Grotewal. No supplementary archival material relating to the portraits has been found, but the œuvre of Rembrandt's preserved portraits does provide new points of departure. The fact that the portraits survived the first generations and that such pieces increasingly attracted attention in the eighteenth century – not merely as family documents but 'as art' – certainly plays a part. The market value of family portraits meant that owners did not get rid of them lightly, so that relatively many of them were preserved. In 1633, precisely in the period that he worked for Uylenburgh, Rembrandt produced the portrait of a 41 year-old man (fig. 87) and in 1634, most probably at the beginning of the year, the pendant of a 40 year-old woman (fig. 88).[93] On the basis of the age given, the man must have been born around 1592, precisely the year that one can calculate as Pieter Sijen's year of birth from his deed of marriage of 1613. On the publication of her marriage banns, Marretje van Grotewal gave her age as 20, and therefore she must have been born around 1593, which coincides near enough with the year of birth of the woman on the portrait. Because they were both Mennonites – and therefore only baptized as adults – their year of birth is not exactly known.

What needs now to be investigated is whether there are any other pairs of portraits with which Sijen and his wife could be identified. There is, in fact, in Rembrandt's œuvre another very good candidate for the man, viz. the *Portrait of a man with a beard* in New York,[94] which originated in 1632 and bears the inscription 'AET. 40', so that – like Pieter Sijen – the man was born around 1592. The crucial question is whether there is a match-

ing pendant. There is a portrait of a woman dated 1633 that is a possible counterpart,[95] but in view of the difference of format and scale it is not eligible as a pendant to the New York painting.[96] Yet another portrait, this time of a 39 year-old woman, is in two respects significant as a potential counterpart:[97] in the first place because the year of birth, 1593, corresponding to that of Marretje van Grotewal; and secondly because the woman's simple costume leads one to surmise a Mennonite background.[98] The conclusion of the Rembrandt Research Project, however, is that the difference in scale of the two portraits and the different manner in which the man and the woman are

93 Br. 177 and Corpus II A 86, and Br. 344 and Corpus II A 87. The portraits are now housed in different museums, but up to 1960, when they were sold, they were a pair together. Their provenance traces back to the nineteenth century.
94 Br. 160 and Corpus II A 59.
95 Br. 335 and Corpus II A 83.
96 Corpus II, p. 242.
97 Br. 334, Corpus II A 62 and Copenhagen 2006, no. 8.
98 Bruyn in: Corpus II, p. 92.

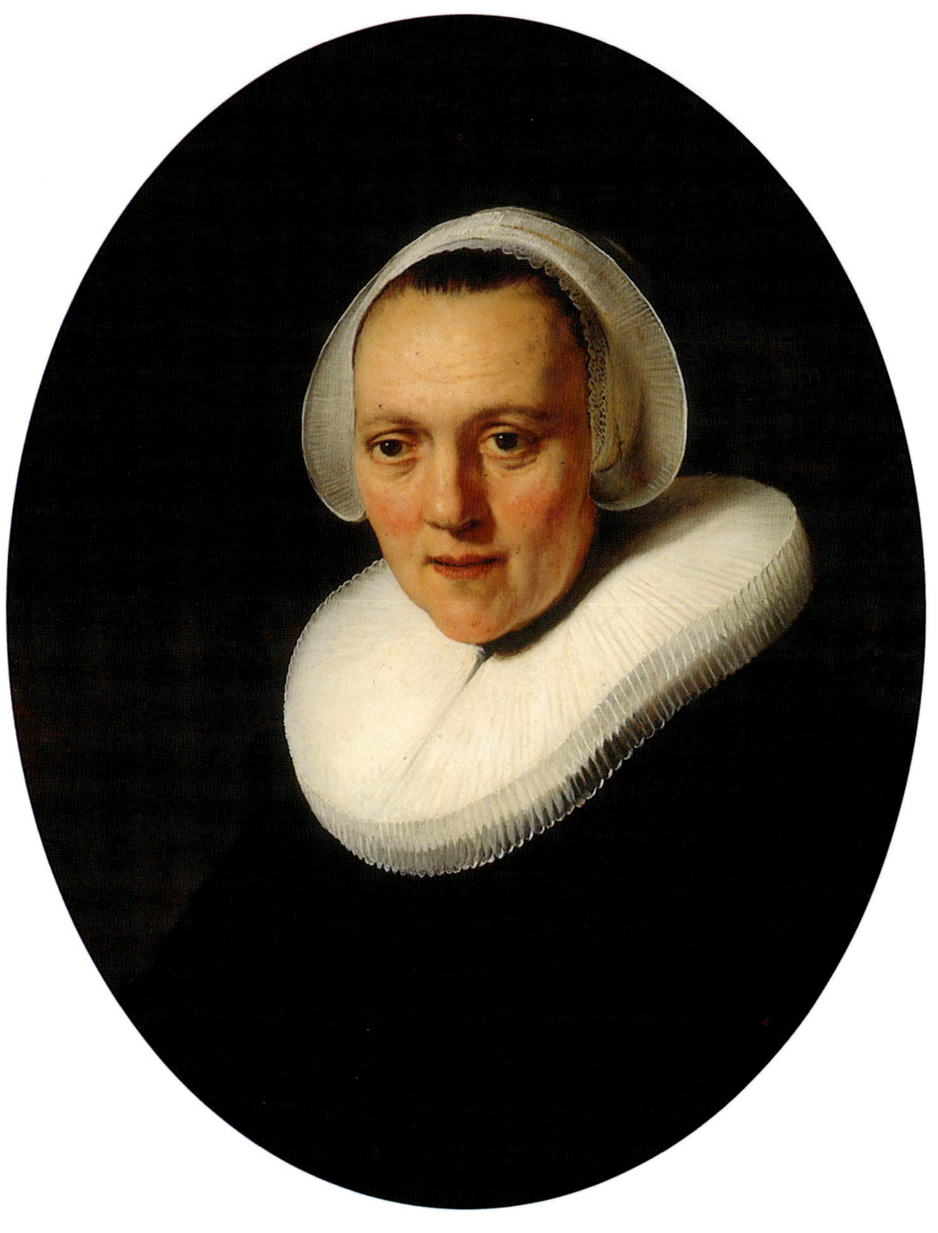

inventory of a descendant are sufficient to conclude the argument for this identification, but the combination of the data seems to me fairly decisive: the contemporary report of a pair of portraits of the forebears of Pieter Pietersz Sijen painted by Rembrandt, the use of the term 'voorouder' here, the business relations both Rembrandt and Pieter Sijen maintained with Hendrick Uylenburgh over a long period, the survival of the pieces into the eighteenth century, the ages given on the paintings of both man and woman that correspond with those of Sijen and his wife, and the inheritance that appears to have followed an obvious course, viz. a straight line from father to eldest son or grandson.

The identities of about half the subjects of the portraits that Rembrandt produced with Uylenburgh remain unknown. This is true, for example, of a portrait of a man from 1633 (fig. 89),[100] a striking feature of which is the man's red doublet. It was more usual at that time for men to have themselves portrayed in darker attire; a red jacket such as this evokes associations with the decorative dress of the higher ranks of the French, English or German military, while the man's hairstyle also suggests a foreigner. It is known from various sources that foreign visitors to the Republic had themselves immortalized by one of the many skilled portrait painters; evidently one of them managed to find his way to Uylenburgh's workshop.[101] The man's attitude leads one to assume that there must have been a pendant, for which role the portrait of a woman, similarly painted in 1633 – moreover, of almost the same measurements as the man's portrait – would seem to be eligible (fig. 90).[102] Both were painted on panel, but the wood was not derived from the same tree. The fact that the woman was not portrayed by Rembrandt but by one of his assistants is not decisive evidence, since it was frequently the case that a portrait would be executed by the master and the pendant by an assistant in his workshop.

99 This conclusion is accepted by Liedtke; the idea that Br. 160 and Br. 334 are pendants, in his view, 'has rightly been rejected', see New York 1995, vol. 2, p. 42. There are no dendrochronological data relating to these paintings.
100 Br. 176 and Corpus IV Add. 4.
101 See also pp. 198-199 and fig. 143.
102 Br. 337 and Corpus II C 81.

placed in the pictorial plane rules out the case for their being pendants.[99]

The *Portrait of a man with a beard* is dated 1633, that of the woman a year later. Rembrandt would have been commissioned to paint the pendant portraits in 1633 and would have completed the portrait of the woman in the early months of 1634. I find it more than plausible that the Pasadena portrait of the 41 year-old man is that of Pieter Sijen and that of the 40 year-old woman, now in Louisville, portrays his wife Marretje Cornelisdr van Grotewal. In themselves, neither the indication of the subjects' ages on the paintings nor the record of a pair of pendants in the

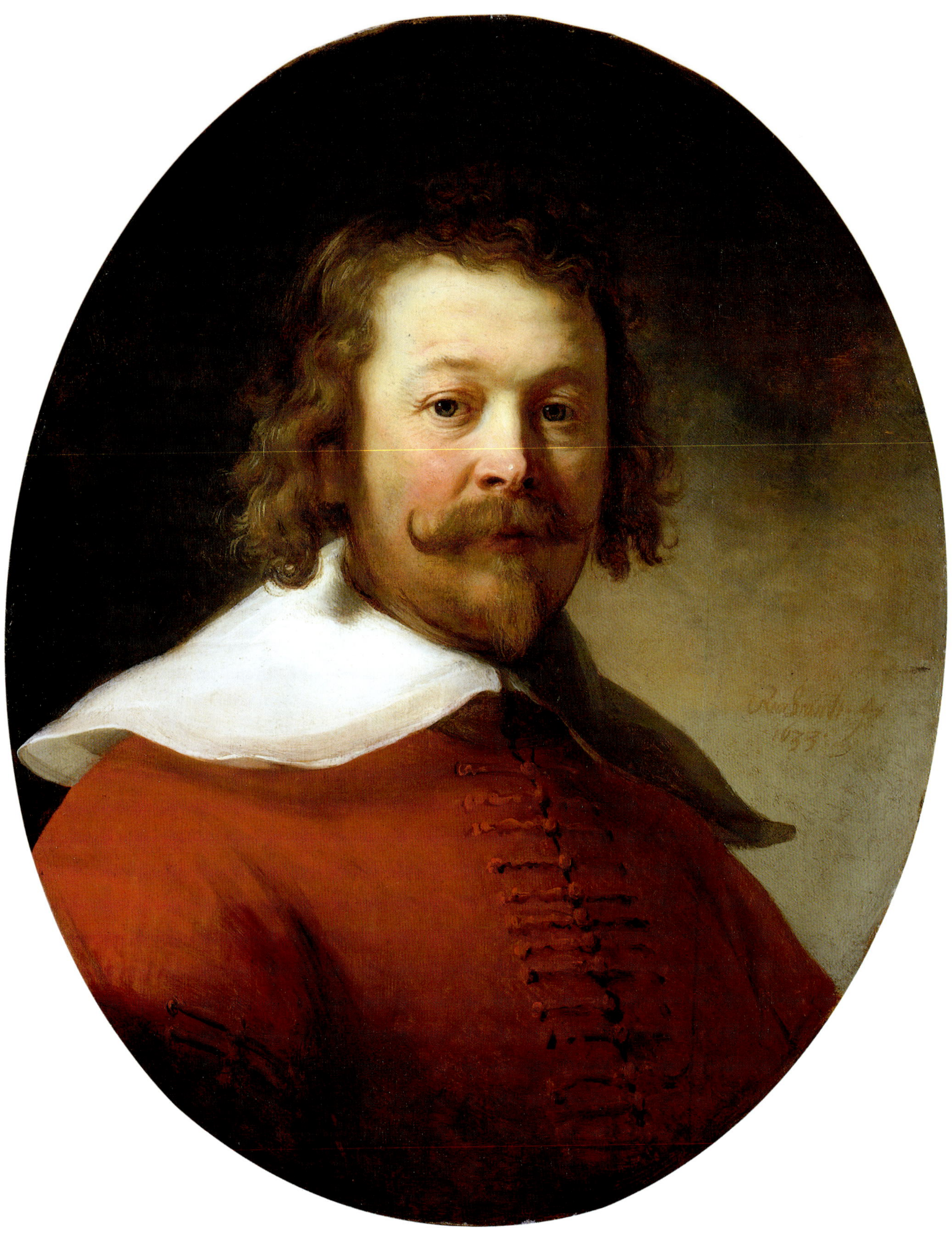

89 Rembrandt van Rijn, Portrait of a man in a red doublet, signed and dated 'Rembrandt. ft 1633', panel, 63.5 x 50.5 cm (oval), Maastricht, Noortman Master Paintings (Br. 176; Corpus ıv Add. 4)

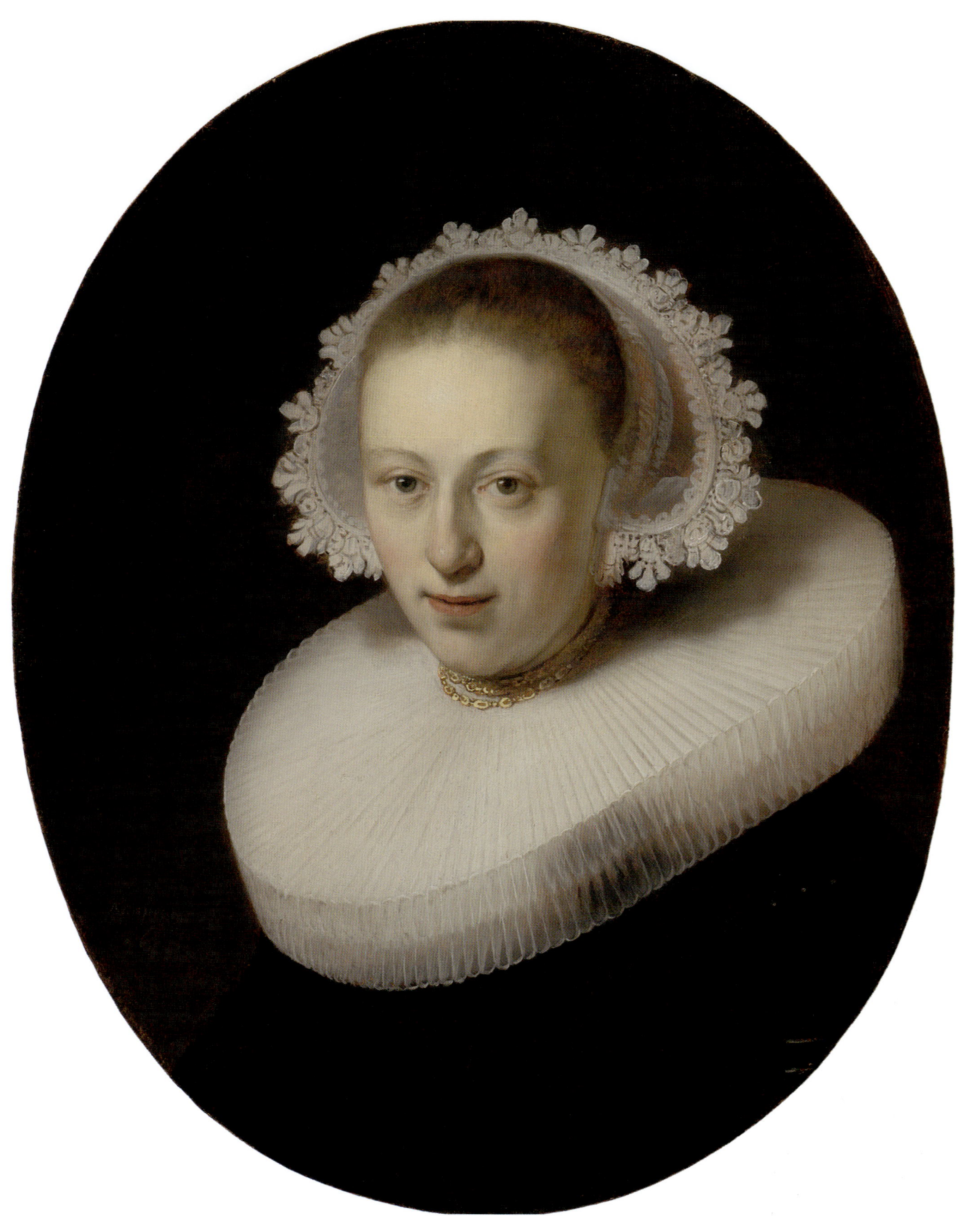

90 Anonymous, probably painted by a anonymous artist in the workshop of Rembrandt van Rijn, *Portrait of a young woman*, signed and dated 'Rembrant f. 1633', panel, 62.4 x 50.4 cm, private collection, United States (Br. 337; Corpus II C 81)

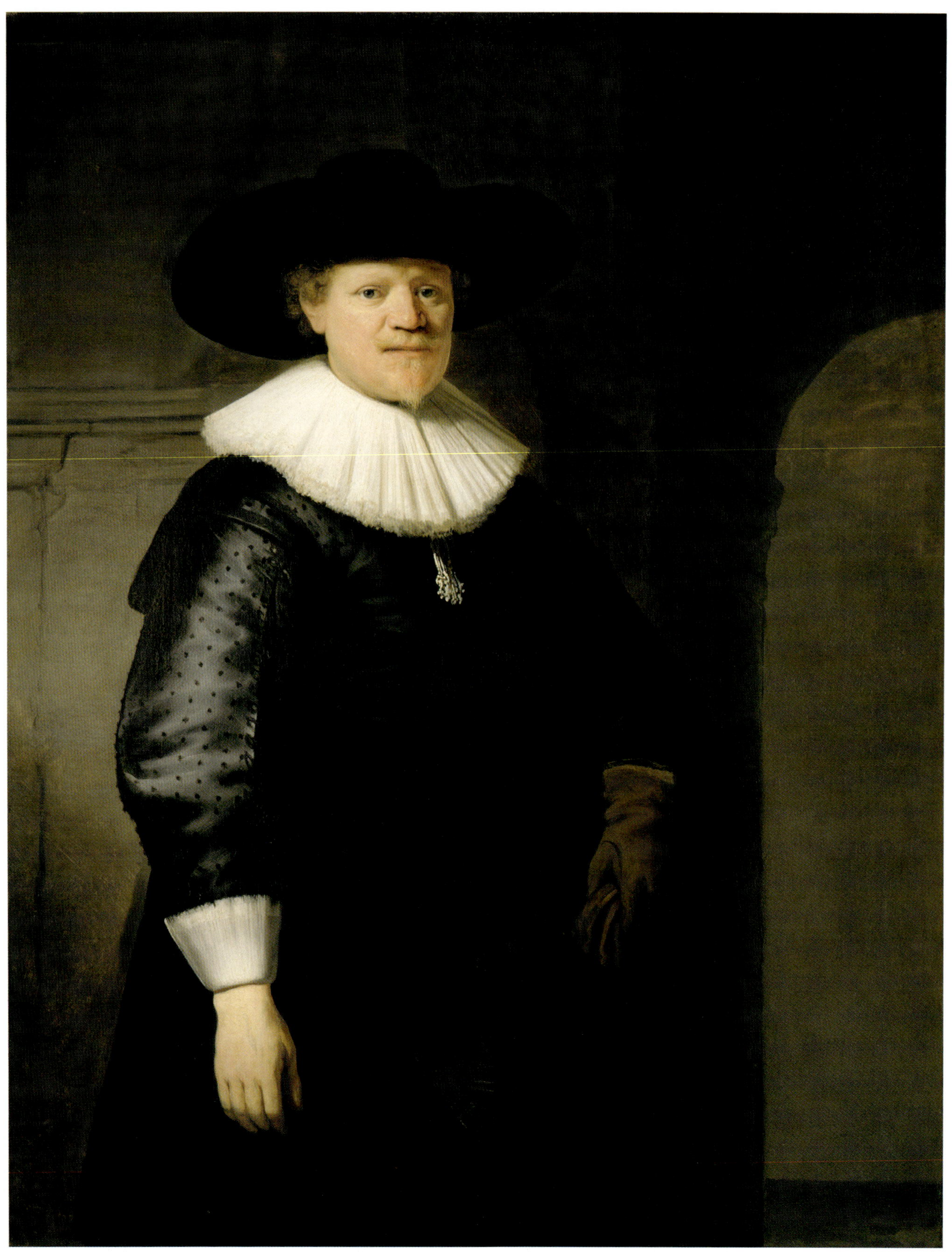

91 Rembrandt van Rijn, Portrait of a man, probably Jan Harmensz Krul, signed and dated 'Rembrandt f... 1633', canvas, 128.5 x 100.5 cm, Kassel, Staatliche Museen Kassel, Gemäldegalerie Alte Meister (Br. 171; Corpus II A 81)

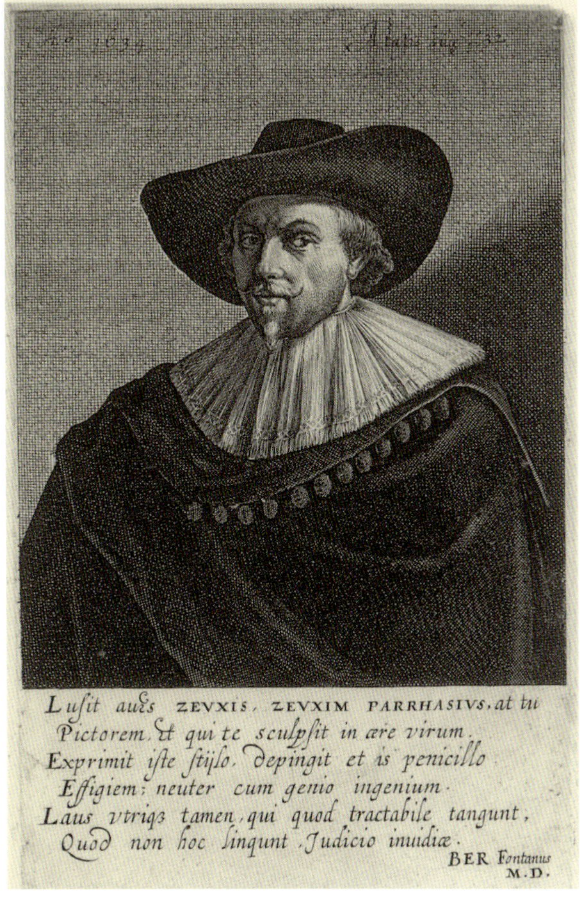

103 Br. 171, Corpus II A 81 and Frankfurt/Kyoto 2002-2003, no. 15.
104 Salomon Saverij brought out prints of several paintings by Rembrandt. The portrait painted by Rembrandt need not necessarily have served as the exemplar for this engraving.
105 Br. 172 and Corpus II A 78 ; and Br. 341 and Corpus II A 79.
106 Br. 199 and Corpus II A 100 ; and Br. 342 and Corpus II A 101.
107 Doc. 1659/9 and Doc. 1660/8 and 8a; respectively Br. 544 and Corpus II A 88.

Another fine example of a life-size portrait is that of a man in very elegant attire. This three quarter-length portrait was also painted in 1633 (fig. 91).[103] There are reasons for identifying the man, with certain reservations, as Jan Harmensz Krul. In 1749 the painting was described in Kassel as the portrait of the 'holländische Poët Croll', by which Krul must have been meant. Krul was born around 1601/02 and was successful in Amsterdam as a poet and playwright. The identification from the mid-eighteenth century must have been based on information provided by the previous owner, probably communicated when the piece was sold by the Amsterdam owner to the Landgrave of Hessen-Kassel in 1738. The poet would not have been known in eighteenth century Germany. There is an engraved portrait of Krul that was made in 1634 by Salomon Saverij and originally intended for one of his publications, although the print does not bear the name of its maker (fig. 92).[104] There is a certain likeness between the two portraits, not forceful enough to be able to conclude definitively that they are of one and the same individual. It has been wondered whether Krul could have afforded such an expensive acquisition, although little is known about his financial position in the early thirties and, after all, it would not necessarily have been Krul himself who ordered the portrait. It could have been commissioned by admirers of the poet, perhaps by the wealthy members of the 'Musyck-Kamer' of which Krul had been one of the founders. His portrait might have adorned the meeting room of this Chamber, which was opened in 1634. Certainly, the man portrayed stands in an appropriate setting: an interior whose architecture puts one in mind of a theatre.

In the same year as the man's portrait in Kassel, the pendant portraits of a man and a woman were also painted (figs. 93 and 94)[105] that demonstrate very clearly why Rembrandt was in such demand as a portraitist: the unusual composition, the way in which the two figures respond to each other – Rembrandt introduced action through the posture of the man who is rising from his chair – and the subtlety of the manner of painting. We do not know the identity of the subjects of these portraits, but the opulence of their dress tells us clearly that they belonged to the wealthier Amsterdam bourgeoisie. In 1634 Rembrandt portrayed another distinguished Amsterdam couple whose identity has survived: Marten Soolmans and Oopjen Coppit, depicted life-size and full-length.[106] We saw earlier that patrons commissioning portraits sometimes proceeded to further purchases. The Soolmans-Coppit couple did just this – at least, according to a document drawn up in 1660 in which the possessions are specified that the widow was allowed to keep, including 'a painting of Joseph and Maria done by Rembrant' that is unquestionably Rembrandt's *Holy family* (fig. 95) painted in the same year as the portraits.[107] We don't know whether this work was painted on commission. It could have already been standing in the workshop – whether or not in a finished state – and seen by Soolmans and his wife. Uylenburgh could also have bought such pieces from Rembrandt, of course, just as he regularly did from Govert Flinck a few years later; in which

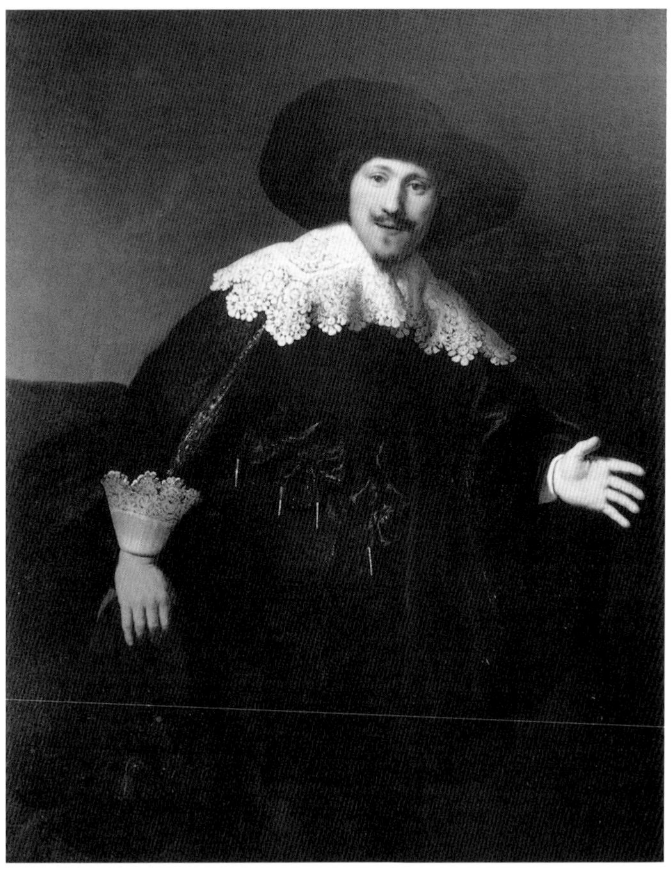

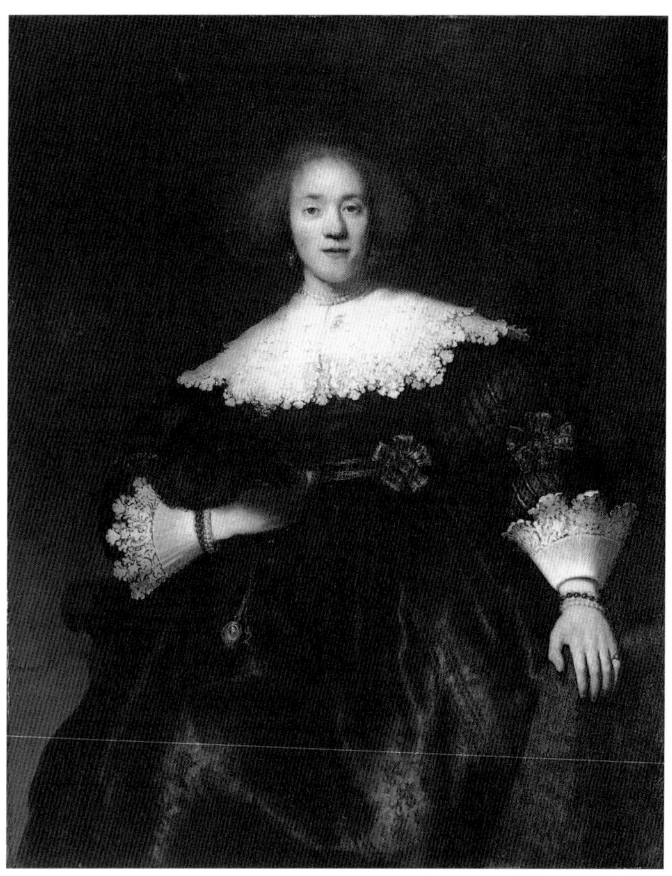

93 Rembrandt van Rijn, Portrait of a man rising from his chair, signed and dated 'Rembrandt. f 1633', canvas, 124 x 98.5 cm, Cincinnati, Ohio, The Taft Museum (Br. 172; Corpus II A 78)

94 Rembrandt van Rijn, Portrait of a woman in an armchair, signed and dated 'Rembrand. f. 1633', canvas, 125.7 x 101 cm, New York, N.Y., The Metropolitan Museum of Art (Br. 341; Corpus II A 79)

case Rembrandt must have been given the opportunity to paint such large biblical subjects for the open market.

In the above, we considered in detail particularly those portraits that Rembrandt painted between 1631 and 1635 in Uylenburgh's workshop. His production was not limited to these; some patrons who commissioned portraits also bought a history piece or a 'tronie' by Rembrandt that in several cases originated in the same year as the portrait.[108] Rembrandt was also producing etchings during this period. In fact, the nature of his etched work quickly changed after his entry into Uylenburgh's workshop. The number of prints declined and the repertoire changed: no more tronies or beggars, but mainly biblical subjects (figs. 96-101). There is also a difference in technical terms: the etchings are in most cases exceptionally carefully and tonally worked out while,

as Hinterding has pointed out, they appear to be closely tied to his paintings.[109]

Jan van Vliet produced reproduction prints after paintings by Rembrandt. The idea to bring out print versions of paintings was possibly inspired by the practice in Antwerp workshops where inventions by Rubens and Van Dyck had been put on to the market by printmakers and had reached a wide public. There were certainly contacts between the two Antwerp masters and artists in the Republic: for example, Van Dyck was in The Hague during the winter of 1631-1632, while Van Vliet visited Antwerp in 1632.[110] Hendrick Uylenburgh did business in Antwerp in the twenties and must have known the art market there well. Van Vliet worked during the first half of the thirties, making prints after eleven paintings by Rembrandt and in close collaboration with him. Rembrandt also entrusted him with

108 See note 53 and here figs. 72 and 73, and p. 149, note 106 and fig. 95, while Maurits Huygens (fig. 76) could have had in his possession Rembrandt's self-portrait from 1632 (fig. 78).
109 Hinterding 2001, vol. I, pp. 92-96.
110 Dickey 2004, pp. 23-27, and Amsterdam 1996, p. 6 and note 10 and passim.

95 Rembrandt van Rijn, The holy family, signed and dated 'Rembrandt f 163.', canvas, 195 x 132 cm, Munich, Bayerische Staatsgemälde-sammlungen, Alte Pinakothek (Br. 544; Corpus II A 88)

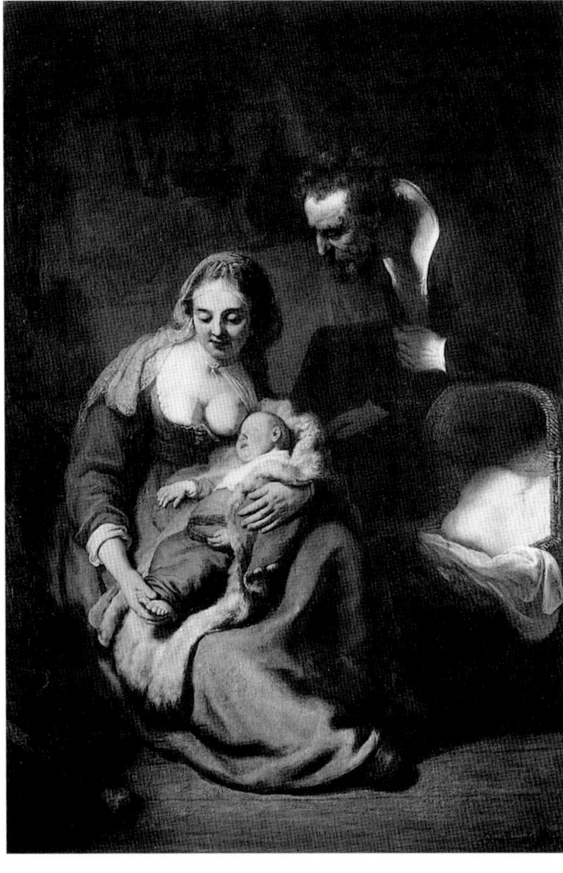

the completion of 'tronies' that he had himself first roughly outlined on the etching plate. Van Vliet was not only an engraver but an artist with both pencil and paintbrush and could well have studied with Rembrandt. An eighteenth century auction catalogue records a painting of an old man 'very fine, in the manner of Rembrandt, by Van Vliet', while on the reverse side of a drawing in black chalk depicting a rembrandtesque head of an old man is written 'van vliet fc'.[111] The question of whether Van Vliet remained in Leiden and made the etchings there or whether he did it in Uylenburgh's workplace has not been definitively answered. However that may be, during the years 1634 and 1635, Rembrandt and Van Vliet were both using paper with the same watermark, which would seem to suggest that during those years Van Vliet was with Uylenburgh.[112]

In the mid thirties Rembrandt produced various monochrome paintings in Uylenburgh's workshop – mainly on paper – in preparation for ambitious etchings. These grisailles are not thought to have been intended for sale in the first place, even though, one assumes, art lovers would have been highly interested in them because these oil sketches were so freely executed. Remarkably enough, no etchings were ever made from some of the oil sketches – for whatever reason. For example, no print was ever made after the grisaille *Joseph relating his dreams* in the Rijksmuseum (fig. 102).[113] A very nice study in red chalk of the seated Jacob, dated 1631, has been preserved (fig. 103).[114] The grisaille, one suspects, was made two years later; but only in 1638 would Rembrandt make an etching of this subject, and when he did so his composition was rather different from that of the oil sketch (fig. 104).[115] The *Deposition* in Glasgow, which can be dated to around 1633-1635, is another grisaille that must have been intended as a preparatory design for an etching that was never executed (fig. 105).[116] Van de Wetering has pointed out that several oil sketches from this period had an almost identical format, which would seem to suggest that Rembrandt had planned a series of biblical scenes. The *Joseph relating his dreams* is almost as large as the *Ecce homo*, a grisaille after which an etching was indeed executed (see fig. 101).[117] The oil sketch for the *Ecce homo* is from 1634, while the first (incomplete) state of the print is dated 1635 and the second (complete) state one year later. The *Descent from the cross*, an etching from 1633, has the same format, while the *Preaching of John the Baptist* also originally had the same size.[118]

If, as suggested, we are looking at a planned series, one may – following Van de Wetering – wonder in what way Uylenburgh could have been involved in the project. In this context, it is highly interesting that the third state of Rembrandt's etched *Descent from the cross* from 1633 bears Uylenburgh's publisher's address: 'Amstelodami Hendrickus Ulenburgensis Excudebat' (fig. 106),[119] which could well be taken to mean that Rembrandt's graphic work and the reproduction prints by Van Vliet were produced under Uylenburgh's aegis.[120] Too little, in fact, is known over the production of prints in his firm but in larger workshops it was not unusual for the production of paintings to go hand in hand with the production and publication of graphic work (cf. fig. 107). We know for certain that Uylenburgh possessed

111 Sale catalogue Schwencke, The Hague, 6-7 October 1767, no. 5, respectively Enklaar 2005, p. 44, note 3.
112 Van de Wetering 2000, pp. 50-51.
113 Br. 504 and Corpus II A 66.
114 Ben. 20.
115 B. 37.
116 Br. 554 and Corpus III A 105.
117 Br. 546, Corpus II A 89 and Amsterdam 1996, nos. 16a-c and B. 77.
118 Van de Wetering 2000, p. 48 and p. 49, table IV.
119 B. 81.
120 Van de Wetering 2000, p. 50.

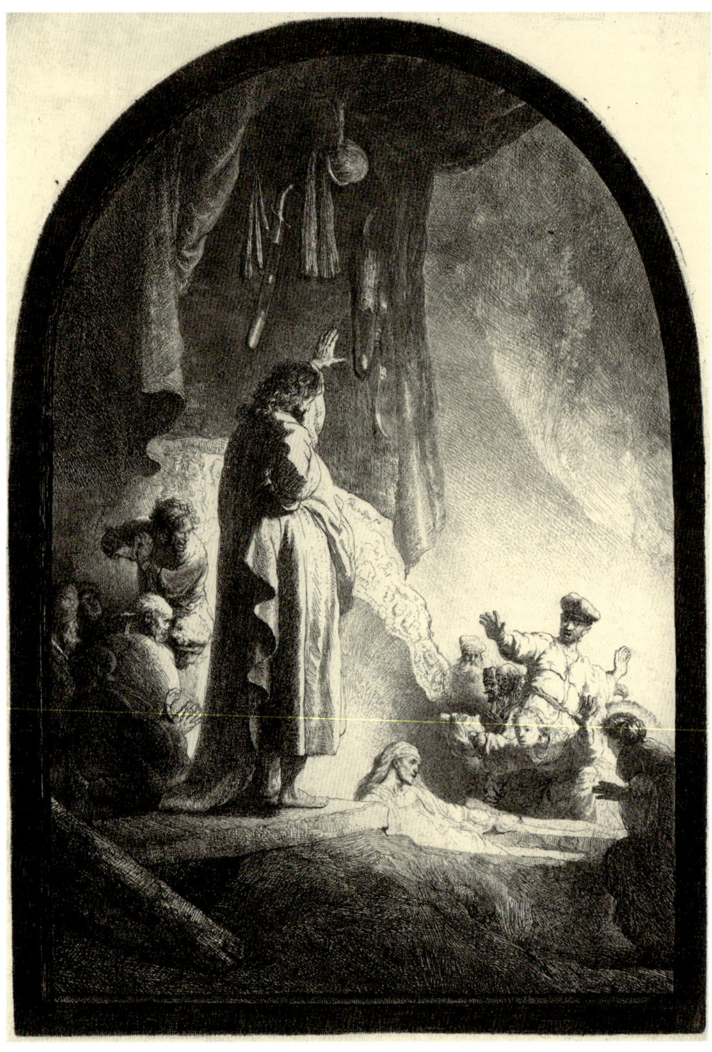

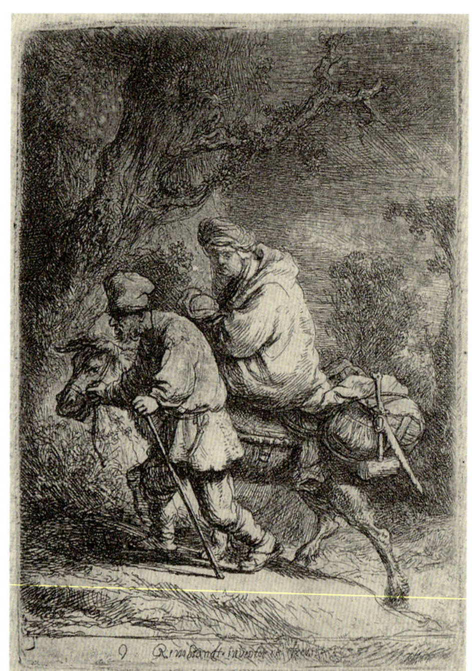

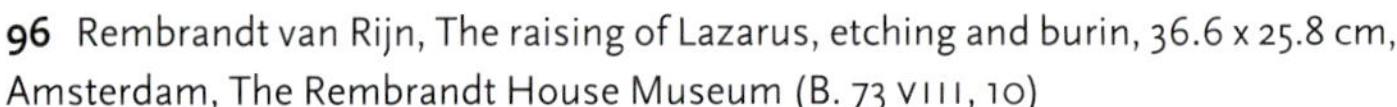

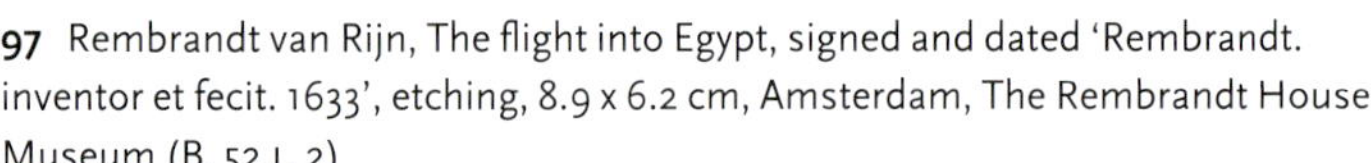

96   Rembrandt van Rijn, The raising of Lazarus, etching and burin, 36.6 x 25.8 cm, Amsterdam, The Rembrandt House Museum (B. 73 VIII, 10)

97   Rembrandt van Rijn, The flight into Egypt, signed and dated 'Rembrandt. inventor et fecit. 1633', etching, 8.9 x 6.2 cm, Amsterdam, The Rembrandt House Museum (B. 52 I, 2)

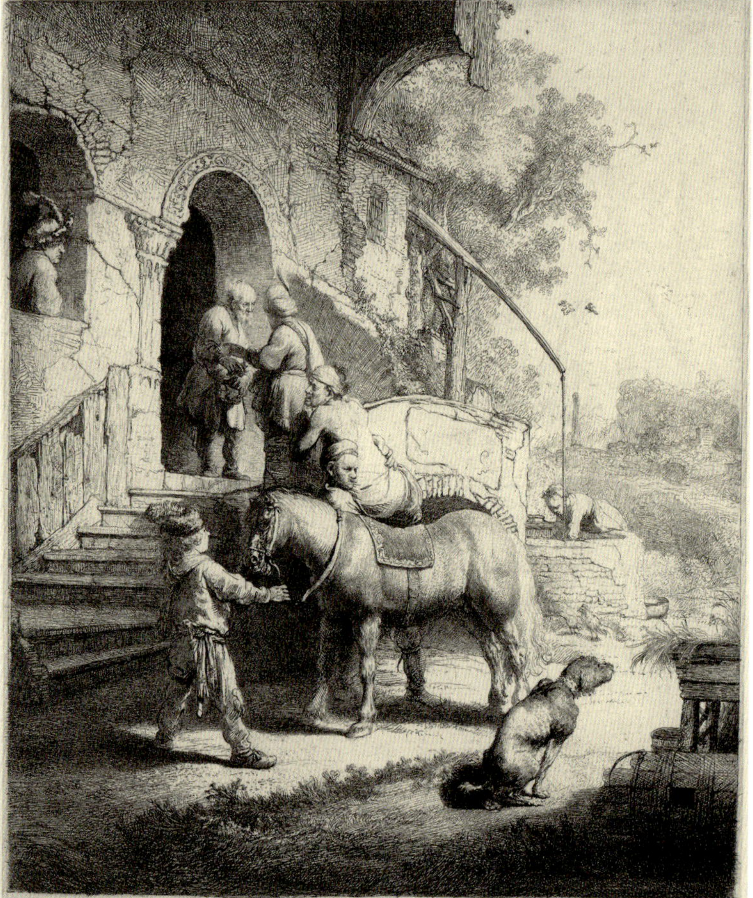

98   Rembrandt van Rijn, The good Samaritan, etching and burin, 25.8 x 21.8 cm, Amsterdam, The Rembrandt House Museum (B. 90, I, 4)
The fourth state is signed and dated 'Rembrandt. inventor et feecit. 1633'

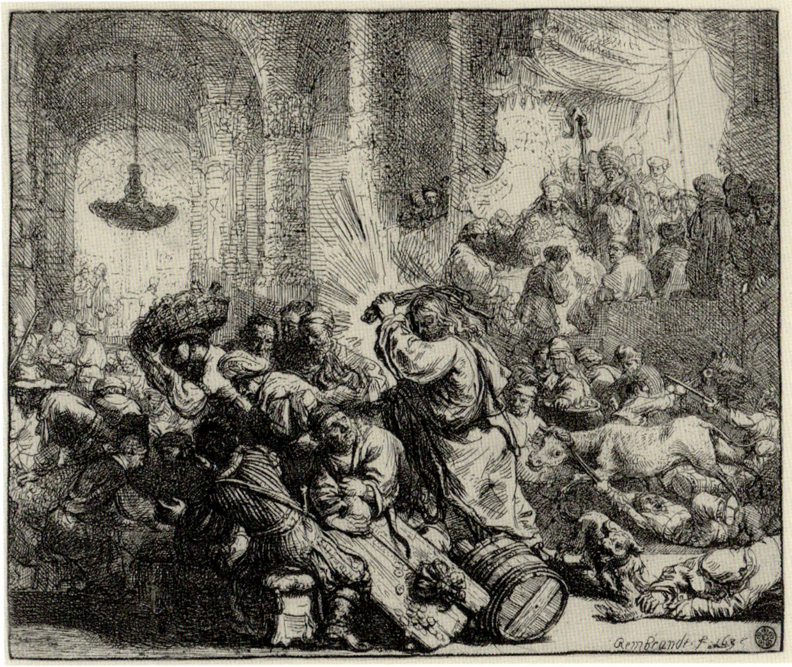

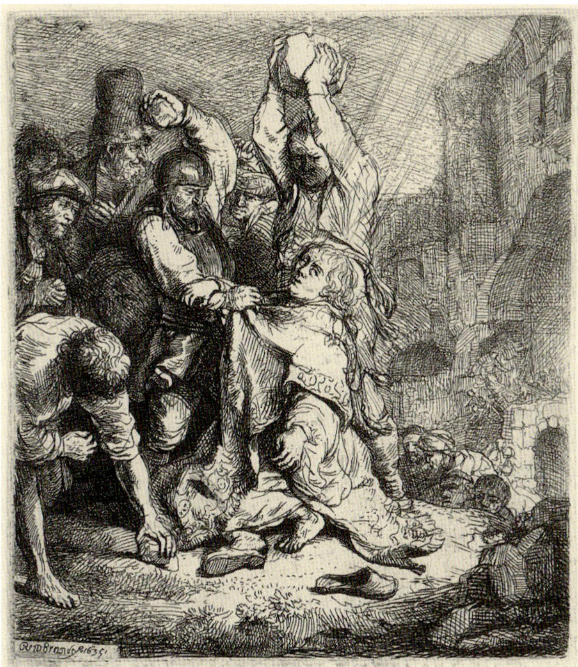

99 Rembrandt van Rijn, Christ chasing the moneychangers from the temple, signed and dated, 'Rembrandt. f. 1635', etching and drypoint, 13.6 x 16.9 cm, Amsterdam, The Rembrandt House Museum (B. 69 I, 2)

100 Rembrandt van Rijn, The stoning of St Stephen, signed and dated 'Rembrandt. f. 1635', etching, 9.5 x 8.5 cm, Amsterdam, The Rembrandt House Museum (B. 97 I,2)

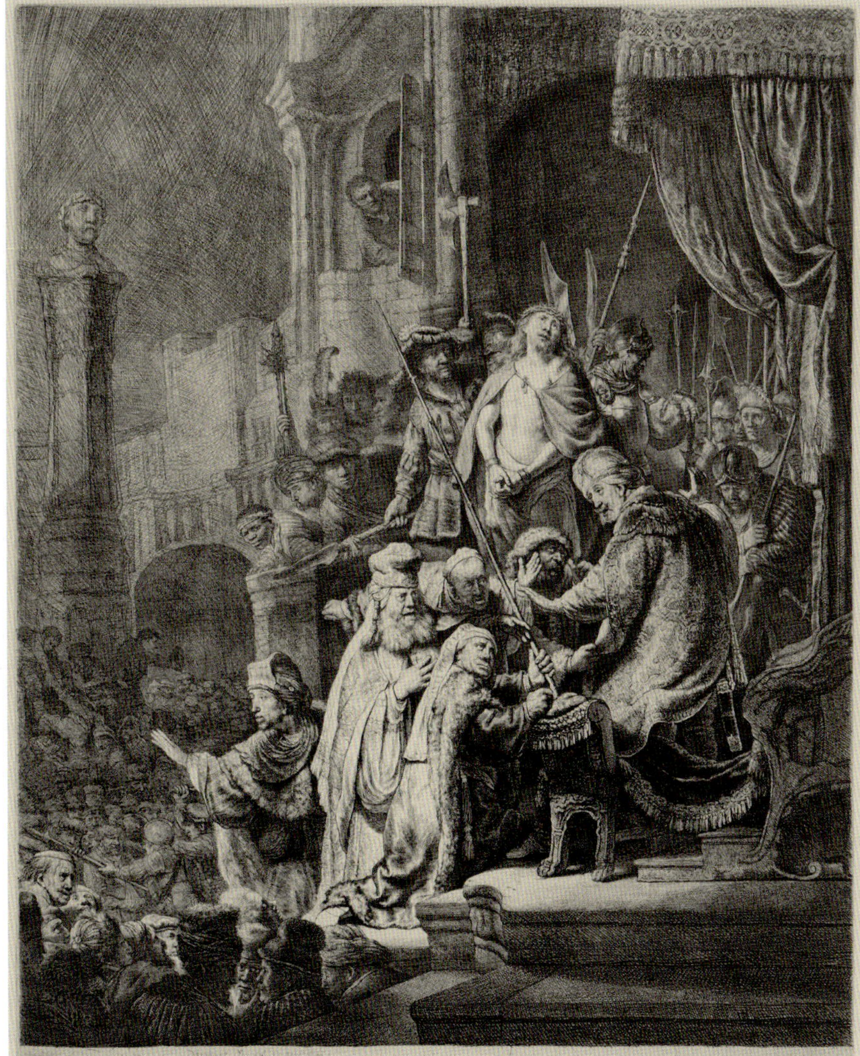

101 Rembrandt van Rijn and Jan van Vliet, Christ before Pilate (Ecce homo), signed and dated 'Rembrandt f. 1636 cum privile', etching, burin and drypoint, 54.9 x 44.7 cm, Amsterdam, The Rembrandt House Museum (B. 77 IV, 5)

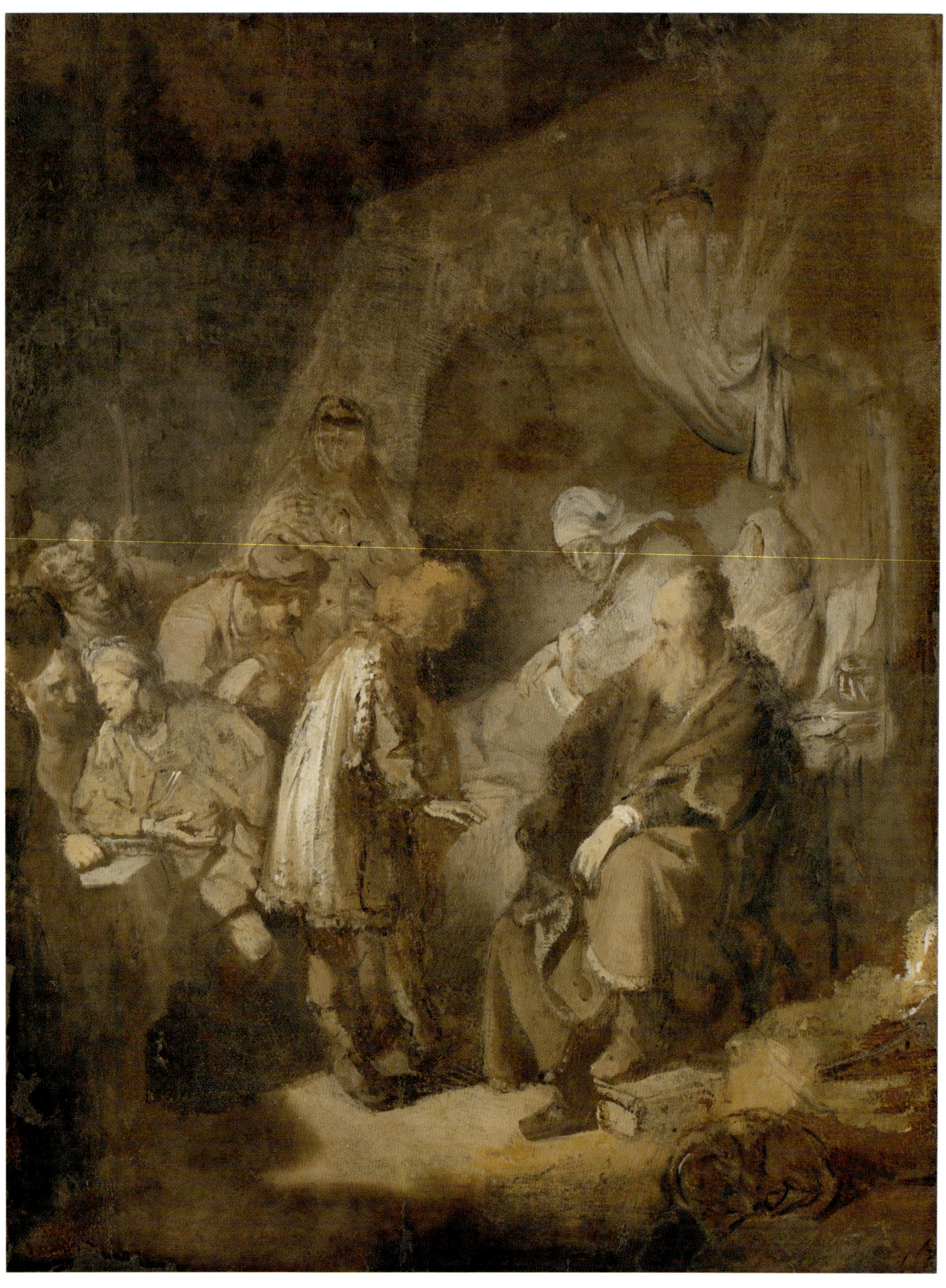

102 Rembrandt van Rijn, Joseph telling his dreams, signed and dated 'Rembrandt f. 163.', paper stuck on panel, 51 x 39 cm, Amsterdam, Rijksmuseum (Br. 504; Corpus II A 66)

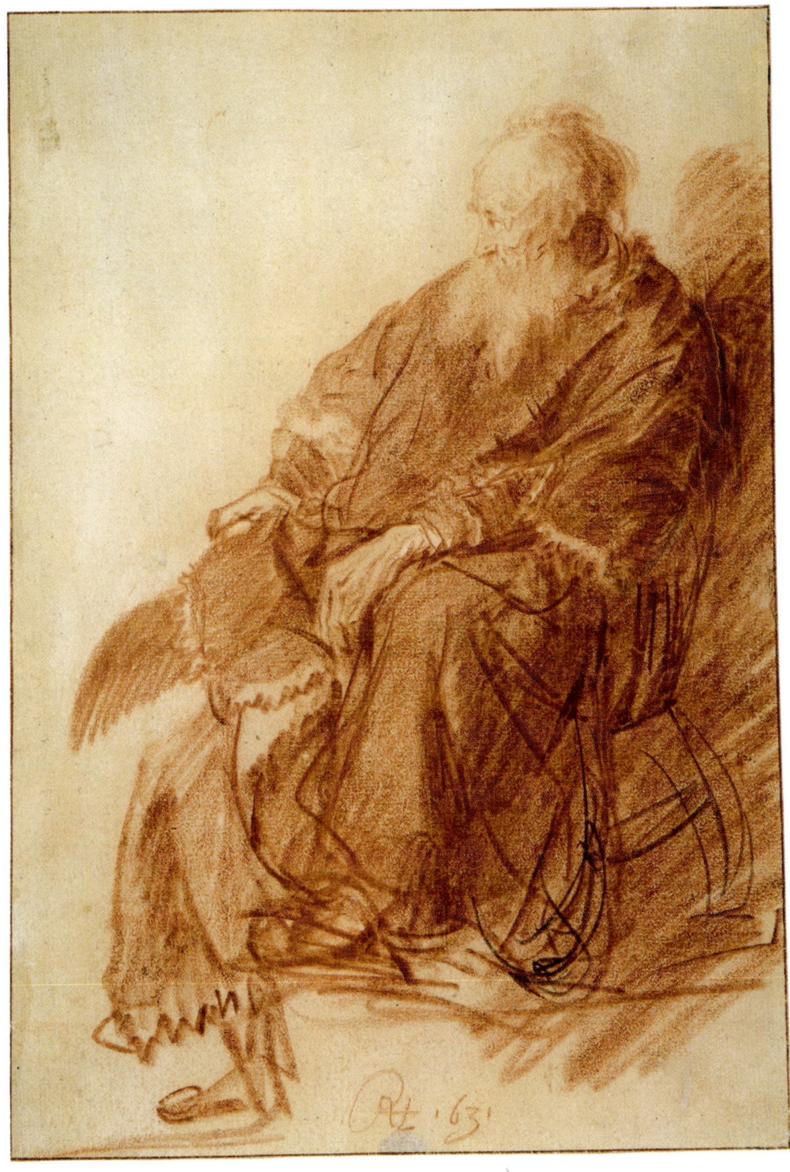

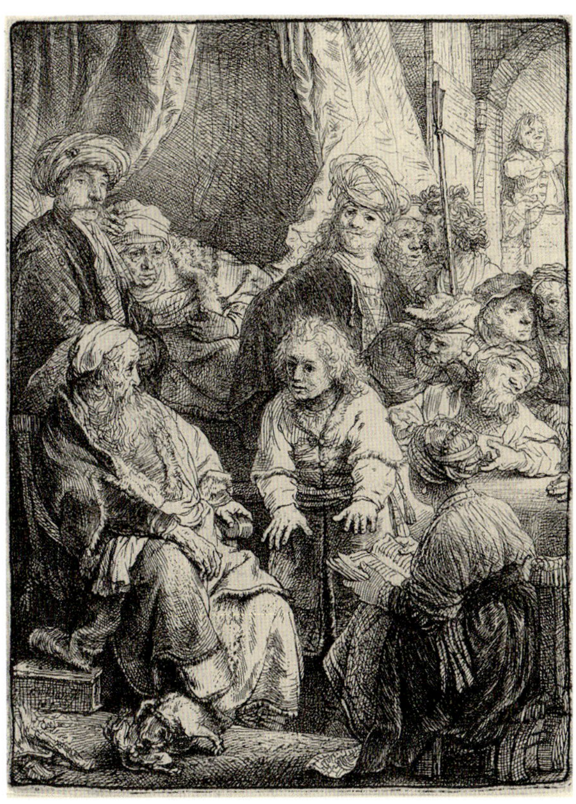

103 Rembrandt van Rijn, Bearded old man seated in an armchair, signed and dated 'RH 1631', red and black chalk on yellow prepared paper, 23.3 x 16 cm, private collection (Ben. 20)

104 Rembrandt van Rijn, Joseph telling his dreams, signed and dated 'Rembrandt. f. 1638', etching and drypoint, 11 x 8.3 cm, Amsterdam, The Rembrandt House Museum (B. 37 II)

etching plates. In 1638 he bought a plate by Bartholomeus Spranger at a sale and in 1641 he gave as security for a loan no less than 125 etching plates.[121] In view of the fact that the loan involved the considerable sum of a thousand guilders, these would undoubtedly have been worked plates. But no further prints bearing Uylenburgh's address are known. Van de Wetering explains Uylenburgh's involvement with the presumed series

of prints as being connected to his religious affiliation: the biblical subjects mentioned above, which were in fact often depicted, could have had a particular significance for Mennonites.[122] This also applies to the story of the doubting Thomas, a story also depicted by Rembrandt in 1634 in a painting which – not by chance – was owned by the Mennonite merchant Ameldonck Leeuw (see figs. 128 and 129).[123]

121 Below pp. 199-200 and 196.

122 Van de Wetering 2000, pp. 52-56.

123 Other examples include the paintings owned by Jan Pietersz Bruyningh, among which was a *Descent from the Cross* by Govert Flinck (see fig. 111), Rembrandt's etchings *Christ's circumcision* and *Ecce homo* owned by Jarich Lubberts and Reijncke Gerrits (see p. 171), an anonymous painting of *The incredulity of Thomas* owned by Reijer Claesz (see p. 41) and a similarly anonymous *Annunciation to the shepherds* owned by de Flines de Younger (see p. 188). All these individuals were Mennonites. Van de Wetering 2000, pp. 53-55 and fig. 18, also discusses Rembrandt's pen and ink drawing of *Jesus in Gethsemane* (Ben. 89) from 1634, a subject that was painted by Rombout Uylenburgh (see p. 26-27 and notes 53 and 54), while in Mennonite circles there was considerable interest in the subject of his grisaille in the Rembrandthuis, taken from the biblical Book of Kings (see pp. 29-32 and fig. 13).

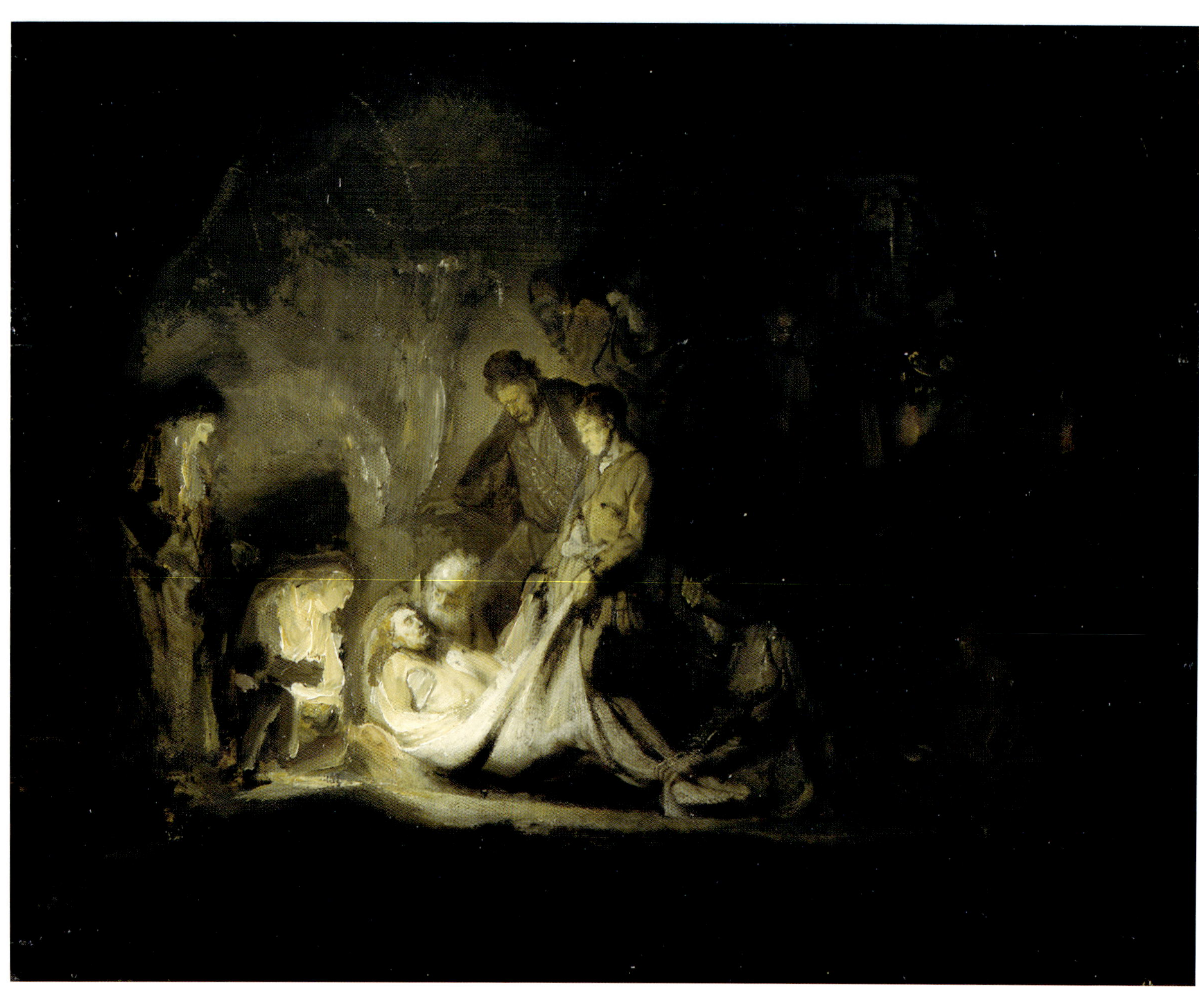

105 Rembrandt van Rijn, The entombment, panel, 32.1 x 40.3 cm, Glasgow, Hunterian Art Gallery, University of Glasgow (Br. 554; Corpus III A 105)

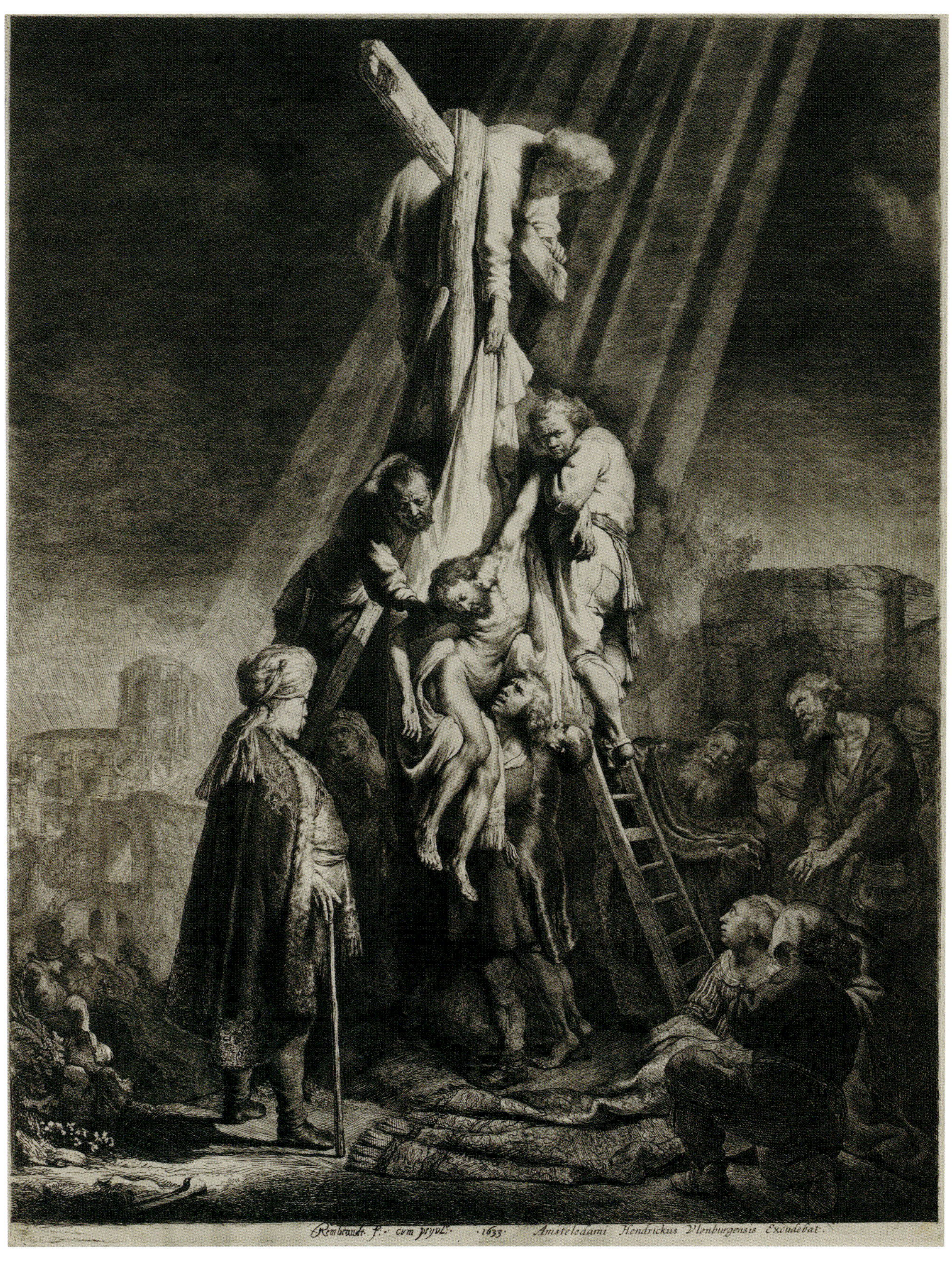

106 Rembrandt van Rijn and Jan van Vliet, The descent from the cross, signed and dated 'Rembrandt. f. cum pryvL°:. 1633', etching and burin, 51.5 x 40 cm (cropped), Amsterdam, Rijksprentenkabinet (B. 81 III, 5)
With the address 'Amstelodami Hendrickus Ulenburgensis Excudebat'

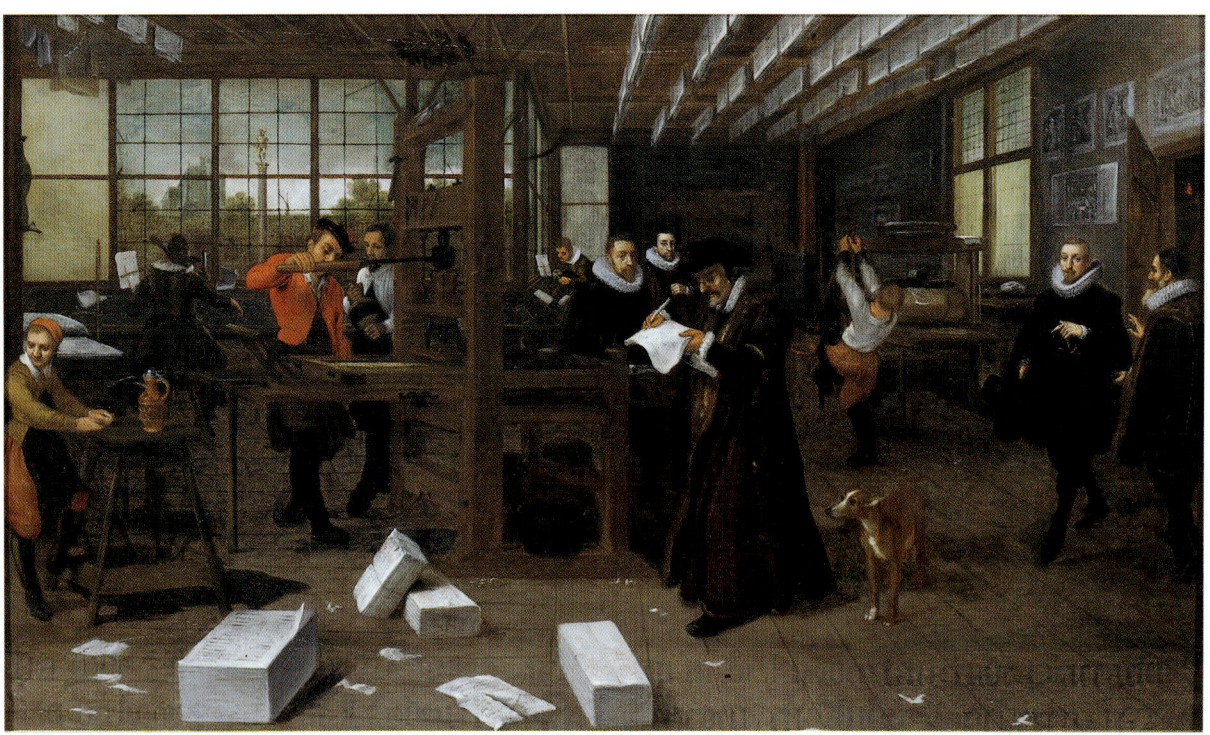

107 Adriaen van de Venne, Interior of an art business, dated 1623, panel, 46.5 x 76.2 cm, London, Daily Mail and General Trust plc

A last example of a grisaille that did not lead to the subsequent making of a print is the impressive *Preaching of John the Baptist* (fig. 109).[124] The sketch was transferred to panel and is of large format but was originally much smaller, roughly the same size as the *Joseph relating his dreams*, the *Ecce homo* and the sketched *Descent from the cross*. Rembrandt made the grisaille while with Uylenburgh, but obviously took the work with him when he moved from his house, for he sold the work in 1652 to the art lover Jan Six (see fig. 211), at the same time as his *Portrait of Saskia* (fig. 108).[125] He must also have kept the *Ecce homo*, since the grisaille was still in his possession in 1656.[126] It was acquired by the Amsterdam art lover and painter Jan van de Cappelle, presumably at one of the sales of Rembrandt's possessions.

The precise nature of the separation of the ways of Rembrandt and Uylenburgh is not known. There seems no question of there having been any business or artistic disagreement. Rembrandt was married in 1634, there were children on the way and by then he was almost thirty. His

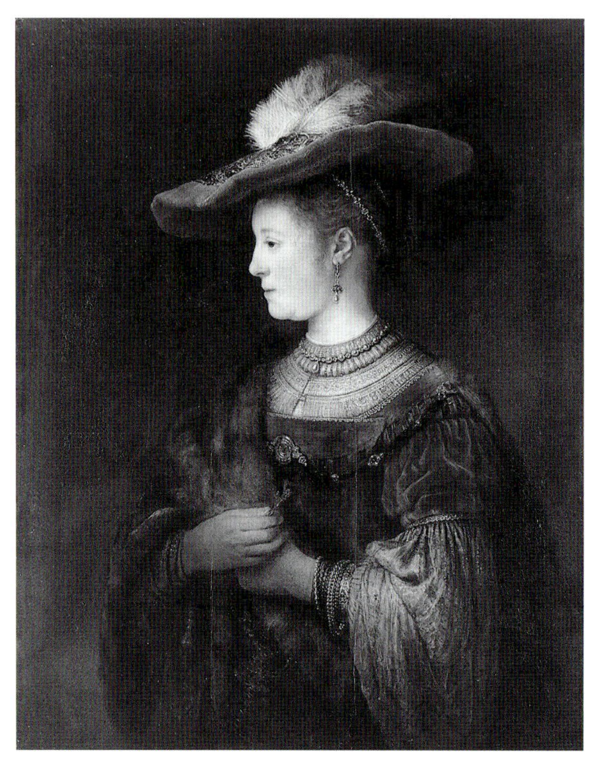

108 Rembrandt van Rijn, Half-length figure of Saskia Uylenburgh, panel, 99.5 x 78.8 cm, Kassel, Staatliche Museen Kassel, Gemäldegalerie Alte Meister (Br. 101; Corpus II A 85)

124 Br. 555 and Corpus III A 106.
125 Doc. 1658/18.
126 Doc. 1656/12, no. 121.

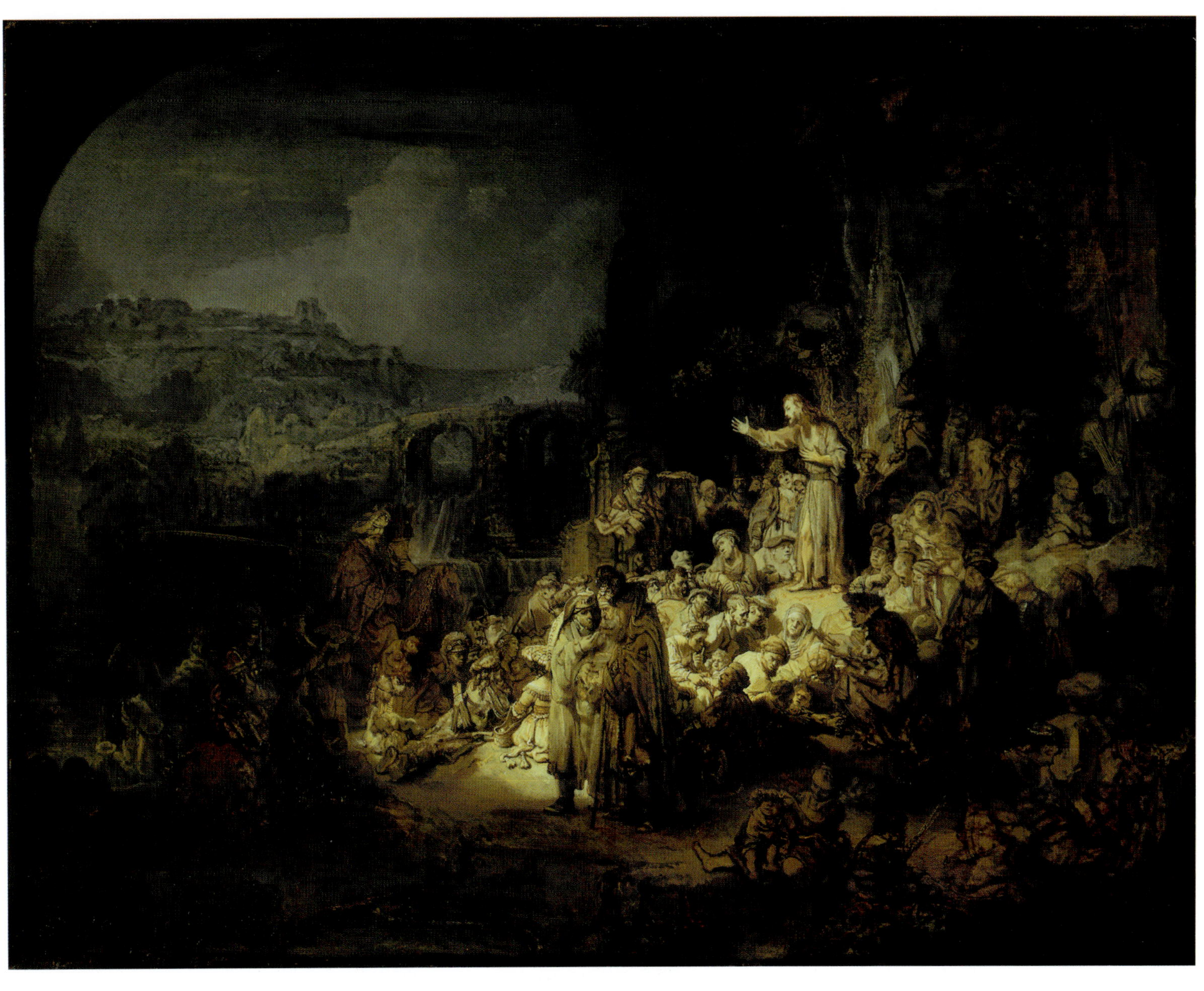

109 Rembrandt van Rijn, The preaching of John the Baptist, canvas, stuck on panel, 62.7 x 81.1 cm, Berlin, Staatliche Museen zu Berlin, Gemäldegalerie (Br. 555; Corpus III A 106)

collaboration with Uylenburgh had lasted quite a long time and indeed it is surprising that he had not set up his own establishment earlier. Rembrandt did not leave a vacancy behind him, for in Govert Flinck he had at once a worthy successor as head of the workshop.

COLLABORATION WITH GOVERT FLINCK, C. 1635 – C. 1638

There are three contemporary printed texts on Govert Flinck, all based on fairly reliable information.[127] Arnold Houbraken, in his *Groote Schouburgh*, owes his precise biography to the information provided by Nicolaes Anthonie Flinck, the son of Govert Flinck born in 1646. Houbraken gives particulars of Flinck's Mennonite background, his training with Lambert Jacobsz in Leeuwarden, his relatives in Amsterdam, his apprenticeship with Rembrandt and the changes that occurred over the course of time in his style of painting. His stay with Uylenburgh, however, is not covered.[128] Joachim von Sandrart, on the other hand, writes explicitly about this episode in his book *Teutsche Academie*, published in 1675.[129] In this book the German painter draws on his own memory, for he lived in Amsterdam between 1637 and 1642 and undoubtedly knew Uylenburgh's firm very well. The third text on Flinck comes from Filippo Baldinucci's *Notizie de' professori del disegno*. In this case, although the author relies on second-hand information, his account can be accepted as reasonably reliable: Baldinucci's source was the painter Eberhard Keil, who was at the time active in Rome but had lived in Amsterdam between 1642 and 1651, where he had worked with both Hendrick Uylenburgh and Rembrandt.[130] Together with supplementary source material and Flinck's paintings that have been preserved, these texts give us a good idea of his earliest years in Amsterdam and his relations with Hendrick Uylenburgh.

Houbraken writes that Flinck was apprenticed by his father to Lambert Jacobsz, who was a creditable painter and a leader among the Waterland Mennonites at Leeuwarden. Flinck worked there with the somewhat older Jacob Backer, another Mennonite. According to Houbraken, Flinck moved to Amsterdam together with Backer. We know that Backer settled in Amsterdam in 1633,[131] but it remains to be seen whether in fact Flinck came at the same time, and until we know for certain, his arrival can perhaps better be placed 'around 1635'. If Flinck did also move to Amsterdam as early as 1633, his collaboration with Uylenburgh lasted at least five years.[132] In Amsterdam, he first worked for almost a year with Rembrandt in order to master the latter's style and then – late in 1635 or early in 1636? – we find him working with Hendrick Uylenburgh. If this chronology is correct, Flinck's training with Rembrandt must also have taken place in Uylenburgh's workshop and Uylenburgh would then have taken him on to work for his firm. Flinck's stay with Uylenburgh is documented for 1637 in the archives: on March 13th of that year, at an auction of the effects of the painter-cum-art dealer Jan Bassé, he bought a lot of prints for twelve *stuivers*. The entry in the sale records reads: 'Govert Flinck tot Hendrick Uylenburch', 'tot' possibly meaning 'residing with'.[133] He stayed with Uylenburgh for some time. Sandrart writes that Flinck first trained with Rembrandt and thereafter 'remained several years with the famous art-dealer Ulenburg, leaving him many truly magnificent portraits from his hand'.[134]

The texts referring to Flinck are both highly informative and credible, but that is not to say that they are, without further qualification, correct in every detail. In the case of Keil, for instance, his memory may have sometimes let him down, while Baldinucci may have misunderstood him or have confused some of the facts – and this does indeed seem to have happened in his biographies of both Rembrandt and Flinck. For example, Baldinucci says that Rembrandt was a Mennonite and that Flinck adhered to the Calvinist faith. In fact, it was Flinck who was a Mennonite during these years and later, in 1651, transferred to the Remonstrant Church; while Rembrandt, although he was never a member of the Dutch Reformed Church, was in all probability of the reformed faith. Baldinucci must have got the denominational affiliations of the two painters the wrong way round. Despite this, his text on 'Guobert Flynk' deserves the closest scrutiny.[135]

127 For the following see also Meijer 1983.
128 Houbraken 1718-1721, vol. 2, pp. 18-27.
129 Sandrart 1675/Peltzer 1925, p. 194.
130 Baldinucci 1681-1728, quoted from the seven-volume edition published in Florence between 1845 and 1847, vol. 5, pp. 322-323.
131 In that year he was commissioned to paint a group portrait of the regentesses of the Burgerweeshuis in Amsterdam.
132 The authors of *A Corpus* assume that Flinck arrived in Amsterdam in 1633 and attribute to him several early rembrandtesque works, *Corpus* II C 48 and II Corrigenda and Addenda I C 6; also several suggestions on pp. 88-89.
133 GAA, arch. no. 5073, inv. no. 962, 9-30 March 1637; Bredius 1915-1922, vol. I, p. 128 and vol. 7, p. 9.
134 'Sich lange Jahre auf bey dem berühmten Kunsthändler Ulenburg, dem er viel ausbündige herrliche Contrafäte von eigner Hand hinterlaßen', Sandrart 1675/Peltzer 1925, p. 194.
135 See above, note 130. I am grateful to Prof. dr Henk van Veen who made a free translation of the crucial passages. Jaco Rutgers allowed me to see the manuscript of his dissertation.

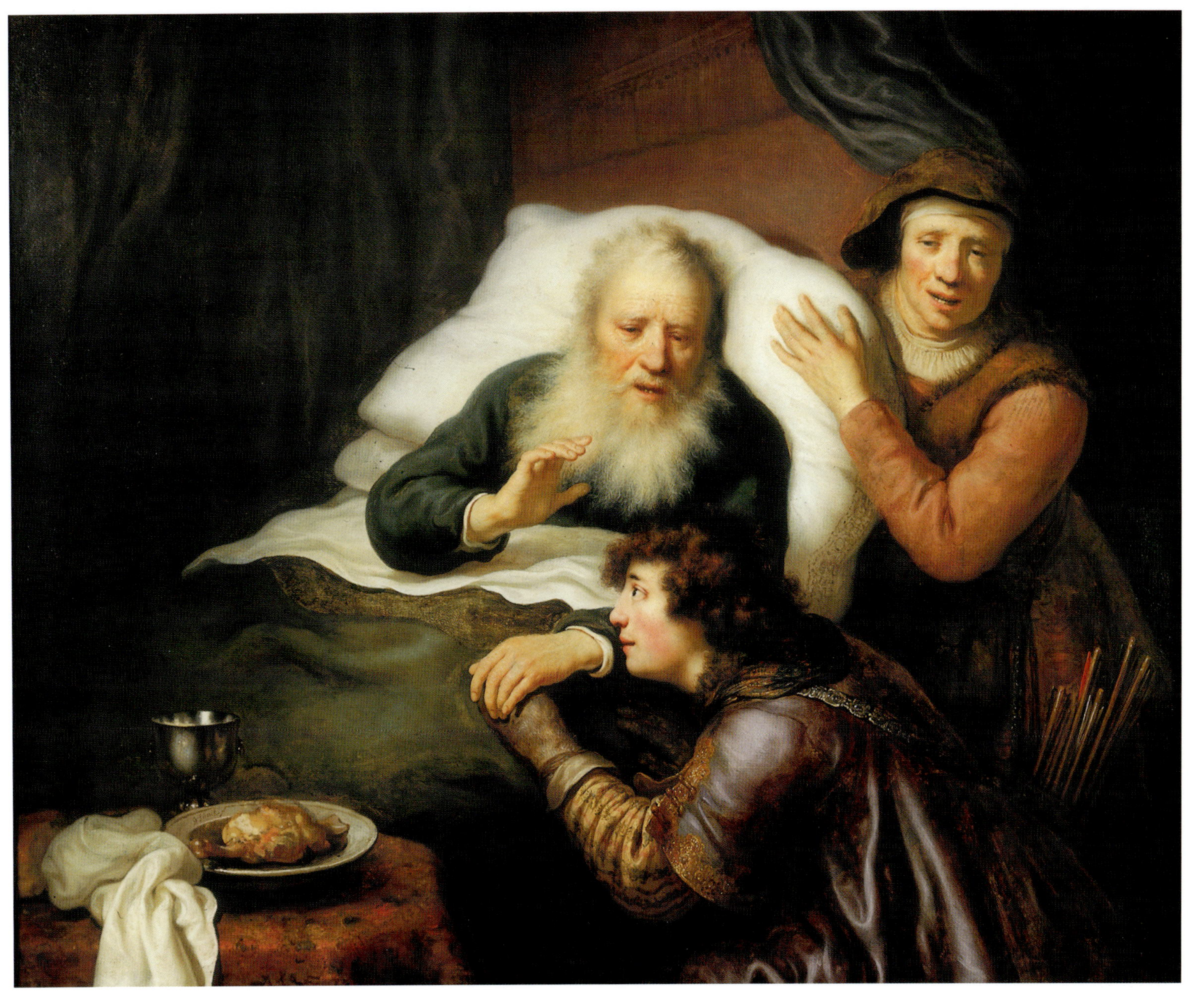

110 Govert Flinck, Isaac blessing Jacob, signed 'G. Flinck f.', canvas, 124 x 151 cm, Utrecht, Museum Catharijneconvent (on loan from Instituut Collectie Nederland) (Sum. 11 613)

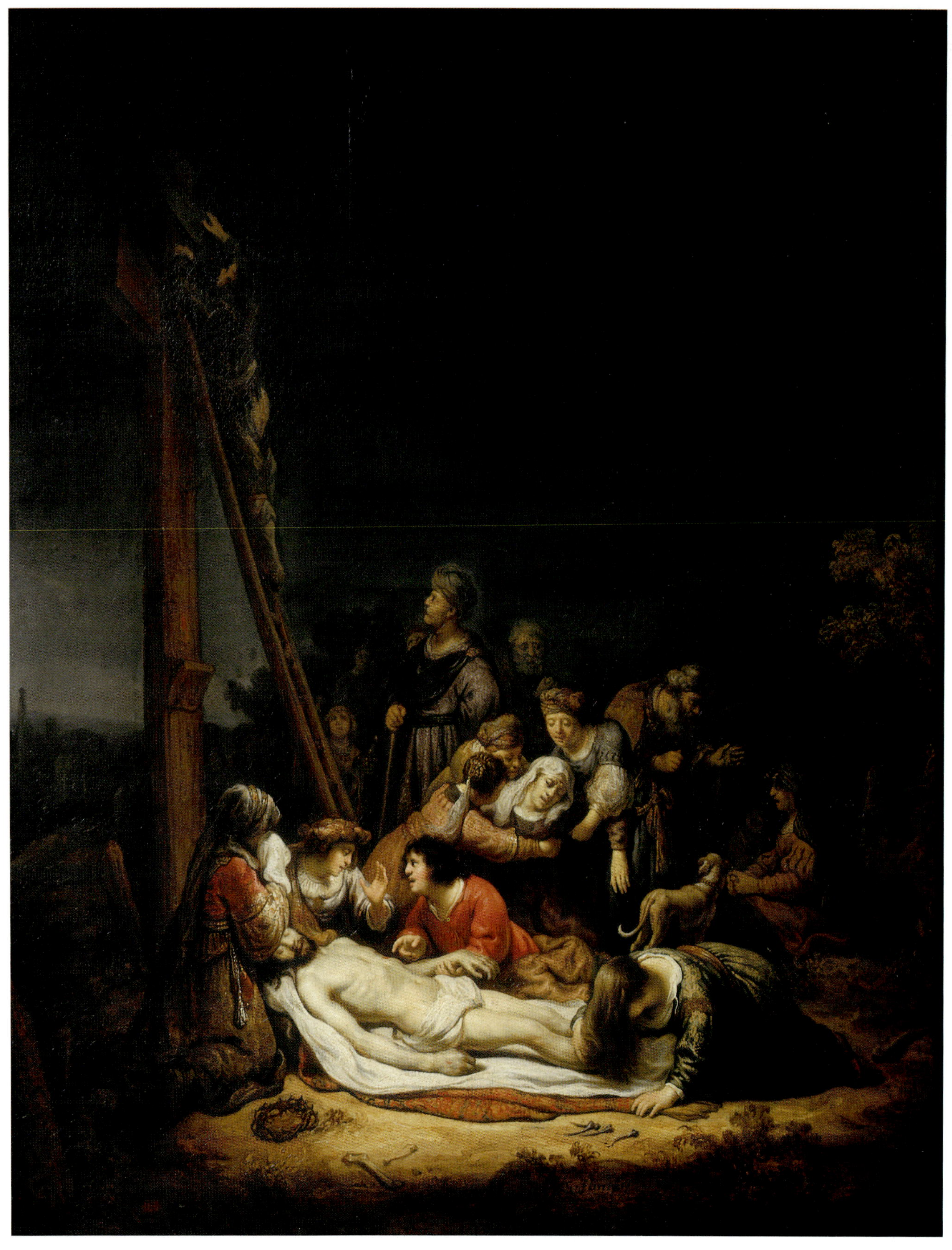

111 Govert Flinck, The lamentation over the dead Christ, signed and dated 'G. Flinck. f 1637', canvas, 90.1 x 71.9 cm, New York, Jack Kilgore & Co., Inc. (Sum. II 612)

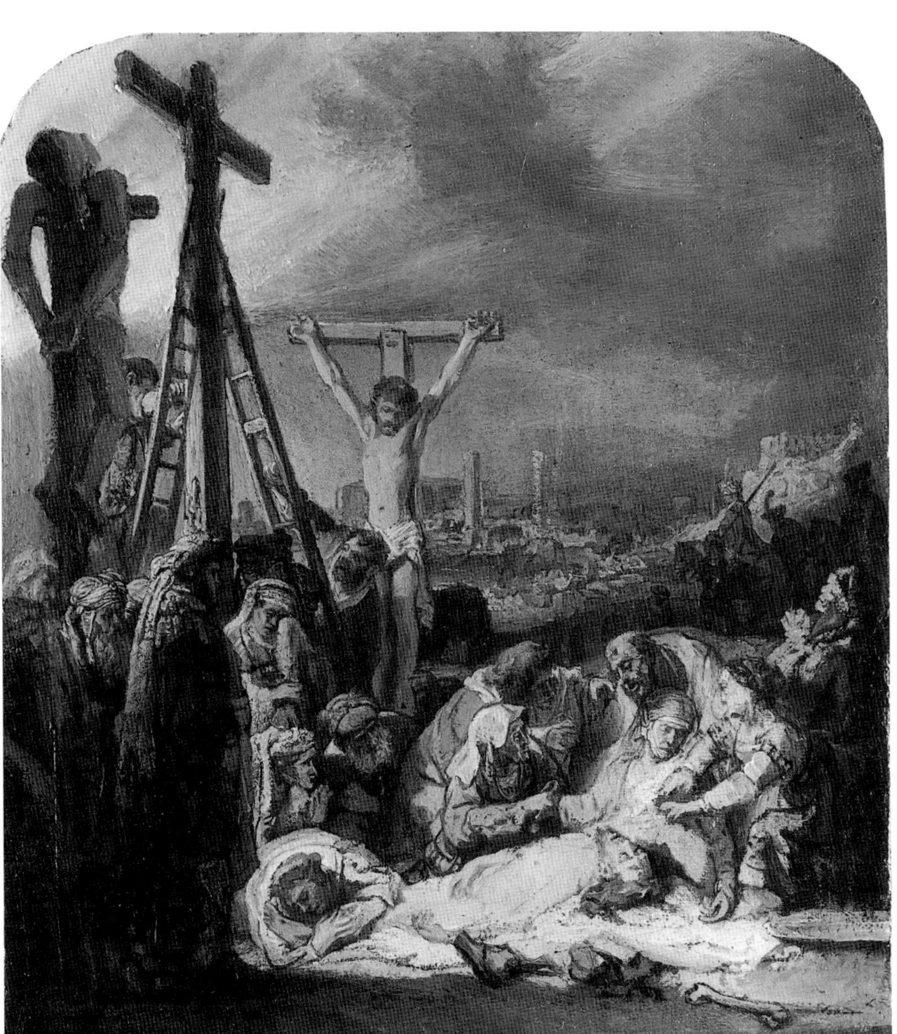

in which a great many animals are depicted in an exceptionally life-like manner, won the admiration of connoisseurs of the time. According to Baldinucci, while still in his youth Flinck 'put himself in the hands' of a certain merchant who, by providing him with a considerable amount of money, had him work 'almost continuously … at the dictate of his own imagination'. This merchant had bought from him the painting mentioned above for a good price. After a certain time Flinck attracted so much attention that, having already acquired the reputation of being the best painter in Amsterdam, he decided to stop working for the merchant and go independent. His work was in great demand with art-lovers and he was evidently very well paid: for a painting of four palms in width Flinck received 60 scudi.[137]

The dealer in whose hands Flinck had placed himself was of course Hendrick Uylenburgh. It is interesting that Uylenburgh had the painter working almost full-time for him and that Flinck painted whatever his own imagination suggested. Flinck could apparently on his own account produce paintings at regular intervals and himself determine the subjects of the works he made. That is, if we can believe Baldinucci, Uylenburgh did not always dictate the subjects to Flinck. The comment that Uylenburgh left the artist free to choose his own subjects should perhaps refer to history pieces and landscapes. We don't know for certain any works from Flinck's earliest Amsterdam period, when he was still training with Rembrandt and would not yet have signed works as his own.[138] The *Isaac blessing Jacob* (fig. 110) is an early history piece from his hand. This work, neither signed nor dated, betrays the influence of Lambert Jacobsz and would therefore have been painted either in Leeuwarden or during Flinck's earliest period in Amsterdam. His first known signed and dated history piece is the *Lamentation* from 1637 (fig. 111), which indicates that it was done in Uylenburgh's workshop. In painting his

136 Flinck appears to have actually been in Antwerp, probably around 1645. See Bruyn 1984-1995, II, p. 226. In his text, Baldinucci makes a leap in time without giving any indication.

137 Four palms is roughly equal to a metre, 60 scudi is roughly 150 guilders.

138 Van de Wetering 2005, pp. 216-217, correctly points out that Flinck's early work is still problematic.

First of all, Baldinucci says that Flinck was a pupil of 'Rembrant del Reno'. Although Flinck wanted to acquire fame as an artist, he never went to Italy, but contented himself with the study of painters from north of the Alps, and in particular the work of his master. In his use of colour he followed in Rembrandt's footsteps, although Flinck would have been much better at 'drawing contours'. In this connection Baldinucci points out that Flinck had visited the southern Netherlands and made a thorough study of the Antwerp artists.[136] He painted an *Annunciation to the shepherds* – on panel, according to Badinucci – with a large number of shepherds, some of whom have been woken by the voice of the divine messenger while others are shown still asleep. This painting,

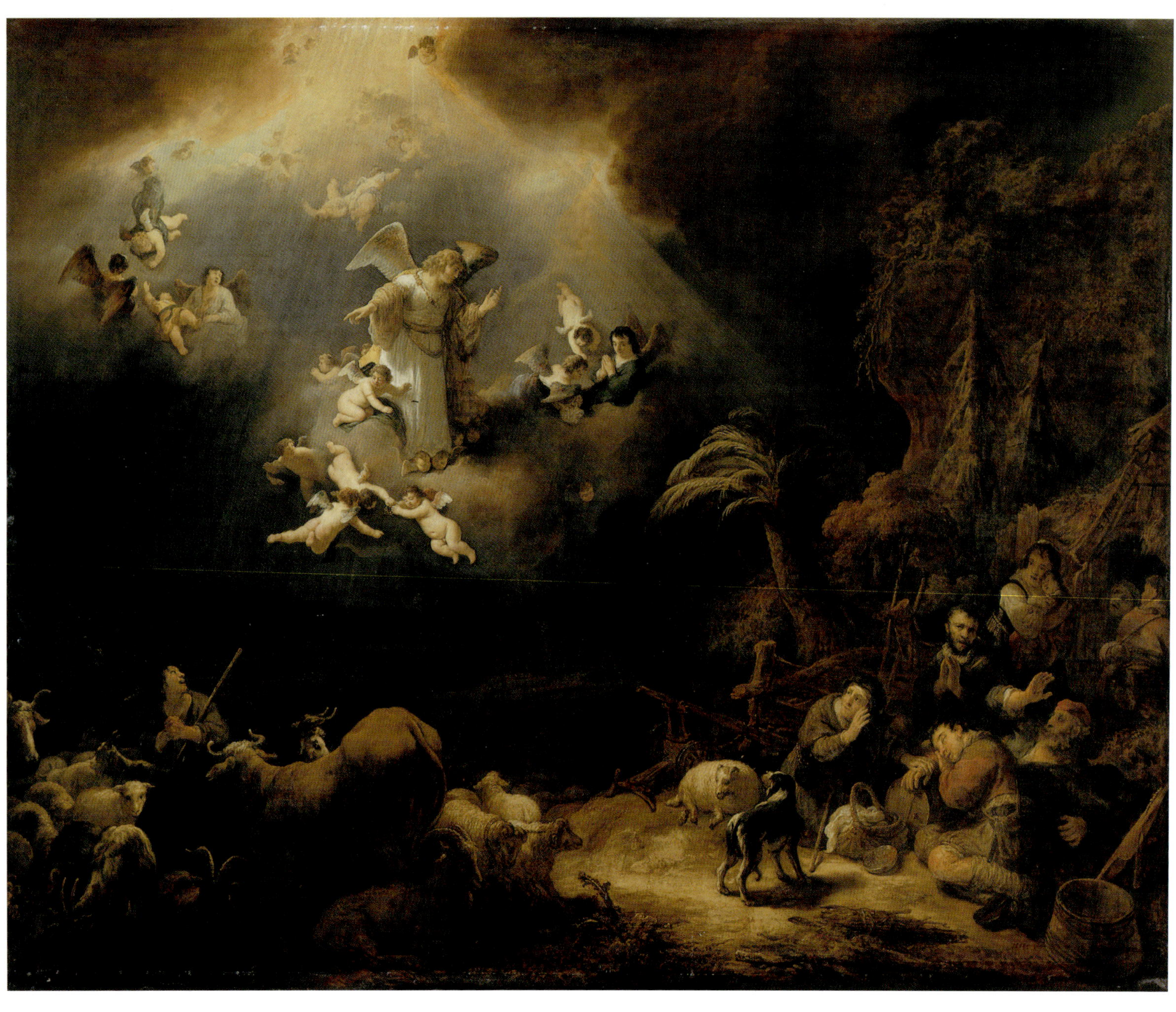

113 Govert Flinck, The annunciation to the shepherds, signed and dated 'G. Flinck f 1639', canvas, 160 x 196 cm, Paris, Musée du Louvre (Sum. 11 615)

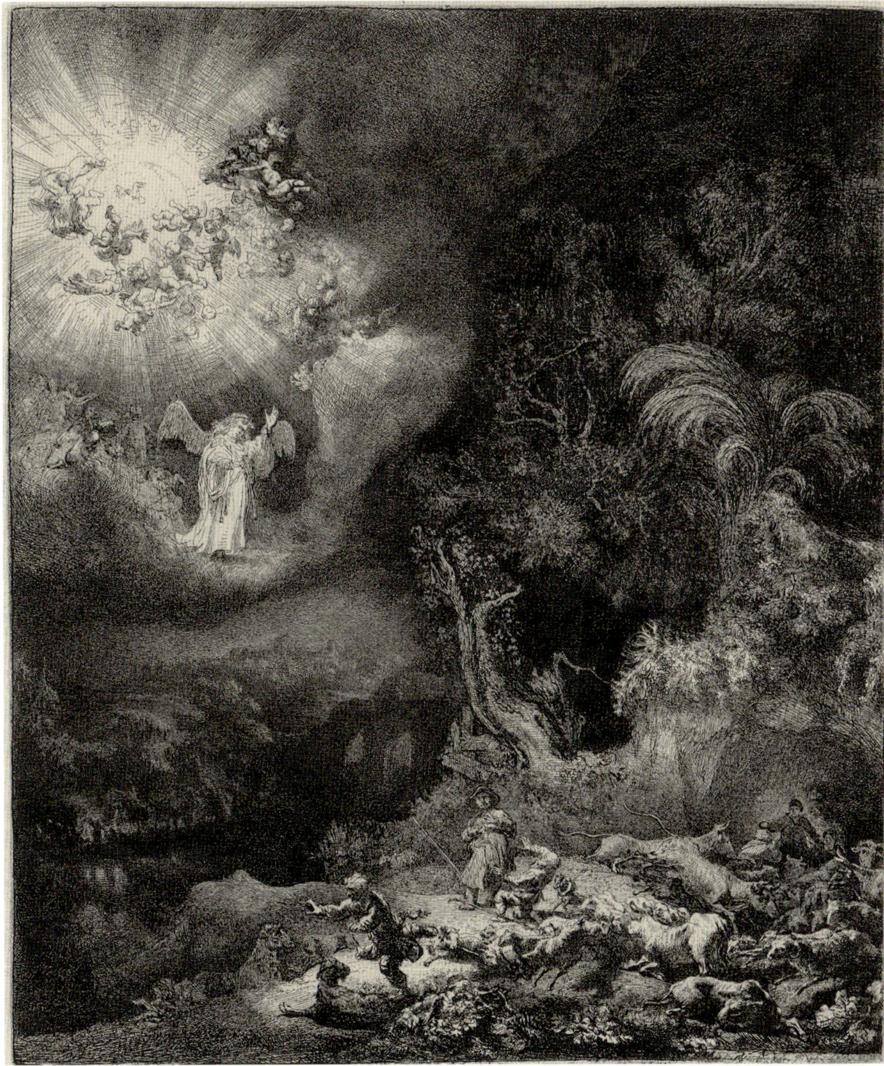

Lamentation, Flinck must have had Rembrandt's grisaille of the same subject (fig. 112) in mind. It is highly significant that this latter grisaille must have been produced in the years 1633-1635,[139] perhaps even originating during the period of Flinck's apprenticeship with Rembrandt. In any case, Flinck's version of the subject is very heavily influenced by it: in the elevated viewpoint, in the placing of the figures – one of which, Nicodemus, the man with the turban and a stick in his right hand looking at the cross, is taken from an other history piece by Rembrandt – and in the han-dling of light and shade. An unusual feature of this painting is that we almost certainly know who was the original owner. When he died, the Amsterdam art-lover Jan Pietersz Bruyningh

bequeathed no less than eight paintings by Flinck, including a Descent from the cross. We know of no other early painting by Flinck of the Descent from the cross, or of the Lamentation – the event immediately following the Descent – and there are certainly no other archival references to this biblical scene. Like Flinck and Uylenburgh, Bruyningh was also a Mennonite. Relations between this art-lover and Uylenburgh's art busi-ness seem to have been particularly close. When Rembrandt was working with Uylenburgh, dur-ing the period 1631/2-1635, he painted a double portrait of Bruyningh and his wife, probably the portrait from 1633, now in Boston (see fig. 122), and also a portrait of her father separately.

The painting that Baldinucci twice mentions is

139 Corpus II A 107; in the sale catalogue of Christie's Amsterdam, *Old Master Pictures and Drawings*, 16 November 2005, no. 152, it was incorrectly stated that Rembrandt's gri-saille was made in the period 1637-1643.

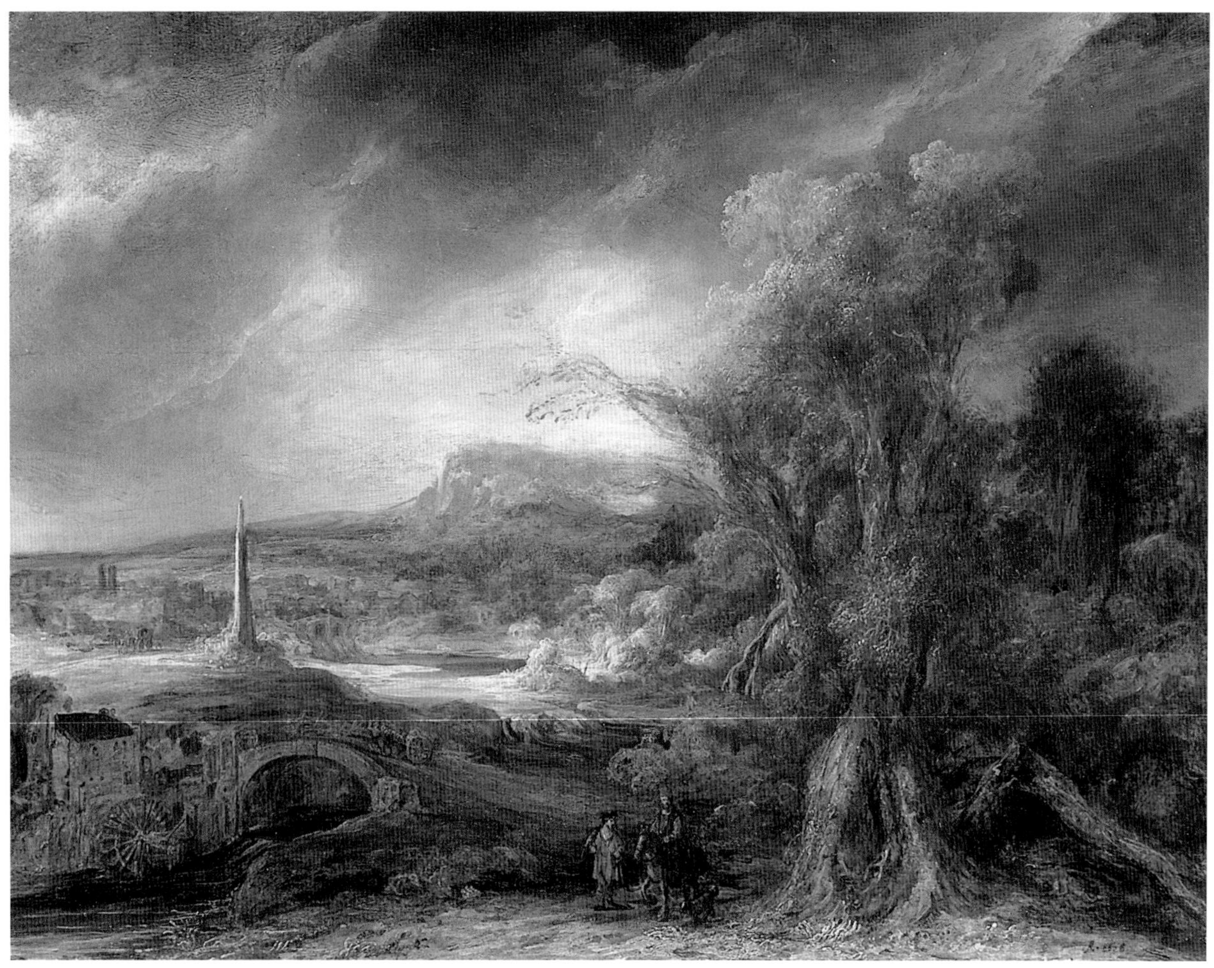

in fact Flinck's excellent *Annunciation to the shepherds* dated 1639 (fig. 113).[140] Although the painter had by then built up a considerable reputation, he still sold this painting to Uylenburgh, who must have seen the opportunity to sell the painting at a profit. In all probability he already had in mind a buyer from outside Amsterdam – possibly beyond the Republic – since any resident of Amsterdam who wanted to purchase a painting could easily have found his way to Flinck's studio, in which case sale through an intermediary would have been unnecessary. The *Annunciation to the shepherds* corresponds closely to Rembrandt' work. There is a clear relation with Rembrandt's etching that shows the same bible scene (fig. 114): although Flinck has changed the format from vertical to horizontal, and although there are differences in composition, the borrowings from the 1634 etching are abundantly clear, particularly the angel

who brings the good tidings, the palm tree and the cow in the foreground.

During his apprenticeship with Lambert Jacobsz, Flinck must also have become adept at painting landscape as an aspect of the history piece.[141] In Amsterdam Flinck painted several landscapes. For a long time, very little was known about his production of painted landscapes. The discovery of the remains of Flinck's signature on the *Landscape with obelisk* was a crucial breakthrough: until then the painting, which must have originated around 1638, had been attributed to Rembrandt (fig. 115). Following this discovery there surfaced a *Landscape with bridge and ruin* by Flinck, fully signed and dated 1637 (fig. 116). On the basis of these pieces a landscape in Berlin, also once taken to be a Rembrandt, could similarly be attributed to Flinck (fig. 117).[142] We can safely assume that he would not have painted a

140 As far as I am aware, this was first pointed out by Meijer 1983, p. 25.
141 In this connection, one can point to a *Landscape with ruins* attributed to Flinck, now in a private collection in Chicago. See Bruyn 1984-1995, II, p. 226 and p. 227, fig. 2, and Schneider 1990, p. 132, fig. 105.
142 Corpus III, pp. 39-50 and Schneider 1990, pp. 128-145.

166

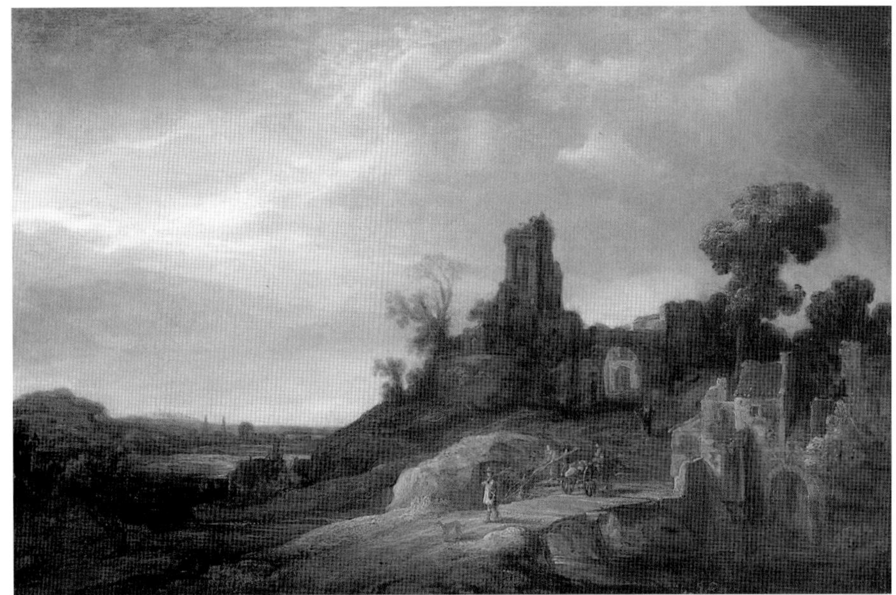

116 Govert Flinck, Landscape with a bridge and ruins, signed and dated 'G. Flinck f. 1637', panel, 49.5 x 74.9 cm, Paris, Musée du Louvre (Sum. 11 718)

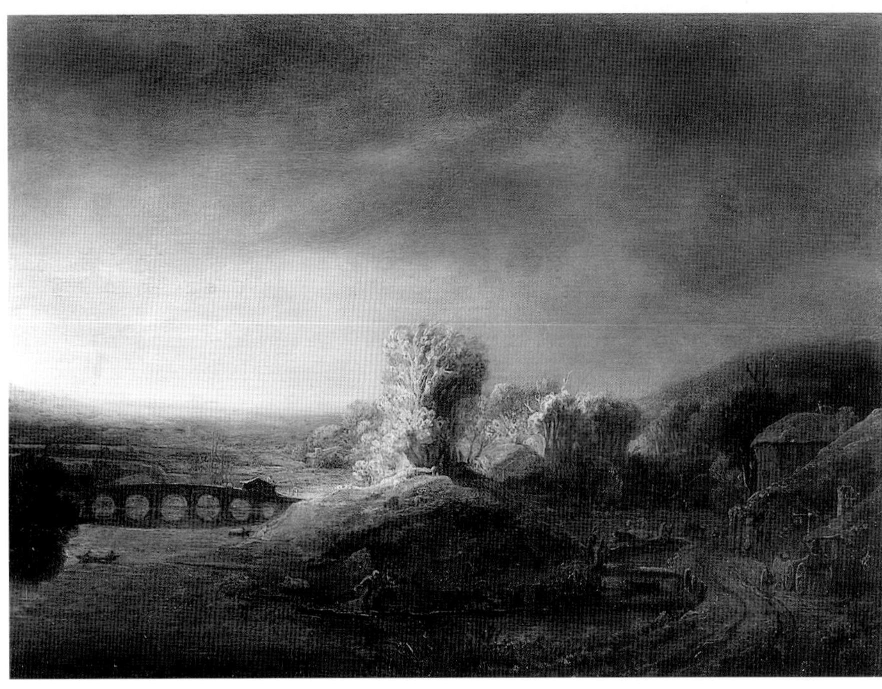

117 Govert Flinck, attributed to, Landscape with a bridge, panel, 28.5 x 39.5 cm, Berlin, Staatliche Museen zu Berlin, Gemäldegalerie (Br. 445)

large number of landscapes; besides, it is striking that they seem to have circulated in a restricted circle, for as far as we know all the owners were Mennonites. There seems therefore to have been a fairly exclusive public for these landscapes. The Jan Pietersz Bruyningh mentioned above possessed two landscapes by Flinck and a further 'copy of a landscape after Flinck'; while his fellow-Mennonite Ameldonck Leeuw, on his death in 1653, had nine painting by Flinck hanging in his house, including two landscapes and a painting of cattle at pasture to be discussed below.[143]

Although Flinck seems to have had a free hand in his choice of history pieces and landscapes, Uylenburgh would certainly have got him to paint portraits, just as he had done earlier with Rembrandt. Sandrart actually mentions Flinck's activity as a portraitist for precisely these years. Houbraken knew that Flinck had well-to-do relatives ('bloedvrienden') living in Amsterdam

143 See p. 174-175.

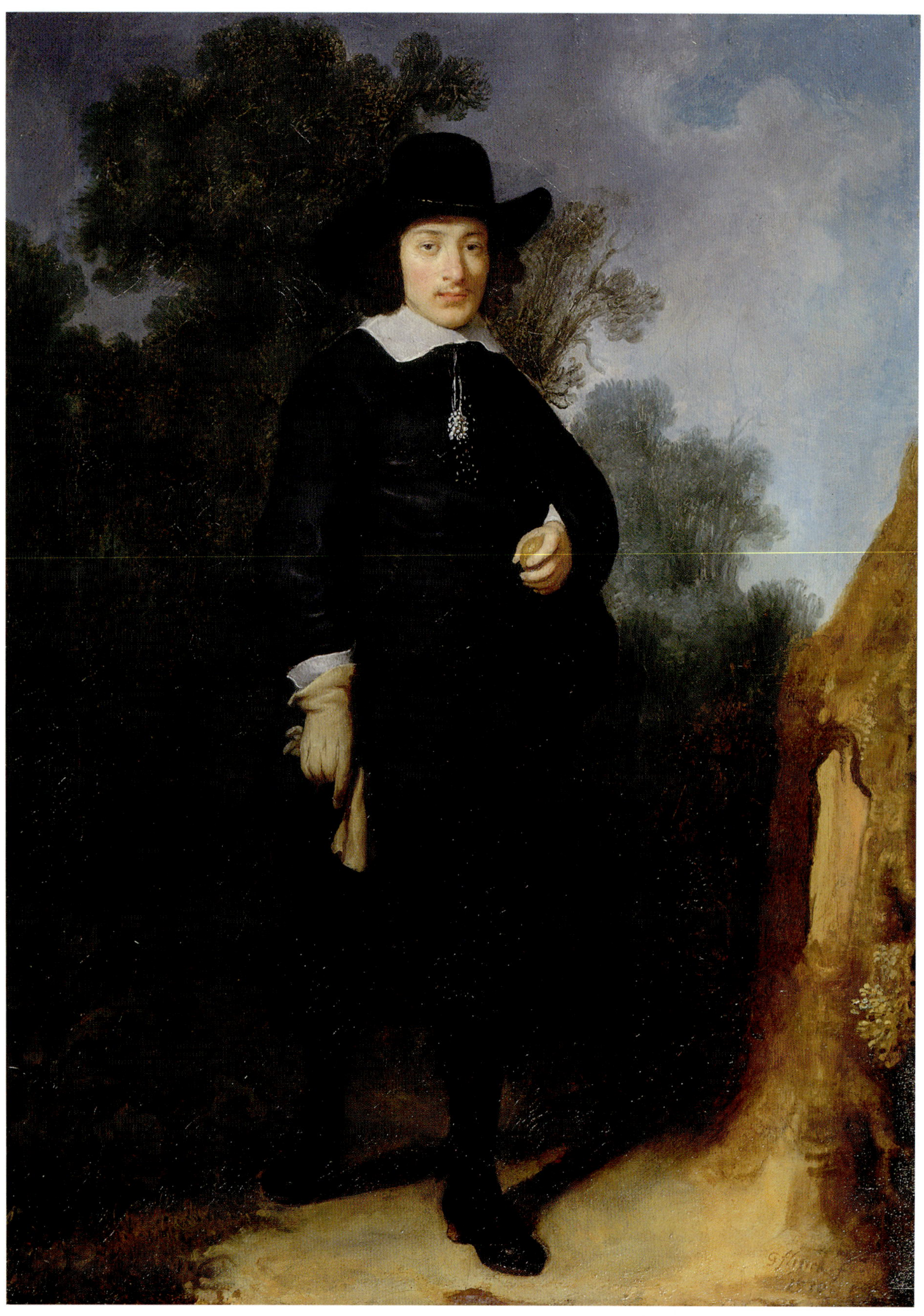

118 Govert Flinck, Portrait of Dirck Jacobsz Leeuw, signed and dated 'G. Flinck f. 1636', canvas, 65 x 47.5 cm, Amsterdam, Verenigde Doopsgezinde Gemeente (Sum. II 685)

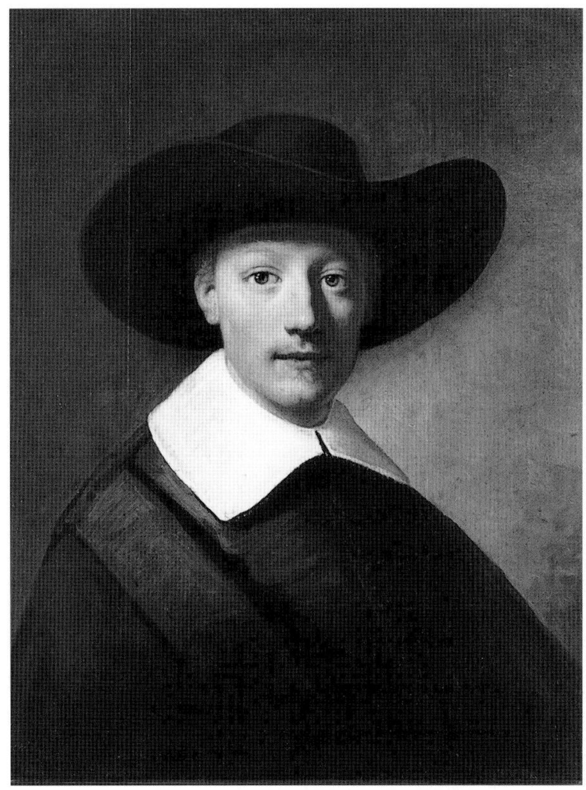

144 For the close relationship
between the painting styles of
Backer and Flinck, see Van den
Brink 1997.
145 Van der Veen 2005, p. 18
and note 81.
146 Schwartz 1984, p. 134; a
list of Huydecoper's paintings
from 1622 has also been preserved, in which appears a
Europa by Veronese valued at
250 guilders, possibly the same
painting as the work of the
same name previously in the
collection of Melchior Wijnt-
gis. It is also evident from his
administration that Cornelis
van der Voort had painted his
portrait for 150 guilders; ibid.,
p. 138.

with whom he 'found the first opportunity to
give proof of his art'. These relatives were the
Mennonite Jacob Leeuw and his family. The
full-length portrait of one of Jacob's sons, Dirck
Jacobsz Leeuw (fig. 118), dated 1636, is one such
early proof of his ability as a portrait-painter.
This portrait would have been one of the pieces
to which Houbraken alluded. Thanks to Martin
Bijl's restoration of this painting in March 2006,
the sky has regained its clear blue and one can
now see that the subject of the portrait is holding
some kind of (citrus?) fruit. The greatest surprise
is the degree of mobility in the portrait. The left
leg is thrust forward, while the right heel is in
process of being raised. The man's posture is comparable to that of the two main figures in Rembrandt's *Nightwatch* from a few years later. This
introduction of 'movement' into a portrait is
something that Flinck must have picked up from
Rembrandt shortly beforehand. Flinck portrayed
various members of the Leeuw family, but other
Mennonites too, the portrait of Gozen Centen
(fig. 119) being a fine example.

In both the choice of his subjects and in his

style, Flinck followed Rembrandt's example.
During his apprenticeship he succeeded in making
Rembrandt's manner of painting entirely his own,
and to imitate him to such an extent 'that several
of his pieces were considered to be – and sold as
– authentic paintings by Rembrandt'. This could
certainly have applied to his rembrandtesque
landscapes and 'tronies'. Flinck has been characterized as an eclectic – not unjustly, since his style at
different times shows the imprint of various influences. There is of course a kinship with the work
of his teachers, but also that of Jacob Backer,[144]
while in the mid-forties his style clearly shows
the influence of Rubens. Govert Flinck must
have maintained contact with Rembrandt and his
work: for years he continued quite openly to borrow motifs from the work of his former master.

CIRCLE OF CLIENTS

Because no record of Hendrick Uylenburgh's
bookkeeping has survived, any insight we might
have into his circle of clients is necessarily limited.
We need other sources if we are to be able to identify them. Art-lovers sometimes wrote up their
purchases in notebooks, noting their price and
provenance after a description of the object. Unfortunately such notebooks from the first half
of the seventeenth century have rarely been
preserved,[145] and in such registers as do exist the
name of Uylenburgh does not occur. Housekeep-
ing books or cashbooks belonging to private individuals can also contain details of art purchases.
A nice example is the cashbook of the Amsterdam
regent Joan Huydecoper, who on June 15th 1628
recorded that he had bought a *Venus* after Rubens
for 25 guilders and a 'tronie' by Rembrandt for
29 guilders,[146] although he gives no indication
of where he acquired either of these works. One
would like to think that Uylenburgh could have
supplied them, of course, but that is pure speculation. There is no record to this effect, nor does
Uylenburgh's name as the supplier of art appear
in any other records of household administration
known to me from this time.

One of the most important sources of our
knowledge of the ownership of paintings in early

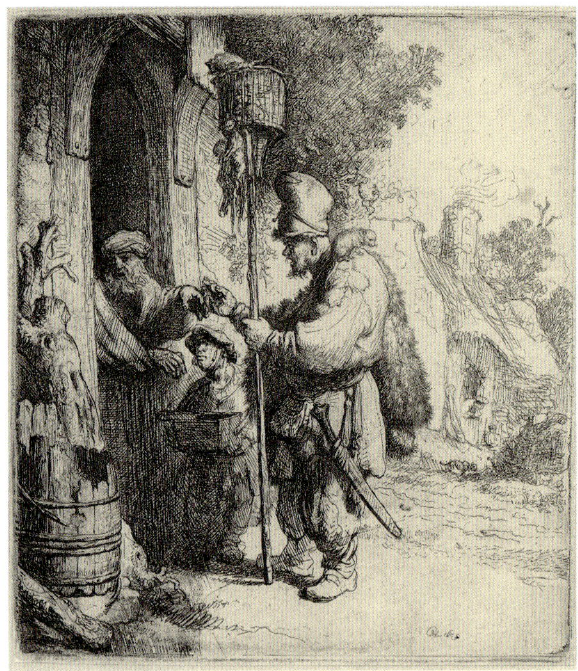

120 Rembrandt van Rijn, The rat catcher, signed and dated 'RHL 1632', etching, 14 x 12.5 cm, Amsterdam, The Rembrandt House Museum (B. 121 III, 3)

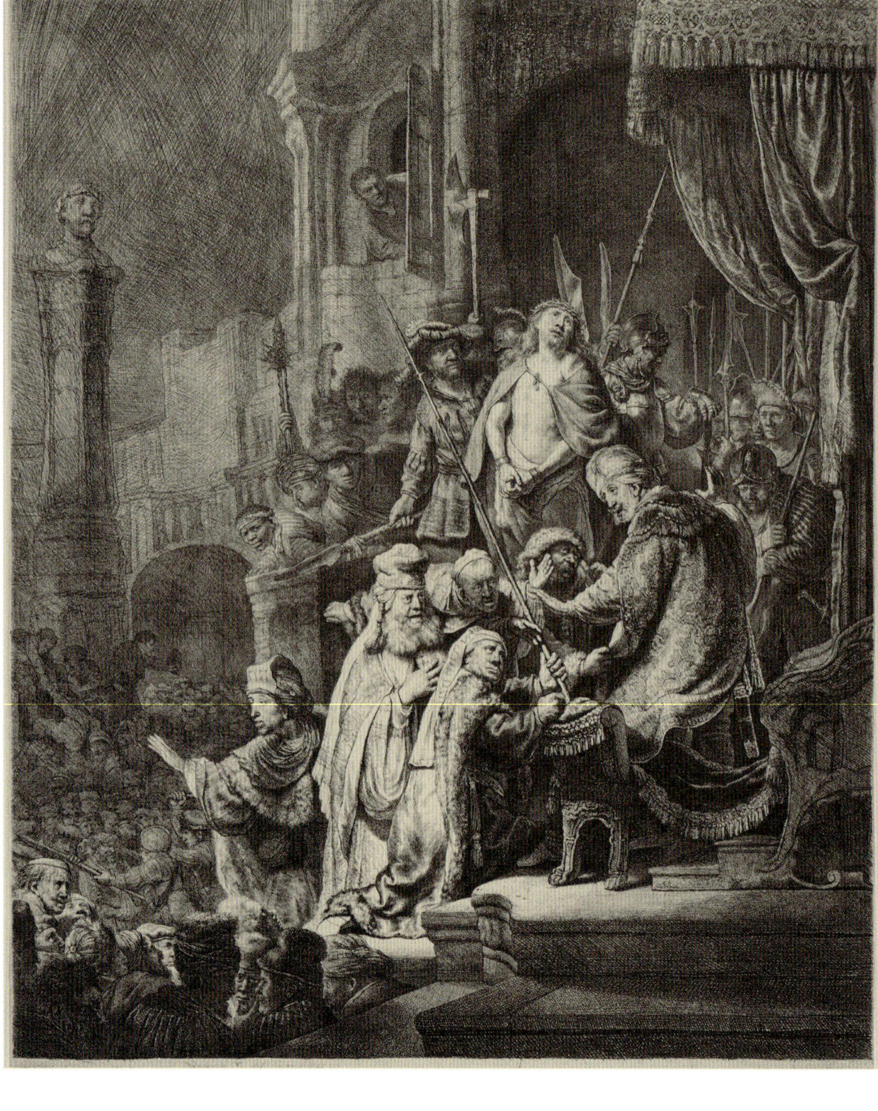

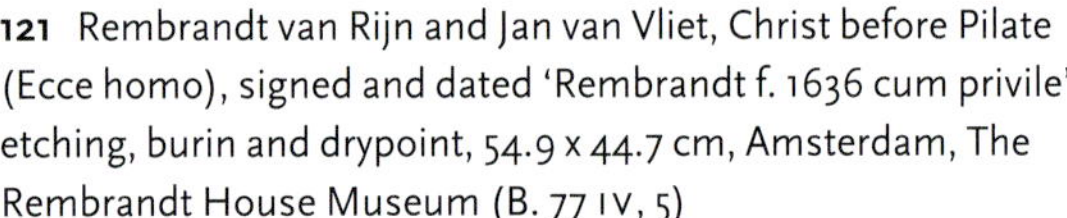

121 Rembrandt van Rijn and Jan van Vliet, Christ before Pilate (Ecce homo), signed and dated 'Rembrandt f. 1636 cum privile', etching, burin and drypoint, 54.9 x 44.7 cm, Amsterdam, The Rembrandt House Museum (B. 77 IV, 5)

modern times is the inventory of household effects. Paintings are often described in the probate inventories of wealthy Amsterdam citizens from the second and third quarters of the seventeenth centuries, giving the subject and occasionally the name of the work's (presumed) author. Unfortunately, the origins of artworks and the way in which the owner had acquired them is almost never given; this only happens in the exceptional case. Thus, in a specification of the dowry a woman had brought with her when she married

a silversmith in 1662, a number of paintings are listed including 'the pickled herring with an armozeen curtain in front, *bought from Cretser, done by Van de Bos*'.[147] A second example comes from the inventory of the household effects of an Amsterdam art-lover in which one finds 'a small thunderstorm by Pieter Mollijn, *bought from Lodewijck van Ludick*'.[148] The dealers Marten Kretzer and Lodewijck van Ludick were both active in the art trade. Again, however, no such record has so far been found relating to Uylenburgh.

147 'Den pekelharingh, *van Cretser gecocht*, bij Van de Bos gedaen, met een armosijne gardijn daervoor', G A A, not. J. Quirijnen Spithoff, N A 1763, pp. 468-472, 8 September-10 October 1662, particularly p. 468; the list was compiled by the woman herself, who would have known how she acquired the still life. 'Cretser' is Marten Kretzer, who had the painter Pieter van den Bosch working for him.

148 'Een onweertje van Pieter Mollijn, *is gekocht van Lodewijck van Ludick*', G A A, not. J. de Winter, N A 2299, prot. no. 99, pp. 57-71, 24 July 1670, particularly p. 69; in this document the paintings and other art works are described 'volgens twe distincte specificatien bij wijlen Cornelis Dircksz. Kool', ibid., p. 60. This latter is the art-lover Cornelis Dircksz. Cool (c. 1593-1669), who thus had described his own art possessions, which explains the exact account given in the inventory. For Lodewijck van Ludick, see Van den Boogert/ Broos/Van Gelder/Van der Veen 1999, p. 143.

149 GAA, not. L. Lamberti, NA 570, pp. 257-270, 29 June 1647; the inventory ends abruptly and is unsigned, but is probably complete.
150 After 'een trony' was inscribed 'van Rembrant' but this was changed (probably at Uylenburgh's instigation!) to 'after Rembrant'.
151 A son-in-law paid 700 guilders to the poor of the Flemish Mennonite community, see the deed of donation of their estate which also gives an idea of the wealth this couple had amassed, GAA, not. L. Lamberti, NA 603, pp. 387-393, 11 May 1648.
152 GAA, arch. no. 5073, inv. no. 973, document no. 4, 30 January 1647.
153 According to the Rembrandt Research Project the double portrait dates from around 1632/3 and was painted by one of Rembrandt's associates, Corpus II C 67; Slatkes 1992, no. 194 considers that Rembrandt was responsible for the work's execution but does not exclude the possibility that some of the work is by an assistant, especially the woman's costume.
154 For instance a black worsted cloak valued at 20 guilders and 'een pack gekepert bratte kleeren met sattijne biesjes' (a suit of cotton twill clothes with satin edging), also valued at 20 guilders; gloves are also recorded.

Inventories of household effects can nevertheless contain important clues. Firstly there are those estates with paintings that were valued by Hendrick Uylenburgh – these will be discussed later – or containing works by artists who worked for him. In particular, one thinks here of Rembrandt and Flinck. Secondly, there are the inventories of the estates of those deceased Mennonites who, we suspect, had had contact with their fellow-believer Uylenburgh. These are also of interest. For example, there was the inventory of the estate of the deceased couple Jarich Lubberts and Reijncke Gerrits. In 1647 Hendrick Uylenburgh valued the paintings in their house,[149] among which were a storm by Simon de Vlieger (at 90 guilders the most valuable painting in the estate), a fight by Pieter de Neyn and, of more relevance here, three works by Govert Flinck: two portraits of family members (ovals valued at 36 and 30 guilders) and a hunter with a falcon (40 guilders). Quite apart from the valuation that he carried out, it is likely that Uylenburgh had had contacts with the Lubberts-Gerrits couple, for the inventory also lists 'a tronie by Rembrandt' (valued at 60 guilders) and also four etchings by this artist: 'a small tronie print by Rembrandt with an ebony frame' (16 stuyvers), 'two prints on board by Rembrandt, a rat-catcher and Christ's circumcision' (16 stuyvers) and 'an Ecce homo print by Rembrandt with an ebony frame' (6 guilders). The second print is the *Rat-catcher* from 1632 (B. 121; fig. 120), the third is the *Circumcision* from c. 1630 (B. 48), the fourth must be the same as the etching of *Christ before Pilate* (B. 77), whose first, unfinished state is dated 1635 and the second state a year later (fig. 121). This Mennonite couple also posssessed a 'tronie' of a young boy by Dirck Dircksz Santvoort (worth 12 guilders) and 'a tronie *after* Rembrandt by Dirck van Santvoort' (10 guilders).[150] As suggested earlier, it is well possible that Santvoort, who lived close by Uylenburgh, could have worked for him, perhaps even under Rembrandt. Like this couple, many wealthy Amsterdam Mennonites spent considerable sums on their art and had their portraits painted by the foremost – and most expensive – artists of the day. Jarich Lubberts and Reijncke Gerrits probably belonged to the Flemish community which, as we have seen in the first Chapter, was more conservative than the Waterland community.[151]

Jan Pietersz Bruyningh, a fellow-Mennonite, was certainly one of Uylenburgh's Amsterdam clients. The inventory of his effects, compiled after his death in 1646, reveals that this merchant draper had built up a collection of art, not that large, but highly selective, with works by Lucas van Leyden, Pieter Lastman, Jan Porcellis and other Dutch masters, including Jan Jansz Treck, who in 1640 was one of Hendrick Uylenburgh's financial sponsors. Six paintings by Salomon Koninck are listed, two portraits and a small landscape by Rembrandt and as many as eight works by Govert Flinck (see figs. 111 and 127) and a copy after another work by him.[152] The first painting in the inventory is a double portrait of Bruyningh and his first wife Hillegond Pietersdr Moutmaker by Rembrandt. Double portraits are almost non-existent in Rembrandt's œuvre, and such a work from 1633 that long bore his name has been removed from his œuvre (fig. 122).[153] Yet there is a strong possibility that it ought to be attributed to Rembrandt, which would make the old identification with the Bruyningh-Moutmaker couple once again possible. Against this identification it has been argued that a Mennonite couple at the time would not be dressed in such a luxurious fashion. There were, however, great differences between Mennonites, particularly with regard to their way of life, their consumption and their ostentation. The internal criticism one reads of the excessive life-style of some members can hardly have been without basis; in this light, therefore, it is interesting that Bruyningh's inventory also lists exceptional items of clothing.[154] If the identification is correct, the contact with Uylenburgh would have begun in the first half of the thirties. The portrait of Bruyningh's father-in-law, which according to the inventory was also painted by Rembrandt, would have originated in the same period.

The Mennonite relations were unquestionably extremely important for Uylenburgh – one of the most important will be discussed below – but his circle of clients was by no means restricted to this religious community. Jacques Specx, for instance,

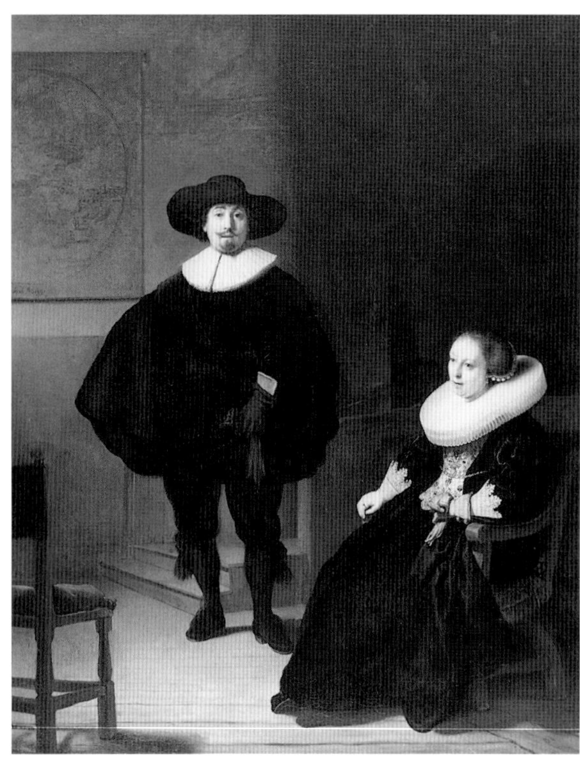

122 Rembrandt van Rijn, attributed to, Double portrait of a couple (Jan Pietersz Bruyningh and his wife Hillegond Pietersdr Moutmaker?), signed and dated 'Rembrandt. f. 1633', canvas, 132.2 x 109.5 cm, Boston, Massachusets. The Isabella Stewart Gardner Museum (Br. 405; Corpus II C 67)

on the Sea of Galilee (fig. 124).[157] The painting depicting 'een Europa van Rembrant' is certainly the same as his *Abduction of Europa* from 1632 (fig. 125).[158] The 'St Paul by Rembrandt' is perhaps the *Paul at his writing table* (fig. 126) painted around 1630.[159] It is conceivable that Specx bought the paintings from Rembrandt after the latter had left Uylenburgh, but certainly Specx was buying paintings in the years 1633-1635. After Specx arrived in the Dutch Republic in July 1633 he acquired at a sale (on August 8th of the same year!) *The reckoning with the steward* by Jacob Backer.[160] Also worth mentioning are a landscape by Pieter de Neyn with the city of Nijmegen in the distance, two versions of a *Hieronimus* from the hand of Johan van Staveren and two pieces by Simon de Vlieger – all three of them investors in Uylenburgh's enterprise in 1640 – and two evangelists (in two paintings) by Govert Flinck. In 1639 Specx had portraits of himself and his sec-

a rich citizen of Calvinist persuasion, owned various paintings by Rembrandt from the period while the artist was still with Uylenburgh. Specx left Holland for the East Indies as a young man and made a career there, eventually succeeding to the highest position of Governor-General and at the same time amassed a fortune. In 1632 Specx left the East-Indies and on arrival in Amsterdam he purchased a canal house that he then richly decorated with paintings. After Specx' death in 1652 the valuable contents of this house were listed.[155] In this inventory one finds the portraits that Rembrandt had painted in 1635 of Specx' brother-in-law Philips Lucasz (fig. 123) and his wife shortly before this couple sailed to Batavia in April 1635.[156] It looks as though Specx, whether in that same year or earlier, bought further paintings from Uylenburgh. Among other paintings, he possessed 'een scheepgen Petri van Rembrant', most probably the 1633-dated *Christ in the storm*

123 Rembrandt van Rijn, Portrait of Philips Lucasz, signed and dated 'Rembrandt 1635', panel, 79.5 x 58.9 cm (oval), London, The National Gallery (Br. 202; Corpus III A 115)

155 GAA, not. P. de Bary, NA 1698, 3 September 1652, concluded 13 January 1653; Doc. 1653/4 and cf. 1655/5.
156 Br. 202 and Br. 349 respectively; according to the Rembrandt Research Project the man's portrait was painted by Rembrandt (Corpus III A 115), while the pendant, the portrait of Petronella Buys (Corpus III C 111, now in a private collection in France), was painted by an assistant. Others hold that the woman's portrait is also an autograph work, see London 1988-1989, pp. 52-57.
157 Br. 547 and Corpus II A 68.
158 Br. 464 and Corpus II A 47.
159 Br. 602 and Corpus I A 26; Rembrandt's *Paul in prison* from 1627 (Br. 601 and Corpus I A 11) is a less obvious candidate.
160 At Petrus Scriverius' auction. In Specx' inventory from 1652 it is described as 'een stuck van den onbermhertigen schuldenaer van Backers' (a painting of the cruel debtor by Backer). The last record of this history piece is from 1716.

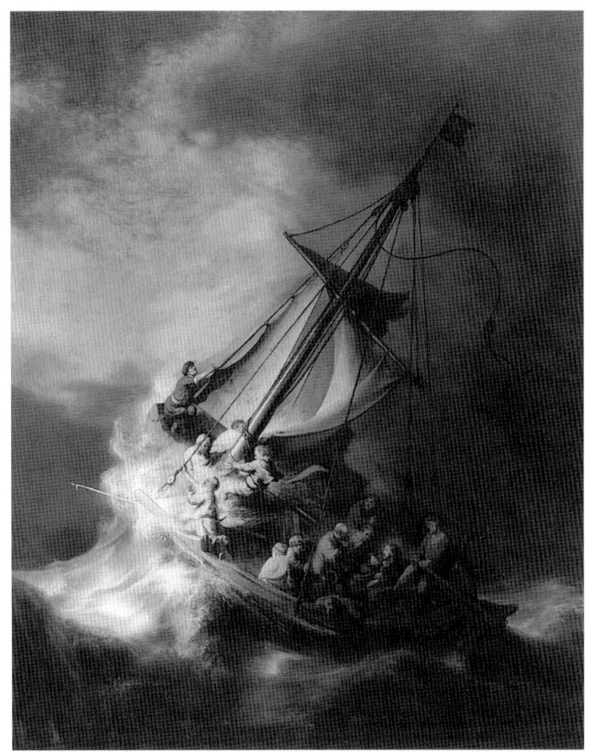

124 Rembrandt van Rijn, Christ in the storm on the sea of Galilee, signed and dated 'Rembrant. f 1633', canvas, 160 x 127 cm, Boston, Massachusets, The Isabella Stewart Gardner Museum (Br. 547; Corpus I I A 68)

ond wife painted by Flinck, who by that stage was no longer working with Uylenburgh, but certainly still maintained close relations with him.[161]

So far, we have looked at individuals whose art possessions and Mennonite affiliation indicate that they could well have belonged to Uylenburgh's circle of clients. But in the case of the Leeuw family we are more certain. The founding father of this Amsterdam family was Jacob Leeuw the Elder, a prominent merchant who died in 1635. Both he and members of his family had very close ties with Hendrick Uylenburgh: in the first place most members of the Leeuw family were attached to the Waterland Mennonite community; and furthermore the Leeuws were related to such Waterland families as the Schoutens, Anslos, Bruyninghs and Flincks, who were all close acquaintances of the Uylenburgh family. Govert Flinck's father, for example, had married the sister of Jacob Leeuw the Elder.[162] The family also had connec-

161 In 1651 Jürgen Ovens painted this couple again. It will be shown below that Ovens worked for Uylenburgh's enterprise, see pp. 212-214.

162 Jacob Leeuw the Elder and Grietgen Jacobsdr, in their last will and testament, name Lambert Cornelisz Schouten (see Genealogy 2, p. 292) and their brother-in-law Theunis Govertsz 'Vlincken' (Flinck) among others, in connection with the guardianship of their under-age children, G A A, not. L. Lamberti, N A 578, 13 August 1632.

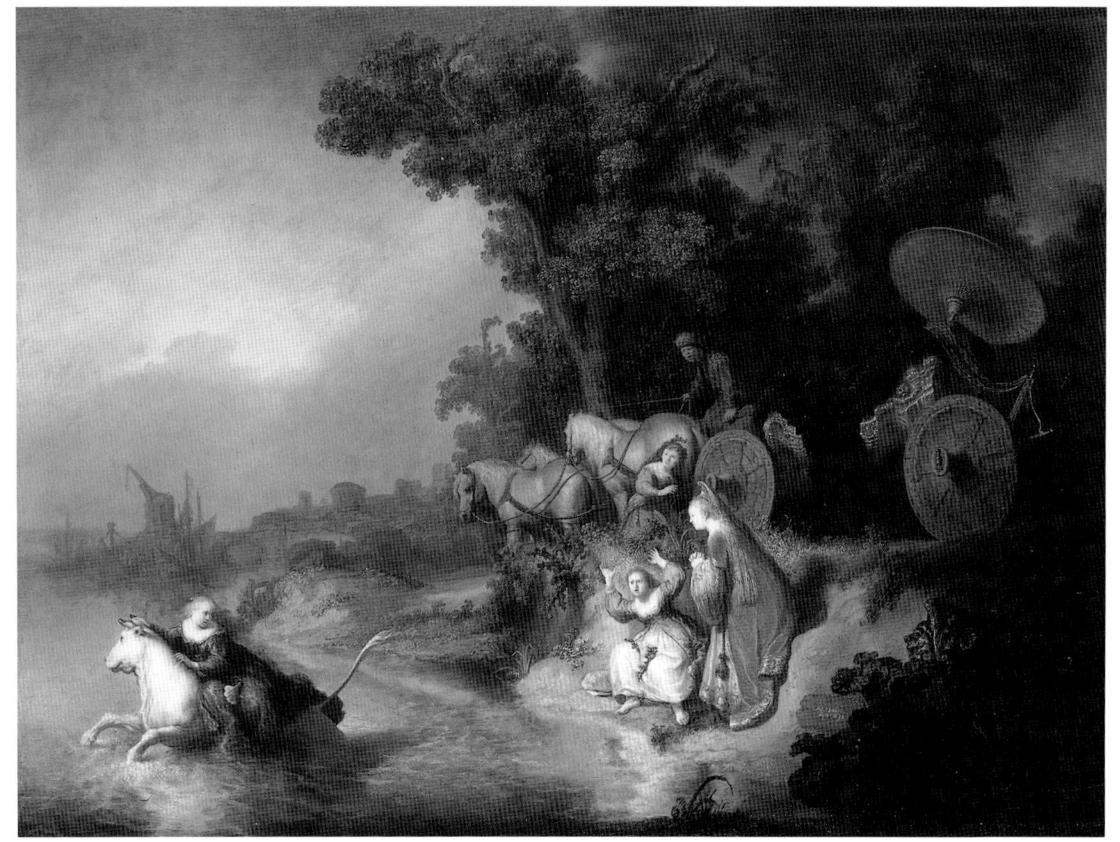

125 Rembrandt van Rijn, The rape of Europa, signed and dated 'RHL van Ryn. 1632', panel, 62,2 x 77 cm, Los Angeles, California, The J. Paul Getty Museum (Br. 464; Corpus I I A 47)

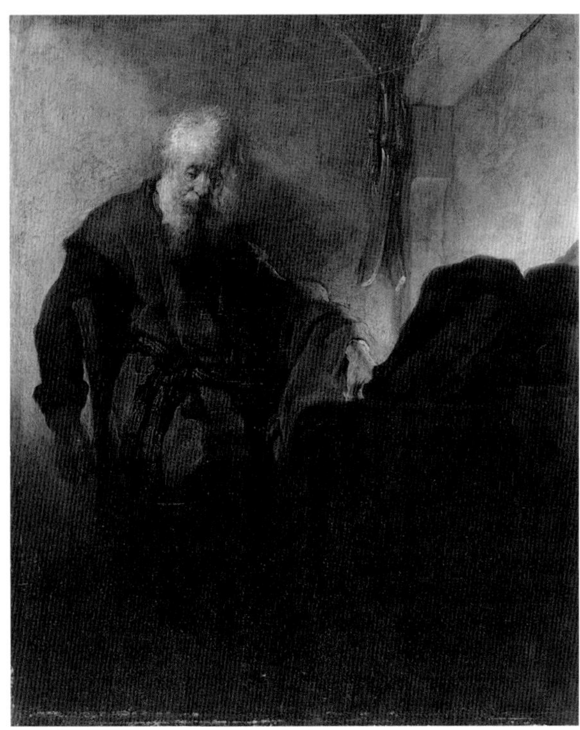

126 Rembrandt van Rijn, St Paul at his desk, panel, 47.2 x 38.6 cm, Nuremberg, Germanisches Nationalmuseum (Br. 602; Corpus I A 26)

tions in Weesp, where several of Jacob Leeuw's children lived.[163] Jacob Leeuw's widow was, as we will see, part of the consortium that granted Uylenburgh a major loan in 1640. They would all have done businesss with Uylenburgh previously, but it is especially the Leeuw family's art possessions that point to close relations with him.

No inventory is known for Jacob Leeuw, or for his widow who died in 1641, but we do have the legal deed of bequest of his eldest son Ameldonck Leeuw, whereby the paintings went to his children.[164] In this 1653 document there are no less than nine paintings by Govert Flinck listed, including 'a crucifix by Govert Flinck', most probably the work dated 1649 (fig. 127) that Leeuw would have bought for the house in Amsterdam he had had built for himself a few years earlier. Flinck portrayed several members of the Leeuw family, including his cousin Dirck Jacobsz Leeuw, a portrait painted in 1636 and in fact Flinck's earliest dated portrait (see fig. 118). This painting is also striking for its element of landscape. During

this period Flinck painted a handful of landscapes under the influence of Rembrandt, two of which Ameldonck Leeuw possessed along with a further 'piece by Flinck being a cattle pasture done after the life'. To date, virtually no attention has been paid to this work in the literature. The rather insistent specification that the landscape had been painted from real life is especially interesting, for Ameldonck Leeuw was involved with cattle and cattle pastures and it is very well possible that he expressly commissioned Flinck to portray his profitable business. In this same context, another painting from Leeuw's effects should also be mentioned: 'a landscape being the bleaching ground, by Gerrit Uyllenburgh'. In my own view, it is not insignificant that the text here attaches the definite article to the bleachery.[165] It was not previously mentioned that the Leeuw family owned property at Bennebroek, including a house and a bleachery; so this painting too may well have been specifically commissioned.[166] That Gerrit Uylenburgh had painted it confirms the relation between Leeuw and Uylenburgh. Another work referred to in the 1653 deed of bequest is 'a piece done by Wlenburgssoon, in which my tronie by Ovens appears'. This was a landscape painted by a son of Hendrick Uylenburgh – certainly Gerrit – that included a painted portrait of Jacob Leeuw the Younger by Jürgen Ovens.[167]

Other paintings in Ameldonck Leeuw's legacy that could have been acquired from Uylenburgh include the two beach scenes by Simon de Vlieger and a history piece and a landscape with the rest on the flight to Egypt by Claes Moyaert. As will be shown below, both painters belonged to the same consortium mentioned above that lent Uylenburgh money in 1640. Yet another painting in the legacy also certainly came out of Uylenburgh's shop: 'a piece by Rembrant being Thomas with Christ', which must be the work from 1634 (fig. 128).[168] In the context of the other paintings, it would seem an obvious inference that either Jacob Leeuw the Elder or his son Ameldonck acquired this history piece not very long after it had been painted. Rembrandt was still working with Uylenburgh in 1634. There exists a free copy after that painting which unquestionably originated at the same time as the prototype

163 Their daughters married the sons of Lambert Cornelisz Schouten. Relationships can be followed further. For instance, in 1651 David Leeuw, a son of Ameldonck Leeuw, married Cornelia Hooft, a daughter of Pieter Gerritsz Hooft and Weijntje Schouten (see Genealogy I, p. 291).
164 GAA, arch. no. 88 (Family archive Brants), inv. no. 809, 7 February 1653; Van Eeghen 1953, pp. 173-174, and Dudok van Heel 1980, pp. 119-121. The document was compiled by Jacob Leeuw de Jonge. Ameldonck Leeuw died in 1647, his widow Maria Rutgers in 1652.
165 Meticulousness is required here. A correct reading of this entry is in Van Eeghen 1953, p. 173.
166 A comparable case is presented by a painting in the inventory of Jan van der Heyden the Younger (1662-1726) and Christina Leeuw (1668-1731), a grand-daughter of Ameldonck Leeuw, showing 'een gesigt van een buytenplaets and *een bleeckerije daervoor*' (an outside view of a countryhouse *with a bleachery in the foreground*) (my italics) by Jan van der Heyden and Adriaen van de Velde, Van Eeghen 1973, p. 130. Commissions given to artists were not uncommon in the Leeuw family. In his will, a grandson of Ameldonck Leeuw bequeathed several paintings (GAA, not. J. Ardinois, NA 9211, deed 501, 21 August 1750), including a piece by Flinck and 'een leggende leeuw door Jan Liewesz.' (a recumbent lion by Jan Lievens.). The choice of subject is certainly no co-incidence.
167 See further p. 213.
168 Br. 552 and Corpus II A 90.

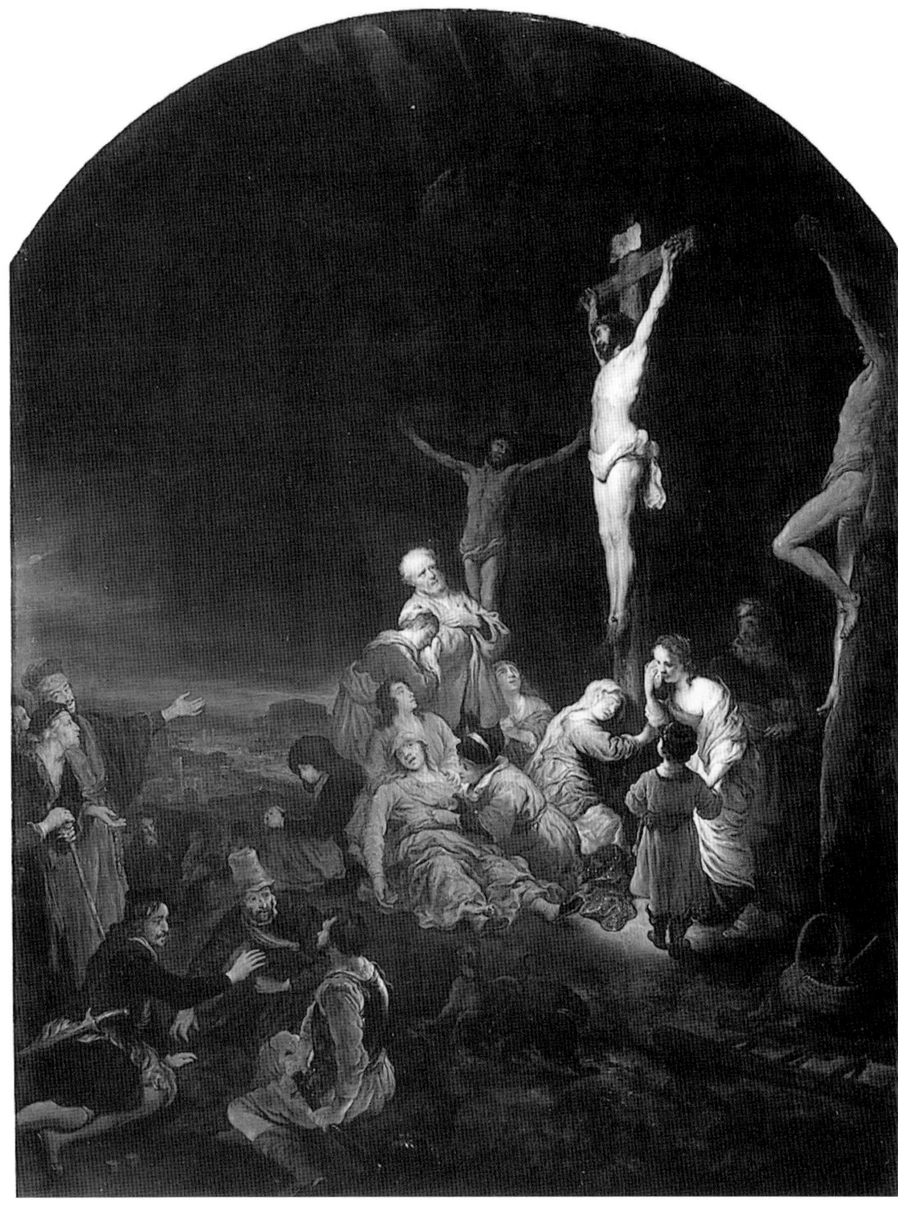

noting that the man who appears in both paintings in the right-hand group, praying and looking to the right, also appears in Flinck's *Annunciation to the shepherds* (see fig. 113). The appearance of two drawings by Rembrandt in Leeuw's legacy is particularly exceptional: these are hardly ever seen in the inventories of private persons' possessions before the middle of the seventeenth century. Finally, Ameldonck Leeuw also possessed 'een groote koocken van Ulenborch', undoubtedly a kitchen piece by Rombout Uylenburgh (see pp. 24-32). In short, this all indicates a fairly close connection between two generations of the Leeuw family and the Uylenburghs – father and son – over many years. Shortly before the widow of Ameldonck Leeuw re-married in 1650, Hendrick Uylenburgh valued the paintings in the estate of her second husband.[169]

BUSINESS CONTACTS BEYOND AMSTERDAM

The foregoing discussion was restricted to the Amsterdam clients of Uylenburgh's shop. In fact, less is known about buyers and commissioning patrons from further afield. The most we know on that score concerns the business dealings that Uylenburgh had with Lambert Jacobsz in Leeuwarden. When the latter died in June 1636, an inventory of his possessions was drawn up which gives us a very clear insight into the stock held by his shop, the production in the workshop and his relations with Uylenburgh. It turns out that they sent each other art works to sell on the other's account. Thus, Uylenburgh had paintings by Jacobsz on consignment in his shop in Amsterdam, while the latter had works in his own shop that came from Uylenburgh's workshop. Beside an item for 22 guilders is written 'due to Hendrick Ullenburgh dealer in paintings in Amsterdam, booked too'.[170] This small sum would have

169 'Schilderijen berustende tot Amsterdam, gestelt achtervolgende de prisatie door Hendric Uylenburch' (Paintings in Amsterdam, according to the valuation by Hendrick Uylenburch). R A L, not. K. Outerman, N A 444, deed 173, 17 August 1651. The most expensive piece was a landscape by Jan van Goyen valued at 100 guilders.
170 'Hendrick Ullenburgh schilderijhandeler tot Amsterdam, oock te boeck', Straat 1925, p. 67.

(fig. 129). The two groups of three figures to the right and the left follow Rembrandt's original accurately; but the middle group differ in several respects from that painting: in the bearing of some of the figures, for example, while the young man kneeling in the foreground of the Chicago painting has a clearly visible left hand which is lacking in the Moscow painting. However, the greatest difference lies in the way the middle group is painted. In the copy, this middle group of figures has not been worked out, but executed rather as a sketch. One wonders whether it has even been done by the same hand. It is worth

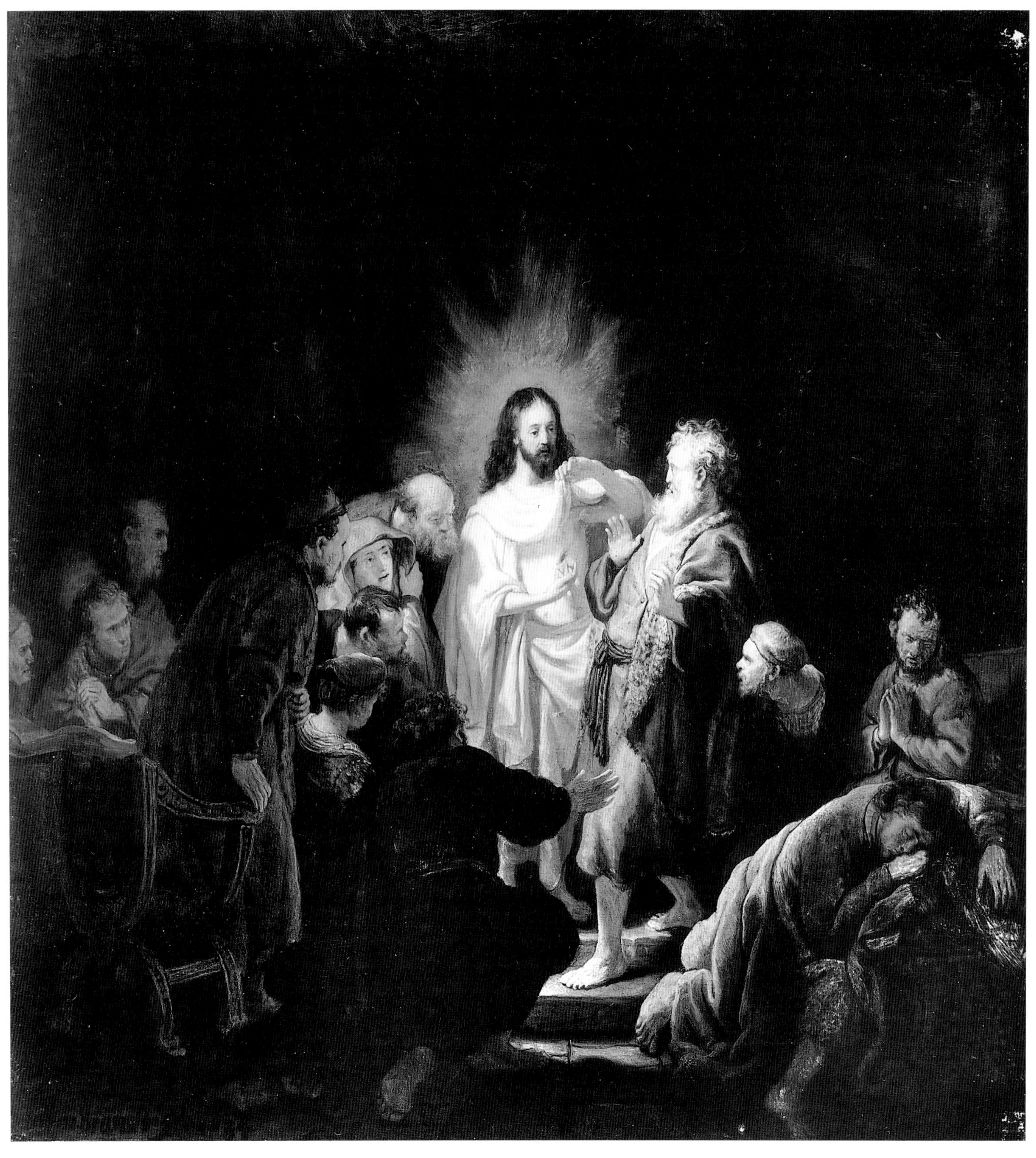

128 Rembrandt van Rijn, The incredulity of Thomas, signed and dated 'Rembrandt. f 1634', panel, 53.1 x 50.5 cm, Moscow, Pushkin State Museum of Fine Arts (Br. 552; Corpus II A 90)

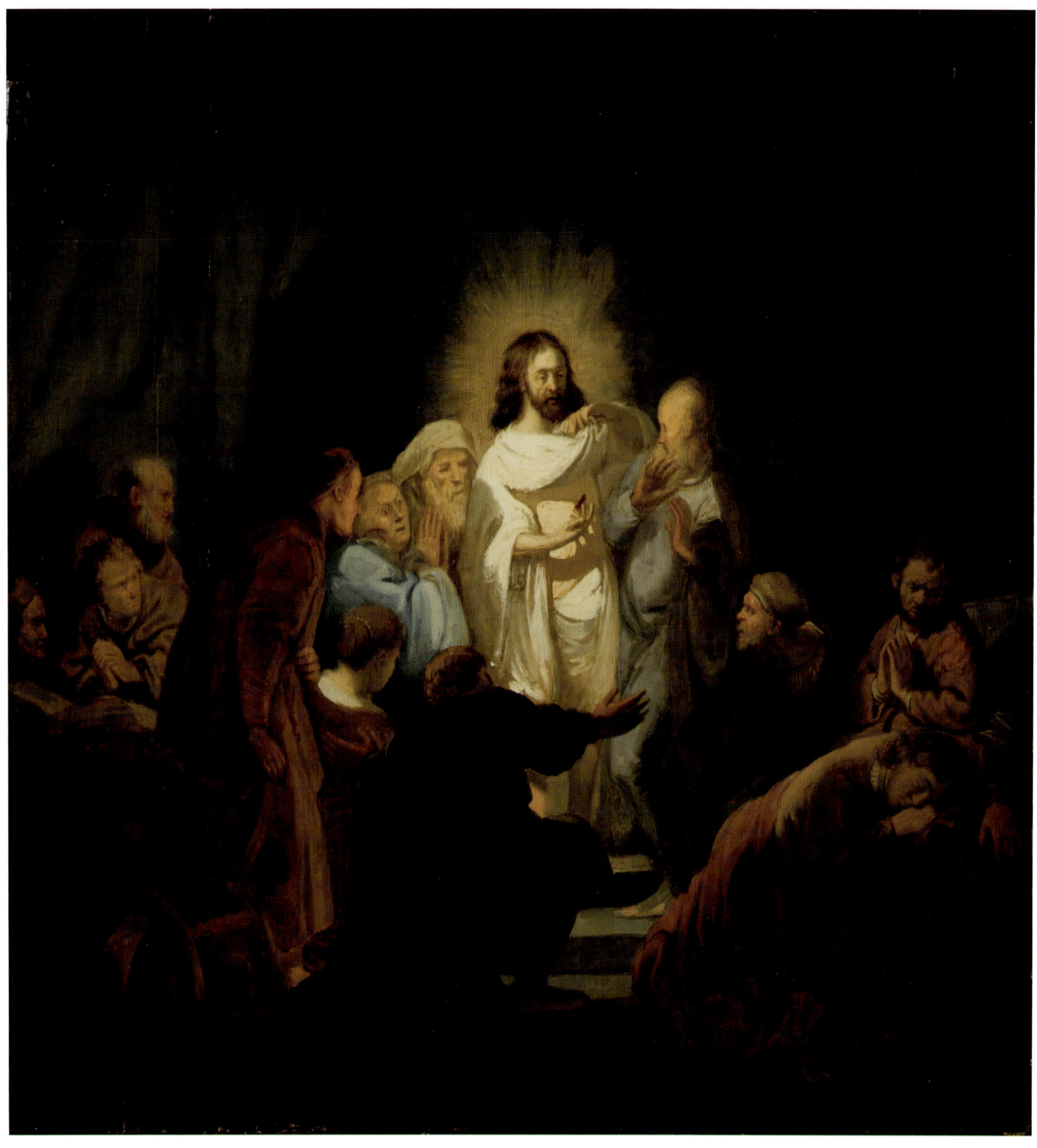

129 Anonymous, from the workshop of Rembrandt van Rijn, The incredulity of Thomas, panel, 54.2 x 51.2 cm, private collection, United States

been the amount outstanding from their current account.

There was a close link between these two men. To start with they were both Mennonites: Lambert Jacobsz preached as a leader of the Waterland Mennonite community in Leeuwarden, while Uylenburgh originally came from this Frisian city and still had relatives there. Jacobsz, who was born in Amsterdam, was a son of a merchant draper who had been deacon of the Waterland community there and associated with such Mennonite families as the Anslos, Schoutens and Munters, who can also be linked to Uylenburgh. As already mentioned, Mennonites sought by preference their business partners from within their own circle. The business relation must have been profitable to both parties and in 1640, just a few years after the death of Lambert Jacobsz, the administrators of his estate put money into Uylenburgh's business enterprise.[171]

In Lambert Jacobsz's shop there were various pieces from his own hand and from his former pupil Jacob Backer, including 'the showing of the tribute money in seven tronies by Mr. Jacob Ariens', i.e. Jacob Adriaensz Backer, while under the heading 'with Hendrick Ulenburch art seller in Amsterdam' was entered 'a large life-like painting, with Christ, among the Pharisees with Herod's servants accompanied by his disciples whom he shows the tribute money, painted by Mr. Jacob Ariens'.[172] The unsigned *Tribute money* in Stockholm (fig. 130), attributed to Jacob Backer, corresponds exactly with the latter description.[173] This piece would have been painted in Leeuwarden shortly before Backer moved to Amsterdam sometime during 1633. There was thus one version of this biblical subject in Uylenburgh's shop and a second painting that remained in Leeuwarden. There must have been a lively interest in such large-format history pieces in Amsterdam. The inventory of the shop contains yet another remark-

able painting, 'a brown rock through which a strong light falls on Democritus who while sitting studying is visited by Hippocratis dressed in a red cloak. L. J.'.[174] This is a wonderfully apt description of Backer's *Hippocrates visiting Democritus in Abdera* (fig. 131), possibly also painted in Leeuwarden.[175] The inventory gives Jacobsz as the author of this painting, which could well mean that Backer painted a copy or variant of it; but it is also conceivable that the master and his pupil have been confused here.[176] Backer's large figure history pieces are closely similar to the work of his master both in style and their use of colour, with striking purple tones. He also painted disciples after the example set by Lambert Jacobsz, whose *Paul* from 1629 is a particularly fine example (fig. 132). This painting by Jacobsz shows close similarity with the *Apostle Paul* by Jan Lievens from the same period and also with a work by his own pupil Govert Flinck that is dated to around 1630.[177] Paintings by Lievens circulated in Leeuwarden as well as in Amsterdam and were assiduously copied, both with Uylenburgh and possibly also with Jacobsz.

In total, there are about sixty paintings in Lambert Jacobsz's inventory listed as unsold. The inventory, however, was only drawn up almost a year and a half after Jacobsz's death, so that several pieces could have been sold out of the deceased's house in the intervening period. There are various paintings listed by other artists, including works by (Jacob or Jan) Pynas, Claes Moyaert and Cornelis van Poelenburch and work by and after Gerrit van Honthorst and Jan Lievens. These include 'a tronie of a boy with long curly hair [and] plump, pale cheeks', immediately followed by 'a tronie of a young girl, its companion piece, after Jan Lievens'.[178] The Rijksmuseum possesses a small painting that fits this description (fig. 133). The painting bears an inscription that has been read as 'Rembrandt geretuceer ... [naar?] Lieve..', which could be

---

171 See below p. 188-196. For Lambert Jacobsz see.: Wijnman 1930a, Wijnman 1934 and Bruyn 1984-1996, VI, pp. 167-168.
172 Straat 1925, p. 71, no. 1, and p. 76, no. 54.
173 Sum. vol. 6, p. 3916 and fig. 2318, assumes this to be a work by Lambert Jacobsz, but Cavalli Björkman (most recently in Copenhagen 2006, no. 23) and Van den Brink 1997, p. 180, see the hand of Jacob Backer in it.
174 Straat 1925, p. 75, no. 42.
175 Van den Brink 1997. If, in fact, as has several times been remarked, the model of the man on the right in Backer's *Hippocrates visits Democritus in Abdera* is identical with the model used by Rembrandt for his *Man in oriental costume* (see fig. 173), then Backer must have painted the work in Amsterdam and had it sent to Leeuwarden to sell. Jacob Backer also made a drawn study of the same model (Sum. Drawings vol. 1, no. 2) and a painted study, see Van den Brink 1997, fig. 7.
176 In one case in the inventory, Lambert Jacobsz is named as the author of a painting, but in a first edition this was followed by 'off J.A.', i.e. by Backer, Straat 1925, p. 71, no. 5.
177 Manuth 2005, pp. 51-52 and figs. 11-13.
178 Straat 1925, p. 73, nos. 21 and 22; the portrait of the girl could have been a copy of Lievens' *Laughing girl with long blond hair* in the Museum der bildenden Künste in Leipzig (panel, 43.3 x 34.8 cm), which is dated to around 1625-1629 and in 1641 was probably in the possession of Jacques de Gheyn (fig. 77), see Melbourne/Canberra 1997-1998, cat. no. 34 and pp. 108-111.

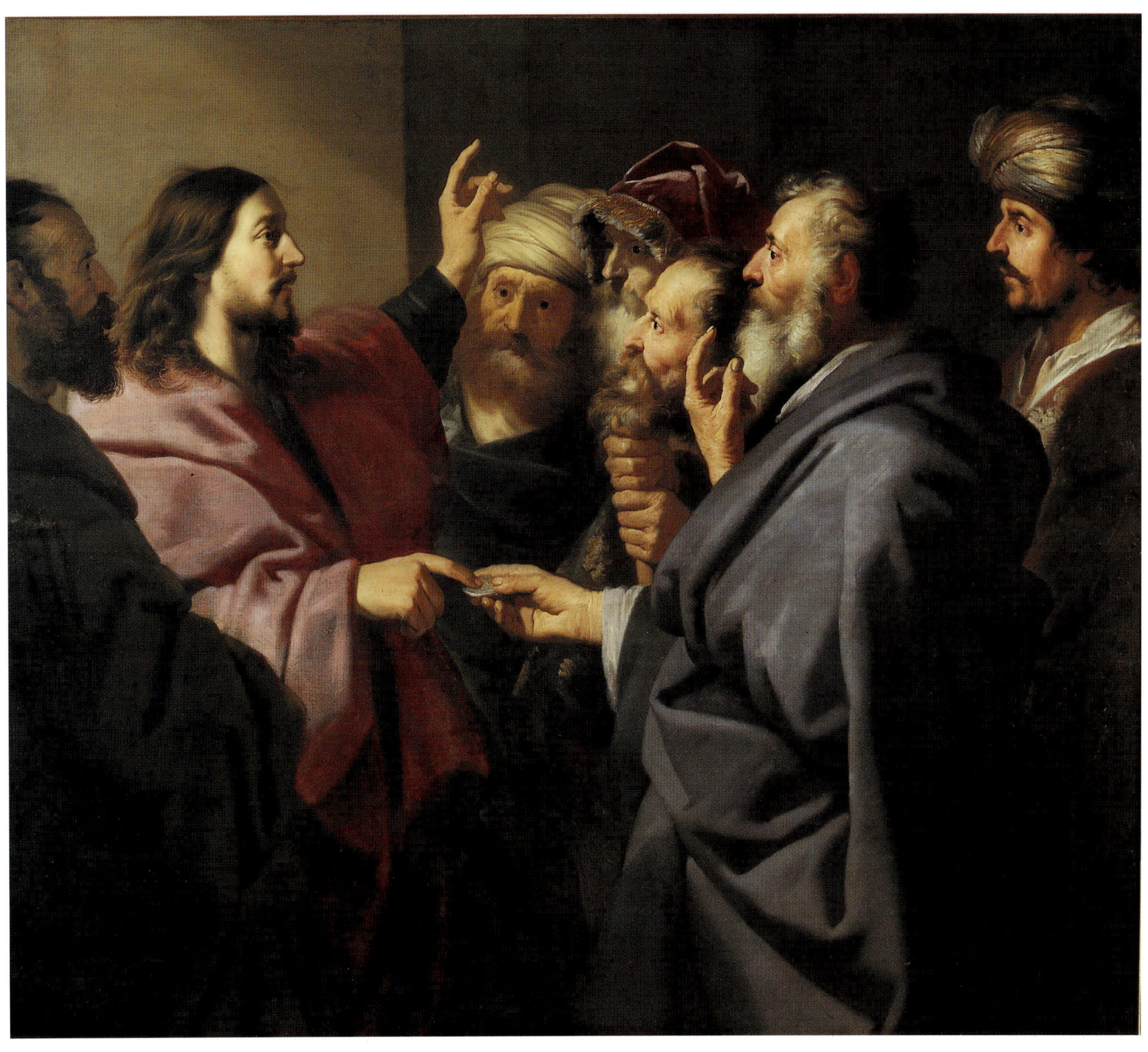

130 Jacob Backer, The tribute money, canvas, 139 x 159 cm, Stockholm, Nationalmusem

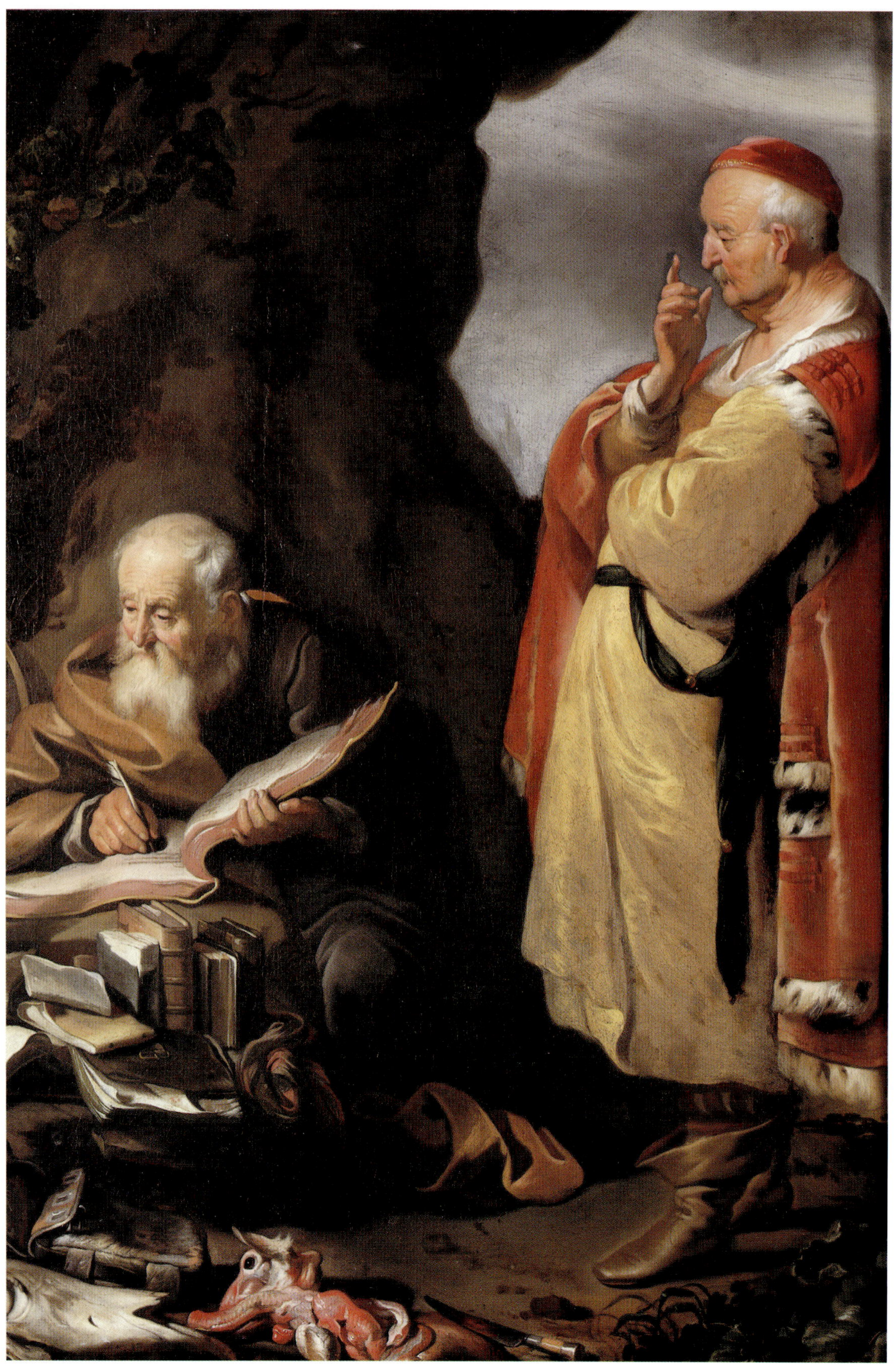

131 Jacob Backer, Hippocrates visiting Democritus in Abdera, canvas, 94 x 64 cm, Milwaukee, Dr Alfred and Isabel Bader

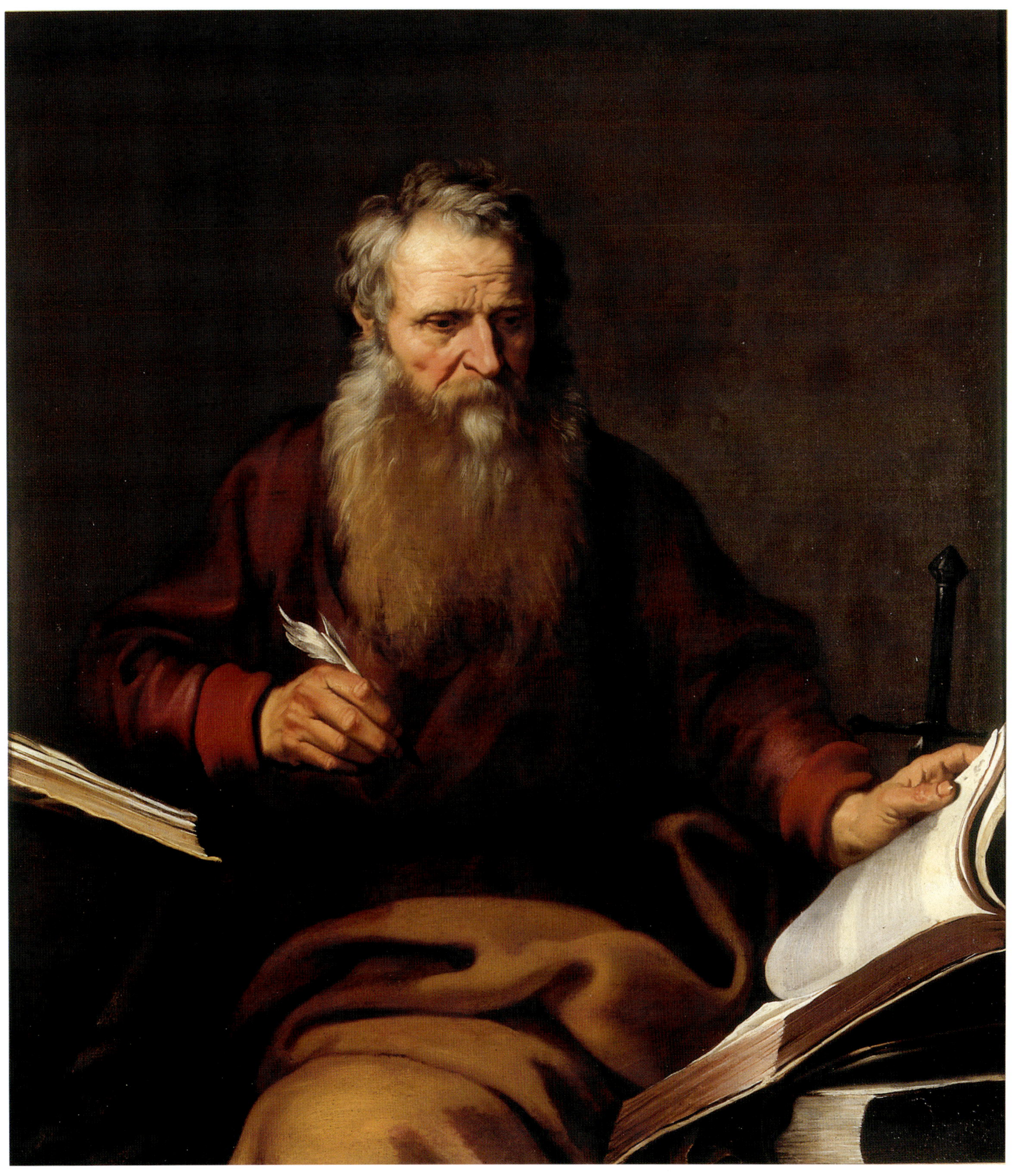

132 Lambert Jacobsz, The apostle Paul, signed and dated 'Lambert Jacobsz. f 1629', canvas, 114 x 101 cm, Leeuwarden, Fries Museum

taken to mean that it is a workshop copy after a
work by Jan Lievens, retouched by Rembrandt.
Technical research carried out in the Rijksmuseum, however, has produced new information
bearing on this question: the dendrochronological data show that the very earliest date the panel
could have been painted is the late thirties.[179]
Since Jacobsz's inventory was drawn up in 1636,
it is thus impossible that the small painting in his
shop was the painting now in the Rijksmuseum.
The description of 1637, however, fits so well that
it raises the possibility that both could have been
copies after the same prototype, now lost. Besides,
the remains of the inscription are found on the
cracked paint layer, so that the inscription would
have been added some time after the completion
of the painting. It was thus not only works by
Rembrandt that were copied in Uylenburgh's
workshop, where this 'tronie' retouched by Rembrandt must have originated, but evidently also
the works of other artists. The inventory always
distinguishes between originals and copies. It is
incorrect to assume that contemporary purchasers
would have 'expressed little preference' for originals.[180] On the contrary: why otherwise would
one have gone to the trouble of making that distinction so carefully?[181]

Apart from the history piece by Backer mentioned above, there were another three paintings
belonging to Jacobsz in Uylenburgh's shop. Firstly there was an *Adam and Eve* by Gerrit van Honthorst, the figures almost life-size, and 'a satyr
making love to a beautiful young woman after
Master G. Honthorst' (a personification of lasci-
viousness?). The second work can be identified
with a high degree of probability: it would have
been copied after a prototype by Van Honthorst
from 1623 that is now in Pommersfelden (fig.
134).[182] A version is also known of the *Ruth and
Naomi* by Pieter de Grebber, a painting dated
1628 (fig. 135), whose figures are slightly less than

life-size.[183] What strikes one about these works
is the large format of the paintings that Uylenburgh had for sale. The same is true of the *Tribute
money* by Backer (fig. 130), the *Annunciation to
the shepherds* by Flinck (fig. 113) and to a lesser
extent of the *Meleager and Atalante* by Janssen
(fig. 66).

133 Anonymous (after Jan
Lievens?), Head of a boy, panel,
27.5 x 20 cm, Amsterdam,
Rijksmuseum

179 I am grateful to Arie
Wallert who allowed me to see
the text of his article on the
Tronie of a boy for the *Bulletin
van het Rijksmuseum*. See also
Van der Veen 2005, pp. 27-28
and notes 133-135, with older
literature. The same model was
used for a tronie dated 1634
(Bredius 191), which according
to the Corpus (11 c 64), 'may
have been produced in Rembrandt's workshop'.
180 Wijnman 1959, p. 3.

181 Van der Veen 2005.
182 Straat 1925, p. 76, no. 57.
For the original see:
Judson/Ekkart 1999, no. 122;
the authors mention several
copies, of which the one in
Kassel has virtually the same
measurements as the painting
in Pommersfelden.
183 Straat 1925, p. 76, no. 56;
the painting reproduced here
was last auctioned by Lem-
pertz in Cologne on 28 April
1965, no. 48.

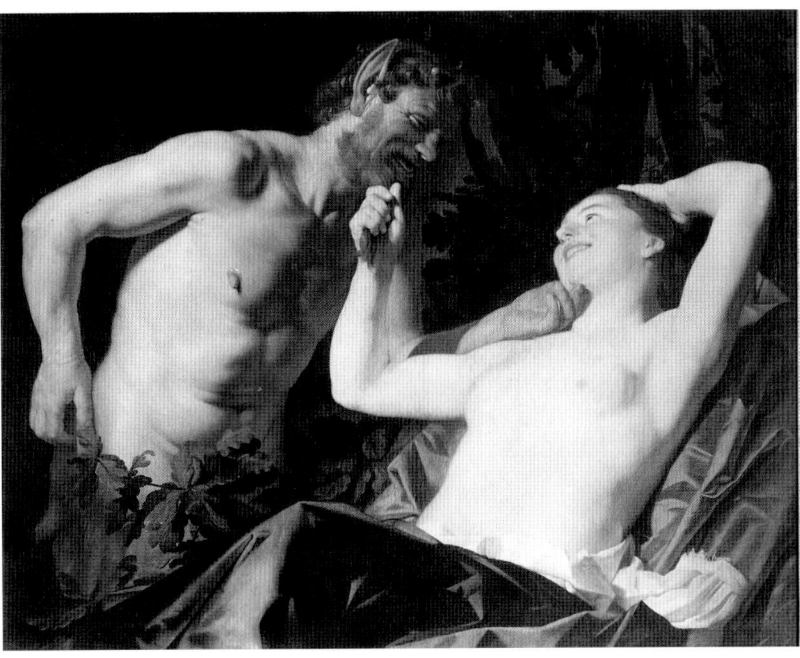

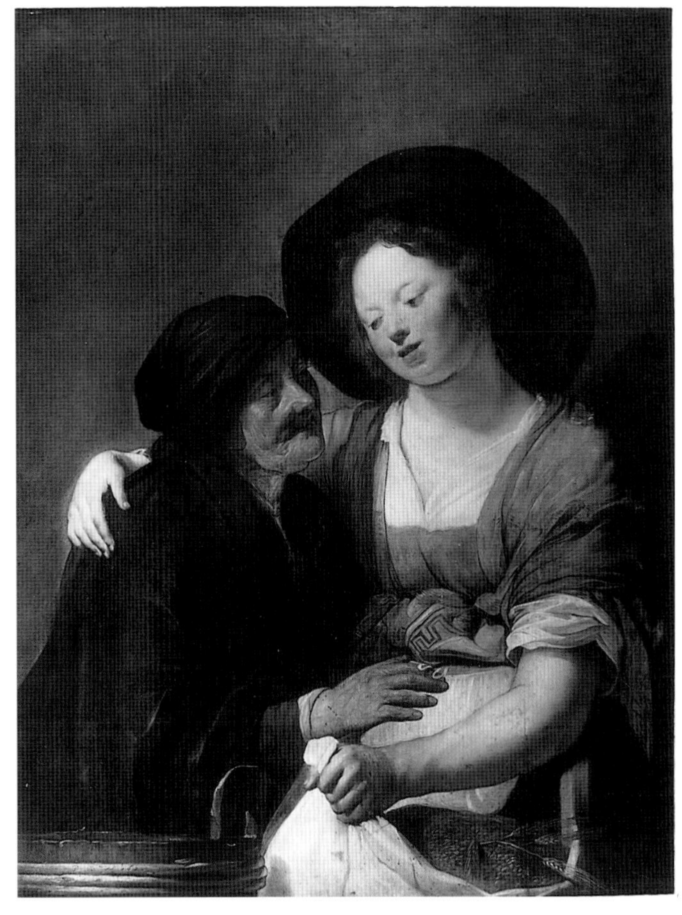

134 Gerrit van Honthorst, Satyr with nymph, signed and dated 'G. v. Honthorst: fe 1623', canvas, 104 x 131 cm, Pommersfelden, Schloss Weissenstein, Graf von Schönborn Collection

135 Pieter de Grebber, Naomi gives counsel to Ruth, monogrammed and dated 'P D G An 1628', panel, 96 x 74 cm, present whereabouts unknown

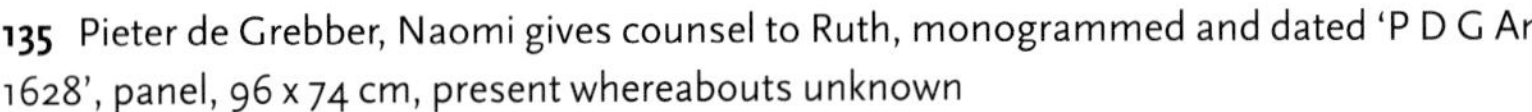

184 Straat 1925, p. 72, nos. 7, 8, 11, 14 and 15 and p. 73, nos. 20 and 34.

185 Straat 1925, pp. 59-60, thought it well possible and referred to Eekhoff 1862, where it was claimed that Lambert Jacobsz. got to know Rembrandt in Amsterdam in the company of Wybrand de Geest. This must have been invented by the author; at least there is no documentary evidence for the assertion. Wijnman 1934, p. 251, assumes that all copies were made at Uylenburgh's workshop.

186 Bredius 147 and Corpus III, p. 24 and fig. 11.

187 Leiden 2006, nos. 3-6 and 8, works from 1628-1630.

188 Corpus II C 54 as 'attributable to Isaack Jouderville'.

189 Corpus II C 55.

190 Bredius 605 and Corpus I C 16 (as a copy after Rembrandt).

Uylenburgh must in turn have sent paintings from his own workshop to Leeuwarden. The six copies after Rembrandt and one original work by him immediately stand out.[184] It is unlikely that the copies were done in Jacobsz's workshop, or that he would have painted them whilst on a visit to Amsterdam;[185] they would rather have been produced in Uylenburgh's workshop under the supervision of Rembrandt himself. There is one called 'a tronie of an old man with a long wide beard, by Master Rembrandt van Rijn himself', a description that fits perfectly the *Old man with a long wide beard* from 1632 (fig. 136). This painting was for a long time held to be an autograph work by Rembrandt, but was subsequently removed from his œuvre and is now considered to be a workshop copy.[186] The relation to the master's work, however, is clearly evident. The same model – in mirror image – appears in an etching by Rembrandt (fig. 137). Following this original, the inventory lists the copies after Rembrandt.

The first is called 'an old woman with a black headdress after Master Rembrandt', several versions of which have been preserved, painted by unknown artists in Rembrandt's immediate working environment.[187] The 'tronie of a woman after Rembrandt, il re de mendici' is not so easily identified, but 'a handsome young Turkish prince after Rembrandt' is possibly identical with the *Young man with a turban*, a painting attributed to Isaack Jouderville, one of Rembrandt's Leiden pupils who possibly transferred with him to Uylenburgh's workshop in Amsterdam.[188] The 'a soldier with black hair [with] an iron gorget [and a] scarf around the neck after Rembrandt' puts one in mind of a work in San Diego from Rembrandt's earliest years in Amsterdam.[189] Further down the inventory there is 'a hermit studying in a cliff-face after Master Rembrandt in a gilded frame', which one can relate to the *Hermit reading* in the Louvre that can be dated to around 1630-1631.[190]

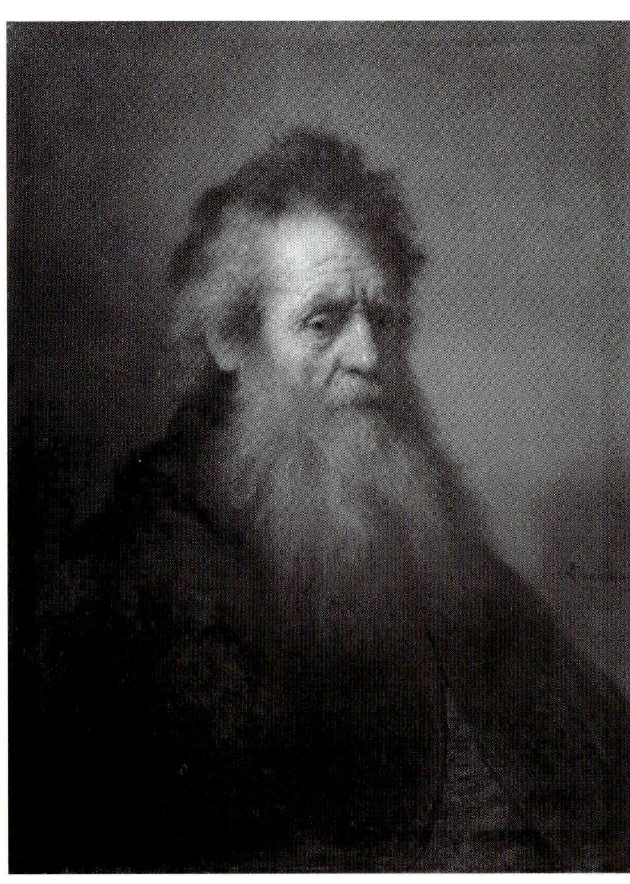

136 Anonymous, workshop of Rembrandt van Rijn, Old man with a long wide beard, signed and dated 'RHL van Ryn 1632', panel, 67 x 50.8 cm, Cambridge, Massachusets, Fogg Art Museum, Harvard University (Br. 147)

137 Rembrandt van Rijn, Old man with long beard, etching, 6.8 x 6.6 cm, Amsterdam, Rijksprentenkabinet (B. 315 II, 2)

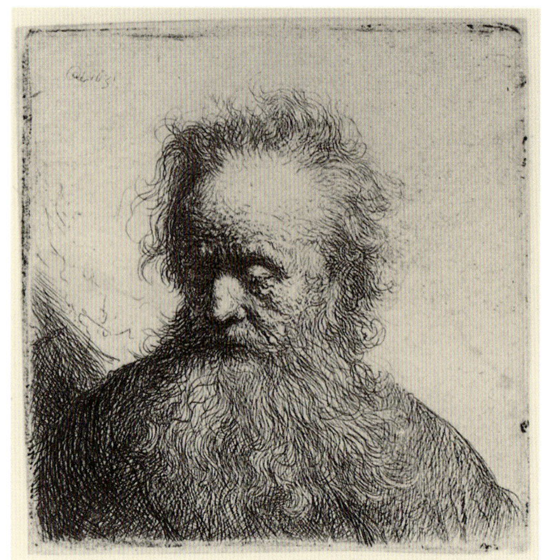

The last Rembrandt copy in Lambert Jacobsz's inventory is the highly intriguing painting, 'noch een cleine Oostersche vrouwen troni, het conterfeisel van H. Ulenburgh huysvrouwe nae Rembrant' (a small oriental troni of a woman, the likeness of H. Uylenburgh's wife, after Rembrandt). Maria van Eyck must have sat as a model for Rembrandt – undoubtedly between 1631 and 1635 – for a painting that was then copied and this copy sent to Leeuwarden. But the work referred to cannot be convincingly identified among any paintings that have been preserved, whether by Rembrandt or his pupils. It was certainly not unusual in the seventeeenth century painters' workshops to use members of the family as models.[191] Rembrandt also did it. Thus, in the estate of a Leiden citizen one finds recorded in 1644 'a tronie of an old man, being the likeness of the father of master Rembrandt' and again in 1722, in the description of an art collection in Haarlem there is an entry for 'Rembrandt van Rijn the portrait of father with his beard'.[192] Such reports lead one to suspect that there was a relation between the painting's owner and either the painter or the model. In the case of the tronie of Maria van Eyck in the possession of Jacobsz this was certainly so.[193] The fact that her facial features were 'recognized' in Leeuwarden is readily explicable: the compiler of this inventory could simply have made use of the deceased's bookkeeping, for the inventory itself makes it plain that the latter recorded his purchases and sales.

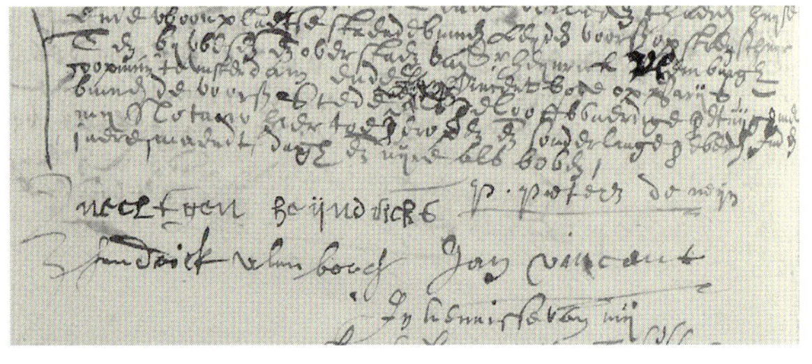

138 Hendrick Uylenburgh's signature witnessing the will of Pieter de Neyn of 15 December 1638, Leiden, Regionaal Archief Leiden

191 Költzsch 2000 and Leiden 2006, pp. 36-37.
192 Recorded in the inventory of Sybout van Caerdecamp, Doc. 1644/1. The report from 1722 in: Biesboer 2001, p. 343, no. 11; the reading of the record here is correct but I assume that 'zijn' (his) should be read before 'vader', since in view of the year the inventory was drawn up one can almost certainly exclude the possibility that a portrait of the deceased's father was painted by Rembrandt.
193 In 1654 Jan van Caerdecamp lent a sum of money to the widow of Rembrandt's brother Adriaen van Rijn (c. 1597-1652), Bredius/De Roever 1887, p. 219. The precise relationship between Sybout and Jan van Caerdecamp has still to be investigated.

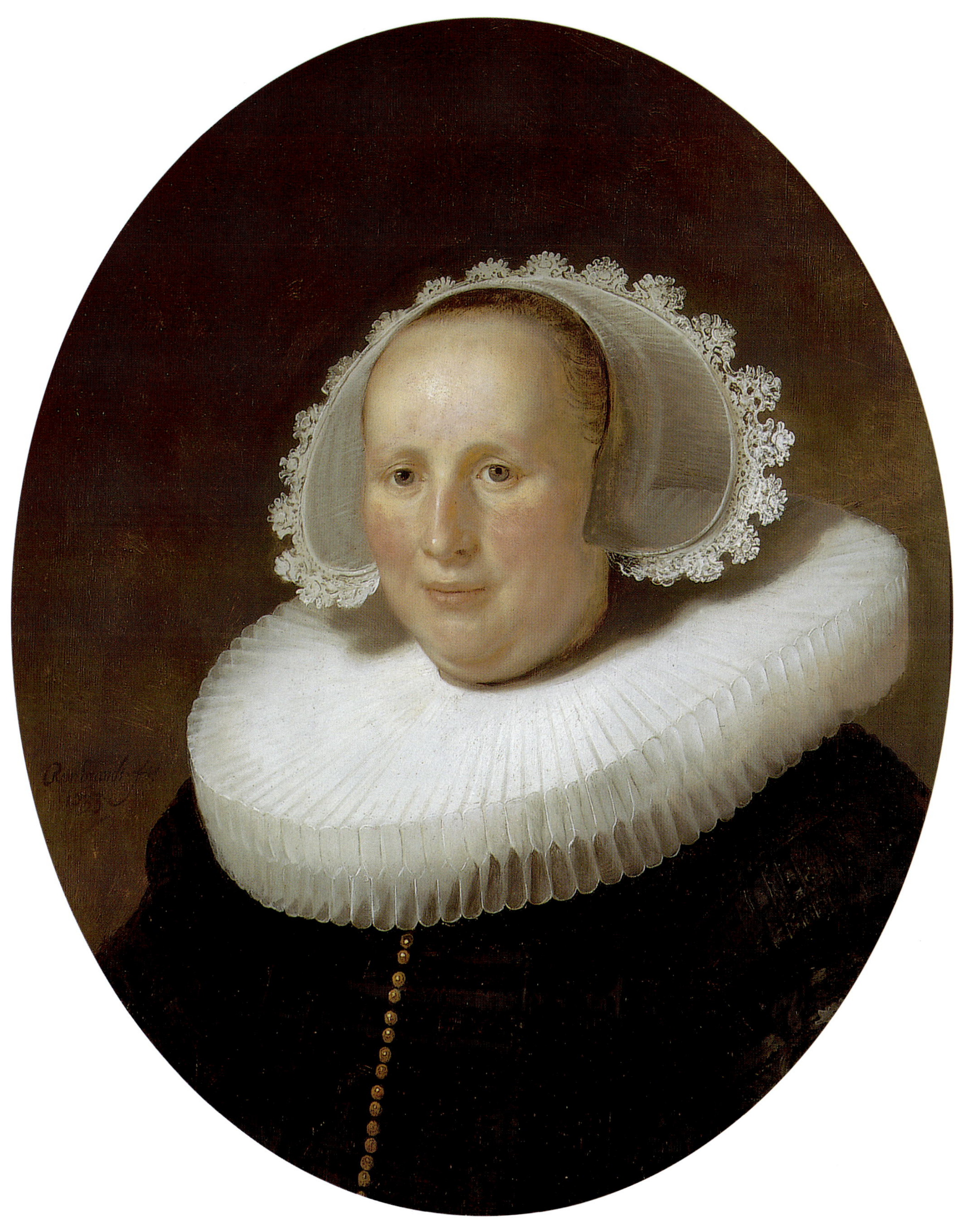

139 Rembrandt van Rijn, Portrait of Maertgen van Bilderbeeck, signed and dated 'Rembrandt. ft: 1633', panel, 67.5 x 54.9 cm, Frankfurt am Main, Städelsches Kunstinstitut (Br. 339; Corpus II A 82)

Was Leeuwarden the only place where Hendrick Uylenburgh had a 'branch manager'? Probably not. He seems to have collaborated in a similar way with Pieter de Neyn in Leiden. In 1640, after the death of this wealthy Leiden painter and art dealer in 1639, his widow invested money in Uylenburgh's business,[194] from which one can infer that she and her husband must have known him well. Indeed, their will of 1638 confirms this: in the presence of a notary, this document was signed by 'Heynrick Ulemburgh, merchant of Amsterdam' as a witness (fig. 138).[195] This reference to the latter's profession seems to bear out the supposition that his presence in Leiden would have been for commercial reasons. It is likely that the men had had business relations with each other for some time. Rembrandt, in fact, painted the portrait of Pieter de Neyn's sister-in-law, Maertgen van Bilderbeeck (fig. 139), in 1633 while he was working with Uylenburgh.[196] This painting is a typical example of Rembrandt's carefully executed portraits from the first half of the thirties. In this case it seems possible that an assistant executed the lace parts of the headgear.[197] We have no other documented Leiden portraits commissioned from Rembrandt. This commission would surely have been conveyed via Uylenburgh, particularly in view of the fact that some members of the Van Bilderbeeck family belonged to the Waterland community in Leiden. Pieter de Neyn, it should be said, was not one of these, for he was married in 1617 in the Reformed Church. He was a successful entrepreneur: besides running an art dealership he was a prominent stone-cutter and had learned the ropes of landscape painting from Esaias van de Velde.[198] One suspects that the landscapes and cavalry battles that De Neyn painted would also have been traded by Uylenburgh in Amsterdam.

It is a fairly obvious assumption that Uylenburgh would also have taken the work of independent painters on consignment, not an unusual practice in the seventeenth century.[199] There is one document that specifically records this in the case of Uylenburgh. One item, taken from the deceased's account book, appears in an Amsterdam inventory of household effects from 1645, in which is written that Volckert (Wolfert) van Lier owed him a small sum of money, which sum '[must be] collected from Hendrick Oulenborgh, painter, who has several of Volkert's paintings in his possession for sale'.[200] Van Lier, who as far as is known painted exclusively landscapes, had thus placed paintings in Uylenburgh's shop for the latter to sell. I assume that these were paintings from Van Lier's hand. As will be shown below, Gerrit Uylenburgh also took works of art on consignment.[201]

Trade and production, 1639-1655

On various occasions, Hendrick Uylenburgh borrowed money to fund art purchases for his shop. Rembrandt lent him money in 1631 and a few years earlier someone stood surety for him to enable him to complete a transaction for which he did not have ready funds. Between 1639 and 1641, however, these loans involved large sums of money. The documents relating to these loans will be discussed in detail below; they provide insight into the way in which the business functioned and they give us the names of the investors, some of whom also belonged to Uylenburgh's circle of clients. These documents often furnish valuable information. For example, as collateral for a loan in 1641, the art dealer gave the other party to the deal copper plates from his stock. I have tried always to follow such transactions, to see whether the debts are paid off and if so, when and how.

It seems that the trade in art works was at this stage more important for Uylenburgh than production. From the second half of the thirties he valued paintings and was several times involved in expert appraisals – his contemporaries evidently had considerable faith in his expertise. But the workshop continued to exist: more specifically, Baldinucci's oft-quoted reference to 'the famous academy of Uylenburgh' certainly refers to the mid-thirties, when his informant Eberhard Keil worked there for three years. It is questionable, however, whether Uylenburgh's business enterprise should be classified as an 'academy' in the sense of an establishment with organized sessions where nudes were drawn from the life.

194 See below p. 188-196.
195 'sr. Heynrick Ulemburgh, coopman te Amsterdam', R A L, not. J. Jansz. Verwey, N A 112, deed 5, 15 December 1638.
196 Pieter de Neyn married Neeltgen Hendricksdr van Bilderbeeck in 1617 in Leiden; the latter's sister Maertgen Hendricksdr van Bilderbeeck married the corn merchant Willem Burchgraeff (c. 1604-1647) in 1625 in Leiden. For the presumed portrait of Burchgraeff, see: Corpus II C 77 and p. 411, fig. 6, and for her portrait Corpus II A 82 and Frankfurt/Kyoto 2002-2003, no. 16. Liedtke 2004, p. 66, believes the man's portrait in Dresden is also an autograph work.
197 Corpus II, p. 410 and p. 75.
198 Houbraken 1718-1721, vol. I, pp. 172-173, Gerson 1947 and Briels 1997, p. 363.
199 Thus, in the 1653 inventory of the Delft painter Anthonie Palamedes, several entries suggest this practice, Van der Veen 1996, p. 127 and note 14.
200 'Bij Hendrick Oulenborgh, schilder, gesocht [moet] worden, diewelcke verscheiden schildereyen van Volckert in hande heeft om te verkopen', G A A, not. J. Jansz Westfrisius, N A 565(A), fols. 16-35, 23-25 March 1645, specifically fol. 32; first published in Montias 1996, p. 152 and note 52, also in Montias 2002, p. 125 and notes 380-382.
201 See pp. 241-242.

There is a deed, dated April 2nd, 1639 and signed by Hendrick Uylenburgh, which records a loan of 1,600 guilders from the merchants Gilbert de Flines and Pieter Sijen. This loan was 'had already been granted to Uylenburgh a while' (though apparently not yet confirmed in writing) and was made, as was explicitly stated, with an eye to 'the purchase of paintings'. The annual interest was six percent. As surety for the loan already granted and for the money 'if afterwards there should be a further loan or before making it good and repaying it'. Uylenburgh offered them all the paintings that he possessed 'and that he declared he had bought for the aforementioned sum, and the cash from the sale of any of the paintings bought, declaring in this connection all the paintings that he had and would still be able to get' with the outstanding debt, and any 'proceeds from any paintings sold'. To allay any anxieties they might have, the financiers could remove the paintings from his house and at such a time as a sale should be made, the proceeds would be deducted from the debt. Further, De Flines and Sijen would be able to demand cash and recall outstanding debts.[202]

The further history of this loan can to some extent be followed. Uylenburgh certainly did not pay off his loans quickly, but then there was no particular pressure on him to pay. On December 12th, 1650 Uylenburgh announced that he had transferred the loan of 1,600 guilders that he had 'owed up to now [...] without having deducted anything from the capital'.[203] In the case of Pieter Sijen the loan remained on the books for a very long time. In 1666 the heirs of Sijen's widow, Marretje Cornelisdr van Grotewal, had her estate inventoried in a legal document which includes a survey of her real estate and securities, of her assets and her debts. She possessed considerable wealth – houses, land and security bonds – and among her assets, taken from a book of debts that was also present in her household effects, are found the following: 'fol. 2 of Hendrick Uylenburgh on account of capital still remaining with the accumulated interest up to December 2nd, 1666 219 guilders and 10 stuyvers'.[204] This sum

must have been the remainder of the loan from 1639. Given that Uylenburgh had died in 1661, Sijen's heirs would have had to recoup the sum from Gerrit Uylenburgh, who had taken over the business. On the list of the latter's creditors from 1675, however, Sijen's name does not appear,[205] so perhaps the outstanding debt had been paid off in the intervening years or even written off by the heirs as an ancient debt.

In Marretje Cornelisdr's inventory only her stocks are detailed. There is no description of household effects, furniture etc., nor are they entered – as was usually done – *pro memorie*. Perhaps this elderly woman had latterly given away part of her household belongings; in any case, nothing is said about her personal goods in the will she drew up shortly before her death. The absence of an inventory of household effects at the time of her death means that we know nothing of the couple's art possessions – which is a great pity, for Pieter Sijen and his wife had their portraits painted by Rembrandt in 1633 while the latter was working with Uylenburgh (fig. 87 and fig. 88).[206] Their contact with Uylenburgh must therefore date back to that time, which means that they had dealings with each other over almost three decades.

Hardly anything is known about the second financial backer, Gilbert de Flines. In the literature he is identified as one Gilbert Philipsz de Flines without further information provided.[207] But it would seem far more likely that Uylenburgh's backer is the latter's uncle of the same name, who in 1612 married Annetje Cornelisdr van Grotewal, a sister of the Marretje who married Pieter Sijen the following year. If so, the two financial backers would have been brothers-in-law.[208] And yet it is not absolutely certain that this De Flines was in fact Uylenburgh's creditor. One cannot tell this from the original bond of 1639, because that document was only signed by Sijen. The deed of 1650, which records that the debt had not yet been paid, is equally unhelpful in identifying De Flines: Sijen accepted the contents of the document 'on behalf of himself and his consort'. The elder De Flines had died in 1648, but Sijen could well have taken care of the interests of his beneficiaries. Sijen and his brother-in-law De

202 GAA, not. L. Lamberti, NA 599, pp. 600-602, 2 April 1639; this act of conveyance is first reported, albeit in concise form, in Bredius 1915-1922, vol. 5, p. 1687(f).
203 GAA, not. L. Lamberti, NA 604, p. 20, 12 December 1650; published for the first time in Van der Veen 2001, p. 48 and note 18.
204 GAA, not. C. Hoogeboom, NA 2661, pp. 709-716, 3 October 1666; first published in Van der Veen 2003, p. 57 and note 64.
205 See p. 285.
206 See p. 142-145.
207 Schwartz 1984, p. 140, no. 21.
208 The order of sequence in the document of 1639 – according to seniority – argued for this identification: first Gilbert de Flines and then the three years younger Pieter Sijen.

Flines were wealthy Amsterdam merchants, who could easily allow themselves a financial investment of this kind.[209] Both were associated with the Waterland community and so would in fact have known Uylenburgh well. No inventory is known from the De Flines-van Grotewal couple, so one has to look at the estates passed on by their children, six of whom survived into adulthood. In 1669 their eldest son Gilbert de Flines and his wife Heijltje Lambertsdr Schouten (see Genealogy 2, p. 292) bequeathed, among their household effects, some 35 paintings, including several with the artists' names supplied.[210] Two anonymous pieces in particular attract one's attention: 'een schilderije van een kooken' and 'een schilderije van de kersnacht van de herders' that hung in the entrance hall. The kitchen piece suggests Rombout Uylenburgh. Could the second work have been Flinck's *Annunciation to the shepherds* from 1639? Further investigation of the De Flines family art possessions is needed here.[211]

THE 1640 LOAN BY A CONSORTIUM

In 1640, Hendrick Uylenburgh, the 'coopman van schildereyen ende kunststucken' (dealer in paintings and art works), acknowledged that various persons had granted him 'eene goede somme van penningen tot beneficie ende bevorderinge van sijne neringe ende handel' (granted him a goodly sum of money to assist and promote his business and trade). These financial backers were 'Jan ende Pieter Hooft', 'Pieter Beltens', 'Jan Carels wegen Jasper Tongerlo', 'Claes Moyert', 'Sijmen de Vlieger', 'Johannes Staveren', 'Jacob de Wet', 'Johan Coelenbier', 'Wijbrant Claeszen', 'Jacob Hero', 'Rembrandt van Rijn', 'Nicolaes van Bambeeck', 'Claes Arents van Neerden', 'Lambert Jacobs erffgenamen (heirs)', 'Jan Jansen Treck', 'de weduwe van (the widow of) Jacob Liewen' and 'de weduwe van (the widow of) Pieter Denijn'. Uylenburgh declared that these creditors had done him 'a great service and convenience' and to 'allay any anxieties' he gave in surety 'in proportion to the amount invested by each his entire shop of paintings and art works with all means of outstanding debts or credits relating to them', nothing ex-

cepted, 'thus should they now or hereafter be used or sold by him'. He assents to any of them, at any moment they wish, seizing 'his aforementioned paintings, art works and the accounts thereof' and trading them as they see fit 'without having to resort to any legal claim'; nor has Uylenburgh or anyone else the right to resist this. The deed includes an additional clause to the effect that Uylenburgh committed his person and his goods to ensure the observance of the contracted obligations. Pieter Gerritsz Hooft then declared that he accepted this conveyance in his own name and on behalf of the other named creditors, signing the document together with Hendrick Uylenburgh, two witnesses and the notary.[212]

Why this consortium of eighteen parties should have lent this money is not clear. Merchants normally cooperated – in the chartering of ships, for example – in order to spread the risk as far as possible; but that is highly unlikely to be the reason here. The duration of the loan is not specified, and even more remarkably, the amount of the loan is not fixed either. In any case, it was clearly not the same for each investor: 'De rato caverende' (according to the proportion stipulated) the document says literally. The amount involved can be roughly estimated if we look at the other loans: that of 1631 involved 1,000 guilders, in 1639 the sum was 1,600 guilders and in the loan of 1641, still to be mentioned, it was 1,000 gulden. The painters could have lent an average of 500 guilders, Claesz and Hero 250 guilders each and the merchants (or their heirs) an average of 750 guilders each. If these assumptions are not too remote from the truth – and the sums suggested are more likely to be an under- than an over-estimate – then the loan in all would have amounted to some 8,500 guilders. The investors can be divided into two groups: artists and other persons associated with the art enterprise, and wealthy merchants, some of whom were members of Uylenburgh's Mennonite circle or his neighbours.

The list of the investors begins with the brothers Jan and Pieter Gerritsz Hooft, both rich merchants, the latter being the signatory of the document on behalf of all the others. His business contact with Uylenburgh is not difficult to ex-

209 Pieter Sijen was assessed in 1631 for 150 guilders (indicating wealth to the tune of at least 30,000 guilders), Gilbert de Flines for 130 guilders (26,000 guilders), Kohier 1631, p. 30, fol. 126, no. 190, and p. 33, fol. 141, no. 25, respectively.
210 Four pieces by Jan van Goyen, two by (Adriaen) van de Velde, two by Jan Miense Molenaer and one each by 'Savrij' (Roelant Saverij?) and (Gillis de) Hondecoeter. GAA, not. Jac. Hellerus, NA 2483, pp. 590-603, 30 January-14 March 1670.
211 The couple De Flines-Schouten were married in Weesp in 1638. Their wedding contract was also signed by Pieter Sijen as the bridegroom's uncle and by Sijbrant Haye Fries as uncle of the bride, GAA, arch. no. 5073, inv. no. 1067, transcript of the wedding contract of November 21st 1638 in the presence of not. Gijsbert Louff in Weesp.
212 GAA, not. J. Jansz Westfrisius, NA 557(A), fols. 21-22, 20 January 1640 (minute) and NA 523, fols. 224-225, 20 January 1640 (transcript), and Doc. 1640/2.

plain: the parents of Jan and Pieter Hooft lived in Danzig until 1595 and the brothers conducted trade with that city from Amsterdam during the period that Rombout Uylenburgh lived there. They were both, moreover, members of the Waterland community of Mennonites (both were deacons) and both became related to the Uylenburgh family through marriage: in 1624 Pieter Hooft married a daughter of Laurens Cornelisz Schouten, the brother-in-law of Sijbrant Haye Fries, who in turn became a brother-in-law of Rombout Uylenburgh. Was Pieter Hooft the organizer of the whole venture? In 1642 he went bankrupt and one can assume that his administrators pressed for the recovery of outstanding debts. Subsequently, he established himself with his wife in Weesp. There is very little information about their estate,[213] but we know much more about his brother Jan Gerritsz Hooft, because in 1654 an inventory was drawn up of the goods in the house where his widow died. The art possessions were restricted to a few works that bear no further description, the most expensive of them a seascape valued at twelve guilders.[214] Given that the roughly 70-year-old woman had been a widow for ten years, the usual household furnishings could have already been passed on to her children before she died. For example, there are no portraits mentioned among her effects. The list of debts and credits finally comes out at credit extended to Hendrick Uylenburg of four hundred guilders.[215] That sum would presumably have been the remainder of the loan of 1640.

At first sight, it may not seem surprising that Rembrandt joined the consortium, since in 1631 he had already invested money in the enterprise and subsequently worked there for almost four years. Yet it is rather remarkable, given that in 1640 Rembrandt hardly had cash to spare. He had only the previous year put himself deeply into debt for the purchase of his house.[216] It is not known how the group of investors came together, but it is well possible that Rembrandt joined only at a late stage. In the original deed the name 'Rembrandt van Rijn' has been added in the margin, with Uylenburgh's signature below it to authorize this change in the document. Rembrandt could of course have been simply

forgotten, but it is surely more likely that he came forward later than the other investors. Although Rembrandt had a heavy mortgage to pay off within a few years, this loan of money to Uylenburgh suggests interesting possibilities. Whether Rembrandt got his money back again within the short term we don't know. The matter could have been settled through other means.

Another investor was Simon de Vlieger. This painter of sea- and riverscapes, originally from Rotterdam, worked in Delft between 1634 and 1638, and thereafter until around 1650 in Amsterdam, where he purchased his citizenship in 1643. He subsequently moved to Weesp, where he lived until his death in 1653 (see fig. 18).[217] His art was well sought after. In 1637 he bought a house in Rotterdam from an art dealer and undertook to pay the purchase price of 900 guilders with monthly deliveries of paintings worth 31 guilders. He sold the house again in 1644 and in 1650 bought a house in Weesp, for which purpose he borrowed 1,500 guilders from a citizen of Amsterdam. De Vlieger was not without means, certainly, but the data do not suggest that he had a large sum of money at his disposal to lend to Uylenburgh in 1640. Perhaps the latter took his paintings.

We have no precise information on Jan Jansz Treck's financial position around the relevant time of 1640, but this still-life painter seems to have been comfortably well-off. His parents were wealthy; he had remained a bachelor and lived in rooms, so he had no expensive overheads, and when he died his beneficiaries had almost 10,000 guilders to share between them after the deduction of costs and bequests.[218] Treck certainly had the financial resources to be able to lend money. In 1643 he sold a house for 6,000 guilders. A few weeks before that he had lent a merchant 1,800 guilders at a rate of interest of five percent, a debt that was repaid eighteen months later. However, things did not always run so smoothly for him. Another document shows that Treck had told the woman in whose house he lodged that he had lent money to various persons from whom he had sought in vain for repayment. He had not even been paid the interest.[219] But whatever these set-backs, the painter could afford to put money

213 Pieter Gerritsz Hooft and Weyntje Laurensdr Schouten named in their will of 1652 their daughter Nelletje (Cornelia) Hooft as their sole heir. No particularities concerning personal property were given, NHA, Weesp, not. S. Jansz Verlaen, NA 5192, 12 November 1652. This daughter was married to David Leeuw (c. 1631/2-1703), possibly the boy whose portrait was painted in 1640 by Govert Flinck (Sum. II 692). Their other daughter Maria Hooft was not mentioned in the will of 1652.
214 GAA, not. Joh. Hellerus, NA 2088, pp. 798-808, 29 July 1654.
215 'Hendrick Uijlenburgh, schilder, is schuldich p. reste van reeck. f 400:-:-', ibid., p. 806; first published in Van der Veen 2001, p. 48 and note 21.
216 Doc. 1639/1.
217 Haverkorn van Rijsewijk 1891-1893.
218 GAA, not. C. Tou, NA 1442, 27 September 1652 and 24 December 1652-5 July 1653; Bredius 1915-1922, vol. 6, pp. 2085-2096, and vol. 7, p. 235.
219 Bredius 1915-1922, vol. 6, p. 2093(o).

into Uylenburgh's enterprise. By 1652, since Uylenburgh's name does not appear in Treck's list of debitors in 1652, the debt must have been repaid.[220]

Johannes van Staveren was also well-off and unmarried, but he too came from a wealthy patrician background; his father was a burgomaster of Leiden.[221] He enrolled as a student at Leiden University and took lessons in painting, possibly with Gerrit Dou in Leiden, and following his period of study he continued to paint, albeit not as his means of livelihood. Like his father, he assumed public office. As a young artist he had sufficient means to join the consortium. How he came into contact with Uylenburgh is not exactly known, but one need not seek far. Van Staveren's father had been commissioned to represent the city of Leiden at the Admiralty of Amsterdam since 1637, while Uylenburgh maintained business relations with persons in Leiden.

Like Treck and Van Staveren, the painter Claes Moyaert is recorded as a man of considerable means.[222] Various deeds witness to his growing wealth and in the period 1635-1645 he was especially productive and flush with money. Not only did he possess several properties in the city; when he bought a house in Amsterdam in early 1639, he was able to pay the purchase price of 4,500 guilders in full.

Two of Hendrick Uylenburgh's backers lived in Haarlem. Jan Coelenbier is recorded as being a painter there from 1632 (see also fig. 200), but he put his main energies – not without success – into the art trade. When he married in 1638, in addition to clothes and the 'morgengift' (payment for the bride's consent), his father gave him the handsome sum of a thousand guilders.[223] Coelenbier evidently granted loans more often: in 1655 he demanded from somebody the interest on a loan of 400 guilders; in 1656 he was one of Jan van Goyen's creditors, and in 1667 he was claiming repayment of another loan he had made of 2,000 guilders.[224] The second Haarlem contact was Jacob Willemsz de Wet, who had been a productive history painter since the beginning of the thirties.[225] His possessions of houses and lands around 1642 reveal him to be artist of some means. It is possible that De Wet maintained connections with Uylenburgh in the mid-thirties (perhaps at the same time as his fellow Haarlemer Willem de Poorter?). He was active on the Amsterdam art market and could well have established the contact with Uylenburgh there.

From the above data it is evident that Uylenburgh was not restricted to Mennonite circles when he needed to find investors. Treck, Van Staveren and Rembrandt did not belong to this persuasion; they are likely to have been Reformed. Moyaert and De Wet were Catholics, while the denominational allegiances of De Vlieger and Coelenbier are not known with certainty. It is an obvious assumption that these painters supplied works for Uylenburgh. Treck painted still lifes, Coelenbier landscapes (we know landscapes from his hand dating from the years 1640-1646), Moyaert and De Wet painted history pieces, De Vlieger seascapes, and Van Staveren painted anchorites at prayer and genre pieces in the style of Dou.

Undoubtedly, Wybrand Claesz and Jacob Heeremans (Hero) had dealings with Uylenburgh by reason of their craft: as ebony workers and frame-makers they would have supplied wood and frames and possibly also canvas to his workshop and no doubt they would have done work for him. Wybrand Claesz, originally from Leeuwarden, was a pre-eminent ebony-worker who is recorded in 1649 as 'overman' (headman) of the guild of cabinet-makers. On his death in 1651, he left considerable wealth, part of it tied up in houses. The inventory also records the debts that were still outstanding at the time of his death, including 70 guilders owed by Hendrick Uylenburgh.[226] This sum could certainly have derived from the 1640 loan, but it could equally be the sum owed for a delivery of materials. His colleague Jacob Heeremans had no further claim on Uylenburgh in 1655 – at least, none that is mentioned in the inventory of his effects drawn up at the time of his death. But this should not be taken to mean that contact had been broken, for members of the family had had dealings with Uylenburgh over several decades. This connection could well have begun with Heere Jansz, the father of Jacob Heeremans, a cabinet-worker who owned a frame-maker's workshop and was also a near neighbour of Uylenburgh. When the latter

220 It is possible that Treck produced work for art dealers more often: it appears from the inventory of a milliner who dealt in paintings that Treck had given him two still-lifes from his own hand to sell, Bredius 1915-1922, dl. 6, p. 2092.
221 The data concerning Johannes van Staveren are taken from Leiden 1988, p. 226.
222 See for the following, Dudok van Heel 1976.
223 Haarlem, Archiefdienst voor Kennemerland, not. J. Steyn, NA 160, fol. 401r-v, 21 March 1638.
224 Goosens 2001, pp. 265-267 and 425.
225 Goosens 2001, pp. 98-100, 202-203 and 437.
226 'Sr. Oulenborgh op ten Dam in de Bril, debet 70 gl.', GAA, arch. no. 5073, inv. no. 1371, lade 179, 3 and 4 March 1651, transcript from the inventory of Wybrand Claesz and his (fifth) wife, cited in Van der Veen 2001, p. 49 and note 24, and in Montias 2002, p. 124 and note 376.

moved to the Breestraat, Heere Jansz lived 'near the Anthonissluys'.[227] He was moreover the pastor of the Oude Vlamingen (the Old Flemish), the more orthodox branch of Mennonites. Lambert Jacobsz, the painter in Leeuwarden whom we have already encountered, was another Mennonite with communal business relations. His inventory records a debt for frames and panels in the name of Heere Jansz, cabinet-maker of Amsterdam.[228] It is not certain whether his son, who was baptized in the Waterland community, actually lent money in 1640; his participation in the consortium could well have been a way of transferring outstanding debts on existing accounts without insisting on immediate payment. But whatever the case, after the death of his first wife in 1648, when their possessions were inventoried, the unspecified debts remaining on the books barely amounted to 90 guilders.[229] If Uylenburgh still owed him money, it could only have been a small amount. The extent of the household effects was rather modest. The 'shop with its tools, benches and shelves therein' was valued at 50 guilders, the house contents at slightly more than 800 guilders. The cost of the house on the Singel, bought by Heeremans in 1634 and assessed in 1648 at 7,500 guilders, had only partly been paid off. But Heeremans cannot be called a man without means: in 1648 he was able to put aside a sum of 1,500 guilders for his five children from the inheritance from their mother.[230] It seems that his finances did not fare so well subsequently, for after his death in 1654 his children's guardians judged that there were so many debts, they were only willing to accept the estate under benefit of inventorization.[231] The inventory that was compiled of the household effects includes two planing benches and a number of cabinet-maker's tools in the hall and, apart from the house furniture, a list of debts.[232]

In Jacob Heeremans' inventory there is no credit against the name of Uylenburgh, but that does not mean that the professional contact had been ended. His much younger half-brother Pieter Heeremans, who continued the family business, actually worked for Gerrit Uylenburgh. Like his father Heere Jansz, Jacob Heeremans is variously described in different documents as either 'schrijnwerker' or 'kistenmaker', more or less equivalent terms for a cabinet-maker.[233] Apart from selling panels and frames, therefore, he was clearly a cabinet-maker. In Amsterdam, the cabinet-makers came under the St Joseph's Guild, the frame-makers under the St Lucas Guild. In 1688 Pieter Heeremans appears among the members of the St Lucas guild,[234] suggesting that he concentrated on making frames for paintings and prints and the supply of painters' materials. At least, the documents concerning his activities, without exception, all refer to this line. In 1665 Pieter Heeremans authorized someone to demand money for him from Caesar van Everdingen in Alkmaar.[235] A year later, the 'frame- and panel-maker' Heeremans declared at the request of Emanuel de Witte that someone had commissioned him – i.e. Heeremans – to make two canvases and to deliver them to De Witte for him to paint them. The commissioning client had said that he would pay for the canvas, but apparently he had forgotten his promise.[236] There are also records of supplying frames from later years. The inventory drawn up on the death of the painter Willem Schellincks contains an item of 25 guilders and 4 stuyvers, an amount owed to Heeremans 'for the making of frames'.[237] The claim that he had on the effects of Clement de Jonghe dates from the same period. In the household inventory compiled on the decease of this print publisher and art dealer a payment is recorded of 175 guilders and 18 stuyvers to Pieter Heeremans 'for frames supplied paid according to verdict'.[238] In 1681, Heeremans supplied the frame, the canvas

227 Heere Jansz declared that address when he remarried that same year, GAA, DTB 670, p. 121, 17 January 1626.
228 'Voor lysten, panelen etc. aen Heere Jansz. kistermaker tot Amsterdam', Straat 1925, p. 71. The sum of 20 guilders that was claimed for this also included the calculated cost of six months' lodgings with Jan Pouwelsz, a Mennonite merchant draper of Amsterdam, for Abraham, the son of Lambert Jacobsz, later calling himself Van den Tempel (1622/3-1672). The young man was apprenticed in Amsterdam by his guardians, probably with Jacob Backer, which does not exclude a contact with Uylenburgh's workshop. In 1640 the brothers Abraham and Jacob inherited from their father Lambert Jacobsz.
229 GAA, arch. no. 5073, inv. no. 974, no. 47. This is a transcript of the inventory that was drawn up on August 26th 1648 in the presence of the not. J. van Speenhoven; the protocols of this not. have not been preserved.
230 GAA, arch. no. 5073, inv. no. 27, fol. 229v, 28 August 1648.
231 The Hague, Nationaal Archief, Hoge Raad (3.03.02), inv. no. 59, 1655.
232 GAA, not. N. Kruijs, NA 1856, pp. 749-752, 17 March 1655, and Van der Veen 2001, p. 49 and note 25; this inventory concerns the estate of Jacob Heeremans. The effects of his second wife Anna Cornelisdr van Geresteyn are described separately. Her inventory lists a number of paintings, including a 'King Solomon's idolatry' by (Jan) Tengnagel and a work that is not further described by (Pieter) Quast; ibid., pp. 753-756, 17 March 1655. His second wife was reformed. If only because of his 'marrying out', one can exclude the possibility that Jacob Heeremans would

be a deacon in the Waterland community in 1648, as claimed by Wijnman 1959, p. 47 and note 2. It was Dirck Heeremans.
233 'Schrijnwerker' is the North-Nederlands term for a cabinet-maker; 'kistenmaker' was apparently the South-Netherlands equivalent; Prijst de lijst 1984, p. 30 and note 3.
234 Van Eeghen 1969b, p. 97.
235 GAA, not. J. van de Ven, NA 1152, fol. 8v, 9 August 1665.
236 GAA, not. S. van der Sluijs, NA 3512, 3 August 1666, and

Bredius 1915-1922, vol. 5, p. 1834. In the sequel to this matter Heeremans was not mentioned further; ibid., 6 September 1666, and Bredius 1915-1922, vol. 5, p. 1835.
237 GAA, not. D. Ypelaer, NA 2663, 13 December 1679.
238 GAA, not. J. Backer, NA 4532, p. 378, 22 June 1679. De Jonghe's inventory mentions among the charges to the estate, 'Pieter Heromans f 175:- :-'; ibid., NA 4528, pp. 117-146, 11 February 1679, especially p. 145.

and the stretcher for a coat-of-arms for the room of the church warden's room in the Old Church. The canvas, to be painted by Jacob Colijns, was fixed by Heeremans on the stretching frame while he also gilded and varnished the frame of the painting. Three years later, Heeremans supplied a new frame for a painting that was hung in the same room and carried out certain repairs to the canvas.[239] At the end of the 1680s he received an assignment from the city governors of Enkhuizen, supplying the canvas that would be painted by Theodoor Ferreris. In 1689 and 1692, according to the cashbook of the Enkhuizen treasurer, payments were made to Heeremans of 125 guilders and 16 stuyvers, and of 38 guilders and 8 stuyvers.[240] In 1675 Pieter Heeremans was in credit to the tune of 364 guilders in the accounts of Gerrit Uylenburgh.[241] Given the nature of his activities, it would seem a fair assumption that this credit derived from the supply of painters' materials or frames. It is striking that Heeremans worked for such artists as Schellincks and Ferreris, who had connections with Gerrit Uylenburgh.

Two other backers from the circle of artists can be briefly dealt with. The first is the widow of Lambert Jacobsz, the painter and art dealer in Leeuwarden who was for years such an important business partner of Uylenburgh.[242] Although less well documented, there was similarly a business contact between Pieter de Neyn and Uylenburgh.[243] The fact that after the deaths of both men their widows put money into Uylenburgh's enterprise surely indicates that they had always enjoyed good business relations. The loan from Grietgen Jacobsdr, since 1635 the widow of Jacob Leeuw, also argues for confidence in Uylenburgh's way of conducting his business.[244] Uylenburgh's and Govert Flinck's relations with the Leeuw couple, who also belonged to the Waterland Mennonite community, and with other members of their family have already been dis-

cussed.[245] In view of their long involvement with Uylenburgh's business, these investors must have had a good insight into the way it was run and they too must have been convinced that their capital was well invested.

The listing of 'Pieter Beltens' as one of the investors is somewhat puzzling. It must refer to Pieter Belten the Younger, son of the merchant already mentioned above, Pieter Belten the Elder. Belten the Younger died in 1639, so that the money must have been lent by his widow, Constantia Coymans. The Beltens lived in the house in the Breestraat immediately next to the corner-house of the Zwanenburgwal that Uylenburgh rented. Just prior to the loan, Uylenburgh valued paintings in the estate of some family relatives,[246] so the family would have been familiar with Uylenburgh's business. The same goes for Claes Arentsz van Naerden, a brother of Jan Arentsz van Naerden, who had died in 1637 and had named him in his will as co-beneficiary.[247] Jan van Naerden had bought the house in the Breestraat called 'Cronenburgh' in 1636 and lived there up to his death, after which his brother Claes took over the property and let it (from 1638?) to Hendrick Uylenburgh.[248] In 1640, thus, Uylenburgh was borrowing money from his landlord. Relations between the Catholic Van Naerdens and Uylenburgh stem from further back, for in 1637 Uylenburgh together with Lucas Luce had valued the paintings in the house of the deceased Jan van Naerden.[249] It seems likely, although one cannot be certain, that Van Naerden had bought a number of those paintings from Uylenburgh's shop. He could certainly afford to purchase art works, for the Van Naerden's were wealthy merchants: Jan was assessed in the tax register of 1631 at 50,000 guilders, his brother Claes at 'only' 15,000 guilders, but the latter's wealth would have been far higher in 1640 after inheriting from his brother. Whatever the details, in 1640 Claes van

239 Bijtelaar 1969, pp. 40-41, and Prijst de Lijst 1984, p. 32.
240 To 'Pieter Heromans tot Amsterdam over gelevert doeck tot de schilderijen van T. Ferreris', see pp. 222-224.
241 See p. 284.
242 See pp. 175-184.
243 See pp. 184-186.
244 Montias 2002, p. 282, note 374, identifies 'Lieuwen' incorrectly with the Jewish merchant Jacob Lievensz.
245 See pp. 174-175.
246 The estate of Samuel van Swol (deceased 1639) and Catharina Thijs (deceased sometime after 1642). Catharina was a sister of Christoffel Thijs (1603-1680), who was married to Pieter's sister Magdalena Belten (1610-1659).
247 In his will, Jan van Naerden laid down that, in the event of his dying childless, his brothers and sisters or their children should inherit from him, GAA, not. J. Meerhout, NA 429, 16 April 1627. This was confirmed in a codicil, GAA, not. L. Lamberti, NA 580, fol. 934, 31 January 1637.
248 The exact date of Uylenburgh's moving in is unknown.
249 GAA, not. L. Lamberti, NA 569, pp. 310-322, 11 December 1637.

Naerden had enough room for manœuvre to be able to put money into Uylenburgh's business.

The 'Jan Carels' who appeared 'on behalf of Jasper Tongerlo' has up to now never been properly, or correctly, identified – nor the individual he represented.[250] The first was Jan Carelsz Rousé, who together with Jacob Haesbaert was a guardian to the sons of Jasper van Tongerlo for the time of their minority.[251] Jasper van Tongerlo, a prominent Amsterdam merchant, had died around 1637, leaving four sons. According to the estate, they would inherit the considerable capital of at least 75,000 guilders.[252] The household effects – including paintings – were estimated at around 3,000 guilders, a respectable sum for those days. By the time proceedings reached the division of the inheritance the two eldest sons had reached their majority. Between 1637 and 1642, with successive divisions of the estate they were paid their share of the inheritance.[253] Because the two other sons were still minors, their guardians looked for the best possible investment for the capital that was now available and for which they bore the responsibility. Apparently, Uylenburgh's business enterprise offered a solid prospect. The elder of the two minors, however, died in the autumn of 1640, after which his inheritance of more than 12,000 guilders was divided among the two elder brothers and their half-brother Christiaen.[254] From that moment on, the loan to Uylenburgh involved only this youngest son.

Jasper van Tongerlo was a member of the Flemish community of Mennonites and a man of capital. He conducted business with his brother-in-law (and neighbour) Jacob Haesbaert. In the tax register of 1631, these two companions are assessed at 25,000 guilders each.[255] Jan Rousé was married to a sister of Jasper van Tongerlo's second wife. All three brothers-in-law, Rousé, Haesbaert and Van Tongerlo, were deacons of the Flemish Mennonite community. Jasper van Tongerlo's father was a successful merchant draper who also dabbled in property and land speculation both in Amsterdam and in Weesp.[256] Together with Van Tongerlo, Haesbaert also had interests in the latter town.[257] Another possible link with Uylenburgh is Pieter Gerritsz Hooft, who acted on behalf of his fellow-investors in 1640 and lived in Weesp. How close the contact was between Uylenburgh and Rousé or Haesbaert one cannot yet say: I have found Rousé and Uylenburgh recorded together on one occasion: in 1626 they both bought porcelain at the same auction.[258]

No household inventories at the decease of Van Rousé or Haesbaert have been found, so we know nothing of any art possessions they may have had. We do have this information, however, for the two eldest sons of Jasper van Tongerlo, and here Uylenburgh's name crops up. The inventory of the unmarried Hendrick van Tongerlo contains little of particular interest. Among the household goods are recorded seven paintings and four drawings, but there is no further description.[259] In Cornelis van Tongerlo's inventory, on the other hand, the paintings are specified: besides a painting with lobsters and two landscapes by Jan Looten we find 'two octagonal paintings by Uijlenburgh',[260] but because the subjects of these pieces are not given, we cannot say for certain which member of the Uylenburgh family had painted them. One thinks of Rombout Uylenburgh or, more probably, Gerrit Uylenburgh since the same estate contains an item in which the latter is specifically mentioned: among the debts recorded in a financial ledger, two third of which were due to Cornelis and the rest to his brother Hendrick, is recorded: 'Gerret Uijllenburgh f 66:10:-'.[261] This sum could relate to merchandise purchased, since Cornelis van Tongerlo was a merchant draper – there are, for example, several painters on the list of his debtors who owed small amounts.[262] But when it comes to their younger half-brother Christiaen, part of

250 Montias 2002, p. 124, wrongly identifies Jan Carels with Jan (Jansz) Carels (the Younger), owner of a glass factory in Amsterdam. The suggestion of Van Tongerlo for the investor in Van der Veen 2001, p. 55, note 26, is also incorrect unless, in the text, one thinks 'the Elder' after the name of Cornelis van Tongerlo.
251 With the deed of 25 March 1637 Jacob Haesbaert, Christiaen de Coningh, surgeon of Leiden, and Jan Carelsz Rousé were appointed testamentary guardians of the under-age children of the *late* Jasper van Tongerlo, GAA, not. L. Lamberti, NA 598, pp. 146-147, 25 March 1637. I have been unable to find the record of burial of Jasper van Tongerlo, but it must have been shortly before. In 1642 Rousé appeared again together with a co-guardian and the two elder minor sons (mentioned below) of Jasper van Tongerlo, GAA, not. L. Lamberti, NA 601, pp. 322-323, 18 February 1642.
252 GAA, not. L. Lamberti, NA 569, pp. 327-329, 25 May 1638; the household effects with the 'paintings' were valued by two assessors, but this valuation gives no details. The personal property was valued according to the will of Jasper van Tongerlo in order that it be divided between his children, GAA, not. L. Lamberti, NA 579, pp. 587-592 and 592-593, 16 February 1635.
253 GAA, not. L. Lamberti, NA 601, pp. 322-323, 18 February 1642; according to this deed, some 9,140 guilders were shared out. It appears that a division of Jasper van Tongerlo's wealth had taken place in 1639 and in 1640. See also: GAA, not. L. Lamberti, NA 600, pp. 453-454, 26 October 1640.
254 GAA, not. L. Lamberti, NA 601, pp. 323-324, 18 February 1642.
255 Kohier 1631, p. 33, fol. 140v, nos. 19 and 20.
256 Wijnman 1932 mentions many transactions in the two cities.
257 GAA, not. L. Lamberti, NA 595, p. 112, 29 April 1633.
258 See p. 48 and note 137.
259 GAA, not. B. Coornhart, NA 2861, deed 318, 24 March 1659; his will of 20 June 1657 contains no specific instructions about paintings.
260 GAA, not. B. Coornhart, NA 2858, fols. 307-331v, 17/24 August 1657; first pointed out in Van der Veen 2001, p. 55, note 26.
261 Ibid., fol. 329v.
262 Among others, Elias Vonck (1605-1652) and Simon Luttichuys (1610-1661).

140 Rembrandt van Rijn, Portrait of Nicolaes van Bambeeck, signed and dated 'Rembrandt f. 1641' and the inscription 'AE 44', canvas, 108.8 x 83.3 cm, Brussels, Koninklijke Musea voor Schone Kunsten (Br. 218; Corpus III 144)

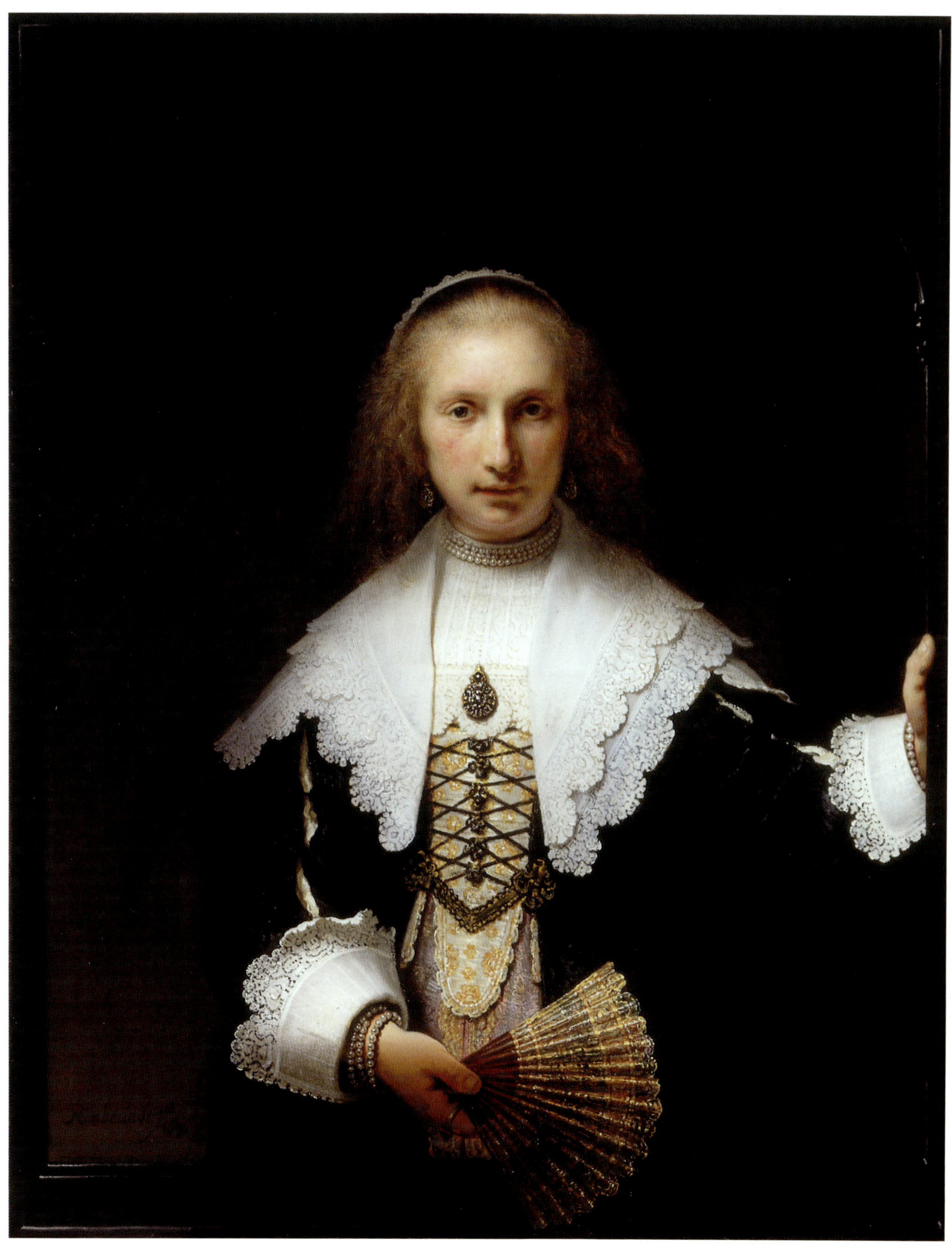

141 Rembrandt van Rijn, Portrait of Agatha Bas, signed and dated 'Rembrandt f. 1641' and the inscription 'AE 29', canvas, 105.2 x 83.9 cm, London, The Royal Collection, Her Majesty Queen Elizabeth II, Buckingham Palace (Br. 360; Corpus III A 145)

whose inheritance had been invested with Uylenburgh (as we have seen), we know of no inventory. He married in 1649 and it may be that Uylenburgh was asked to pay him back.

The investor Nicolaes van Bambeeck, a merchant, was another of Uylenburgh's neighbours. In the thirties, together with his mother and a brother, he lived in the parental house 'Aäron' in the Breestraat, obliquely opposite Uylenburgh's house (see fig. 21). In the mother's tax assessment for the year 1631, her wealth was estimated at 175,000 guilders, the highest assessment of anyone living in the street.[263] In 1638 Nicolaes van Bambeeck married Agatha Bas. Two years later he invested in the firm of Uylenburgh, at the same time as Rembrandt. It could well have been this business contact that led to the commission from Rembrandt of two pendant portraits, which were finished in 1641 (figs. 140 and 141). It was a regular occurrence for a portrait commission to lead to the purchase of other art works from the same workshop, as was outlined earlier. No household inventory has survived for Van Bambeeck and his wife, but we do have one from their eldest son, which includes many paintings – with the artists identified – that he could have inherited from his parents. That is certainly the case for a pair of portraits of the parental couple Van Bambeeck-Bas (painted by Govert Flinck!) and possibly also for the beach scene painted by Simon de Vlieger and a history piece by Jacob Backer, while there is also mention of a painting of Abraham and Hagar by a 'discipel van Rembrant'.[264] This history piece, possibly the same painting from Rembrandt's workshop that is now in London (fig. 142), would have been bought from Uylenburgh.

Nicolaes van Bambeeck allowed the loan to Uylenburgh to stand for fifteen years. In 1655 he reached an agreement on repayment with 'father and son' Uylenburgh. It says in the deed that Hendrick Uylenburgh owed him 2,250 guilders, fifteen stuyvers and eight pennies, which would be paid off in instalments. Starting from 1655, there would be annual payment of about 330 guilders, gradually increasing until the debt was paid off around 1660.[265] This seems to have happened, or at least there are no known documents to indicate the contrary. The size of this debt is considerable, though we don't know what the figure was in 1640. It could have been higher; Uylenburgh could have paid some of it off in the intervening years. In theory, it is also possible that Van Bambeeck took over the credit of another investor. The agreement states explicitly that the debt stood to the account of Hendrick Uylenburgh, but his son Gerrit also assumed responsibility for the repayment. Gerrit took over the business and with it the responsibility for its debts. The same seems to have happened with the repayment of the debt to the Mennonite community.

THE LOAN OF 1641 BY THE WATERLAND MENNONITE COMMUNITY

In 1641 Hendrick Uylenburgh borrowed 1,000 guilders from the Waterland community of Mennonites in Amsterdam at an annual rate of interest of five percent, proposing to hand over as collateral '125 copper plates'.[266] It was not entirely usual to have to give security; at least, with other loans recorded in the 'book of debts' concerned, there is seldom or never mention of such securities. The repayment of this loan can be followed: at the beginning of 1646 the amount owed remained intact, but up to April 1644 Uylenburgh had managed to pay off the interest. Not until 1654 did Uylenburgh pay off half the loan, after which his son Gerrit completed repayment of the outstanding 500 guilders three years later.[267] The trustees of the capital belonging to the Waterland community invested the money for which they were responsible as advantageously as possible and would only have lent money – normally to members – if they were guaranteed six-monthly payments of interest and an eventual repayment of the loan.[268] Evidently, Uylenburgh was able to provide them with this guarantee.

UYLENBURGH'S FINANCES

One needs capital to maintain a business enterprise of some size or to expand it, but it would seem that Uylenburgh was short of liquid assets.

263 Kohier 1631, p. 36, fol. 157v, no. 105.
264 GAA, not. P. Padthuijsen, NA 2910, pp. 1133-1180, 7 February 1676, especially p. 1160, no. 41, and Bredius 1915-1922, vol. 3, p. 1022.
265 GAA, not. A. Eggericx, NA 1823, p. 1008, 3 November 1655, and Bredius 1915-1922, vol. 5, p. 1689(p).
266 GAA, arch. no. 1120, inv. no. 148, fol. 73, 22 April 1641, and Wijnman 1959, p. 15 and note 3.
267 GAA, arch. no. 1120, inv. no. 149, fol. 24, 1 and January 1646, 6 September 1654 and 12 July 1657, and Van der Veen 2001, p. 49.
268 See also Sprunger 1993, pp. 194-195.

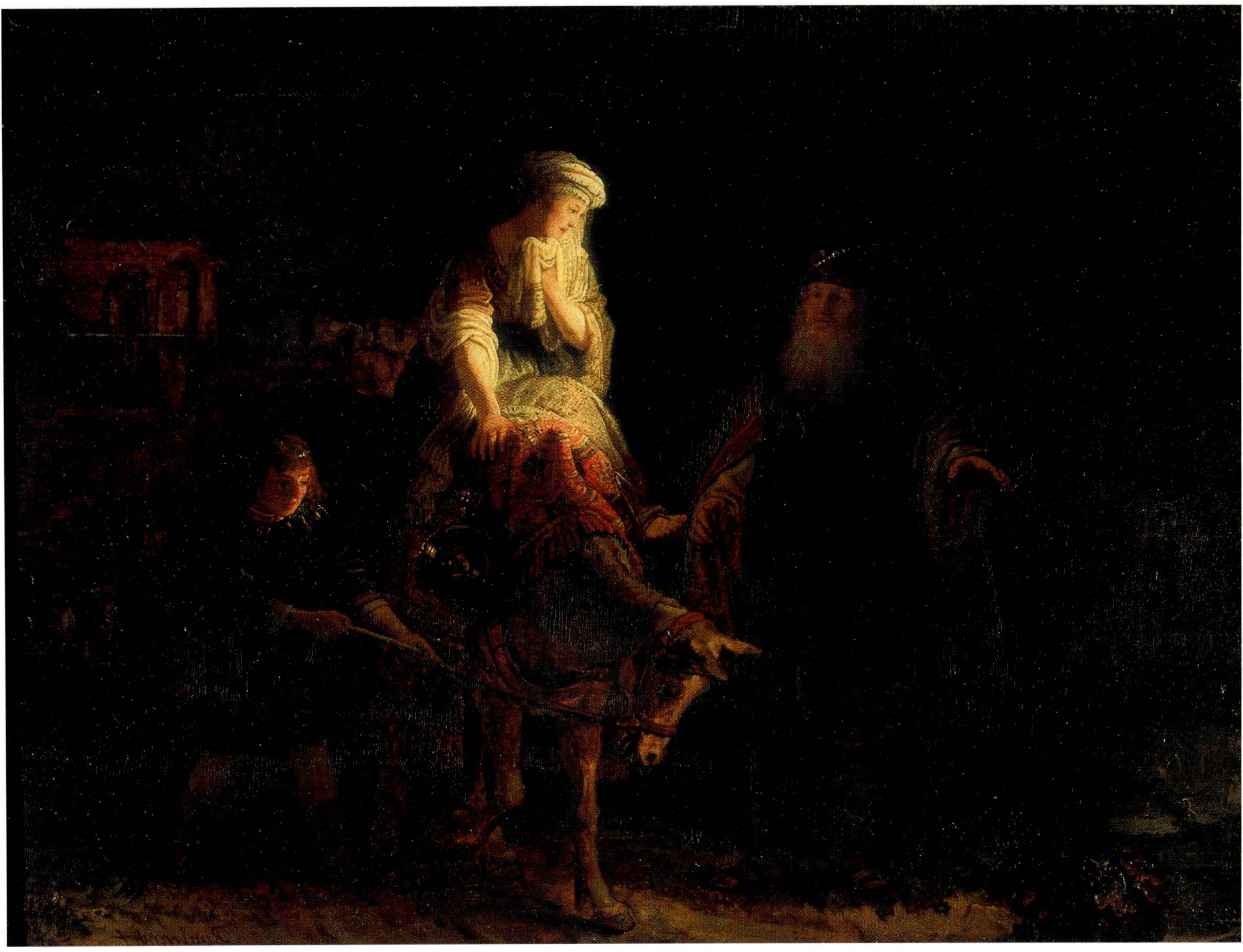

He never possessed his own house in Amsterdam; to the end of his life he lived in rented houses. Around 1631 he had some wealth – probably in bonds – to which the tax assessment for that year refers. After 1630 he no longer had an account with the Bank of Exchange. Uylenburgh inherited his portion from his father's estate, but there could have been no question of a significant family fortune. His capital was invested in his stock and his workshop – and he continued to invest in it. Given that he needed to find considerable sums of money for his purchases, there was little alternative but to take out loans. It is evident from the documents discussed above that these loans were concluded with an eye to purchases for his art trade and not, for example, for acquisitions of real estate. A rough estimate suggests that around 1640 Uylenburgh borrowed in the region of 10,000 guilders. Those extending him this credit must have had confidence in the business, although what strikes one is that securities or guarantees were always given. The stock seems to have been considered a sufficient surety. But if he was not pressed, Uylenburgh certainly did not hurry to pay off his debt: in the early fifties he still owed at least 5,000 guilders.

For a business such as Uylenburgh's, it was essential to keep accounts: one thinks of cashbooks and records of correspondence and the business administration. But very little concerning the art trade has been preserved from the early modern period of the Dutch Republic. It is evident that Uylenburgh did keep accounts from a passage from the deed of the 1640 loan, where 'paintings, art works *and the accounts thereof*' are mentioned, which Uylenburgh's creditors could take with them if they so wished. On the occasion of the 1639 loan there was mention of outstanding debts that Uylenburgh had, for which an administration was needed. But as far as we know, nothing relating to this has been preserved; we have to make do with such fragmentary evidence as there is and with incidental finds that are sometimes difficult to interpret. For example, on the 16th April 1641, Uylenburgh was in the red to the tune of 26 gulden and 10 stuyvers with the Amsterdam 'Weeskamer'.[269] The reason is unclear. Either he had bought goods at an auction organized under their auspices and only later paid the full purchase price, or perhaps he himself had organized a sale and still owed money to the auctioneer. Nothing much is known about such sales organized by painters or art dealers, for which permission had to be granted by the city authorities. It is not known whether Uylenburgh involved himself with these.[270] There are further debts. In 1653 he had to pay some 100 guilders to the Amsterdam art dealer Pieter van Melder, possibly for art supplied by the latter, but Van Melder also dealt in painters' canvas.[271] In 1654 Uylenburgh was two years behind with the rent for his house on the Dam, which he rented from the city government for 700 guilders a year. After consulting with the burgomasters he paid up 1,000 guilders on the 18th January 1658, the rest being written off, perhaps in connection with work undertaken in lieu of payment.[272]

Taking all these debts together, it has often been assumed that Uylenburgh was continually short of cash and not altogether successful.[273] In the case of the loan from Rembrandt, Bredius observed that the latter had shown himself a warm-hearted financial supporter of a friend in difficulties. He suggested that things had not gone well for Uylenburgh and characterized him as probably a mediocre painter – though he did wonder whether anyone had ever seen anything by him – who *had to* make the dealing in art his main concern.[274] But this judgement is based on a misunderstanding. Trade was in general much more profitable than production and the borrowing and lending of money was entirely normal in the seventeenth century. The fact that so many were willing to put money into the enterprise in fact shows that people had confidence in it. Another question is whether Uylenburgh's art business in the first half of the fifties could have suffered from the maritime war with the English, as has been suggested was the case with Rembrandt.[275] There is no concrete evidence for this. The loans all date from at least ten years earlier and there is nothing to indicate that they were not eventually paid off.

We know hardly anything about Uylenburgh's income and assets. The legacy of 1,000 guilders from his aunt Sas Remmerts Uylenburgh had nothing to do with the business, although undoubtedly the money came in handy. We learn of it only because problems arose over its payment.[276] It is evident from the texts of the 1639 and 1640 loans that he did have assets. A concrete example is the bond given by a Polish nobleman in 1641. The man had a notary draw up a document to the effect that his father in Amsterdam owed money to various persons and that Hendrick Uylenburgh, 'painter', was still owed 50 guilders for a portrait of his father.[277] The fact that Andrzej Rej, the subject of this portrait, had approached Uylenburgh to paint his portrait is understandable, given the latter's Polish past; but did Uylenburgh himself carry out this commission or did he get an associate to do it? Another

269 GAA, arch. no. 5073, inv. no. 965, fol. 83, 16 April 1641.

270 In a conflict Rembrandt had in 1654 with a principal over a commissioned portrait, he threatened not to deliver it, but 'als hij vendu hout van sijn schilderijen 't selve alsdan mede sal vercoopen', Doc. 1654/4.

271 GAA, not. J. de Vos, NA 1202, fols. 270-286, 1-3 October 1653, and Bredius 1915-1922, vol. 6, pp. 1968-1973. Among the debtors, as well as Uylenburgh there appear also Marten Kretzer and Johannes de Renialme, though for small amounts. The inventory lists 'nogh tweehondertsesseda[r]-tich ellen ruw lijwaet ende doeck, soo op ramen als anders'. The large number of painters with small debts, including Bartholomeus van der Helst (1613-1670), Simon de Vlieger, Bartholomeus Breenbergh (1598-1657) and Johannes Lingelbach, will have related to supplies of canvas. Incidentally, Van Melder was married to the widow of Isaac Jouderville, Rembrandt's former pupil.

272 See p. 56.

273 Montias 2002, pp. 121-126.

274 Bredius 1910a, p. 2.

275 Dudok van Heel 2001(a), pp. 25-26.

276 See p. 15, note 3 and p. 16, note 5. In 1634, a number of beneficiaries in this affair, including Hendrick Uylenburgh, complained to the Court of Friesland; Leeuwarden, Tresoar, Civiele sententies, inv. nr. 16503, 20 May 1634.

277 GAA, not. J. Warnaertz., NA 685, pp. 125-127, 27 and 29 April 1641, and Bredius 1915-1922, vol. 5, p. 1688(i).

143 Rembrandt van Rijn,
Man in a foreign costume,
signed and dated 'Rembrandt f.
1637', panel, 96.6 x 66.1 cm,
Washington, D.C., The National
Gallery of Art (Br. 211; Corpus
III A 122)

278 The Rembrandt Research
Project considers the work to
be a 'tronie', a picturesque type
perhaps in the role of an East
European potentate' and
rejects an identification with
Rej, Corpus III A 122. Wheelock 1995, pp. 222-226, concurs
with this view of the Corpus.
279 Thijssen 1992, p. 159, pro-
poses that the man 'in all probability' portrays Andrzej Rej
with the golden chain that he
had previously been given by
the States-General. Nothing
here is said about the costume.
280 Van de Wetering 2002, p.
8.
281 We know from a demand
presented to Isaac van Ruys-
dael (c. 1599-1677), painter,
ebony worker and art dealer in
Haarlem, that the latter had
bought paintings at this sale,
C.W. Fock in Lunsingh
Scheurleer 1986-1992, vol. 5a,
p. 28.
282 GAA, arch. no. 5073, inv.
no. 961, 22-28 February 1635,
and Bredius 1915-1922, vol. 3,
pp. 796-800. Various artists and
art-lovers bought art works at
this sale, including Rembrandt
(see pp. 126-127), the print
dealer and publisher Cornelis
Danckerts (1603/4-1656),
Pieter de la Tombe, and
Marten Kretzer.

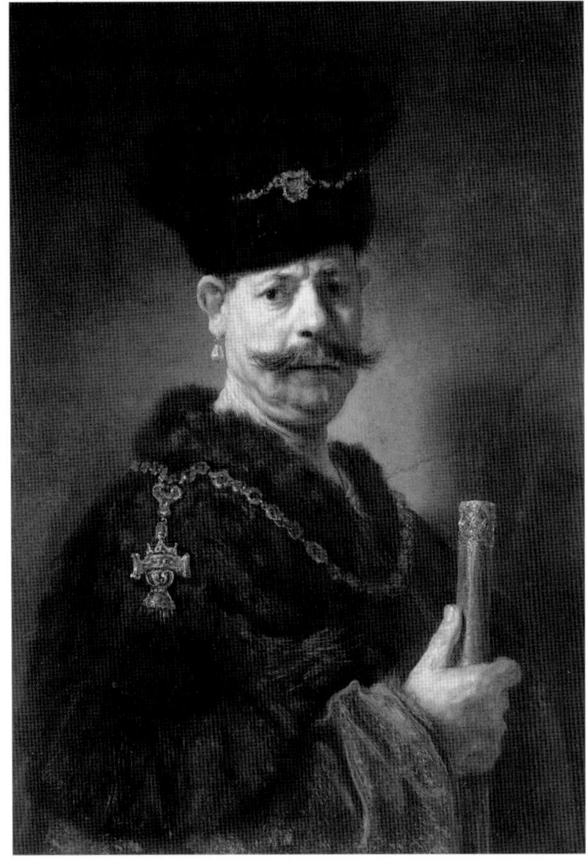

possibility is that he passed the commission on to Rembrandt. In this context, one is reminded of a work by Rembrandt from 1637, depicting a man in East European dress (fig. 143). Is this a 'tronie' of a man in foreign attire?[278] Or is it a portrait? And if so could it be the portrait of Rej?[279] Because it was precisely in that year that Rej travelled in the Republic and stayed in Amsterdam during November, 1637. The size of the debt is not much for the price of a portrait by Rembrandt – if such it was – but it was not unusual in the case of such commissions for part of the price to be paid in advance and Uylenburgh could have put down money as a pre-payment. The man's costume has been described as 'Polish' but 'Russian' has also been suggested as an alternative. In the latter case the man would have been a Russian boyar, a member of the high nobility, recognizable by a tall fur hat, a shaven head and a large mous-tache.[280] This makes an identification with Rej problematic, but what one needs now is further research on the costume and hair styles of the

Polish-Lithuanian aristocracy. If the painting by Rembrandt is indeed a portrait, it is exceptional in his œuvre, because between 1635 and 1641 he painted – if at all – hardly any portraits, which would again argue for the identification with Rej.

ART PURCHASES

The fact that we find Uylenburgh arranging loans between 1639 and 1641 may perhaps be explained by the arrival on the market of highly important art during precisely those years. An auction that attracted enormous attention was held in Amster-dam in April 1639: the public sale of the famous collection of Lucas van Uffelen, a Dutch mer-chant who had settled in Amsterdam after a long sojourn in Venice. His art collection contained major works by Raphael, Titian, Ribera and Van Dyck. We only know the names of two buyers at this sensational sale, Gerard Reynst and Alfonso Lopez, but Rembrandt and Sandrart were also present, the latter as a bidder. In view of the fact that, on the one hand, the 1639 loan emphatically stated that the money was being lent for the pur-chase of paintings, and on the other that the sale of Van Uffelen's paintings took place just one week after the signing of the deed of conveyance, one can infer that Uylenburgh wanted to buy art works on this occasion. Slightly less than 60,000 guilders were spent on art, the most expensive pieces going for a few thousand guilders. Uylen-burgh may have joined the bidding. One might also think of the public sale in Leiden on August 10th, 1639 of paintings left by the death of Pieter de Neyn, with whom Uylenburgh had done business.[281]

There are two documented purchases at public auctions by Hendrick Uylenburgh for his busi-ness. In 1635 he bought from the estate of the painter and art dealer Barent van Someren several lots of prints and drawings, a few drawings by Adriaen Brouwer, 'a piece of work in the round – a relief', 'a man's head in plaster or stone, in view of the other objects for sale' and '4 tronis', in total for 18 guilders and 7 stuyvers.[282] In view of the low prices for art works on paper and plaster works

199

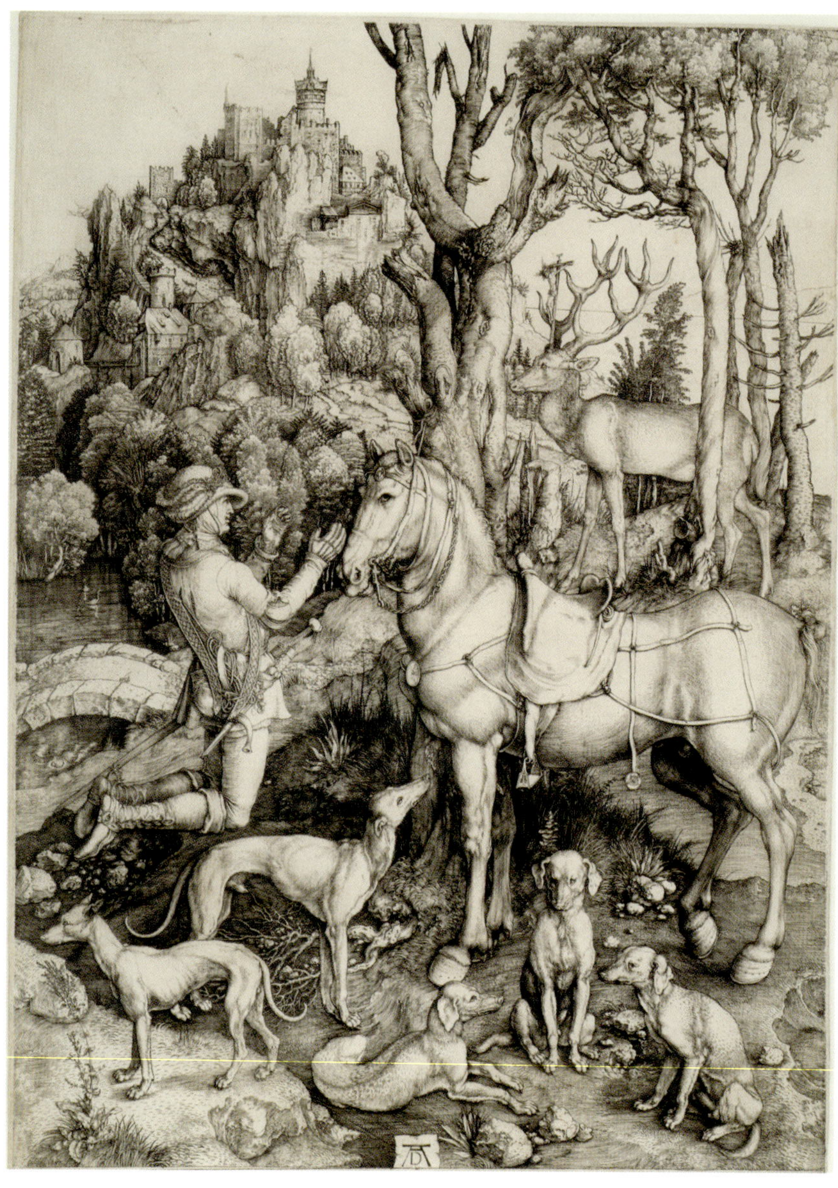

these purchases would have been made with an eye toward their use in the workshop. Three years later, Uylenburgh bought various works at the public sale of art works that had been in the possession of the merchant Gommer Spranger. With the first purchase, eight Italian prints, he is referred to as 'painter in the Breestraat'. There then follow five prints by Albrecht Dürer, a 'St Hubert' by the same master (for 4 guilders and 4 stuyvers) (fig. 144), another two prints by Dürer, thirteen anonymous drawings in different lots, two versions of the 'Life of the Virgin', a series by Dürer consisting of 21 woodcuts, and another 12 'Dreamers', also by Dürer. At this same auction, plates by Dürer (most probably copies) and many prints, probably made shortly beforehand, were listed for sale. Uylenburgh also bought '1 etched plate by [Bartolomaeus] Spranger' for 1 guilder and 16 stuyvers.[283] His most expensive acquisition was a drawing by Raphael. One may doubt whether this sheet was correctly attributed to Raphael, but the price of 25 guilders and 10 stuyvers leads one to think that it must have been a rather special Italian drawing.[284] Uylenburgh also obtained several large batches of graphic work: '140 images of Mary' (4 guilders and 16 stuyvers), '160 St Johns' (3 guilders and 10 stuyvers), '96 small images of Mary' (2 guilders and 4 stuyvers) and '104 coat-of-arms' (1 guilder and 11 stuyvers). Because a plate 'of St John' by Spranger was being sold, Uylenburgh could have acquired a packet of impressions (fig. 145). The large number of prints suggests that Uylenburgh also dealt in art work on paper, but little more is known of this. In total, Uylenburgh paid out 66 guilders and 4 stuyvers at this sale.

We have no knowledge of other purchases made by Uylenburgh.[285] We do know that in 1637, for example, he passed over the sale of the art dealer Jan Bassé. We find no trace of connections with fellow-art dealers – with a single exception. In 1658 Matthijs Musson bought from 'sieur Ulenborch' an 'Emous' (*Christ at Emmaus*) by Sotte Cleef for 120 guilders (and sold the piece

283 '1 geëste plaett van [Bartholomeus] Spranger', GAA, arch. no. 5073, inv. no. 962, 9-12 February 1638.
284 This was a high price, but not exceptional: the item was immediately followed by '1 dito', knocked down to Claes Eliasz for 45 guilders, while Rembrandt paid comparable prices for drawings by Hendrick Goltzius (1558-1617). In 1654 the painter Jan Miense Molenaer (c. 1610-1668) had negotiated with Abraham de Cooge, art dealer of Delft, to buy 'een grote teeckeningh van Rafel Urbyn, represen- teerende een kindermoort van Herodes... voor de somme van driehondert gulden', Bredius 1915-1922, vol. 7, p. 156. In the inventory of the widow of the painter and art dealer Nicolaes Rosendael a drawing on paper 'door Raphael de Urbin' is mentioned, GAA, not. J. de Winter, NA 2413, 23 November 1686. The last-mentioned drawing could well have been earlier in Uylenburgh's posses- sion. For the relation between Rosendael and Gerrit Uylen- burgh, see p. 216.
285 Montias 2002, pp. 123-124.

145 Bartholomeus Spranger, St John the Evangelist, signed 'B Sprangers ANTvs F', etching, 15.3 x 20.5 cm, Amsterdam, Rijksprentenkabinet

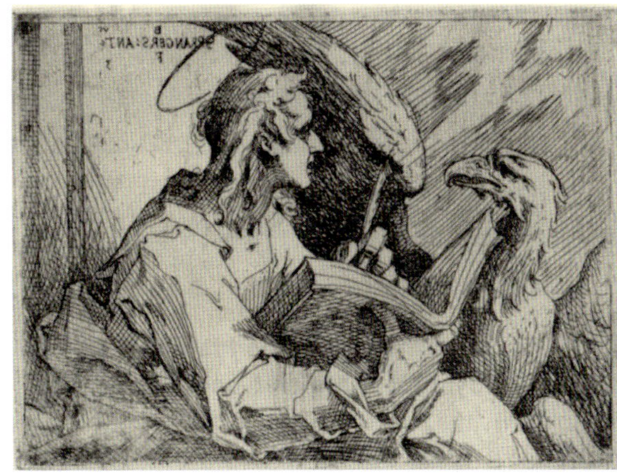

within a week for a profit of 20 guilders); a year later he sold 'menheer Ulenborch tot Amsterdam' a hunt scene by Frans Snyders for 175 guilders.[286] The 'Ulenborch' referred to here could have been Gerrit as well as Hendrick Uylenburgh. But this was an incidental transaction: the name Uylenburgh reappears only once more in the meticulously maintained accounts of this Antwerp art dealer.

ARBITER AND VALUER

The trade in works of art requires expert knowledge.[287] An art dealer must be able to judge paintings, know how to distinguish copies from originals and be capable of ascertaining their value. As a renowned art dealer, Hendrick Uylenburgh was on many occasions involved in the valuation of paintings – in the first place as a kind of referee, an arbiter in disputes. He assumed this role in 1639, c. 1642, 1653 and 1657, in two such cases settling a dispute over the price of a delivered portrait. The first question concerned a disagreement between an Amsterdam art dealer and someone who was owed around 2,100 guilders. The dealer

promised to pay this but first he was to give 'complete insurance' within two days in the presence of Hendrick Uylenburgh.[288] Uylenburgh was thus fulfilling the role of expert witness and valuer, since together with a professional colleague he was assessing the art works that would serve as collateral.[289] Uylenburgh was especially active during these years as a valuer, as will be seen below.

From the declaration given by Uylenburgh in 1659 at the request of the guardian of Titus van Rijn, it appears that around 1642 he had arbitrated in a dispute between Andries de Graeff and Rembrandt over a portrait that the latter had painted for De Graeff. Together with other, unnamed arbiters, it was decided that De Graeff must pay Rembrandt 500 guilders.[290]

In 1653 a number of experts gave their judgement on a landscape with hills, trees and a valley with figures and animals. Several Antwerp painters and art dealers had denied that the painting was an autograph work by Paulus Bril; but the Amsterdammers unanimously agreed that it was a 'pure original, painted by the hand of Pouwels Bril'.[291] The first to declare a judgement was the 'consthandelaer' (art dealer) Hendrick Uylenburgh who, together with his professional colleagues Marten Kretzer and Lodewijck van Ludick, 'beyden lieffhebbers ende eervaaren kenders van de schilderkonst' (both art-lovers and experienced connoisseurs of the art of painting), justified their judgement by declaring that all three had seen various works by Bril and '*selffs in eygendom gehadt*' (*even had work by him in their possession*). The passing mention of Uylenburgh having had work by Bril in his shop is a significant indicator: many paintings would have passed through his hands in this way.

In 1657 Hendrick Uylenburgh and Guilliam de Ville, 'painters and art dealers in Amsterdam', gave a declaration at the request of the 'commis-

286 Duverger 1969, pp. 102 and 107.

287 For problems of authenticity in the seventeenth century see Van der Veen 2005 and below Chapter 4.

288 GAA, not. B. Jansen Verbeeck, NA 935, 13 May 1639.

289 GAA, not. J. van de Ven, NA 1056, fols. 263v-264, 24 October 1640, and fols. 267v-268, 19 November 1639, Doc. 1640/10, and Montias 2002, pp. 75-76.

290 GAA, not. N. Listingh, NA 2613, p. 429, 1659, and Doc. 1659/21, where the names of the witnesses (two sons of Hendrick Uylenburgh!) are omitted, See Bredius/De Roever 1885, p. 93, and Urk. no. 208; the date of this deed and the statement of age after Uylenburgh's name have been lost as the result of a fire. The document does not state that it concerned a portrait *of* Andries de Graeff himself. However,

that this Amsterdam burgomaster actually was portrayed by Rembrandt is clear from the inventory of one of his nephews from the beginning of the eighteenth century, in which a portrait painted by Rembrandt is listed: see the commentary on Doc. 1659/21. This monumental portrait has been identified by Dudok van Heel with Rembrandt's full-length *Portrait of a man*, dated 1639, in Kassel (Br. 216). The Rembrandt Research Project has disputed this identification, Corpus III A 129. The identification proposed in the Corpus, however, is not very convincing. In Frankfurt/Kyoto 2002-2003, no. 27, the Kassel portrait is once again considered to be that of Andries de Graeff.

291 'Een suyver originael, geschildert bij de hant van Pouwels Bril', GAA, not. J. van der Hoeven, NA 1649, pp. 1239-1240, 16 September 1653; first published in Bredius 1889, p. 42. See also Blankert 1968.

sarissen van de Kleine Zaken' (Commissioners of Petty Sessions). They appeared as expert witnesses in the matter of a dispute between the painter François Dancx and an Amsterdam surgeon who had commissioned from Dancx a portrait of his wife. There was disagreement over the price. After a 'thorough and serious study' of the portrait, Uylenburgh and De Ville concluded that in any case it was worth the 18 guilders that both parties had originally agreed and that in the portraitist could well have asked more.[292]

Three of the four documents relate to an assessment of the value of a work of art. Valuations of personal property in Amsterdam were conducted by sworn assessors, but from the beginning of the seventeenth century, valuers were increasingly often used who had expertise in the relevant areas. They were paid for this, of course. I know of 188 inventories in Amsterdam between 1601 and 1700 in which paintings were valued by experts. The valuations were carried out by (former) 'over-lieden' (guildmasters) of the St Lucas Guild, by painters actively involved with the art trade, or by professional art dealers – in short, the people in the trade.[293] This was articulated in a legal document of 1628, in which two artists valued paintings and pronounced themselves 'as being painters, having a very good knowledge of this [field]'.[294] Since Uylenburgh took no part in the guild's government, the fact that he was asked so many times to undertake valuations must have to do with his position as a prominent art dealer; in addition to which his presumed training as a painter would also have been significant. In his early career between 1625 and 1637, as far as we know, Uylenburgh valued nothing. It is possible that he would first have had to obtain a position in the art market. From 1637, however, he built up a commanding position, as the following statistics demonstrate: between 1637 and 1640 one finds seven valuations and Uylenburgh is involved in six of them; between 1641 and 1650 there are seventeen valuations, six of them conducted by Uylenburgh; between 1651 and 1660, 23 valuations, ten of which were conducted by him. That is, out of a total of 47 such cases, Uylenburgh was the expert who conducted the valuation on 26 occasions and in ten of these cases he was the sole

valuer. Those who asked him must have had great confidence in his expertise, while Uylenburgh himself must have viewed hundreds of paintings by many artists among people's household effects, many of these works having also previously passed through his shop.

It would be impossible here to discuss all the valuations Uylenburgh carried out, but an illustrative example is the procedure followed with the following inventorization of household effects in 1657. Two assessors had been asked to carry out a valuation of the personal effects in the house of their client's father-in-law. The father-in-law was not satisfied with the result and asked Uylenburgh to assess the paintings again. The six works were re-valued by him, with attributions. Uylenburgh's revisions can be seen noted in the margin of the document: for instance, he saw the hand of Cornelis Ketel in one painting of the three Christian virtues (Faith, Hope and Charity) and doubled its value as estimated by the assessors to 60 guilders. A painting first described as a 'Brabans lantschapje' (a small Brabants landscape) was, according to him, a work by the Fluwelen Bruegel which he valued not at 8 but at 42 guilders.[295] It is worth mentioning here that the individual at whose request the valuation was carried out was a Mennonite and connected by marriage to the De Flines family. He would thus have known Uylenburgh and it is well possible that some of these pieces had originally been bought in the latter's shop.[296] We saw earlier that Uylenburgh carried out valuations for acquaintances – fellow-believers or neighbours – in a number of cases. One can safely assume that many of them, if not the majority, belonged to his circle of clients.

UYLENBURGH'S 'FAMOUS ACADEMY'

Hendrick Uylenburgh's activities discussed so far, from 1639 onward all relate to his profession as an art dealer: the buying in of art works with an eye to future profit. To make purchases for the shop he borrowed money; he served as an arbiter in disputes and he gave expert opinion. We don't know whether he was an advisor or intermediary

292 'Wel behoorlijck ende serieusel[ijk] hebben besichticht', GAA, not. P. de Bary, NA 1707, p. 1385, 7 June 1657, and Bredius 1915-1922, vol. 3, p. 965. Uylenburgh and De Ville worked together more than once during this period. In 1658 they valued the paintings that had belonged to a deceased burgher. In 1667 Guilliam de Ville referred to himself as a 'conterfeytschilder' (portrait painter).
293 Too little is known of the role of the guildmasters' valuations. Van Eeghen 1969b, p. 71, writes that she knew of only two valuations by guildmasters and although she assumed that there were more to be traced she concluded that they probably did not play an important role in this area. Montias 2004-2005, p. 336, on the contrary, rightly attributes a significant role to the guildmasters.
294 *Als schilders sijnde* seer goede kennisse daervan te hebben', GAA, not. J. Jacobs, NA 396, p. 144, 18 February 1628.
295 GAA, not. J. van Loosdrecht, NA 1996, pp. 745-749, 28 August-23 October 1657; it is stated that the father-in-law had had the painting '[laten] priseren door Hendric Uijlenburch, cunstvercoper binnen dese stadt'.
296 Beside '1 ouwe tronie' valued at 5 guilders was written in the margin 'van Lubbert Gerritsz' (1535-1612), and further on in the same document is mentioned 'de afbeeldinge van Lubbert Gerritsz.'. Lambert Jacobsz had a portrait of this well-known leader of the Waterland community, who was also his grandfather, in stock, Straat 1925, p. 73, no. 25. Michiel van Mierevelt (1567-1641) in Delft – similarly a Mennonite painter – had among the (copies of) portraits in his shop ('conterfeytsels raeckende de winckel [...] alle wesende copie') a 'conterfeitsel van Lubbert Gerritsz.' and 'een rondeken van deselffde'. The latter was sold for 5 guilders, Bredius 1908, p. 9. It is conceivable that Uylenburgh was also able to supply portraits of Mennonite preachers.

for art collectors, nor whether he had clients or colleagues beyond the Netherlands. His recognition by contemporaries as an expert in the field of the art of painting is evident from the sheer number of valuations he was asked to carry out. Beginning (as far as we know) in 1637, he served this role on many occasions in the years that followed – that is, in the period during which he was active as a merchant. This is not to say, however, that Uylenburgh closed his workshop: during this period too the workshop continued to function, although little is known about it. The part in the production played by his children must have been considerable, certainly sufficient for one to speak of it as a family business.[297]

During the 1640s and thereafter, besides the Uylenburghs there must have been painters 'from outside' who were also active in this family business. This much is clear from the biography of Eberhard Keil in Filippo Baldinucci's *Notizie de' professori del disegno*,[298] a book that contains highly interesting observations on the years the Danish painter spent in Amsterdam and his employment by Uylenburgh.[299] Keil was trained as a painter in his own country, but his father sent him at the age of eighteen to Amsterdam to qualify further in the art of painting. This Amsterdam period lasted from 1642 to 1651. Keil obtained a place 'in de school of Rembrant van Rein', remained there for two consecutive years and subsequently moved to 'the famous academy of Uylenburgh'. The latter, writes Baldinucci, was a talented individual who, having assembled a large collection of paintings by the most important masters of Europe, offered places to a great many young painters in his house whom he got to copy these paintings and to learn from them, not least to his own advantage on account of the good business he made with these copies. Keil worked for three years in this 'academy', but he also remained on excellent terms with Rembrandt. When Keil thought he could work independently, and because he longed for that 'freedom which youth so ardently desires' he set up school in his own house: he himself painted and at the same time also had pupils. In 1651 Keil decided to travel to Italy 'in order to be able to see the beautiful things of that country'.

The account of Eberhard Keil's life gives a strong impression of reliability, partly because the information was provided first-hand. The passages concerning his stay in Amsterdam include various salient details. After his two-year period with Rembrandt there followed a period of three successive years with Uylenburgh: the duration of this association could indicate that Uylenburgh's painters worked with him over a long periods, perhaps even contracted to do so. Rembrandt, after all, was with him for four years, Flinck for about three years and Keil similarly for three years. Apparently he offered his painters favourable working conditions, for otherwise they would surely not have stayed so long. Baldinucci reports that Flinck was allowed to paint whatever he wished and that he was always well paid. But it does seem, in the case of Keil at least, that the constraints of fixed employment can become oppressive; he wanted freedom, to stand on his own two feet. We don't know how many painters there were to be found in the workshops of Uylenburgh and Keil. When Keil worked with Uylenburgh between 1644 and 1647, the latter was living in 'Cronenburgh' in the Breestraat, a house not much smaller than the dwelling on the corner of the Zwanenburgwal and certainly big enough to provide room for all the painters' workplaces. The painter Pieter Isaacxz had had his workshop in the same house.[300]

It is significant that Keil is alleged to have had pupils, young men whom he himself must have trained. In the case of Uylenburgh, on the contrary, Baldinucci writes that there were 'a great many young painters in his house whom he had copy these paintings', and who, one assumes, had already largely completed their apprenticeships. That would certainly chime with the age of the painters whom we know for certain worked with Uylenburgh: Rembrandt was 25 years old in 1631, Flinck was 20 when he began with Uylenburgh around 1635 and Keil was similarly about 20 in 1644. The young painters contributed to the production of the workshop and their education consisted of copying paintings from Uylenburgh's shop. The art dealer in turn did very good business with these copies. While Keil painted for Uylenburgh, he remained on good terms with

297 See pp. 211-212.
298 Baldinucci 1681-1728, vol. 5, pp. 365-374.
299 Ibid., p. 366.
300 See pp. 56-57.

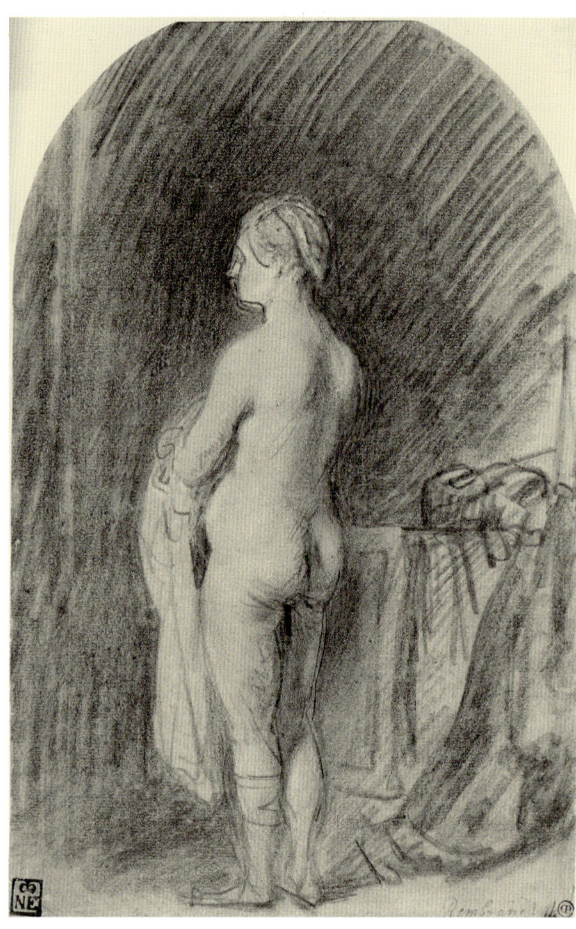

146 Anonymous, pupil of Rembrandt, Nude model, black chalk heightened with white, 25.3 x 16.2 cm, Budapest, Szépmüvészeti Museum (Ben. 713)

derived from the Greek word 'Akademos', the garden where Plato taught, suggests a fellowship of the practice and advancement of learning, letters and arts and also the space where the members associate together. The word is frequently employed in relation to the visual arts in the early modern period: an 'academy' was an organized gathering of artists who got together to draw or paint from the life, usually after a nude model and not necessarily in an artist's studio. One constantly comes across this combination of group-working after a nude model in contemporary texts. Joachim von Sandrart uses the term frequently in his book *Teutsche Academie*; he remarks about Johann Liss: 'er zeichnete viel auf unserer Academie zu Venedig nach den nackenden Modellen'.[301]

There is a nice illustration of an academy, whose origin lay in Italy, in the engraving by Agostino Musi of the sculptor Baccio Bandinelli and six pupils, with the inscription 'academia di Bacchio Brandin in Roma' and the date 1531. The print shows small naked models of stone or plaster being drawn by candlelight under the supervision of the master.[302] In the sixteenth century, Italy had several academies, often associations of artists who were friends and had a common interest in classical literature or sculpture. At the beginning of the seventeenth century, academies were also set up in the Dutch Republic, first in Haarlem and subsequently in Utrecht.[303] The important point is that these academies in the Republic were intended to give extra training in drawing and were independent of the training given within the traditional guild system.[304] According to some, Uylenburgh's 'academy' – as Baldinucci calls it – can be seen as a natural development of the academies in Haarlem and Utrecht. Huys Janssen, referring to Uylenburgh's academy, suggests that a third academy was founded not long after those of Haarlem and Utrecht, although suggesting that it may have functioned in a different way. According to Huys Janssen, Rembrandt would also have had an 'academy' when he began working independently in 1635.[305]

But the term 'academy' is used all too easily. The definition given above would not really seem

his former teacher, Rembrandt. One wonders, naturally, whether Uylenburgh also maintained friendly relations with Rembrandt during these years, and whether he more often took over his pupils from him. The account of Uylenburgh's young painters copying paintings by the most important masters of Europe leads one to assume that, as well as Dutch art, Italian and Antwerp art must also have been represented in his shop. This would figure, since Uylenburgh had, after all, borrowed between 1639 and 1641 large sums of money in order to buy paintings.

Baldinucci's account of the 'academy' that was alleged to have been run by Uylenburgh has been repeatedly cited in the literature. But what did he actually mean by an 'academy'? This term,

301 Sandrart 1675/Peltzer 1925, p. 188. See also Költzsch 2000.
302 Thomas 2005.
303 Bok 1994, pp. 108 and 178-182.
304 According to Miedema 1987.
305 Huys Janssen 1992, pp. 23 and 27 and passim. Goldstein 1996, pp. 37-40, points to the significance of the study of the nude in Rembrandt's training, but not from his Uylenburgh period.

306 Sandrart 1675/Peltzer 1925, p. 207.
307 No less than four painters who all worked for Sandrart at the same time are mentioned in a document of 1641: Marten Coren, 19 years old, Jan Benningh, 21 years old, Dudley Calandrini, 16 years old, and Hendrick Bosch, 38 years old, Klemm 1986, pp. 355-356. Mattheus Merian the Younger stayed with Sandrart between 1637 and 1640, and the latter's nephew Jacob Sandrart around 1640.
308 Ben. 713.
309 B. 198 and B. 201, respectively, Vienna 2004, no. 59.
310 B. 192.
311 Valuation of the paintings by 'sieurs Henderick Ulenburch ende Gerbrant Ban, schilders ende kunsthandelaers deser stede', G A A, not. G. Borsselaer, N A 1496, fols. 36v-56v, 14 August-19 December 1640; among other paintings they valued a *Fruit Market* by Joachim Beuckelaer (c. 1533-c. 1575) at 100 guilders and various pieces by the marine painter Bonaventura Peeters (1614-1652), including *The City of Antwerp*, also at 100 guilders.
312 Ekkart 1991, p. 430, fig. 4.
313 See pp. 136-137.
314 See p. 173, note 161 and pp. 212-214.

to apply to Uylenburgh's business enterprise. If we look at what exactly went on there, it is evident that any learning consisted mainly in the copying of paintings by young, but advanced painters. Similarly, one finds Sandrart using the term repeatedly – also in relation to Utrecht – as, for example, when he writes about a painter from Augsburg who at the age of 17 was sent by his father to Amsterdam. Sandrart took him, he says, 'zu mir in meine Behausung'. The young man made progress, also through 'fleißige Besuchung der Academien' and became 'ein schöner Copist allerhand großer Historischen Tafeln ins Lebensgröße'.[306] The young painter thus worked in Sandrart's studio and also attended academies. Sandrart had a number of young painters working for him in Amsterdam.[307] In the case of Uylenburgh, there are no indications that nude models were painted or drawn in his house at arranged times, nor did Sandrart use the term 'academy' in relation to Uylenburgh. A further circumstantial argument is that we know of no academy drawings from Uylenburgh's workshop. Rembrandt and Flinck both drew after nude models, but neither of them during their times with Uylenburgh. The sole drawing that has been cited in this connection is a sketch in black chalk with white high points of a female nude drawn obliquely from behind, holding some delicate material in both hands, formerly attributed to Rembrandt but nowadays attributed to one of his pupils (fig. 146).[308] The dating of this sheet is problematic. Previously, a dating to around 1645 was accepted, but recently it has been suggested that the drawing is correlated with two etchings of female nudes that Rembrandt made around 1631, while the drawing, on stylistic grounds, has also been placed to the early thirties, i.e. to the time when Rembrandt was working with Uylenburgh.[309] In my own opinion, however, the drawing is related to Rembrandt's etching *The artist drawing a naked model*, in which one sees unmistakably the same model, only seen from a slightly different viewpoint. This print originated around 1639.[310] If the drawing is indeed connected to the print, it could not have been made in Uylenburgh's workshop.

It would seem, then, that it is better not to speak of 'Uylenburgh's academy' but rather of his 'winckel' (his shop), the term used to refer to his workshop or workplace, the place where his art wares were also housed and offered for sale. The art business of Uylenburgh father and son was exceptional for the way in which both the productive and the commercial sides functioned side by side for so long. We need further investigation before we can say whether more art dealers combined commerce and production in the same way. The Uylenburghs, in any case, were pre-eminent for half a century by virtue of their ability to contract such exceptional artists as Rembrandt, Flinck and De Lairesse and to buy in art works on a large scale, with all the risks that entailed. The fact that, apart from Keil, we are unable to name any of the copyists from the forties onward, or the new head of the workshop, should not be regarded as too significant. Data on Amsterdam workshops are simply extremely scarce and what does exist is based on chance finds. We don't know, for example, exactly what Keil did during his time in the workshops of Rembrandt and Uylenburgh, there are no known paintings that have survived from his Amsterdam period. One can speculate, though, about painters who may have been involved with the Uylenburgh business and one such candidate is Gerbrand Ban, who in 1640, while still relatively young, valued paintings together with Hendrick Uylenburgh.[311] It is the only valuation by him that we know of. Did he accompany his (former) employer? It is striking that Ban's earliest known, dated work, a child's portrait from 1647, is reminiscent of the work of Dirck Santvoort,[312] a painter who also probably had connections with the Uylenburgh workshop.[313] The mention of a painting by the son of Hendrick Uylenburgh in which a portrait of Jacob Leeuw by Jürgen Ovens can be seen suggests that Ovens worked with the Uylenburghs in the forties. This portrait must have been made around 1650 or shortly before. In 1651 Ovens painted the portraits of Jacques Specx and his wife. Both families belonged to the circle of Uylenburgh's clients.[314] Ovens later worked closely together with Govert Flinck and Gerrit Uylenburgh. With the latter, the business entered a new phase.

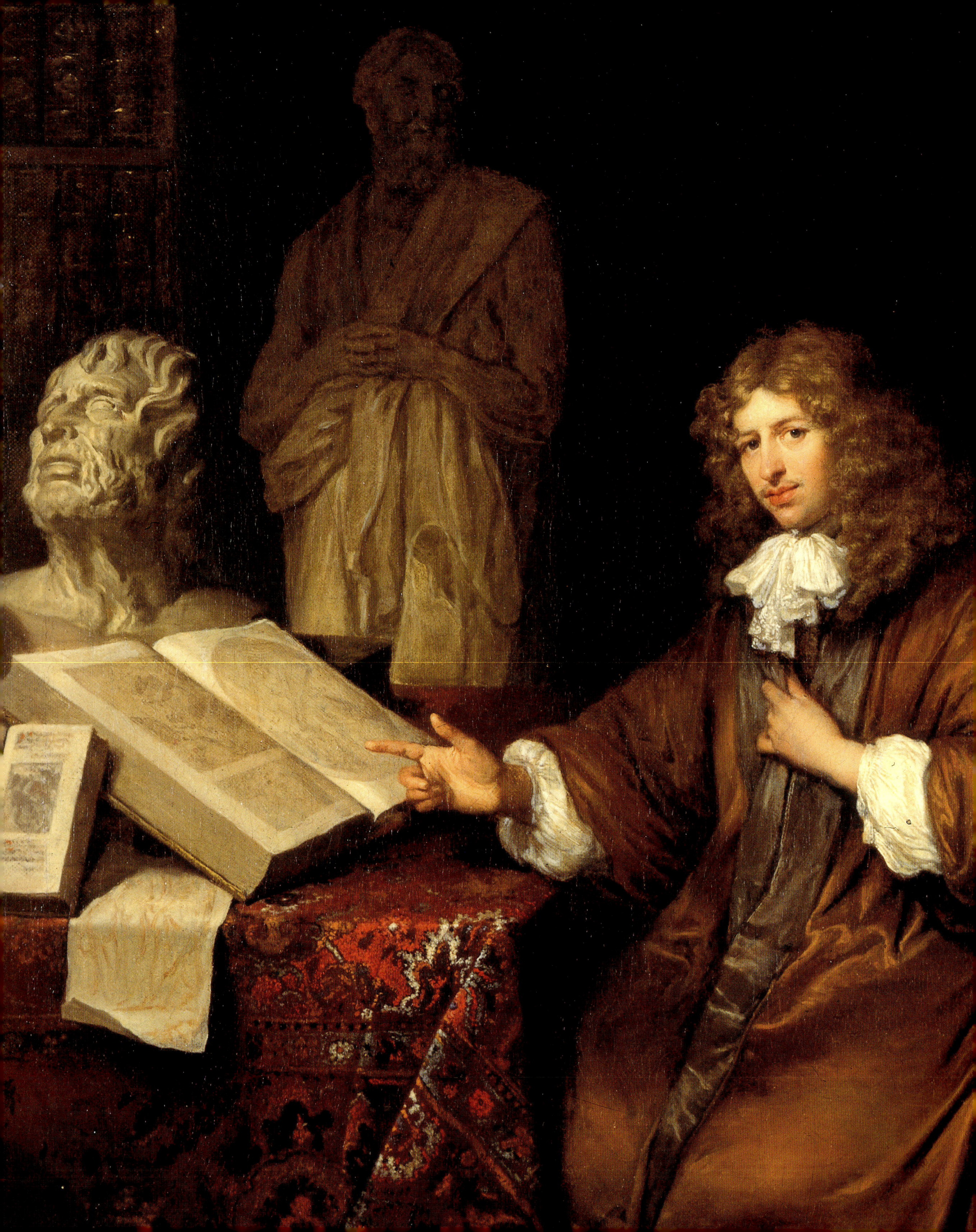

4 Gerrit Uylenburgh's art business between 1655 and 1675

FRISO LAMMERTSE

The children of Hendrick Uylenburgh and Maria van Eyck grew up in close contact with the painters who worked for their father and saw the works he sold in his shop every day. So it is not surprising that some of them became artists themselves. Not only Gerrit but also his younger brothers Isaack and Abraham took up painting, and at least one of his sisters must have done so too. His other siblings may have helped out in the business. Before discussing Gerrit's career as an art dealer, we shall look first at his work, and his family's, as painters. Their endeavours in this field – meagre though the information on them may be – must have been an important part of the business. Painting was in any event something they could always fall back on.

GERRIT UYLENBURGH THE PAINTER

'A work by Uylenburgh's son, with my portrait painted by Ovens', 'A landscape being the bleaching-field by Gerrit Uyllenburgh',[1] 'A landscape with figures in ditto frame by G: Uylenb.'[2] 'Landscape by me and Lingelbagh',[3] 'A small figure by Uijlenborg with a curtain',[4] 'of Ulenburg, a Landskip',[5] 'Ruin by Uijlenburgh',[6] 'a ditto [small painting] of a horse by Uijlenburg',[7]

'A large landscape by Uijlenbergh',[8] 'four seasons by Uylenberg with staffage by Lingelbagh', 'Rome by Uylenberg',[9] 'Large landscape by Uylenborgh'.[10] Paintings by Gerrit Uylenburgh regularly feature in seventeenth- and early eighteenth-century inventories.[11] This tells us that Gerrit, unlike his father, continued to work as a painter and dealer. None of the paintings mentioned here are known today. They have all been lost, concealed behind another name or recorded as anonymous. The list of paintings by Gerrit Uylenburgh derived from inventories, short as it is, would seem to indicate that Houbraken was right when he observed that Uylenburgh worked primarily as a landscape painter.

We do not know who taught Gerrit. Around twelve was the usual age for a boy to begin training as a painter in the seventeenth century.[12] When Gerrit was that age – in about 1637 – Govert Flinck was the foreman in Hendrick Uylenburgh's workshop. It seems obvious that he would have been Gerrit's first teacher. It was at precisely this time, in the late 1630s and early 1640s, that Flinck painted a number of landscapes. After this he painted virtually none. Gerrit's knowledge and love of landscape painting may well have been inspired by Flinck.

In his biography of Uylenburgh, Houbraken

---

1 GAA, archive no. 88, inv. no. 809, 7-14 February 1653. See further p. 174. See Van Eeghen 1953, pp. 170-174. See for Ovens, Schmidt 1922 and Drees 1997 and below pp. 212-214.

2 GAA archive no. 5072, DBK, inv. no. 372, fol. 60-70v, 26, 27 May, 20 October 1666, inventory of goods in the estate of Govert and Pieter Boogardt; the painting was valued at 36 guilders.

3 Valuation of Gerrit Uylenburgh's paintings, 19 April 1675, see p. 302.

4 Inventory of Jan van Wickevoort, see p. 278. Rijksarchief Utrecht, court archives for 1811, see inv. no. 1059, 26 June 1679 (The Getty Provenance Index).

5 Editorial, 'Sir Peter Lely's Collection', *The Burlington Magazine* 83 (1943), p. 187. Sale catalogue Sir Peter Lely's collection, 18 April 1682. The painting does not appear in the French edition of the sale catalogue. See Ogden/Ogden 1944, p. 154.

6 GAA, NA 5220, not. D. Doornick, dated 12 February 1691, p. 155. Inventory of Abraham Velters and Helena de Haze.

7 GAA, NA 4249, not. D. van der Groe, fol. 468. Inventory of the estate of Barbara Mirou, widow of Balthasar van der Perre. The painting was valued at 10 guilders.

8 GAA, NA 5335. Inventory of Adolf Visscher, widower of Louise Blaeu, dated 7 February 1702, fol. 37-182. The painting was valued at 15 guilders (The Getty Provenance Index). The painting was in the corridor of the manor of Driemont near Weesp.

9 GAA, not. J. Lansman, NA 4720, fol. 655. Inventory of Pieter Six. See Dudok van Heel 1982, p. 77, note 36. See also below, p. 278.

10 GAA, not. W. Denijs, NA 6670, inventory of Geertruyd Bicker and Joan Deutz the Elder, dated 16 April 1712, fol. 597-667 (The Getty Provenance Index).

11 If no forename is stated in the inventories, it has to be borne in mind that the painting might have been by one of the other members of the Uylenburgh family and not by Gerrit. However, Gerrit appears to have built up the greatest reputation not only as an art dealer but also as an artist.

12 See for the painter's training chiefly De Jager 1990, p. 70.

13 Houbraken 1718-1721, vol. 2, p. 294.

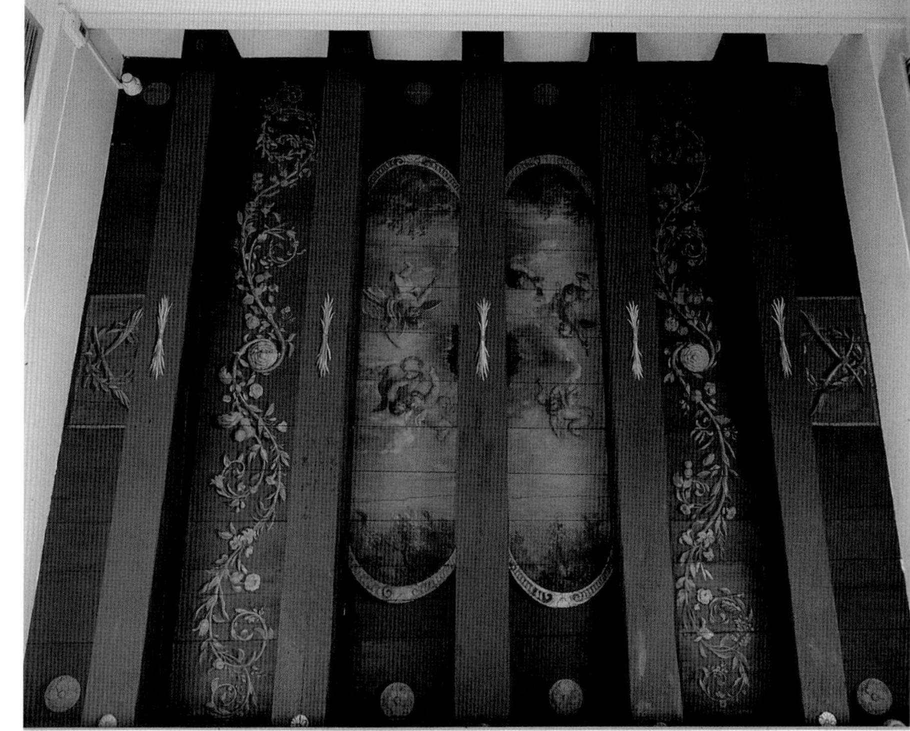

refs to a 'large painted room' by him, which could be seen in the Amsterdam house of the 'Lord of Kerkwyk'. The decorations, which have not survived, must have been landscapes because Houbraken mentions them to prove that Uylenburgh was a landscape painter.[13] When Houbraken published the second volume of his collection of biographies of artists in 1719, the Lord of Kerkwijk was Justus Ranst Kemp, an Amsterdam merchant who had inherited the title from his father, Joost Kemp. Joost had had a large house built on the Herengracht in 1665 (the present-day number 554).[14] It seems likely that it was he who commissioned the wall hangings.

It is clear from a contract that Kemp entered into in October 1665 with Mattheus van Pellecum, who had a reputation for painting wreaths, garlands and borders, that he embarked on the decoration of his new house as soon as it was built. In 1674 there was a dispute about payment, and the art collector Herman Becker and the painter Jan Blom were appointed to act as arbiters.[15] A painted ceiling that was revealed in the house not long ago is very probably Van Pellecum's work (fig. 147).[16] Kemp may have asked Uylenburgh to paint his landscapes at the same time. It is equally conceivable, though, that this did not happen until several years later.

In the third volume of his *Groote Schouburgh*

of 1721 Houbraken wrote that in Mr Roeters's house on the Herengracht in Amsterdam there was a room with paintings by Theodoor Ferreris.[17] The house that best qualifies is the one that belonged to Kemp.[18] Justus Ranst Kemp had leased the property to Jacob Roeters for some time. We know from a deed that Roeters was in any event living there in 1716, in other words around the time that Houbraken was writing his book. This document related to Kemp's sale of the house to Quirijn van Strijen, who acquired

described it as Mr Roeters's house is probably because the house had been let in the meantime: the biography of Uylenburgh is in the second volume and that of Ferreris in the third volume. Another house on the Herengracht that was occupied by a Roeters around this time was no. 48, which came into the possession of Hendrick Roeters (1617-1699) and then passed to his son Ernst Roeters. However, he died in 1710, and in 1712 the house was sold to Willem Gerrit Dedel. At the time Houbraken's book was published it was therefore no longer in the hands of a Roeters, which makes it unlikely that this was the house with the Ferreris room. See *Vier eeuwen Herengracht* 1976, pp. 410-411.

14 See *Vier eeuwen Herengracht* 1976, p. 600. As noted below, in 1716 Justus Ranst Kemp sold the house to Quirijn van Strijen. When Houbraken published his second volume in 1719 the house therefore no longer officially belonged to Kemp. However, number 554 Herengracht seems to be the only house that Houbraken can have meant.

15 See Bredius 1915-1922, vol. 5, p. 1717 (deeds of 18 September, 26 October and 10 December 1674). See for Becker, pp. 275-276. Becker was also mentioned in connection with Kemp on one other occasion. Both men are mentioned in connection with a dispute between Philips Koninck, another acquaintance of Uylenburgh's, and Dirck Duijsent. Both Becker and Kemp had been present when Duijsent commissioned Philips Koninck to paint a portrait of his daughter and 'two pieces for the whole ceiling of the hall'. Although the works were finished and Koninck asked his principal to come and see them and take them away, this never happened. These ceiling pieces were a great nuisance to the painter because they were so large that they took up most of the space in his studio, making it very difficult for him to work. GAA, not. A. Lock, NA 2229, p. 1185-1186, dated 27 April 1669; Bredius 1915-1922, vol. I, pp. 161-162.

16 Cf. for instance the signed decorations in the regents' room in the Amsterdamse Burgerweeshuis (municipal orphanage) of 1656 and 1657 (now the Amsterdams Historisch Museum). See Meischke 1975.

17 Houbraken 1718-1721, vol. 3, p. 184.

18 The fact that in his entry on Uylenburgh Houbraken referred to the house as belonging to the Lord of Kerkwijk and in the Ferreris entry

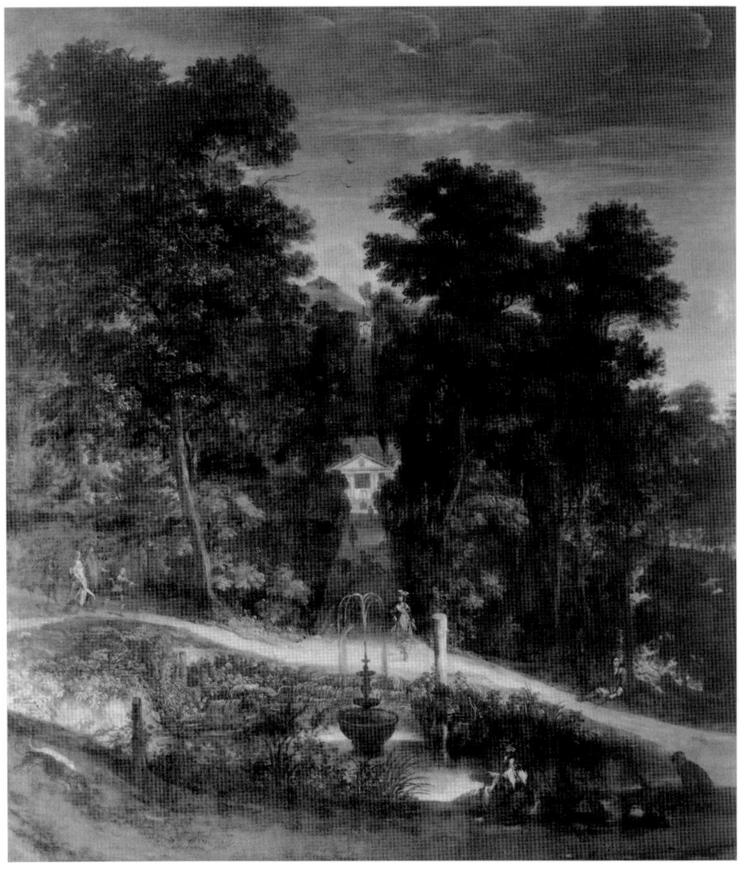

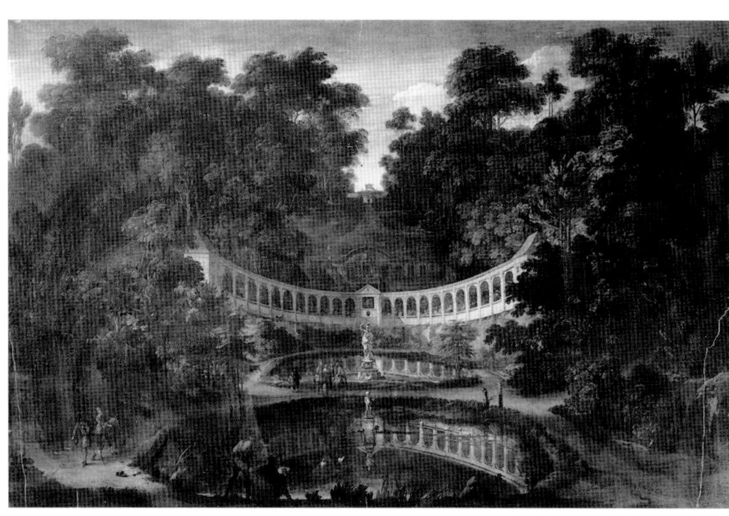

148 Gerrit Uylenburgh, attributed to, View of the Butterberg in the Tiergarten in Cleves, canvas, 218.4 x 194.3 cm, collection of Her Majesty Queen Elizabeth II

149 Gerrit Uylenburgh, attributed to, The amphitheatre in the Tiergarten in Cleves, canvas, 221.6 x 335.3 cm, collection of Her Majesty Queen Elizabeth II

it with 'all the paintings, and decorations, moreover gold leather, the large carpet, and the six gilt eagles serving as chairs in the painted Ulysses Room [...]'.[19] It is tempting to assume that the paintings of scenes from the story of Odysseus were painted by Ferreris. It is even possible that it was a collaboration between him and Uylenburgh, with the latter responsible for the landscapes. By the same token, however, the two painters could have worked on separate rooms in the large house. Ferreris did not return from a trip to Italy until the end of 1666 or perhaps in the course of 1667, so his contribution cannot have been made before then.[20]

Although no signed paintings by Uylenburgh have surfaced to date, there are five paintings that can, with a degree of caution, be attributed to him.[21] These are large landscapes with views of Cleves and the surrounding area, which have belonged to the British royal family since the days of King Charles II (figs. 148-152). In the 1688 inventory of Charles's successor, James II,

they are described as 'Being large Landskips with several Houses of Prince Maurice's in them – All five done by Oldenbergh'.[22] At that time the paintings hung in Windsor Castle, where Uylenburgh worked a great deal during the brief period he spent in England. It seems likely that when he wrote 'Oldenbergh' the Englishman who compiled the inventory in 1688 meant Uylenburgh.

Charles II had little to do with Cleves and it would therefore seem unlikely that he specifically commissioned Uylenburgh to paint the views in the environs of this German town. Might Uylenburgh have painted them previously in Holland, taken them with him to England and succeeded in palming them off on the king? It is also conceivable that Charles II acquired the canvases from Johan Maurits. In 1677 'six large paintings showing the fine views around Cleves' were listed as being in the Prinsenhof, Johan Maurits's residence in Cleves.[23] These works may well have been made especially for the new Prinsenhof,

19 Gemeentearchief Alkmaar, not. Kaspar Seullijn, NA 344, deed no. 6, dated 18 March 1716. See Belonje 1972, p. 188.
20 See below, p. 224.
21 The attribution of these landscapes to Uylenburgh was suggested for the first time in an unpublished dissertation by J. Postma, *Gerrit Uylenborch*, Rijksuniversiteit Leiden, 1981.
22 See White 1982, nos. 270-274, pp. 161-164, as 'anonymous'.
23 White 1982, 'sechs grosse schildereyen, representiren den schonen prospect von der Clevischen Situation'.

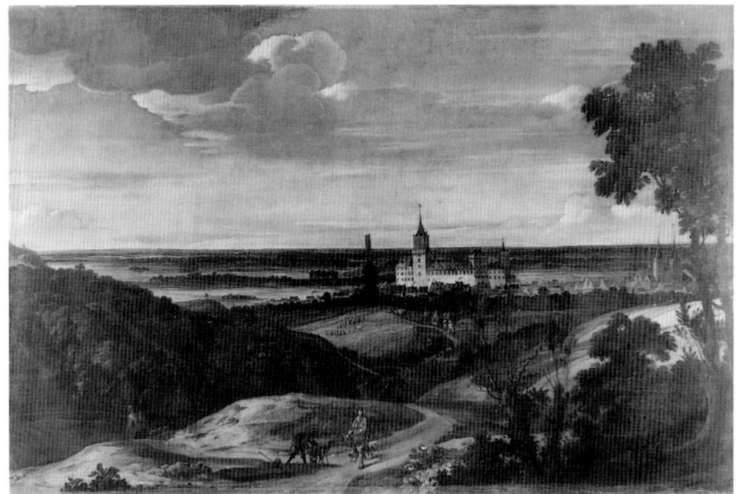

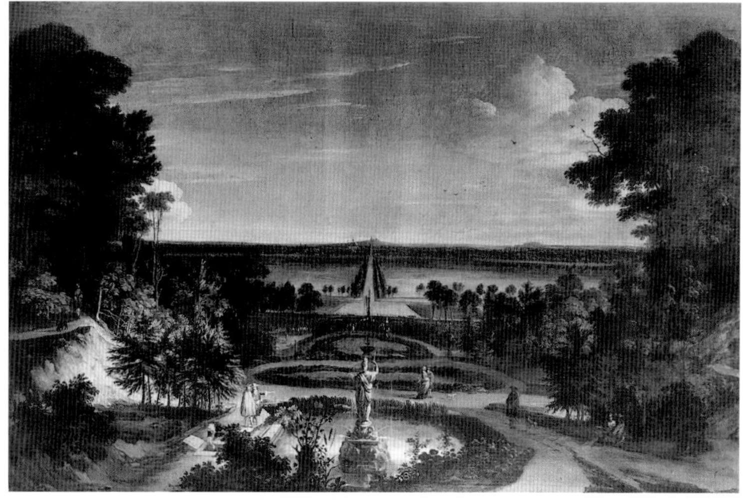

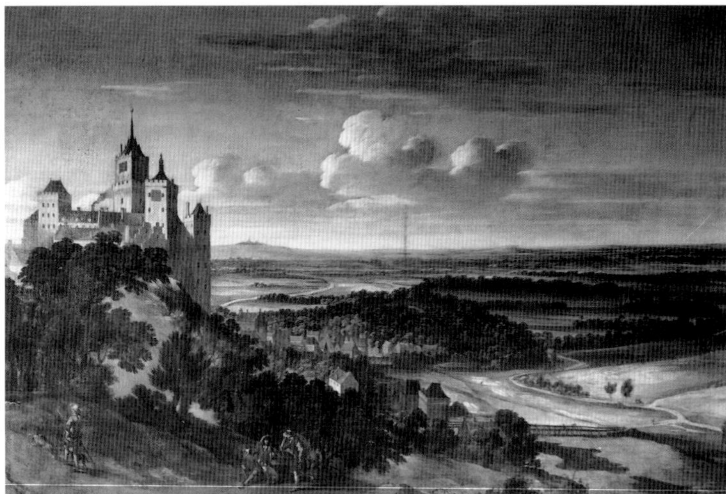

150 Gerrit Uylenburgh, attributed to, View of Cleves with the castle, canvas, 221.6 x 337.8 cm, collection of Her Majesty Queen Elizabeth II

151 Gerrit Uylenburgh, attributed to, View from the amphitheatre looking towards the Eltenberg, canvas, 219 x 333.4 cm, collection of Her Majesty Queen Elizabeth II

152 Gerrit Uylenburgh, attributed to, Cleves Castle, canvas, 219.7 x 332.7 cm, collection of Her Majesty Queen Elizabeth II

which was built in 1671.[24] In 1677 or earlier Johan Maurits had wanted to commission Uylenburgh to restore a number of paintings, but Uylenburgh's departure for England meant that the commission did not go ahead.[25] As Stadholder of the Electorate of Brandenburg, moreover, he would certainly have heard of Uylenburgh in connection with his notorious sale of paintings to the elector. It remains unclear, however, as to how the works turned up in England in such a short space of time.

The paintings in the British Royal Collection reveal an artist who was skilled at making large, decorative pieces. Although the brushwork is not as loose as in the majority of works by Roeland Roghman, they nonetheless show a certain kinship with them. In a valuation conducted in 1702 two appraisers confused Uylenburgh with this painter. They attributed a landscape to Roghman, and then subsequently to Uylenburgh.[26] We may infer from this that the two artists worked in a similar manner.

24 In the light of certain topographical particulars the paintings must have been done after 1666. The *View of the Amphitheatre* (fig. 149) depicts several small buildings that were originally designed by Van Campen but never built. The painter must therefore have known of these designs and may even have seen sketches. See White 1982.

25 See p. 110.

26 GAA, not. G. Ypelaer, NA 5335, fols. 37-182, 7 February 1702; the valuers were Jan Pietersz Zomer and Anthony de Vos, see Van der Veen 2005.

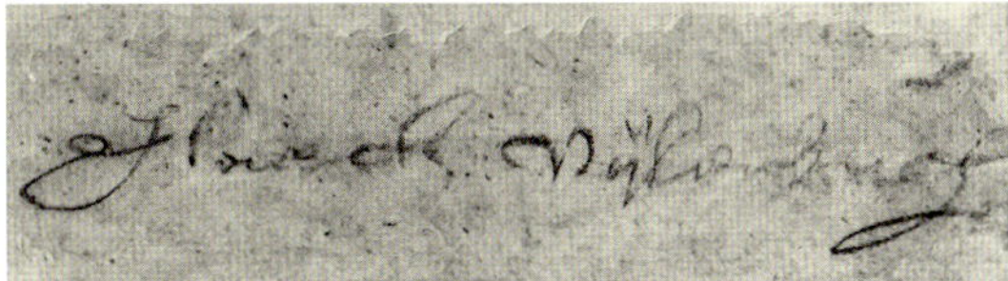

153a Isaack Uylenburgh, Landscape with trees, figures and cattle, black chalk, 40.3 x 31.2 cm, London, British Museum

153b Inscription on the back of 153a: 'Isaack Uijlenburch'

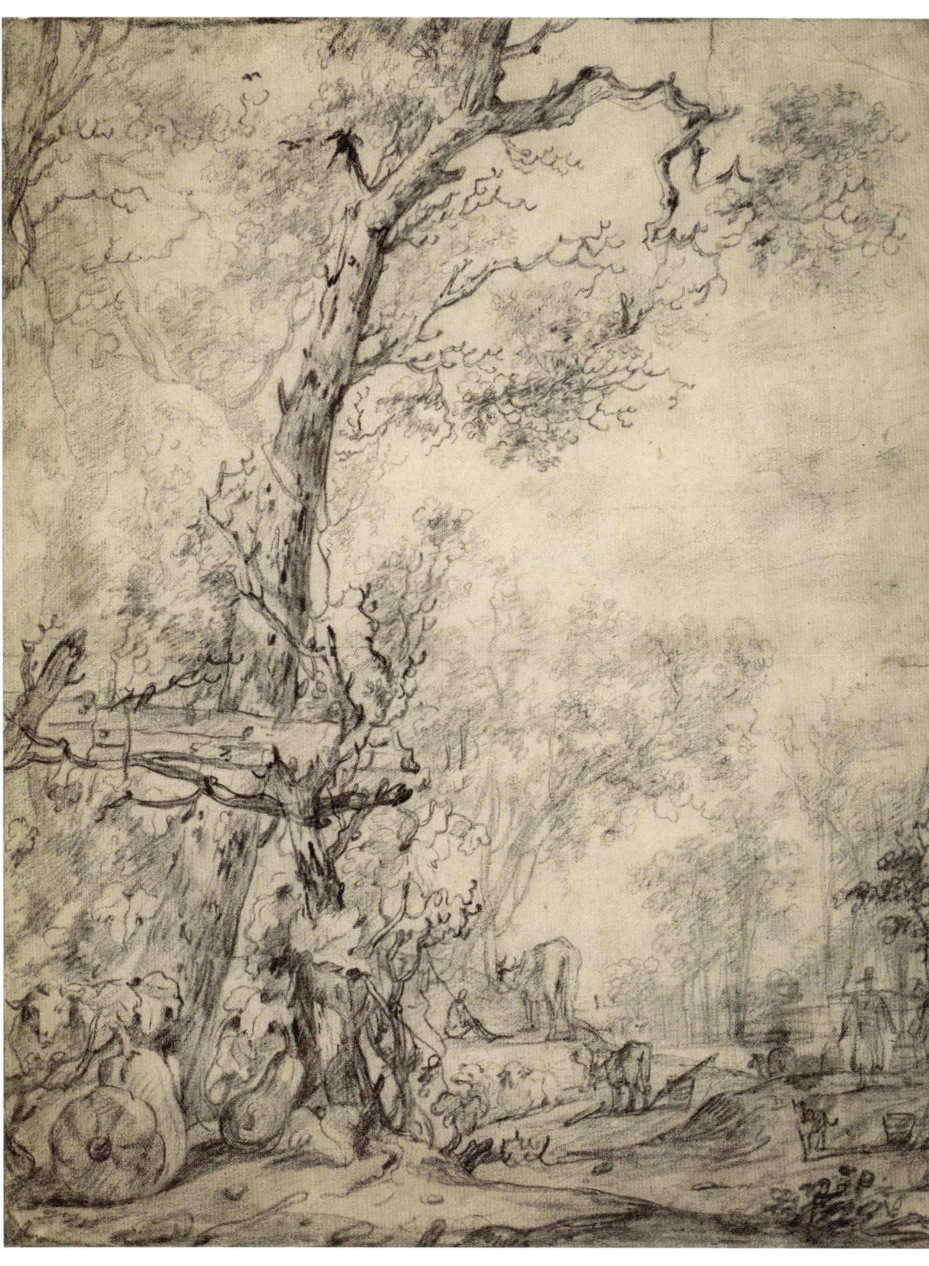

BROTHERS AND SISTERS

Among Gerrit Uylenburgh's brothers and sisters we know that in any event Isaack and Abraham worked as artists. Isaack, Hendrick Uylenburgh's second son, who was probably born in about 1627, enrolled as a master in the Guild of St Luke in Alkmaar in 1658. In September 1661 he was baptised in the Waterland Mennonite church. He was given priority because he and his brother Rombertus were planning to go abroad. There is no further information about Isaack and Rombertus

and it is not known whether they ever returned from their travels.[27] Only one landscape drawing by Isaack has survived. On the back there is an inscription, possibly a signature, in a seventeenth-century hand: 'Isaack Uijlenburch' (figs. 153a and b).[28] The sheet betrays an accomplished hand and must have been done in the late 1650s or early 1660s. It would at any rate appear to date from before Isaack's departure in 1661.

No works by Abraham have survived and we are therefore completely in the dark as to what sort of paintings he made. He is not mentioned

27 See for this p. 71. Neither is mentioned in the deed of 1668 in which Gerrit and his sisters requested Peter Lely to take care of the goods left by Abraham Uylenburgh (see p. 77), which means that they had probably died before this.
28 Recognized for the first time in Van der Veen 2001.

by name in the will drawn up by Hendrick Uylenburgh and Maria van Eyck in 1634 and must consequently have been born after that date. Towards the end of his life he was painter to the Irish Duchess of Ormonde. He died in Dublin at the end of 1667 or the beginning of 1668.[29]

At least one of Gerrit's sisters also painted. An Amsterdam inventory drawn up in 1662 lists 'a flower still life by Uylenburch's daughter, in a gilt frame'.[30] In the 1690 inventory of the widow of Jürgen Ovens there is 'A flower piece by Miss Uylenburg'.[31] It is not clear which of Hendrick's daughters is meant by this. Sara, Anna and Susanna are all candidates.[32] When they were baptised by the Waterlanders in 1661 they were described as 'young daughters', in other words unmarried. It also appears that they did not marry later. Many women who painted in the early modern age came from an artistic background and often worked in the family business.[33] It is interesting to note that both references relate to flower still lifes, a genre that was considered in the seventeenth century to be ideally suited to women. Two of the most prominent female artists in the Republic of the United Provinces in the seventeenth century, Maria van Oosterwijck and later Rachel Ruysch, specialised in the same genre.[34] As we shall see, Uylenburgh dealt in flower pieces and sold work by Maria van Oosterwijck. The still-life painter Hendrick Fromantiou must have worked at Uylenburgh's in the 1660s.[35] It is consequently quite possible that the paintings by Gerrit's sister (or sisters) were executed under his supervision.

The family's painting activities must have been at their height in the 1650s and 1660s. In other words the business flourished under Hendrick Uylenburgh. It is striking that, aside from one of his own works, there are no paintings by any members of his family in the inventory of Gerrit Uylenburgh's possessions in 1675, probably because most of his brothers, if not all of them, had passed away. It is also possible that he had himself specialised in large decorations for specific rooms, which were always commissioned and consequently did not appear in his stock.[36]

ARTISTS IN THE WORKSHOP

Many other artists besides the members of his own family worked for Gerrit Uylenburgh. Information about them is limited. Ten are known to have worked for Uylenburgh (to a greater or lesser extent).[37] At first sight this seems like a great many, but it is nonetheless probable that they are only some of painters who were actually involved with the firm. It is unfortunate that we know so little about the employment practices in the firm. There are no surviving contracts that reveal the nature of Uylenburgh's relationship with his assistants, and we can moreover be fairly confident that these arrangements would differ from one artist to the next. The painters whom we can assume would have been part of Uylenburgh's workshop for varying lengths of time are discussed below in the order in which they probably worked for him for the first time.

Jürgen Ovens – Jürgen Ovens (fig. 199) twice spent lengthy periods in Amsterdam: from the 1640s to 1651 and from 1657 to 1663. For a talented and ambitious painter from Northern Germany, it made sense to go to the Republic with its flourishing art culture. There was, moreover, a large Dutch colony in his home town of Tönning.[38]

29 See for this pp. 76-77.
30 GAA, not. N. Listingh, NA 2617, dated 17 March 1662. Van der Veen 2001.
31 Schmidt 1914.
32 It is even possible that the artist was Magdalena, who died young in 1661.
33 See Kloek et al. 1998. This is nicely illustrated by an entry in the 1640 inventory of Jan Jansz Orlers of Leiden: 'a small round banquet still life painted by a painter's daughter'. See Leiden 1976-1977, p. 18.
34 Other female painters also specialized in flower still lifes, among them the sisters Maria Theresia, Anna Maria and Françoise Katharina van Thielen, about whom Houbraken wrote, 1718-1721, vol. 3, pp. 105-106, evidently with some surprise, that according to a verse they painted not just flower still lifes but sometimes figures, too. Maria van Oosterwijck trained her maid, Geertje Pieters, as a painter of flower still lifes. See Houbraken 1718-1721, vol. 2, p. 216.
35 See p. 222.
36 See also below, p. 237.
37 We can assume that among the artists mentioned in the inventory of 1675 there were painters who were closely associated with the firm. In the absence of any information, nothing can be said with certainty on this subject and it has therefore been decided to deal with them individually in the discussion of the inventory. There is a similar lack of information about the large group of painters that supported Uylenburgh in 1672 in his dispute with Fromantiou. They undoubtedly included artists who had worked for Uylenburgh. Among them were young artists like Herman Collenius and Abraham Begeyn, while Philips Koninck is known to have had contacts with Uylenburgh.
38 Schmidt 1922, pp. 9, 14. See p. 63.

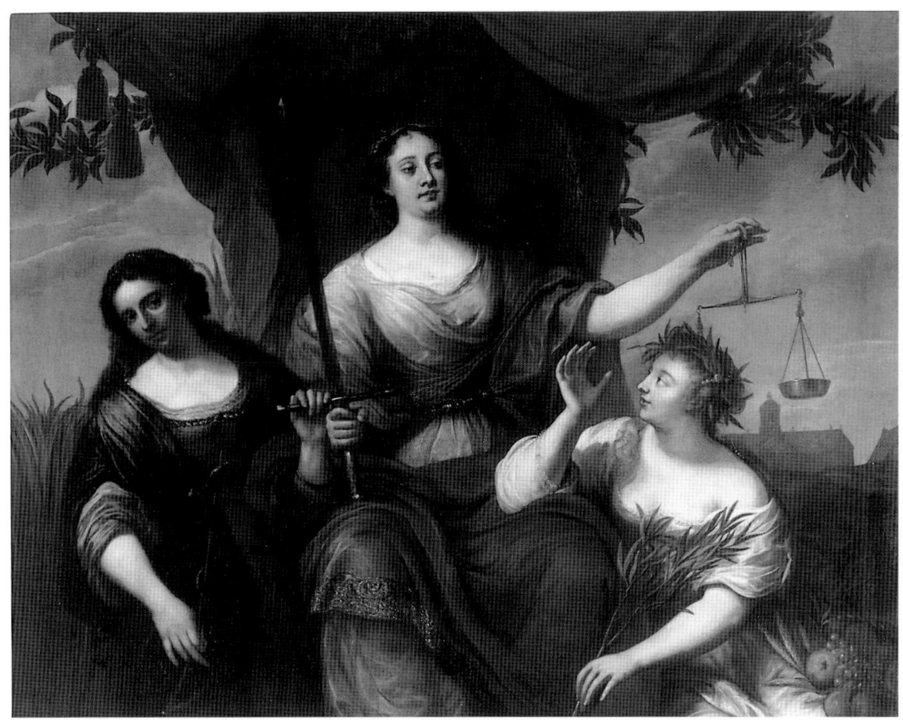

154 Jürgen Ovens, Prudence, Justice and Peace, canvas, 172 x 220 cm, Amsterdam, Koninklijk Paleis

were excellent.[42] Ovens was probably the Uylenburghs' neighbour from 1661 to 1663 or perhaps he lodged with them on the Lauriergracht, in one of the houses that had previously belonged to Govert Flinck.[43] He may have been there during the last months of Hendrick Uylenburgh's life. Uylenburgh was buried on 22 March 1661.

Ovens must have been the first artist with whom Gerrit Uylenburgh worked closely after his father's death, although it is difficult to determine the precise nature of their collaboration. Ovens was not an apprentice any more, he was a fully-fledged artist. As a history painter and, above all, a portraitist, he must have wanted to take over Flinck's position as one of the most eminent painters in the city. He also closely approached the master in style. Ovens's reputation was probably such that he did not necessarily need Uylenburgh as a dealer. He was, moreover, at least as wealthy as Uylenburgh. They must have worked together in the belief that they would both benefit as a result.

During his second stay in Amsterdam, Ovens painted portraits of Nicolaes Tulp, Margaretha Tulp (Jan Six's wife) and Dirk Tulp and his wife, as well as large group portraits of the regents of the civic orphanage and the Oudezijds almshouse.[44] The Grand Pensionary Johan de Witt considered commissioning him to paint portraits of his parents-in-law on the basis of a painting by Jan Lievens and a preliminary drawing for it. The prepared canvases were even standing ready in Ovens's studio. However he was then – May 1663 – on the point of returning home, so De Witt eventually had the paintings done by Lievens.[45]

Among the most prestigious commissions Ovens received in Amsterdam was to paint a chimney-piece for the Magistrates Chamber of the newly built Amsterdam Town Hall (fig. 154),[46] although Ovens had probably been hoping for even more. It was at this time that the commissions were awarded for eight huge paintings for

Houbraken describes Ovens, Christoph Paudiss and Frans Wulfhagen as German pupils of Rembrandt's.[39] However, there is no evidence that this was the case. Ovens may have worked for Hendrick Uylenburgh in the late 1640s. The portrait of the Mennonite Jacob Leeuw in a painting by Gerrit Uylenburgh that must have been made in or before 1651 would tend to support this.[40] In 1651 Ovens painted the portraits of Jacques Specx and his wife. Specx was a loyal customer of Hendrick Uylenburgh's and it seems probable that the commission came about through the intermediary of the art dealer.[41] Around 1651 Ovens returned to Schleswig-Holstein. In 1657, however, he was back in Amsterdam. He stayed there until May 1663 and then settled permanently in Friedrichstadt, although we cannot rule out the possibility that he did come back later for a brief stay in Amsterdam. The thriving shipping sector meant that connections between the two cities

39 Houbraken 1718-1721, vol. I, p. 273.
40 See p. 174.
41 See for Specx p. 172. See for a reference to the two portraits in an inventory, Schmidt 1922, pp. 194-195.
42 Ovens may also have spent time in Amsterdam in 1674/1675. This was suggested by Schmidt 1922 on the basis of some portraits.
43 See p. 71.
44 Schmidt 1922. The portraits of the Tulp family are in the Six Collection in Amsterdam. The group portrait of the Regents of the Oudezijds Huiszittenhuis is supposedly

dated 1656. However, the date is now very difficult to read. If this date is indeed correct, it would mean that Ovens came back to Amsterdam in 1656 not 1657. See for this painting and

that of the Regents of the Burgerweeshuis (both in the Amsterdams Historisch Museum), Blankert 1975-1979, pp. 233-236.
45 Fruin 1922, pp. 489-490.

Letters from Pieter de Graeff to Johan de Witt, dated 13 April and 2 May 1663 and from Johann de Witt to Pieter de Graeff, dated 7 May 1663. The portraits that Lievens painted

are now in the Amsterdams Historisch Museum, see Blankert 1975-1979, pp. 186-190.
46 Schmidt 1922, pp. 160-161, no. 139.

the galleries, depicting scenes from the Batavian uprising against the Romans. Govert Flinck had been engaged to do the work in 1659, but by his untimely death in 1660 he had got no further than an initial design for the *Conspiracy of Claudius Civilis*. In January 1663 Ovens was paid for 'working this up' into a finished painting (fig. 155). This, though, was to be Ovens's only contribution to the prestigious series. The other paintings were done by Jacob Jordaens, Jan Lievens and Rembrandt. We know from drawings that Ovens also made sketches for other episodes from the struggle of the Batavians, but they were never executed (see fig. 201).[47]

During his second stay in Amsterdam Ovens must have become close friends with Johannes Lingelbach. When Ovens's son Jorgian was baptised in the Lutheran Church on 12 September 1662, Lingelbach's wife was a witness. Ovens in turn was present on 16 January 1663 at the baptism of one of Lingelbach's children in the same church.[48] Lingelbach also had contact with Uylenburgh.

Johannes Lingelbach – The suggestion that Johannes Lingelbach worked for Gerrit Uylenburgh is based on the mention of two paintings on which they collaborated. In 1675 Uylenburgh owned a 'Landscape by me and Lingelbach', and in 1704 a 'four seasons by Uylenberg with staffage by Lingelbagh' was listed in an Amsterdam inventory.[49] In the case involving the Berlin elector, Lingelbach was one of the painters called by the magistrates to testify on Uylenburgh's behalf. It is difficult to pinpoint the moment when their collaboration began. They must in any event have known each other in the period around 1662/1663 when Ovens and Uylenburgh lived together in Flinck's former houses on the Lauriergracht and the Ovens and Lingelbach

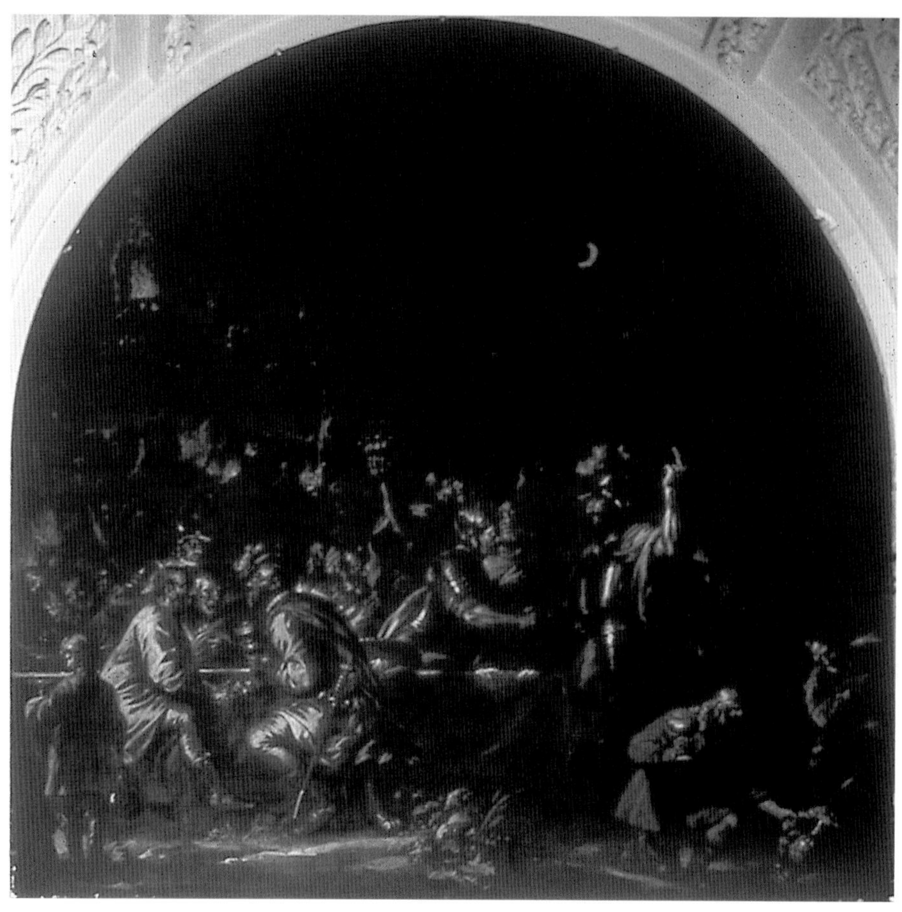

families were witnesses at the baptisms of each other's children.

Lingelbach was born in Frankfurt am Main in 1622, and must have moved to Amsterdam with his parents in about 1634. In 1642 he went to France, where he stayed for two years before travelling on to Italy. Houbraken tells us that he was back in Amsterdam by 1650. Throughout his life Lingelbach painted genre works inspired by his visit to Italy. He also frequently added the figures in landscapes by other masters. His collaboration with Uylenburgh was consequently nothing out of the ordinary.[50]

155 Jürgen Ovens over a design by Govert Flinck, The conspiracy of Claudius Civilis, canvas, 600 x 550 cm, Amsterdam, Koninklijk Paleis

---

47 Von Zesen 1664, p. 209. Von Zesen, who lived in Amsterdam at the same time as Ovens, appears to be very well informed about Ovens's work and probably met him. Ovens was given the commission to finish Flinck's canvas after a painting by Rembrandt of the same subject was rejected for reasons that remain obscure. Rembrandt's painting is now in the museum in Stockholm.
48 GAA, DTB 146, pp. 58, and 147, p. 4; Dudok van Heel 1982, p. 77.
49 See p. 277.
50 In the 1704 inventory of Pieter Six alone, where the painting of the four 'seasons' made by Uylenburgh in which Lingelbach had painted the figures was mentioned, there are also the following paintings with staffage by Lingelbach: 'Two Antiques, by De Momper [probably Philips], with staffage by Lingelbagh', 'A landscape by Rochman with staffage by Lingelbach', 'A landscape by Moucheron, with staffage by the same [Lingelbach]', 'A landscape by Jan Wijnands with staffage by Lingebag'; GAA, not. J. Lansman, NA 4720, pp. 655-657, dated July 1704.

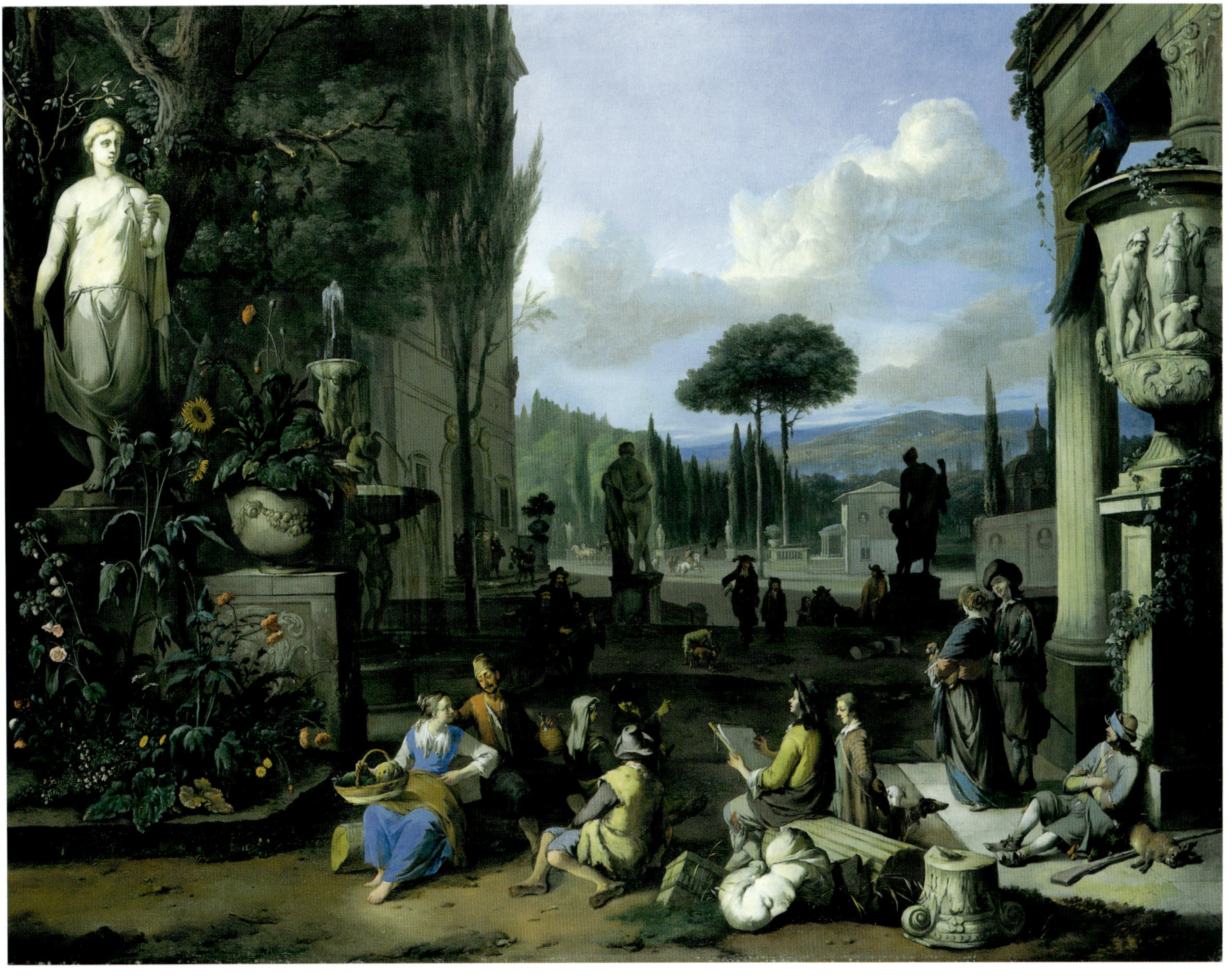

156 Johannes Lingelbach, *A Roman garden: figures among classical ruins with an artist sketching*, (twice) signed and dated 'I: Lingelbach 1668', canvas, 85.3 x 111.2 cm, Maastricht, Noortman Master Paintings

In 1675, as well as the painting that he and Lingelbach had done together, Uylenburgh also owned a work that the German artist had painted alone. At 180 guilders a 'Roman garden' was valued at considerably more than the painting that both had worked on, which was listed at just 45 guilders. The painting is described in Uylenburgh's inventory as 'a Roman garden full of sculptures' and is probably the same work of 1671 that is now in Nuremberg, or a similar but earlier work in the art trade (figs. 156 and 157).[51]

It is hard to tell just how closely Lingelbach was involved in Uylenburgh's business. He occasionally painted the staffage in landscapes by Uylenburgh and the art dealer bought work from him, but there is no reliable information about any further contact between the two men. Lingelbach was also sometimes involved in the trade in old Italian masters. In 1662 he declared that eight-

51 See Inventory, no. 137 and Valuation, no. 5.

een months previously, 'having instructions from his master to buy some excellent paintings', he had gone to Cornelis van der Cruyssen, who had shown him a 'large painting, being an Ecce Homo, done by Titian'. Lingelbach had offered 1,100 guilders, but in the end the sale did not go ahead.[52] We do not know the identity of the 'master' for whom he wanted to buy this expensive work. It might have been Uylenburgh, or a wealthy collector.

Nicolaes Rosendael – Nicolaes Rosendael may have worked for Gerrit Uylenburgh around 1663. He was in any event present as a witness when one of the art dealer's servants made her will. The deed was drawn up in Uylenburgh's house and Rosendael declared that he knew the maid well.[53] Uylenburgh himself was in Italy at the time. It seems likely that Rosendael was lodging in Uylenburgh's house on the Lauriergracht before Uylenburgh went to Italy.

Rosendael was born in Hoorn in about 1634-35.[54] The document dating from 1663 is the first record of his presence in Amsterdam. In 1665 the painter was living in rented accommodation on the Rozengracht. He was working as an independent artist and had pupils.[55] In the same year he gave notice of his intended marriage.[56]

A painting of Christ Carrying the Cross of 1664, which Rosendael probably made for a clandestine Catholic church, shows that the painter was inspired by Italian examples (fig. 158).[57] The work seems to have been influenced by Jacopo Bassano's *The Way to Calvary*, a painting in the Reynst brothers' collection that Uylenburgh selected as part of the Dutch Gift (fig. 31). It was not until 1670 that Rosendael, in company with Jacob Torenvliet, actually went to Rome, where he stayed for three years.[58]

Rosendael was wealthy and had a house built on the Herengracht. In 1674 he was taxed on assets

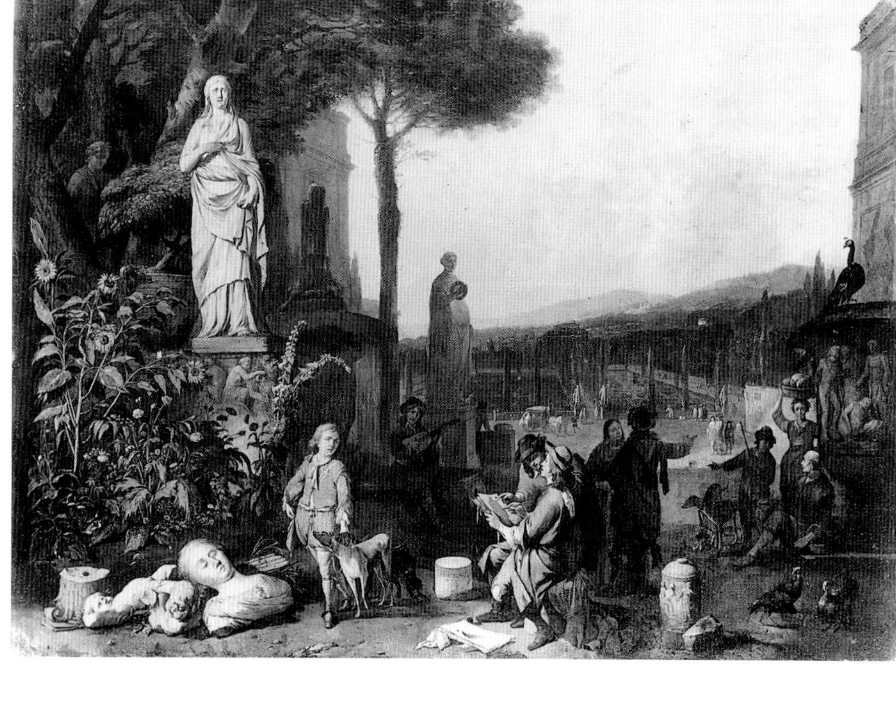

157 Johannes Lingelbach, A Roman garden, signed and dated 'J. Lingelbach fecit 16[71]', canvas, 100 x 136 cm, Nuremberg, Germanisches Nationalmuseum

of 11,000 guilders.[59] When he died in 1686 he had a considerable number of paintings.[60] Interestingly, at that moment two of the works listed were with Hendrick Fromantiou in Berlin so that he could sell them. The two painters may have met at Uylenburgh's.

Gerard de Lairesse – The notarial deeds, our principal source of information about Gerrit Uylenburgh's life, usually provide commercial data. Stories that give us a slightly more colourful picture of him are few and far between, but Houbraken's description of how Uylenburgh discovered the talented Gerard de Lairesse is one such exception. Houbraken appears to have heard the anecdote, recounted with great attention to detail, from a reliable source.[61]

must also have been in touch with Caspar Barlaeus the Younger (see below, pp. 285-286), GAA, NA 3672, not. A. van den Ende, fol. 78r, dated 6 April 1677; Bredius 1915-1922, vol. 2, p. 548.
59 Dirkse 1984; GAA, archive no. 5028, inv. no. 662, tax register 200th penning, district 60, fol. 557v, Rosendael had to pay 55 guilders, that is on assets worth 11,000 guilders.
60 Bredius 1915-1922, vol. 2, p. 545.
61 Houbraken 1718-1721, vol. 3, pp. 109-111. The story appears to have been written down from the perspective of a certain Grebber and Jan van Pee. Since Grebber's forename is not even mentioned, it seems probable that Jan van Pee was the source. Houbraken may have heard the tale from Jan's son Theodorus van Pee, also a painter, whom Houbraken mentions and about whom he intended to write more than he ultimately did (ibid., vol. 3, p. 89).

52 GAA, not. J. de Winter, NA 2290, dated 7 December 1662. The painting had been given to Van der Cruyssen as collateral by the Haarlem painter Dirck Bleeker. See for other documents concerning this sale Van der Veen 1992, p. 124.
53 See p. 72.
54 See for Rosendael, esp. Dirkse 1984. The date and place of birth (1636 in Enkhuizen) given by Houbraken 1718-1721, vol. 3, p. 164, are wrong.
55 Bredius 1915-1922, vol. 2,

pp. 546-547; see also GAA, not. A. Lock, NA 2223, dated 25 April 1667, pp. 877-878; in this deed Johannes Worm ('XVIIJ years old') and a gardener testified about the garden at the back of the house on the Rozengracht where Rosendael lived. In the
56 Bredius 1915-1922, vol. 2, p. 546; GAA, DTB 686, p. 243, dated 1 June 1665, betrothed to Catharina Deyl.
57 Dirkse 1984.
58 Dirkse 1984. Rosendael

deed it says that Worm 'goes to paint' with Rosendael.

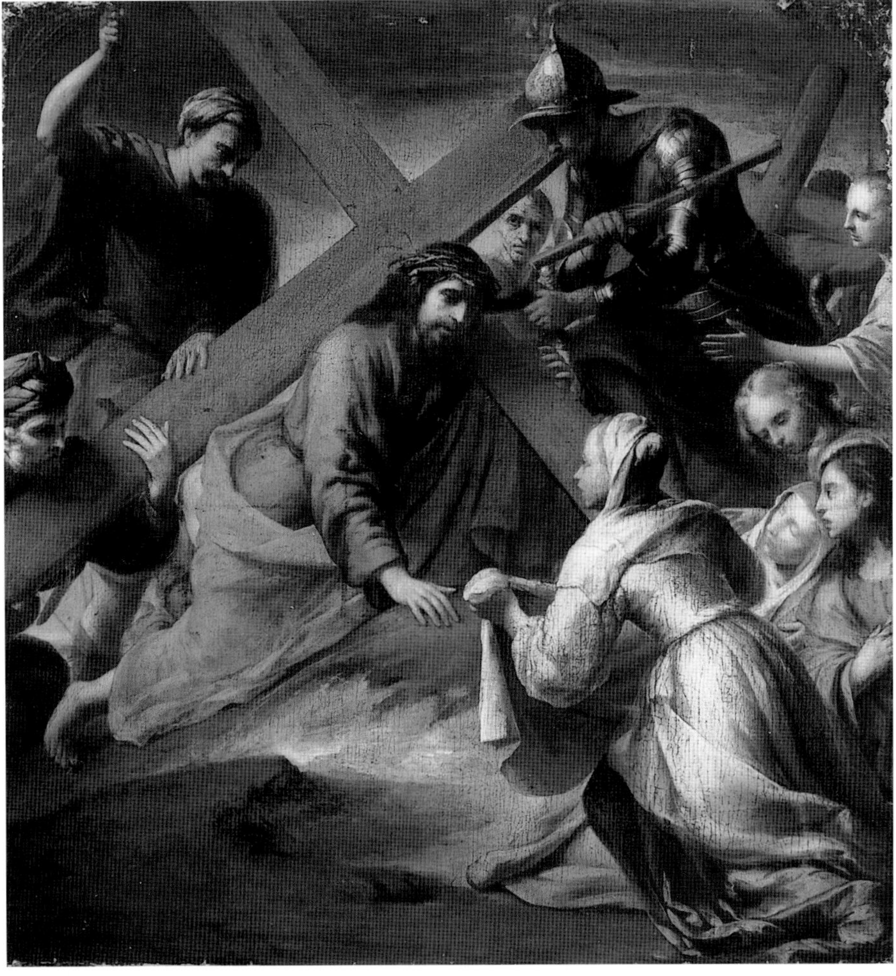

painting for Uilenburg, and between them made out so much French that they understood and could answer the woman who brought the two works and who spoke no Dutch. And seeing these two pieces in the presence of Uilenburg, praising the same for their worth, wondering that such an artistic light could have been shrouded in stupidity as if by a dark mist, and advised Uilenburg to buy the same, and thereupon asked the woman who brought them how much money she was asking for them? Who answered thus: as much as he wants to give. Uilenburg offered her 60 guilders for the piece, and asked whether she was satisfied with this, and whether this master might want to come to Amsterdam to paint for him; the answer was yes. She left with the take, and Uilenburg, urged on by Van Pée and Grebber, followed her that same evening (so that this Hare should not escape him) by the night boat to Uitrecht, and talked about this himself with Laires, who declared himself willing to leave there, which could be easily done, since he did not need a barge to move his things. He then came straight to Amsterdam, and one morning at about nine o'clock to Uilenburg's, where Van Peé and Grebber were, and they stood staring at him because of his repellent person.' De Lairesse had a badly disfigured face, which obviously shocked Uylenburgh's assistants. This is evident in a drawn self-portrait (fig. 159) and in the painting that Rembrandt made of him in 1665 (fig. 160).

De Lairesse was born in Liège in 1640. In April 1664 he fled his native city after a knifing involving two sisters, one of whom he had promised to marry. He settled in Utrecht, where according to Houbraken he had little success.[62] However, someone advised him to show a couple of his paintings to Uylenburgh, which he duly did. 'At that time,' writes Houbraken, 'Jan van Peé and Grebber were

<hr>

62 Aside from Houbraken, there are two other contemporary biographies that describe the 'discovery' of De Lairesse. The accounts vary in the details and only Houbraken refers to Uylenburgh by name. The Liège painter Louis Abry (1643-1720), who worked with De Lairesse for some time, writes that De Lairesse fled not to Utrecht but to Den Bosch, where he rented a small room.

De Lairesse displayed his paintings at the window. An art dealer came past, recognized the quality and asked De Lairesse to go with him to Amsterdam, 'where he gave him work, working only for him and for very little' ('à le suivre à Amsterdam, où il lui donna de l'ouvrage chez soi, travaillant tant seulement pour lui et pour peu de chose'). Abry tells us that, acting on the advice of

some friends, De Lairesse then started to work for himself. See Abry 1867, pp. 248-249 (first edition of the manuscript of 1715). The second description is by Joachim Sandrart and dates from 1675/ 1683. He says that during his flight De Lairesse was laid low by an illness in Utrecht and his wife went into labour. Because he could not speak Dutch he got into dreadful difficulties. When he had

regained some of his strength he displayed one of his paintings 'in a public place, where people offer paintings for sale. The painting was greatly admired by all and on the third day found a buyer in the person of Mr Hooft of Amsterdam. On his recommendation he was summoned to Amsterdam soon afterwards...' (Quamprimum enim vires paululum recollegisset, pictam

quandam a sese tabulam loco illo exponebat publico, ubi picturae venales conspici solent. Quae cum ab omnibus mire probaretur, tertia mox abhinc die emtorem reperiebat Dominum Hooftium Amstelodamensem, quo commendante paulo post Amstelodamum vocabatur...'). See Von Sandrart 1675/ Peltzer 1925, p. 365. It is not clear which Hooft Van Sandrart meant.

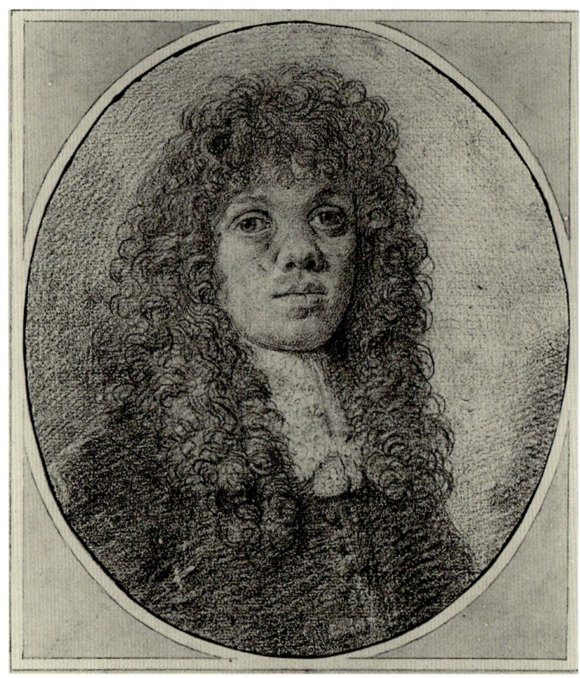

159 Gerard de Lairesse, Self-portrait, black chalk, pen and brown ink, 16.5 x 13.9 cm, Berlin, Staatliche Museen zu Berlin, Kupferstichkabinett

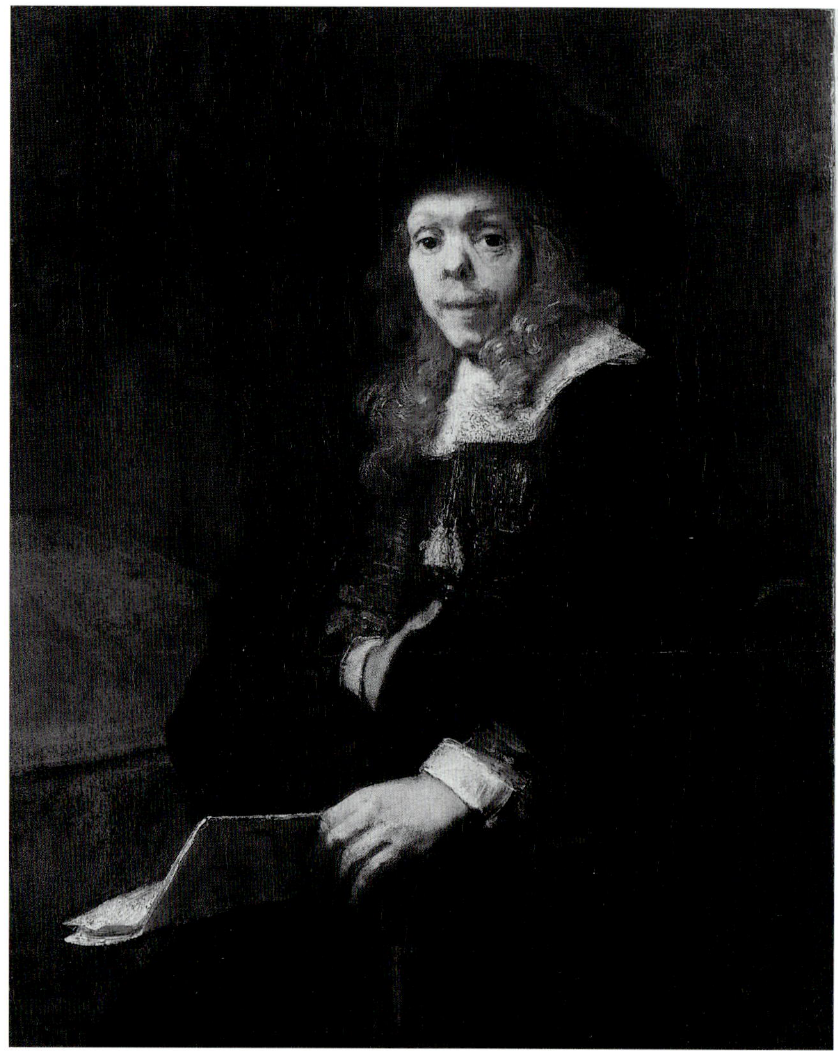

160 Rembrandt van Rijn, Portrait of Gerard de Lairesse, signed 'Rembrandt', canvas, 112.7 x 87.6 cm, New York, N.Y., The Metropolitan Museum of Art, Robert Lehman Collection (Br. 321)

Uylenburgh showed the young painter a canvas and asked him when he could start. According to Houbraken, De Lairesse replied 'right away' and asked the art dealer what he should paint. 'That is of no importance to me, said Uilenburg, make whatever you please. At once he was given a palette with paint and a stick of chalk, and he sat down at the Easel. Until then he had kept one hand inside his coat, which everyone had their eye on, curious as to what he was concealing there, until he brought out his Violin from under there, tuned the strings, and played a melody so skilfully that Grebber, who understood playing, was astonished by it, and even more when having set down the violin, he took up the chalk, and in an instant made the sketch or design for his work, which depicted a stall, and in it Joseph and Mary with her Child. Then he picked up his Violin again and played a piece of music, but soon exchanged the violin for the palette, and that same morning painted the Child, the Virgin and Joseph's head, and the head of an Ox complete, and so skilfully that those who had stood beside him the whole time were astonished by it.'[63]

The story reveals Uylenburgh's single-mindedness in getting hold of the artist and recognises his nose for talent; seemingly he was always on the lookout for good painters and afraid that a competitor would beat him to it. Probably to Uylenburgh's great regret, the painter remained with him for only a short while. Houbraken mentions a period of eight weeks. During this time, Uylenburgh had shown and praised various of De Lairesse's paintings to connoisseurs. The upshot

63 Houbraken 1718-1721, vol. 3, pp. 109-111.

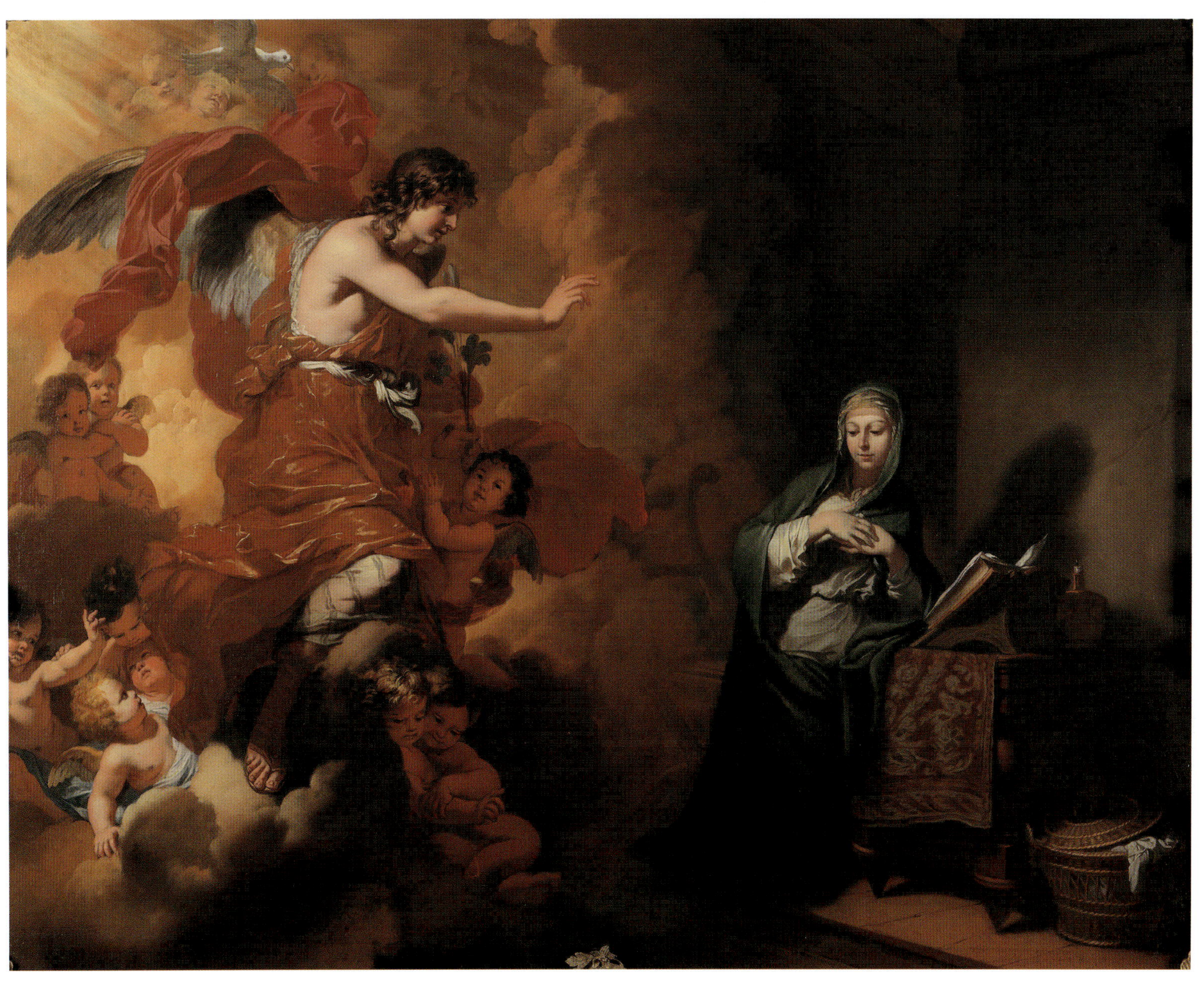

161 Gerard de Lairesse, The annunciation, monogrammed 'GL', canvas, 133 x 168 cm, Brussels, Koninklijke Musea voor Schone Kunsten

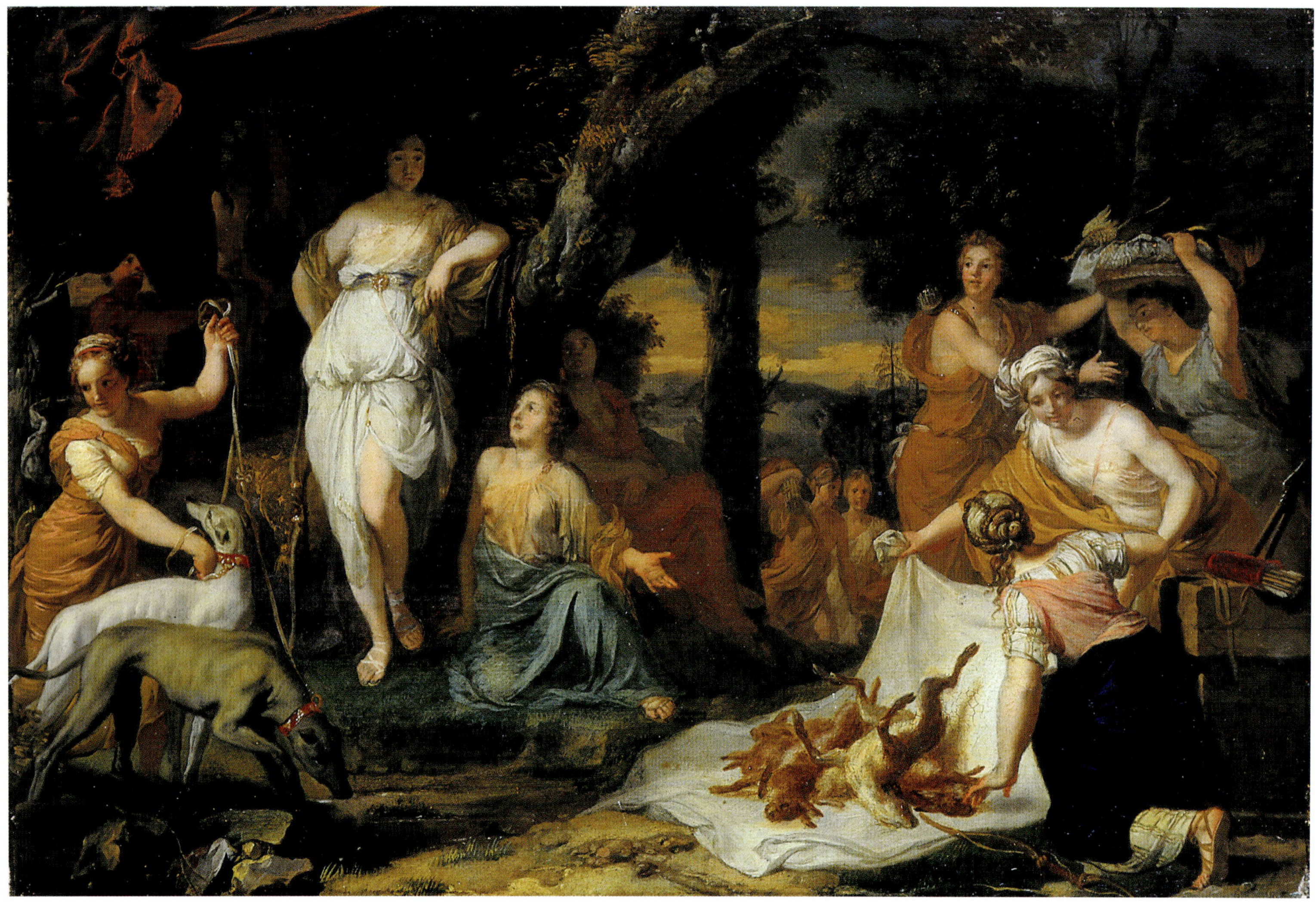

162 Gerard de Lairesse, *Diana and her Nymphs*, signed 'G. Lairesse', panel, 31.5 x 46.5 cm, Schwerin, Staatliches Museum Schwerin

was that the painter immediately received offers that were more attractive than Uylenburgh's. The fact that De Lairesse was able to leave without notice tells us that he was not bound by a contract.

De Lairesse's arrival in Amsterdam can probably be dated to 1665. He must have gone to Utrecht in the course of 1664,[64] and been discovered by Uylenburgh not long afterwards. We do not know what De Lairesse painted during the brief time he worked for Uylenburgh. As far as the style is concerned, the sample he painted of the Virgin and Child probably resembled the *Annunciation* (fig. 161), which is an early work.

De Lairesse probably made small, easy to sell history paintings for Uylenburgh, like *Diana and her Nymphs* (fig. 162), a work that probably dates from the beginning of his career in Amsterdam.

Jan van Pee – From Houbraken's story about De Lairesse, it is clear that at that time Jan van Pee and 'Grebber' were working for Uylenburgh. Van Pee was the son of a myopic Amsterdam art dealer who sold cheap works by the dozen. He started out working for his father, but then went on to train as a proper artist.[65]

Jan van Pee got married in the Reformed church in Leiden in 1657, but probably converted

64 In April 1665 a 'Ludovicus, filius pictoris Leodensis' was baptized in Utrecht; it is not certain that this was indeed De Lairesse's son. Note by Marten Jan Bok referred to in De Vries 1998, p. 4, note 6. Two later sons of De Lairesse's were baptized in the Reformed faith in the Oude Kerk in Amsterdam (Abraham, 2 October 1670; Johannes, 24 September 1673). 65 Houbraken 1718-1721 vol. 3, p. 85.

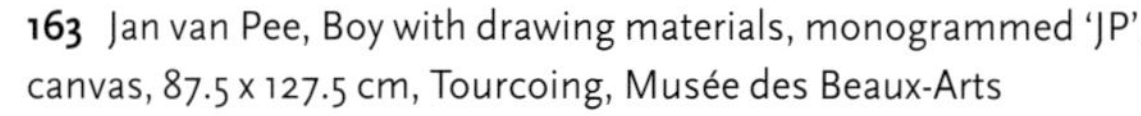

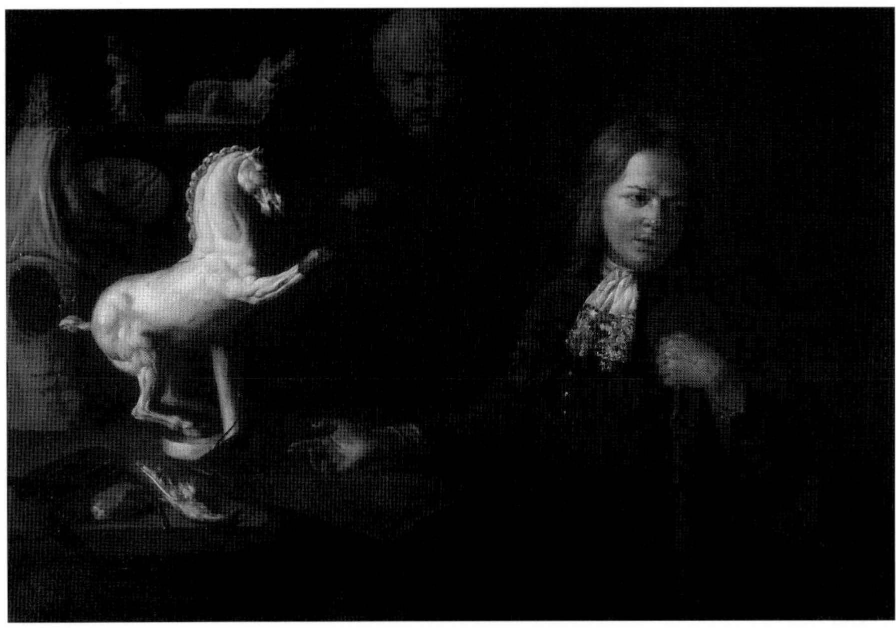

burgh's when De Lairesse turned up. He must have been a member of the large De Grebber family of artists, who originally came from Haarlem. The most likely candidate is Anthonie Claesz de Grebber.[69] He was the son of a silversmith and first cousin to the Haarlem painter Frans Pietersz de Grebber. Born in Haarlem, he moved to Leiden where he married a woman from Amsterdam in 1651.[70] In the 1640s and early 1650s he lived in Leiden, and in 1652 he became a burgher in Amsterdam. In Leiden he probably taught Gabriël Metsu, who was later to marry into the family.[71] We know of only a handful of works by Anthonie de Grebber. His earliest known painting is a *Lamentation* of 1651, which was painted for the Roman Catholic parish of St Bavo in Oude Ade, near Leiden. His *Dido and Aeneas* of 1677 is a classicist work strongly reminiscent of De Lairesse (fig. 164).

Like Van Pee, Anthonie de Grebber was a Catholic. They had both lived in Leiden and may therefore have already known each other. De Grebber, who was probably born around 1622, was already past his prime when he worked at Uylenburgh's. In the 1660s he must have been a reasonably well-known painter, and one who received important commissions.[72] This tells us that the art dealer did not confine himself to seeking out talented young artists to work for him; he also engaged more experienced people.

Hendrick Fromantiou – According to Houbraken, the painter Hendrick Fromantiou – Uylenburgh's adversary in the transaction with the elector – had

to Catholicism later.[66] When he was already married and had children, he went to Antwerp to study the paintings of Rubens, Jordaens and Van Dyck, returning eight months later.[67] Houbraken says that Van Pee 'particularly imitated famous Italian and other works of art, which he could imitate so wonderfully well that people could hardly tell them apart; and the art dealers, for whom he painted a great deal, often played the scoundrel with them'.[68] Apparently Van Pee worked not just for Uylenburgh, but for other art dealers who appreciated his abilities as a copyist.

Only a few works by Van Pee have survived and it is difficult to form a picture of his qualities as an artist (fig. 163). He seems to have painted primarily figure pieces.

Grebber – Houbraken tells us that, as well as Van Pee, a certain 'Grebber' was working at Uylen-

---

66 RAL, DTB, inv. no. 12 (Dutch Reformed banns), fol. 25. Johannes van Pee, residing in Breedestraet, painter, and Heyndricktgen Matthys, residing in Breedestraet, banns dated 14 April 1657. Two years later a daughter born to them was baptized a Catholic in Amsterdam. GAA, DTB 304, p. 38; baptism in the Moses and Aaron Church on 14 April 1659 of Jannetie, daughter of Jan van Pee and Hendrica Matthijse.

67 Houbraken 1718-1721, vol. 3, pp. 84-89, where we also find the amusing account of how Van Pee, having got the key to the cash box from his wife so that he could take out some money to buy fish at the market, took a considerably larger sum and some clothes and set out for Antwerp with a friend. He had to resort to this subterfuge because his wife had consistently refused to let him undertake the trip.

68 Ibid., pp. 88-89.

69 The only other De Greb-

ber who would seem to qualify is Willem de Grebber, Anthonie's brother. The brothers Anthonie and Willem are mentioned together in a deed dated 26 June 1671. In a deed dated 1683 they are both described as 'skilled painters' (GAA, not. R. Duee, NA 2470, p. 114, dated 27 June 1671; not.

J. Matham, NA 4496, p. 364, dated 20-21 September 1683). It is therefore possible that it was Willem that Houbraken is referring to in this context. However, since Anthonie is also mentioned as one of the painters who examined the works for the elector, and gave a positive opinion, he would

seem to be the more likely of the two. See p. 85.

70 RAL, DTB, inv. no. 3 (marriages before magistrates), fol. 94v, Anthony Grebber, Haerlem, residing at Hoygraft, painter, Grietgen Pieters van Troyen residing in Amsterdam'.

71 See Waiboer 2005.

72 De Grebber was the teacher of Guilhelmo van Ingen, Houbraken 1718-1721, vol. 3, p. 315. With Cornelis Brisé he painted two works for the Oudemannenhuis in Amsterdam, see ibid., vol. 2, pp. 341-342. He is also said to have a painted a chimney-piece for the Burgerweeshuis.

221

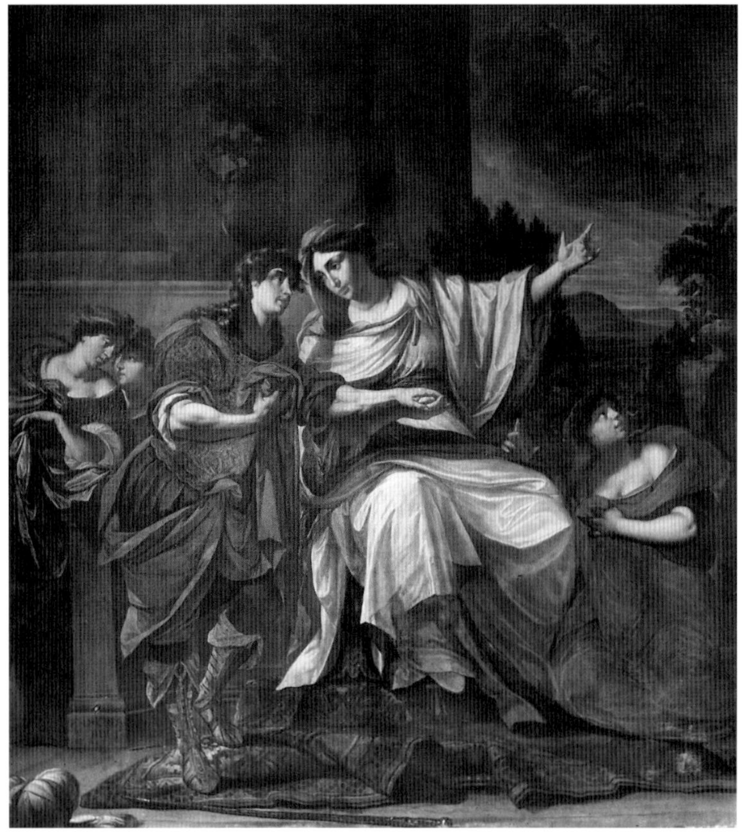

164 Anthonie de Grebber, *Dido and Aeneas*, signed and dated 'A. D. Grebber. F. A°. 1677', canvas, 198 x 183.5 cm, Dunkirk, Musée des Beaux-Arts de Dunkerque

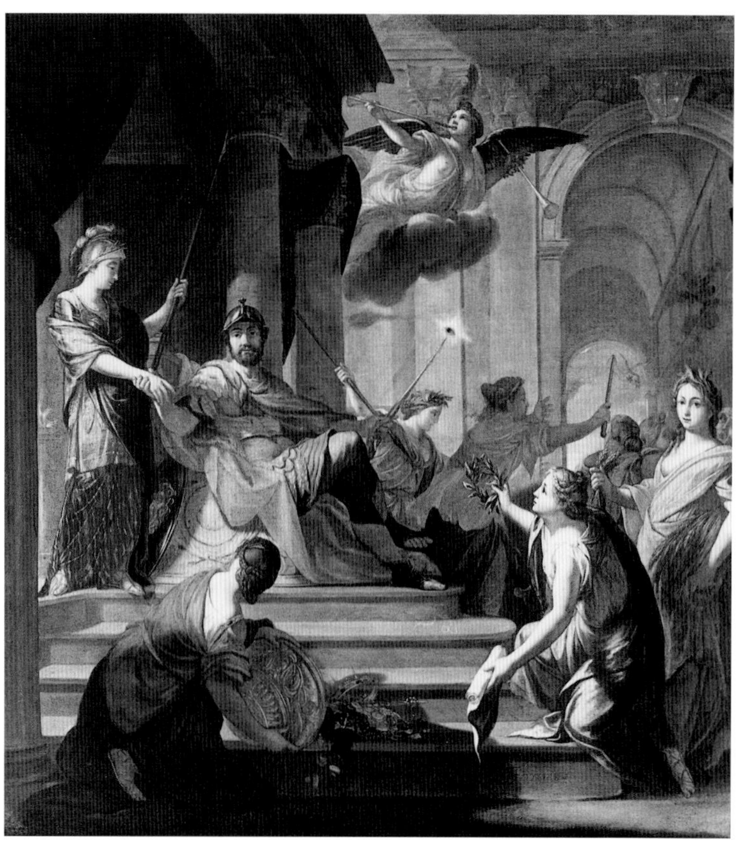

165 Theodoor Ferreris, *Wisdom, Prudence and Strength support a Roman consul*, signed 'Td Ferreris. Ft.', canvas, 190 x 180 cm, Haarlem, Stadhuis

previously worked with the art dealer.[73] Constantijn Huygens the Elder observed that Uylenburgh and Fromantiou had been friends for a very long time ('sincere et ancienne amitié').[74]

It is impossible to establish exactly when Fromantiou worked for Uylenburgh. In 1658, the Maastricht-born painter was in The Hague. The first record of him in Amsterdam dates from 1662; in 1670 he was appointed painter to the elector.[75] This means that he must have worked for Uylenburgh at some point in the 1660s. In view of Huygens's comment, it seems likely that the two had known each other for many years and worked together. Fromantiou was a gifted still life painter. His earliest known works date from 1661.[76] The high standard of his paintings is particularly evident in a magnificent little flower still life in a private collection (fig. 166).

Theodoor Ferreris – Theodoor (Dirck) Ferreris belonged to Gerrit Uylenburgh's circle of friends. He was born in Enkhuizen in 1639. Houbraken says that he came from 'an old and respected family, and had private means on which to live, aside from his practice of art'. We do not know to whom he was apprenticed. He is said to have spent 'many years' in Italy and to have been there with Adriaen Backer in 1666. Houbraken reports that he lived as frugally as possible and spent only thirty guilders during a whole year he lived there. He leaves us in no doubt that this was because of Ferreris's 'wilfulness' and not from necessity.[77] While in Rome Ferreris drew classical statues. In his *Icones*, Jan de Bisschop published a drawing by Ferreris depicting the back of a Hermes (the so-called Belvedere Antinous), which stood opposite the famous Laocoön group in the Vatican. He must have copied paintings as well during his visit

73 Houbraken 1718-1721, vol. 2, p. 294. See p. 82.
74 See p. 88, note 171.
75 See for the biography of Fromantiou, Lammertse 2005.
76 *Still life with nuts and mouse* and *Still life with oysters*; both on panel, signed and dated 1661. Antwerp, Museum Mayer van den Bergh.
77 Houbraken 1718-1721, vol. 3, pp. 184-186.

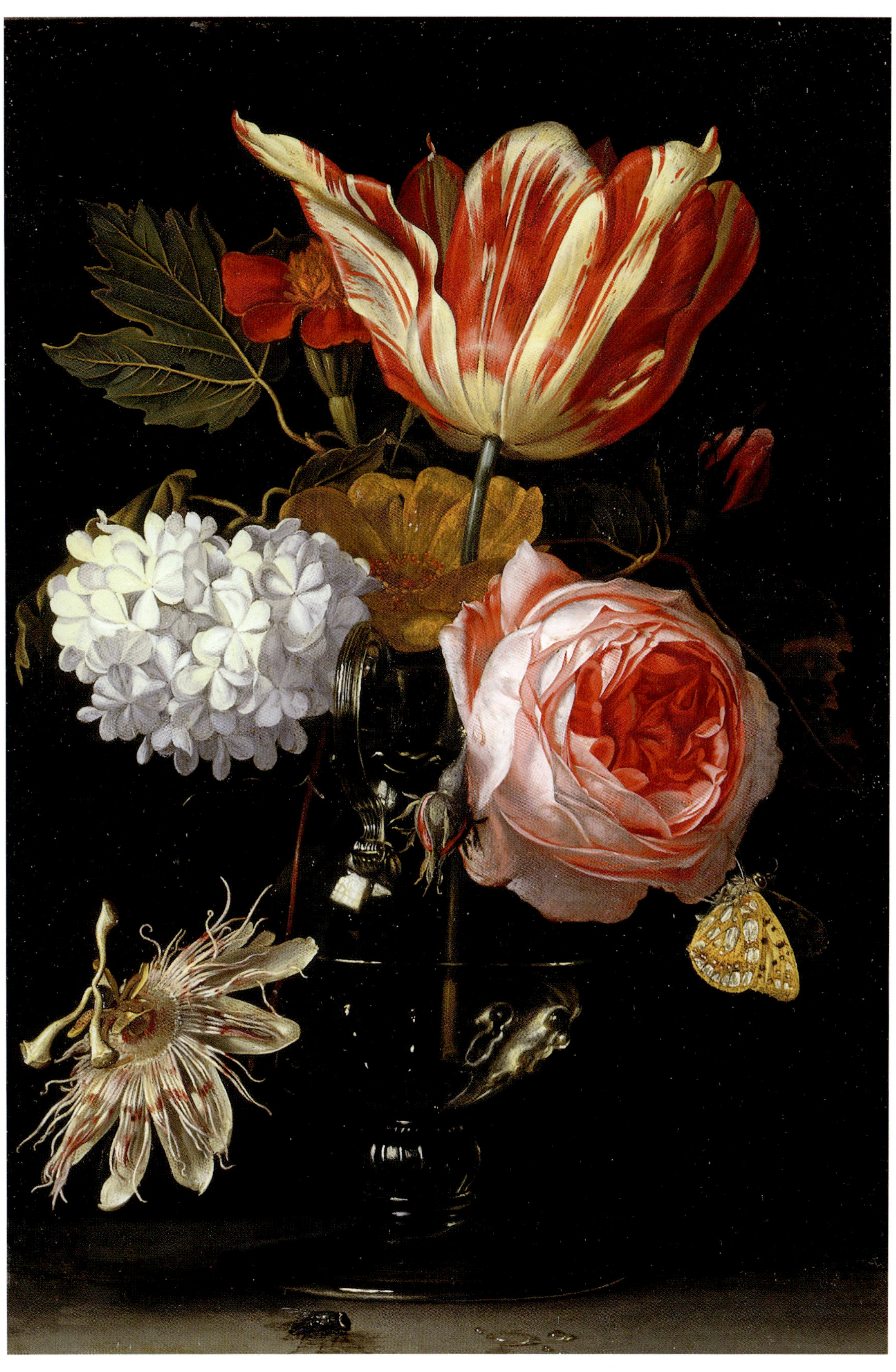

166 Hendrick Fromantiou, Flowers in a vase, with a passion flower, signed and dated 'HDF.romantiou i668', copper, 27 x 19 cm, private collection United States to Italy. In October 1685, when Christiaan Huygens was carrying out trials with his pendulum clock on the Zuyder Zee, he dropped anchor in Enkhuizen one evening and paid Ferreris a visit. He was much impressed by the painter's house and reported that he possessed several 'fine paintings besides the copies he had made in Italy after originals by the best masters'.[78]

By December 1667 Ferreris was back from Rome and living in Amsterdam.[79] A couple of months later, in February 1668, he was the only person who was not a member of the family to sign the deed in which Gerrit Uylenburgh and his sisters asked Peter Lely to claim the estate of their brother Abraham, who had died in Dublin.[80] In 1674 Ferreris was a witness at the baptism of one of Uylenburgh's daughters in the Amstelkerk.[81] When Uylenburgh moved to England for good, he asked Ferreris (with Jan Six and Pieter Deldeijm) to look after his affairs in Amsterdam. A year later, in 1678, the Enkhuizen artist himself went to London, persuaded by Lely and probably Uylenburgh. After working there for a year or two he returned to the Republic and settled in his birthplace. We do not know when Uylenburgh and Ferreris met for the first time; it is possible that it was during Uylenburgh's stay in Italy in 1663. According to a deed dating from 1669 Ferreris knew the art collector and Uylenburgh's financier, Herman Becker.[82] In 1672 the painter lived on the Herengracht, not far from Uylenburgh's house on the Keizersgracht.[83]

In the light of these contacts it seems likely that Ferreris painted in Gerrit's workshop. After Ferreris's return from Rome, Uylenburgh may have been a good starting point for him in the unfamiliar city of Amsterdam. With his abilities as a copyist that Huygens had remarked on he would certainly have been useful. In his own day Ferreris had a reputation as a painter of large, fixed decorations for ceilings, walls and chimneybreasts.

He was the less talented competitor of Gerard de Lairesse. It is conceivable that Uylenburgh, who as we have seen also painted large wall decorations, acted for Ferreris in getting commissions. After De Lairesse's brief stay, Uylenburgh may well have seen Ferreris as an excellent successor – someone, moreover, whom he got on well with and numbered among his friends.

Ferreris was also highly regarded at the stadholder's court, and his commissions included works for the palaces of Soestdijk and Honselaarsdijk. Very little of his substantial output has survived. In 1671 he made a chimney-piece for the Burgomasters' Chamber in Haarlem Town Hall, which hangs there to this day (fig. 165). His friend Adriaen Backer made a work for this building in the same year.[84] There are also still a number of paintings by Ferreris in the town hall of his birthplace, Enkhuizen. In 1674 Ferreris's fortune was assessed at 13,000 guilders for the purposes of municipal taxes. He was thus considerably wealthier than Uylenburgh, who was taxed on 7,000 guilders.[85] This would seem to confirm Houbraken's observation that Ferreris did not have to paint for a living. According to the author he only consorted with 'people of standing and honour'.

Ferreris was a friend of Adriaen Backer and Jan van Neck. The three painters – Backer, Van Neck and Ferreris – worked in the classicist style, which characterised much of Uylenburgh's stock of paintings. In 1675 Uylenburgh had work by both Van Neck and Adriaen Backer in stock.[86] There was nothing by Ferreris, but this was probably because he chiefly painted large works on commission.

Johannes Glauber – Following his apprenticeship as a painter, Johannes Glauber, who was born in Utrecht in 1646, studied with Nicolaes Berchem for nine months.[87] This was probably at the end of

78 Huygens 1888-1950, vol. 9, 1685-1690, pp. 30-31, letter from Christiaan Huygens to his brother Constantijn Huygens, dated 3 October 1685 '… et vus voir le Sr. Fereris, qui est fort proprement logé, et a quelques beaux tableaux, outre les copies qu'il a faites en Italie apres des originaux des meilleurs maitres.' Ferreris also showed Huygens a chimney-piece that he had made for Soestdijk. It featured a good female figure, but her arm was much too clumsy and Huygens had persuaded the painter to do something about it.
79 G A A, not. Jacob de Winter, N A 2295, pp. 70 and 71, dated 19 December 1667. From the two deeds it appears that 'Sr. Theodoris fereeris, residing in this city [Amsterdam]' wanted to transport 'fifty lengths of sawn oak' from Amsterdam to Enkhuizen, but that the ferryman to Enkhuizen, Aris Mulder, had refused this on that day.
80 See for this, p. 77.
81 G A A, D T B 119, p. 33. See also p. 76.

82 G A A, not. Jacob van Loosdrecht, N A 1983, fol. 2v, dated 4 January 1669. Ferreris testified with Philips Koninck that while they were visiting Becker they had seen Becker and Joost de Ruijser agree the purchase of a house by clapping hands.
83 G A A, not. D. Danckerts, N A 2847, p. 941, dated 23 March 1672. This was probably a newly-built house. Ferreris filed a complaint against the owner of the house, the notary Hendrick Rosa, listing all sorts of defects, such as fireplaces that did not work, bad floors that had subsided, missing sinks, shutters and window frames that were badly painted or not painted at all, and the lack of a fence in the garden.
84 Biesboer 1983, p. 56. In 1671 Ferreris received 350 guilders for the chimney-piece; in 1672 Backer received 750 guilders for a chimney-piece in the courtroom (this painting is dated 1671).
85 G A A, archive no. 5028, inv. no. 662, tax register 200th penning, fol. 545v.
86 See below, pp. 246-247.
87 Houbraken 1718-1721, vol. 3, pp. 216-217.

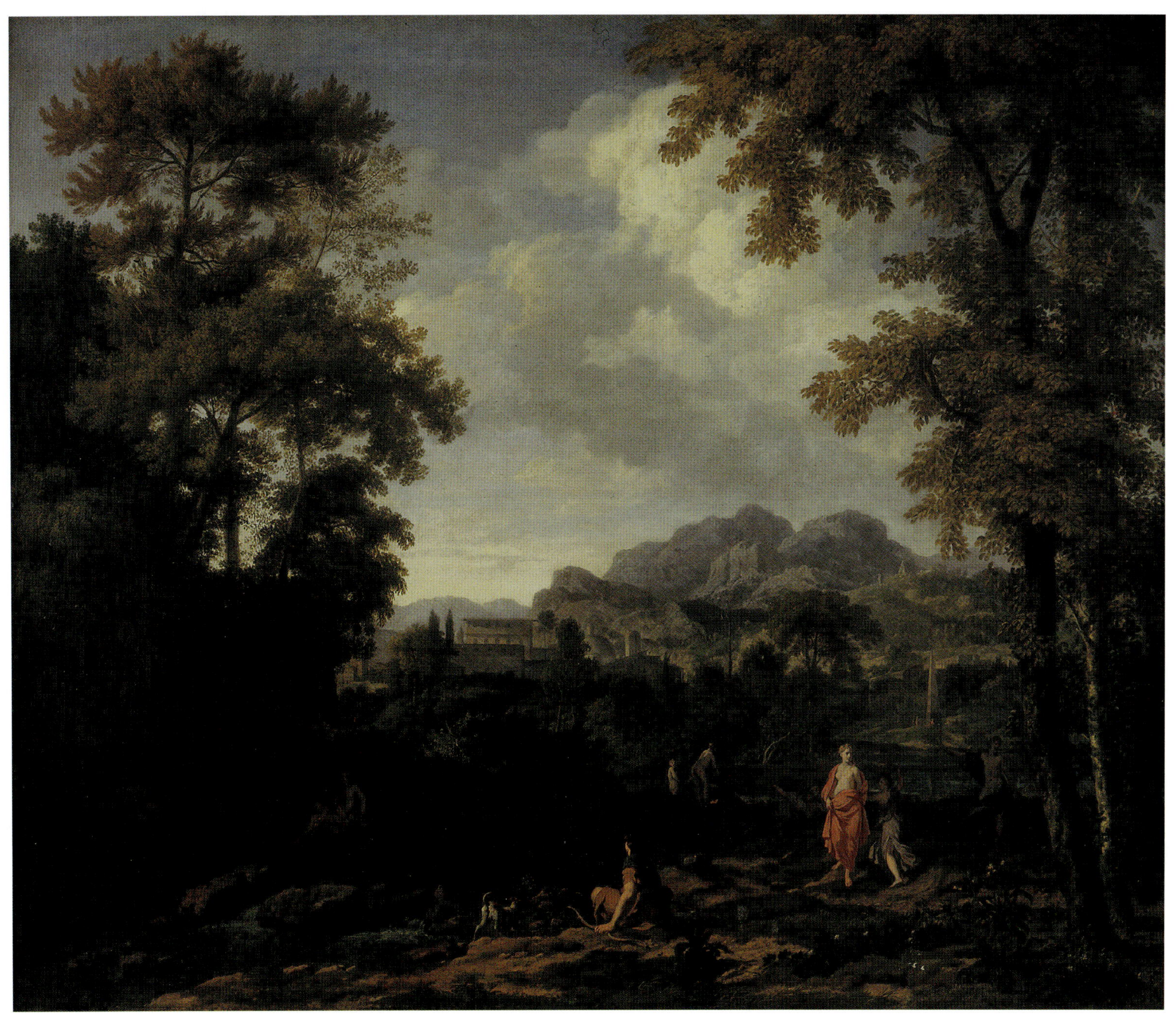

167 Johannes Glauber, Landscape with a classical scene (Diana and her nymphs?), signed 'Glauber', canvas, 70 x 85 cm, Copenhagen, Statens Museum for Kunst

the 1660s, when Berchem was living in Amsterdam.[88] Glauber then, so Houbraken tells us, went 'to board' with Uylenburgh, 'and practised after those fine examples [that is to say Italian paintings], which at the same time aroused a desire in him to go and see Italy. He went on this journey in the year 1671 [...]'. Glauber did not return to Amsterdam until 1684, when he went to live in 'a room' in Gerard de Lairesse's house.[89] He specialised in landscapes and painted both small cabinet pieces and large wall decorations. He worked a great deal with De Lairesse, who painted the figures in his landscapes. A landscape now in Copenhagen is a fine example of this collaboration (fig. 167). Houbraken must have got his information about Glauber from the man himself. When the author published the third volume of his biographies of artists in 1721, Glauber was living in the Proveniershuis in Schoonhoven, 'where he delighted in a pipe in his garden'.[90]

Houbraken does not say how long Glauber remained with Uylenburgh. He probably worked there from the end of the 1660s to 1671, when he went to Italy. Glauber did not go straight to the south. He went via Paris, where he worked for the art dealer Picart for a year.

Houbraken begins the paragraph about Glauber's time with Uylenburgh, 'the greatest dealer in Italian paintings that there was in Holland', by reporting that he 'kept various young painters at work, copying these pieces'.[91] It would seem, therefore, that Glauber started by making copies. In the light of his training with Berchem, it is also possible that he painted landscapes while he was with Uylenburgh and collaborated on large wall decorations, a genre in which he was to achieve considerable fame later.

Horatius Paulijn – One of the last painters who was probably active in Uylenburgh's workshop was Horatius Paulijn. His carefully executed

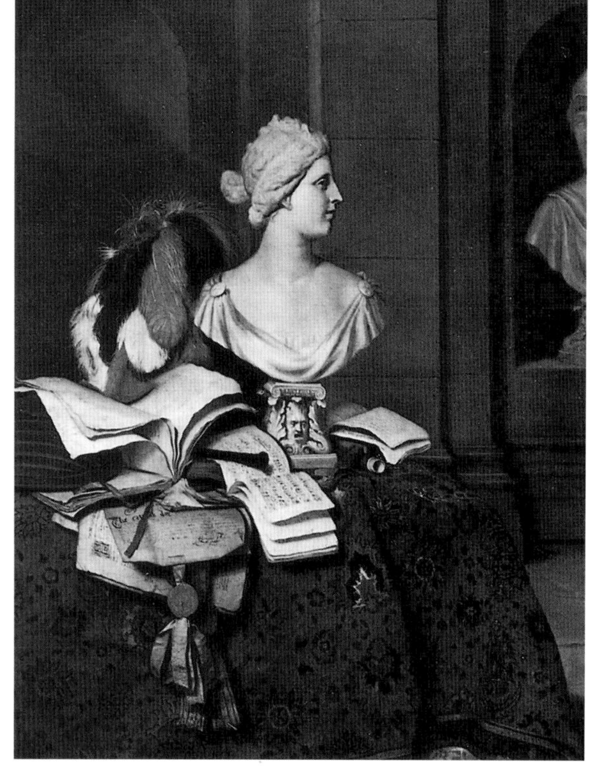

168 Horatius Paulijn, Still life with musical instruments and a bust of Venus, signed 'Horatius Paulijnus Pinxit', canvas, 50.7 x 38.5 cm, Sør Rusche Collection

works are now extremely rare (see fig. 168). His paintings fetched high prices in his own day. Houbraken tells us that Uylenburgh had 'a piece by him that he valued at 200 ducats'.[92]

Little is known about Paulijn. He married in Amsterdam in 1668, on which occasion he gave his age as 27 and his place of birth as 'Baet', possibly Bath in England.[93] He married in the Reformed faith and his children were baptised in the Reformed church. One of the witnesses at the baptism of his daughter Barbara was the painter Toussaint Gelton.[94] Paulijn probably lived near Uylenburgh in the early 1670s.[95] There is a surviving deed dating from April 1674 relating to a loan Uylenburgh took out with a merchant, which Paulijn witnessed.[96] We know little about

88 Berchem lived in Amsterdam between 1660 and 1670, see the biography of Berchem by Irene van Thiel in Blankert, Giltaij, Lammertse 1999-2000, pp. 236-243.

89 Houbraken 1718-1721, vol. 3, p. 217.
90 Ibid., p. 218.
91 Ibid., p. 217.
92 Houbraken 1718-1721, vol. 3, p. 186. There were different types of ducats. A silver ducat

was 2 guilders and 10 stivers, so 200 ducats was 500 guilders.
93 GAA, DTB 491, p. 441.
94 GAA, DTB 44, p. 321, Nieuwe Kerk, dated 28 July 1671.
95 Paulijn's daughter Maria

was baptized on 10 September 1673 in the Amstelkerk, the church where Uylenburgh had his children baptized after he moved to the Keizersgracht. GAA, DTB 119, p. 22.
96 See p. 104, note 236.

the relationship between Uylenburgh and Paulijn.

In 1674 Paulijn went to Hamburg as a member of a sect that wanted to establish a new kingdom there.[97] He remained there for a short while, and then appears to have gone on to Denmark.[98]

WORK AND WORKING RELATIONSHIPS

We can identify considerably more artists who worked for Gerrit Uylenburgh than for his father. Nonetheless we cannot get as clear a picture of what they did. A great deal of the output of artists like Rembrandt and Flinck from the period when they were associated with Hendrick Uylenburgh's firm has survived. We only know roughly when the ten painters referred to above, who are known to have been involved in the workshop in one way or another, actually worked there. It is in any event clear that Ovens was closely involved in the production in 1662 and 1663. Interestingly, his work is very similar to what Rembrandt and Flinck were doing in the years when they were working for Hendrick Uylenburgh. Like them, he painted history pieces and portraits. Gerrit Uylenburgh's importance to Ovens is harder to determine, though, since there is no question of a typical (Mennonite) clientele as there was with Hendrick. Ovens painted for the Reformed regent class, with which both he and Gerrit had good contacts. He was affluent, so that he certainly did not have to depend on Uylenburgh for money. It is quite possible that Uylenburgh took a proportion of Ovens's output, while Ovens may have undertaken portrait commissions for him. Like Rembrandt and Flinck, he must have been free to seek and accept commissions on his own behalf.

The collaboration between Ovens and Gerrit Uylenburgh is more or less in the tradition of the relationship that Hendrick had with his painters. It is striking that none of the other artists we know to have been involved with Gerrit's firm were portraitists. Under Hendrick Uylenburgh, portraits were an important aspect of the business. Its is conceivable that Gerrit abandoned this ele-

ment, although it is equally possible that he did have portrait painters working for him and that we simply have no documentary evidence of them.

Gerrit Uylenburgh clearly continued the firm's copying operations. As we have seen, Baldinucci wrote about Hendrick's 'accademia', where many 'young painters' copied works by masters from all over Europe.[99] Houbraken reported that Gerrit kept 'various young painters' at work by getting them to paint copies of the Italian paintings he owned.[100] Elsewhere he noted that Uylenburgh took on 'various good painters and young men and got them to copy works by esteemed masters, each according to his skill [...]'.[101] He wrote that Jan van Pee was very skilled in copying 'famous Italian and other works of art'.[102]

Hendrick Uylenburgh must also have had Italian paintings copied, but the emphasis nonetheless most probably lay on copying the work of Dutch contemporaries. Gerrit, however, appears to have concentrated almost exclusively on having copies made of works by Italian masters and possibly also renowned Flemish artists. In the inventory of 1675, for instance, there are copies after painters like Titian, Guido Reni, Rubens and Van Dyck, but not one after a contemporary Dutch artist.

Copying evidently played a crucial role in the Uylenburghs' art business. It was also an important part of a painter's training. Pupils would copy work to improve their technique and learn to recognise the manner of a particular master. Baldinucci emphasised that the practice of copying was not simply beneficial to Uylenburgh – the young painters also learned from it. It was with good reason that Houbraken described Glauber's work for Uylenburgh as practice. Through copying, Glauber became so fascinated by Italian art that he went to Italy.[103]

Copying was thus a generally accepted and respected activity. It even occasioned admiration if it was impossible or extremely difficult to distinguish between the original and the copy. Houbraken relates how Isaac de Moucheron made a copy after Poussin. Van Swoll, a collector who visited him in his studio, bought it without

169 Anonymous, after Andrea Schiavone, The presentation in the
temple, canvas, 156 x 176 cm, Amsterdam, Amstelkring Museum

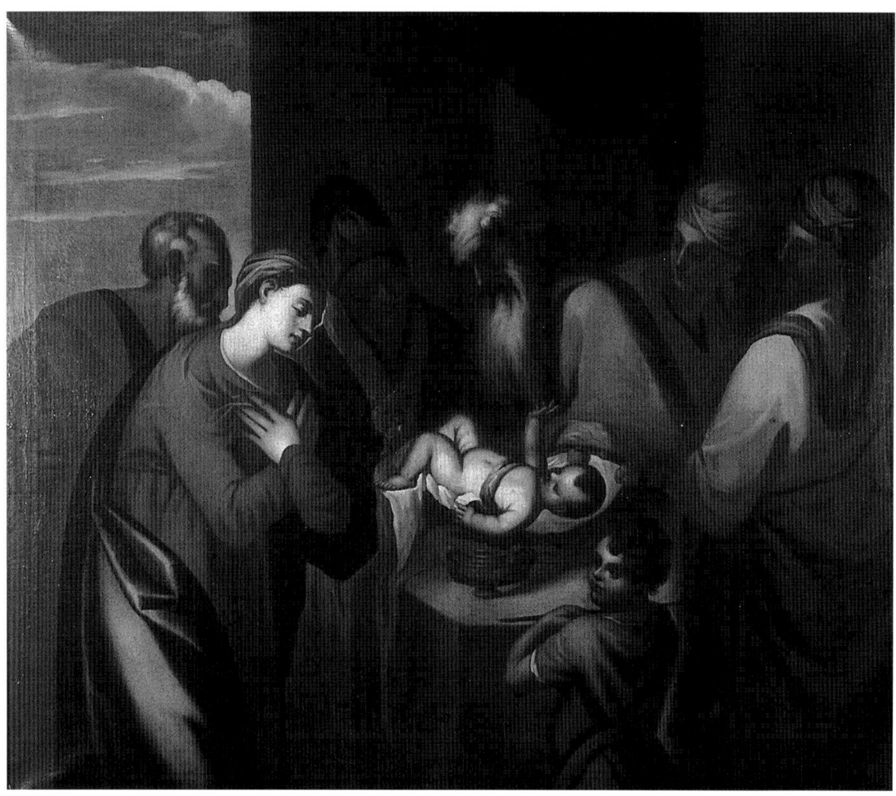

asking about the artist, taking it to be one of the
best works by the French master. Later, however,
De Moucheron admitted frankly and probably
not without some pride that he had painted it
himself.[104]

Forgery, however, is something altogether
different. The deliberate selling of a copy as an
original was strongly condemned. Uylenburgh's
unprecedentedly fierce attacks on Fromantiou
in the case with the Great Elector suggest that
Uylenburgh, at least by his own account, did not
hold with these practices. At any rate he asserted
that he was a reputable dealer and the Amsterdam
burgomasters confirmed this. Houbraken, however, writes that now and again Uylenburgh let a
'spurious work slip through. If it went unnoticed,'
says Houbraken, 'he just let it pass'.[105]

As early as the seventeenth century paintings
were being deliberately aged to make them look
more like the originals. Information about this is
scarce. One contemporary recorded how a forger
tempered the colours with soot from the chimney
so that the painting became darker and consequently looked older. He then rolled the painting
up to produce a visible craquelure.[106] We do not
know whether Uylenburgh engaged in such practices.

By their nature, copies are difficult to date and
to place. Although many hundreds of them must
have been made, there are virtually no known
examples that can be identified with certainty
as having been executed by seventeenth-century
Dutch artists after Italian examples. The painting
in Museum Amstelkring in Amsterdam, which

was made around 1663 as a chimney-piece for
the principal room in the house, is very probably
one such imitation. It is a copy after Andrea
Schiavone's *Presentation in the Temple* (fig. 169).
The original was in the Reynst brothers' collection (cf. fig. 170).[107] The hard execution and the
fact that it is painted on a canvas with a fine weave
make it likely that the work was created in Holland.[108] Given the good relations that existed
between Uylenburgh and the Reynst family, it
is tempting to assume that it was done in his
workshop.

Original work was also done in Uylenburgh's
workshop – by Ovens among others. Houbraken's
story about De Lairesse reveals that Uylenburgh
gave him a free hand in choosing a subject. It

104 Houbraken 1718-1721,
vol. 2, pp. 297-298. Houbraken
probably heard this story
from De Moucheron himself.
The painting is listed in the
sale of Van Swoll's estate in
1699, see Hoet/Terwesten
1752-1770, vol. 1, p. 51, as no.
86 'A Pagan Sacrifice, by De

Moucheron, after Poussin,
painted in Italy'.
105 Houbraken 1718-1721, vol.
2, p. 294.
106 Sanderson 1658, pp. 16-17,
'It is said that *Laniere* in *Paris*,
by a cunning way of temper-
ing his Colours with Chimney
Soote, the Painting becoms

duskish, and seems ancient;
which done, he roules up and
thereby it crackls, and so mistaken for an old Principall,
it being well copied from a
good hand'. This was probably
Jerome Lanier, the painter and
restorer, and brother of the
collector Nicholas Lanier.

Another painter who was
known in his own day for
his imitations, particularly
of Giorgione, was the seventeenth-century Venetian
painter Pietro dellla Vecchia,
see Aikema 1990, pp. 32-36.
107 The original is no longer
known, see Logan 1979, p. 144.

The copy must have been
bought by Jan Hartman when
he renovated the house on the
Oudezijds Voorburgwal. The
house was later bought by
Joan Reynst (Gerard's son). It
does not, however, seem likely
that he installed the painting
there; Logan 1991, pp. 153-155.

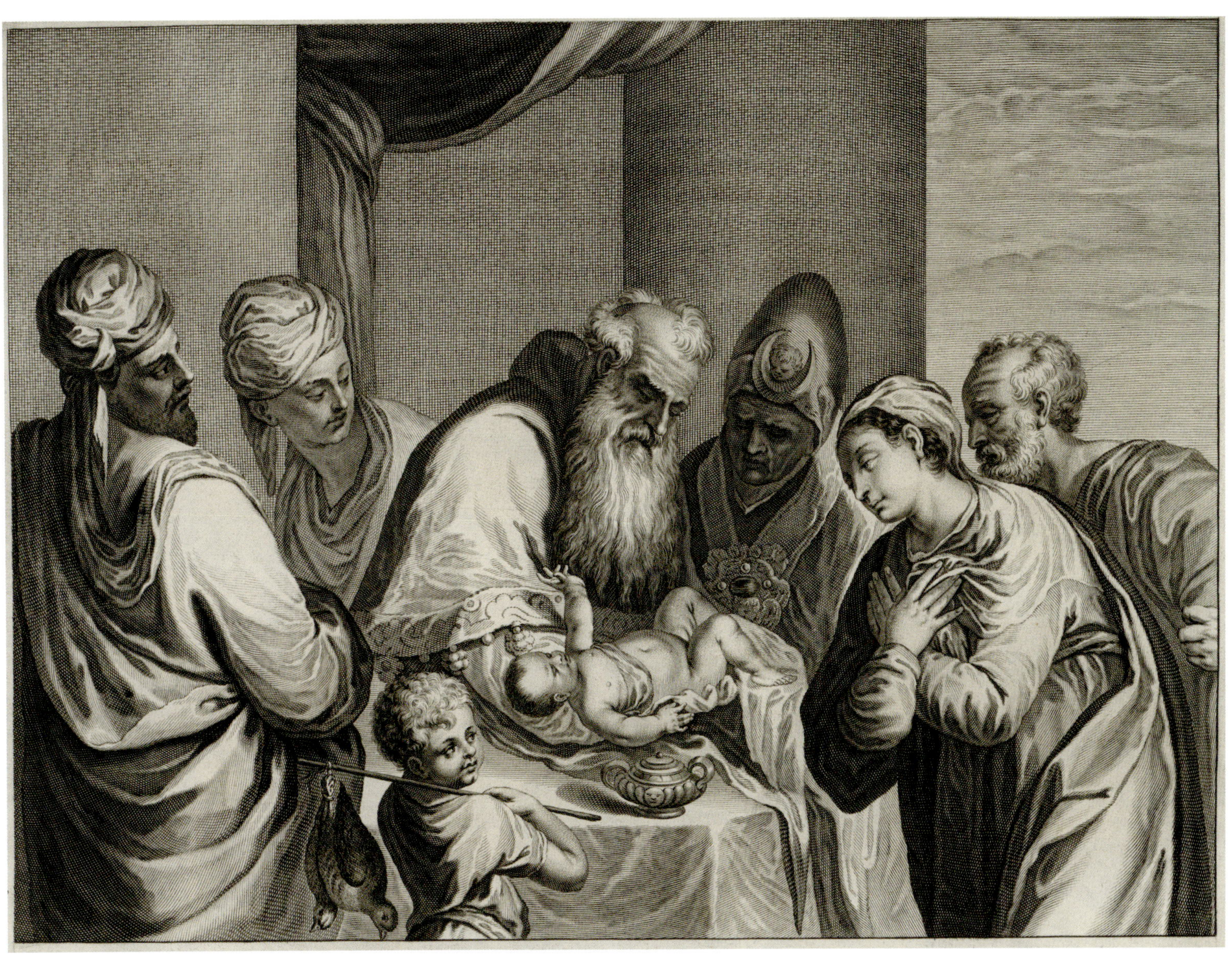

170 Jeremias Falck after Andrea Schiavone, The presentation in the temple, engraving, 27.3 x 37.2 cm, in: Variarum imaginum a celeberrimis artificibus pictarum caelaturae elegantissimis tabulis repraesentatae imaginum, Amsterdam, Rijksprentenkabinet

must have been clear to him from the outset that De Lairesse was someone who could make his own, eminently saleable inventions. Uylenburgh would never have gone to so much trouble if he had just wanted to use De Lairesse as a copyist. Houbraken's image of De Lairesse as a hare that might escape from Uylenburgh suggests that there was cutthroat competition between the Amsterdam art dealers in their quest for young talent. Sadly, we know next to nothing about who these potential rivals might have been.

De Lairesse was a history painter who emerged as the pre-eminent maker of large ceiling and wall decorations of his age. In the 1660s it became increasingly fashionable to have houses decorated. The wealthy Amsterdam citizens who built their magnificent homes along the newly-dug sections of the canals in the 1660s and 1670s often commissioned complete decorations for their finest rooms. The walls and ceilings were covered with painted canvases. For the walls, the subjects were often landscapes or scenes from history. The ceilings were usually decorated with allegorical images. Uylenburgh appears to have responded to this new trend. At any rate he himself painted landscapes for a house on the Herengracht. It is possible that painters like Ferreris and Adriaen Backer got similar commissions through him.

Another area of production in Uylenburgh's firm must have been flower paintings and still lifes. Hendrick Fromantiou, who worked for the firm at some point during the 1660s, specialised exclusively in still lifes – primarily flower pieces. One or more of Uylenburgh's sisters must also have made flower paintings. In the inventory of 1675, though, there are few flower paintings. We do know that in 1671 Uylenburgh sold the Great Elector a flower still life by Maria van Oosterwijck.[109] He had probably purchased

this work directly from the artist herself. There is no indication that she was associated with the business.

One of the hardest points to ascertain is the working relationship between Uylenburgh and his artists, because there is essentially no information about it. Houbraken mentions relatively few dealers in his biographies. When he does write about them, it is almost always in pejorative terms. They were 'bloodsuckers', who paid far too little for the paintings done by the artists.[110] In connection with Uylenburgh, he compares working for dealers with slave labour in the galleys.[111]

Poorly as they may have paid, however, the art dealers must nonetheless have been the salvation of countless painters. Houbraken himself talks of artists 'who otherwise could not have survived' and who went to work for Uylenburgh.[112] There appears to be good reason why none of the painters associated with Gerrit Uylenburgh's firm came from Amsterdam. Like those who had worked for his father Hendrick, they came from other towns and cities in the Republic or from abroad. It seems that, like Hendrick, Gerrit Uylenburgh had no apprentices in his service who still had to be trained. Baldinucci and Houbraken refer to 'young painters'. Young men, in other words, who had already completed their training. As well as the young painters, who used working for Uylenburgh as a step towards gaining a reputation in Amsterdam, there were also artists who were already married and had children, but for various reasons went on working for art dealers. Painters like Van Pee and De Grebber probably only worked for Uylenburgh now and then, possibly at times when they were not selling much themselves or had no commissions and when Uylenburgh needed them.

These painters could work at home in their own studios or in Uylenburgh's 'shop'. From

108 As a rule the canvas used in Venice had a coarse weave.
109 See p. 82, note 143.
110 Houbraken 1718-1721, vol. 3, p. 94. Houbraken made the comment in connection with Fromantiou and Netscher, see p. 250.

111 Van Gool 1750-1751, vol. 2, p. 472, explains the expression used by Houbraken, working 'in the galleys', to describe painters who worked for 'bloodsuckers', in other words art dealers. According to him the 'painters' galley' was a

'notorious painting shop' in Rome, 'whose supreme commander was an art dealer; of whom there were many living in that celebrated city in former times and offering work to the young painters who came over and otherwise had no liv-

ing: either by day wages or by piece, according to the man's skill, and as fat or as lean as each one's artistic merit was judged to be, according to the generosity or meanness of the supreme commander ... To those who were too tight-

fisted, the Bentvueghels gave the name *bloodsuckers*; and thus this honorary title of self-interested art dealers owes its origins to *Rome*, and blew this way from there...'.
112 Houbraken 1718-1721, vol. 3, p. 294.

Houbraken's story about De Lairesse we know that Van Pee and De Grebber painted in Uylenburgh's house. In the contract drawn up in 1670 for the building of the houses on the Keizersgracht where Uylenburgh was to live and work it was clearly stated that the large room 'will be to hang paintings in and also to be able to paint in at his [Uylenburgh's] discretion'.[113] In Flinck's former house on the Lauriergracht, the assistants reportedly worked in the 'large painting room with tall windows'.[114]

There were also artists who boarded with Uylenburgh, among them Glauber and probably also Rosendael. Here, too, Gerrit was continuing a tradition started by his father. It is not clear how he paid his assistants. Art dealers often paid per painting – or at least the Antwerp art dealer Musson adopted this approach.[115] In the case of the young painters living in the house, it is possible that they were not paid for each work they painted, but had a contract that tied them to Uylenburgh for a specific period. There are several instances in the seventeenth century of painters and dealers who engaged artists on a contract basis. In 1662, the then 23-year-old Leendert van der Strate had undertaken to go and paint for someone. He had second thoughts, however, and asked the art dealer Lodewijk van Ludick and the painter Frederick de Moucheron if they would 'give him copying to do and put him to work'. Initially they refused and said that he had to honour his contract, but eventually Van Ludick relented and 'set him to work and had him make copies'.[116]

The still-life artist Pieter van den Bosch had a contract for a year with the collector and dealer Marten Kretzer. In the winter he had to paint 'from daybreak in the morning until dusk in the evening' and in the summer from seven in the morning to seven at night. He had Sundays and feast days off. If he arrived late or left early, or if he was ill, he would have to make up the time later and he was not allowed to work for anyone else. Kretzer decided what Van den Bosch should paint. The salary was 1,200 guilders for the year.[117]

Houbraken stresses that it was predominantly young painters who worked for Uylenburgh. As far as we can tell, De Lairesse and Glauber were

about 24 when they came to him. Rosendael, Fromantiou and Ferreris were in their late twenties when they first came into contact with him. Ovens and De Grebber were considerably older.

It is hard to establish how many painters actually worked in Uylenburgh's studio at any one time. The 1675 inventory lists three easels, two of which were in the attic, typically the place where assistants worked. When De Lairesse arrived, there were two artists there. Perhaps we may therefore assume that there were never more than two or three painters at a time working at Uylenburgh's.

Although all ten of the artists discussed here worked for Uylenburgh, we must bear in mind that 'worked for' will have meant something very different for each of the ten, ranging all the way from some sort of employment contract to making the occasional painting.

The stock

Besides the paintings of the artists who worked for him, Gerrit Uylenburgh also sold countless other works of art. Our knowledge of these is based primarily on the inventory and the valuation of his property in 1675, when he ran into financial difficulties. At that point various people who had left works on consignment with him came to retrieve their paintings. Let us look first at what we know about Uylenburgh's stock prior to this time.

THE STOCK BEFORE 1675

The first information about paintings owned by Uylenburgh dates from 1663. In that year he returned from Italy with all sorts of works of art. We do not know for certain exactly what he brought back with him, but there was in any event a painting by Palma Vecchio – probably of a female nude.[118]

In 1668 Uylenburgh paid the Antwerp art dealer Matthijs Musson 80 guilders for a 'Battaelieken' (a battle scene) by Jacques Courtois,

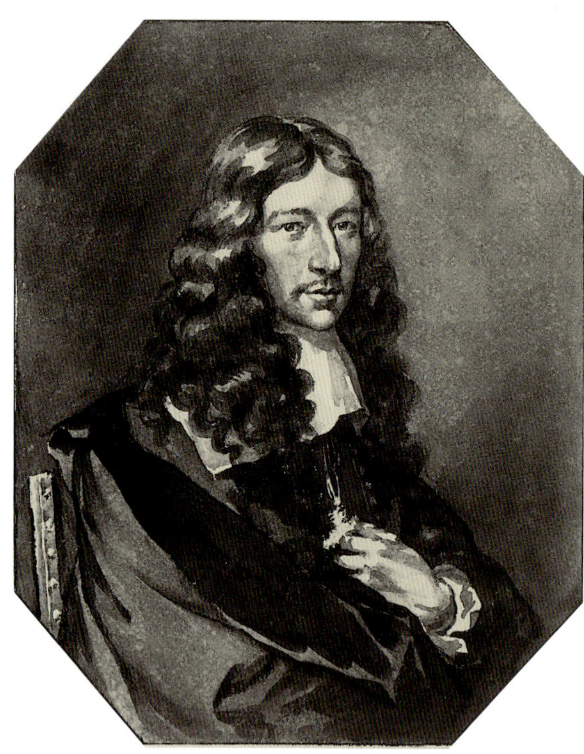

171 Jan de Bisschop after Jürgen Ovens, Portrait of Jan de Bisschop, pen, brush and brown ink, 19.6 x 16 cm, inscription stuck on below: 'J: Ovens pinxit J. Episcopius fecit.', Amsterdam, Rijksprentenkabinet

'il Borgognone', a painter working in Italy.[119] The Uylenburghs had done business with Musson before.[120] Gerrit Uylenburgh must have dealt with other colleagues in the same way, but to date no archive documents have been found to substantiate this.

Elsewhere in this book there is an exhaustive account of the way Uylenburgh tried to sell thirteen paintings to the Elector of Brandenburg in 1671-1672. A significant proportion of them came from the Reynst brothers' collection. Uylenburgh must without a doubt have bought more from this collection, but aside from a probable self-portrait by Palma Vecchio there is no further information about it.[121]

In about April or May 1660 Uylenburgh took an album of etchings by Jacques Callot to sell for Constantijn Huygens the Younger. In the following months he was unable to get an offer of more

than 50 livres for it, a price that was evidently too low for Huygens, whereupon Uylenburgh returned the album to him.[122]

Between 1657 and 1663 Gerrit and his friend Peter Lely must have acquired a collection of drawings from Walter van der Voort, an Antwerp merchant who had amassed his collection in Venice. We shall look at this sale in more detail later. What is relevant here is that it involved more than 1,100 drawings, including 66 by Titian, 98 by Raphael, 53 by Parmigianino, 30 by Giorgione, 40 by Tintoretto, 18 by Palma Giovane, 36 by Giulio Romano, 13 by Mantegna and 12 by Dürer. We do not know how the sheets were shared out between Uylenburgh and Lely. Lely himself said that he had taken the best pieces, but he may simply have been boasting.[123]

In 1665, through Ovens, Uylenburgh sold three rare books and engravings to the Duke of Gottorf. This is the only indication that Uylenburgh also supplied special books, probably late medieval breviaries.[124]

As well as paintings, in 1671-1672 Uylenburgh also offered the elector a number of statues. These were Roman portrait busts and small sculptures. Like the paintings, the statues came (for the most part?) from the Reynst brothers' collection,[125] but even before this it was possible to buy classical statuary from Uylenburgh.

Jan de Bisschop (fig. 171) included a number of statues that were with Uylenburgh at the time in the second volume of his *Icones*. This book, the first volume of which appeared in 1668 and the second in 1669, was a sampler of important classical statues.[126] De Bisschop got most of his examples from Italy, but also showed statues that were in France and England at that time. The only examples in Dutch collections that he included belonged to Uylenburgh and Hendrick Scholten.[127] These were also the only ones that De Bisschop drew himself.[128] The first work from Uylenburgh's collection that he illustrated was a Dionysus and Hermaphrodite (fig. 172).[129] The group is a Roman variant of a lost Hellenic original that probably dated from the third century BC. The statue had already been drastically restored in De Bisschop's day. The second sculpture he put in his

119 Duverger 1969, pp. 102, 107, 150.
120 See p. 200.
121 See for this, p. 103.
122 Huygens 1888-1950, vol. 3, p. 200, letter from Constantijn Huygens the Younger to Christiaan Huygens, 1 December 1660, in which Huygens writes that it was more than eight months since he had given the album to Uylenburgh on consignment. See below, pp. 284-285.
123 See below, p. 268.
124 Schmidt 1922, p. 93. See p. 63 and p. 263, note 234.
125 See pp. 91-94.
126 De Bisschop 1668-1669, see Van Gelder/Jost 1985.
127 See below, p. 280.
128 For the etchings of the other sculptures he worked from examples by Salviati, Cornelis van Poelenburch, Jacques de Gheyn III, Adriaen Backer, Theodoor Ferreris, Nicolaes Willingh and Willem Dodijns. See Van Gelder/Jost 1985.
129 De Bisschop 1668-1669, describes the group as no. 63 'Bacchus supported by a Faun'. The statue is now in the Rijksmuseum voor Oudheden in Leiden (inv. no. Pb 88). See Van Gelder/Jost 1985, p. 147-148, no. 63. Dionysus's left arm and hand and the lower part of his right arm and hand, the legs and feet of both figures and the greater part of the base, the panther and the tree trunk are not original.

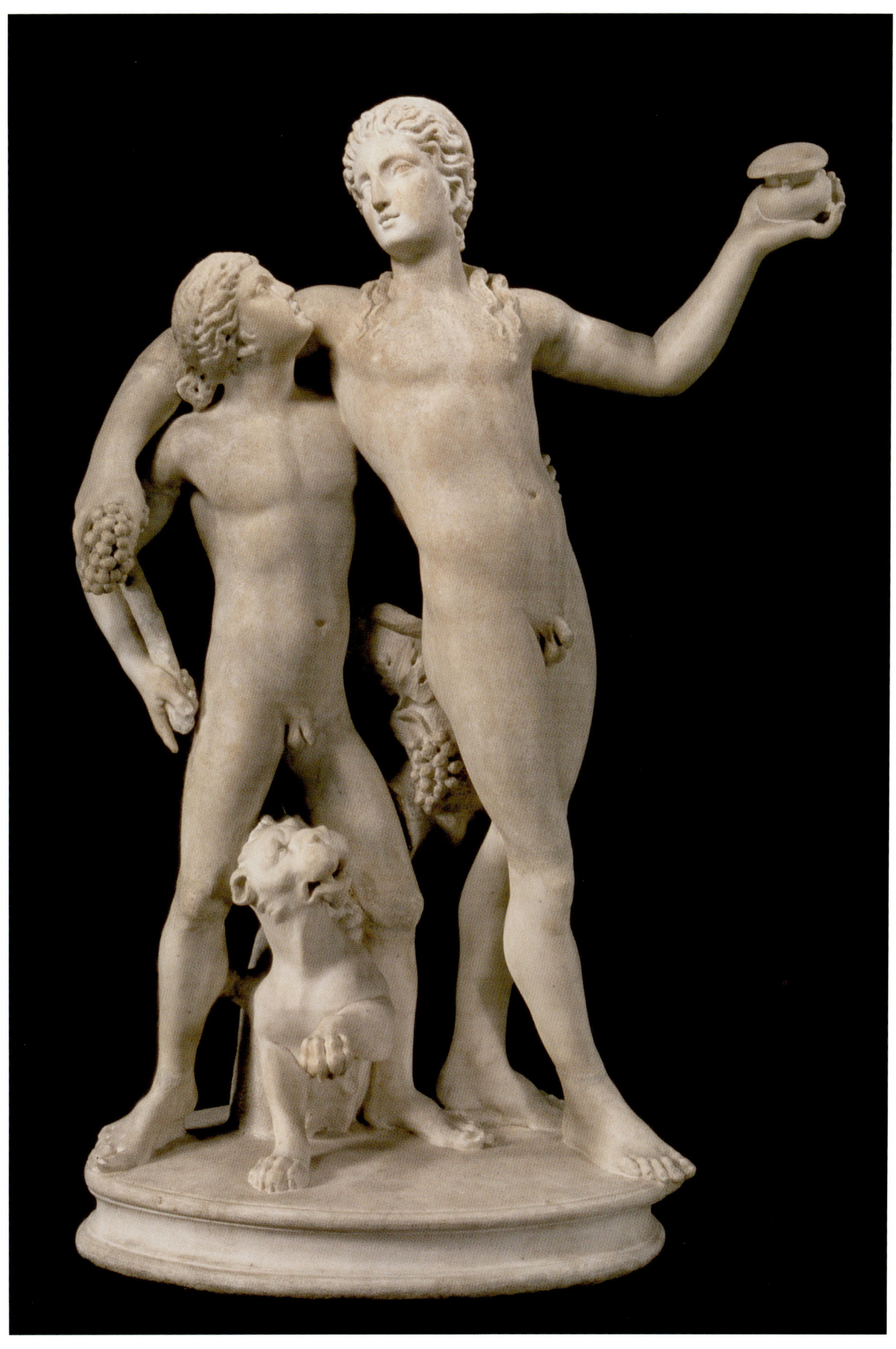

172 Roman, Dionysus and
Hermaphrodite, marble,
height 94 cm, Leiden,
Rijksmuseum van Oudheden

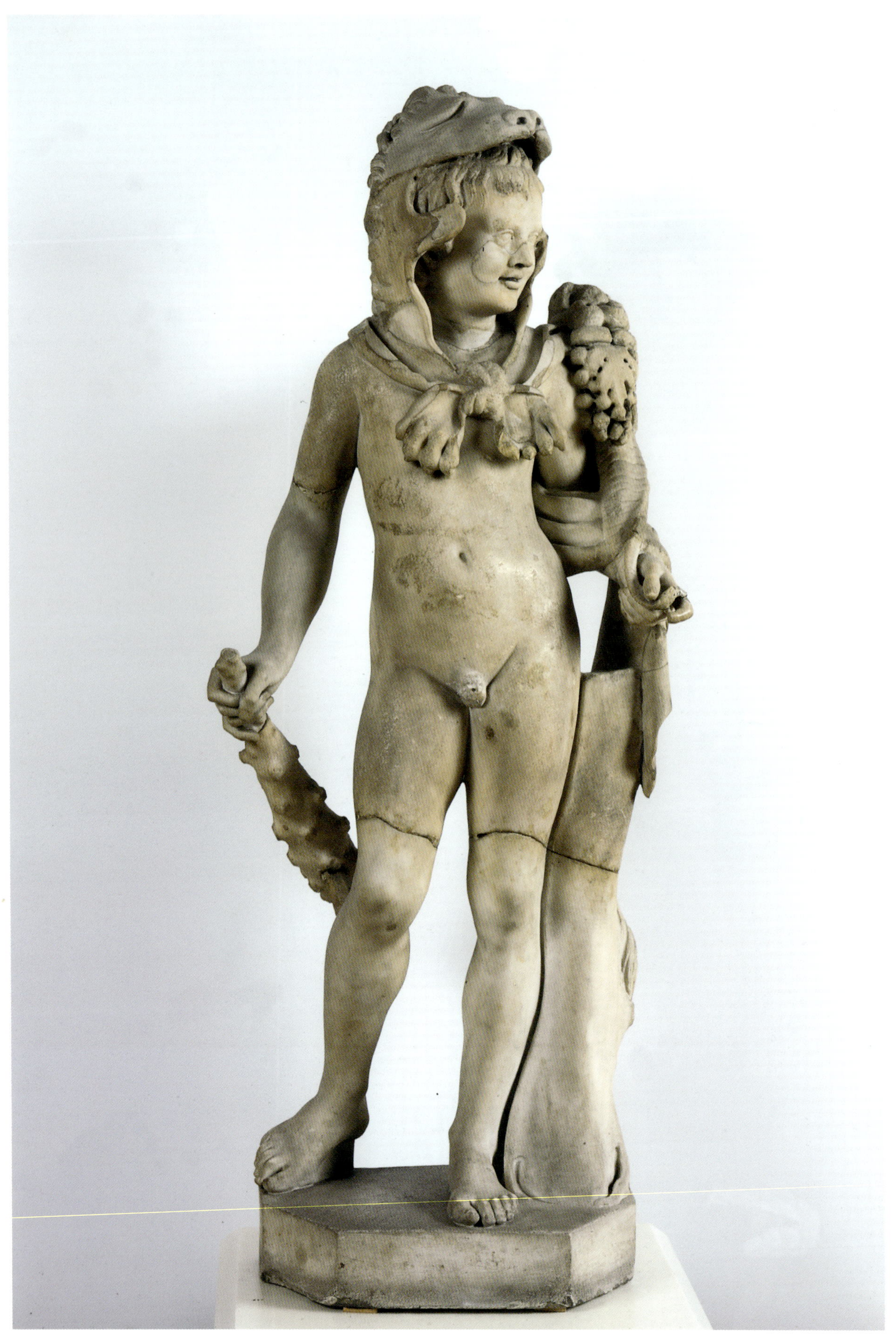

173 Roman, The infant
Heracles, marble, height
70 cm, Braunschweig,
Herzog Anton-Ulrich
Museum

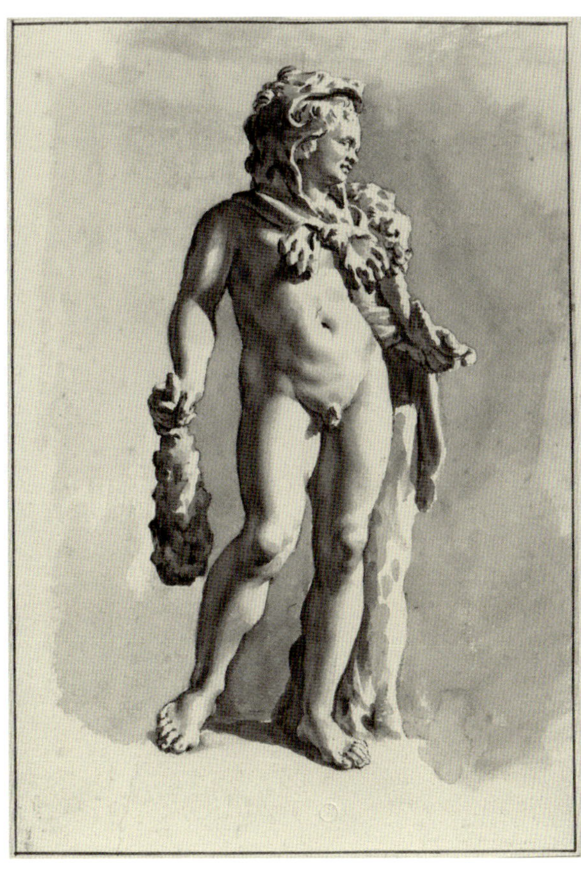

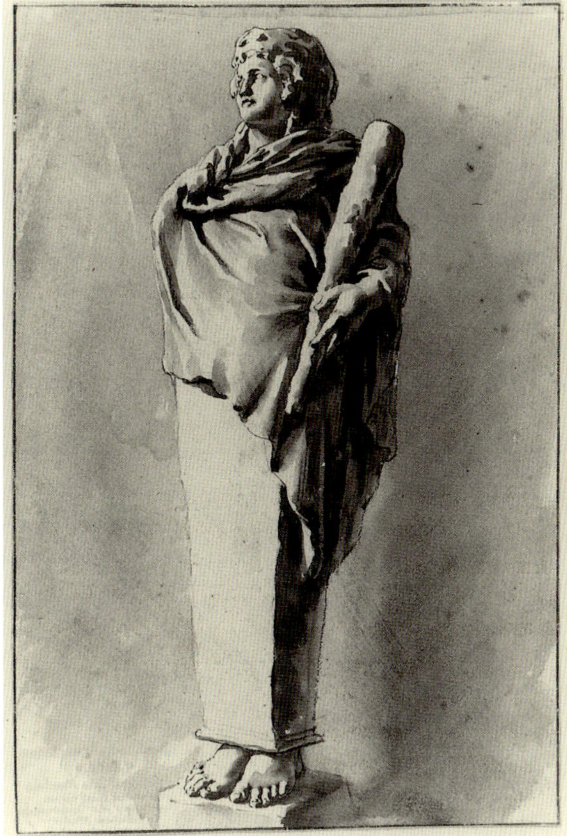

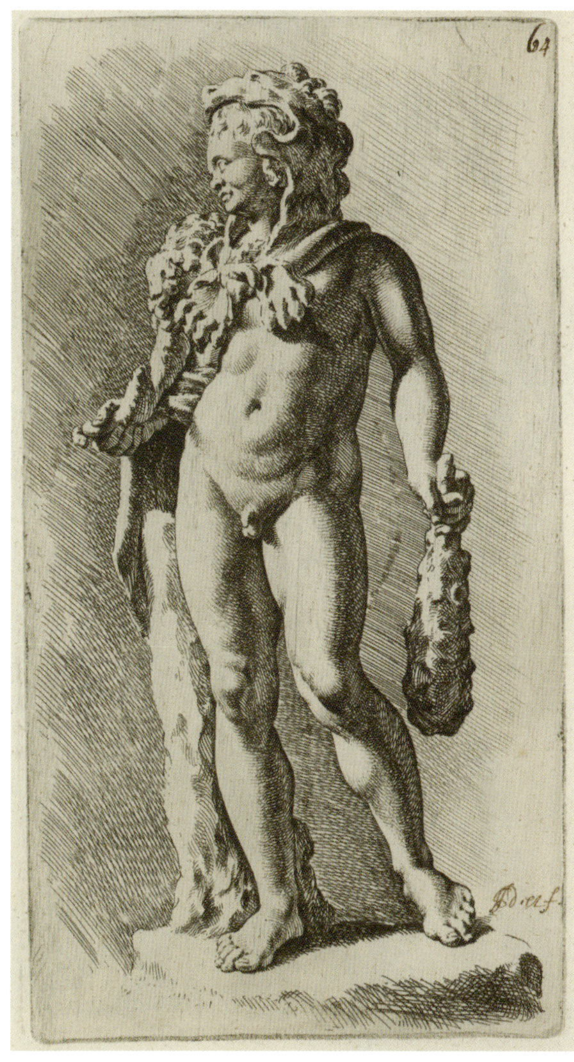

175 Jan de Bisschop, The infant Hercules, etching, in: Signorum
veterum icones, vol. 2, pl. 64, Amsterdam, Rijksprentenkabinet

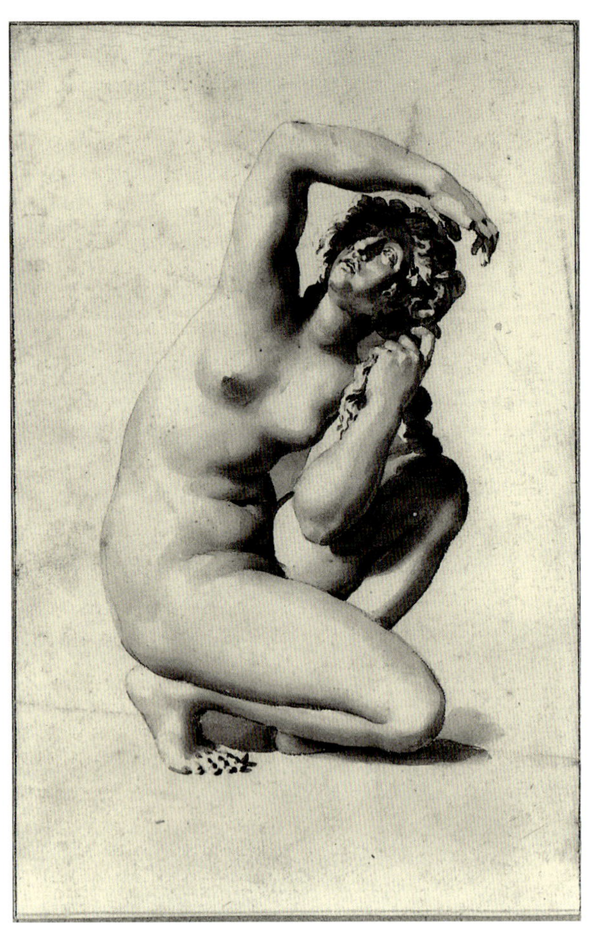

177 Jan de Bisschop, Kneeling Venus, pen and brush, washed, 21.5 x 13.8 cm, Paris, Fondation Custodia (coll. F. Lugt), Institut Néerlandais

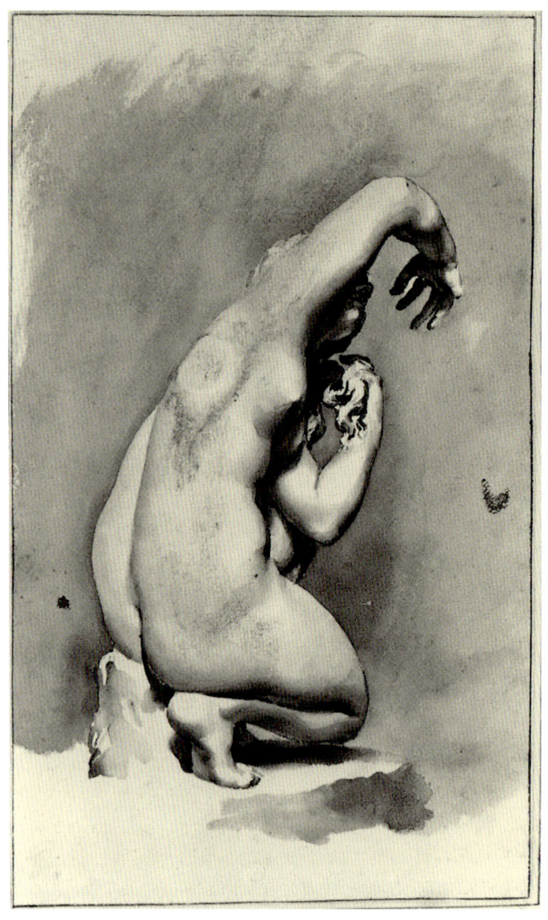

178 Jan de Bisschop, Kneeling Venus seen from behind, pen, brown wash, London, Victoria & Albert Museum

book was a Hercules as a child (fig. 173).[130] Here again this was a much restored Roman statue derived from a lost Hellenic example. It is probable that only the torso is genuinely classical. The drawing of the statue that was made in preparation for the etching, which De Bisschop must have done at Uylenburgh's workshop, has survived (figs. 174 and 175).[131]

The third statue from Uylenburgh's collection that De Bisschop illustrated was a herm of Hercules. The statue is no longer known, but the drawing that De Bisschop did of it is (fig. 176).[132] The last of Uylenburgh's statues that De Bisschop pictured has likewise not survived. It represented a kneeling Aphrodite and must have been a heavily restored Roman variant of a Hellenic

original.[133] De Bisschop made at least three drawings of the statue (figs. 177 and 178).[134] He also included in his book another version, unrestored, which was probably in Rome at that time. The author noted in the caption that he knew a third version 'in the house of the skilful Sir Pieter Lely, Painter to his Royal Majesty'.

In one of his notebooks Christiaan Huygens recorded that he had written Uylenburgh a letter on 8 April 1666: 'Ulenburg. Whether he knows of coins for sale'.[135] The letter itself has not survived. A letter written from Paris to his brother Constantijn on 2 July of that year reveals why he had approached the art dealer.[136] The coins were not for Christiaan himself but for Louis

130 Listed by De Bisschop 1668-1669, as no. 64 'A young Hercules'. See Van Gelder/Jost 1985, pp. 148-149. The statue is now in Brunswick, Herzog Anton Ulrich-Museum (inv. no. As 10) and is first mentioned there in 1753. It is a pair with the young Dionysus that De Bisschop illustrated as no. 66 and which was then with Hendrick Scholten. Ibid., pp. 150-151. See fig. 213.
131 London, Victoria and Albert Museum, in an album of drawings by De Bisschop (Dyce 1212.9-1889).
132 De Bisschop 1668-1669, no. 65. Van Gelder/Jost 1985, p. 150, suggest that the herm is probably the same as the statue that is first mentioned as 'A Hercules, bust' in Uylenburgh's inventory of 1675 (see p. 298); the drawing is reversed relative to the etching.
133 De Bisschop 1668-1669, nos. 79-80. Van Gelder/Jost 1985, pp. 165-166.
134 Two in the album in the Victoria and Albert Museum (Dyce 1212.10-1889 and 1212.11-1889) and one at the Fondation Custodia, Paris.
135 Huygens 1888-1950, vol. 6, p. 22. Leiden, Universiteitsbibliotheek, Hugeniorum, codex 3 (Hug. 3, book C), p. 269. He had written to Carcavy on the same day. The summary of this letter reads: 'Carcavy, que je partiray dans 8 ou 10 jours et que j'auray soin de ses livres et des medailles'.
136 Huygens 1888-1950, vol. 6, pp. 56-58.

236

xiv's librarian, Pierre de Carcavy, who had a
large library and coin collection. Uylenburgh
had sent Huygens a list of coins from a collection
that was apparently available. Huygens had taken
this 'memoire' to the collector and translated it
for him. Carcavy was only interested in part of it,
but wanted to have the whole collection sent to
Paris so that he could better make his selection.
However, Huygens doubted whether the owner
would be prepared to do that. It can be seen from
Huygens's letter that Uylenburgh did not have
coins in stock, but that he was willing to go looking for them on request.

THE STOCK IN 1675

The main sources for our knowledge of the paintings and statues that Uylenburgh owned are the
inventory and the valuation drawn up in 1675.
The inventory is dated 27 and 28 March and 26
and 27 April. It includes the household effects and
the trade stock and is printed here in full (p. 295-
300). Uylenburgh's own valuation of 19 April,
which is also reproduced here (fig. 179), covers
a large selection from his holdings of paintings
and statues, which he transferred to his creditors
in order to discharge his debts.[137] Almost all the
paintings that appear on the valuation list can be
found in the inventory, with the exception of a
large Jordaens (fig. 188), a work by Anthonie van
Hoeck, a painting done by Uylenburgh himself
in collaboration with Lingelbach, and seven
works that were with Lely in England.

Although it would be hard to overestimate
the significance of the inventory, it is important
to emphasise that it is a snapshot of a moment
in time, when the glory days of the firm were
already in the past. Moreover, Uylenburgh had
staged a sale a few months earlier but there are
no records of what he was offering.[138] The fact
that there are works in the valuation that do not
appear in the inventory tells us that the latter
does not represent the full extent of Uylenburgh's property. Strikingly, there are no drawings or prints listed in the inventory and no
works by Uylenburgh himself. The latter could
be an indication that Uylenburgh had effectively

given up painting or confined himself to making large works as commissions. The family
portraits, which are not mentioned anywhere
but must certainly have existed, had probably
already been 'secured'. It is conceivable that
Uylenburgh had already disposed of the cheaper
studio work and/or the prints and drawings at
an earlier sale.

We will now look first at the statues and then
at the paintings. For clarity, we shall deal briefly
with the paintings by their country of origin and
the century in which they were created, devoting
the greatest attention to the Dutch works by contemporaries. Aside from the works in the inventory we shall also discuss the paintings that
Uylenburgh had on consignment in 1675.

Sculptures

In 1675 Uylenburgh had 52 sculptures, around
half of which were portrait busts. The descriptions of these works are minimal, making it
impossible to get a good insight into exactly what
he had. In the valuation he described his statues as
'all my marble statues, and modelled in the round,
by Quellinus, pander and bronze'. So there were
marble, terracotta and bronze statues. It is not
clear what is meant by 'pander'. Most of the statues will have been regarded as antique, although
there were some contemporary sculptures among
them. The only two sculptors mentioned by name
are Artus Quellinus and Rombout Verhulst.
Uylenburgh owned three 'modelled statuettes',
'two portals of the town hall' and a 'children
and a goat' by Quellinus, and a relief of the same
subject by Verhulst (fig. 180).[139]

From 1650 to 1664-1665 the Antwerp sculptor
Quellinus had worked on the decorations for the
Amsterdam Town Hall (now the Royal Palace).
In 1660, with Uylenburgh, he had made a selection from the Reynst brothers' collection for the
Dutch Gift.[140] Most of his terracotta designs for
the Town Hall remained the property of the
city, but some were intended for the free market.
Quellinus moreover made different versions of
some designs. The 'two portals of the town hall'
were probably designs for the semi-circular decorations above the entrances to the offices in the
Town Hall. The reliefs of children and a goat,

137 Hereafter the numbers
in the inventory and the valuation will be given for the
paintings that are mentioned.
See Appendices, pp. 295-300
and pp. 301-305.
138 See p. 106.
139 See Scholten 2003 for a
terracotta relief of this subject
by Verhulst, which is now in
the Rijksmuseum and may
be the work in Uylenburgh's
inventory (inventory 1675,
statue no. 49).
140 See p. 67.

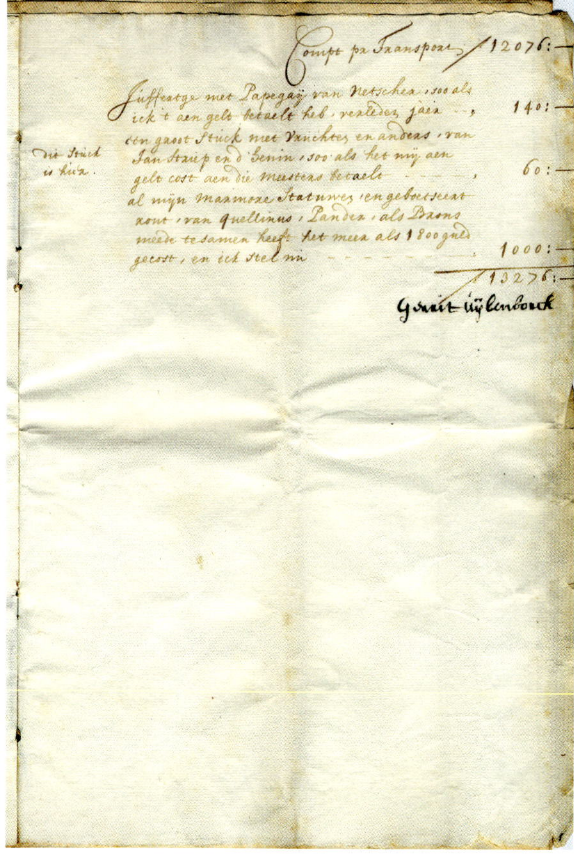

179 1675 valuation of Gerrit Uylenburgh's paintings, Amsterdam, Gemeentearchief

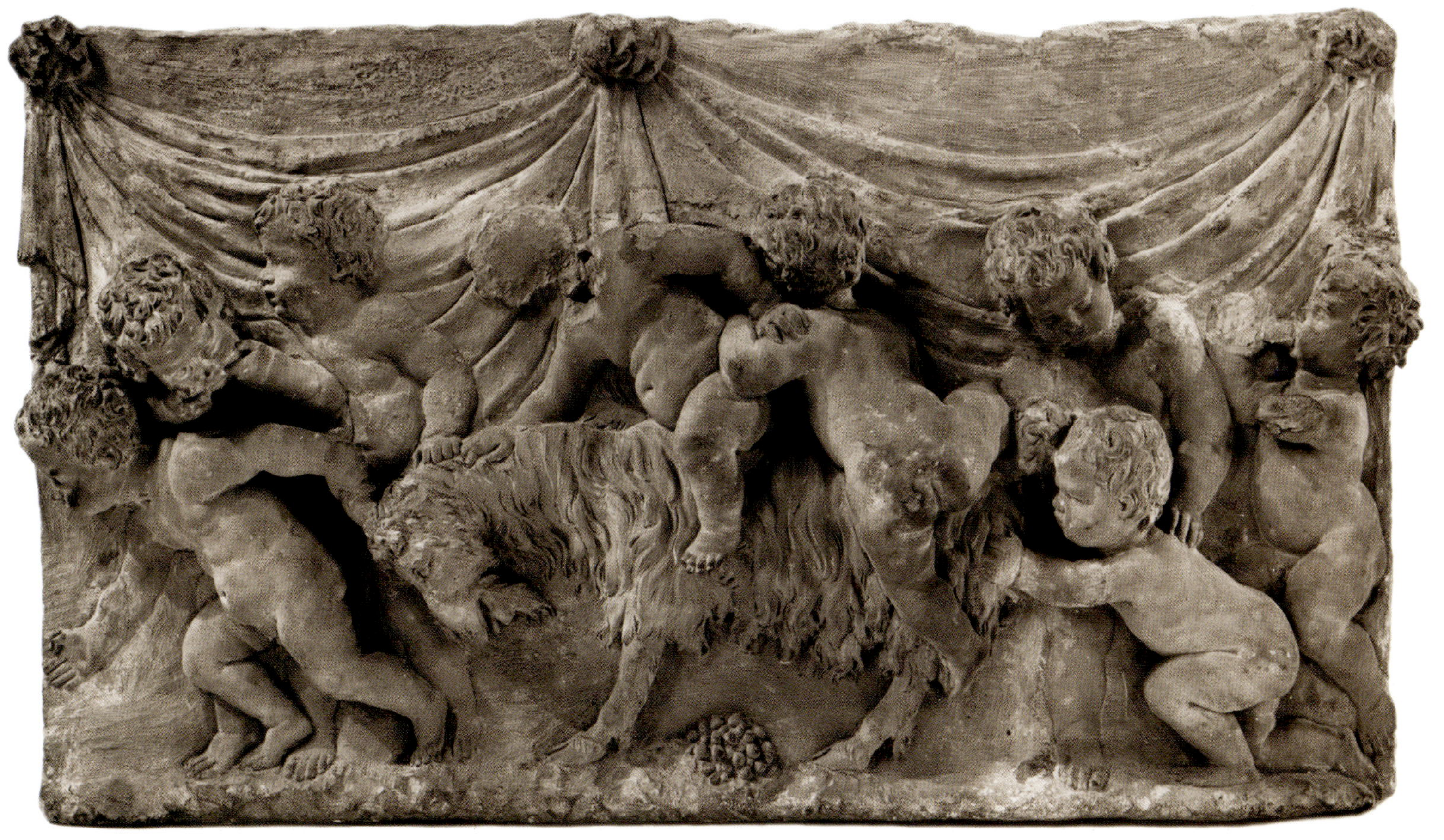

180 Anonymous, attributed to Rombout Verhulst, Children with a goat, terracotta, with traces of gilding, 36 x 64 cm, Amsterdam, Rijksmuseum

which Uylenburgh had in versions by both Quellinus and Verhulst, must have been inspired by François du Quesnoy's famous relief, a sculpture that was extraordinarily popular in the seventeenth century.[141]

In the valuation Uylenburgh assessed his statues at 1,000 guilders, with the comment that he had paid more than 1,800 guilders for them. In 1675, therefore, the average price of a statue was less than 20 guilders.

Italian and French paintings of the sixteenth and seventeenth centuries

The inventory lists 163 paintings; there are about 123 paintings in the valuation.[142] Nine of the works in the valuation do not appear to have been recorded in the inventory, so that we can assume that in 1675 Uylenburgh had at least 172 paintings in stock.

Uylenburgh had around twenty paintings that he attributed to sixteenth-century Italian masters such as Giovanni Bellini, Giorgione, Palma Vecchio, Titian, Il Pordenone, Paris Bordone, Parmigianino and Tintoretto. He had one or at most two works by the different artists. Most of them were Venetian masters and it is striking that more than half of them were portraits or 'tronies' (character heads). In comparison with the other paintings in Uylenburgh's valuation and given the illustrious artists to whom they were attributed, the average price of around 97 guilders was not very high. Uylenburgh also had six copies after sixteenth-century Italian masters. Four were after Titian (three of them after a portrait of a woman – the same one?), one after Tintoretto and one after Raphael.

The merchant Jan Bardewits had given him a number of early Italian works on consignment.

141 The relief is in the Galleria Doria Pamphilj in Rome. See Boudon-Machual 2005, pp. 276-279.

142 The paintings described in the inventory as '144 Three female heads' and '148 Three small heads', where in both cases it is not entirely clear whether this is one painting or three, have each been counted as one work. The precise number in the valuation cannot be determined because in one place it refers to 'about 20 items'.

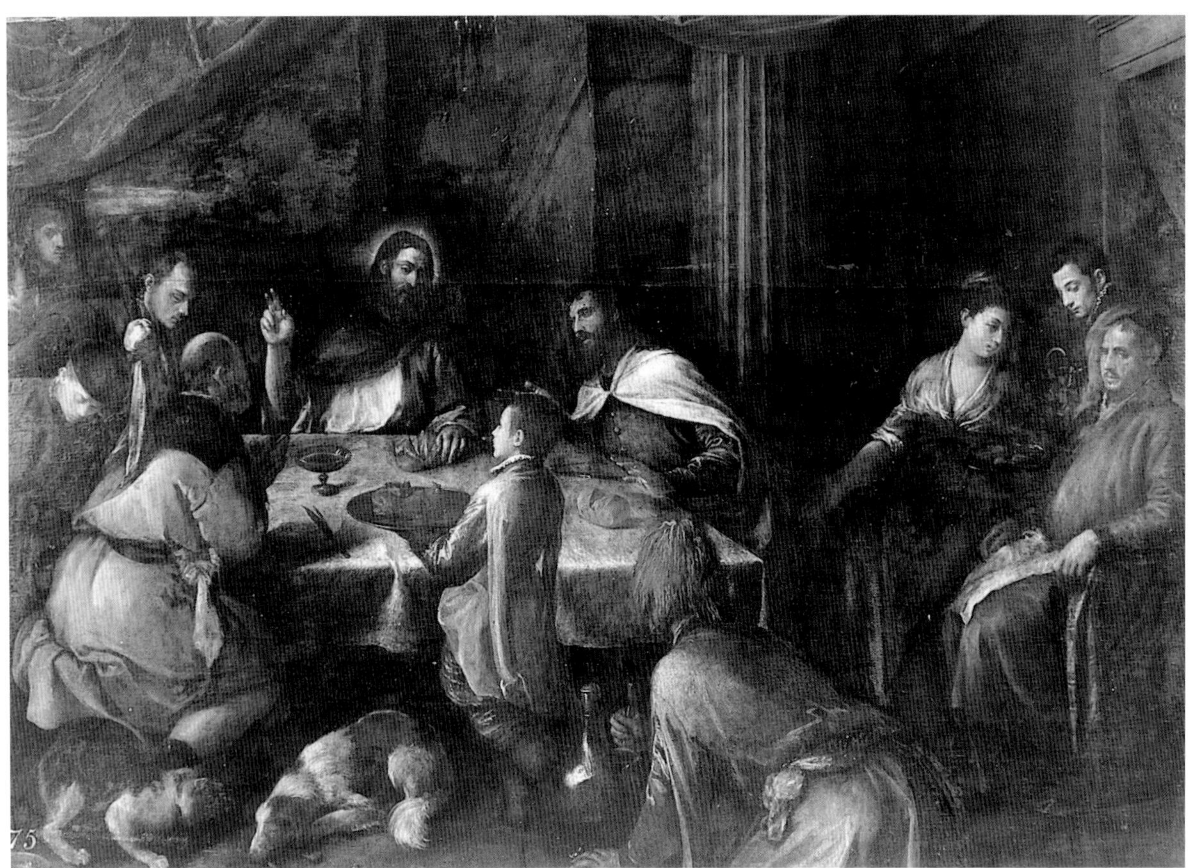

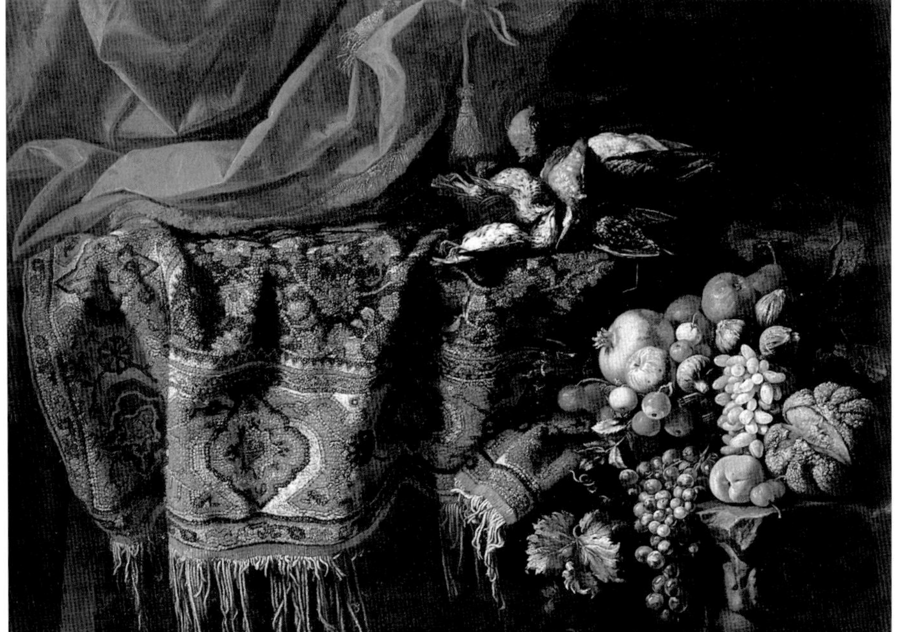

These were Bassano's Supper at Emmaus, a David and Goliath by Veronese, a head of a boy by Giorgione and a Minerva by Parmigianino.[143] The Bassano was probably the painting of the *Supper at Emmaus* that is now in Hampton Court (fig. 181) or a work very similar to it. There is only one known *Minerva* by Parmigianino, the painting that was part of the Dutch Gift (see fig. 34). This may have been a copy, but it could also have been a lost work, or a painting by another master who employed a style similar to Parmigianino's. The Veronese and the Giorgione cannot be identified.[144]

Uylenburgh had ten paintings by seventeenth-century Italian masters. At an average price of about 230 guilders each this was the most highly-valued part of his holding. There were works by

143 See p. 107, note 259.
144 See for the Parmigian-ino, p. 68. See for the Bassano, Shearman 1983, pp. 27-28. The provenance of this painting goes back no further than the Capel Collec-tion, *c.* 1720. See also Ballarin 1997, figs. 881, 882. There are several copies of the painting (among others in Dijon, Musée des Beaux-Arts, from the collection of Everhard Jabach). There is also an early painting of the same subject by Bassano (now Fort Worth, Kimbell Art Museum). Veronese's *David and Goliath* in Hampton Court has been part of the English royal col-lection since 1660. It is more-over the pendant to a *Judith with the Head of Holofernes.* See Shearman 1983, pp. 287-289.

240

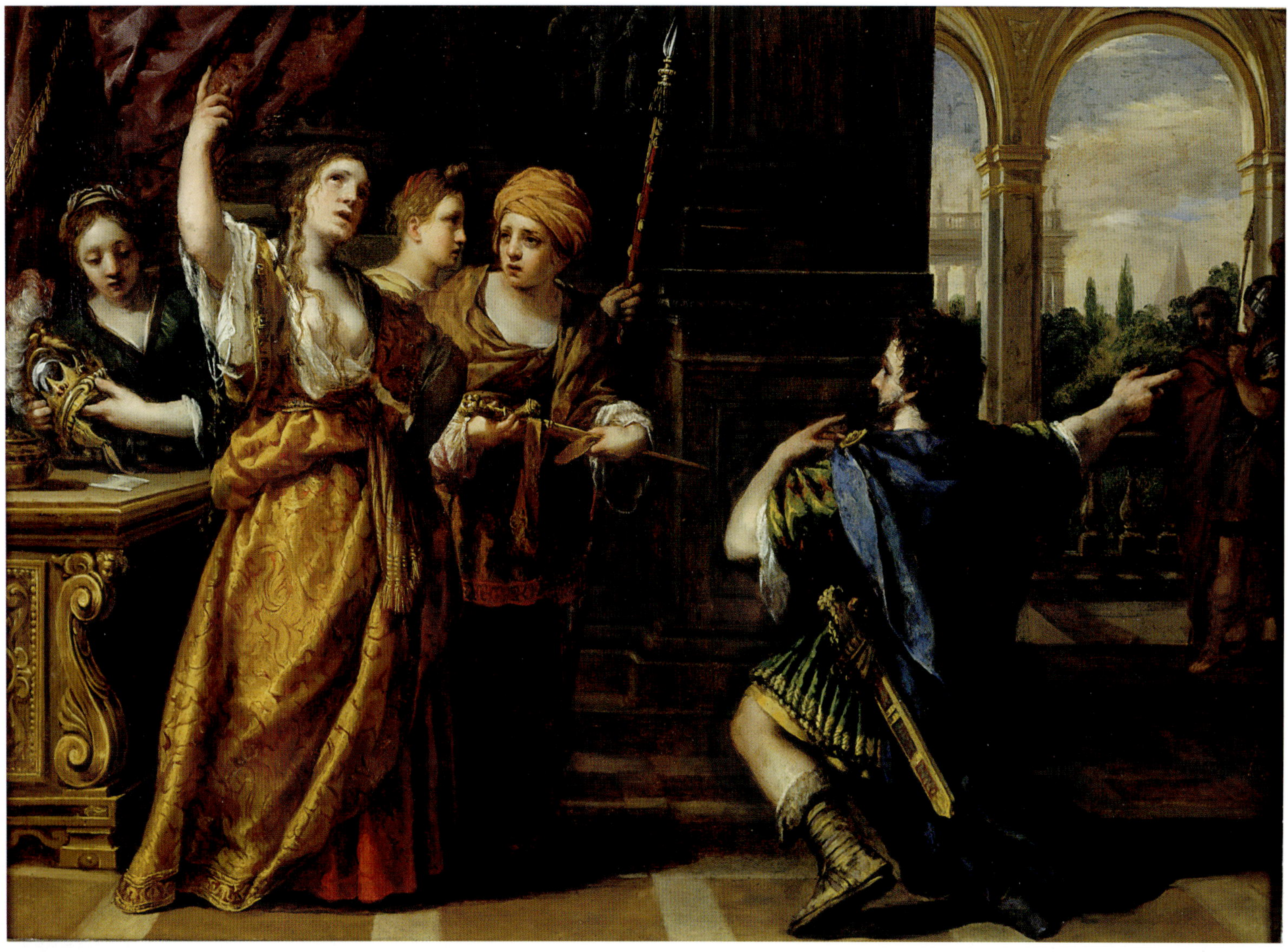

all sorts of different masters, among them a still life by Francesco Maltese (at 500 guilders the second most expensive work in the valuation, cf. fig. 182), Pietro da Cortona's *Semiramis* (400 guilders) (see fig. 183), Alessandro Turchi's *Lot and his Daughters* (300 guilders) (see figs. 184 and 185) and a *Woman with Satyrs* by Francesco Albani (150 guilders).[145] Uylenburgh also had a work by the Spanish-Italian master Jusepe de Ribera. Jean Lemaire was the only French painter represented in his stock in 1675.

Of the six copies after seventeenth-century Italian masters there were four after Guido Reni (two Mary Magdalenes, a Saint Sebastian and a Virgin with Christ). The other two were after paintings by Francesco Albani and one of the Carraccis.

Uylenburgh also had paintings by foreign artists of the seventeenth century on consignment from various people. Jan Bardewits had brought in a *Noah in the Ark* by Nicolas Poussin and a head by Caravaggio to be sold.[146] Jan Six had

145 The Francesco Maltese illustrated is intended to give an idea of his work; there is no reason to think that this particular painting is the one that Uylenburgh had, see Inventory no. 1 and Valuation no. 1; see for the Cortona, Inventory no. 43 and Valuation no. 44; see for the Turchi, Inventory no. 46 and Valuation no. 45 (there are currently two known paintings of this subject by Turchi, it is not clear which of the two Uylenburgh owned – and it may even have been another painting altogether); see for the Albani, Inventory no. 44 and Valuation no. 79. 146 See p. 107, note 259. Neither of these paintings can be identified.

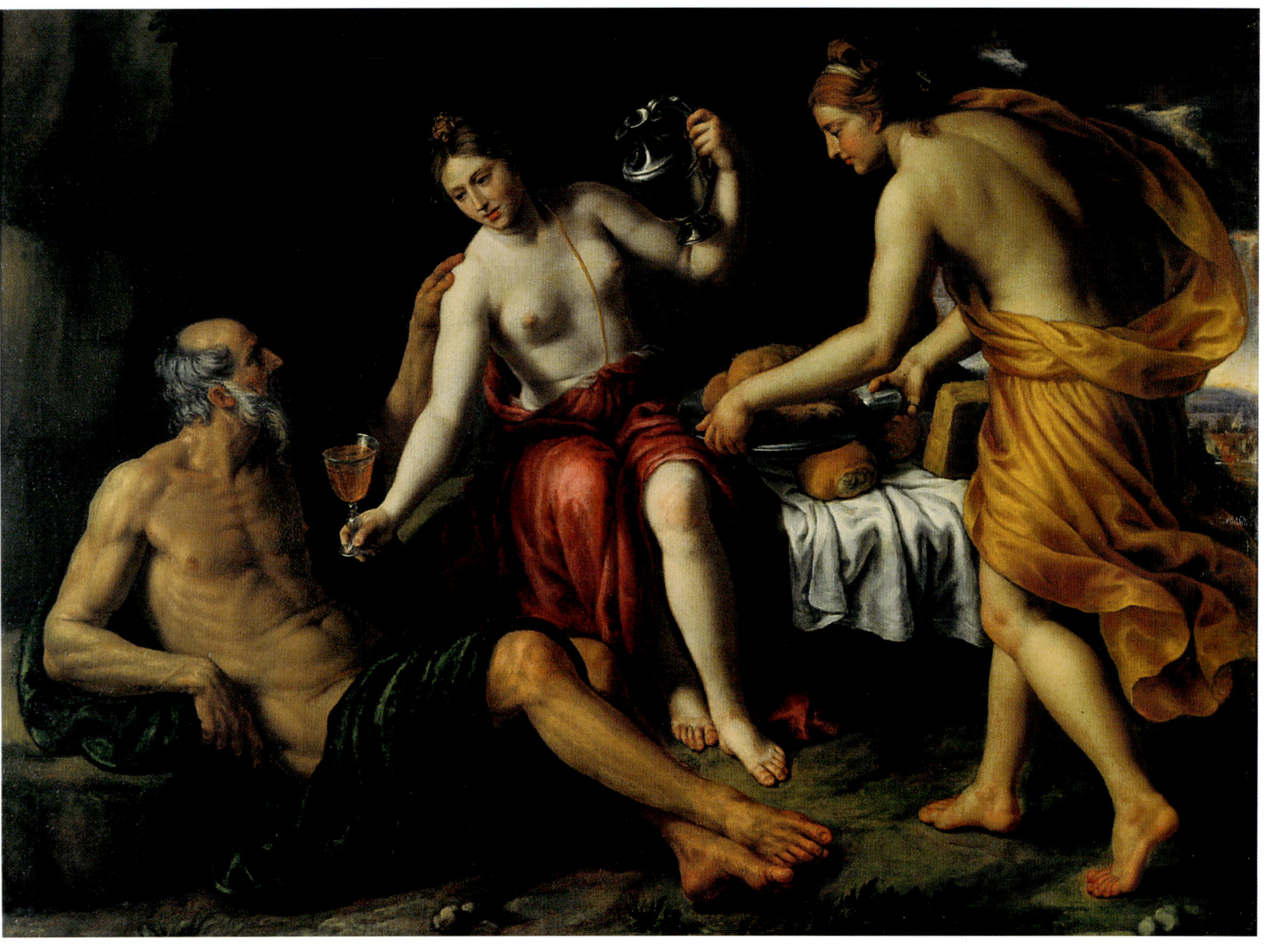

184 Alessandro Turchi, Lot and his daughters, canvas, 99 x 133.4 cm, Kingston, Canada, Agnes Etherington Art Centre, Queen's University, gift of Dr Alfred and Isabel Bader

borrowed against a *Vulcan* by Giovanni Benedetto Castiglione.[147] In 1675 the Hague painter Jean Gericot demanded the return of a landscape painted on copper by Pier Francesco Mola and a landscape by Agostino Carracci, which he had left with Uylenburgh a year earlier. He had also sold two other paintings to Uylenburgh, but the painters of these works are not known.[148] As well as work by himself and his brother Jacques, Wallerant Vaillant had brought in a 'Venus with a Cupid by Carel Lorijn', by which was meant Charles Mellin (le Lorrain).[149] It is not possible to link any of these paintings with extant works.

147 See for the other paintings he had also pawned, p. 106. There is no known painting by Castiglione that can be identified with this. Castiglione's only picture of Vulcan is now in Palazzo Doria in Genoa and is one of a pendant pair representing the four seasons; it cannot possibly have been the work that belonged to Six. With thanks to Timothy Standring for his information.

148 See p. 107, note 260.

149 See p. 108, note 261. There is no record of whether Vaillant owned any other foreign art besides the Mellin. We do know that for some time he was the owner of a small sketchbook containing copies of drawings by Parmigianino. Some of these are now in the British royal collection. Rogeaux 1999 regards the drawings as not by Vaillant. From the legend on the title page, which Rogeaux 1999 in fact misreads, it is at any rate clear that it belonged to Vaillant ('ce livre apparten a W. Vaillant pinter a este aupres le lecteur le 5 decembre 1655'). For this little book see also Popham/Wilde 1949, pp. 286-287.

242

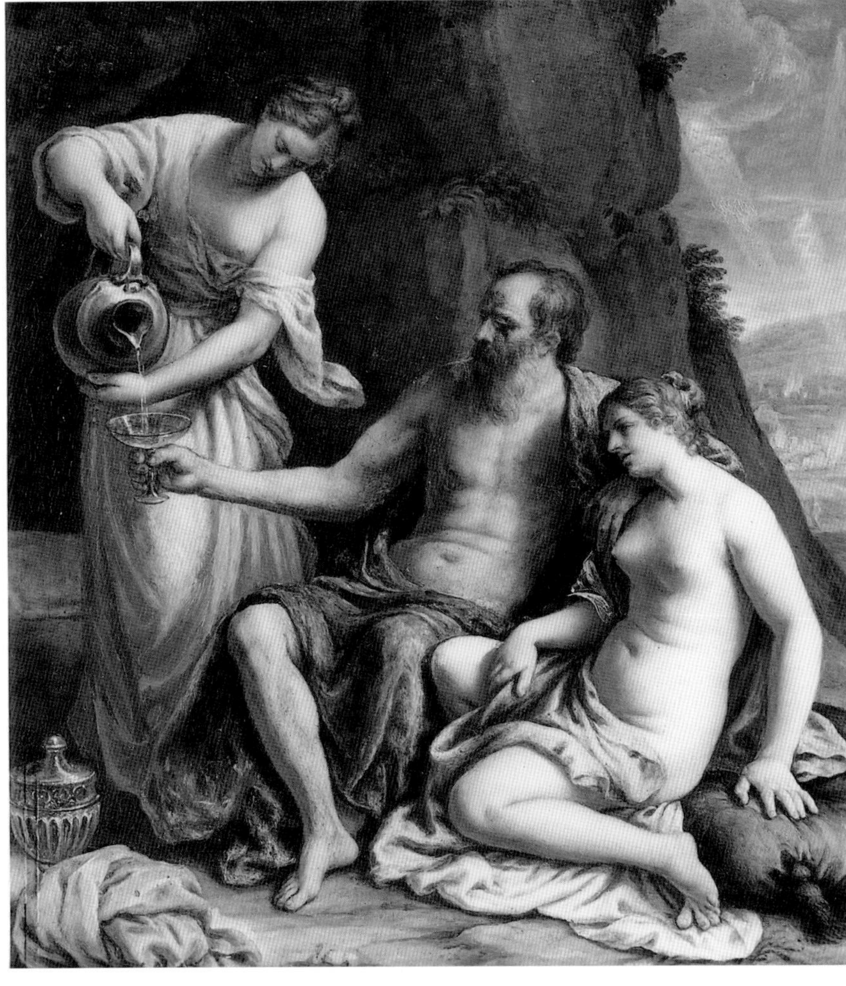

golden age of Flemish art, such as Rubens (three works, including the most expensive painting that Uylenburgh owned in 1675: 'a Capital piece by PP Rubens, Peace' for 650 guilders), Jan Brueghel the Elder, Frans Snyders, Adriaen Brouwer (three paintings, cf. figs. 187 and 209) and Jacob Jordaens.[151] Jordaens was the only one still living in 1675. Uylenburgh had two paintings by him, a *Visitation* and a portrait or tronie. Jordaens must have had longstanding ties with the Uylenburgh firm. In 1661 he declared that he had 'known' Hendrick Uylenburgh and had 'undertaken various transactions with him'.[152] Alongside the *Visitation*, Uylenburgh added the note 'cost me f 225.- at the time without frame'. This would seem to suggest that he had had the work in his possession for some time. The painting is probably the canvas that is now in Dayton (fig. 188). It is a late work that Jordaens probably painted in the 1650s or 1660s. Jordaens had regular contact with Amsterdam patrons during this period. For instance, he made an altarpiece for the clandestine church known as De Krijtberg in Amsterdam and in the early 1660s he painted four large canvases for Amsterdam Town Hall.[153]

The average price of the seventeenth-century Flemish paintings was around 165 guilders. Uylenburgh had three copies after Flemish masters (two after a portrait of a woman by Anthony van Dyck and one after a *Diana Hunting* by Rubens).[154]

In 1675 Jan Six redeemed a *Bear Hunt* by Frans Snyders and a flower still life by Brueghel (probably Jan Brueghel the Elder or Younger) that he had pawned with Uylenburgh.[155]

Dutch and Flemish masters of the fifteenth
to seventeenth centuries

Uylenburgh had only a handful of works by fifteenth- and sixteenth-century Netherlandish artists. Among them were paintings by R. van Bruggen, Aertgen van Leyden, Lucas van Leyden, Frans Floris (cf. fig. 186), Michiel Coxie and Willem Key.[150]

He owned some twenty works by Flemish masters of the seventeenth century. They were almost exclusively works by dead masters from the

150 See the Inventory, nos. 116, 23, 51, 113, 131 and 160. The painting by Frans Floris illustrated is probably not the painting that Uylenburgh had, but is intended to give an idea of the tronies that he painted.

151 In the Inventory, respectively nos. 54, 55, 135 (Rubens), 20 (Brueghel), 62, 128 (Snyders), 92, 106 and Valuation no. 88 (Brouwer), 136 and Valuation, no. 2 (Jordaens). The landscape by Brouwer illustrated is intended to give an idea of the sort of painting Uylenburgh may have had.
152 See p. 33.
153 D'Hulst/De Poorter/ Vandenven 1993, pp. 18-19, 279-281.

154 Inventory, nos. 12 (Rubens), 14 and 16 (Van Dyck).
155 See p. 106. Because of the brief descriptions, neither of the paintings can be identified.

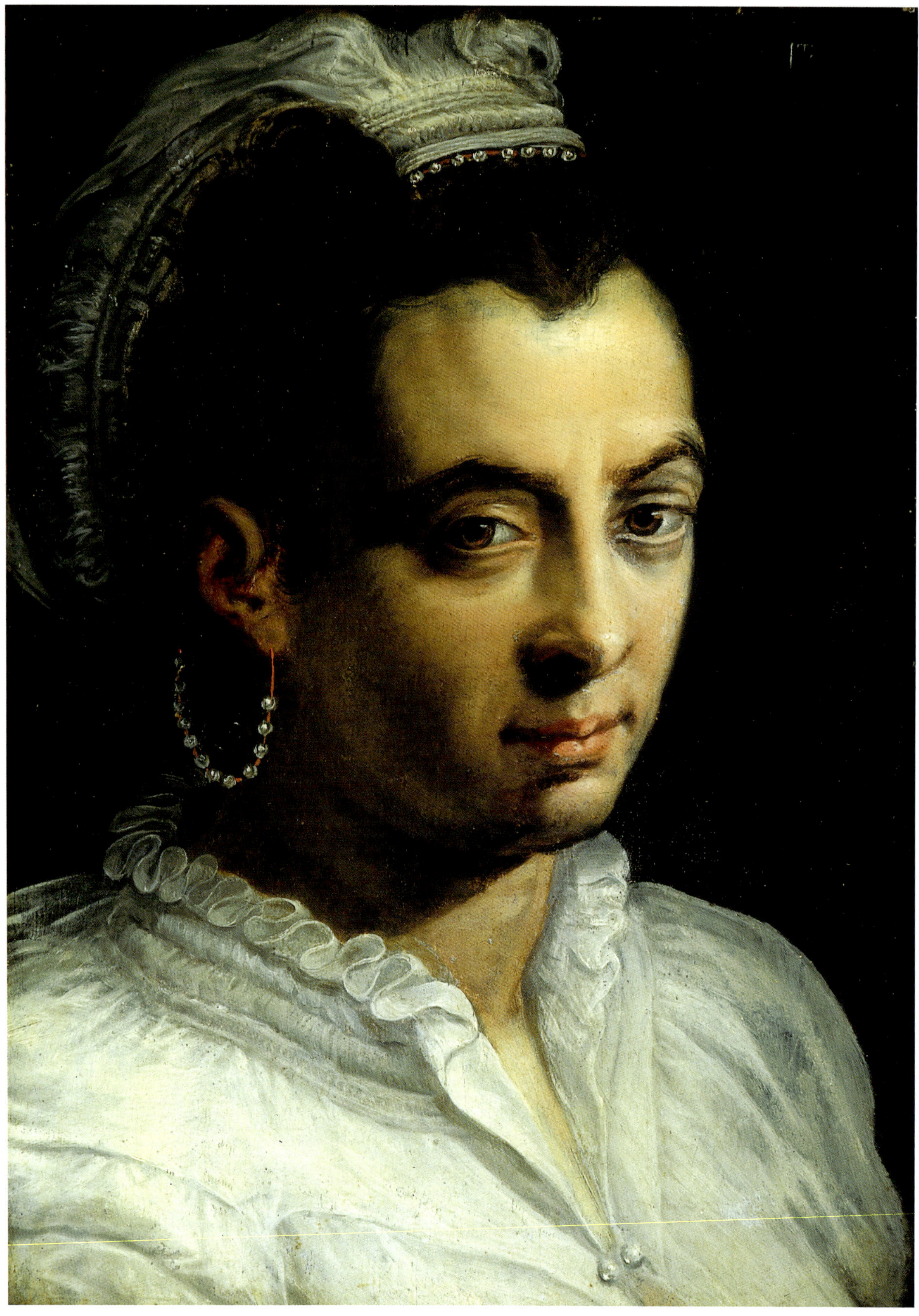

186 Frans Floris, Portrait of a woman, monogrammed 'FF', panel, 46.5 x 32.5 cm, Heino/Wijhe, Museum de Fundatie

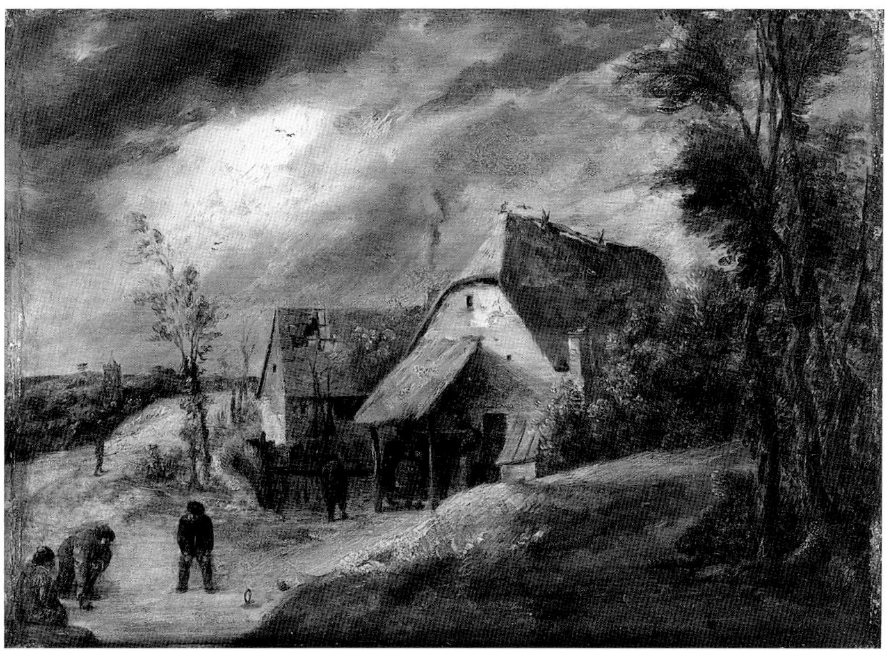

187 Adriaen Brouwer, Landscape with skittle players, monogrammed 'AB', panel, 24.8 x 33.9 cm, Staatliche Museen zu Berlin, Gemäldegalerie

188 Jacob Jordaens and workshop, The visitation, canvas, 162.5 x 111.8 cm, Dayton, Ohio, The Dayton Art Institute, gift of Mr and Mrs Elton F. MacDonald

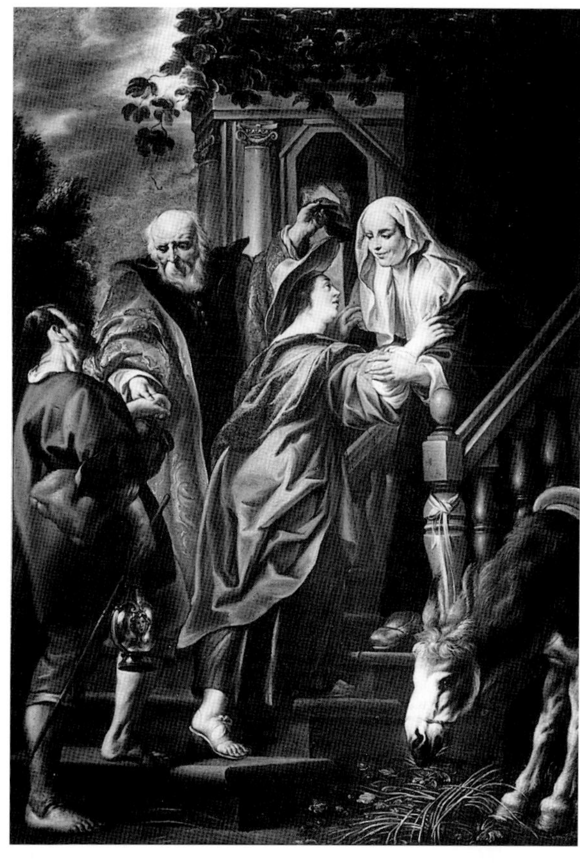

Dutch masters of the seventeenth century

The majority of the paintings, at least 56, were the work of seventeenth-century Dutch painters. Most of them were by artists who had been working since Gerrit Uylenburgh took over the business from his father, although he also owned works by earlier masters like Porcellis, Hendrick ter Bruggen, Jacob Pynas, Hercules Segers (three paintings), Pieter Lastman, Karel van Mander and Jacob Backer. The average price for the seventeenth-century Dutch paintings was about 129 guilders. What is striking is that, according to the inventory and the valuation, Uylenburgh did not own any copies after seventeenth-century Dutch masters.

Uylenburgh must have kept in touch with some of the artists who were still alive in 1675 or who had died not long before. There were also painters who came to collect their own paintings when he got into financial difficulties. Let us look briefly at the most important artists from the various towns and cities and their possible further contacts with Uylenburgh.

Amsterdam: On 26 April 1675 Wallerant Vaillant asked for a number of paintings back. He came for a 'music piece' of his own and an *Apollo with a Satyr*, a *Bacchenale* and a *Narcissus* by his younger brother Jacques. This last work was most likely the painting that was in Schwedt Castle, but was very probably destroyed in a fire there in 1945 (fig. 189).[156] At that time Jacques was living in The Hague and he must have asked Wallerant to go to bankruptcy chamber on his behalf. Vaillant also asked for a large landscape by Jan Looten, an artist who was then living in London.[157]

Vaillant, a member of the same generation as Uylenburgh, came from Lille to Amsterdam with his parents in about 1642. His earliest known painting is a portrait of Jan Six dating from 1649. He was in Paris between 1659 and 1665, after which he returned to Amsterdam where he had great success primarily as a printmaker. He made innumerable mezzotint engravings after Italian paintings, often working from drawings by Jan de Bisschop. A number of these paintings belonged to Uylenburgh, among them two works attrib-

156 The date of the painting is difficult to read on a photograph. It could be 1671 or 1677. With thanks to Gerd Bartoschek.

157 See p. 108, note 261. See for the painting by Mellin that Vaillant also came to collect, p. 242.

158 See pp. 96 and 97.

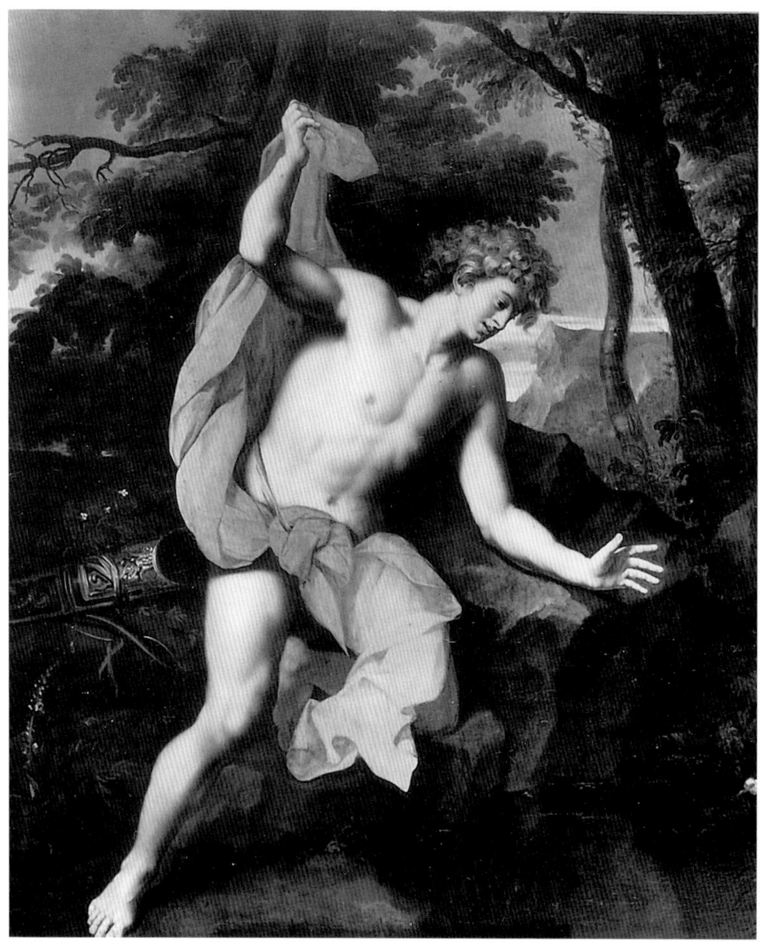

189 Jacques Vaillant, Narcissus, signed and dated 167[1], canvas, in Schwedt Castle before 1945, most probably lost in the Second World War

uted to Titian, which were part of the transaction with the elector.[158] He also made prints after the work of contemporaries, including Theodoor Ferreris and Caspar Netscher. Among his engravings after Netscher were his portrait of the art collector (and Vaillant's neighbour across the street) Abraham van Lennep (fig. 194).[159] Both the Vaillant brothers, Wallerant in Amsterdam and Jacques in The Hague, made statements supporting Uylenburgh in the case involving the paintings for the elector.[160] Wallerant also left his work on consignment with other art dealers besides Uylenburgh.[161]

In 1675 Uylenburgh owned two works each by the painters Adriaen Backer and Jan van Neck, which were valued relatively highly. He owned a *Diana* by Backer that had cost him 140 guilders (without a frame) and which he valued at 180 guilders. He also had an *Atalanta*, for which he had paid 250 guilders and which he thought would fetch 260 guilders.[162] By Van Neck he owned a *Europa* (purchased for 125 guilders and now priced at 150 guilders) and a *Venus*, which he estimated at 110 guilders.[163] Both were life size. Although it does not say this in so many words in the valuation list, it seems likely that Uylenburgh bought the paintings from the artists themselves. In 1675 Backer was one of his creditors, owed the sum of 76 guilders, probably for paintings he had supplied.

Van Neck and Backer must both have been apprenticed to Jacob Backer.[164] Adriaen was a nephew of this master, who had dealings with Hendrick Uylenburgh. Van Neck and Adriaen

Backer must have known Theodoor Ferreris well. Backer was with him in Rome, where they both lived for many years. They also both gave Jan de Bisschop drawings of classical statues for his sample books. De Bisschop's brother-in-law, Gerard Brandt, wrote a poem on the occasion of Backer's marriage in 1669.[165] Both Backer and Ferreris received a commission for a large painting in Haarlem Town Hall in 1671.[166] In the case involving the Berlin elector, Backer and Ferreris were on Uylenburgh's side.

According to Houbraken, Van Neck was 'a

159 Hollstein, vol. 31, 1987, no. 42, p. 87. The *Hebe and Cupid on a Cloud* bears the inscription 'Fareris Invent'. This must refer to Ferreris and not, as Hollstein thought, to Luca Ferrari da Reggio. See for the print after the portrait of Van Lennep, Van Gelder 1978.

160 See pp. 85 and 87.
161 After his death in 1677 Vaillant's stepmother demanded the money 'for the paintings and other art by the late Walrand Valjant given during his lifetime to Melchior Liedel for him to sell'. GAA, not. Jacob Matham, NA 4493,

pp. 461-464, dated 11 August 1678; Rougeaux 1999. We hope to return to the art dealer and agent Melchior Liedel in a later publication.
162 Valuation, nos. 51 and 67.
163 Valuation, nos. 56 and 57.
164 Houbraken 1718-1721, vol. 3, p. 75, says that Van Neck was

apprenticed to Jacob Backer. Adriaen Backer's training with his uncle is assumed in view of the family relationship and the somewhat similar style.
165 Brandt 1688, pp. 301-302: 'To the artist Adriaan Bakker on his marriage to Miss Eliza Kolyn'. While the opening

lines of the poem may be lacking in grace, they are undeniably informative 'Oh Bridegroom, who spent many days and years/ In Rome, the school of the greatest artists'. Brandt and De Bisschop, who had a 'fraternal friendship' for each other (De Haes 1740), had each married one of Caspar Barlaeus the Elder's daughters. On 19 September 1659 Adriaen Backer made his will in Amsterdam 'in order to go on a journey outside the country' (GAA, not. Nicolaes van Born, NA 2131, dated 19 September 1659).
166 See p. 224.

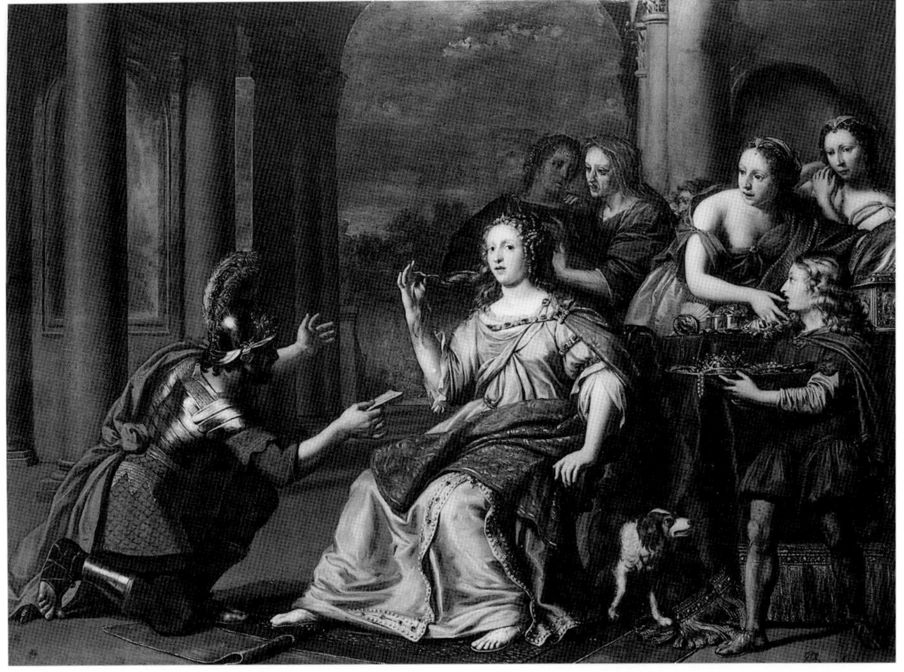

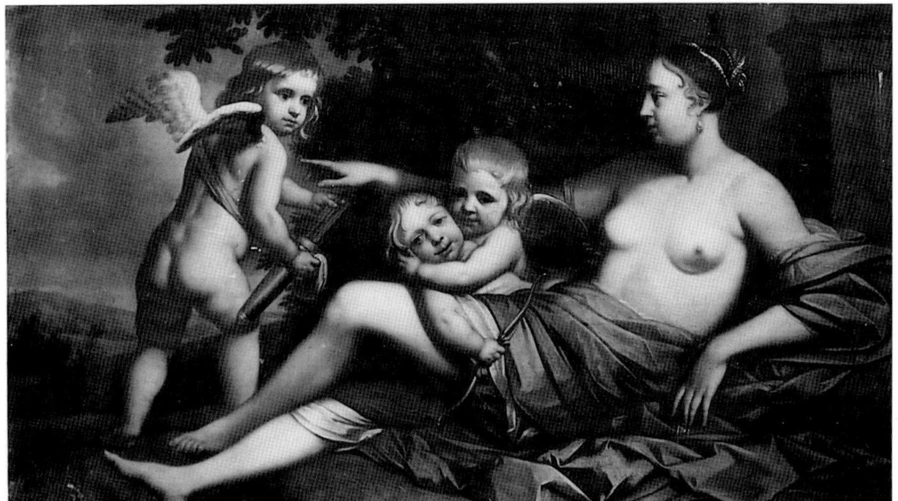

190 Adriaen Backer, Semiramis, signed and dated 'AB. 1669.', canvas, 122 x 166 cm, Haarlem, Frans Halsmuseum (on loan from the Elisabeth van Thüringen Fonds)

191 Jan van Neck, Venus with Cupid and putti, signed and dated 'J. van Neck 1670', canvas, 82 x 145 cm, Cognac, Musées de la Ville de Cognac

not been traced. Backer's *Semiramis* of 1668 gives a good idea of his style (fig. 190). The composition is also reminiscent of Pietro da Cortona's painting of the same subject, which may have belonged to Uylenburgh (fig. 183). Van Neck's *Venus* (fig. 191) dated 1670 must be similar to the work depicting the same goddess that Uylenburgh owned, but it cannot be the actual painting, since the one in Uylenburgh's inventory is described as 'a sleeping woman'.

In 1675 Uylenburgh also had paintings by many other contemporary painters who lived in or near Amsterdam, and works by artists who had died not long before, including Rembrandt, Jan van der Does, David Colijns, Jan Lievens and Gabriël Metsu. He may have bought them from the painters themselves. Those still living were Roeland Roghman, Frederick de Moucheron, Willem van Aelst, Willem Kalf and Cornelis van Everdingen.[168] Roghman must have painted in a style similar to Uylenburgh's; in 1672, however, he sided with Fromantiou. There is no information about any contact between Uylenburgh and the other painters.

The Hague: When Uylenburgh followed Fromantiou to The Hague in 1672, he succeeded in persuading a great many artists there to testify in his favour about the paintings he had sold to the Berlin elector. In 1675 he had paintings by three of them in his shop. The most important was Caspar Netscher, who with five works was also the best

great friend' of Ferreris.[167] The author also tells us that he inherited much of Ferreris's 'art on paper and drawings'. The three painters – Backer, Van Neck and Ferreris – worked in a similar classicist style. Sadly, the works listed in the inventory have

167 Houbraken 1718-1721, vol. 3, p. 76. Houbraken's information about Van Neck will be reliable, because he writes that he often visited Van Neck when he was bedridden.
168 'An antique tronie by the young Eeverdinge' appears as number 86 in the inventory. This must be a work by Cornelis van Everdingen, the son of the landscape painter Allart van Everdingen and the nephew of the history painter Caesar van Everdingen. He must have painted in his uncle's manner. Like his father he knew Rembrandt and it has been suggested that he was one of his last pupils. See for this Bredius 1909 and Van Eeghen 1969A. Both Jan Six and his cousin Pieter Six had work by him in their collections. Cornelis thus seems in any event to have moved in the same circles as Uylenburgh; see Davies 2001, pp. 28-29, Huys Janssen 2002, pp. 134-135. Sale Jan Six, 6 April 1701, 'Gods in the clouds by Kornelis van Everdingen; A Battle, by the same; sale Pieter Six, 2 September 1704, 'A woman etc in the Clouds by K.V.E.; Mercury and Juno in Heaven by ditto'. There was also a work by Cornelis in Het Loo Palace ('Heemeltje van Everdinge').

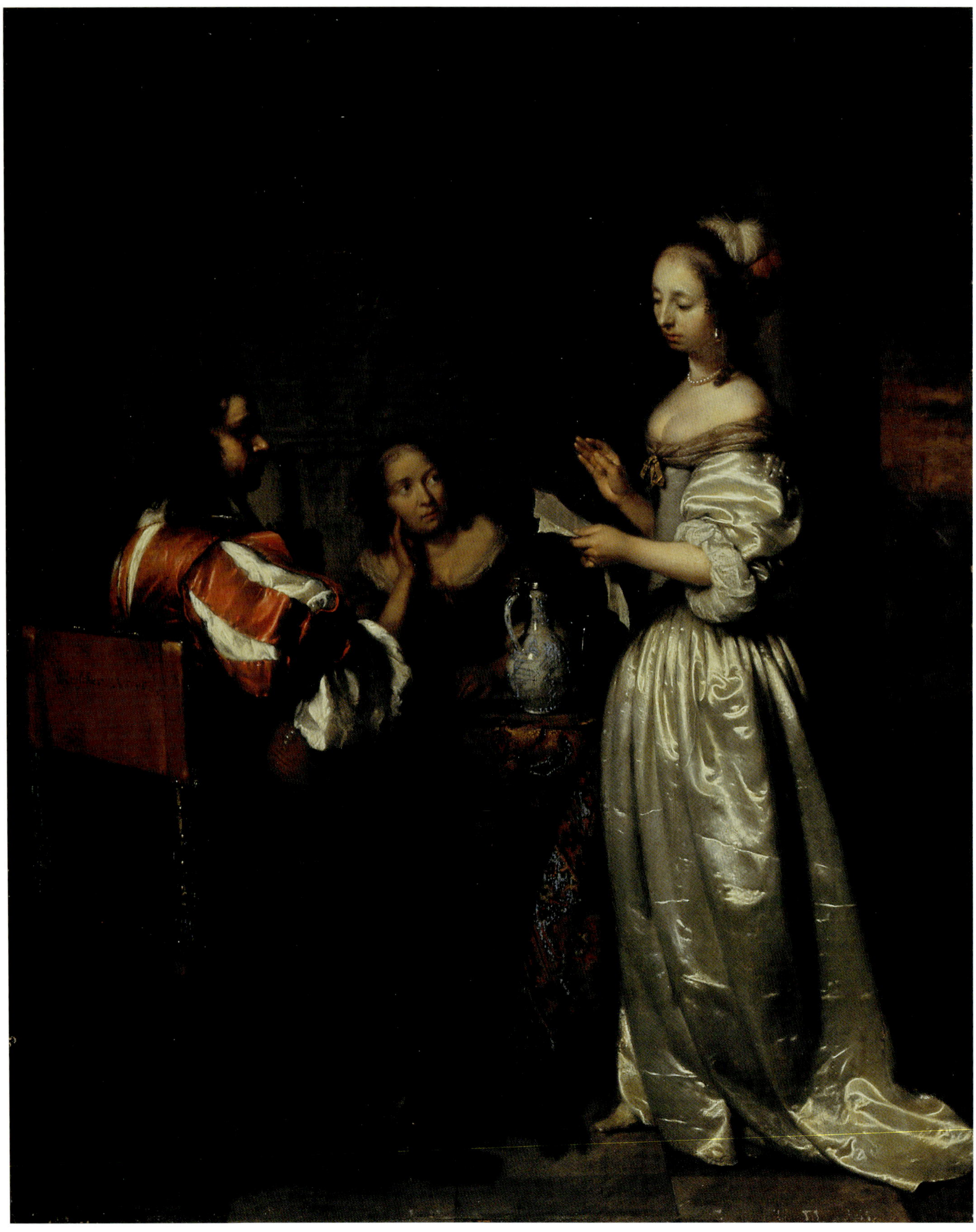

192 Caspar Netscher, Musical company, signed and dated 'C Netscher. Ao 1665', panel, 44 x 36 cm, The Hague, Mauritshuis

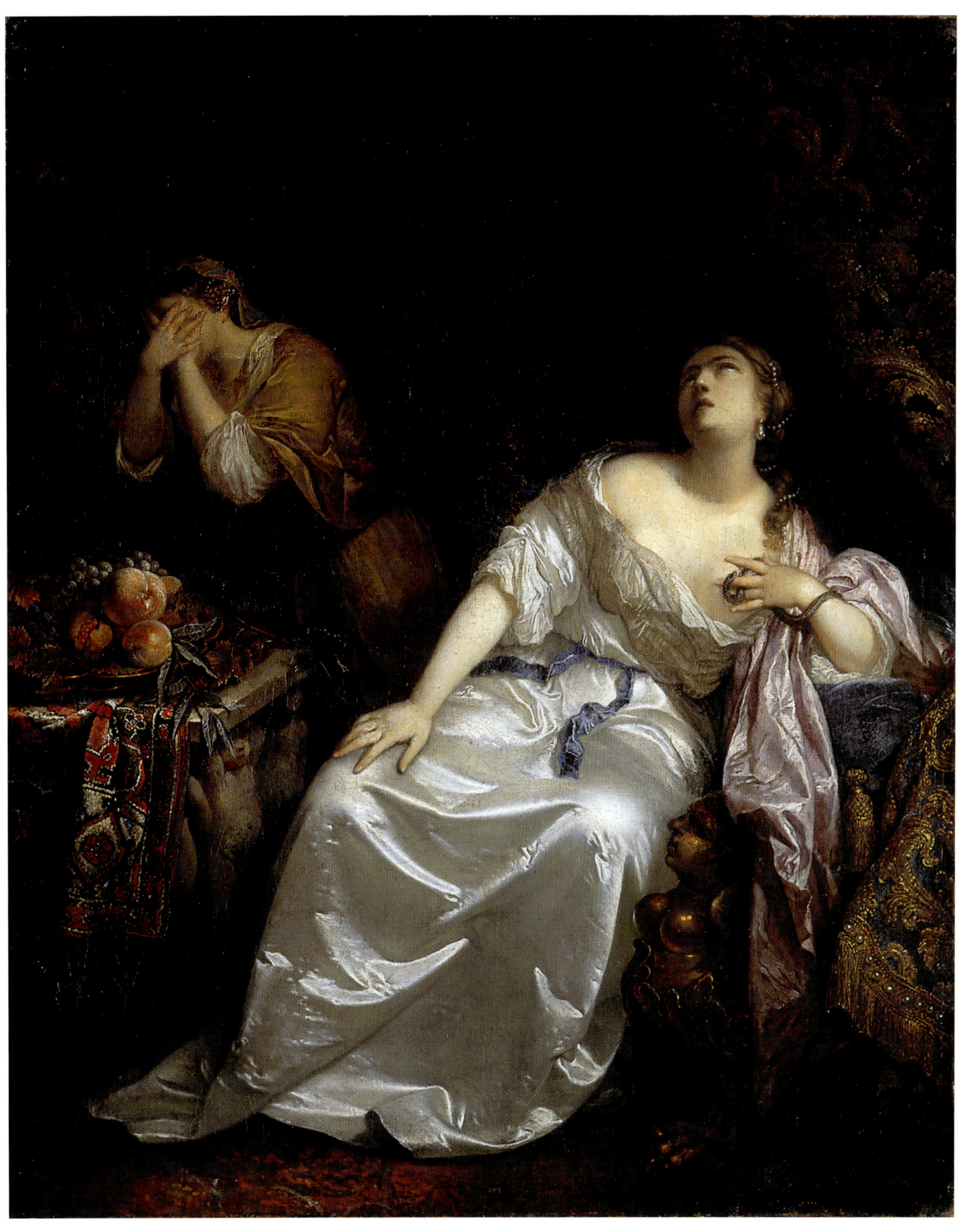

193 Caspar Netscher, The death of Cleopatra, signed and dated 'C. Netscher f. 1673', canvas, 53.5 x 44 cm, Karlsruhe, Staatliche Kunsthalle

represented artist. The paintings were given high valuations with prices ranging from 140 to 500 guilders. At 500 guilders, the 'excellent painting of singers' was – aside from the Rubens and the Francesco Maltese – in fact the most expensive item in Uylenburgh's possession (cf. fig. 192).[169] In 1675 four of the five paintings were not in Amsterdam, but were with Peter Lely in London.[170]

Uylenburgh explicitly stated that he had purchased Netscher's *Cleopatra* for 315 guilders cash from the artist himself in 1674. The work is without doubt the canvas dated 1673 in Karlsruhe (fig. 193). In the case of two other works Uylenburgh noted the purchase price but not who he had bought them from.[171] If he had acquired them directly from the artist, one would expect that, like the *Cleopatra*, they would be recent works. It seems, however, that Netscher had essentially given up painting genre scenes by the 1670s.[172] The works known today that fit the descriptions in Uylenburgh's inventory all date from the 1660s.[173] It is possible that Netscher still had early work in stock, but it must be borne in mind that Uylenburgh may have obtained these paintings, or at least some of them, from other people.[174]

In April 1675, at Jean Gericot's request, Netscher and Theodoor van der Schuer made a statement that a year before Gericot had handed over to Uylenburgh two landscapes by Carracci and Mola.[175] We can see that in the 1670s at least, Netscher had close contact with Uylenburgh. At that time he was one of the most eminent painters in the United Provinces and could command high prices. It had not always been so. Houbraken recounts how at the start of his career in Holland Netscher painted 'for the bloodsuckers, art dealers that is to say, who paid him low wages for his work, as well as buying in the same for a trifling price and peddling it for a high price: which unfair treatment did not please him, as a means of extinguishing the spirit and delight of artists, instead of encouraging the same'.[176] Houbraken does not tell us who exploited Netscher in this manner.

Although he lived and worked in The Hague, Netscher was also much sought-after as a portrait painter in Amsterdam. Leading art collectors and clients of Uylenburgh, among them Hendrick Scholten and Abraham van Lennep, had their portraits painted by him (see figs. 194 and 212).

Theodoor van der Schuer was another Hague painter whose work Uylenburgh owned in 1675. The work listed in the inventory as 'Time clipping the wings of a young boy' was described in the valuation as 'Two figures, Time'. Uylenburgh noted that he had paid 120 guilders for it and now valued it at 100 guilders.[177] It seems likely that he had bought the painting from Van der Schuer himself. He also owned a 'small landscape' by the artist.[178]

Aside from Netscher, Van der Schuer and Jacques Vaillant, we do not know whether the other Hague artists who testified on Uylenburgh's behalf in 1672 had any further contacts with the art dealer. Painters like Johanna van Aerssen, Daniel Haringh and Johan van Haensbergen were good friends of Netscher's, and it may have been at his urging that they spoke up for Uylenburgh.[179]

Leiden, Delft and other towns: Frans van Mieris and Gerrit Dou were the only two living painters from Leiden whose names occur in the 1675 inventory. Uylenburgh owned a 'woman sleeping' by Van Mieris and a 'St Francis' by Dou. He valued both works at 250 guilders.[180] The two artists were among the most famous of their day and had an international clientele. Uylenburgh had known Dou since at least 1660, when he collected paintings from him for the Dutch Gift.

In 1675 the virtually unknown Delft painter Pieter Ruyven asked for the return of two paintings that he had left with Uylenburgh on consignment. In the deed that he had drawn up by a Delft notary, he left Uylenburgh's forename open. This tells us that he did not know the art dealer well and was therefore not an old contact. Ruyven was the headman of the guild in 1674 and a man of standing in his day.[181]

Uylenburgh had one work by the Haarlem painter Theodoor Helmbreker, who lived mostly in Rome and had returned to Haarlem temporarily just around that time, in about 1674.[182] The art dealer owned two works by the Utrecht artist Cornelis van Poelenburch (cf. figs. 195 and 208), who had died in 1667.[183]

169 The painting in the Mauritshuis illustrated is one of the several extant paintings by Netscher that are candidates for the work that belonged to Uylenburgh. See the comment to the Valuation, no. 83.
170 See p. 268.
171 See Valuation, nos. 87 and 89.
172 Wieseman 2002.
173 See the valuation of 1675, nos. 66, 83, 84, 87 and 89.
174 The sums Uylenburgh mentions would seem to be on the high side when they are compared with the notes on drawings that Netscher made after his paintings. For the genre scenes they range from 50 to 140 guilders. These notes must date from the sixteen-sixties when the paintings were done. It is possible that the prices had risen significantly during the sixteen-seventies. There is a drawing after the *Woman with a Parrot* in Wupperthal (see fig. 207), which according to the inscription was sold for 100 guilders. If this is indeed the painting that Uylenburgh had in 1675, we can see that the price had gone up to 140 guilders. See for Netscher's drawings Wieseman 2004, pp. 251-257.
175 See p. 107, note 260.
176 Houbraken 1718-1721, vol. 3, p. 94.
177 Inventory, no. 129 and Valuation, no. 68.
178 Inventory, no. 120.
179 See p. 87, note 170.
180 Inventory, nos. 105 and 110 and Valuation, nos. 64 and 34.
181 See p. 108. Montias 1982, pp. 216, 374.
182 See Inventory, no. 96
183 See Inventory, no. 104 and Valuation, nos. 29 and 85.

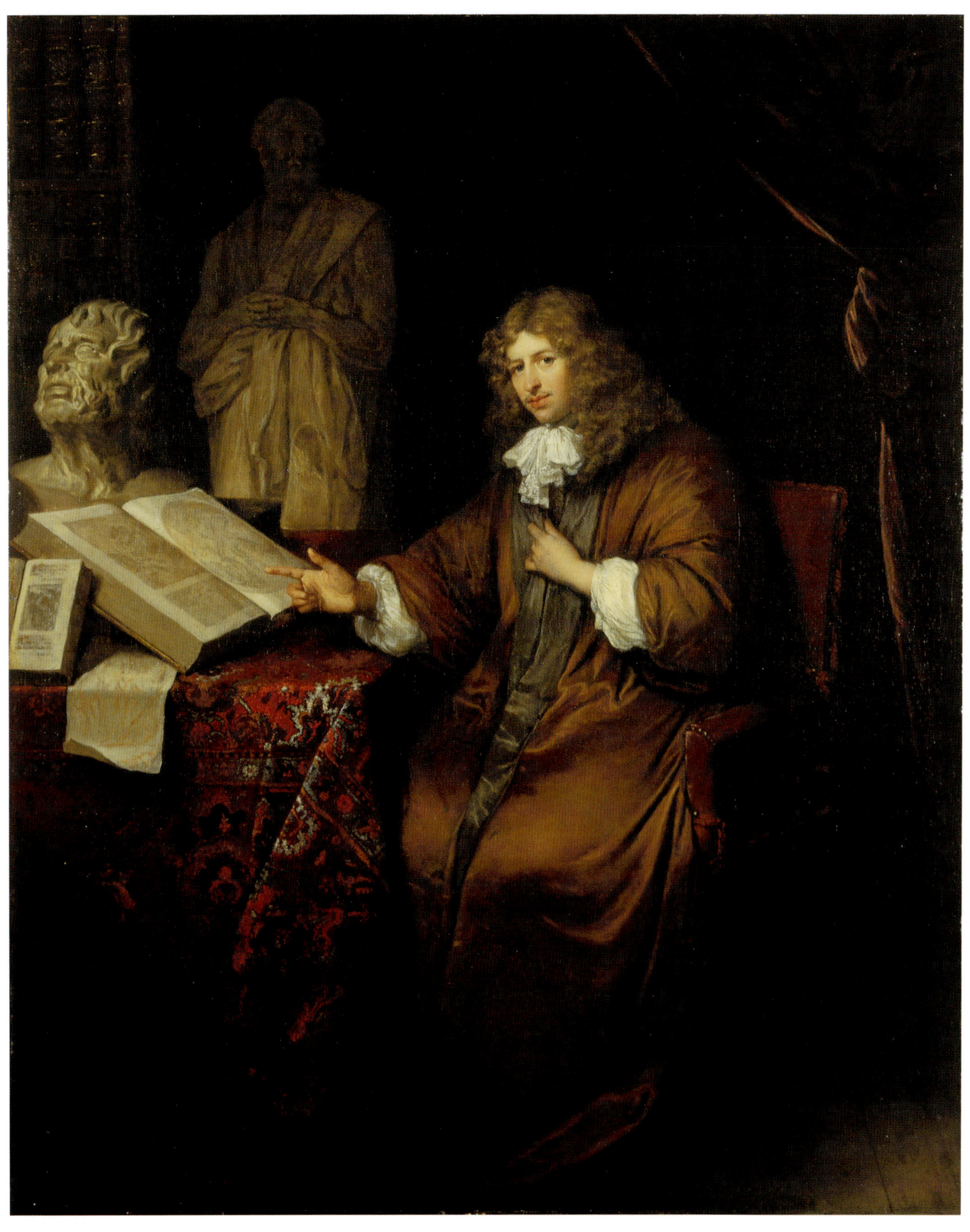

194 Caspar Netscher, Portrait of Abraham van Lennep, signed and dated 'C Netscher 1672', canvas, 55 x 45.3 cm, Paris, Fondation Custodia (coll. F. Lugt), Institut Néerlandais

Summing up the stock, we can say that customers could go to Uylenburgh primarily for original paintings by Dutch contemporaries, works by Italian masters of the sixteenth and seventeenth centuries, Flemish paintings by Rubens and his contemporaries, classical and modern statues, drawings – probably chiefly by Italian masters – and prints. They could also buy copies of the works by the Flemish and Italian painters, which would have been significantly cheaper than the originals. In terms of works by his Dutch contemporaries, Uylenburgh appears to have had a certain preference for classicist paintings by masters like Adriaen Backer and Jan van Neck. The Dutch and Flemish Italianates were well represented, with works by Lingelbach, Frederick de Moucheron, Cornelis van Poelenburgh, Alexander Petit and Jan van der Does. He owned a few genre scenes by Netscher, Metsu and others. As a good dealer Uylenburgh kept pace with the tastes and fashion of the day, and he may also have influenced trends through the work he chose to stock. He appears to have been especially authoritative in the Republic in the field of Italian and Flemish masters. He must also have had a particular liking for Dutch painters who had been to Italy or at least drew their inspiration from Italian art.

As early as 1660, Constantijn Huygens the Younger had lamented that 'the Italians are so much in fashion here that compared with their prices the rest is nothing'.[184] Uylenburgh seems to have taken advantage of this partiality. However, we must not forget that he also had countless other paintings. He kept a varied range in his shop, although customers going to him could expect to find mainly paintings in the higher price brackets.

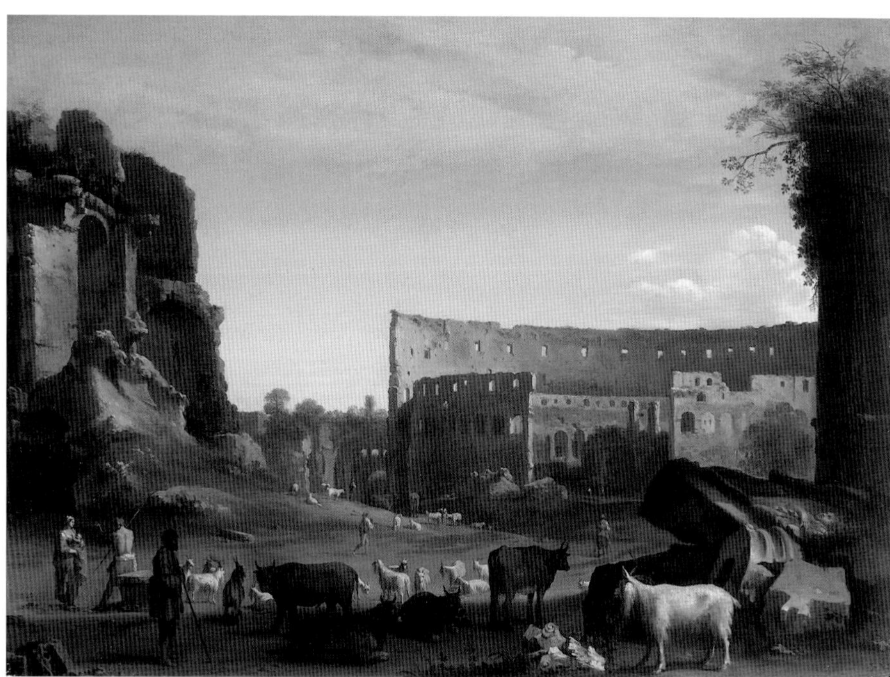

195 Cornelis van Poelenburch, The Colosseum in Rome, panel, 44.4 x 60 cm, Toledo, Ohio, The Toledo Museum of Art

Courant of 13 March 1666, for instance, there was an advertisement about the sale of the collection of Johan Heurnius, 'counsel in ordinary of the Court of Utrecht'. His heirs wanted to sell the collection of 'most excellent and rare art of Paintings and Print Albums by all the most admired masters [...] as a whole or separately'. According to the notice, the 'Sale Bill' could be obtained from 'Gerrit van Uylenburg' in Amsterdam.[185] More important to Uylenburgh, however, were the many valuations he undertook, and he was also sometimes called in for his expertise. Before we discuss this aspect of his business, we shall look briefly at his work as a restorer.

Restorations, valuations and expertise

As an art dealer, Gerrit Uylenburgh did more than just sell paintings and have painters working for him. There were various other activities directly related to his profession. You could go to him for information about public sales in Amsterdam and elsewhere. In the *Oprechte Haarlemsche*

RESTORATIONS

In the seventeenth century paintings were usually restored by artists who were also active in the art trade and by art dealers with their own workshop. In the previous chapter we saw that Hendrick Uylenburgh was given a major commission by the city to restore and revarnish paintings.[186]

184 See p. 285, note 392 ('les choses italiennes ont tellement la vogue que toute la reste n'est rien au prix d'icelles').
185 Among the prints specifically listed were 'the large Tobias and the Angel by Adam Elshamer, the book of prints by Raphael of Urbyn, Lucas van Leyden, Georgius Pens &c. all very fine and dark'.
186 See p. 56.

Before 1677 Gerrit Uylenburgh was asked by Johan Maurits, Stadholder of Cleves, to 'lift' paintings (in other words to renew the varnish and possibly to restore them).[187] This commission confirms that the restoration activities started under Hendrick were continued, although the firm did not do this particular job after all because Gerrit went to England, where in his capacity as keeper of the king's paintings he was also to undertake this type of work.[188] Nevertheless we will look at the project in some detail, because the surviving source material provides a picture of the kind of restoration that Uylenburgh would have done.

The works that Johan Maurits wanted to have restored were paintings of Brazilian landscapes and natives by Frans Post and Albert Eckhout. He intended to present them to the French king, so they needed to be smartened up. The paintings had been packed up for more than twenty years. In a letter, Johan Maurits's Amsterdam agent, Jacob Cohen, advised the stadholder against having the canvases refreshed with oil ('the oiling of the paintings'). He does not explain his objection to this practice. When the paintings eventually emerged from the crates they proved, according to Cohen, to be 'almost totally ruined'. There were creases in them and the paint had flaked off. The reason for their poor condition was said to be that in the past the works had been washed 'with blueing' ('met blauwsel'). The damaged areas were retouched and the arms of Johan Maurits depicted on them were removed with a view to the new owner. The restorations were carried out by two painters in The Hague. Cohen was delighted with the result: 'As good as new,' he wrote in a letter to the stadholder.[189] Although Johan Maurits presented the paintings as a gift, he did so in the hope of receiving significant reimbursement for them, so it was important that the works looked good.

The surviving sources tell us that paintings were often restored and, above all, revarnished when they were put up for sale. Parry Walton, who succeeded Gerrit Uylenburgh as keeper of the English Royal Collection, was asked to varnish the paintings from Peter Lely's collection before they were sold in 1681 and 1682.[190] Uylen-

burgh undoubtedly also did this sort of work. Like art dealers today, he will have seen to it that his paintings looked as attractive as possible.

VALUATIONS AND EXPERTISE

The success of an art dealer is determined to a considerable degree by his expertise. He must be able to see quality, recognize the hand of a particular master so as to make the correct attribution, tell a copy from an original and have a good understanding of the value of paintings. Gerrit Uylenburgh was regarded as an expert in his own day. Even after the debacle with the Elector of Brandenburg his standing in this regard does not appear to have diminished. During his career his assistance was called upon by the States of Holland, by the Amsterdam city government and by Amsterdam citizens when they wanted their collections valued, or to settle a dispute about the author of a painting. We shall look briefly at these functions before going in somewhat greater depth into the attribution of Italian paintings and drawings, which played such an important role in Uylenburgh's art business.

The first major sign of recognition for Uylenburgh was the request for his assistance in choosing the paintings for the Dutch Gift in 1660. The fact that former burgomaster De Vlaming van Oudtshoorn asked him to make a selection from the famous Reynst Collection demonstrates that he was seen as an expert on Italian painting – and as someone, moreover, who had an eye for quality. The point, after all, was to pick out the best of the collection for the English king.[191]

In 1671 the Amsterdam burgomasters wrote that they had used Uylenburgh for various 'important dealings with art and paintings'. We do not know precisely what they were referring to, but it does show that Uylenburgh was held in esteem by the city authorities.[192]

In 1673 Uylenburgh was asked by the Amsterdam magistrates to act as referee or arbiter in a quarrel between Pieter de la Tombe and his brother Isaac. Pieter was a bookseller, art dealer and collector who had, in his own words, a collection of 'exceptionally fine and outstanding paintings,

187 See for this p. 110.
188 See for this p. 112.
189 The Hague, Koninklijk Huisarchief, I V, 1463. See Lemmens 1979. The quotations were also taken from there. The first restorer was Jacobus de Lange. The other is referred to in a letter as 'Pieter de Mellij'; Lemmens identifies him with some reservations as Paulus de Milly.
190 Dethloff 1996, p. 17, 47 note 19. Walton was paid for valuing Lely's collection and for 'varnishing the collection'.
191 See p. 67.
192 See p. 83.

prints, drawings, shells and other rarities and antiquities'. With Rembrandt, who made two portraits of him, Pieter owned paintings by Palma Vecchio and Giorgione. Isaac had worked with his brother a great deal. The dispute between the brothers was that, according to Pieter, Isaac had never paid for a great many things. Pieter demanded more than 6,800 guilders from his brother for board and lodging, for the use of his shop and for books he had supplied. In 1643 Pieter had transferred his 'whole trade and custom' to Isaac. He demanded compensation for this, too, to be determined by an arbitration committee. Lastly, he wanted the immediate return of his collection, which at that moment was with his brother.[193] Isaac countered by claiming that he had money to come from his brother, because Pieter had eaten his breakfast and midday meal with him every day from 1653 to 1668.[194] We do not know what Uylenburgh and the other arbiters decided. Doubtless Uylenburgh was appointed because of his experience with art and the value of art. Daniel Elsevier, one of his fellow arbiters, will have been asked because of his knowledge of books.

After his father's death, Gerrit Uylenburgh took over his role as one of the city's leading valuers.[195] In the 1660s and, particularly, the early 1670s he was repeatedly asked to appraise works of art.[196] The heirs to an estate could personally appoint a particular painter, dealer or expert to value the art.[197] Often two or even three people were approached for this work. Uylenburgh worked with, among others, painters like Ferdinand Bol, Jan Blom, Dirck Matham, Dirck Santvoort and Allart van Everdingen, as well as with the art collector Herman Stoffelsz van Swoll.

If a valuation concerned an insolvent estate, it was the commissioners of the bankruptcy chamber who appointed an appraiser. For ordinary household effects there were accredited estate valuers who could be called in, but painters or art dealers were often appointed separately for paintings and other works of art. They were usually brought in after a clerk had drawn up an inventory under the supervision of the official receiver. Because these people's knowledge of paintings was often limited, the valuers sometimes had to correct the attributions.

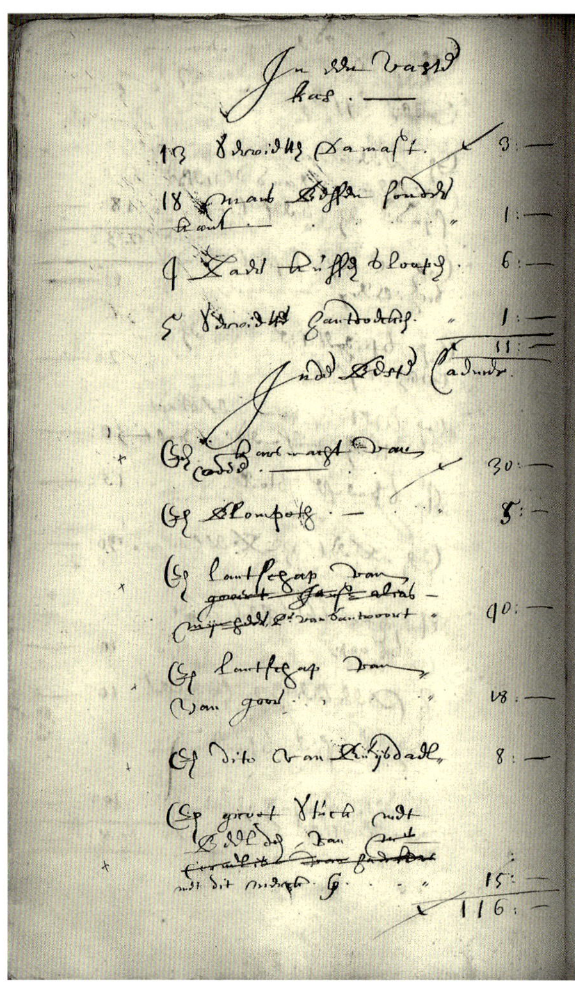

196 Inventory of the estate of Egbert Schut of 15 February 1666, Amsterdam, Gemeentearchief
The illustration shows a page from the inventory (fol. 23v) on which the corrections made by Gerrit Uylenburgh can clearly be seen

It is beyond the scope of this book to examine all of Gerrit's valuations individually, but the inventory of the estate of the Mennonite Egbert Schut can serve as an example. Schut had run into financial problems and on 15 February 1666 his possessions were described on the instructions of the bankruptcy chamber.[198] A day later the art collector Abraham van Lennep, who was Schut's brother-in-law, stood surety for the whole of the property (see fig. 194). It was only two months later, on 17 April, that two assessors valued all the household effects apart from the paintings. Five days later the paintings were examined by Gerrit Uylenburgh, who changed the previously noted attribution of several of the works. In the 'best room', for instance, there hung a landscape that the clerk had noted as being by Govert Janszoon alias Mijnheer. At Uylenburgh's instigation, this name was crossed out and replaced with that of

193 GAA, archive no. 5061, inv. no. 1348, fol. 32r and v., court of justice 16 May 1673. See for Pieter de la Tombe, Van den Boogert/ Broos/ Van Gelder/ Van der Veen 1999, pp. 144-145; Van Eeghen 1956.
194 Van Eeghen 1956, pp. 46-47.
195 See for valuations esp. Van der Veen 2005.
196 In the 1661-1670 period Gerrit undertook seven valuations with, among others, Lodewijck van Ludick, Marten Kretzer and Ferdinand Bol. From 1671-1676 Gerrit was involved in nine of the ten valuations we know of in this period. This would seem to indicate that he had a dominant position in the field at this time. See Appendices, pp. 293-294.
197 See pp. 201-202.
198 GAA, archive no. 5072, DBK, inv. no. 594, fol. 22-29v.

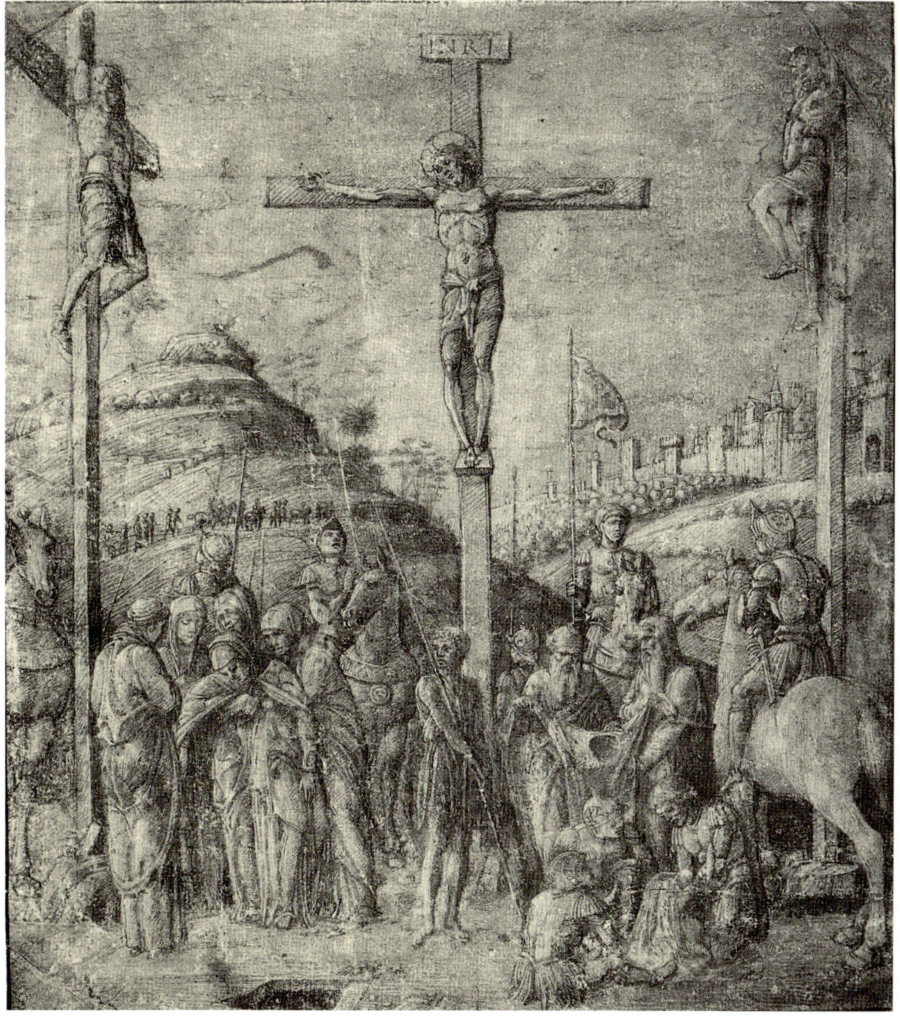

197a Giovanni Bellini attributed to, The three crosses, pen, brown ink, brown wash on grey paper, heightened with white, 24 x 21.5 cm, London, British Museum

197b Inscription by Philips Koninck which was probably stuck on an earlier cardboard mount or frame of the drawing

In the British Museum there is a drawing that is now attributed to Giovanni Bellini. The painter Philips Koninck wrote the following couplet, which must have been attached to the mount: 'dit is montanges hand, wie hier noch tegen streeft/ en is niet waert dat hij als kunstbeminner leeft/ P. Ko' (this is Mantegna's hand, and whoever may demur/ is not worthy to be called a connoisseur) (figs. 197 a and b).[199] The drawing was probably once part of Koninck's own collection. He certainly did own a collection of 'outstanding Italian drawings'.[200] The verse leads us to suspect that not everyone in his circle agreed with the attribution to Mantegna. The inscription is a splendid illustration of the lively interest in making attributions that existed at the time. First and foremost this was for financial reasons. The attribution would after all largely determine the value of a work of art. But it would also seem that art lovers and artists debated these matters with genuine interest – indeed with delight.

Uylenburgh's standing as an expert is evident from the numerous valuations he undertook, and for example from the fact that on 27 May 1667 he and Philips Koninck were asked for their opinion of a particular painting. The Delft confectioner and art dealer Gerrit Maertens had sent Koninck a work that was purportedly by Adriaen Brouwer. It showed a sleeping peasant 'whose money is being taken from his purse by a boy, with a woman holding her finger to her nose'. Having examined the work thoroughly, both Uylenburgh and Koninck concluded that the work could not be by this artist.[201] As we saw in the previous chapter, Hendrick Uylenburgh was consulted in a similar case involving a work by Paulus Bril.[202] The Uylenburghs, father and son, must undoubtedly have been asked for their opinions on countless other occasions, but without this being recorded by a notary.

199 See for the drawing Popham and Pouncey 1950, no. 15, pp. 9, 10.
200 In the *Amsterdamsche Courant* of 15 October 1689 it was described as such in an advertisement for the sale of the collection of 'art on paper' left by Philips Koninck. See Dudok van Heel 1975B, p. 157.
201 GAA, not. J. Hellerus, fol. 265, NA 2078, dated 27 May 1667; Bredius 1915-1922, vol. I, pp. 160-161.
202 See p. 201.

Pieter van Santvoort. In the same room there was a 'large work with figures' that was attributed to Cornelis Cornelisz van Haarlem. This name was also crossed out and the note 'with the mark G P' was added (fig. 196). In other words the painting bore the monogram of Gerrit Pietersz, a pupil of Cornelis van Haarlem. In another room there was a painting of peasants that was taken to be an Adriaen Brouwer, but according to Uylenburgh was by Jan Miense Molenaer. The attributions and valuations were obviously very important when the paintings were subsequently sold at auction by the creditors.

Whereas people nowadays are inclined to give credence to contemporary attributions of seventeenth-century Dutch and Flemish paintings and drawings, the opposite is true when it comes to seventeenth-century Dutch assessments of Italian art. The numerous attributions to Raphael, Michelangelo and Titian in this period often seem far too optimistic. What should we make of the paintings that Gerrit Uylenburgh wanted to sell the elector? Studies show that at best they may have been sixteenth-century Italian paintings, but they were not by the artists to whom Uylenburgh attributed them. We should however bear in mind that this was already clear to those in the know at the time. With the exception of Philips Koninck, none of the painters who testified for Uylenburgh referred to the attributions, they simply stressed that these were good pieces. They probably realized that not all of the paintings were by the masters concerned. And anyone with any knowledge would also have been able to see this from the prices that were asked for them. This is clear from the comment of Jacques Vaillant and Theodoor van der Schuer that if the paintings had been genuine masterpieces, 'they would be worth not hundreds but thousands'.[203] An authentic, undisputed work by Raphael, such as his portrait of Baldassare Castiglione, which is now in the Louvre, fetched 3,500 guilders in Amsterdam in 1639.[204] The 140 rijksdaalders that Uylenburgh asked for an 'old man's likeness' by Raphael must certainly have awakened some suspicion among connoisseurs.

Not every art dealer was quite as dogmatic in his attributions as Uylenburgh initially was with the elector. Johannes de Renialme, for instance, occasionally expressed some doubt in the list he sent to the same Friedrich Wilhelm in August 1650. The first and most important painting in his lengthy summary was 'I Christ in the garden by Anttoni de Coinegio [Correggio] or Hanlibal Carrats [Annibale Carracci] taken by the experts to be the rarest item in Holland'. The second painting was 'I Danae by Carrats or Paduanino [il Padovanino], very rare'. In the portraits he offered one that was by 'or as good as Albert Durer'. To the entry for a portrait by Holbein he added 'reputedly'.[205] Sometimes the customer was given time to consider, and to find out whether a work was indeed authentic. The Antwerp art dealer Matthijs Musson noted in his records on 6 February 1660 that he had sent someone in Utrecht a painting by Brouwer 'and that he shall keep it for a month to see whether it is the original, if not he will return it to me undamaged and I shall give him back the hundred and twenty guilders'.[206] As they do today, however, many art dealers displayed no hint of uncertainty, clearly acting from the conviction that customers would be less keen to buy paintings whose makers were not known beyond a doubt.

Attribution to a particular hand and the recognition of the identifying style of a master is one thing. A related aspect is distinguishing between a copy and an original. The precise arguments for or against an attribution were seldom recorded in writing. In the dispute about the paintings for the elector, most of the artists expressed themselves only in general terms. Only Dujardin and Dodijns made an attempt to explain their opinions. They rejected most of the works because they lacked quality. The 'Michelangelo' lacked 'drawing and grace'; the children with a hermit 'by Titian' had neither 'strength nor clarity of colour'; the children dancing 'by Palma Giovane' displayed none of the master's qualities in 'colour, drawing, action, composition or the handling of light and shade'. They thought the Saint Paul by Palma Vecchio was 'badly drawn, in particular a hand incapable of holding the sword'.[207] The brushwork, the use of colour and shade, the composition and similar factors thus all played a role in their appraisal.

In Uylenburgh's day, publications explaining how to tell a copy from an original were few and far between. The Englishman William Sanderson, who wrote an informative book for art lovers and amateurs in 1658, devoted some attention to the question.[208] He described how one could recognise an original. A copy, he said, would always be an imitation of someone else's ideas. An original had a natural power and expressed the genius of the true artist, whereas the copyist could only produce an imperfect and borrowed grace. An original revealed a freedom in the handling of the brush that one would not find in a copy.[209]

203 See p. 87.
204 See for the sale of Lucas van Uffelen's collection, where the Raphael was offered, p. 199. The sum was noted on a drawing by Rembrandt which he made after the portrait of Castiglione. Vienna, Albertina.
205 Berlin, Geheimes Staatsarchiv, Preussischer Kulturbesitz, Rep. 76 alt III no. 167, fol. 26-29.
206 Duverger 1969, p. 108. The painting was sent to Johan Casembroot.
207 See for this, pp. 94-99.
208 Sanderson 1658. Abraham Bosse had previously treated the subject briefly in a slim volume. See Bosse 1649.
209 Sanderson 1958, p. 16-17, 'Originalls have a Natural force of Grace Rising; Copies seem to have, only a imperfect, and borrowed comlinesse .... An Imitator, does never come neer the first Author ... a similitude ever more, comes short of that truth, which is the Thing themselves: The Copier being forced to accommodate himself to another mans intent .... In Copies you shall not find such freeness of the hand and Pensill'.

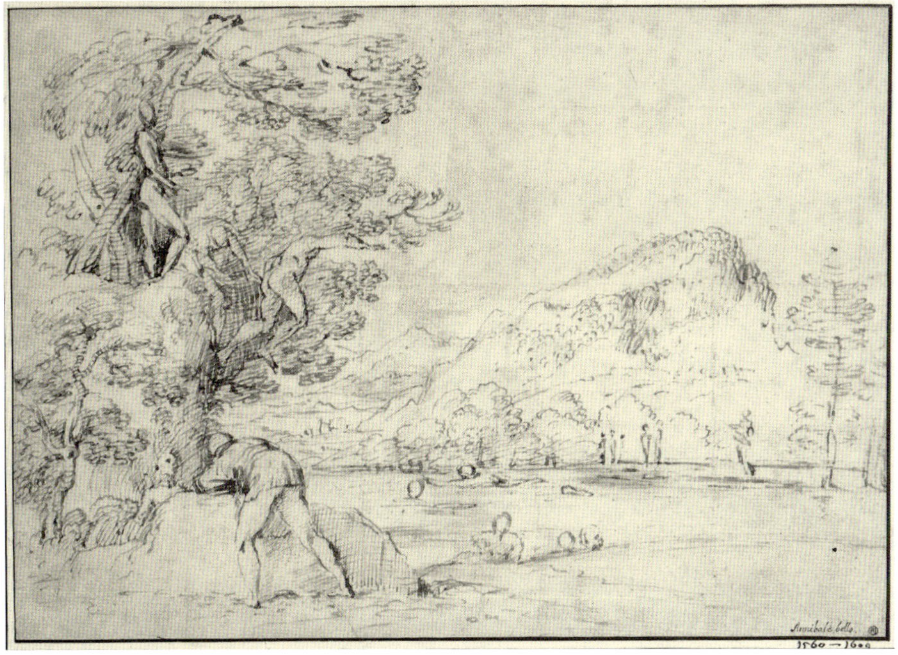

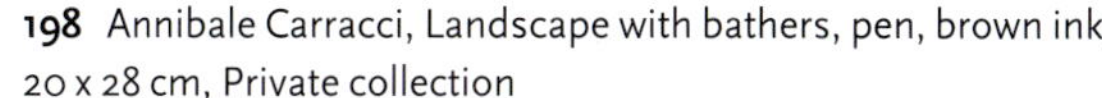
198 Annibale Carracci, Landscape with bathers, pen, brown ink, 20 x 28 cm, Private collection

One of the problems when copying an old work was having to take account of changes in the colours. In time the air, said Sanderson on the authority of 'many masters', had such an effect on the colours that it faded their 'oiliness'. The colours then, according to him, became fleshier and more natural than they were originally. He asserted that this was said to be particularly true of Titian and his master Giorgione.[210] The copyist therefore has to adjust his colours. In old paintings, the author continued, we are delighted by the decay of the colours.[211] Around 1658, in other words, there was already a liking for the discoloured and muted tones of the old masters. Sanderson goes on to tell us that experts sometimes had a special way of looking at old paintings. They held their fingers spread before their eyes and inspected the work as if they were looking through a lattice. This enabled them 'by a

secret mystery' to see how an old work once looked – in the same way, says Sanderson, as we can look at a comely older woman and see the beauty she must have been in her youth.[212]

Koninck's little verse tells us that people also disputed the attribution of drawings. Our knowledge of Uylenburgh's expertise with drawings comes to us indirectly. In a letter dated 6 December 1663, Constantijn Huygens the Younger asked his brother Christiaan to visit Jabach and look at a sheet by Annibale Carracci. He had heard from Uylenburgh that among the fifty landscape drawings by Carracci that Jabach owned, there was one with 'a lot of water and small figures bathing'. Rembrandt had a similar drawing and Huygens wanted to know whether or not it was a copy. He did not believe it was because of the 'skill of the pen'.[213] Jabach's sheet is probably the drawing that is now in an English private collection (fig. 198).[214]

It is interesting to note that in 1665, referring to the Carracci drawings he had seen at Jabach's, the renowned sculptor Bernini said that they were very difficult to copy because they were so little worked out. In his view there were 'no drawings in which it would be harder to be mistaken'.[215] It was seemingly easier to recognise the hand of the master in a rapid sketch than in finished and worked up sheets.

It was in fact many years later that Christiaan Huygens finally succeeded in visiting Jabach. In a letter dated 1 June 1668 he was able to tell

210 Ibid., p. 17, 'Ancient *Originalls*: that the ayre, by time and age works so much upon the Colours, that the Oilynesse thereof, being vaded, the Colours become more fleshy, more Naturall, than at the first. So they say of *Tityans,* and of *Jurgiones* being his Master'.

211 Ibid., p. 16, 'But in old Pictures we are delighted, with their decayings, horridnesse of the Colours'.

212 Ibid., p. 17, 'Painters express the difference; they judge of old pieces and their decayes from what they were at the first, by viewing them through their fingers as through a Lattice or Vale, by a secret Mystery in that Art. Like as to a good Judgement we usually may guesse of the Beauty of her *Youth* in an ancient well formed *Matron*.

213 Huygens 1888-1950, vol. 4, p. 456. 'Vous ne devriez pas aussi negliger de voir à Paris le cabinet de Sieur Jabach qui est un des plus beaux du monde pour les tableaux aussi bien que pour les desseins ... Il a ce dit on entre autres choses environ une cinquantaine de passages desseignés à la plume d'Annibal Caracci, et Uylenburg dit que parmy ceux la il y en a un ou il y a beaucoup d'eau et des petites figures de gens qui se baignent. Je voudrois que si vous voyez cela vous en fissiez vistement un petit brouillon n'importe quelque mauvais qu'il soit pourveu [sic] qu'on y puisse aucunement discerner ou sont les figures et combien il y en a, pour scavoir un peu au vray si celuy qu'a Rembrant a Amsterdam ou il y a semblablement des gens qui nagent du mesme maitre n'est pas une copie, ce que je ne croy pourtant pas pour l'hardiesse de la plume'.

214 Py 2001, pp. 77-78. There are several copies of the sheet.

215 According to Chantelou in his description of Bernini's trip to Paris in 1665. 'Le Cavalier a dit qu'il n'y avait aucuns dessins où l'ont pût être moins trompé que ceux d'Annibal Carrache, pour ce qu'ils étaient moins finis et pourraient plus difficilement être copiés'. Chantelou 1981, p. 276.

his brother that he and some friends and connoisseurs had dined with Jabach.[216] He had had a splendid time. First they had looked at a great many drawings at Colbert's that had been offered for sale to the French king. 'It would have given you the utmost pleasure,' he wrote to his brother, 'to see how Jabach pronounced on the authenticity of the pieces with magisterial self-importance.' Of the three hundred drawings that were attributed to Raphael, only two remained after Jabach had passed judgement. 'I would give a great deal,' continued Huygens, 'to watch him appraise yours [in other words the drawings in Constantijn Huygens's collection] while you hid behind the curtains.' Huygens then went with the assembled company to Jabach's house, where the host flew into a rage when his guests questioned his attribution of some drawings to Giulio Romano and Raphael.

We shall shortly examine the contact between Uylenburgh and Jabach, one of the greatest collectors of and dealers in Italian paintings and drawings of his day. Perhaps Uylenburgh debated with his rich Parisian acquaintance in the manner so graphically described in Huygens's letter.

Uylenburgh was clearly valued for his expertise even after he left the United Provinces. The fact that he was appointed keeper of the king's art collection in London was probably due in some measure to his friendship with Lely, but must first and foremost have been because of his standing as a connoisseur.

Business contacts abroad

Hendrick Uylenburgh had important business contacts in several cities in the Republic, but there are no indications of any contacts in other countries. The reverse is true of Gerrit Uylen-

burgh. There are no indications of collaboration with dealers in other cities in the United Provinces, but there are various documents from which it emerges that he had contacts in various town and cities in Europe. We shall look at three of them: Jürgen Ovens in Friedrichstadt, Peter Lely in London and Everhard Jabach in Paris. These three were not his only foreign contacts. Through his wife, Uylenburgh was related to the Momma's, a leading family of merchants who had settled in Sweden.[217] However, nothing is known about any dealings in art with them.[218] We have also seen how Gerrit travelled to Italy, where he gave the painter Jan Houwaert, who had settled in Genoa, money to buy paintings that he was supposed to send to Amsterdam. In the end nothing came of this.[219] As we shall see, Uylenburgh also had good relations with Amsterdam merchants who traded with Italy. It is possible that he worked with them to import art, but there is no definite evidence of this. In the cases of Ovens, Lely and Jabach, however, there were contacts lasting many years in which the trade in art was a major factor.

JÜRGEN OVENS, SCHLESWIG-HOLSTEIN

Jürgen Ovens (fig. 199), who spent some time painting in the Uylenburghs' workshop, must also have worked with them as a dealer. After his first spell in the Republic in the 1640s, around 1651 he returned to Friedrichstadt, where he maintained close contact with the court in Gottorf. He received commissions for paintings from the Duke and Duchess of Schleswig-Holstein and supplied them with all sorts of works of art. Shortly after his return, in November 1652, Friedrich III paid him for a copper plate that had been engraved in Amsterdam, evidently an

216 Huygens 1888-1950, vol. 6, 1666-1669, p. 219-220, letter dated 1 June 1668. 'Nous avions examiné auparavant avec luy chez Monsieur Colbert une grande quantité de desseins qu'un gentilhomme de Flandre a porté icy, et qu'il offre a vendre au Roy. Vous auriez un plaisir nompareil [sic] a voir comme Jabach determine sur l'authenticité de ces pieces avec un suffisance magistrale; concluant en fin que de 300 desseins qu'on donnoit pour des Raphaels il n'y en avoit que 2 d'originaux. Je donnerois quelque chose de bon pour le voir censurer les vostres et que vous fussiez derriere la tapisserie'.
217 See p. 75.
218 We should like to thank Kenneth Awebro who at our request carried out research in the National Archives in Stockholm into the contacts between the Mommas and Juyst. Momma-Reenstiernas Samling E 2526. There are references to paintings in letters of 22 November 1656 from Hendrick Juyst to Jacob Momma and of 25 August 1660 from Jacob Momma to Hendrick Juyst, but these are exceptions.
219 See p. 72.
220 Schmidt 1922, pp. 95, 118.

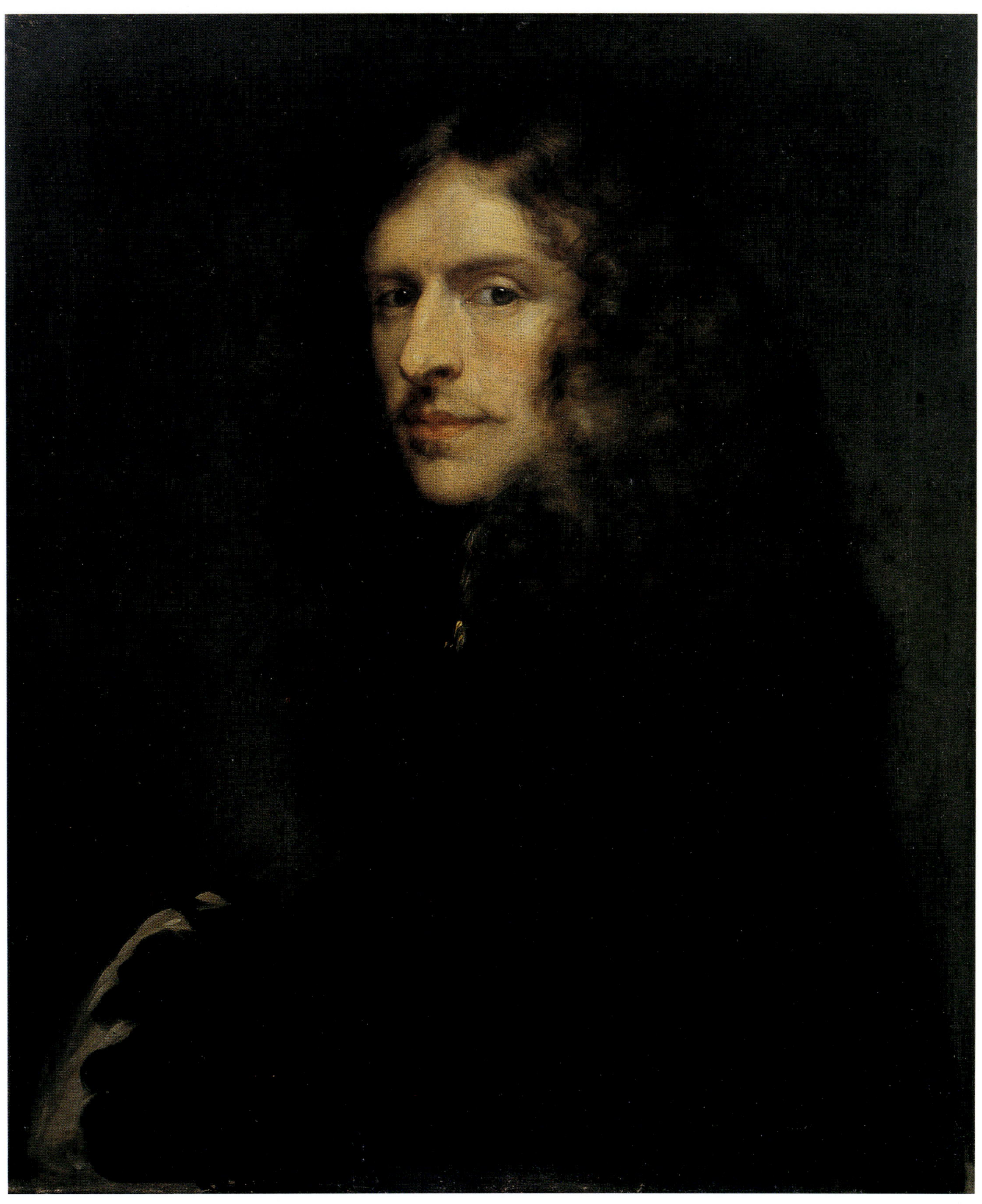

199 Jürgen Ovens, Self-portrait, canvas, 64.6 x 55 cm, Hamburg, Hamburger Kunsthalle

engraving commissioned by the duke. The following year he received 1,100 rijksdaalders for paintings and 'other things' he had supplied. In 1654 Ovens was paid 200 rijksdaalders for 'daß grosse Stück von Sileno so P.P. Rubens gemacht'.[220] It can be seen from the bill that he had actually asked more for it. In the same year he was also paid for unspecified paintings and marble statues.[221] As well as selling to the duke, Ovens also supplied art works, chiefly prints, to Friedrich's wife Maria Elisabeth.[222]

It seems likely that Ovens got these works from Amsterdam. It is tempting to suppose that the Uylenburghs acted as intermediaries in at least some of these transactions. In 1655 Gerrit Uylenburgh himself appeared at the court. On 13 June there is an entry in the account book of the Gottorf court showing that he received 250 rijksdaalders for paintings supplied.[223] In the Statens Museum for Kunst in Copenhagen there is a set of seventeenth-century Dutch paintings with the seal of Gottorf on the back. Some of these works, including paintings by Balthasar van der Ast, Hendrick van Balen, Maerten Stoop and Jan Coelenbier, undoubtedly entered the collection in the time of Friedrich III.[224] The *River Landscape* by Coelenbier (fig. 200), who was one of Hendrick Uylenburgh's financiers in 1640, might be one of the paintings acquired through Uylenburgh.

Two weeks after Gerrit was paid for the paintings, a 'Davidt Uhlenburg' received a further 74 rijksdaalders for prints and 'engraved pictures' supplied to the duchess.[225] 'David' is probably a slip of the pen for Gerrit.[226] It seems likely that these were not two separate shipments, and that Gerrit Uylenburgh stayed with Ovens in Schleswig-Holstein for this short interval.

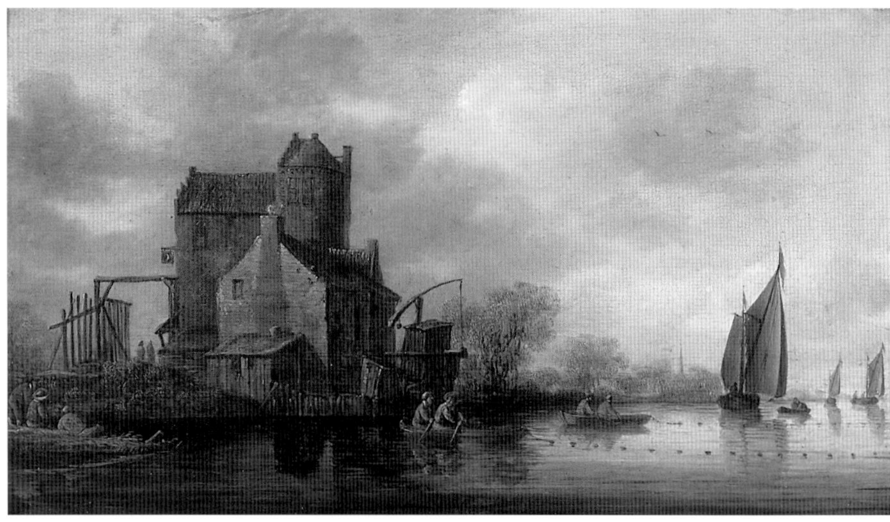

200 Jan Coelenbier, River landscape, panel, 31.5 x 56 cm, Copenhagen, Statens Museum for Kunst

In 1657 Ovens and his family went back to Amsterdam, where he maintained close ties with Gerrit Uylenburgh. On the verso of one of Ovens's sketches for the Batavian series in Amsterdam Town Hall there are three brief draft letters, one of which is dated 6 September 1662 (figs. 201 and 202), in other words at a time when Ovens was either living next door to Uylenburgh or staying with him. The art dealer is also mentioned in two of the three notes. Unfortunately the name of the addressee is not given and the text is not very clear. In the first draft Ovens asks the unknown recipient to make a payment directly to Uylenburgh because he has paid Ovens something that the addressee owed him.[227] In the second it says that Ovens had heard from Uylenburgh that the unknown addressee had arrived and asks him to send the rest of the payment.[228]

In the middle note Ovens wrote that he had a very important painting by Pieter Lastman in his possession.[229] It is impossible to say for certain whether the three fragments of text were indeed

obligatie, wenste ik well dat ued: ge: Ulenb: geliefden mit de betalingen te begonstigen. Den is mij tegenwoordig, niet wel anders bequaem is, mit versoek ued: dit memorial my niet sinistre gelieven te duyden, en verwahte hirop resolutie. Den ik ben naer befehelingh Godes, - Mijn Heer ued. seer dienstwillige dienaer.'
228 Mijn Heer. ued: ankompst heb uijt M. Ulenburg verstaen, maer de eere van ued: te sijn niet ghadt en twijffel niet of ued. sal glieven d rest mit den ersten over te senden, den ick jeegenwoordig wat veel uyt te leggen heb, sal mijn g...'.
229 'Het frayste dat oyt van P. Lasman int landt geweest heb ick jegenwoordigh: so alst fray is; so capiteel ist ock Ambsd. 6 7br 1662'.

221 Schmidt 1922, p. 95.
222 On 20 January 1654 he received 78 rijksdaalders and 43 shillings for engravings he had supplied, and on 16 April of the same year he was paid 52 rijksdaalders. On 6 January 1655 he also received money for engravings. See Schmidt 1922, p. 95.
223 Landesarchiv Schleswig-Holstein, Schleswig, LAS

Abt. 7 no. 2316, fol. 93r [13 June 1655] 'Vermöge bey verwahrtenn von E[uer] Fürst [lichen] Durch [laucht] Meinem gnedigstenn Fürstenn unndt Herrn selbst subscribirtenn Zettels und der quitung no ... Gerrit Ulenborch, contrafaictern für vonn demselbenn erhandelte Schildereyenn bezahlt 250 [Reichstaler]'. With thanks

to Johannes Rosenplänter of the archives in Schleswig, who was kind enough to hunt down and transcribe the references in Schmidt 1922. See further Schmidt 1922, p. 93.
224 See for these paintings, Spielmann/ Drees 1997, p. 594-595.
225 Landesarchiv Schleswig-Holstein, Schleswig, LAS Abt. 7 no. 4765, 'den 26. J [uni 1655]

Auff gnedigster Befehl Ihr Durchl. Einen Holländischer Painter, namens Davidt Uhlenburg wegen abgehandelte kupfferstücken und eingeschnittenen bildern lauth Quittung zahlt 74 [Reichstaler].' Schmidt 1922, p. 93.
226 See p. 63.
227 'Mijn Heer, also M. Ulenburg mij contentement gedaen heeft, voor de rest van ued:

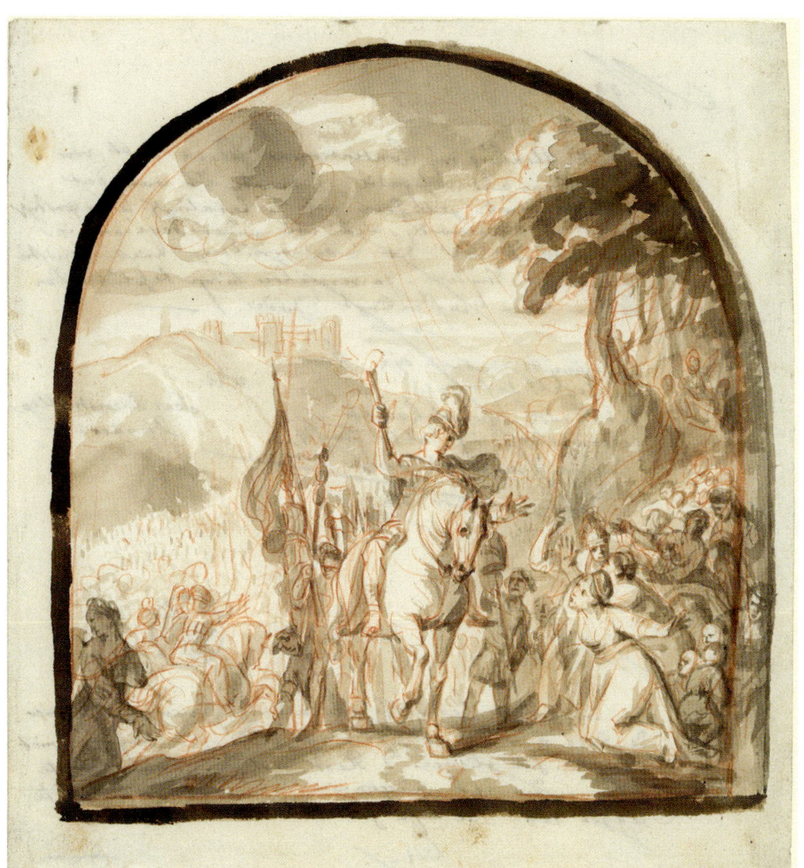

201 Jürgen Ovens, Julius Civilis departs for the Battle of Xanten, red chalk with grey wash, 18.5 x 17.5 cm, Hamburg, Hamburger Kunsthalle

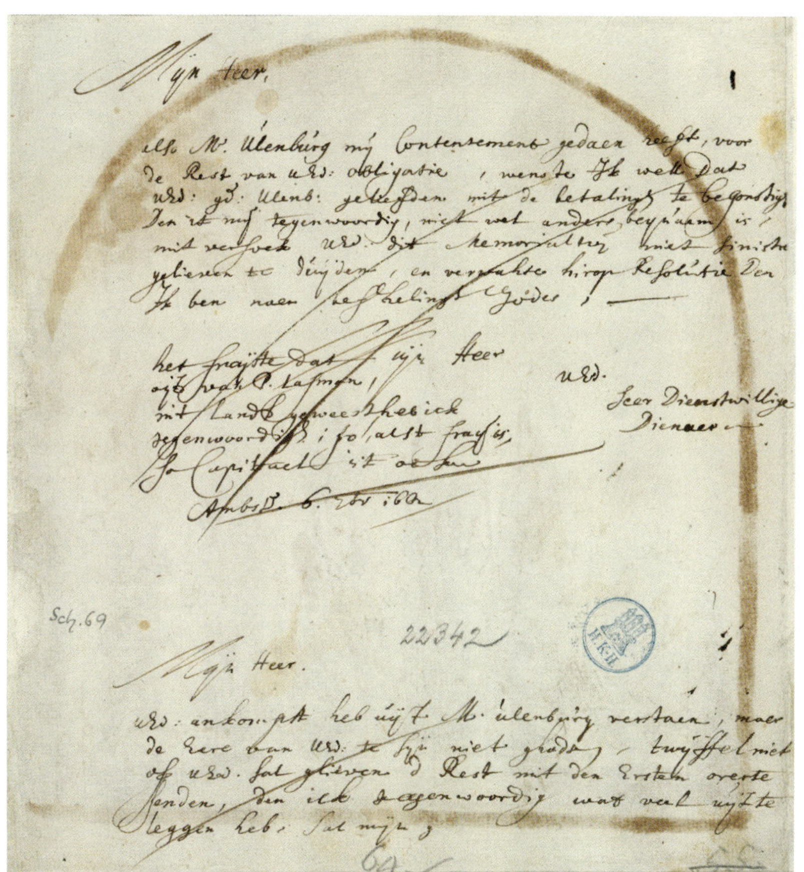

202 verso of fig. 201, with rough drafts of letters by Jürgen Ovens

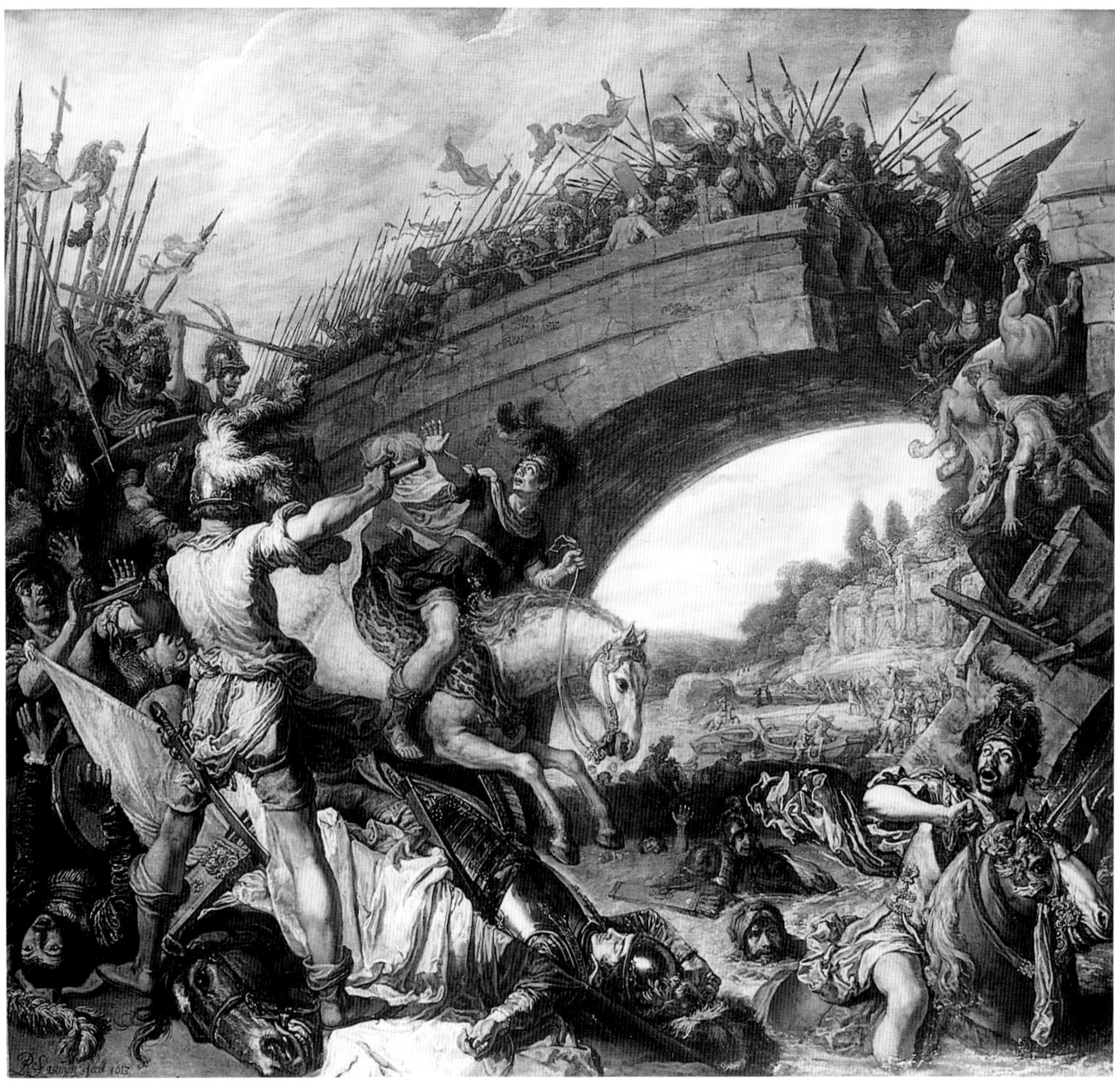

all part of one and the same letter. The painting
by Pieter Lastman was very probably the *Battle
at the Milvian Bridge* (fig. 203). The painting is later
listed as belonging to the Duke of Gottorf, so that
it seems obvious that Ovens sold the work to him.
However, the letter Ovens was drafting cannot
have been meant for the duke, because had it
been he would certainly have written it in German.[230]

During his second stay in Amsterdam, Ovens
kept in touch with the ducal couple in Schleswig-
Holstein. For instance, he organised the greater
part of the order to Artus Quellinus for sculptures
for the entrance to the ducal crypt in the cathedral
in the capital of Schleswig-Holstein.[231] Ovens also
sent prints, Italian stones, slate and glass to
Duchess Maria Elisabeth.[232]

In May 1663 Ovens returned to the region of
his birth. He lived in a large, lavishly appointed
house in Friedrichstadt. His wealth came from
legacies, his marriage (his wife brought with her
a dowry of no less than 60,000 rijksdaalders), his
success as a painter and from earnings in the art
trade. He owned a great deal of land around
Tönning and Friedrichstadt.

Houbraken paints a nice picture of Ovens as
an art dealer in his biography of Johannes Voorhout. In 1672, because of the unrest in the Republic, this artist went to Friedrichstadt, where
his wife had friends. He soon made a name for

230 '1 Römische Bataille von
Laßman' appears in the 1694
inventory of Duke Christian
Albrecht in the Castle of Gottorf. This painting probably
went with the duke's daughter,
Sophia Amalia, when she
married August Wilhelm of
Brunswick. Later it found its
way into the museum in Bremen. See Schmidt 1922, pp. 96-
97.
231 Schmidt 1922, pp. 88-92.
232 Schmidt 1922, pp. 36-37.

himself and came into contact with Ovens, who showed him his 'large room with art by the most esteemed Masters, with which he did business at the Court [...] and also sounded him out as to whether he wanted to paint for him'. Voorhout did not take him up on his offer.[233]

As he had done in the 1650s, after his return Ovens again supplied works of art to the court in Gottorf. On 5 January 1665 he received 71 rijksdaalders 'on behalf of Gerrit Uylenburgh' for 'rare books' and engravings.[234] On the same day he received 130 rijksdaalders himself for four frames or 'Contrafaiethramen aus Ambsterdam'.

The inventory compiled after the death of Ovens's widow in 1690 gives us a good idea of what Ovens had in his 'large room'. The inventory was divided into originals (99 items) and copies (97). More than half of the originals were by Ovens himself. At a total of six paintings, the work of Anthony van Dyck was remarkably well represented. He also had works by Jordaens (three of them, including an *Arrest of Christ*, which at 240 marks was among the most expensive paintings), Rubens, Frans Snyders,[235] Roeland Saverij, Jan Lievens, Jacob Backer, Pieter van Laer, Joan van Noordt, Philips Wouwerman, Parmigianino, Giorgione and Poussin. And he owned a flower painting by one of Uylenburgh's sisters, which was valued at 10 marks.[236] The works classified as copies had probably all been done recently, even those after sixteenth-century artists. More than twenty were done after paintings by Ovens himself. Among the copies there were also works of which Ovens had the original, including a Wouwerman, the expensive Jordaens and a Parmigianino.[237] There was a relatively high proportion of copies after Italian masters such as Titian, Veronese, Giovanni Benedetto Castiglione and Mattia Preti.

If we compare Ovens's collection with Uylen-

burgh's, what strikes us is that Ovens owned a relatively large number of copies and that the standard of his works that were classified as 'original' was probably not as high as that of the Amsterdam art dealer. The large number of his own works clearly shows that Ovens was first and foremost an artist and only in the second place a collector and dealer.

It seems likely that a significant proportion of Ovens's collection came from Amsterdam. In Friedrichstadt, off the beaten track as it was, the artist must have had to rely on his contacts in the United Provinces. It is therefore obvious that some of it will have come to him through Gerrit Uylenburgh. The copies after Italian masters might well have come straight from his shop. Copies were also made in Ovens's own studio. When he asked Johannes Voorhout whether he wanted to work for him, he must have had in mind that Voorhout could at any rate have made copies.

Ovens was a painter, he was rich and he had good connections at the court in Gottorf. The surviving documents suggest a flourishing trade in art with Amsterdam. Ovens was thus an ideal partner for Uylenburgh.

SIR PETER LELY, LONDON

Peter Lely (fig. 204) was much more than an important business associate of Gerrit Uylenburgh's; he was also a good friend.[238] They had a very close relationship from the 1650s (possibly even earlier) until Uylenburgh's death in 1679.

Lely, who trained in Haarlem, probably went to England in 1641. He was to establish a glittering career there.[239] He started by painting landscapes with small figures and history works, but rapidly switched to portraiture.[240] Few of his early

233 Houbraken 1718-1721, vol. 3, p. 225. Houbraken must have heard this story from Voorhout in person.
234 Schmidt 1922, p. 93. '1665 5 Januar Noch demselben [Jürgen Ovens, Contrafaietern in Friederichstadt] wegen Gerrith Uhlenborg für 3 zur Fürstl. Bibliothec gelieferte rare Bücher für Jahren und Kupferstücken vermöge gleichmäßig subskribirten Zettels und der Quittung entrichtet 71 Reichstaler'. See also pp. 63 and 232.
235 The painting by Snyders was described as a 'groszer Hundt' and may be identical to the 'hondt' (dog) by Snyders that is listed as no. 62 in the 1675 inventory of Gerrit Uylenburgh's property. See for the inventory of Ovens' widow, Schmidt 1914.
236 See p. 212.
237 The originals included a painting by Ovens after Palma [Vecchio] and a *Sacrifice to Priapus* by Ovens that was very probably based on Giovanni Benedetto Castiglione's painting of the same subject, of which Ovens owned a copy. These paintings were probably classified among the originals rather than the copies because only the composition was derived from these masters, the style was Ovens's own. This was certainly true of a *Virgin and Child* that was based on a work by Sebastiano del Piombo in Hendrick Scholten's collection (see fig. 215);

Ovens's version, which appears as an original in the inventory, hangs to this day in the memorial tablet to him and his wife in the church in Tönningen.
238 See p. 77.
239 Lely studied with Frans Pietersz de Grebber, see Miedema 1980, p. 456. On 6

October 1637 it was noted in the finders' book of the Haarlem Guild of St Luke that Frans de Grebber would be asked to enrol all his pupils, such as 'Pieter lelij. Van Campen ...', whom he had not yet registered or for whom he had not yet paid. It seems

probable that Lely was studying with De Grebber at the time, but this is not necessarily the case. De Grebber still had to pay fees for no fewer than 16 apprentices. In view of the number, there must have been pupils among them who had already left the studio.

Houbraken 1718-1721, vol. 2, p. 47 writes that Lely studied with De Grebber for two years.
240 Graham wrote in 1695 that Lely went to England in 1641 and began working there as a landscape painter, but soon switched to portraits. See Millar 1978, p. 9.

history paintings have survived. His masterpiece is *Nymphs by a Fountain,* which must have been painted during the 1650s and was clearly influenced by Dutch classicism (fig. 205). The portrait of a woman, which may be a depiction of the penitent Magdalene, is another of Lely's early works (fig. 206). Lely soon had success with his portraits, but it was not until the restoration of Charles II in 1660 that his career really took off. In 1661 he was appointed court painter at an annual salary of 200 pounds. Contemporaries were impressed by his lavish lifestyle. Houbraken tells us that he rose late and 'never started to paint before nine o'clock'. He had several servants and valets, one of whom kept the diary of whose turn it was to have their portrait painted. He stopped working at four, when he dined 'seldom without company; for he always had food served for twelve people [...] while in another room there was artful playing and singing'.[241]

Lely maintained contact with Holland all his life and his paintings must have been known there.[242] In the summer of 1656 he travelled to the Republic with the English architect Hugh May.[243] As far as we know, this was the only time he ever went back to Holland.

Lely was a passionate art collector. At the sale of Charles I's property between 1649 and 1653 he acquired works by Veronese, Breenbergh and Tintoretto.[244] It is possible that Everhard Jabach was also in London at this time to look at the former king's paintings. He had two portraits of himself painted by Lely around this time (fig. 210).[245] On his death in 1680 Lely owned an impressive collection of works by first and foremost Van Dyck (more than 25, 'being his best Pieces'), but also by Titian, Veronese (8 works), Tintoretto, Rubens, Antonio Mor (7 works),

Jacopo Bassano, Pieter van Laer (5 works), Van Poelenburch and many others.[246]

As well as paintings, Lely had an extensive collection of drawings and prints, which he himself regarded as the best in Europe – at least so we learn from Charles Beale's notebook. After a visit to his friend Lely on 14 July 1677 Beale wrote: 'Mr Ulemberg had made an estimate of his [that is to say Lely's] Collection of Paintings Drawings and Prints, and that at a very moderate rate sett upon them came to about £ 10000. I say Ten thousand pounds. He said yt for Drawings & Prints his was the best Collection in Europ. He told me at ye same time that rimbrant had given £ 100 for ten prints, & that himself had most of those ten prints in his Collection'.[247] Mr Ulemberg was, of course, Gerrit Uylenburgh. The story about Rembrandt buying ten prints for £100 probably came from him.

According to Roger North, who organised the sale of Lely's property after his death, the collection comprised more than 10,000 prints and drawings.[248] The collection of drawings was particularly strong in Italian masters of the sixteenth century, such as Parmigianino, Correggio, Raphael and Veronese. Lely also owned work by seventeenth-century artists like Pietro da Cortona, Carracci, Claude Lorrain and Poussin, and by Dutch and Flemish artists like Rubens, Van Dyck (his Italian sketchbook) and Jan de Bisschop. The print collection had a similar emphasis on Italian art.[249]

We know from various sources that Lely acquired his drawings from, among other places, the famous Arundel Collection and from Nicholas Lanier.[250] When Constantijn Huygens the Younger looked at the Italian drawings owned by the English king in 1690, it appeared to him that

241 Houbraken 1718-1721, vol. 2, p. 43. In a letter of 24 August 1663 Christiaan Huygens told his brother Constantijn that three days before 'le dit Signor Pittore [Lely] nous traita a diner fort splendidement' ('the said Signor Pittore [Lely] treated us to a truly splendid dinner'). Huygens 1885-1950, vol. 4, p. 394.

242 Paintings by Lely were mentioned in seventeenth-century sales by the Hague painters' guild, see Bredius 1915/22, vol. 2, pp. 493, 504, 516, 520. It is also assumed that Johannes Vermeer owned a painting of *The Finding of Moses in the Bullrushes* by Peter Lely, which is depicted in two of his paintings. This was first pointed out by Willem van de

Watering, see Blankert/Montias/Aillaud 1992, p. 193.
243 London, Public Record Office, State Papers, domestic 25/77, 150. Permission dated 29 May 1656 for a passport for Holland for 'Peter Leley, and his Servt. Hugh May'. See Millar 1978, p. 28, note 22.
244 Millar 1978, Dethloff 1996.
245 Vey 1967, pp. 163-165.

Both paintings are in in the Wallraf-Richartz-Museum in Cologne.
246 See Dethloff 1996; and Editorial, 'Sir Peter Lely's Collection', *The Burlington Magazine* 83 (1943), pp. 185-191.
247 Quoted from Kirby Talley, p. 280.
248 Dethloff 1996, p. 19.
249 See Dethloff 1992, 1996 and 2003.

250 The fact that he had drawings from the Arundel Collection was stated by Evelyn, when he visited the Duke of Norfolk on 9 May 1683. Roger North said that Lely had acquired some of Lanier's drawings after the latter's death in 1666. See Dethloff 1996, p. 24 and Dethloff 2003, and for Lanier, Wood 2003.

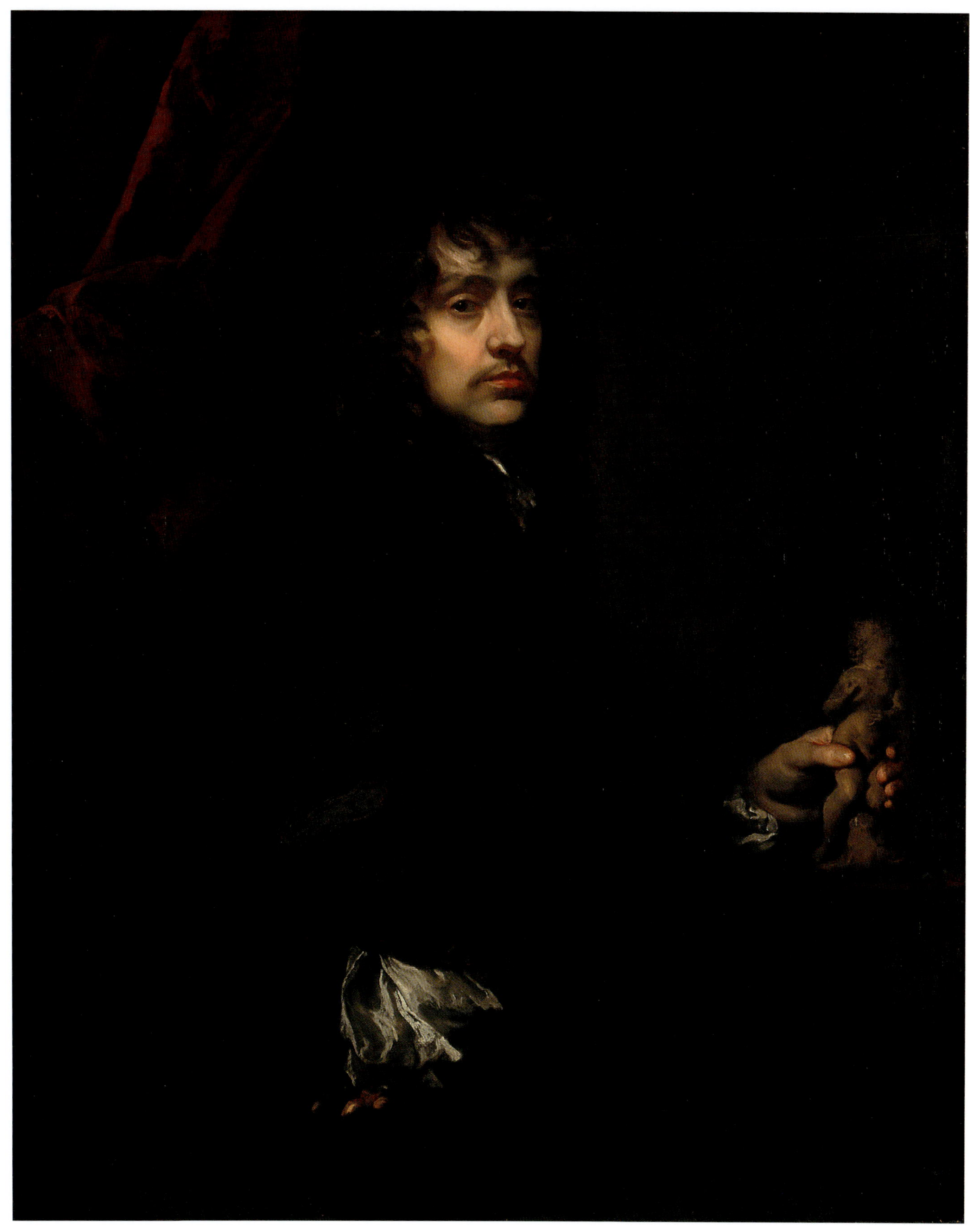

204 Peter Lely, Self-portrait, monogrammed 'PL', canvas, 108 x 87.6 cm, London, National Portrait Gallery

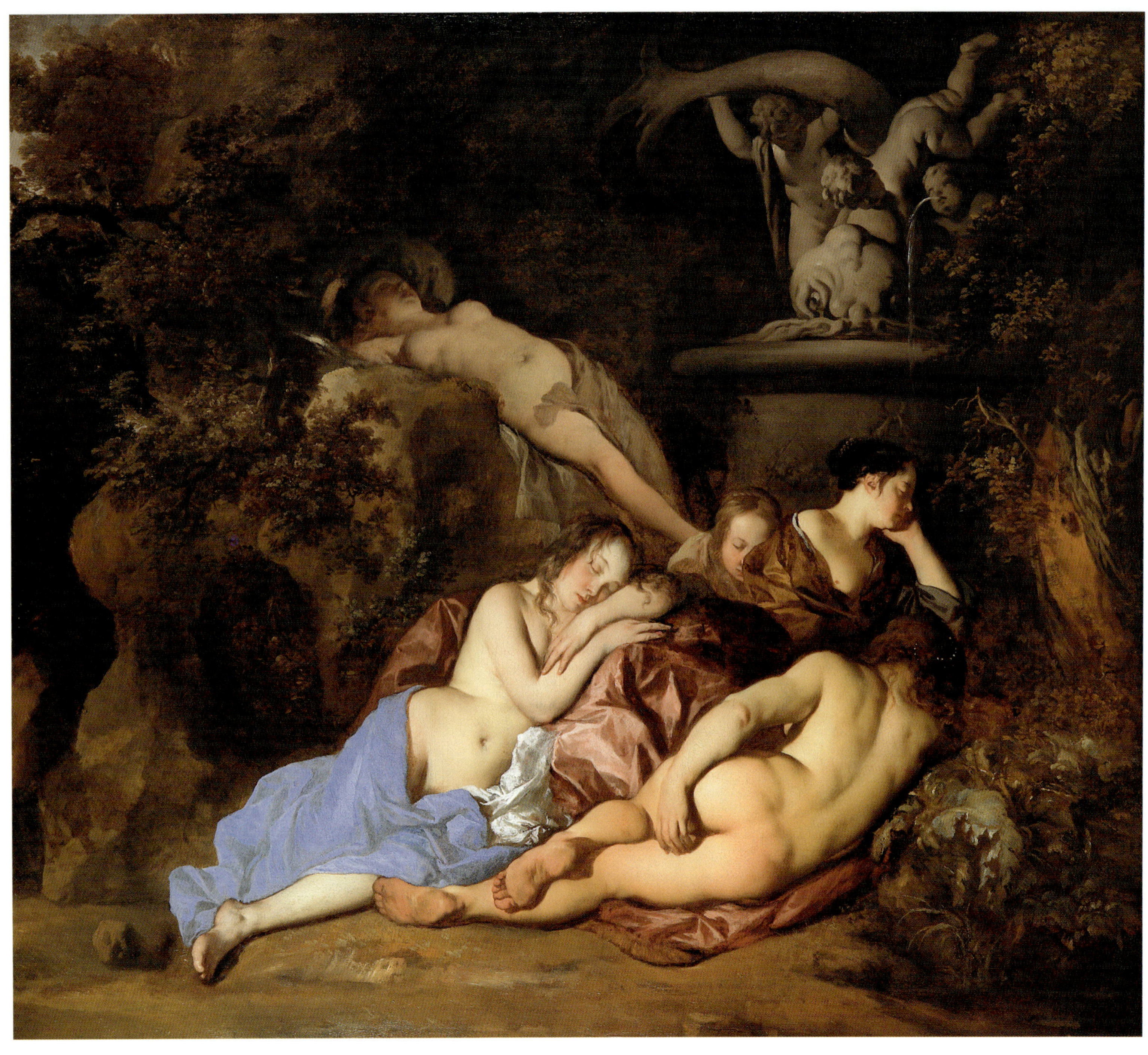

205 Peter Lely, Sleeping nymphs by a fountain, canvas, 128 x 144.5 cm, London, Dulwich Picture Gallery

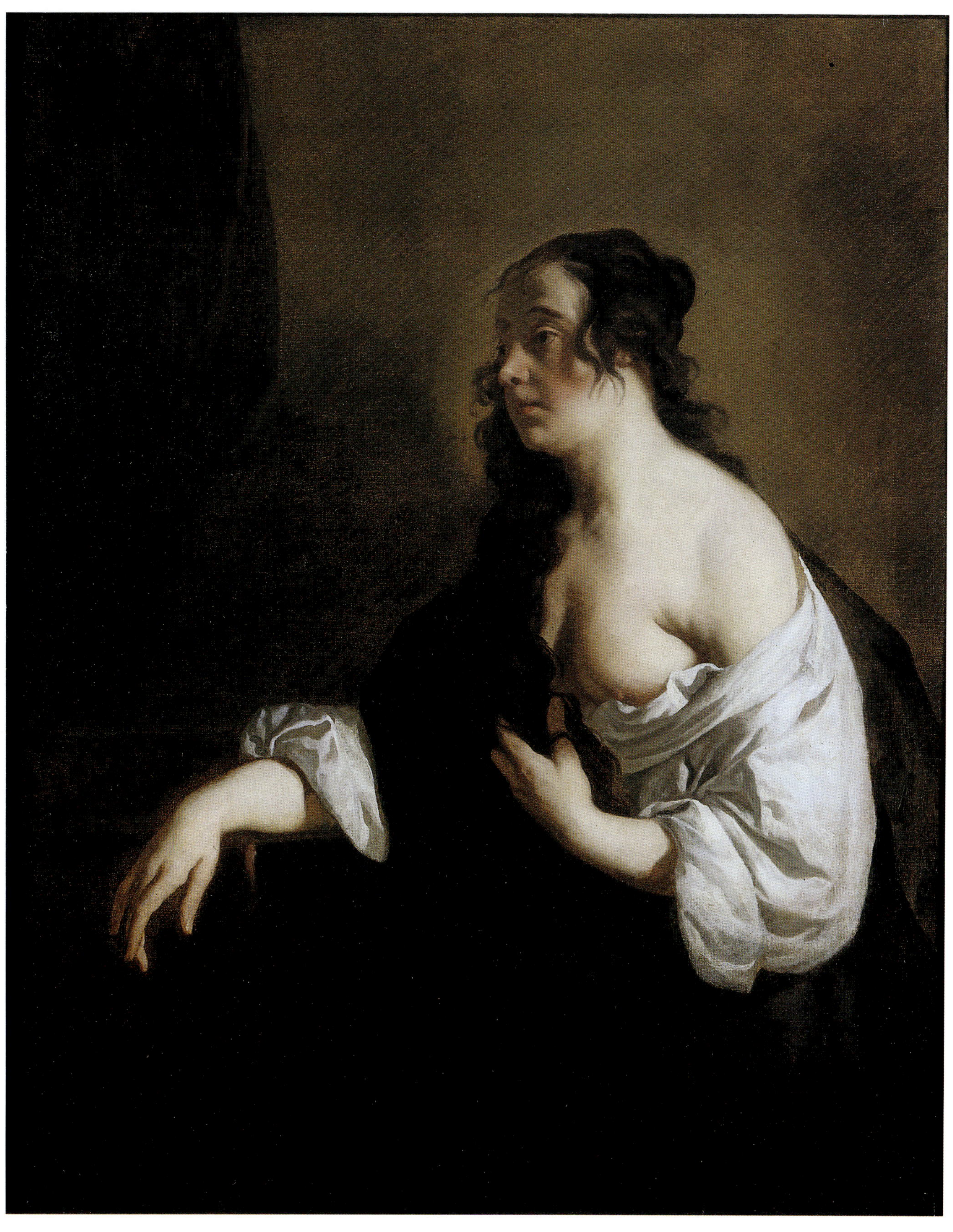

206 Peter Lely, Portrait of a young woman (the penitent Magdalen?), canvas, 105.5 x 91.2 cm, London, Dulwich Picture Gallery (on loan from a private collection, Canada)

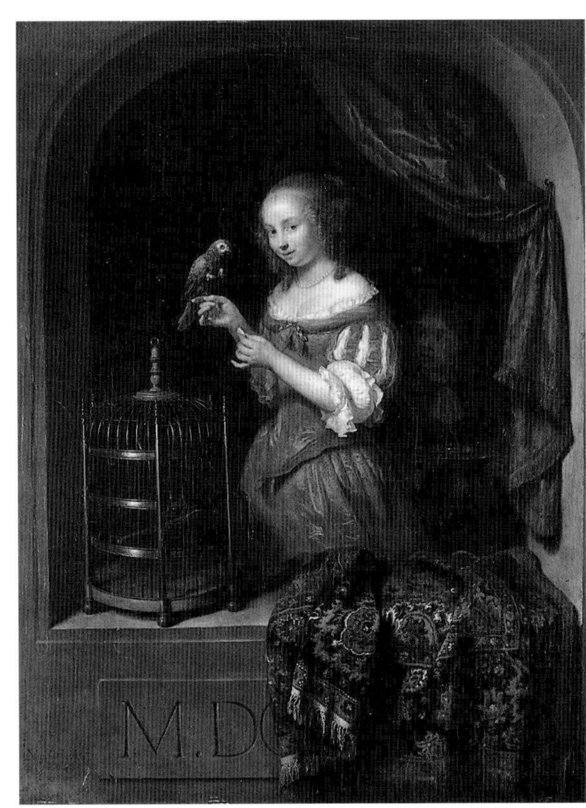

207 Caspar Netscher, *Woman with a parrot*, signed and dated 'CNetscher. Ao. 16.66', panel, 46 x 37 cm, Wuppertal, Von der Heydt Museum

Venice that Van der Voort's son – his father had died in 1654 – was at that moment offering the collection for sale. It appears from the letter that there were ten albums, with numerous sheets by Titian, Raphael, Parmigianino, Giorgione, Tintoretto, Palma Giovane and many other Italian Renaissance artists. Del Sera wrote that the Cardinal would have to make up his mind quickly because the young Van der Voort had been summoned back to Flanders by his uncle and would be taking the collection with him. However, the price of 4,000 scudi was too high for the Florentine cleric and so Van der Voort must have returned to Flanders with the albums. It seems very probable that Lely and Uylenburgh acquired the collection not long afterwards.[253] This could have happened in Antwerp, perhaps in 1657 when Lely may still have been in the Netherlands, or in London, but that would mean that Van der Voort's collection was taken there.

In 1660 Uylenburgh accompanied the delegation that went to present the Dutch Gift to Charles II. Without doubt he visited Lely. In 1668 Uylenburgh and his sisters asked Lely to look after their affairs in connection with the death of their brother Abraham in Dublin.[254]

The most important document relating to the business dealings between Uylenburgh and Lely is the valuation of Uylenburgh's paintings of 1675.[255] At the end of the list there is a note that the following works were with Peter Lely in England: four paintings by Netscher (an 'excellent painting of singers' (cf. fig. 192), a 'Cleopatra' (fig. 193), a 'Conversation of young ladies and others by Netscher' and a 'Young woman with a parrot' (cf. fig. 207), a Danaë by Cornelis van Poelenburch (fig. 208), a portrait by Antonis Mor and a *Temptation of Saint Anthony* by Adriaen Brouwer (cf. fig. 209). Lely probably had these paintings to sell, although he may have had his eye on some of them for his own collection. The majority of the seven paintings were by Netscher.

things had been stolen from the albums. When he asked about this he was told that 'Lilly, having borrowed the books from Chiffins [one of the keepers of the English royal collection], had really set to work on them, taking originals out and putting in copies made by his people ...'.[251]

How the foundations of Lely's collection of drawings were laid emerges from a letter of 13 July 1663 from Christiaan Huygens in London to his brother Constantijn. He said that he had been to see Lely and examined his collection of Italian drawings and was very much impressed by it. Most of the sheets, according to the letter, came from the 'cabinet of Vander Voort'. 'He [that is Lely],' continued Christiaan, 'says that he picked all the best ones out *and left the rest for Uylenburgh, who took them with him to Holland*' [my italics].[252] This was Walter van der Voort's collection of more than 1,100 drawings, which the Antwerp merchant had amassed in Venice. Around 1650 Van der Voort had exchanged a number of drawings with Cardinal Leopoldo de' Medici in Florence. In January 1657 Leopoldo's agent, the painter Paolo del Sera, wrote from

251 Huygens the Younger 1876-1888, vol. I, p. 326.
252 Huygens 1888-1950, vol. 4, pp. 456-457.
253 Gaetela Bertela 1987, p. 477-481. See for Van der Voort also Ridolfi 1648, p. 238, who calls him 'Signor Gualtieri Vander Voort' and writes that he 'fatto raccolta di molte pitture, e numerosi disegni di eccelenti autori', including a painting by Andrea Schiavone of the *Contest Between Pan and Apollo*.
254 See pp 76-77.
255 See Appendices p. 302.

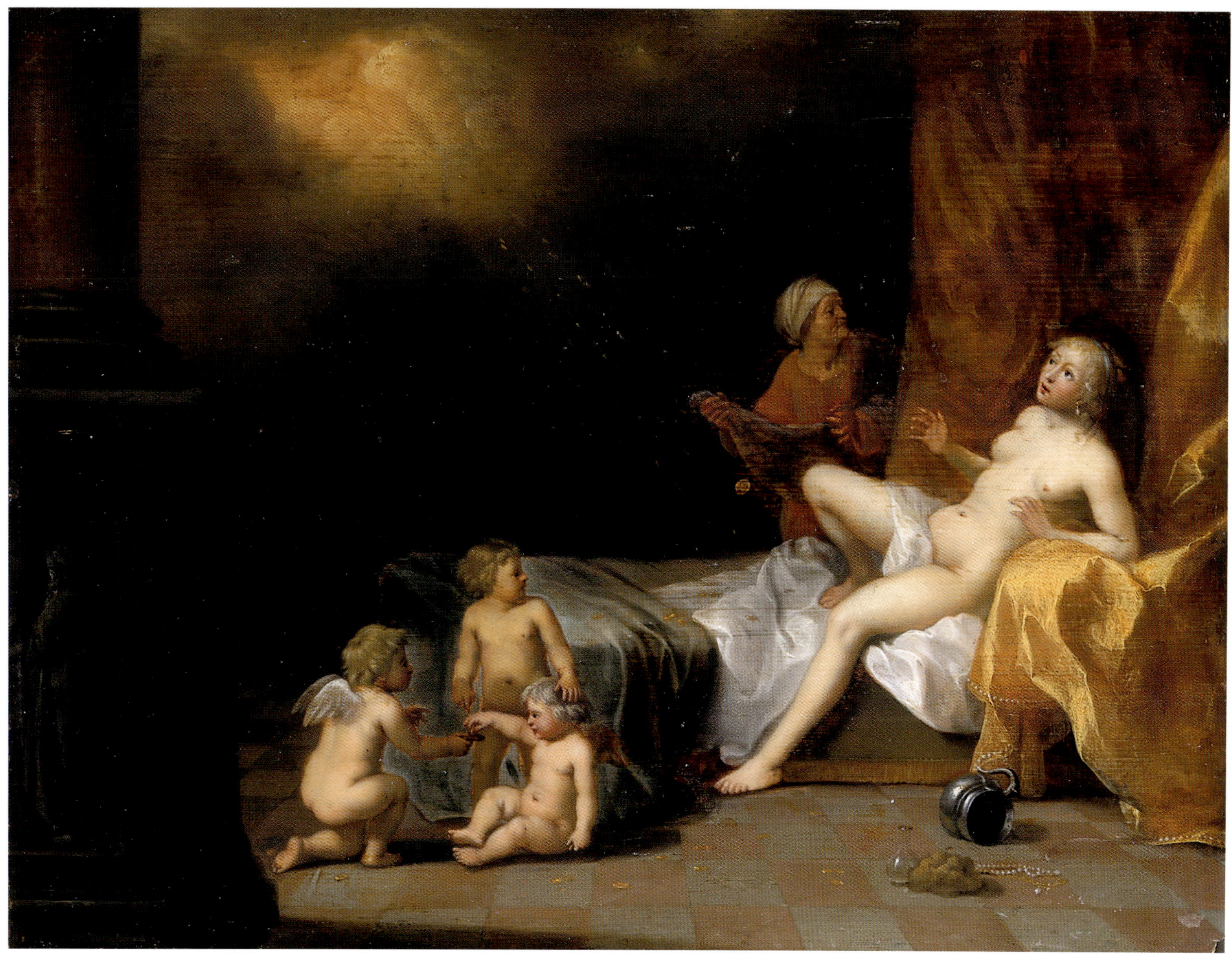

208 Cornelis van Poelenburch, Danaë, panel, 26 x 34,1 cm, private collection Great Britain

256 Houbraken 1718-1721, vol. 3, p. 95. The ambassador at the time was Sir William Temple; Vertue dates Temple's activities to 1668 (see *The Twentieth Volume of the Walpole Society* 1931-1931, p. 53); see also Wieseman 2002, p. 28, note 31.
257 Sluijter-Seijffert 1984, pp. 31-32.
258 Millar 1978, p. 9.

Lely and Uylenburgh evidently thought that there were good prospects of selling his work in England. Houbraken says that Charles II was very fond of the artist's paintings and had tried several times, through the intermediary of the English ambassador in The Hague, to persuade Netscher to come to his court. The artist had, however, politely refused the invitations.[256] Van Poelenburch's work was also known at the English court. He had been employed by the court between 1637 and 1641,[257] and Lely's his-

tory pieces were inspired by his work.[258] Lely, and possibly other English collectors too, must have admired Mor's work. There were, as we have said, no fewer than seven works by this sixteenth-century portrait painter in Lely's estate.

We know that Lely had dealt in paintings from Holland before. Prior to 1659 he sold Sir Ralph Bankes, who was an admirer of Lely's portraits, a large landscape by Nicolaes Berchem painted in 1655 and a copy after a night piece by Gerrit Dou, the original of which Lely himself

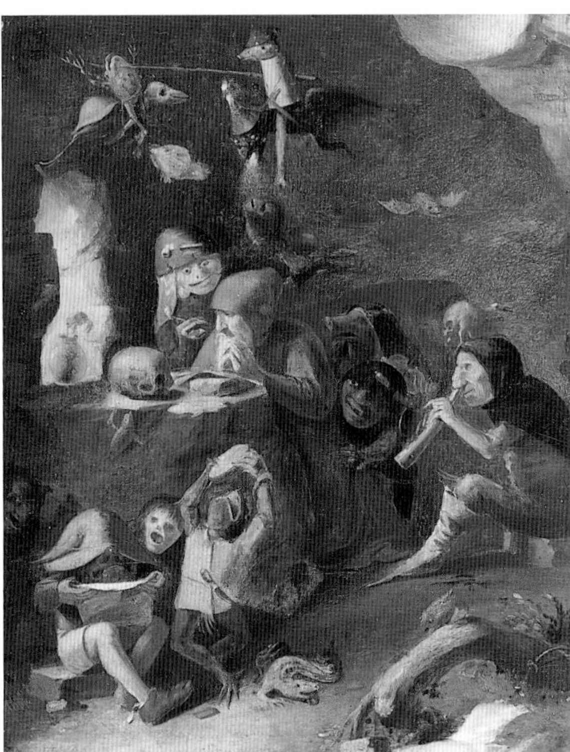

209 Adriaen Brouwer, circle of, The temptation of St Anthony, panel, 27.2 x 21 cm, Berlin, Staatliche Museen zu Berlin, Gemäldegalerie

owned.[259] Bankes also possessed a copy of Rembrandt's *Man in Oriental Dress* of 1639. Just how *au fait* the collector was with the art scene is clear from his note that at that time (1659) the original was with Cardinal Mazarin (in Rome).[260]

As we have seen, shortly after his financial collapse Gerrit Uylenburgh went to England, where thanks to Lely's good offices he became keeper of the royal collections. Whether the two men continued to do business together in England we do not know, but on his death Lely owned a large landscape by his friend.[261]

Almost half of all Uylenburgh's debts in 1675 were owed to one man: the French banker, merchant, collector and art dealer Everhard Jabach (fig. 210). He was owed more than 5,100 guilders – probably for works of art he had supplied to Uylenburgh which had not been paid for. We cannot rule out, though, the possibility that this was a loan; Jabach's principal business was, after all, banking. In the same year Jabach also submitted a list of paintings and drawings that he had left on consignment with Uylenburgh and which he now wanted back. This list has not survived, but it is safe to assume that it contained a considerable number of works. Like the works left on consignment by other people, they do not appear in the 1675 inventory.

Jabach was a man of the grand gesture, or as he himself put it, 'comme je vais toujours le grand chemin'.[262] He was born in Cologne in 1618, the son of the wealthy merchant, banker and collector of the same name.[263] In July 1636, shortly after the death of his father, he and his brother-in-law Johan Hunthum (who was married to Jabach's older sister) travelled through the Netherlands.[264] He then went on to London, where the family had influential business contacts.[265] There he had his portrait painted by Van Dyck and visited the leading collections.[266]

In 1638 Jabach settled in Paris. He became a naturalised Frenchman in 1647 and married a year later.[267] In 1659 he bought a large house, where he had his office; it also provided enough room for his constantly growing art collection. Jabach had a network of contacts throughout Europe – for the most part family – with whom he did business.

One of the first signs of Jabach as a collector were his purchases at the sale of Charles I's paint-

259 Laing 1992. Berchem's landscape appears on the third list of his paintings, compiled by Bankes on 23 December 1659, as 'A Greate Landskip of Bergens mr. Lilly' and was valued at 33 pounds. The copy after Dou appears on this list as 'A Coppy of a night Peice bought of mr lilly after...'. In

an earlier list it is recorded as 'A dutch peice of A man & woman singing, night peice on A small board of Dows of Leyden mr Lylly hath the Originall twas copied by one'. The original is now in the Queen's collection. Since it was not in the sale of Lely's estate, it seems probable that Lely had

already sold it to Charles II. The king's partiality for Dou's work is clear from his comment about the painting by Dou in the 'Dutch Gift', see p. 70.
260 Laing 1992. On the 1659 list the work appears as 'A coppy of A Turks head from Rainebrand/ the Orriginall is

Cardinal Mazarins'. The original is now in the Duke of Devonshire's collection. The copy is still in Kingston Lacy (National Trust). It may be a copy made in Italy, and Bankes may have acquired painting through N. Wray, who bought various paintings for him in Italy. With many thanks to

Alastair Laing of the National Trust for the information.
261 See p. 207, note 5.
262 Lettre from Jabach to M. de Metz, dated 10 March 1671, quoted from Monbeig Goguel 1988, p. 828, note 31.
263 See for Jabach the Elder esp. Vey 2000 and Grossman 1951.
264 Vey 2000, p. 142; on 7 June 1636, shortly after his father's funeral, Jabach and his brother-in-law Johan Hunthum were granted passports by the Cologne authorities for a journey through the Netherlands.
265 Vey 2000.
266 There are two known portraits of Jabach by Van Dyck, both of which must have been painted around 1637. One is in the Hermitage, St Petersburg, and the other in a private collection. See Barnes/ De Poorter/Millar/ Vey 2004, pp. 537-538.
267 He married Anna Maria de Groote, daughter of Hendrick de Groote and Sibille Duysterlo, in Cologne.

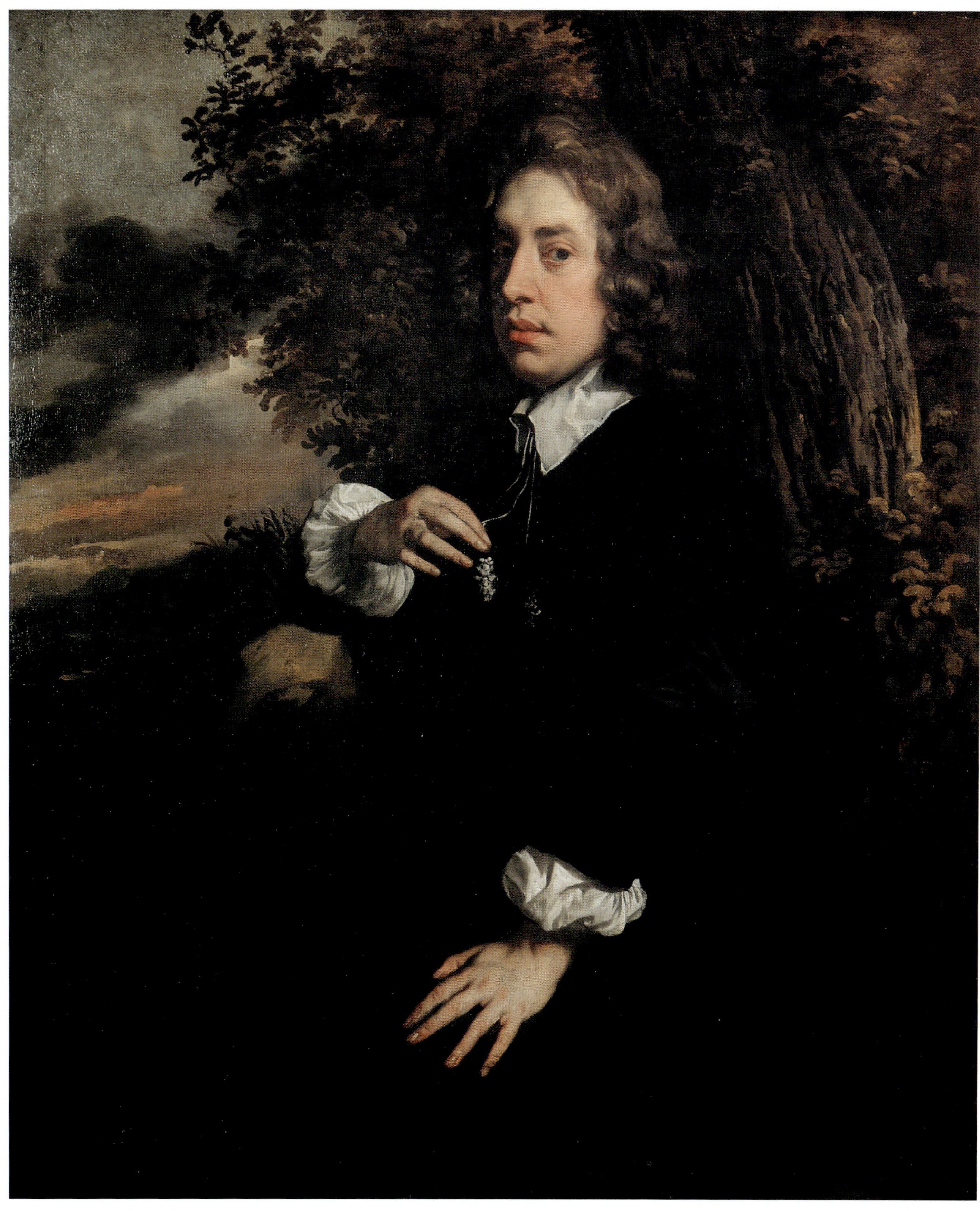

210 Peter Lely, Portrait of Everhard Jabach, canvas, 124 x 105 cm, Cologne, Wallraf-Richartz-Museum

ings in London between 1649 and 1653, although he was never mentioned as a buyer himself. The paintings he sold to the French king ten years later were acquired in London by various people. It seems unlikely that they were all working as his agents.[268] Jabach therefore probably bought many of the paintings afterwards.[269] It is, though, conceivable that he spent some time in London to make his selection and had his portrait painted by Peter Lely while he was there (fig. 210).

The pride of Jabach's collection were his paintings by sixteenth-century Italian masters, luminaries like Raphael, Titian, Leonardo da Vinci and many more. But he also owned works by Italian artists of the seventeenth century like Guido Reni, Carracci and Domenichino. In his drawings, too, the emphasis was on the Italian Renaissance. Jabach's collection rapidly became one of the most important in Europe. Christiaan Huygens gives an idea of the size of his collection of drawings in a letter dated 1664. Someone had told him that a man had already been engaged for four years in putting Jabach's drawings into albums and that it would take him at least another ten years to finish his task.[270] Jabach must have regarded his collection as trade goods and they represented a significant proportion of his possessions. In 1671 he estimated his total assets at 2 million livres, of which he stated that more than 500,000 livres were accounted for by his paintings, drawings and sculptures.[271]

Jabach's best customer was Louis xiv. In 1661-1662 he sold him 'paintings, busts and bronzes' for the huge sum of 330,000 livres. They included around a hundred paintings, some twenty of which had originally been part of Charles i's collection.[272] In 1671 Jabach transferred another 101 paintings and 5,542 drawings to the French king for 220,000 livres. He then started building up his own collection again.

Jabach had copies made of many of his paintings. These were for his own use, as a sort of record, but also for sale. According to contemporaries he sometimes omitted to mention that they were not originals. The French collector Loménie de Brienne recounted how Jabach sold a Virgin by 'Annibale Carracci' for 1,500 livres and a portrait of Gaston de Foix by 'Giorgione' for a similar sum. Both works, however, had been done by the French seventeenth-century painter Sebastien Bourdon. Only Loménie de Brienne had seen that they were forgeries. He noted that he had recognised Bourdon's hand in some of the folds of the draperies.[273] More than 150 copies are listed in the inventory drawn up after Jabach's death, most of which were made by 'Francisque', otherwise known as Jean-François Millet.[274]

Jabach also had his own drawings copied – he said himself that this was so that he could use them when 'he no longer had the originals'.[275] But there are indications that he sometimes sold the copies as originals. Among the drawings acquired by Louis xiv, for instance, there were copies of originals that Jabach had retained for himself.[276] He also had old drawings by Raphael and others extensively worked up.[277]

Jabach proved not always to have been entirely upright when it came to his statues too. A Swedish collector, who bought works from his collection at the sale held after his death, in 1696, wrote that there was virtually no difference in price between modern and antique busts. This was because all the old statues were composites. 'When Mr Jabach had an antique head, he had the garments or the armour of another marble attached to it. Furthermore, he likewise called a great many busts antique that in truth were modern, but he buried them in the ground, and he did many more things of this kind.'[278]

268 See for an overview of the paintings owned by Charles i that ultimately ended up with Jabach, Brejon de Lavergnée 1987. The paintings that Jabach later sold to the French king were purchased in London by various people, among them 'John Linchbeck'. This was probably a relative of one of Jabach's partners, Hans Cornelis Linterbeck (suggested by Raimbault 2002, p. 40.) See also Millar 1970-1972.

269 This is certainly true of Correggio's *Allegory of the Virtues*. It was acquired in 1651 at Charles i's sale by De Kritz, who subsequently sold it to an otherwise unidentified dealer 'Oudancour' or 'Adamcourt'. In 1653 this person took it to France, where it must have been acquired by Jabach. The dealer 'Oudancour' or Adamcourt' is referred to in the correspondence between Antoine de Bordeaux and Cardinal Mazarin, see Brejon de Lavergnée 1987.

270 Huygens 1888-1950, vol. 5, 1664-1665, letter dated 25 January 1664, pp. 20-21.

271 Schnapper 1994, p. 276

272 Brejon de Lavergnée 1987.

273 Hourticq 1905, p. 332.

274 Grouchy 1894.

275 Letter from Jabach to M. de Metz, dated 10 March 1671, '… copies que j'avais fait faire pour m'en servir à défaut des originaux'. Quoted from Monbeig Goguel 1988, p. 828, note 31.

276 Bacou 1978; Monbeig Goguel 1988, p. 830; Py 2001, p. 13.

277 Monbeig Goguel 1988. The working up of drawings was a very common practice in the seventeenth century.

278 Weigert/ Hernmarck, pp. 109-110. Letter from Daniel Cronström to Nicodemus Tessin the Younger, dated 2/12 March 1696: 'La raison en est que les "modernes" sont entièrement de marbre, alors que les autres sont faits de pièces ajustées. Ainsi, quand le bonhomme Chabac avait une tête antique, il faisait ensuite ajuster au mastic un revêtement ou une armeure [sic] d'un autre marbre. En outre il a également donné pour antiques nombre de bustes qui en vérité étaient modernes, mais il les enterrait dans le sol et faisait des tas de choses semblables'.

Although Jabach concentrated on collecting paintings and drawings by old masters, he also bought work by living artists and he had painters working for him.[279] When he saw a painting by Le Brun, which he had done in a day, he wanted to hire him immediately. He offered the young artist 20 pistolets a day and the freedom to choose what he wanted to make. Le Brun appears to have turned down the offer.[280]

As we have seen Jabach travelled through the Republic in 1636, when he was eighteen years old. He may have been there again a year later. In letters written in 1637 by the painter Daniel Mijtens to the Earl of Arundel's secretary there are references to a 'Mr Everard', probably Jabach.[281] This Mr Everard had gone to Dordrecht to look at a work by Leonardo da Vinci. In his opinion, however, it was only a copy after Jan Gossaert. Mijtens and Mr Everard also acted as intermediaries in the Earl of Arundel's purchase of works of art from the collection of Joachim van Wickevoort in Amsterdam, including paintings by Holbein, Titian and Dürer.[282] In March 1637 Mijtens and his companion also attended Jan Bassé's sale in Amsterdam. Rembrandt and Govert Flinck were present as well.[283]

When Jabach settled in Paris, he maintained close contact with people in his birthplace, Cologne, and Amsterdam. There were members of his family living in both cities and he did a great deal of business with them. His grandfather, his father and he himself had a trading house with the Hunthum and Duysterlo families.[284] In 1646, Jabach set up a trading company in Amsterdam with Pieter Hunthum, Hendrick Duysterlo, Hans Cornelis Linterbeck and Joan de Licht.[285] These people were all related to one another and most of them lived in Amsterdam.[286] In 1653 Jabach bought 1,000 drawings for 10,000 guilders from Lady Arundel, who was living in Amsterdam at that time. It is not clear whether he bought them from her directly or through a middleman.[287]

On 16 September 1668 Jabach wrote to the French minister Colbert about 'twelve crates of paintings' that he had had sent from Cologne and Amsterdam on Colbert's instructions.[288] They included works that had belonged to Charles I or to one of the English nobles at his court. Jabach's contact in Cologne was probably his nephew Franz von Imstenraedt, whose mother was Jabach's sister. Von Imstenraedt himself collected on a large scale from the 1650s onwards and had a magnificent collection of Italian, Flemish and Dutch paintings.[289] When Von Imstenraedt married in 1662, Vondel wrote a poem on the marriage.[290] We do not know who Jabach's contact in Amsterdam was. The most likely would seem to be a member of the Hunthum or De Licht families. Or might Uylenburgh have been involved? They had probably known each other since at least 1663.[291] The hefty sum of 5,142

279 Monbeig Goguel 1988, p. 832.
280 Jouin 1889, p. 103. Jouin took the information from the unpublished biography of Le Brun by Claude Nivelon, which dates from about 1695.
281 Hervey 1921, pp. 404-405, letters dated 18 February and 12 March 1637 from Daniel Mijtens to Edward Walker (see also Grossman 1951); Van Gelder/Jost 1985, p. 203, write that 'Mr Everard' could also have been Everard Quirijnsz van der Maes, but they too think it likelier that it is Jabach who is meant.
282 They were a portrait of a woman that was attributed to Andrea del Sarto, but according to Mijtens and Mr Everard was more probably by Titian, a portrait of a man by Holbein, a Madonna and a drawing of a dead man by Dürer and a Raphael, which according to the buyers was not authentic. They also bought six books. These were early editions of Greek and Roman authors, a number of which had been illustrated by Dürer. The paintings and books cost 1730 guilders altogether. The books had probably previously been owned by Matthys van Overbeke of Leiden, who had personally acquired from the Imhoff family in Nuremberg fourteen books from Pirckheimer's library. Van Overbeke had already sold eight of these volumes directly to the Earl of Arundel in 1636. See Van Gelder/ Jost 1985, p. 204.
283 See p. 160.
284 Vey 2000.
285 Grouchy 1894, p. 223. In the will of Aernout Hunthum (GAA, not. J. Thielmans, NA 2108, pp. 8-11, dated 9 January 1647, there is a reference to the contract between him, his brother Pieter Hunthum, Hendrick Duysterlo, Hans Cornelis Linterbeck and Joan de Licht. It was entered into on the last day of August 1646. The will specifically stipulates that Aernout Hunthum's children must also honour the contract. Jabach is not mentioned.
286 Joan de Licht was married to Catharina Hunthum (GAA, DTB 679, p. 126, banns dated 13 September 1647; GAA, not. J. Thielmans, NA 2108, p. 87, dated 14 November 1650, will of Joan de Licht and Catharina Hunthum); Aernout Hunthum was married to Maria de Licht (GAA, DTB 684, p. 208, dated 25 July 1659). In 1613 Margriet Jabach married Heijnrik Duysterlo (GAA, DTB 667, p. 106, dated 21 December 1613). Of importance to the contacts of the Uylenburghs is the fact that the Hunthum family was related in various ways to the Kerckrinck family. Pieter Hunthum was married to Cornelia Kerckrinck (GAA, DTB 673, p. 45, banns dated 30 September 1630) and Willem Kerckrinck (1616-1668) to Clara Hunthum (1620-1673), a daughter of Aernout Hunthum (he of the will of 1647 in the note mentioned above; GAA, DTB 676, p. 97, banns dated 20 September 1641). Willem Kerckrinck was a brother of Anna and Maria Kerckrinck, who together owned a painting 'made by Uylenburgh', see p. 124, note 134.
287 Howart 1998, p. 135.
288 Grouchy 1894, pp. 231-232. 'Je ne suis en peine que des douze caisses de tableaux que j'ai fait venir par vos ordres, Monseigneur, et qui sont parties de Cologne et d'Amsterdam il y a plus de trois semaines, tant par terre que par mer, sans en avoir eu depuis aucune nouvelle. S'ils arrivent heureusement ici, je ne fais nul doute que vous y trouverez de très belles choses, la mémoire me restant toute fraiche de quelques-uns que j'ai vus en Angleterre et trouvés alors fort beaux, il y a trente-trois ans, ce qui est bon signe'.
289 See for Von Imstenraedt, Seyfarth 1995 and Seyfarth 2000.
290 Verwey 1937, p. 878.
291 See p. 72.

guilders that Uylenburgh owed Jabach points to a high volume of business dealings. Jabach did not go to Amsterdam himself in 1675; instead he sent Gideon Cruydenier to take care of his business for him. Cruydenier's sister Judith was married to Joris de Kaersgieter and his other sister Hesther to Christiaen de Kaersgieter. The Kaersgieters were eminent art dealers in Amsterdam. Jabach sent Cruydenier on similar missions during this period. In 1672 Cruydenier was given the mandate to recover 8,840 livres from a person in Poitiers. This was a debt that Jabach had taken over from someone else and had nothing to do with art. At this time Cruydenier was living in Jabach's house in Paris.[292]

BUSINESS PARTNERS

Business contacts or agents were extremely important in selling art abroad. This is perhaps most clearly illustrated by the story of the sale of paintings to the Great Elector. Uylenburgh's decision to arrange the transaction on his own initiative in 1671, without involving his old friend the court artist Fromantiou, was one that he must have come to regret.

In many respects Ovens and Lely were ideal trading partners for Uylenburgh. Both were court painters and close friends of his. Thanks to their good relations with the courts in Schleswig and London respectively, Uylenburgh was able to sell works of art through them. Aside possibly from his own work, Ovens is unlikely to have sold paintings through Uylenburgh in Amsterdam. It is also debatable whether Lely ever sent art from London to Amsterdam, although there was considerably more available in London than in Schleswig. Uylenburgh also worked with Lely when they jointly purchased a collection of drawings.

Jabach's contacts with Uylenburgh must have been confined to supplying him with paintings and drawings. Unlike Lely, Ovens and Uylenburgh, Jabach was a banker, not an artist, which put him higher up the social ladder. Although Uylenburgh, Ovens and Lely were well-to-do, their assets paled into insignificance beside the wealth of the Parisian.

Paintings and drawings may also have been sent, not just for sale but with a view to having them copied. Copying was, as we have seen, an important activity in Uylenburgh's business. It must have been much easier to find talented copyists than to get hold of original Italian paintings to serve as examples. As far as original masterpieces were concerned, Jabach's collection must have looked like a treasure trove. Taking paintings and drawings on consignment from Jabach gave him the opportunity to have them copied. It is possible that this was done in consultation with the Frenchman and that copies made in Amsterdam went back to Paris. Something of the kind was in any event suggested in a French sale catalogue of 1755. By a drawing of Galatea that was attributed to Raphael, it states that this was a copy 'made by Allaert van Everdingen in Holland, who copied drawings for M de Jabac'.[293]

Creditors and clients

When Gerrit Uylenburgh got into financial difficulties in 1675, twenty-seven people applied to the bankruptcy chamber for money he owed them. A note was made of how much was due to them, but there is no record of why they believed they were entitled to it. The list of creditors is the most important document giving us an insight into Uylenburgh's business associates and possible circle of clients. It would be going beyond the scope of this book to deal with all of them individually. We have therefore decided to select the people who had an evident interest in art. This group includes Amsterdam art collectors, painters and a dealer in art supplies. Together with Everhard Jabach, they accounted for more than ninety percent of the total debt. Among the small group of Amsterdam art lovers we have included three who do not appear on the list of creditors, but whom we know from other sources to have had close relations with Uylenburgh – they are Pieter Six, Isaac Jan Nijs and Hendrick Scholten. And lastly we look at a number of art lovers in The Hague, who have already been mentioned because they maintained contact with Uylenburgh.

292 Paris, Archives Nationales, Minutier Central des notaires parisiens, étude C X X I, liasse 88, dated 2 October 1672; see also étude C X, liasse 145, dated 24 August 1662. With many thanks to Christine Raimbault, who drew our attention to this. She searched in vain for Jabach's warrant of attorney for Cruydenier to collect what Uylenburgh owd him.
293 See Py 2001, p. 21, note 45. This is a note in the Tallard sale, Paris 1755, 'faite en Hollande par Allaert van Everdingen, qui copiait des dessins pour M de Jabac'. It is tempting to suppose that this may have been done under some sort of supervision by Uylenburgh. Although there is no concrete evidence, it seems likely that Uylenburgh had contacts with the Van Everdingen family. At any rate, he owned a painting by Cornelis, Allaert's son, and Isaac Uylenburgh was a member of the Guild of St Luke in Alkmaar, where the Van Everdingens came from, see p. 211.

Pieter Schaep – After Everhard Jabach, Pieter Schaep – owed 1,420 guilders – was Uylenburgh's principal creditor. Schaep belonged to Amsterdam's regent class; he was a magistrate and a member of the town council. He was married to Constantia Reynst, daughter of the collector Gerard Reynst. Schaep himself was not known as a great collector; paintings in his country house 'Schapendoorn' on the River Vecht are listed in the inventory of his estate that was drawn up in 1686, but none with the name of the artist.[294] In the hall was the 'stone table with the tomb of Aristotle' from the Reynst Collection, which Schaep and his wife had doubtless inherited.[295] Uylenburgh bought extensively from this collection and it therefore seems likely that the money Schaep was claiming was an outstanding sum that he owed for these purchases.[296]

Herman Becker – In 1675 Uylenburgh owed Herman Becker 1,195 guilders. The Lutheran Becker was a merchant and ship charterer, he dealt in stocks and shares and acted as a financier.[297] In 1674 he was taxed on assets of 80,000 guilders.[298] In the 1650s he had dealings with the art dealer Johannes de Renialme. In exchange for a significant sum, De Renialme had pledged jewellery and a number of paintings by Jan Lievens and Philips Koninck.[299] In the 1660s Becker lent Rembrandt money on several occasions, again with paintings as collateral and this time with albums of prints too.[300] Painters like Frederick de Moucheron, Jan Lievens and Philips Koninck also borrowed money from him.[301] The latter's name appears in deeds together with Becker's several times.[302] Becker also knew the painters Ferreris and Jan Blom.[303] On more than one occa-

sion he had dealings with Joost Kemp, the man who probably commissioned wall decorations from Gerrit Uylenburgh.[304] On his death in 1678 Becker left a large collection of paintings – 231 works in all.[305] He had primarily Dutch masters, particularly Rembrandt, Jan Lievens and Philips Koninck, who were represented by fifteen, sixteen and six paintings respectively.[306] Although the notice of the sale of his possessions mentions 'Italian and Netherlandish Masters', he cannot have been particularly fond of Italian painting.[307] With the exception of a *John the Baptist Preaching* attributed to Tintoretto, he had only a few Italian works of art, listed without artists' names in the inventory. He did own two 'capital' landscapes by Claude Lorrain. Becker had no classical statues and in his large library there were no books relating to painting.[308]

Becker was the second person (Gerrit Hooft was the first) to go to the Amsterdam magistrates to demand his money back from Uylenburgh.[309] Two weeks later Uylenburgh's affairs were taken over by the bankruptcy chamber. It appears that Becker's step was the last straw needed to bring about Uylenburgh's bankruptcy. In March 1674 he had loaned Uylenburgh 1,710 guilders at six percent annual interest.[310] The sum that Becker was claiming must have been the balance of this loan. In 1675 he declined to sign the agreement in which Uylenburgh offered his creditors almost his entire collection of paintings to pay off his debts. Even after he had discussed the matter with the commissioners, he still did not sign. It was not until 20 July 1677, when Uylenburgh was already in England, that he finally signed the deed.[311] He probably realized that no more money would be forthcoming after all.

'A cockerel with a young woman by Gabriel Metsu' which appears in Becker's inventory may be the painting described by Uylenburgh in 1675

294 NHA, Weesp, not.. C. van Drosthagen, NA 5217, dated 19 February 1686.

295 See for the tomb, Logan 1979, p. 55, fig. 10. Aristotle's tomb originally came from the Vendramin Collection, most or all of which Reynst probably acquired; see p. 94.

296 In the Backer family archives (GAA, no. 172) there are various documents relating to the settlement of Gerard Reynst's estate. However, there are no specific indications of a settlement between Schaep and Uylenburgh; no. 570 (settlement of the estate of Gerard Reynst and Anna Schuyt), and no. 567 (will of Pieter Schaep and Constantia Reynst, dated 17 October 1669). See also Logan 1979, pp. 27-28.

297 See for Becker esp. Postma 1988.

298 GAA, archive no. 5028, inv. no. 662, tax register 200th penning, fol. 325v (district 33).

299 Postma 1988.

300 Doc, pp. 531, 533-534, 554-558, 567, 568, 577-579.

301 GAA, NA 4767, not. S. Pel-

grom, fol. 276 v. (Koninck), fol.277v (Moucheron). Becker's inventory, dated 19 October, 23 November 1678, was published in part for the first time by Bredius 1910, pp. 193-204, later Postma 1988 published a full transcription of the books and paintings, but not of the rest.

302 See for Philips Koninck p. 208, note 15 and p. 224, note 82.

303 See note 302.

304 See p. 208, note 15.

305 See note 301.

306 Postma 1988, p. 13, note 49, thinks that a breakdown can be made into six paintings by Jan Lievens and ten by his son Jan

Lievens the Younger, suggesting that all the paintings that are listed as Lievens the Elder are by the father and all those without this suffix are by the son. I believe that this is debatable.

307 Advertisement in the *Oprechte Haerlemse Dinsdaegse*

Courant of 21 March 1679; Postma 1988, p. 9.

308 See for the library, Postma 1988.

309 See p. 106.

310 Listed in Becker's inventory of 1678, fol. 275v. See for the inventory note 301.

311 See p. 109.

as 'A peasant with a cock by Gabriel Metsu', which means that Becker might have acquired this work at the sale of Uylenburgh's art holdings.[312]

Jan van Weert and Jan Bardewits – With 853 guilders owing to him, Jan Bardewits, who came from Bremen, was one of Uylenburgh's larger creditors.[313] In 1675 he collected eight paintings that had been left on consignment. These were chiefly works attributed to Italian masters such as Veronese, Bassano, Caravaggio and Giorgione. Bardewits was probably acting not for himself but for his wife Adriana de Vogelaer. In the books of the bankruptcy chamber he was described as the husband of the widow of Jan van Weert.[314]

Bardewits does not appear to have been very affluent in his own right. In 1674 he was assessed for tax on just 4,800 guilders.[315] In that year, however, he married Adriana de Vogelaer, who came from a considerably wealthier family.[316] She had previously been married to the merchant Jan van Weert, who had died in 1673.[317] His precise relationship to Hendrick or Henrico van Weert, who traded with Genoa, was appointed consul there in 1673, and was certainly living there by 1667, is not (as yet) known.[318] In 1667 Gerrit Uylenburgh gave him a mandate to claim the money that he had given the artist Jan Houwaert in 1663 to buy paintings.[319]

Bardewits's Italian paintings and the money owed by Uylenburgh must originally have been Jan van Weert's. The balance that was still outstanding may have been for paintings that Uylenburgh had bought from Van Weert or that he had been given to sell after Van Weert's death in 1673. Van Weert acted as a middleman, sometimes in dealings involving paintings. In 1678 Johan Maurits wrote to his agent Jacob Cohen in Amsterdam that it was such a shame that 'Vogelaer, Jan de Weert and now H. Piso are all dead'. He would have liked to ask one of them 'for a fee' to look for 'Brazilian paintings' in Amsterdam collections. By Vogelaer he probably meant Daniel de Vogelaer, Jan van Weert's father-in-law.[320]

Pieter and Jan Six – In 1675 Jan Six was owed 640 guilders by Uylenburgh. With his brother Pieter he was one of his most important and probably most loyal customers.[321] In February 1656 the art dealer acted with Pieter Six as surety for a house that Jan Six was selling.[322] In 1670 Jan Six's wife Margaretha Tulp was a witness at the baptism of Uylenburgh's daughter Sara. A year later Pieter Six was in attendance when another of Uylenburgh's children, Maria, was baptised.[323] When Uylenburgh went to England for good, he asked Jan Six, together with Theodoor Ferreris and Pieter Deldeijm, to look after his affairs in the Republic for him.[324] In 1675 Jan Six was the first person to be given permission by the commissioners of the bankruptcy chamber to retrieve works from the estate – he collected three paintings that he had pawned with Uylenburgh.[325]

the Hiole family, Hioolen 1915. A family portrait of Rutger van Weert with his wife and children by Jacob van Loo of 1644 is in a private collection, see Ekkart 2002, p. 37.

318 See Heeringa 1910/1917, vol. 2, pp. 57, 59, 109, 121, 455; Schutte 1976. Henrico van Weert was the consul in Genoa from 1673 to 1685. Notice of his marriage to Maria Reijniers was registered in Amsterdam on 1 January 1687, in the presence of his brother Rogier. This Rogier may be Ruggieri van Weert, who was in Livorno in 1655. When Rogier van Weert, 'merchant', gave notice of his marriage on 28 June 1668, his 'brother' Jan van Weert was a witness. Rogier and Jan van Weert lived next door to each other on the Herengracht (now nos. 70-72, see *Vier eeuwen Herengracht* 1976, p. 418). This Jan van Weert was certainly the husband of Adriana de Vogelaer, because the house had belonged to her father Daniel de Vogelaer. The only problem in identifying Jan, Rogier and Hendrick van Weert as brothers is that we cannot prove directly that the latter two were children of Rutger van Weert and Belitje Kempen.

319 See p. 72.

320 Quoted from Lemmens 1979, p. 275. Daniel de Vogelaer was related to Constantijn Huygens, so Johan Maurits probably knew him through Huygens. See for the family relationship, Unger 1885, appendix F.

321 See for Pieter Six esp. De Boer 1948; see for Jan Six esp. Van Eeghen 1984 and Möller 1984.

322 See p. 64.

323 See p. 76.

324 See p. 110.

325 See p. 106.

312 See for a possible identification, p. 304, note 62. Becker also owned 'A large work of Peace with much ornamentation'. This painting may have been the one referred to in Uylenburgh's valuation (no. 50) as 'an capital piece by PP Rubens, Peace', which at 650 guilders was the most expensive work the art dealer had.

313 Jan Bardewits may have been the 'Bardewits' who held meetings of the Labadists in his house in Amsterdam after Jean de Labadie went to Herford in 1670, see NNBW, vol. 6, columns 70, 71.

314 See p. 107, note 259.

315 GAA, archive no. 5028, inv. no. 662, tax register 200th penning, fol. 358r (district 38).

316 In 1674 as 'Jan de Waert's widow' she was taxed on 100,000 guilders (GAA, archive no. 5028, inv. no. 662, tax register 200th penning, fol. 443v. (district 48)). Notice of the marriage of Bardewits and De Vogelaer was given on 3 August 1674 (GAA, DTB 689, p. 241). Bardewits had previously been married to Catrina Dupré.

317 Jan van Weert was the son of the furrier Rutger van Weert and Geertruij Wijers.

This Rutger remarried in 1627; his second wife was Belitje Kempen. To this marriage was born, among other children, a Hendrick, who was baptized in 1635. This Hendrick does not however seem to be the same person as the later Henrico, consul in Genoa, since when he published the banns for his marriage in 1687 he gave his age as 44. It is possible that Hendrick died young and that a second Hendrick was born around 1643. In Rutger van Weert's will of 1648 Jan van Weert and five other unnamed children are mentioned (GAA, not. J. Westfrisius, NA 508, fol. 198v-200v, dated 7 February 1648). When Jan van Weert gave notice of his marriage to Adriana de Vogelaer on 24 July 1657, one of the witnesses was the Amsterdam grocer Isaac Hiole, who was married to Walburgh Wijers, a sister of Geertruij, the mother of Jan van Weert (GAA, DTB 477, p. 357). Adriana de Vogelaer was then the widow of Dirck van der Gal. At the baptism of Jan van Weert and Adriana de Vogelaer's son Johannes on 8 September 1658, Rutger van Weert the Younger and Jan's half sister Magdalena van Weert were witnesses. See for

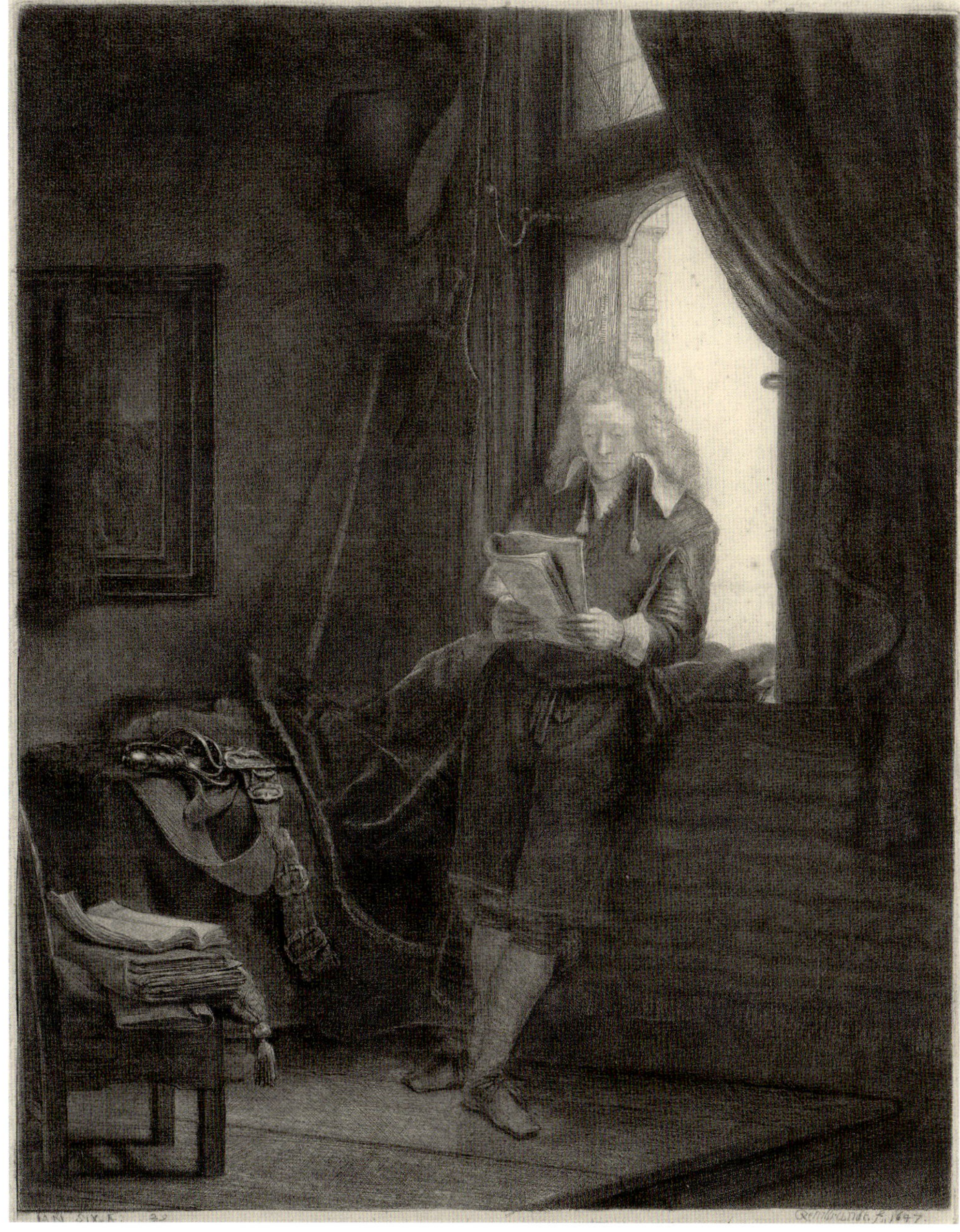

Both brothers collected art. The tax assessment for 1674, when his assets were estimated at 650,000 guilders, gives an indication of Pieter's immense wealth. Jan Six, although assessed for the far from inconsiderable sum of 280,000 guilders, was appreciably less well off.[326] Houbraken tells us that after church on Sundays Govert Flinck was in the habit of visiting 'artists and art lovers', among them Pieter and Jan Six, who, writes Houbraken, 'afterwards owned many superb Italian paintings and also outstanding art on paper'.[327] One of the paintings Pieter Six possessed was Rubens's *Leander and Hero*, which had previously belonged to Rembrandt.[328] There is no known inventory for Pieter himself, but there is one for his son, who bore the same name. At his manor in Lisse, which had previously belonged to his father, there was a 'Rome by Uylenberg' and the 'four seasons by Uylenberg with staffage by Lingelbagh'. He also owned paintings that were attributed to Raphael, Palma Vecchio, Palma Giovane, Ribera, Titian, Rembrandt, Frederick de Moucheron, Roghman and many others.[329] It is quite possible that a significant proportion of these paintings had been bought by his father.

Jan Six, who was six years younger than his brother Pieter, is now much better known. He studied law at Leiden and went on a Grand Tour to Italy in 1641. Between about 1645 and 1655 he saw a great deal of Rembrandt. In 1647 the artist made an etching of Six (fig. 211) and seven years later he painted the famous portrait.[330] Six also owned several paintings by him, including *The Preaching of John the Baptist* (fig. 109). In 1654 Six married Margaretha Tulp, the daughter of the renowned physician Nicolaes Tulp. In 1671 Jan de Bisschop dedicated his survey of important Italian drawings, the *Paradigmata*, to Jan Six. Vondel wrote several poems for Six and said of him that he 'was in love with Art and Scholarship'.[331] Six himself also wrote poetry and a tragedy, for which Rembrandt did an illustration.

There is a surviving catalogue of Six's collection dating from 1702, which reveals that he had a large collection of paintings, many of them Italian, and antique statues.

Jan van Wickevoort – The Amsterdam merchant Johan or Jan van Wickevoort was claiming 585 guilders from Uylenburgh in 1675. He came from a family that was extremely interested in art.[332] His brother Joachim, in particular, was an eminent collector and art agent. He owned, among other things, rare objects, paintings, classical statues and manuscripts illustrated by Dürer.[333] Jan must also have had an interest in art, but we know less about the size and importance of his collection. An inventory of his manor house, Steevliet near Eemnes, was compiled after his death in 1678. He had around forty paintings there, but

regrettably an artist is named in only two cases: Pieter Aertsen (a kitchen scene) and, much more important for our purposes, a small painting by Uylenburgh. It was described as 'A small figure by Uijlenborg with a curtain'.[334] He must have acquired it from Gerrit Uylenburgh himself.

Herman Stoffelsz van Swoll – In 1675 Herman Stoffelsz van Swoll was owed 200 guilders by Uylenburgh. In 1656 he had been keeper of the Exchange Bank and in 1678 he landed the lucrative job of postmaster for the postal traffic with Hamburg. In drawing up his marriage contract he was assisted by 'his good friend', the collector Gerard Reynst.[335] He got Nicolaes Verkolje to make copies of paintings by Gerard de Lairesse and other masters, which he paid for by the piece.[336] When his property was sold in 1699, an advertisement stated that he had amassed his collection 'with great effort and expense over many years'.[337] Van Swoll owned paintings by De Lairesse, Anthony van Dyck, Nicolaes Berchem, two capital pieces by Lingelbach, Guercino, Veronese, Titian, Vouet, Rubens and many others. He also had a collection of classical statues.[338] In 1671 he and Uylenburgh together valued the paintings in an estate, from which we may infer that he was respected as an art expert.[339] In 1674 he was taxed on assets of 12,000 guilders.[340] He was not one of the very wealthy regents but rather a member of the prosperous middle class. At that time his assets were comparable to those of someone like Theodoor Ferreris.[341]

Cornelis van Gheel – Cornelis van Gheel was not one of the major creditors. In 1675 Uylenburgh owed him a mere 75 guilders. Little is known about Van Gheel as a collector. He was, however,

329 The catalogue of the sale of 2 September 1704 in Amsterdam is printed in De Boer 1948. An inventory of Pieter Six of July 1704 in G A A, not. J. Lansman, N A 4720, pp. 653-658. According to this inventory Pieter Six the Younger had exchanged the painting of Mary Magdalene by Titian, which fetched 410 guilders, for a Saint Francis by Carracci and a King David by Lastman.

330 The painting is still in the Six Collection in Amsterdam.

331 Verwey 1937, p. 830.

332 Jan van Wickevoort was a Lutheran; in 1651 he married Elisabeth Rulandt (or Reelandt). He dealt with people in Riga, Hamburg and elsewhere. See Utrechts Archief, not. H. Vyandt, inv. no. U 78a1, deed

no. 1, dated 28 March 1667 (in this he authorized his brother Joachim to collect a debt from Baron Henrick Cronestern in Riga); not. H. Vyandt, inv. U 78a1, deed 5, dated 14 April 1667 (power of attorney to collect a debt in Hamburg). However Wickevoort also bought, for example, a flock of 68 sheep for 306 guilders (not. H. Vyandt, inv. no. U 78 a1,

333 Van Gelder/Jost 1985, pp. 39, 40, 200-204. In 1646 Casper Wickevoort bought classical statues at the same sale where Hendrick Scholten and Rembrandt also bought works. See also p. 280.

334 Inventory Jan van Wickevoort, Utrechts Archief,

deed no. 13, dated 8 November 1667). He was buried in Amsterdam in 1678.

333 Van Gelder/Jost 1985, pp. 39, 40, 200-204. In 1646 Casper Wickevoort bought classical statues at the same sale where Hendrick Scholten and Rembrandt also bought works. See also p. 280.

334 Inventory Jan van Wickevoort, Utrechts Archief,

Court archives for 1811, see inv. no. 1059, 26 June 1679 (The Getty Provenance Index). Small curtains were usually hung in front of valuable paintings or works with a risqué subject. Given that Uylenburgh's paintings were never very expensive, this may have been a somewhat saucy piece.

335 See for a brief summary Bergvelt/Kistemaker 1992, p. 329.

336 G A A, not. P. Schabaelje, N A 6004, dated 8 July 1698, writ by Stoffelsz Van Swoll in which he declared that he had agreed with Verkolje that the latter would copy some paintings, 'both by Larissen and other masters and that he would give 12 guilders for each copy'; G A A, not. C. van Loon, N A 6972, dated 28 October 1700, statement that Jan Verkolje's widow had agreed on behalf of her son Nicolaas that he would make copies for 12 guilders each, but he had demanded twice the amount.

337 Dudok van Heel 1975B, p. 160, nos. 53, 58.

338 Hoet/Terwesten 1752-1770, vol. 1, pp. 47-52, sale of 22 April 1699.

339 See Appendices, p. 294.

340 G A A, archive no. 5028, inv. no. 662, Tax register 200th penning, fol. 322v (district 33)

the son-in-law of one of the leading Amsterdam art collectors, Joannes Wtenbogaert, whom Rembrandt portrayed in an etching in 1639.[342] Wtenbogaert owned a collection of paintings (with works by Rubens, Jordaens, Van Dyck and Flinck) and inherited from his cousin Jacques de Gheyn III (see fig. 77) his collection of natural history specimens and paintings by Rembrandt, Brouwer, Jan Lievens and Holbein. His pride and joy was his collection of drawings and prints.[343] De Bisschop borrowed drawings of Roman statues by Salviati and Jacques de Gheyn from him to use in his *Icones*, and dedicated the second volume of the book to him. In his introduction De Bisschop praised Wtenbogaert's 'great esteem for art on paper, prints from wood and copper as well as drawings, and besides this a thorough knowledge, a fervent desire to have them, a constant industry in collecting them, ample means, and lastly a heart inclined to do good with all this'.[344] It is almost inconceivable that Wtenbogaert did not know Uylenburgh. On his death in 1680 Wtenbogaert left the collection of drawings to his daughter Maria, who was married to Cornelis van Gheel.[345] It is clear from the will that Van Gheel already had some of the drawings in his possession, which would seem to suggest that he was also interested in art.

Gijsbert van Goor – In the same year that Uylenburgh was forced to go to the bankruptcy chamber, Gijsbert van Goor, to whom he owed 67 guilders, also found himself in serious financial difficulties.[346] Van Goor, who owned the manor

of Tienhoven near Culemborg, must have been an avid collector. He had a collection of important Italian masters.[347] In 1674 he was taxed on assets of 65,000 guilders.[348] His father Cornelis Gijsbrechtsz van Goor, a merchant who traded in Italy, was taxed on almost ten times as much.[349] He acted as middleman for the Sicilian nobleman Antonio Ruffo in the matter of an order from Rembrandt.[350]

In his hall Gijsbert van Goor, who also called himself Ghisberto, had two maps of Italy in gilt frames. As well as paintings he also owned statues, including eight 'statues of Roman emperors'. When his property was inventoried in 1675, he had 44 empty picture frames in the attic.[351] This would seem to suggest that he may also have dealt in paintings.

We can get some idea of what Van Goor had in terms of art from a number of deeds drawn up in 1673.[352] In that year Van Goor's wife wanted to pledge a great many paintings and valuable silverware to her brother, an Antwerp merchant. The works were taken in crates from Amsterdam to a merchant and tapestry maker in Antwerp, who had taken charge of them. The valuables were collateral for a consignment of 'crude sulphur'. Among the paintings were works by Guido Reni, Lorenzo Lotto, Murillo (two beggars), Van Dyck, Mola, Titian and Ribera, and by Dutch artists like Dujardin, Rembrandt, De Heem, Pieter van Laer and Cornelis van Poelenburch.[353] It appears that some of the paintings came from Gerard Reynst's collection. Van Goor owned Reni's *Susannah and the Elders*, Lorenzo Lotto's *Holy Night* and Jacopo

341 Ibid., fol. 545v (district 58), Ferreris was assessed on assets of 13,000 guilders.

342 See for Wtenbogaert, a cousin of the Remonstrant preacher of the same name, esp. Dudok van Heel 1978.

343 Dudok van Heel 1978.

344 De Bisschop, 1668-1669.

345 GAA, NA 2663, not. D. Ypelaer, dated 3 March 1678; Dudok van Heel 1978, p. 165; 'will give all the party's [i.e. Wtenbogaet's] collection of drawings and prints, which consists of various books of drawings and prints, and he declared that he transfers ownership of all of these (that is both the part that will be found in his house on his death and the part that will be with the aforesaid Mr Van Gheel) and that they shall belong to his aforementioned daughter Maria'. Wtenbogaert's collection then passed to the two sons of Cornelis van Gheel and Maria Wtenbogaert, Jan and Jacob van Geel. The collection was sold at auction in 1722. An advertisement for the sale referred to drawings by Titian,

Parmigianino, Veronese, Guido Reni, Claude Lorrain, Rubens and Van Dyck, and by Dutch artists like Schellincks, Lingelbach, Moucheron, De Bisschop and many more.

346 GAA, archive no. 5072, DBK, inv. no. 603, fol. 88v-96v, dated 11 and 12 May, 22 July 1675. Inventory of the property of Gijsbert van Goor. The inventory lists numerous paintings, but almost all of them without an artist's name with the exception of a 'naked woman in a sea triumph' by Holstein. The estate was esti-

mated at something over 3,300 guilders, but this did not include the paintings and jewellery.

347 In the 1680s Van Goor seems to have withdrawn to his country estate near Culemborg, according to a number of deeds in the Utrechts Archief (not. H. van Hees, inv. no. U110a1, deed no. 133, dated 22 August 1684; inv. no. U110a2, deed no. 226, dated 25 August 1688; inv. no. U110a2, deed no. 232, dated 21 September 1688).

348 GAA, archive no. 5028, inv.

no. 662, Tax register 200th penning, fol. 280r (district 29).

349 GAA, archive no.5028, inv. no. 662, Tax register 200th penning, fol. 408r (district 44). Cornelis Gijsbrechtsz van Goor's assets were assessed at 600,000 guilders.

350 Giltaij 1999, pp. 43-44. This was the famous *Aristotle*, now in the Metropolitan Museum in New York.

351 'Eight gilded frames for paintings both large and small 30.-'; 'six and thirty frames for paintings both large and small 75.-'. See the inven-

tory referred to in note 346.

352 Published by Duverger 1984-2002, vol. 9, pp. 439-442. Deeds dated 27-28 March 1673, 28 March 1673, 24 April 1673 and 23 August 1673. See also GAA, not. F. Tixerandet, NA 3681, pp. 569-571, dated 28 December 1673.

353 'A Spiral Staircase with an Old Man sitting on a chair by Rembrant' was very probably the painting that is now in the Louvre (panel, 29 x 33 cm, signed and dated 1633, Br. 431). Van Goor's wife's brother's name was Benedetto Lenaerts.

Bassano's *Entombment*. Gerard Reynst owned paintings with identical compositions by these artists, which were included in the *Caelaturae*, the set of 34 engravings of the most important works in his collection.[354] Had Van Goor acquired them directly from Reynst's heirs or through Uylenburgh, who bought part of the Reynst Collection?

Nicolaes Anthonie Flinck – In 1675 Nicolaes Anthonie Flinck, the son of the painter Govert Flinck, was claiming 66 guilders from Uylenburgh. He was living in Rotterdam at the time and got Theodoor Ferreris to sign the agreement between Uylenburgh and the creditors on his behalf. Flinck was to become one of the most eminent connoisseurs and collectors of his time. In 1675, though, he was not yet thirty and, with the exception of what he might have inherited from his father, his collection cannot have been very large. It is possible that Flinck was owed the money he was claiming in 1675 for works of art he had sold.

Hendrick Scholten – Hendrick Scholten, a merchant trading with Italy and the Levant and a director of the Dutch East India Company (1670), is not listed as one of Uylenburgh's creditors in 1675.[355] He was however one of the witnesses at the baptism of Uylenburgh's daughter Abigael in the Westerkerk in 1668 and must therefore have known Uylenburgh well.[356] In 1674 Scholten was taxed on assets of 210,000 guilders.[357] He seems to have had a particular liking for classical statues. When a group of statues was sent from Antwerp to Amsterdam for auction in 1646, he was one of the buyers.[358] Jan de Bisschop included four of Scholten's statues in the second volume of his *Icones* (1669).[359] In view of his contacts with Italy it is possible that Scholten (perhaps with Uylenburgh?) acquired art directly from there. It was

not unusual for merchants to work with artists in bringing art from Italy. For instance, the Rotterdam collector Reinier van der Wolff got paintings from Italy through David Beck, and Joseph Deutz used Michael Sweerts as his agent in Rome.[360]

There is no known inventory of Scholten's property, but in 1705 'a lot of extraordinary Marble Antique Statues […] collected over many years and left by Hendrik Scholte' were sold at auction.[361] There are indications that he also had an important collection of paintings, but virtually nothing is known about it.[362]

In 1674 Scholten had himself painted with his youngest son Jeronimus by Caspar Netscher (fig. 212).[363] In the painting there are references to two statues the collector owned. Jeronimus holds in his hand a miniature version of the statuette of the young Dionysus, which was illustrated in reverse in De Bisschop's *Icones* (cf. fig. 213).[364] In the background can be seen a large statue of Dionysus and a satyr, which likewise appeared in the *Icones*.[365] It is striking that Netscher showed this statue in the same direction as in the *Icones*, in other words as the mirror image of the original (fig. 214). Netscher evidently worked from the print and not the actual sculpture. A *Holy Family with John the Baptist* attributed to Sebastiano del Piombo can also just be made out in the painting. Ovens drew a copy of the painting, probably the most important Italian work Scholten owned, adding a meticulous and admiring inscription below his drawing (fig. 215).[366]

Isaac Jan Nijs – Like Hendrick Scholten, Isaac Jan Nijs was not one of Uylenburgh's creditors. Nijs was also a dealer trading with Italy and the Levant. In the 1650s he spent some time in Livorno, after which he lived in Amsterdam.[367] He was, among other things, a regent of the old men's and old women's almshouses.[368] Nijs's sec-

354 See for the paintings, without the reference to Van Goor, Logan 1979, nos. 5 (Bassano; there are various versions of the composition known), 18 (Lotto; the painting is no longer known), 23 (Reni; there are still numerous extant versions of the composition).

355 See for a brief biography of Scholten, Bergvelt/ Kistemaker 1992, p. 328; see for Scholten and the Levantine trade, Heeringa 1910-1917, vol. 2.

356 See p. 76.

357 G A A, archive no. 5028, inv. no. 662, Tax register 200th penning, fol. 393 (district 42).

358 Van Gelder/Jost 1976, p. 297.

359 See p. 232; Van Gelder/Jost 1985; De Bisschop 1668-1669, nos. 66, 67, 68 and 69.

360 See Poelmans 1917; Bikker 1998.

361 Advertisement in the *Amsterdamsche Courant*, see Dudok van Heel 1975B. In his will Scholten had stipulated that his house on the Herengracht and his collection were not to be sold until 25 years after his death; Van der Veen 1992, p. 68.

362 For instance Scholten owned Rembrandt's *Old Man Asleep*, which is now in Turin, Galleria Sabauda, see Corpus I, 1982, no. A 17.

363 Wieseman 2002, no. 129.

364 De Bisschop 1668-1669, no. 66, see Van Gelder/Jost 1985, pp. 150-151. The statue now forms a pair in Brunswick with the *Hercules as a child* that belonged to Uylenburgh (see fig. 173).

365 De Bisschop 1668-1669, no.67, see Van Gelder/Jost 1985, pp. 151-152.

366 The painting must have been a version of the so-called 'Madonna del velo' by Sebastiano del Piombo, which is now in the Narodni Gallery in Prague. In 1655 this painting was in the collection of the widow of Thomas Howard and later in the collection of Franz von Imstenraedt. See Volpe/Lucco 1980, no. 65, p. 114, and Hirst 1981, pp. 84-86, 137.

367 See for the Nijs family esp. Van Eeghen 1968; Elias 1903-1905, vol. 2, pp. 645-646; Heeringa 1910-917, vol. 1, p. 116.

368 Nijs appears in Jacob Adriaensz Backer's Regentesses and Regents of the Old Men's and Women's Hospice of 1676 (now the Amsterdams Historisch Museum).

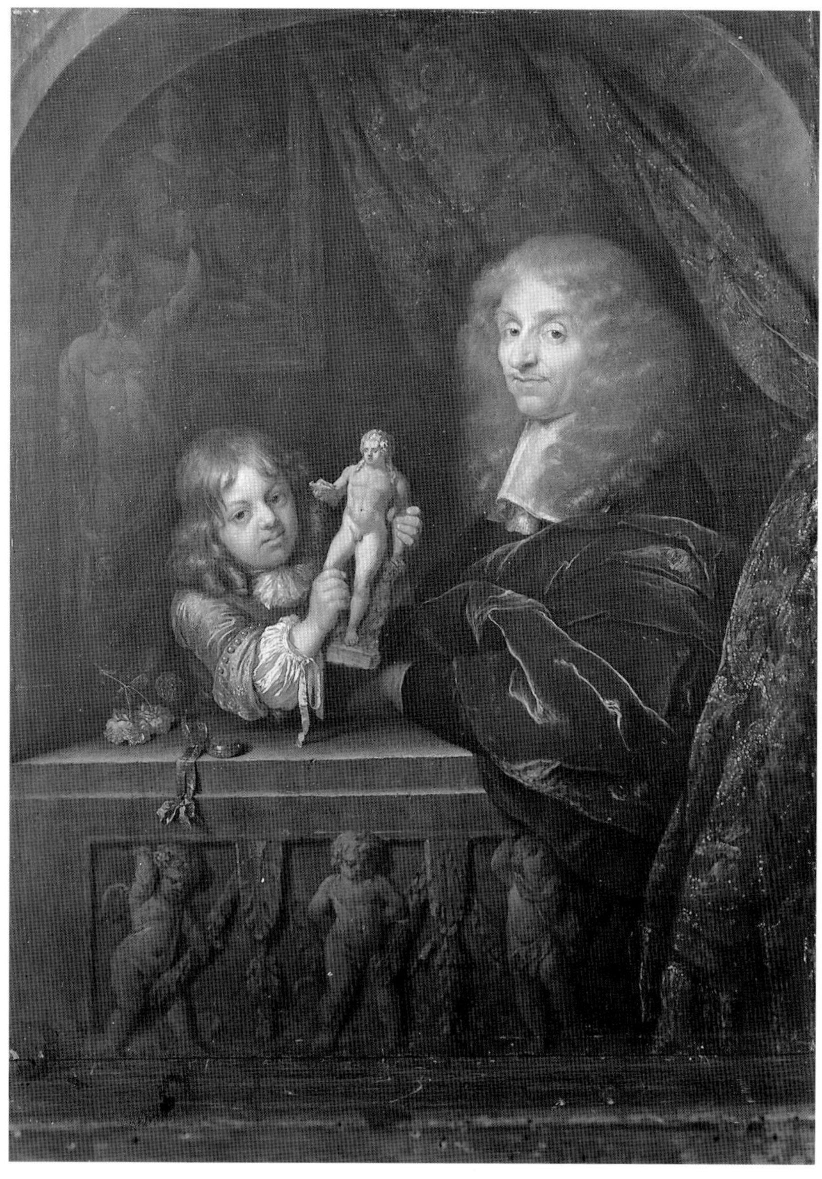

After Nijs's death, his collection with a 'lot of outstandingly fine paintings [...] including many by leading Italian Masters' was sold in 1691.[370] Nijs lived in a palatial house on the Keizersgracht (now number 577), five houses along from Uylenburgh's. It was built for Nijs between 1664 and 1666 to a design by Philips Vingboons.[371]

Nijs was born in Venice; he was the son of Daniel Nijs, a merchant and banker who himself had owned a large collection and sold art to, among other people, famous English collectors like Arundel and Carleton.[372] He also acted as intermediary in the sale of the Duke of Gonzaga's magnificent collection in Mantua to King Charles I.

PAINTERS AND SUPPLIERS OF ARTISTS' MATERIALS

Alongside the predominantly rich art lovers, there are also a several painters on the list of creditors – the brothers Willem and Daniel Schellincks, Adriaen Backer, Jacob Colijn and Jean Gericot. We know that Gericot was claiming 120 guilders which he was owed for two paintings he had sold to Uylenburgh.[373]

Adriaen Backer wanted 76 guilders. This relatively low sum seems to indicate that he was also owed some or all of the money for a painting.

Jacob Colijn(s) was a reasonably well-to-do artist. In 1674 he was taxed on 6,000 guilders, only a little less than Uylenburgh himself.[374] Like Backer, he was claiming 76 guilders. In 1675 Uylenburgh owned a painting of the *Day of Judgement* by David Colijn, Jacob's father, which

ond wife Maria Munter, with Pieter Six, was a witness at the baptism of Uylenburgh's daughter Maria in the Amstelkerk in 1671. In 1669 Nijs helped Uylenburgh recover money he had owing to him in Genoa. It is quite possible that Nijs was not only one of Uylenburgh's customers but also worked with him importing art from Italy. In 1674 Nijs was taxed on assets of 100,000 guilders.[369]

369 GAA, archive no. 5028, inv. no. 662, Tax register 200th penning, fol. 540v (district 57).
370 Dudok van Heel 1975B, p. 157. Advertisement in the *Amsterdamsche Courant*. The sale took place on 11 April 1691.
371 Ottenheym 1989, pp. 99, 232, 252, 253.

372 See for a brief history of the turbulent life of Daniel Nijs, Meijer 1991, pp. 74-79.
373 See p. 107, note 260.
374 GAA, archive no. 5028, inv. no. 662, Tax register 200th penning, fol. 111r (district 12), 'Jacob Colijn fine painter'. See for Colijn Oldewelt 1942B, pp. 101-106.

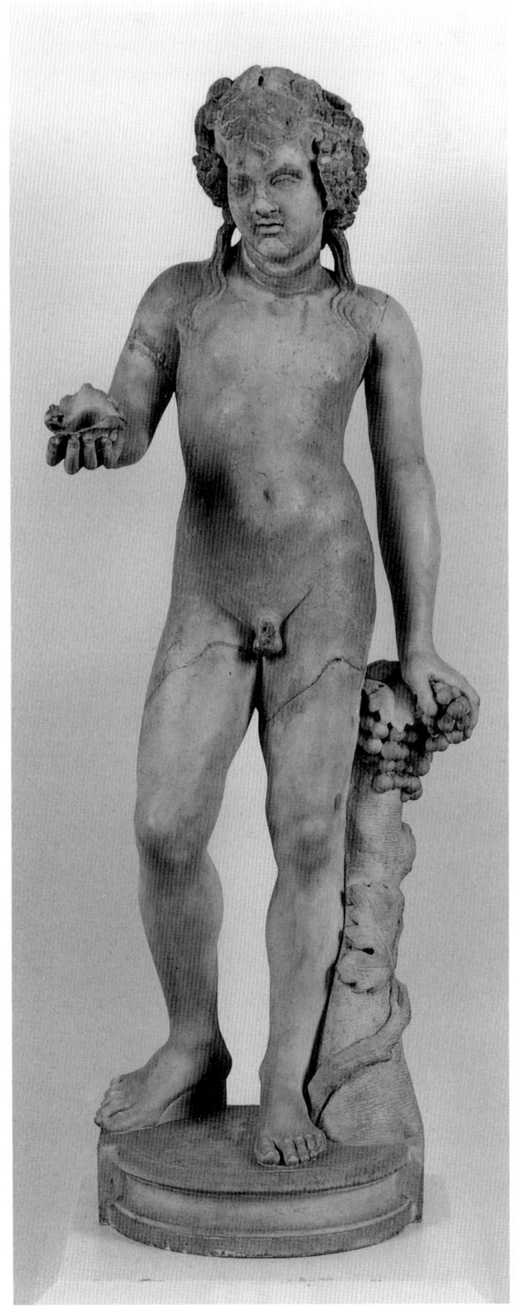

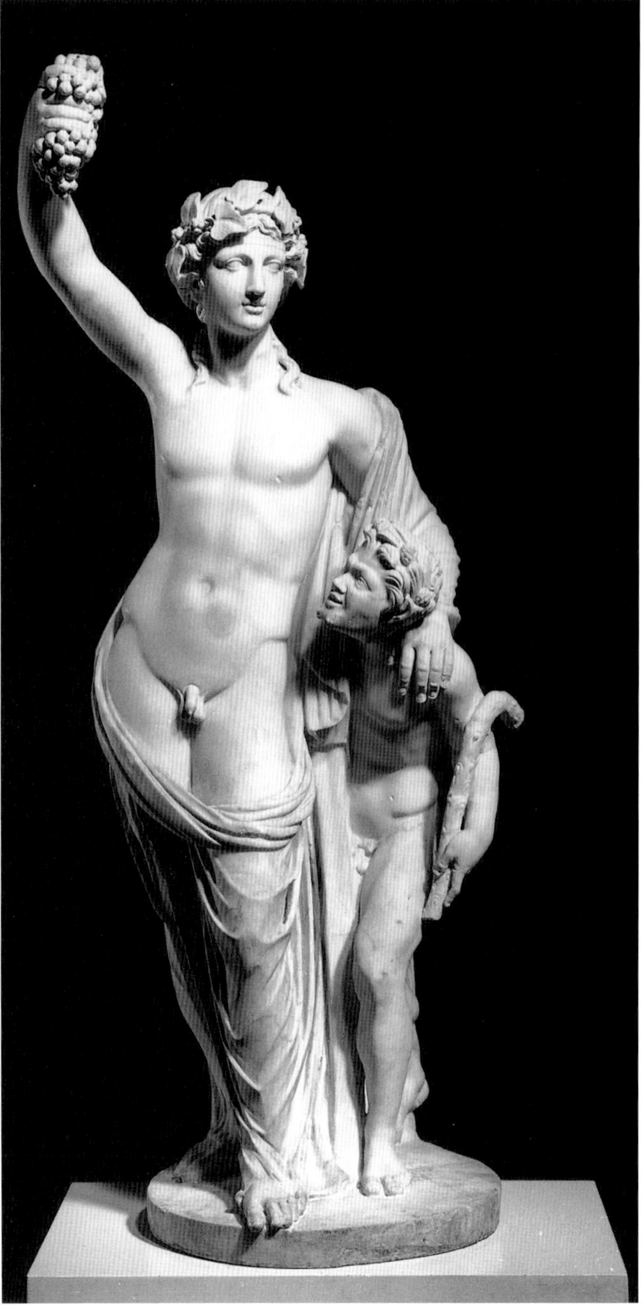

he valued at 80 guilders. The money might have been the payment outstanding for this work.

Among the painters Willem Schellincks was the biggest creditor with a claim for 230 guilders. His brother Daniel wanted 90 guilders. Willem Schellincks was a painter first, but also an amateur poet.[375] Between 1661 and 1665 he had been on a long trip through England, France, Italy, Malta, Germany and Switzerland. Among the people he had met in Rome was Jacques Vaillant.[376] After his return to Amsterdam he lived near Uylenburgh on the Keizersgracht close to the Spiegelstraat. In 1674 Schellincks and his wife were assessed for assets of 4,000 guilders, 3,000 less than Uylenburgh. On Schellincks's death the couple proved to have capital of at least 19,000 guilders. After his death in 1678 his 'paper art' and paintings were sold. The paintings that he left unfinished were completed by Frederick de Moucheron and Nicolaes Berchem before they

375 Like his friend the painter Gerbrandt van den Eeckhout, who wrote a poem to him. See for the Schellincks brothers, De Vries 1883.
376 Houbraken 1718-1721, vol. 2, pp. 263-273.

282

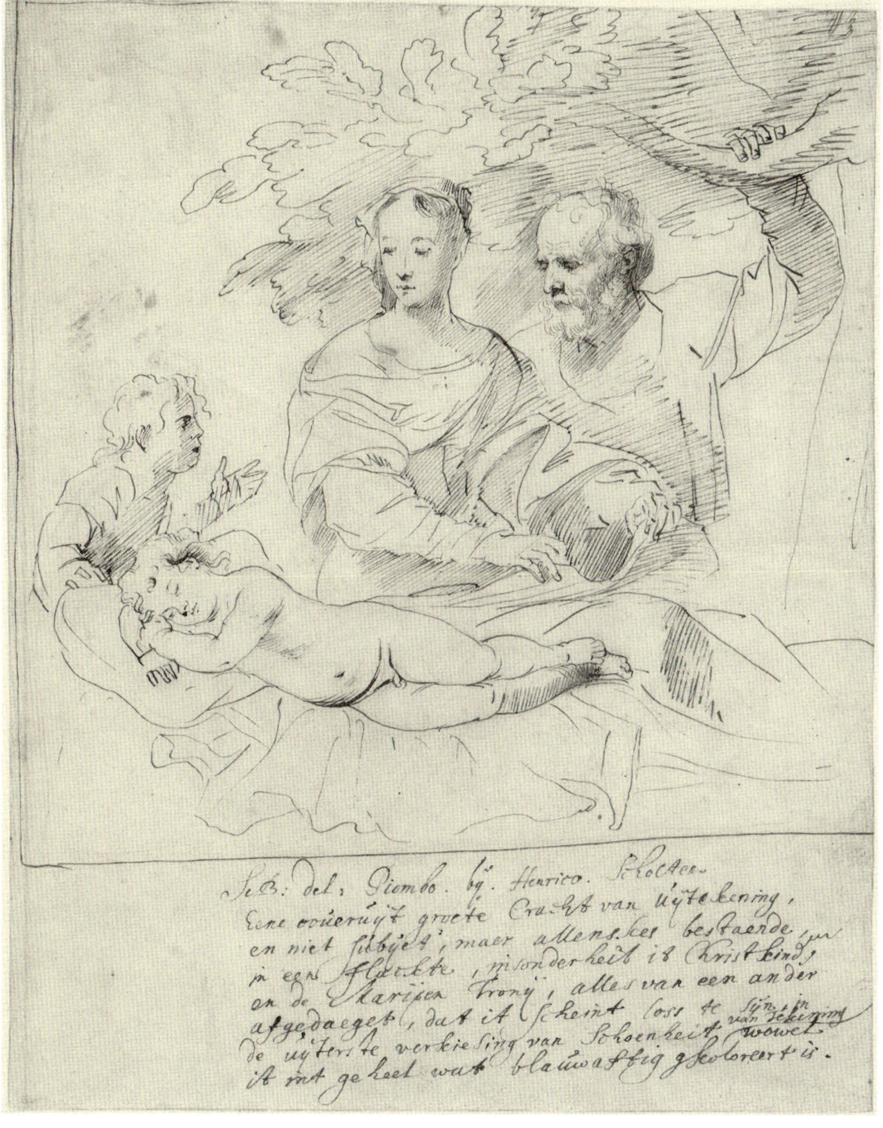

215 Jürgen Ovens after Sebastiano del Piombo, The holy family with the young John the Baptist, pen and brown ink over traces of leadpoint, 25.2 x 20.4 cm, Hamburg, Hamburger Kunsthalle
The inscription reads: 'Seb: del Piombo bij Henrico Scholten. Eene ooveruyt groete cracht van uytekening, en niet subyet, maer allenskes bestaende in een flackte, insonderheit is Christkind en de Maryen trony, alles van een ander afgedaeget, dat it scheint loss te sijn in de uyterste verkiesing van schoenheit van tekening wowel it int geheel wat blauwaffig gkoloreert is'

burgh. The money they were owed was probably for works of art they had sold to him, although there are no paintings by either of them in the inventory.

Besides the painters, there was also a supplier of artists' paraphernalia among the creditors, Pieter Heeremans. His older half-brother Jacob had been one of Hendrick Uylenburgh's creditors.[379] Heeremans took the firm over from his half-brother and must have been one of the leading suppliers of panels, canvases and frames in Amsterdam. He was taxed on assets of 4,000 guilders in 1674.[380] The sum of 364 guilders that he was claiming from Uylenburgh will undoubtedly have been for artists' supplies or frames.

The sums owing to Abraham de Coninck and Jacob de la Tour may also have been for the supply of painting materials. The former was probably the Amsterdam paint merchant of this name.[381] The other was a cloth merchant, from whom Uylenburgh may have bought artist's linen.[382]

Several of Uylenburgh's creditors not discussed so far did have contacts with the art world. Of these, Cornelis Meijer, Anna Becx and Matthijs Crayers must certainly be mentioned.[383] Meijer was a friend of Jan Six's and left part of his collection with him before he went to Rome, where he lived from 1675 until his death in 1701 and earned

were put up for sale.[377] Daniel Schellincks, Willem's younger brother, appears to have been a silk merchant by trade – this at least is how he described himself at the time of his wedding in 1662. Houbraken, however, lists him as 'a good landscape painter'.[378] The Schellincks brothers seem to have moved in the same circles as Uylen-

---

377 In 1678 Schellincks owed Pieter Heereman 25 guilders and 4 stivers for making frames. 'Juffr. Lingelbach' was owed 1 guilder. De Vries 1883.
378 Houbraken 1718-1721, vol. 2, p. 273. GAA, DTB 483, p. 32, dated 8 April 1662, notice of marriage of Daniel Schellincks to Elisabeth van Weerdt.
379 See pp. 190-191.
380 GAA, archive no.5028, inv. no. 662, Tax register 200th penning, fol. 26 (district 27).
381 GAA, not. N. Listingh, NA 2617, dated 20 April 1662. Probably the same Abraham de Coninck was taxed on 6,000 guilders in 1674 (GAA, archive

no. 5028, inv. no. 662, Tax register 200th penning, fol. 223v (district 24).
382 De la Tour was taxed on assets of 14,000 guilders in 1674 (GAA, archive no. 5028, inv. no. 662, Tax register 200th penning, fol. 47v (district 6)).
383 The other creditors were

Daniel van Gheel, the owner of the house on the Keizersgracht where Uylenburgh lived from 1672 onwards; Lourens Charles, who was later to become a counsellor and magistrate in Amersfoort (taxed on 5,000 guilders in 1674, GAA, archive no. 5028, inv. no. 662, Tax regis-

ter 200th penning, fol. 303 (district 31); Abraham Claesz Le Seutre, wine merchant, who was taxed on assets of 36,000 guilders in 1674 (GAA, archive no. 5028, inv. no. 662, Tax register 200th penning, fol. 69v (district 8); Johannes Calckoen Willemsz, a merchant in East

India wares, was owed 200 guilders by Uylenburgh, possibly for Oriental porcelain and lacquerwork he had supplied. Calckoen was taxed on assets of 6000 guilders in 1674 (GAA, archive no. 5028, inv. no. 662, Tax register 200th penning, fol. 218 (district 24)).

his living as an engineer and inventor.[384] Anna Becx, who was owed 153 guilders, was the sister-in-law of the broker Isaack van Beest.[385] In 1660 Van Beest was described as an 'eminent expert on paintings'.[386] He was a friend of Abraham Francen, the apothecary and collector of art on paper who was portrayed in an etching by Rembrandt.[387] After his death in 1672, Van Beest's art holdings were valued by Dirck Matham and Gerrit Uylenburgh.[388] Jacob van Anstenraet, who was owed 154 guilders by Uylenburgh, was a nephew of Anna Becx. Matthijs Crayers was a mirror seller who also dealt in paintings.[389] He was probably the man who was appointed official curator of Uylenburgh's property.

HAGUE CONNOISSEURS;
SONS OF FAMOUS FATHERS

In a letter of 18 November 1660 Constantijn Huygens the Younger wrote to his brother Christiaan in Paris to tell him that he had exchanged his album of etchings by Jacques Callot for a large number of drawings belonging to the painter Jacob van der Does. Because the etchings were incomplete, he asked his brother to look in Israel Henriet's shop to see if the missing prints could be obtained there. He remembered from his stay in the French capital that this dealer had most of Callot's prints in stock.[390] Eight days later Christiaan replied that he had not yet had a chance to go and look for the prints. He wondered how his brother could ever have decided to part with such a fine album and hoped that he had not taken a loss on the deal.[391] On 1 December Constantijn reassured him that he did not regret the exchange in the slightest and that he had only done it after taking advice from people who knew about these things. More than eight months previously he had tried to dispose of the album through Gerrit Uylenburgh. However, Uylenburgh had not been able to get more than 50 livres for it and had consequently returned it. The reasons, according

384 See for Cornelis Jansz Meijer or Maijer, Bergvelt/ Kistemaker 1992, p. 324. Because Meijer was in Rome in 1675, he was included among the creditors who did not sign the agreement with Uylenburgh. He was owed 125 guilders. Meijer was taxed on assets of 6000 guilders in 1674 (GAA, archive no. 5028, inv. no. 662, Tax register 200th penning, fol. 365v (district 38). Bernard Vaillant made a portrait of Meijer in a mezzotint; see Hollstein, vol. 31, 1987, no. 21, p. 47.
385 Anna Becx was taxed on assets of 2000 guilders in 1674 (GAA, archive no. 5028, inv. no. 662, Tax register 200th penning, fol. 212v (district 23)). It appears from her will of 1685 that she was reasonably well-to-do. Among other things, she left interest of 20,000 guilders to her sister Aeltje Becx, and her 'porcelain, paintings, bullion and silverwork' to her nieces Maria and Margaretha van Anstenraet (GAA, not. N. Brouwer, NA 3950, fol. 313v-316v, dated 21 April 1685).
386 Isaack van Beest was married to Aeltje Becx, Anna's sister. Aeltje had previously been married to Gillis van Anstenraet. One of the children born to this first marriage was Jacob van Anstenraet, one of Uylenburgh's creditors. In 1660 Isaack van Beest and Lodewijck van Ludick were called in to value a collection of art, on which occasion they were both described as experts (GAA, not. J. van de Ven, NA 1134, fol. 307-315v, dated 13 September-12 November 1660).
387 See Van den Boogert/ Broos/Van Gelder/Van der Veen 1999/2000, pp. 142-143.
388 GAA, not. A. Voskuijl, NA 4064, deed 134, pp. 255-257, dated 5 July 1672. See Appendices, p. 294.
389 GAA, 5028, no. 662, Tax register 200th penning, fol. 41r (district 5), where he is described as a 'spiegelcooper'. Crayers was taxed on assets of 5000 guilders. In 1697/98 Pieter Sijen bought paintings from Crayers for 750 guilders, see Van der Veen 2003, p. 52.
390 Huygens 1888-1950, vol. 3, letter dated 18 November 1660 : 'J'ai troqué mon livre de Callot pour une bonne quantité de desseins que vous verrez à vostre retour avec un peintre d'icy nommé vander Does. Mais comme ce livre n'est pas complet, je me suis chargé de vous prier de regarder à Paris si lon y pourroit recouvrer quelques pieces dont il manque. Ie vous envoye donc une liste de ces pieces, et vous prie d'aller un peu chez Israel Henrichet qui de mon temps avoit la plus part des planches de Callot ...'.
391 Huygens 1888-1950, vol. 3, letter dated 26 November 1660, p. 192.

to Huygens, were that the album was far from complete and that collectors were no longer interested in Callot's etchings and only wanted Italian things ('choses Italiennes'). He had thereupon exchanged the album with Van der Does. The painter had regretted it the same evening and had suggested making a painting for Huygens worth 40 livres if he would return the drawings, but Huygens had refused. Van der Does then exchanged the etchings with Caspar Barlaeus the Younger for a small painting by Cornelis van Poelenburch and another 'trifle' ('bagatelle'). The prints were still with Barlaeus, who at that moment was having a row about them with his brother-in-law Jan de Bisschop, said the letter writer.[392]

From the correspondence between the Huygens brothers we make the acquaintance of a small group of art lovers in The Hague, all of whom had contact with Gerrit Uylenburgh. In the first place there were Constantijn and his younger brother Christiaan themselves.[393] Both had enjoyed an excellent education, with a considerable emphasis on the arts, and were trained draughtsmen. Constantijn himself had a modest collection of drawings, mainly by Italian masters. The letters reveal that it was here that his interests primarily lay rather than with the contemporary art of his own country. Constantijn made many drawings of his own, mostly landscapes, which are often hard to tell apart from those of his friend Jan de Bisschop. Uylenburgh's name crops up several times in the correspondence. We have already discussed Constantijn's request to his brother in Paris in regard to a drawing by Carracci. We have also already touched on Christiaan's request to Uylenburgh as to whether he knew of coins for sale and his letter from London in which he referred to the joint purchase by Lely and Uylenburgh of Van der Voort's large collection of Italian drawings.[394]

Jan de Bisschop, advocate at the Court of Holland in The Hague, was a good friend of the Huygens brothers. Like them, he was a talented amateur draughtsman. As well as landscapes he made numerous drawings after paintings by predominantly Italian masters. He seems to have kept a sort of drawn archive of painted masterpieces. When Christiaan Huygens saw some magnificent paintings in Jabach's collection in Paris, he wrote to tell his brother that De Bisschop had to leave The Hague immediately and come to him to make drawings of the paintings.[395] De Bisschop may have planned to publish his drawings in print form at some time, but nothing ever came of this scheme. He did, however, publish two books of prints after classical statues and a volume of etchings after Italian drawings – the *Icones* and *Paradigmata*. As we have seen, the *Icones* included statues that belonged to Uylenburgh and Hendrick Scholten. He also used drawings by Adriaen Backer, Theodoor Ferreris and others.[396] In the book of examples of Italian drawings De Bisschop did not mention where the originals were. They appear for the greater part to have come from Dutch collections and some of them could have come from Uylenburgh.[397]

De Bisschop sent copies of his books to Christiaan Huygens, Jabach and probably Lely too. Willem Schellincks was also sent the two volumes of the *Icones* 'in memory of their old friendship'.[398] De Bisschop had his portrait painted by Ovens (fig. 171).

Although he lived in London for most of his life, Peter Lely can also be counted among the group of art lovers in The Hague. His family lived in The Hague and his parents figure in the Huygens brothers' correspondence.[399] But it is predominantly Lely himself who is frequently mentioned in the letters and who helped the brothers with technical aspects of drawing.[400] Lely had drawings by De Bisschop in his collection.

392 Huygens 1888-1950, vol. 3, dated 1 December 1660, p. 200 : '... du trocq que j'ay fait des plans tailledouces de Callot je ne me repens nullement et l'ay fait avec advis de personnes tres intelligentes dans cette matiere. Il y a plus de huict mois que je taschay de me defaire de ce livre par le moyen d'Uylenburg à Amsterdam, lequel n'en put jamais avoir plus de 50. Livres et me le renvoya. La cause est en partie qu'il est fort defectueux y manquant plus de trente pieçes, partie le peu d'estime que les Curieux de par deça font des choses de Callot, lesquelles pourtant en leur espece sont tres bonnes. Mais les choses Italiennes ont tellement la vogue que tout le reste n'est rien au prix d'icelles. J'ay troqué mon dit livre à un Peintre d'icy nommé Vander Does qui fait bien en Animaulx, lequel se repentit du marché le mesme soir et dit qu'il estoit prest de me faire un tableau de quarante livres si je le voulois casser dont je n'eus point d'envie. Il le trocqua donc à Barleus contre un petit tableau de Poulenburg et une autre bagatelle; cestuy la l'a encore, et il en a brouillerie encore à present avec son beaufrere Bisschop'.
393 See for Constantijn Huygens, Heijbroek et al. 1982/1983; see for Christiaan Huygens e.g. Andriesse 1993.
394 See p. 236-237, 257-258 and 268.
395 Huygens 1888-1950, vol. 3, years 1660-1661, letter dated 4 February 1661, p. 233. For the identification of these paintings with the Jabach's first sale to the French king, Schnapper 1994, pp. 273-275. De Bisschop probably did go to Paris. For example, there is a copy by De Bisschop of Giulio Romano's *Tirumph of Titus and Vespasian* (now in the Louvre, Paris), which was part of the sale, in Munich. See Wegner 1973, p. 47, no. 239.
396 De Bisschop must have had reasonably close ties with Backer. In 1669 Adriaen Backer drew a portrait of the Amsterdam Remonstrant preacher Praevostius for De Bisschop, which he sent to him by way of Gerard Brandt, De Bisschop's brother-in-law. This was the Brandt who wrote a poem on the occasion of the painter's marriage (see p. 246, note 165). See De Gelder 1971, p. 248.
397 See Van Gelder/Jost 1985.
398 Letter from De Bisschop to Schellincks, dated 10 August 1669. See De Gelder 1971, p. 248.
399 Huygens 1888-1950, vol. 4, letter dated 8 February 1662, Christiaan Huygens to Lodewijk Huygens, p. 33.
400 Huygens 1888-1950, vol. 4, letter dated 23 June 1663, Christiaan Huygens to Constantijn Huygens, p. 361; letter dated 29 June 1663, p. 363; letter dated 13 July 1663, pp. 370-372; letter dated 3 August 1663, p. 389; letter dated 24 August 1663, p. 394; letter dated 31 August 1663, p. 396.

From the letter about Callot's etchings we know that the album ended up with Caspar Barlaeus the Younger, the son of the famous scholar and poet of the same name.[401] He was the brother-in-law of Jan de Bisschop, who was married to his sister Anna Barlaeus. Between 1641 and 1643 he travelled to England and France. Barlaeus the Younger was a lawyer and then bailiff of Wassenaar and Katwijk, not far from The Hague. Later he became consul in Lisbon. Relatively little is known about him, but he emerges from the Huygens brothers' letters as an avid collector. He was not wealthy in his own right, but he married a rich woman in 1644.[402]

On 12 October 1663 Constantijn Huygens wrote to tell Christiaan that he had borrowed a portrait by Joris Hoefnagel from Barlaeus and that Barlaeus had been able to get hold of it very cheaply. The only thing was that the head needed a little retouching.[403] Constantijn went on to say that Uylenburgh had brought some very beautiful paintings by Palma Vecchio and others back from Italy. Barlaeus, Huygens reported, 'has made an exchange for one of these depicting a nude woman, which is indeed very fine. He so set his heart on it I fear he will go mad because of it.'[404] Huygens does not give the artist's name. It seems likely, though, that it was Palma Vecchio, since he is the only master Huygens mentions in connection with the works brought back by Uylenburgh. Unfortunately Huygens also neglects to say what Barlaeus had exchanged for the painting.

THE TASTE OF THE ART LOVER

We have sketched a picture of a milieu of Amsterdam creditors, collectors and painters in which Gerrit Uylenburgh lived. The collectors were rich merchants, some of whom traded with Italy and the Levant. Interestingly, none of the creditors was a Mennonite. A significant proportion of them were members of the Dutch Reformed Church[405] and belonged to the regent class. Over time, Uylenburgh had gathered a circle of people around him that was very different from his father's. It must however be borne in mind that the list of creditors gives a limited and possibly distorted picture. It seems likely for instance that important Mennonite collectors like Abraham van Lennep (fig. 194) and Philips de Flines, both of whom were interested in Italian art, had contact with Uylenburgh.[406] The latter was moreover an acquaintance of Constantijn and Christiaan Huygens and Nicolaes Anthonie Flinck. It must also be stressed that this is a list of creditors. In reconstructing a circle of customers one would tend to look first at the debtors, but there are virtually no records of them. Uylenburgh's clientele evidently did not buy on tick.

In most cases it is not clear why the creditors were owed the money. Herman Becker was owed the outstanding balance on a loan; in the case of Pieter Schaep it seems virtually certain that the sum he was claiming was for works of art he had sold to Uylenburgh. But as far as the others are concerned we do not know whether these were loans, works of art that had been sold or something else altogether. In the case of relatively large sums, like the 640 guilders owing to Six, one would be inclined to suspect the former, but this is by no means certain.

Some of the Amsterdam contacts, men like Joannes Wtenbogaert and Jan and Pieter Six, as well as the circle of friends in The Hague, belonged to the cultural elite – the people who dictated taste in the Republic. De Bisschop came from an Amsterdam family and appears to have been one of the most important links between the Hague circle and the Amsterdam collectors. But the Huygens brothers and Barlaeus had relatives in Amsterdam and Van Wickevoort, in turn, had family in The Hague.

The art lovers shared a liking for classical statues and old paintings, particularly the work of the Italian masters of the sixteenth century. We get something of an insight into the way they discussed things in De Bisschop's prefaces to his *Icones* and *Paradigmata*. He reminded Constantijn Huygens the Younger how 'unanimous' their sentiments were about the 'great perfection' of classical art. In the preface addressed to Jan Six he admitted that Six's remark that De Bisschop 'would always observe what was beautiful and try to portray it' still seemed 'to ring in my ears'.

401 See for Barlaeus the Elder Blok 1976; the work also treats Caspar Barlaeus the Younger's youth.
402 Blok 1976, pp. 85-88, 94-102. Barlaeus the Younger married the Amsterdam orphan Susanna Pelgrom, who had a fortune of 50,000 guilders and a further 10,000 guilders in property, and was heiress to a wealthy aunt.
403 Huygens 1888-1950, vol. 4, pp. 413-414. According to the letter the portrait was retouched by Blavet, after which Barlaeus valued it at 10 pistolets.
404 Ibid.: 'Uylenburg a porté de forts beaux tableaux d'Italie del Palma Vecchio et d'autres. Barlaeus en a trocqué un de ceux la ou il y a une femme nue qui est en effet tres-excellent, et il est si aise de l'avoir que je crains qu'il n'en devienne fol.'.
405 Pieter Schaep, Jan van Weert, Pieter and Jan Six, Herman Stoffelsz van Swoll, Gijsbert van Goor, Hendrick Scholten, Isaac Jan Nijs and the Huygens brothers were Dutch Reformed. Jan van Wickevoort and Herman Becker were Lutherans.
406 See for Van Lennep's collection Dudok van Heel 1975A; see for De Flines, Bergvelt/ Kistemaker 1992, pp. 318-319.

Although Constantijn Huygens the Younger and Barlaeus the Younger collected art, it was not on a scale comparable with that of some of the foremost Amsterdam merchants. It was consequently not so much as clients, but rather as influential connoisseurs that they were important to Uylenburgh. Italian art had always been very highly regarded in the Republic, but from the 1660s onwards it seems to have acquired an almost sacrosanct status – a status that would only increase in the following decades.

When Huygens became secretary to William III in 1672, it gave Uylenburgh direct access to the stadholder's court. Huygens had a significant say in what the stadholder collected and he must have ensured that he bought expensive Italian paintings and statues from Uylenburgh. It is striking that there was also the same or a similar partiality for contemporary artists. De Lairesse, Ferreris and Glauber, for example, all made paintings for William III's country houses. All three of these artists had been associated with Uylenburgh's workshop for varying lengths of time.

What was relatively new was the interest in drawings. Paintings by the great Italian masters were rare and, if they were good quality, astronomically expensive. But there were drawings in abundance and they were not yet the sole preserve of the extremely rich. They were often bought and sold in large batches. Both Lely and Jabach, two of the leading collectors of their day, owned thousands of sheets and bought drawings by the hundred. Uylenburgh, who had close ties with both collectors, must have had an important position in the Republic as a dealer in drawings. Sadly, the lack of information makes it impossible to pin down his precise role.

Uylenburgh seems to have played a key role for his contacts in Amsterdam and The Hague. He was in a position to provide them with Italian art and classical statues that were so much in vogue. They could talk to him about the beauty, the quality and the attributions of works of art. In consequence, a centre for art lovers and collectors grew up 'in the house of the celebrated Painter and Art dealer Gerard Wlenborgh' [407]

407 De Bisschop 1668-1669, vol. 2.

Appendices

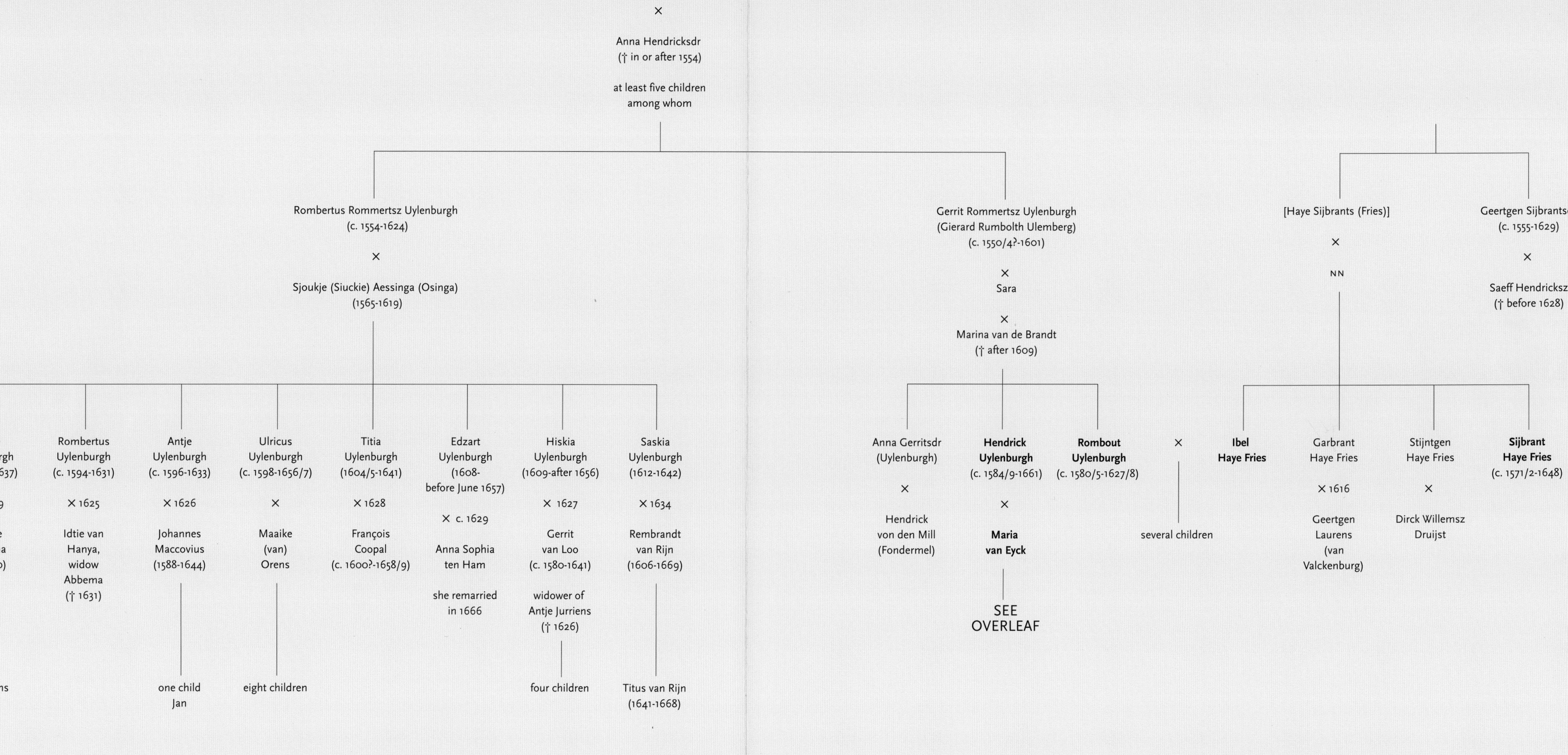

Rommert Pietersz
(† 1555)
×
Anna Hendricksdr
(† in or after 1554)
at least five children
among whom

Rombertus Rommertsz Uylenburgh
(c. 1554-1624)
×
Sjoukje (Siuckie) Aessinga (Osinga)
(1565-1619)

Gerrit Rommertsz Uylenburgh
(Gierard Rumbolth Ulemberg)
(c. 1550/4?-1601)
×
Sara
×
Marina van de Brandt
(† after 1609)

[Haye Sijbrants (Fries)]
×
N N

Geertgen Sijbrantsdr
(c. 1555-1629)
×
Saeff Hendricksz
(† before 1628)

…cke
…burgh
…2-1637)

…609

…ede
…ema
…620)

…sons

Rombertus
Uylenburgh
(c. 1594-1631)
× 1625
Idtie van
Hanya,
widow
Abbema
(† 1631)

Antje
Uylenburgh
(c. 1596-1633)
× 1626
Johannes
Maccovius
(1588-1644)
one child
Jan

Ulricus
Uylenburgh
(c. 1598-1656/7)
×
Maaike
(van)
Orens
eight children

Titia
Uylenburgh
(1604/5-1641)
× 1628
François
Coopal
(c. 1600?-1658/9)

Edzart
Uylenburgh
(1608-
before June 1657)
× c. 1629
Anna Sophia
ten Ham
she remarried
in 1666

Hiskia
Uylenburgh
(1609-after 1656)
× 1627
Gerrit
van Loo
(c. 1580-1641)
widower of
Antje Jurriens
(† 1626)
four children

Saskia
Uylenburgh
(1612-1642)
× 1634
Rembrandt
van Rijn
(1606-1669)
Titus van Rijn
(1641-1668)

Anna Gerritsdr
(Uylenburgh)
×
Hendrick
von den Mill
(Fondermel)

Hendrick
Uylenburgh
(c. 1584/9-1661)
×
Maria
van Eyck
SEE
OVERLEAF

Rombout
Uylenburgh
(c. 1580/5-1627/8)
×
several children

Ibel
Haye Fries

Garbrant
Haye Fries
× 1616
Geertgen
Laurens
(van
Valckenburg)

Stijntgen
Haye Fries
×
Dirck Willemsz
Druijst

Sijbrant
Haye Fries
(c. 1571/2-1648)

Dirck
[van Eyck]

×

NN

Marcus Dircksz van Eyck   ×   Haesje Willemsdr
(† 1627/9)   († in or shortly before 1608)

×   Annitgen Jans
(† before 10-10 1629)

[Isaack Dircksz]
van Eyck

×

NN

probably several
children among whom

SEE
OVERLEAF

Aeltgen Marcusdr   Dirck Marcusz   Isaack Marcusz
(van Eyck)   van Eyck   van Eyck
(c. 1587-1652?)   († in or shortly   (c. 1611-after 1662)
                          before 1656)

× 1614   ×   ×

Bartelt Jansz   Fijdtgen Vincentsdr   NN
(c. 1588-1666)   (van Achtienhoven)
                         († before 1649)

Hendrick   ×   Maria
Uylenburgh   van Eyck
(c. 1584/9-1661)   († 1638)

×
Jannetgen
Thomasdr

Gerrit   NN   Sara   NN   Anna   Suzanna   Isaack   Magdalena   Rombertus   Marcus   Abraham   NN
Uylenburgh   Uylenburgh   Uylenburgh   Uylenburgh   Uylenburgh   Uylenburgh   Uylenburgh   Uylenburgh   Uylenburgh
(1625-1679)   on July 27th 1626 (c. 1626/7-1696) on April 17th 1634 (c. 1628-1681) (c. 1630-after 1697) (c. 1630/2-after 1661) (c. 1634-1661) (c. 1635/6-   (c. 1637/8-   (c. 1637-1668)
                a child of Hendrick   a child of Hendrick   after 1661)   after 1661)
                Uylenburgh   probably   Uylenburgh   probably   probably   probably
                was burried   unmarried   was burried   unmarried   unmarried   unmarried

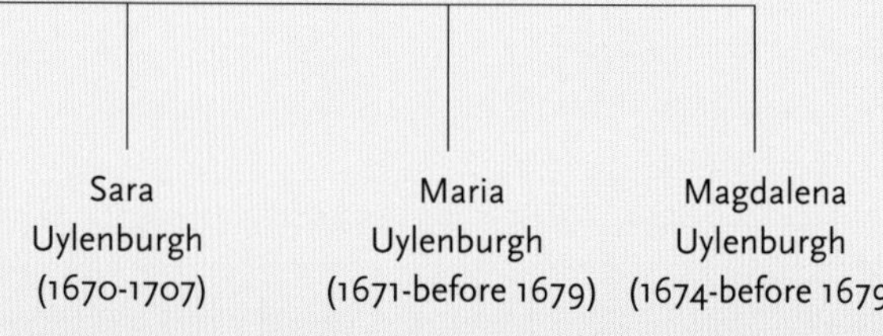

Sara   Maria   Magdalena
Uylenburgh   Uylenburgh   Uylenburgh
(1670-1707)   (1671-before 1679) (1674-before 1679)

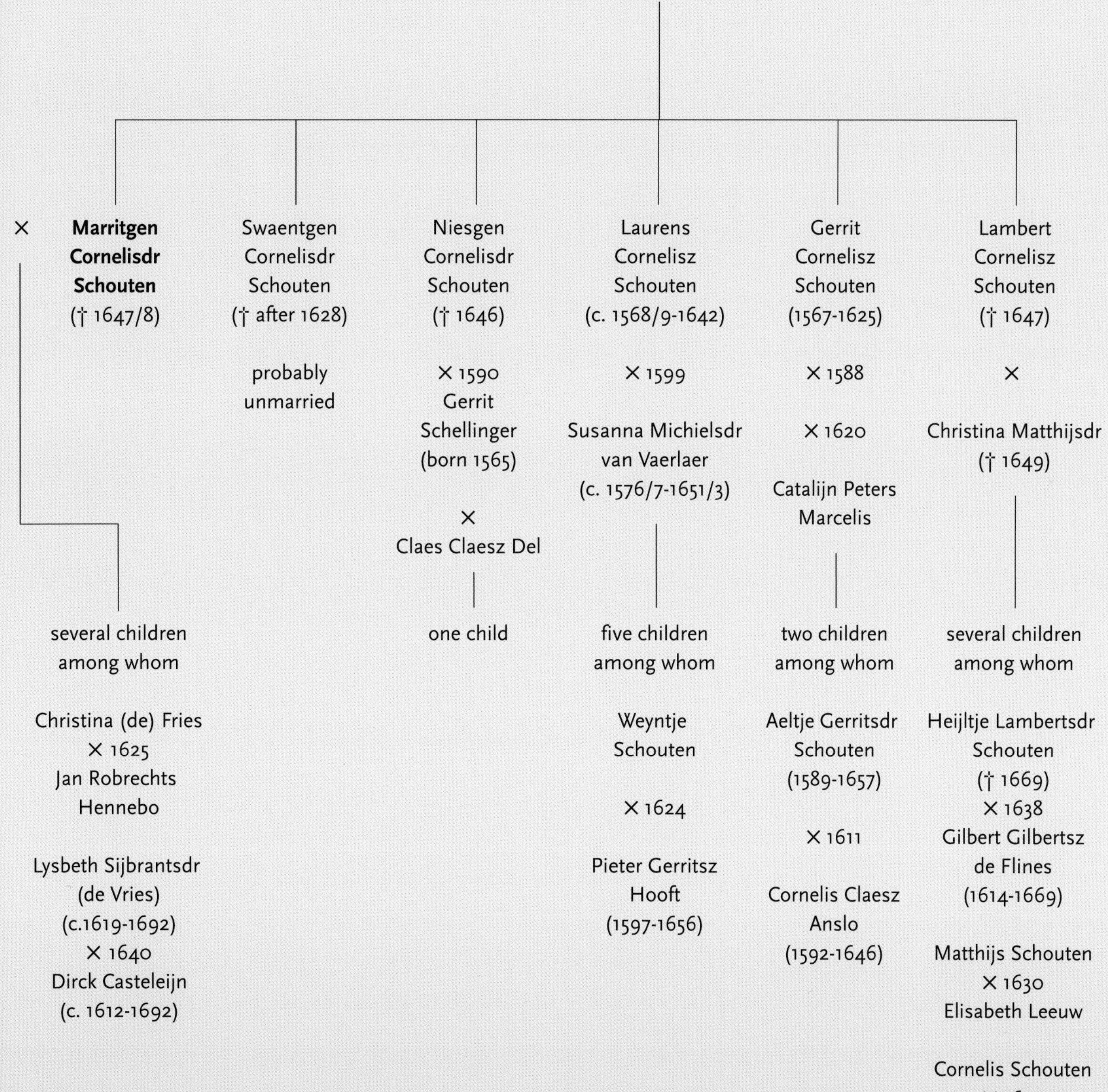

Cornelis Govertsz Schouten,
named van Kleef

×

Weyntgen Lap

| **Marritgen Cornelisdr Schouten** († 1647/8) | Swaentgen Cornelisdr Schouten († after 1628) | Niesgen Cornelisdr Schouten († 1646) | Laurens Cornelisz Schouten (c. 1568/9-1642) | Gerrit Cornelisz Schouten (1567-1625) | Lambert Cornelisz Schouten († 1647) |

×

probably unmarried (Swaentgen)

× 1590 Gerrit Schellinger (born 1565) (Niesgen)

× 1599 Susanna Michielsdr van Vaerlaer (c. 1576/7-1651/3) (Laurens)

× 1588 / × 1620 Catalijn Peters Marcelis (Gerrit)

× Christina Matthijsdr († 1649) (Lambert)

× Claes Claesz Del (Niesgen)

several children among whom (Marritgen)

one child (Niesgen)

five children among whom (Laurens)

two children among whom (Gerrit)

several children among whom (Lambert)

Marritgen's descendants:

Christina (de) Fries
× 1625
Jan Robrechts Hennebo

Lysbeth Sijbrantsdr (de Vries) (c.1619-1692)
× 1640
Dirck Casteleijn (c. 1612-1692)

Laurens' descendants:

Weyntje Schouten
× 1624
Pieter Gerritsz Hooft (1597-1656)

Gerrit's descendants:

Aeltje Gerritsdr Schouten (1589-1657)
× 1611
Cornelis Claesz Anslo (1592-1646)

Lambert's descendants:

Heijltje Lambertsdr Schouten († 1669)
× 1638
Gilbert Gilbertsz de Flines (1614-1669)

Matthijs Schouten
× 1630
Elisabeth Leeuw

Cornelis Schouten
× 1634
Barbara Leeuw

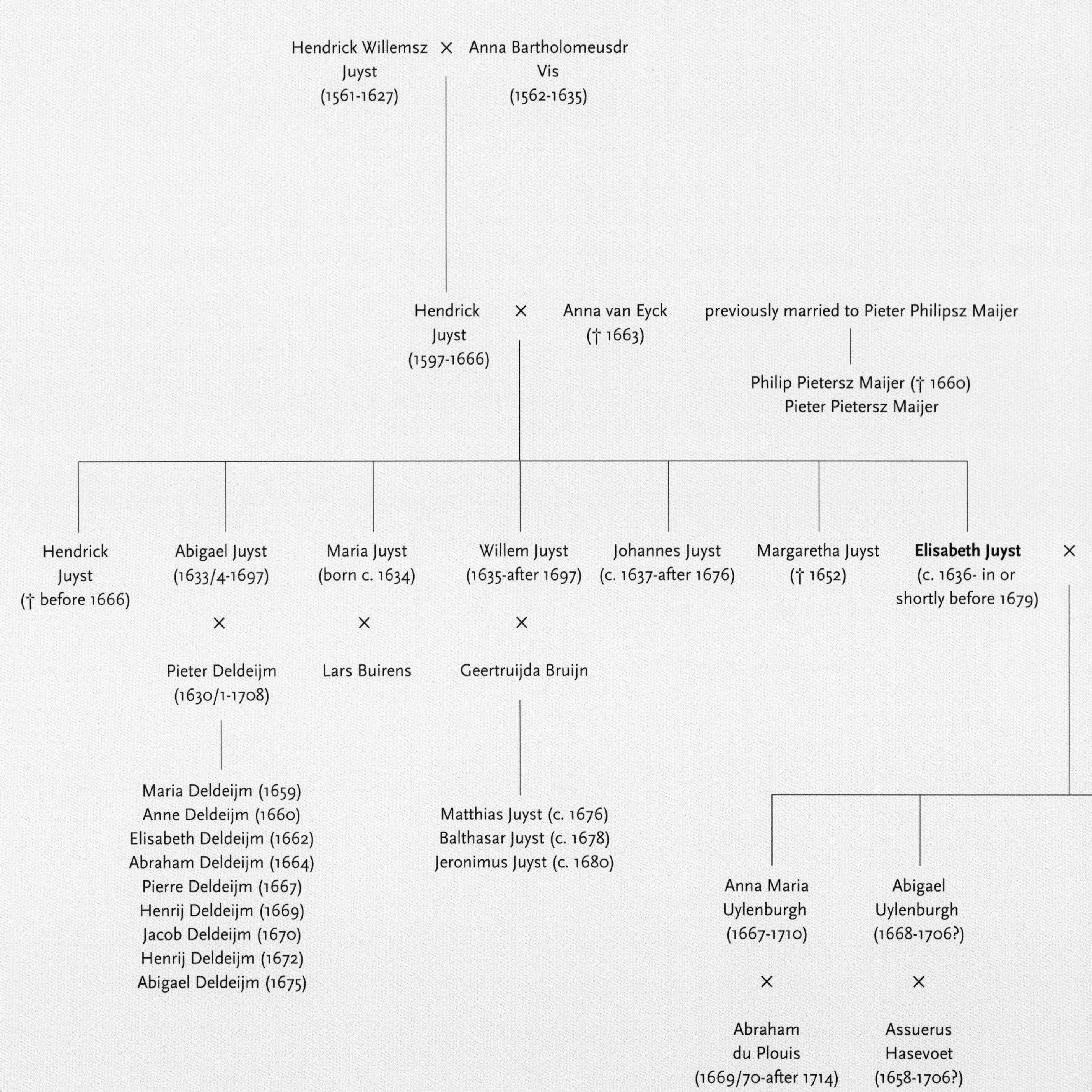

Hendrick Willemsz × Anna Bartholomeusdr
Juyst Vis
(1561-1627) (1562-1635)

Hendrick × Anna van Eyck   previously married to Pieter Philipsz Maijer
Juyst († 1663)
(1597-1666)
Philip Pietersz Maijer († 1660)
Pieter Pietersz Maijer

Hendrick   Abigael Juyst   Maria Juyst   Willem Juyst   Johannes Juyst   Margaretha Juyst   Elisabeth Juyst ×
Juyst   (1633/4-1697)   (born c. 1634)   (1635-after 1697)   (c. 1637-after 1676)   († 1652)   (c. 1636- in or
(† before 1666)   shortly before 1679)
×   ×   ×
Pieter Deldeijm   Lars Buirens   Geertruijda Bruijn
(1630/1-1708)

Maria Deldeijm (1659)
Anne Deldeijm (1660)
Elisabeth Deldeijm (1662)   Matthias Juyst (c. 1676)
Abraham Deldeijm (1664)   Balthasar Juyst (c. 1678)
Pierre Deldeijm (1667)   Jeronimus Juyst (c. 1680)
Henrij Deldeijm (1669)
Jacob Deldeijm (1670)
Henrij Deldeijm (1672)   Anna Maria   Abigael
Abigael Deldeijm (1675)   Uylenburgh   Uylenburgh
(1667-1710)   (1668-1706?)
×   ×
Abraham   Assuerus
du Plouis   Hasevoet
(1669/70-after 1714)   (1658-1706?)

GAA, not. L. Lamberti, NA 569, pp. 231-239 and 245-258, 12 June 1637
Inventory of Jan Arentsz van Naerden with a valuation of the paintings by Lucas Lucasz and 'Hendrick Wlenburch', 'both painters'

GAA, not. J. Cornelisz Hoogeboom, NA 840, 15 April 1639
Inventory of Catharina Thijs, widow of Samuel van Swol, with a valuation of the paintings by 'Hendric Ulenburch'

GAA, not. B. Jansen Verbeeck, NA 935, 12 May 1639
Inventory of Cornelis Rutgers and Anna van Loosvelt with a valuation of the paintings by Lucas Luce and 'Hendrick Uylenbr.'

GAA, not. J. Jacobs, NA 421, fol. 45-56, 16 January 1640
Inventory of Anthony Moens with a valuation of the paintings by 'Henrick Uylenborgh'

GAA, not. J. van de Ven, NA 1056, fol. 263v-264, 24 October 1640
Hendrick Uylenburgh and 'Kee[r]sgieter' value paintings and a book of prints on account of Jan Hendricksz Admirael

GAA, not. G. Borsselaer, NA 1496, fol. 36v-56v, 14 August-19 December 1640
Inventory of Balthasar van Haeften with a valuation of the paintings by Hendrick

Uylenburgh and Gerbrant Ban, 'painters and art dealers'

GAA, not. F. Bruyningh, NA 1416, 22 February-12/13 and 21 March 1641
Inventory of Anthony van der Heeden with a valuation of the paintings by Dirck Pietersz Santvoort and Hendrick Uylenburgh, 'painters'

GAA, not. J. van Zwieten, NA 908, 7 December 1644
Inventory of Jan de Koocker with a valuation of the paintings by 'Hendrick Uijlenburch' and Lucas Luce, 'painters and art dealers of this city'

GAA, not. F. Bruyningh, NA 1416, 7 May 1645, concluded 12 February 1649
Inventory of Margarita van Haelewijn, widow of Anthony van der Heeden, with a valuation of the paintings by 'Louwies Luce and Hendrick Uylenburgh, painters'

GAA, not. L. Lamberti, NA 570, pp. 257-270, 29 June 1647
Inventory of Reijncke Gerrits, widow of Jarich Lubberts, with a valuation of the paintings by 'Hendrick Uijlenburch'

GAA, not. F. Bruyningh, NA 1418, pp. 1-81, 4/22 January 1649
Inventory of Marten van Haelewijn with a valuation of the paintings by Lucas Luce and 'Gerrit Uijlenburgh, painters'

GAA, not. P. de Bary, NA 1692, 13 August 1649
Inventory of Anna du Bois with a valuation of the paintings by 'sr. Henrick Uylenborch'

RAL, not. K. Outerman, NA 444, deed 173, 17 August 1651
Inventory of Jean le Pla and Pieroontgen Henneboo with a valuation of the paintings by 'Hendric Uylenburch'

GAA, not. Joh. Hellerus, NA 2088, pp. 527-537, 22 August 1652
Inventory of Isaac Jacobsz van Horen and Metje Pieters with a valuation of the paintings by 'messrs Hendrick Uijlenburgh' and Dirck Dircksz Santvoort, 'painters of this city'

GAA, not. J. d'Amour, NA 2162, pp. 6-9, 19 February 1654
Inventory of Hans Coymans and Catharina Strijdhoven with a valuation of the paintings by 'sr. Henr. Wlenb.'

GAA, not. P. de Bary, NA 1702, pp. 327-337, 13/18 August 1654
Inventory of Cornelis Jacobsz Weyer with a valuation of the paintings by the 'painter Henrick Uylenborch'

GAA, DBK 13, fol. 98v, 13 February 1657
The commissioners of the Desolate Boedelskamer resolve that the paintings in the estate of Roelof Codde should be

valued by Hendrick Uylenburgh and
Marten Kretzer

GAA, not. C. de Grijp, NA 2605,
pp. 679-690, 9 February 1657
Inventory of Aeltje Gerrits, widow of
Barent Jansz van Kippen, with a valuation
of the paintings by the 'painter
Uijlenburgh'

GAA, not. J. van Loosdrecht, NA 1996,
pp. 745-749, 28 August-23 October 1657
Inventory of Michiel Adriaensz with a
valuation of the paintings by Hendrick
Uylenburgh on 20 September 1657

GAA, not. J. Thielmans, NA 2119, pp. 28-77,
4 June 1658
Inventory of Philips Pelt with a valuation
of the paintings by Hendrick Uylenburgh
and Guillaume de Ville, 'painter[s]'

GAA, DBK 586, fol. 272v-273v and 276-277,
22 April-26 June 1660
Inventory of Abraham Verleth with a
valuation of the paintings by Hendrick
Uylenburgh and Thomas de Keijser

GAA, not. F. Bruyningh, NA 1414,
12/26 October 1660
Inventory of Anthony van der Heeden
with a valuation of the paintings by
Hendrick Uylenburgh, 'painter'

GAA, DBK 592, fol. 236-243, 2 October
1663-21 and 24 April 1664
Inventory of Godefridus de Leeuw with a
valuation of the paintings by Lodewijck
van Ludick and Gerrit Uylenburgh

GAA, DBK 592, fol. 262-263, 9, 25 and
27 September and 7 October 1665
On 25 September 1665 Jan Blom and Gerrit
Uylenburgh valued paintings in the estate
of Isaacq de Braa

GAA, DBK 594, fol. 22-29v, 15 February-
22 April 1666
Inventory of Egbert Schut with a valuation
of the paintings by Gerrit Uylenburgh

GAA, not. N. Kruijs, NA 1843(B),
fol. 517-519, 16 July 1666
Inventory of Grietje Rover, widow of
François Gijsels the Elder, with a valuation
of the paintings by Ferdinand Bol and
Gerrit Uylenburgh

GAA, not. F. Meerhout, NA 2103,
fol. 138-143v, 6 May 1668
Inventory of Catharina Meulenaer, last
widow of Lodewijck de Bas, with a
valuation of the paintings by Marten
Kretzer and Gerrit Uylenburgh

GAA, not. A. Loefs, NA 1605, map VV,
fol. 17v-19v, dated 19 June 1668
Inventory of Jannetge Leonards
Valkenburgh, widow of Claes Jansz
Klopper, with a valuation of the paintings
by Gerrit Uylenburgh, 'art dealer'

GAA, not. G. van Breugel, NA 3505,
pp. 191-200, 5, 6 and 21 February 1669
Inventory of Laurens Maurensz Doucy
with a valuation of the paintings by
Ferdinand Bol and Gerrit Uylenburgh

GAA, not. J. van Loosdrecht, NA 1997,
pp. 264-280, 17 January 1671
Inventory of Adriana Oilarts, widow of
Isaac Swartepaert, with a valuation of the
paintings by Harmen van Swol and Gerrit
Uylenburgh

GAA, not. P. Padthuijsen, NA 2903,
pp. 771-772, 17 March 1671
Inventory of Jeremias van Collen with
a valuation of the paintings by Gerrit
Uylenburgh

GAA, not. J. de Winter, NA 2410,
pp. 117-131, 19 May 1671
Inventory of Catharina de Marez, widow
of Pieter de Marez, with a valuation of the
paintings by Gerrit Uylenburgh, 'painter'

GAA, not. A. van den Ende, NA 3666, fol.
351-371v, 3, 6 and 9 November 1671
Inventory of Jan Moors with a valuation
of the paintings by Gerrit Uylenburgh and
Claes Dommer

GAA, not. A. Voskuijl, NA 4064(A), deed
118, pp. 213-228, 30 May 1672 and deed 134,
pp. 255-257, 5 July 1672
Inventory of Aeltje Becx, widow of Isaac
van Beest, with a valuation of the prints
and the paintings by Dirck Matham and
Gerrit Uylenburgh

GAA, DBK 601, fol. 19v-27, 22 December
1672-25 January 1673
Inventory of Johannes Wijbrants with a
valuation of the paintings by [Gerrit]
Uylenburgh

GAA, not. A. Lock, NA 2262, pp. 621-628,
28 April 1673
Inventory of David van Baerle with a
valuation of the paintings by Hendrick
Velthoen, Allart van Everdingen and
Gerrit Uylenburgh

GAA, not. C. van Poelenburgh, NA 3437,
deed 91, 8 May 1674
Inventory of Joan de Hoest and Catharina
Questiers with a valuation of the paintings
by Dirck Santvoort and Gerrit
Uylenburgh, 'artists'

GAA, not. A. van den Ende, NA 3671,
fol. 234-245v, 29 June 1676
Inventory of Joan van Beaumont with
a valuation of the paintings by Gerrit
Uylenburgh, 'painter'

Inventory of the furniture, household goods
and sundry items in the estate of Gerrit
Uylenburgh, painter, formerly residing
on Nieuwe Keizersgracht

In the room under the side room
One bed and bolster
4 pillows
2 sheets
2 blankets
2 green say curtains
2 velours hangings
One striped dornick bedspread
One serge tablecloth
One iron fire back
[fol.70v]
One small, painted pine table
7 rush seat chairs
7 green dornick velours cushions
One small square mirror
One oak cloth press
One old black woollen coat
A pair of brass tongs
A bible in folio
One ditto in octavo
2 psalm balsos
6 more small printed balsos
3 porcelain parrot dishes
2 ditto bowls
4 ditto cups
One ditto goblet
A pine cupboard
Two fine, yellow curtains
4 pairs of knitted gloves
3 towels
[fol.71]

Eleven bedsheets
7 pillow cases
14 tablecloths
12 napkins
20 aprons
Four women's chemises
4 pairs of sleeves with lace
6 pairs ditto without lace
In the corridor
One small trunk
A small oak press
A rough-hewn pine cupboard
14 porcelain butter dishes
One ditto double
2 ditto bowls
16 items of Delft pottery, undamaged
One rack
In the basement kitchen
One bed and bolster
4 pillows
4 blankets
[fol.71v]
2 sheets
2 striped dornick curtains with two ditto
    hangings
6 rush seat chairs
One small pine table
One small square mirror
3 copper sconces, 4 ditto snuffers, one
    ditto lid, another ditto lid
20 pewter dishes, large as well as small
44 plates
2 pewter candlesticks
2 ditto tin
One copper fish-kettle
One pewter pitcher
One ditto serving platter

6 ditto salt cellars
4 small sauce boats
A ditto mustard pot
[fol.72]
A brass pestle and candlestick
A tin herb caddy
A pewter platter
6 ditto bowls
2 ditto water jars
3 tin sconces, 3 ditto lids and one ditto
    market pail
One pair of tongs, 3 gridirons, ash shovel
    and sundry small kitchen ironware
A small copper basin
A wooden screen
12 items of pottery, undamaged
4 small porcelain cups
6 earthenware jars with pewter lids
17 pewter spoons and 2 small ditto beakers
One iron skewer
A smoothing iron
[fol.72v]
Also found in a small cupboard *in the room
    under the side room*
9 nightshirts
4 small, white linen mantelpiece hangings
6 ditto blue
2 ash cloths
3 neckerchiefs
10 handkerchiefs
One white silk hood
A jewellery box
4 silver spoons
A clothes brush with silver trimming
A black woollen coat with camlet lining
A black silk hood with a ditto veil
An old corset

In the yard
A few pots and pans
A plaster sculpture on a wooden stand
    and a ditto head
One iron pot
[fol.73]
In the side room
4 green velours chairs, one ditto armchair
2 turned chairs with rush seats
5 ash-grey velours cushions
An oak bedstead with green serge
    drapery
A square mirror measuring one el
A fine, white cotton curtain
One Lutheran bible in octave
One ditto psalm book
One ditto testament
One ditto psalm book
One small oak table with a green serge
    cloth
One bed and bolster
2 pillows
2 blankets
One East India cotton blanket
One coverlet and one dornick chair
    cushion
[fol.73v]
In the front room
3 plaster sculptures
One black silk gown
One ditto coloured
One coloured silk suit
One short, black camlet doublet
In the hall
One oak table with a black camlet
    cloth
One large mirror in a gilt frame
12 chairs with yellow velours seats
    and yellow say covers
2 white cotton net curtains
One plaster sculpture
One bronze-plated sculpture on a
    wooden stand
A few more cupids on two black stands
One brass ash shovel
One iron fire back
A large nutwood demi-commode
[fol.74]

In a small box
Four pairs of silver buttons
One mother-of-pearl knife handle
5 linen neckcloths
14 partlets with lace
2 ditto caps
One black armozine jacket
One black woollen skirt
One ditto ras de Cypre
Another ditto skirt
One woollen gown
One ras de Cypre stomacher of a
    gown
One ditto bodice
One red woollen skirt
One small yellow say tablecloth
One length of floral East India chintz
One white silk hood
One black crepe ditto
3 white silk shoulder collars
One lace shoulder collar
[fol.74v]
One black silk ditto
One crepe ditto
One black silk stomacher
In an upstairs back room
One oak chest containing
Eleven pillow cases
18 napkins
7 tablecloths
Six bedsheets
One ticking mattress cover
2 striped dornick curtains and one ditto
    hanging
One ditto tablecloth
2 yellow say curtains, one drape and
    ditto bedspread
18 silk painting drapes
A further four ditto
2 yellow floral curtain drapes, a bedspread
    and small ditto tablecloth, all of floral
    dornick or Haarlem linen
[fol.75]
4 linen underbreeches
One pair of black camlet breeches and
    a doublet
One short, black velvet doublet
One old striped watered costume

Three packages containing children's
    clothing, napkins, skirts and nursery
    goods
6 turned chairs with green velours seats
One ash-grey velours cushion
One plaster sculpture on a wooden stand
In the painting studio or room
One armchair and two turned chairs with
    rush seats
One striped mantelpiece drape
One painter's easel
16 plaster sculptures, both full- and half-
    length as well as heads
In an upstairs front room
A painted bedstead with a striped dornick
    drape and two ditto hangings
Five beds
Four bolsters
[fol.75v]
6 pillows
3 ditto small
4 blankets and one bedspread
One blue stone table with a painted
    wooden leg
One mirror in a gilt frame
8 tapestry chairs with red serge
    cloths
One white cotton net curtain
In the attic
One [deleted: oak] pine trestle table
One ditto bench
2 Delft ember pans
One ditto starching bowl
One stoneware inkwell
One copper kettle
One pine chest
Two painter's easels
One dismantled bedstead
One chest containing
One striped dornick hanging
[fol.76]
One pair of striped bast fabric
    underbreeches, another ditto
One short, serge de Nîmes doublet
One ditto doublet
One pair of black woollen breeches and
    a [deleted: cloak] doublet
One linen bedcover

In an attic above it
28 clothes rods
One pine couch
2 drying racks
Odds and ends of little value
In the cellar
One iron calsoing pot
One iron pot
A few odds and ends of little value

The paintings are as follows
No. 1 A tapestry with Italian fruit by Maltees[2]
2 A sleeping woman by Jan van Neck[3]
3 A seascape by Parcellis[4]
4 A masquerade by Caroselis[5]
5 Diana at the hunt by Backere[6]
[fol.76v]
6 A painting by Juste del Papa[7]
7 Figures by Louis Gentil[8]
8 A landscape by Roghman[9]
9 A Jewess by Rembrant[10]
10 A Judgment by David Colijns[11]
11 Italian fruit by Jan Strijdt[12]
12 Another Diana hunting, after Rubens[13]
13 A portrait after an Italian master
14 Portrait of a woman, after Van Dijck[14]
15 A Crucifixion of Saint Peter
16 Another portrait of a woman, after Van Dijck[15]
17 A Christmas night, after Tintoret[16]
18 A Saint Catherine } after an Italian
19 A Virgin } master

20 A Burning of Troy by the Elder Breugel[17]
21 Another Saint Catherine
22 A small Danae by Rembrant[18]
23 A composition by Aertie van Leijden[19]
24 Portrait of a woman
25 A portrait of Gustavus Adolfs[20]
26 Female tronie by Pordenon[21]
27 Female tronie by Bordon[22]
[fol.77]
28 Tronie of a pope by an Italian master
29 A portrait by Ravesteijn[23]
30 A vanitas

31 A landscape by Muller[24]
32 A figure of a woman by Perments[25]
33 A figure in Turkish costume
34 A winter scene
35 A portrait of an old man
36 and 37 Two nude children
38 An unfinished design
39 Another eight unfinished designs
40 A Saviour by Jan Dalij[26]
41 A Virgin and Saint Catherine by Permens[27]
42 A female tronie by Tietsaen[28]
43 A Semiramis by Pieter Corton[29]
44 A woman with small satyrs by Albaen[30]
45 A landscape by Francisco del Molo[31]
46 A Lot by Alexander Veronees[32]
47 A Ceres with children, by Schorson[33]
48 A tronie of a [deleted: old] woman by Palma the Elder[34]
49 A philosopher by Spanjolet[35]
50 A Judith by Perni del Vadit[36]
51 Mars and Venus by Lucas van Leijden[37]
52 A woman, Jan Bellijn[38]
53 An Atalanta by Ad: Backer[39]
54 Figures by Rubbens[40]
[fol.77v]
55 A small landscape by Rubbens[41]
56 Tronie of a man by the Elder Palma[42]
57 An episode from Ovid by Fransico Saviator[43]
58 A landscape with a boar hunt[44]
59 A landscape by Philip Napolitaen[45]
60 A lute player by Hendrick ter Brugge[46]
61 Two saints by Paulus Fernijs[47]
62 A dog by Franschois Snijders[48]
63 A Ceres by Jacob Pinas[49]
64 Nude figures, after an Italian master
65 A white horse by Bordon[50]
66 A Virgin by Perosin[51]
67 A Mary Magdalene, after Guido[52]
68 A female tronie
69 Portrait of a woman, after Tietsiaen[53]
70 A Saint Sebastian, after Guido[54]
71 A portrait of a woman, after an old master
72 A model by Stockade[55]

73 A landscape by Seegers[56]
74 An unfinished portrait of a woman by Rembrant[57]
75 [deleted: two] Three half-length figures after an Italian master
76 A hunt on paper by Van Aelst[58]
77 A David with Goliath's head
78 A Samaritan
79 Flowers by Luijck[59]
80 A young lady by Netscher[60]

This inventory is continued on folo. 84

[fol.84]
Continuation of the Inventory of Gerrit Uylenburgh, continued from folo. 70

No. 81 A history piece by P. Lasman[61]
82 A peasant with a cock by Gabriel Metsu[62]
83 A landscape by Petit[63]
84 Portrait of a man by Bortiaens[64]
85 A landscape by Moucheron[65]
86 An antique tronie by the Younger Eeverdinge[66]
87 A perspective by Van Baede[67]
88 A Judith after Rafel[68]
89 A portrait by De Haen[69]
90 A landscape by Hercules Seegers[70]
91 A Magdelen, after Gridorin[71]
92 A landscape by Ad. Brouwer[72]
93 A tronie by an Italian old master
94 A dead Christ, after Caras[73]
95 A portrait of an old man by Bardon[74]
96 A landscape by Helembreecker[75]
[fol.84v]
No. 97 A small female tronie by Malo[76]
98 A woman singing by Begga[77]
99 A portrait by Gorgon[78]
100 A round portrait by Willem Cani[79]
101 A small landscape by Momper[80]
102 A small landscape
103 Tronie of a Dominican[81]
104 The Coliseum by Poelenburgh[82]
105 A tronie of a Franciscan friar by Gerrit Douw[83]
106 The big shoe by Ad. Brouwer[84]
107 A monk by Holbeeck[85]
108 A church by the Elder Steenwijck[86]

109 Animals by Van der Does[87]
110 A sleeping woman by Miris[88]
111 A Crucifixion by Carel Vermander[89]
112 A Shrove Tuesday reveller by Frans [deleted: Floris] Hals[90]
113 tronie of a woman by Frans Floris[91]
114 A small painting by Calf[92]
[fol.85]
115 A Burial of Christ by Livens[93]
116 A Virgin, with shutters, by R. van Bruggen[94]
117 A Virgin, after Titiaen[95]
118 A portrait of a woman, after Titiaen[96]
119 A perspective by Vivjaene[97]
120 A small landscape by Van der Schuren[98]
121 A small piece by Gerraeds[99]
122 A Crucifixion by an old master
123 A landscape by Herculus Zeggers[100]
124 A Diana by Ad. Backer[101]
125 A Fall of the Titans by David Vinson[102]
126 A Europa by Jan van Neck[103]
127 A kitchen piece with figures[104]
128 A fowl and fruit by Snijder[105]
129 Time clipping the wings of a young boy by Theodore van der Scheuren[106]
130 A Virgin and a naked Christ [deleted: by] after Guido[107]
[fol.85v]
131 A Venus and cupid by Michiel Cockxi[108]
132 Nude figures after Albaen[109]
133 A landscape by Moucheron[110]
134 A female satyr by Willebords[111]
135 A grisaille by Rubbens[112]
136 A portrait by Jordaens[113]
137 A Roman garden full of sculptures, by Lingelbach[114]
138 A female tronie by Jacob Backer[115]
139 A portrait by Tintoret[116]
140 A Polish trumpeter by Jan Bor[117]
141 A church of Saint Peter by La Meere[118]
142 A model
143 An unfinished shepherd and shepherdess
144 Three female tronies
145 A portrait of a woman, after Titiaen[119]
[fol.86]
146 Four canvases with children
147 A Castor painting of the Descent from the Cross

148 Three portrait studies
149 A marble pot
150 A portrait of Emperor Charles
151 A portrait of his sister
} watercolour
152 A Roman history piece
153 A female tronie by an Italian master

List of sculptures
No. 1 A Hercules, bust[120]
2 A young emperor
3 A Homer, a model
4 Marcus Aurelius
5 Tronie of a boy
6 Tronie of a boy
7 Tronie of a woman
8 A Virgin
9 Tronie of a philosopher
10 A classical tronie
11 A small female tronie
12 Tronie of a philosopher
13 A marble urme [urn?]
[fol.86v]
14 Tronie of a woman, a model
15 A sleeping cupid
16 A sibyl
} full-length figure
17 A classical male tronie, a bust
18 Tronie of a young boy
19 Tronie of an old man
20 A young Bacchus
21 A woman
} half-length figure
22 A small, half-length figure, marble
23 A small figure of a woman
24 A naked body without a head
25 A ditto
26 Another ditto
27 Female tronie
28, 29 and 30 Three female tronies, half round
31 A game hunter, a full-length figure
32 A Triton
33 Tronie of an emperor in a frame, half round
34 Tronie of a young emperor in an ebony frame
[fol.87]
35 A modelled sculpture by Quelinus[121]

36 A ditto by the same master[122]
37 Ditto.[123]
38 and 39 Two models of the entrance of the town hall[124]
40 Tronie of a child in a round ebony frame
41 A small greenish marble pot
42 Ten parts of the body, hands, head, foot, etc.
43 Two tronies of satyrs in a round frame
44 Tronie of a woman, in marble
45 A Venus and cupid
46 A marble tronie lalsoing up, life-size
47 Children and a goat by Quelinus[125]
48 Venus and cupid, in bronze
49 Children and a goat by Verhulst[126]
50 A small marble figure of a woman
51 A Venus, almost life-size, in marble
[fol.87v]
52 A female tronie, larger than life-size

Listed and described on 27 and 28 March and 26 and 27 April 1675

NOTES

1 Amsterdam Municipal Archives, Archive no. 5072, inventory no. 603, fol.70-77v and 84-87v, 27/28 March and 26/27 April 1675.
2 No. 1 in the valuation.
3 No. 57 in the valuation. On Van Neck, see also no. 126.
4 No. 73 in the valuation.
5 No. 28 in the valuation
6 No. 24 in the valuation.
7 No. 27 in the valuation.
8 No. 26 in the valuation.
9 No. 20 in the valuation.
10 No. 30 in the valuation. On Rembrandt, see also nos. 22 and 74.
11 No. 59 in the valuation.
12 Possibly no. 90 in the valuation, where it is attributed to Jan Striep and d'Henin.
13 There are several paintings of this subject by Peter Paul Rubens. On Rubens, see also nos. 54, 55 and 135.
14 Anthony van Dyck. See also no. 16.
15 See no. 14.
16 Jacopo Robusti, called Tintoretto. On Tintoretto, see also no. 139.
17 Either Pieter Bruegel the Elder, who is not known to have painted a Sacking of Troy, or Jan Brueghel the Elder, who executed a painting of this subject, which is

298

now in Munich. See Ertz 1979, p. 130-131, 561, fig. 135. According to Ertz, this is the only autograph Sacking of Troy.

18 No. 19 in the valuation. On Rembrandt, see also nos. 9 and 74.

19 Aertgen van Leyden.

20 Gustav Adolf II Wasa, king of Sweden from 1611 to 1632.

21 No. 22 in the valuation.

22 No. 23 in the valuation. On Bordone, see also nos. 65 and 95.

23 Probably Jan Anthonisz van Ravesteyn or perhaps his brother Anthonie van Ravesteyn or his son Arnoldus van Ravesteyn.

24 Probably Pieter Mulier or his son Pieter Mulier the Younger, called Tempesta.

25 Girolamo Francesco Mazzola, called Il Parmigianino. On Parmigianino, see also no. 41.

26 Possibly Giovanni Bellini; if so, no. 14 in the valuation. On Bellini, see also no. 52.

27 No. 55 in the valuation. On Parmigianino, see also no. 32.

28 No. 63 in the valuation. On Titian, see also nos. 69, 117, 118 and 145.

29 No. 44 in the valuation. Compare fig. 183.

30 No. 79 in the valuation. On Albani, see also no. 132

31 No. 46 in the valuation.

32 No. 45 in the valuation. Compare figs. 184 and 185.

33 No. 58 in the valuation. Compare fig. 58. On Giorgione, see also no. 99.

34 No. 49 in the valuation.

35 No. 43 in the valuation.

36 No. 70 in the valuation.

37 No. 60 in the valuation.

38 No. 42 in the valuation. On Bellini, see also no. 40.

39 No. 51 in the valuation. On Backer, see also no. 124.

40 No. 50 in the valuation. On Rubens, see also nos. 12, 55 and 135.

41 No. 47 in the valuation. On Rubens, see also nos. 12, 54 and 135.

42 Jacopo Negretti, called Palma Vecchio. On Palma, see also no. 56.

43 No. 15 in the valuation.

44 No. 54 in the valuation.

45 Filippo Napoletano.

46 Hendrick ter Brugghen. Several lute players by him are known, see Nicolson 1958, nos. 44-47, 69, 92 and 93.

47 No. 21 in the valuation.

48 No. 53 in the valuation. On Snijders, see also no. 128.

49 No. 52 in the valuation.

50 Paris Bordone. On Bordone, see also nos. 27 and 95.

51 Pietro di Cristoforo Vannucci, called Perugino.

52 Guido Reni. Several Mary Magdalens by him are known. See Pepper 1984, nos. 120, 151, 152, 203, 211; Garboli/Baccheschi 1971, nos. 116, 177, 199. Uylenburgh had a second copy after Reni's *Mary Magdalen*, see no. 91. On Reni, see also nos. 70 and 130.

53 Titian. On him, see also nos. 42, 117, 118 and 145.

54 Guido Reni. Several paintings of Saint Sebastian are known. See Pepper 1984, nos. 155, 194; Garboli/Baccheschi 1971, nos. 63, 64, 205. On Reni, see also nos. 67, 91 and 130.

55 Nicolaes van Helt Stockade.

56 Possibly no. 11 or 12 in the valuation. On Segers, see also nos. 90 and 123.

57 Rembrandt van Rijn. On Rembrandt, see also nos. 9 and 22.

58 Willem van Aelst.

59 No. 17 in the valuation.

60 No. 66 in the valuation.

61 No. 31 in the valuation.

62 No. 65 in the valuation.

63 No. 32 in the valuation.

64 No. 13 in the valuation.

65 Possibly no. 11 or 12 in the valuation. On De Moucheron, see also no. 133.

66 Cornelis van Everdingen, son of the landscape painter Allart. No paintings by him are known. See p. 247, note 167.

67 Hans Juriaensz van Baden, a painter of perspectives, active in Amsterdam.

68 No. 78 in the valuation.

69 Quite a number of painters by this name were active in the seventeenth century. It is difficult to say which one was meant here.

70 Possibly no. 11 or 12 in the valuation. On Segers, see also nos. 73 and 123.

71 Guido Reni. On Reni, see also nos. 67, 70 and 130.

72 No. 37 in the valuation. On Brouwer, see also no. 106.

73 Possibly a copy after Annibale Carracci's *Dead Christ*, canvas, 70.8 x 88.8 cm, in Stuttgart, Staatsgalerie. See Posner 1971, vol. 2, p. 3, no. 3.

74 No. 33 in the valuation. On Bordone, see also nos. 27 and 65.

75 Dirck (Theodoor) Helmbreker, who spent most of his life in Rome. He returned to Haarlem from 1673 to 1676. See Hoogewerff 1913, p. 34.

76 Vincent (Adriaenssen) Malo or his son Vincent Malo II, who was born in Antwerp in 1629 and became a master there in 1652/53.

77 No. 72 in the valuation.

78 No. 35 in the valuation. On Giorgione, see also no. 47.

79 No. 38 in the valuation.

80 Possibly Joos de Momper or another member of this large family of painters.

81 No. 18 in the valuation.

82 No. 29 in the valuation. Compare fig. 195.

83 No. 64 in the valuation.

84 No. 36 in the valuation. On Brouwer, see also no. 92.

85 No. 62 in the valuation.

86 No. 48 in the valuation.

87 No. 39 in the valuation.

88 No. 34 in the valuation.

89 No. 16 in the valuation.

90 No. 41 in the valuation.

91 No. 40 in the valuation.

92 Willem Kalf.

93 Jan Lievens. Possibly an *Entombment*, whereabouts unknown. See Schneider/Ekkart 1973, nos. 38a-b.

94 'Rogier van Bruggen', who is often taken to be Rogier van der Weyden. See Miedema 1994-1999, vol. 2, p. 227-229.

95 Titian. On Titian, see also nos. 42, 69, 118 and 145.

96 See no. 117.

97 Viviano Codazzi. Active in Rome and Naples.

98 Theodoor van der Schuer. On Van der Schuer, see also no. 129 and p. 250.

99 Gerard van Zijl.

100 Possibly no. 11 or 12 in the valuation. On Segers, see also nos. 79 and 90.

101 No. 67 in the valuation. On Backer, see also no. 53.

102 No. 9 in the valuation.

103 No. 56 in the valuation. On Van Neck, see also no. 1.

104 No. 77 in the valuation.

105 No. 69 in the valuation. On Snijders, see also no. 62.

106 No. 68 in the valuation. On Van der Schuer, see also no. 120.

107 Guido Reni. Possibly a copy after the *Madonna with a sleeping Christ*, canvas, 92 x 110 cm. Rome, Galleria Doria Pamphilj. See Garboli/Braccheschi 1971, no. 105. On Reni, see also nos. 67, 70 and 91.

108 No. 71 in the valuation.

109 Francesco Albani, On Albani, see also no. 44.

110 No. 74 or 75 in the valuation. On Moucheron also no. 85.

111 No. 10 in the valuation.

112 Peter Paul Rubens. It was probably an oil sketch. On Rubens, see also nos. 12, 54 and 55.

113 No. 3 in the valuation.

114 No. 5 in the valuation.

115 No. 6 in the valuation.

116 No. 7 in the valuation. On Tintoretto, see also no. 17.

117 No. 8 in the valuation.

118 No. 4 in the valuation.

119 Titian. On Titian, see also nos. 42, 69, 117 and 118.

120 Possibly a herm depicted by De Bisschop. See Van Gelder/Jost 1985, p. 150. See fig. 176.

121 Artus Quellinus. See also nos. 36, 37, 38, 39 and 47.

122 See no. 35.

123 See no. 35.

124 These must have been two terracotta models made by Quellinus for the town hall of Amsterdam, probably designs for the half-round decorations above the doors of the offices. See p. 237.

125 Artus Quellinus. It must have been a relief inspired by François du Quesnoy's relief of the same subject (Rome, Galleria Doria Pamphilj). See also no. 49. See also Scholten 2003.

126 Rombout Verhulst. Like no. 47 (Quellinus) it must have been inspired by the relief by Du Quesnoy. It might be the relief at the Rijksmuseum, Amsterdam, see fig. 180.

19 April 1675[1]

Inventory and appraisal of the paintings in the possession of Gerrit Uylenburgh

	Guilders
[1] A large, capital painting of a Turkish tapestry and Italian fruit by de Maltees, cost over 600 guilders.[2]	500
[2] Mary and Elizabeth and other figures, lifesize, by Jaques Jordaens, cost me at the time, unframed 225 guilders, framed[3]	250
[3] Portrait half-figure by the same master[4]	100
[4] St Peter's Basilica in Rome, by De la Maire[5]	160
[5] A Roman garden by Johannes Lingelbach[6]	180
[6] Tronie of a woman by Jacob Backer, from life[7]	36
[7] Portrait by Jacomo Tintoret[8]	48
[8] Polish trumpeter by Jan Bor[9]	54
[9] Battle of giants by David Finson, cost me 60 guilder at the time without the gilt frame[10]	75
[10] Nymph with children by Willeboorts[11]	150
[11] Landscape by Herculus Segers[12]	40
[12] A smaller, most unusual one by the same master[13]	40
[13] Portrait by Orasius Borgiano[14]	48
[14] Christ by Jan Bellin[15]	75
[15] An episode from Ovid by Francisco Salvoijati[16]	84
[16] Small crucifixion by Carel Vermander, present value[17]	60
[17] Flowers by Luijcas Luijckes[18]	40
[18] Tronie of St Dominic by Michiel Angelo[19]	100
[19] A small Danaë by Rembrant van Rijn[20]	40
[20] Landscape by Rogman[21]	72
[21] Two female saints by Paulo Veronesa[22]	84
[22] Female tronie by Pordenon[23]	30
[23] Female tronie by Bordon[24]	30
[24, 25, 26, 27] Four paintings of the same size, one by Backereel one by Gentil, by Anthonij van Hoeck and Justo del Pape, together[25]	400

Balance brought forward	2696
[28] Masquerade by Caroselli[26]	120
[29] Coliseum of Rome by Cornelio Poelenburg[27]	350
[30] Jewess by Rembrant van Rijn[28]	150
[31] Biblical scene by Pieter Lasman[29]	300
[32] Landscape by Alexander Petit[30]	78
[33] Portrait of an old man by Bordon the Elder[31]	50
[34] Woman asleep by Mires[32]	250
[35] Small portrait by Georgon[33]	30
[36] The peasant with a big shoe by Brouwer, cost me 280 guilders[34]	300
[37] Landscape with peasants by ditto[35]	100
[38] Small portrait by Willem Kaeij[36]	25
[39] Goats by Jan van der Does[37]	120
[40] Female tronie by Frans Flores[38]	36
[41] Shrove Tuesday jester by Frans Hals, cost me[39]	30
[42] Woman by Jan Bellin[40]	40
[43] Philosopher by Spanjoletto[41]	75
[44] Semiramis by Peter de Cortone[42]	400
[45] Lot and his daughters by Alexander Veroneso[43]	300
[46] Small landscape by Francisco del Molo[44]	100
[47] Small landscape by P.P. Rubens[45]	220
[48] Small church by Steenwijck the Elder[46]	70
[49] Female tronie by Palma Vecchio[47]	60
[50] A capital piece by PP Rubens, Peace[48]	650
[51] Atalanta by Adriaan Backer, cost me 250 guilders[49]	260
[52] Ceres by Jacob Pinas[50]	55
[53] Hound by F. Snijders, cost me 120 guilders[51]	100
[54] Landscape with a boar hunt[52]	42
[55] Mary and St Catherine by Francisco Parmitiaen[53]	320
[56] Europa, lifesize figures, J. van Neck, cost 125 guilders[54]	150
[57] Venus, lifesize, by ditto[55]	110
[58] Ceres with children by Georgon del Castelfranco[56]	160
[59] A Judgment by David Colijn the Elder[57]	80
[60] Mars and Venus by Lucas van Leijden[58]	100
[61] 4 to 6 copies after various masters	100

Balance brought forward   8027

[62] 1 portrait of a friar by Hans Holbeen[59]   100
[63] Tronie of a young woman by Titiaan[60]   200
[64] St Francis by Gerrit Douwesz[61]   250
[65] An old peasant couple, by Gabriel Metsu[62]   270
[66] Young woman at her toilet by C. Netscher[63]   326
[67] Diana by Adriaan Backer, cost, unframed, 140 guilders[64]   180
[68] Two figures, Time, by T: van der Schure, cost 120 guilders[65]   100
[69] Fruit by François Snijders[66]   72
[70] Judith by Perin del Vago[67]   150
[71] Venus and Cupid by Michiel Cocxie[68]   45
[72] Peasant woman by Beijga[69]   54
[73] Marine painting by Parsellis[70]   40
[74] Landscape by Moschiron[71]   70
[75] A smaller one by ditto[72]   36
[76] Landscape by me and Lingelbagh[73]   45
[77] A kitchen piece with figures[74]   20
[78] Judith after Raphael[75]   36
[79] Nudes by Francisco Albano, cost me 180 guilders[76]   150
[80] Some 20 pieces, 1 slightly larger than the rest combined   250
[81] The 6 little grisailles by Cornelis Holstijn, together[77]   75
[82] Another 10 small pieces, together   60

Paintings with Mr Pieter Lelij in England
[83] An excellent painting of singers by Casparus Netscher[78]   500
[84] The Cleopatra by the same, paid him cash last year,
unframed, 315 guilders[79]   320
[85] Danaë by Cornelis Poelenburg[80]   300
[86] Portrait by Anthonij Moor[81]   60
[87] Young women and others conversing by Netscher
bought for cash last year, cost me 250 guilders[82]   280
[88] Temptation of St Anthony by Brouwer[83]   60

Brought forward   12076

Balance brought forward   12076

[89] Young woman with a parrot by Netscher, the same
as I paid in cash last year[84]   140
[90] A large painting of fruit and miscellaneous, by
Jan Striep and d'Henin, the same amount I paid in cash
to those masters [in the margin: 'this piece is here'][85]   60
[91] All my marble statues and terracotta models,
by Quellinus, pander and bronze, altogether cost more
than 1800 guilders, and I now propose[86]   1000

    13,276

Gerrit Uijlenborch

BIBLIOGRAPHY:

1 Amsterdam Municipal Archives, archive no. 5072, inv. no. 1573, item 340. The appraisal of 1675 is undated, but the accompanying agreement between Uylenburgh and his creditors is dated 19 April 1675. The final proceeds of the auction are stated on an appended list of the creditors.
'Note: That the paintings specified in the list attached to one of the authenticated copies of the agreement fetched the sum of 5,321 guilders, on which amount the municipality levied 1 percent tax, being 53.4 guilders'.

2 No. 1 in the inventory. There is some debate concerning the identity of this Francesco Maltese. He is generally believed to have been Francesco Fieravino, who was active in Rome. However, it was recently suggested that he may have been Francesco Noletti, who was likewise active in Rome. The painter specialised in large still lifes with tapestries; on Maltese, see Safarik 1999 and Bocchi/Bocchi 2005. The painting documented in Uylenburgh's possession was probably later in the collection of Philips de Flines (see Hoet/Terwesten 1752-1770, vol. 1, p. 55, no. 15).

3 The painting appears not to be listed in the inventory. It may be Jacob Jordaens's late painting of *The Visitation* in Dayton (fig. 188). On contacts between Uylenburgh and Jordaens, see p. 243.

4 No. 136 in the inventory. On Jordaens, see note 3.

5 No. 141 in the inventory. Probably Jean Lemaire, called Le gros Lemaire, an architect and perspective painter who was active in Rome for some time. His son, called Le petit Lemaire or Lemaire-Poussin, was also a painter in Rome, but is not known to have been a perspective painter.

6 No. 137 in the inventory. Johannes Lingelbach. This is probably the signed and dated painting in Nuremburg (fig. 157). The last two digits of the date are no longer legible, but they were formerly said to be '71', see Tacke 1975. An earlier variant of this composition by Lingelbach is at Kunsthandel Noortman, Maastricht (fig. 156). Lingelbach worked with Gerrit Uylenburgh, see no. 76 and p. 214-216.

7 No. 138 in the inventory. Jacob Adriaensz Backer. Hendrick Uylenburgh had contact with Backer, Gerrit Uylenburgh with some of his pupils; see p. 178.

8 No. 139 in the inventory. Jacopo Robusti, called Tintoretto.

9 No. 140 in the inventory. No Jan Bor is known. The person meant was probably the painter Paulus Bor, even though the name Jan appears in the inventory as well.

10 No. 125 in the inventory. David Finson. Nephew and heir of the better known Louis Finson, who died in Amsterdam in 1617.

11 No. 134 in the inventory. Thomas Willeboirts Bosschaert. No painting is known that can be identified with this piece, see Heinrich 2003, vol. 1, no. C 42, p. 325.

12 No. 73, 90 or 123 in the inventory. Hercules Segers.

13 See note 12.

14 No. 84 in the inventory. Orazio Borgianni, active in Rome and Spain. No portraits by him are known today, but a number are listed in inventories.

15 Possibly no. 40 in the inventory 'A Saviour by Jan Dalij'. If so, the name should probably have been Bellien, i.e. Giovanni Bellini, 'Dalij' being a clerical error. This may have been one of the paintings, originally in the Vendramin Collection, that Gerrit Uylenburgh bought from the collection belonging to the Reynst brothers. The drawn catalogue of Vendramin's paintings includes a head of Christ by Bellini. See Borenius 1923.

16 No. 57 in the inventory. Francesco Salviati.

17 No. 111 in the inventory. Karel van Mander. No painting is known that corresponds to the description, see Leesberg 1993/1994. She mentions only a relatively large *Crucifixion in the snow* by Van Mander.

18 No. 79 in the inventory. Possibly Lucas Luce, with whom Hendrick Uylenburgh appraised work, see p. 293. No still lifes by him are known today, but they occur in seventeenth-century inventories, including the inventory of Lely's possessions. See Van der Willigen/Meijer 2003, p. 133, 134-135. The person in question could also be Carstian Luyckx, by whom numerous flower pieces are known.

19 Probably no. 103 in the inventory, 'Tronie of a Dominican', where the painter is not named. The attribution to Michelangelo Buonarotti is improbable.

20 No. 22 in the inventory. It is unclear which painting by Rembrandt this refers to. It is described as 'small' and therefore cannot be the large canvas (185 x 203 cm) at the Hermitage in Saint Petersburg. On Rembrandt, see also no. 30.

21 No. 8 in the inventory. Roelant Roghman. Roghman took Hendrick Fromantiou's side in the dispute with the Great Elector. Some of the landscapes Gerrit Uylenburgh painted must have been similar in style to work by Roghman. See p. 210.

22 No. 61 in the inventory. Paolo Caliari, called Veronese.

23 No. 26 in the inventory. Giovanni Antonis de Sacchis, called Pordenone.

24 No. 27 in the inventory. Paris Bordone. See also no. 33.

25 Three of the four paintings are probably nos. 5, 6 and 7 in the inventory (paintings by Backere, Juste del Papa and Louis Gentil). Strangely enough, the painting by Anthonij van Hoeck does not appear in the inventory. Backereel probably refers to Gillis Backereel. According to Houbraken 1718-1721, vol. 1, p. 218, one or more members of the Backereel family had long been active as artists: 'There have always been one or two living in Rome, and no sooner had the last one died than a couple more moved there from Antwerp to take his place'. Gillis Backereel moved to Rome in 1630 and associated there with Willem Romeyn and Antoine de Wael. Gentil must refer to Luigi Gentile or, more accurately, Louis Cousin. He spent more than 30 years working in Rome, where he went by the name of Gentiel; 'Anthonij van Hoeck' was perhaps meant to read 'Jan van der Hoecke'. He must have arrived in Rome by 1637 and was still living there in 1644. Justo del Pape is Josse de Pape. He is documented in Rome

as from 1633/34. Hence, all four paintings were by Flemish artists who worked in Rome for some time.

26 No. 4 in the inventory. Angelo Caroselli.

27 No. 104 in the inventory. Cornelis van Poelenburch. This is presumably the panel in Toledo (fig. 195), that being the only painting by Van Poelenburch known today in which the Coliseum is pictured clearly. With acknowledgments to Nicolette Sluijter-Seiffert for her help. On Van Poelenburch, see also no. 85.

28 No. 9 in the inventory. On Rembrandt, see also no. 19. This might be a portrait of a young woman called Beatriz Nunes Henriquez, which led to a dispute between Rembrandt and the Portuguese-Jewish art dealer Diego d'Andrade. The principal was unhappy with the painting and insisted that Rembrandt should alter it. Rembrandt agreed to do so on certain conditions and stipulated that if D'Andrade was dissatisfied with the result, the work would be put to auction. See Van der Veen 1997/98, p. 77

29 No. 81 in the inventory. Pieter Lastman. On Lastman. See also p. 262.

30 No. 83 in the inventory. Alexander le Petit, known predominantly for his Italianised landscapes.

31 No. 95 in the inventory. On Bordone, see also no. 23.

32 No. 110 in the inventory. Frans van Mieris. This might be the *Sleeping courtesan*, Florence, Uffizi (copper, 27.5 x 22.5 cm), the only known painting by Van Mieris that corresponds to the description. However, the text 'Francesco Miris 1669' is inscribed on the back of the work. The use of the Italian forename and the date have been taken to mean that Cosimo de' Medici bought the painting during his visit to the Netherlands in 1669, in which case it would not have been in Uylenburgh's possession in 1675. Numerous copies of the work are known, including one by Frans's son Jan van Mieris. See Naumann 1981, vol. 2, no. 75, p. 89-91. With acknowledgments to Quentin Buvelot for his help.

33 No. 99 in the inventory. Giorgione. On Giorgione, see also no. 58.

34 No. 106 in the inventory. Adriaen Brouwer. No painting is known that corresponds to the description. With acknowledgments to Konrad Renger for his help. A peasant with a fairly large shoe can be seen in a mezzotint by Wallerant Vaillant after a work by Brouwer (see Hollstein, vol. 31, no. 141, *The Village Surgeon*). Considering that Vaillant was acquainted with Uylenburgh, the possibility exists that he executed the mezzotint after the painting in Uylenburgh' possession. On Brouwer, see also nos. 37 and 88.

35 No. 92 in the inventory. On Brouwer, see no. 36. The painting must have been similar to the panel presently in Berlin (fig. 187)

36 No. 100 in the inventory. Willem Adriaensz Keij.

37 No. 109 in the inventory. Jacob van der Does. He was acquainted with Constantijn Huygens the Younger, see p. 284.

38 No. 113 in the inventory. Frans Floris. Numerous tronies by him are known (cf. fig. 186). Hendrick

Uylenburgh possessed a grisaille by Floris as early as 1627, see p. 123.

39 No. 112 in the inventory. This could be Peeckelhaering, examples of which are in Kassel, Gemäldegalerie and Leipzig, Museum der bildenden Künste, or the *Buffoon playing a lute* in Paris, Louvre. See Slive 1970-1974, vol. 3, nos. 64 and 65. The inventory of the possessions of the painter Cornelis Dusart dating from 1704 lists as no. 30 'A Shrove Tuesday jester by Frans Hals'. That may have been the same painting as the one in Uylenburgh's list. See Bredius 1915-1922, vol. 1, p. 30.

40 No. 52 in the inventory. On Bellini, see also no. 14.

41 No. 49 in the inventory. Jusepe de Ribera, called Lo Spagnoletto, executed dozens of paintings of philosophers. Gerrit Uylenburgh sold a Ribera to the Great Elector in 1671, see p. 91.

42 No. 43 in the inventory. Pietro Berrettini, called da Cortona. This could be the painting in the collection of Sir Denis Mahon (see fig. 183).

43 No. 46 in the inventory. Alessandro Veronese or Alessandro Turchi, called L'Orbetto. There are paintings of this subject in Dresden, Gemäldegalerie and Kingston (figs. 184 and 185). It is uncertain whether the work in Uylenburgh's possession was one of those two or perhaps another version. A painting of this subject by Turchi was in the Netherlands in the eighteenth century. In 1710 it was in the possession of the Ghent art dealer Francisco-Jacomo van den Berghe and his partner in Paris, who had handed it on to Raoul de Pierre de la Porte. In 1711/12 the Rotterdam dealer Quirijn van Biesum noted that Francisco-Jacomo van den Berghe was still owed money for a painting of this subject by Turchi, Duverger 2004, p. 101, 124-126.

44 No. 45 in the inventory. Pier Francesco del Mola. Jean Gericot had given Gerrit Uylenburgh a landscape by Mola for sale; he collected it in 1675, see p. 107, note 260.

45 No. 55 in the inventory. Peter Paul Rubens. On Rubens, see also no. 50.

46 No. 108 in the inventory. Hendrick van Steenwijk.

47 No. 48 in the inventory. Jacopo Negretti, called Palma Vecchio. This may also have been one of the paintings from the Vendramin Collection that Uylenburgh acquired with the Reynst Collection. Cf. Rylands 1988, no. 35, p. 212-213. Gerrit Uylenburgh had paintings by Palma Vecchio in his collection on several occasions, see p. 231.

48 Probably no. 54 in the inventory. On Rubens, see also no. 47. Several paintings of this subject by Rubens are known, one being the famous work at the National Gallery in London.

49 No. 53 in the inventory. Adriaen Backer. On Backer, see also no. 67.

50 No. 63 in the inventory. Jacob Symonsz Pynas. No painting of this subject by Pynas is known, but Museum Boijmans Van Beuningen in Rotterdam has a drawing of the *Mocking of Ceres*.

51 No. 62 in the inventory. Frans Snijders. Jürgen Ovens may have owned this painting later. In any event, a 'groszer Hundt' by Snijders was listed in the inventory of his widow's estate. See Schmidt 1914. On Snijders, see also no. 69.

52 No. 58 in the inventory.

53 No. 41 in the inventory. Girolamo Francesco Mazzola, called Parmigianino. The painting might be a version of the *Mystic marriage of Saint Catherine* at the National Gallery, London. In 1675 that painting must still have been in the Borghese Collection in Rome, but there were numerous copies in circulation. Charles I, for instance, possessed a version of it. The work in question here could also have been a version of the *Virgin and Child with Joseph and Saint Catherine*, presently at the Louvre, Paris. The original of that work was in Spain around 1675. Charles II may have possessed a version of the same composition; James I is known to have possessed one. See Vaccaro 2002, p. 152-154, 169-170.

54 No. 126 in the inventory. Jan van Neck. On Van Neck, see also no. 57 and p. 246-247.

55 No. 2 in the inventory. See also no. 56.

56 No. 47 in the inventory. On Giorgione, see also no. 35. The painting came from the Vendramin Collection, and Uylenburgh must have acquired it with the Reynst Collection. It was one of the paintings he tried to sell to the Great Elector (cf. fig. 58).

57 No. 10 in the inventory. David Colijn. See also p. 281.

58 No. 51 in the inventory. Lucas van Leyden. An engraving of this subject by Lucas van Leyden is known, but no painting is known (Bartsch 137). The painting may have been executed after the print. That said, readers should note that a great many works are attributed to Lucas in seventeenth-century inventories. He was credited with numerous sixteenth-century paintings that could not otherwise be attributed.

59 No. 107 in the inventory. Hans Holbein. No painting by him is known that corresponds with the description. The painting in question here is one of the works that Uylenburgh offered the Great Elector, see p. 96.

60 No. 42 in the inventory. Titian or, more accurately, Tiziano Vecellio.

61 No. 105 in the inventory. Gerrit Dou. Dou executed numerous paintings of elderly hermits, but no painting of Saint Francis by him is known. Uylenburgh had met Dou by at least 1660, see p. 69.

62 No. 82 in the inventory. Gabriël Metsu. The description in the inventory 'A peasant with a cock by Gabriel Metsu' corresponds to a painting in Dresden (Staatliche Kunstsammlungen. Gemäldegalerie Alte Meister, inv. no. 1733). There, however, the elderly peasant is offering the cock to a sophisticated young woman who could not be mistaken for a peasant. Hence, the painting in question here is probably a work no longer known to us. With thanks to Adriaan Waiboer.

63 No. 80 in the inventory. Caspar Netscher. On Netscher, see p. 250. Netscher executed several paintings of women at their toilet, see, for example, Wieseman 2002, no. 7 (Basel, Kunstmuseum), no. 42 (whereabouts unknown) and no. 44 (Dresden, Staatliche Kunstsammlungen. Gemäldegalerie Alte Meister). On Netscher, see also nos. 83, 84, 87 and 89.

64 No. 124 in the inventory. On Adriaen Backer, see also no. 51.

65 No. 129 in the inventory. Theodoor van der Schuer. On Van der Schuer, see p. 250. His painting must have been a (liberally interpreted?) copy after Anthony van Dyck's already famous *Saturn clipping Cupid's wings* (Paris, Musée Jacquemart-André, see Barnes/ De Poorter/ Millar/ Vey 2004, no. 111.65, p. 299). Jan de Bisschop made a drawing after that painting. Caspar Netscher made two copies after it. See Wieseman 2002, no. B 12, p. 319-320. The whereabouts of Van Dyck's painting in 1675 are unknown. It was later in the collection of Stadholder William III. See Van Gelder 1959, p. 77, who suggests that it may have been in Holland in the 1660s.

66 No. 128 in the inventory. On Snijders, see also no. 53.

67 No. 50 in the inventory. Perino del Vago (Pietro Buonaccorsi).

68 No. 131 in the inventory. Michiel Coxcie.

69 No. 98 in the inventory. Cornelis Bega.

70 No. 3 in the inventory. Jan Porcellis.

71 No. 85 or 133 in the inventory. Frederick de Moucheron. See also no. 75.

72 No. 85 of 133 in the inventory. See also no. 74.

73 The painting appears not to correspond to any work described in the inventory. On Lingelbach, see also no. 5. and pp. 214-216.

74 No. 127 in the inventory.

75 No. 88 in the inventory. This was probably a copy after the *Judith* presently at the Hermitage in Saint Petersburg and attributed to Giorgione. In the seventeenth century it was thought to be by Raphael. Van Gelder maintains that it was in the possession of Everhard Jabach for some time, and that Jan de Bisschop produced a drawing of it (Van Regteren Altena Collection, Amsterdam, reproduced in Van Gelder 1971, p. 215, fig. 49). See Anderson 1996, p. 292-293.

76 No. 44 in the inventory. Francesco Albani. No painting is known that corresponds to the description. It may have borne a resemblance to the *Nymph and a satyr playing a flute* in the British Royal Collection. See Puglisi 1999, no. 124.

77 They appear not to correspond to any paintings in the inventory. Cornelis Holsteyn.

78 The paintings that were in England are not listed in the inventory. On Netscher, see also no. 66 and nos. 84, 87, 89. Several paintings by Netscher fit the description. See Wieseman 2002, no. 31 (Paris, Louvre, dated 1664), no. 49 (Dresden, Staatliche Kunstsammlungen, Gemäldegalerie alte Meister, dated 1665), no. 51 (Munich, Alte Pinakothek, dated 1665), no. 52 (The Hague, Mauritshuis, dated 1665, fig. 192) and no. 53 (Dresden, Staatliche Kunstsammlungen, Gemäldegalerie alte Meister, dated 1666).

79 The painting is now in Karlsruhe, Staatliche Kunsthalle (fig. 193). See Wieseman 2002, no. 121. Numerous copies of it have been made. On Netscher, see no. 83.

80 Cornelis van Poelenburch. The painting is believed
to be a work which is now in a private collection (fig.
208). With acknowledgments to Nicolette Sluijter-
Seiffert for this identification. On Van Poelenburch,
see also no. 29.
81 Antonis Mor van Dashorst.
82 On Netscher, see also nos. 66, 83, 84, 89. Quite a few
paintings by Netscher correspond to the description,
see Wieseman 2002, no. 26 (whereabouts unknown,
dated 1664), no. 27 (Schwerin, Staatliches Museum,
ca. 1664), no. 41 (Belvoir Castle, dated 1665) and no. 50
(New York, Metropolitan Museum, ca. 1665).
83 On Brouwer, see also nos. 36 and 37. A *Temptation of
Saint Anthony* attributed to a follower of Brouwer and
presently in Berlin (fig. 209) may be similar in composition to a work by Brouwer himself. Peter Paul
Rubens also possessed a painting of the same subject
that was attributed to Brouwer, see Belkin, Healy 2004,
no. 42, p. 202-203.
84 On Netscher, see also nos. 66, 83, 84, 87. Of the
paintings known today the most likely candidate is a
work in Wuppertal dated 1666 (fig. 207). See Wieseman 2002, no. 54.
85 No painter by the name of Jan Striep is known.
The artist in question may have been Christiaan Striep,
who took Uylenburgh's side in the dispute with the
Great Elector. D'Henin was probably the landscapist
Adriaen de Hennin, who lived in The Hague in 1664;
he was in Amsterdam in 1667 and again documented
in The Hague in 1675. He must have moved to London
a short time later. The painting could conceivably be
no. 11 in the inventory 'Italian fruit by Jan Strijdt'.
86 The sculptures correspond to those listed individually as nos. 1 to 52 in the inventory.

Begr. reg. Wk Burial register of the Orphanage
DBK Insolvent Estates Office (Desolate Boedelskamer)
DTB Register of Baptism, Marriage and Deaths
GAA Gemeentearchief Amsterdam
Kw. Remissions of Debt (Kwijtscheldingen)
NA Notarial Archives
NHA Noord-Hollands Archief
not. notary
(O)RA (Old) Judicial Archives
RAL Regionaal Archief Leiden

ABRY 1867
H. Helbig and S. Bormans, *Les hommes illustres de la nation Liégoise par Louis Abry,* Liège 1867

AIKEMA 1990
B. Aikema, *Pietro della Vecchia and the heritage of the Renaissance in Venice,* Florence 1990

AMSTERDAM 1996
exh. cat. *Rembrandt & Van Vliet. A collaboration on copper* (Amsterdam: The Rembrandt House Museum), Amsterdam 1996

ANDERSON 1996
J. Anderson, *Giorgione. Peintre de la 'Brièveté Poétique',* Paris 1996

ANDRIESSE 1993
C.D. Andriesse, *Titan kan niet slapen. Een biografie van Christiaan Huygens,* Amsterdam 1993

ANTONIDES VAN DER GOES 1685
J. Antonides van der Goes, *Gedichten van J. Antonides van der Goes,* Amsterdam 1685

ANTWERP 1997
exh. cat. *De prinselijke pelgrimstocht. De 'grand tour' van Prins Ladislas van Polen, 1624-1625* (Antwerp: Koninklijk Museum voor Schone Kunsten), Ghent 1997

B.
A. Bartsch, *Catalogue raisonné de toutes les estampes qui forment l'œuvre de Rembrandt, et ceux de ses principaux imitateurs,* 2 vols., Vienna 1797

DE BAAR 2004
M. de Baar, *'Ik moet spreken'. Het spiritueel leiderschap van Antoinette Bourignon (1616-1680),* Groningen 2004

BACOU 1978
R. Bacou, 'Everard Jabach. Dessins de la seconde collection', *Revue de l'art* 40-41 (1978), pp. 141-150

BAHL 2001
P. Bahl, *Der Hof des Großen Kurfürsten. Studien zur höheren Amtsträgerschaft Brandenburg-Preußens,* Cologne 2001

BALDINUCCI 1681-1728
F. Baldinucci, *Notizie de'professori del disegno da Cimabue in qua...,* 4 vols., Florence 1681-1728

BALLARIN 1997
A. Ballarin, *Jacopo Bassano, Tavole, Parte Prima 1531-1568,* Cittadella (Padua) 1997

BARNARD 2000
T.C. Barnard, Introduction: The Dukes of Ormonde, in: Barnard/Fenlon 2000, pp. 1-54

BARNARD/FENLON 2000
T. Barnard and J. Fenlon (eds.), *The Dukes of Ormonde,* Woodbridge 2000

BARNES/DE POORTER/MILLAR/VEY 2004
S.J. Barnes, N. De Poorter, O. Millar and H. Vey, *Van Dyck. A complete catalogue of the paintings,* New Haven/London 2004

BARTOSCHEK 1988
G. Bartoschek, 'Ein Kurfürstliches Gemäldekabinett', in: Giersberg 1988, pp. 134-148

BARTOSCHEK 2001
G. Bartoschek, 'Die Residenz und Ihre Gemäldesammlung', in: exh. cat. *Zeit der Markgrafen. Die Hohenzollern von Brandenburg-Schwedt* (Schwedt: Städtischen Museen Schwedt im Stadtmuseum 2001-2002), s.l. 2001, pp. 28-41

BAUCH 1926
K. Bauch, *Jakob Adriaensz Backer. Ein Rembrandt-schüler aus Friesland,* Berlin 1926 (Grote'sche Sammlung von Monographien zur Kunstgeschichte, 5)

DE BEER 1955
E.S. de Beer (compiler), *The diary of John Evelyn,* 6 vols., Oxford 1955; vol. 3, Kalendarium 1650-1672

BELKIN/HEALY 2004
K. Lohse Belkin and F. Healy, *Een huis vol kunst. Rubens als verzamelaar,* Antwerp 2004

BELLONI 1988
V. Bellonie, *Scritti e cose di arte Genovese,* Genoa 1988

BELONJE 1972
J. Belonje, 'Interieurversiering van Herengracht 554', *Maandblad Amstelodamum* 59 (1972), p. 188

BEN.
O. Benesch, *The drawings of Rembrandt,* 6 vols., London 1954-1957

BERCKENHAGEN 1964
E. Berckenhagen, *Die Malerei in Berlin vom 13. bis zum 18. Jahrhundert,* Tafelband, Berlin 1964

BERGVELT/KISTEMAKER 1992
E. Bergvelt and R. Kistemaker (eds.), *De wereld binnen handbereik. Nederlandse kunst- en rariteiten-verzamelingen, 1585-1735,* Zwolle 1992

DE BIE 1662
C. de Bie, *Het gulden cabinet van de edele vry schilder-const,* Antwerp 1662 (reprint: Soest 1971)

VAN BIEMA 1906
E. van Biema, 'Nalezing van de stadsrekeningen van Amsterdam vanaf het jaar 1531 (v)', *Oud Holland* 24 (1906), pp. 171-192

BIESBOER 1983
P. Biesboer, *Schilderijen voor het stadhuis Haarlem. 16e en 17e eeuw kunstopdrachten ter verfraaiing,* Haarlem 1983

BIESBOER 2001
P. Biesboer with the assistance of C. Togneri, *Collections of paintings in Haarlem 1572-1745,* Los Angeles 2001 (Documents for the history of collecting: Netherlandish Inventories, 1)

BIKKER 1998
J. Bikker, 'The Deutz brothers, Italian paintings and Michiel Sweerts: new information from Elisabeth Coyman's *Journael',* *Simiolus* 26 (1998), pp. 277-311.

DE BISSCHOP 1668-1669
J. de Bisschop, *Signorum veterum icones,* 2 vols., s.l. s.a. [c. 1668-1669]

DE BISSCHOP 1671
J. de Bisschop, *Paradigmata graphices variorum artificum/Voor-beelden der teken-konst van verscheyde meesters,* The Hague 1671

BLANKERT 1968
A. Blankert, 'Over Pieter van Laer als dier- en landschapsschilder', *Oud Holland* 83 (1968), pp. 117-134

BLANKERT 1975-1979
A. Blankert with contributions by R. Ruurs, *Amsterdams Historisch Museum. Schilderijen daterend van voor 1800, voorlopige catalogus,* Amsterdam 1975-1979

BLANKERT/MONTIAS/AILLAUD 1992
A. Blankert, J.M. Montias and G. Aillaud, *Vermeer,* Amsterdam 1992

BLANKERT/GILTAIJ/LAMMERTSE 1999-2000
A. Blankert, J. Giltaij and F. Lammertse (eds.), exh. cat. *Hollands Classicisme in de zeventiende-eeuwse schilderkunst* (Rotterdam: Museum Boijmans Van Beuningen; Frankfurt: Städelsches Kunstinstitut 1999-2000), s.l. 1999

BLOK 1976
F. Blok, *Caspar Barlaeus, from the correspondence of a melancholic,* Assen/Amsterdam 1976

BOCCHI/BOCCHI 2005
G. Bocchi and U. Bocchi, *Pittori di Natura Morta a Roma. Artisti Italiani 1630-1750,* Viadana 2005

DE BOER 1900
M.G. de Boer, 'Een onrustige geest (Joannes Rothé)', *Tijdschrift voor Geschiedenis, Land en Volkenkunde* 15 (1900), pp. 201-219

DE BOER 1948
M.G. de Boer, 'Vergeten leden van een bekend geslacht', *Jaarboek Amstelodamum* 42 (1948), pp. 10-34

BOERS-GOOSENS 2001
M.E.W. Boers-Goosens, *Schilders en de markt, Haarlem 1605-1635*, s.l. 2001

BOGUCKA 1971
M. Bogucka, 'Zur Problematik der Münzkrise in Danzig in der ersten hälfte des XVII Jh.', *Studia Historiae Oeconomicae* 6 (1971), pp. 66-73

BOGUCKA 1980
M. Bogucka, *Das alte Danzig. Altagsleben vom 15. bis 17. Jahrhundert*, Leipzig 1980

BOGUCKA 1990
M. Bogucka, 'Dutch merchants' activities in Gdansk in the first half of the 17th century', in: J.Ph.S. Lemmink and J.S.A.M. van Koningsbrugge (eds.), *Baltic affairs: relations between the Netherlands and North-Eastern Europe, 1500-1800*, Nijmegen 1990 (Baltic Studies, 1), pp. 19-32

BOK 1994
M.J. Bok, *Vraag en aanbod op de Nederlandse kunstmarkt, 1580-1700*, z. pl. 1994

BOLTEN 1981
J. Bolten (compiler), *Rembrandt and the Incredulity of Thomas. Papers on a rediscovered painting from the seventeenth century*, Leiden 1981

VAN DEN BOOGERT/BROOS/VAN GELDER/
VAN DER VEEN 1999
B. van den Boogert, B. Broos, R. van Gelder and J. van der Veen, *Rembrandt's Treasures*, Zwolle 1999

BORENIUS 1923
T. Borenius, *The picture gallery of Andrea Vendramin*, London 1923

VAN DEN BOSCH 1650
L. van den Bosch, *Kunstkabinet van Maerten Kretzer*, Amsterdam 1650

BOSSE 1649
A. Bosse, *Sentimens sur la distinction des diverses Manieres de Peinture, Dessein & Graveure, & des Originaux d'avec leurs copies*, Paris 1649

BOUDON-MACHUAL 2005
M. Boudon-Machual, *François du Quesnoy*, Paris 2005

BRANDT 1688
G. Brandt, *G: Brandts Poëzy*, Amsterdam 1688

BR.
A. Bredius, *Rembrandt schilderijen*, Utrecht 1935

BREDIUS 1884
A. Bredius, 'De schilder Abraham Uylenborgh', *Oud Holland* 2 (1884), pp. 219-220

BREDIUS 1886
A. Bredius, 'Italiaansche schilderijen in 1672 door Amsterdamsche en Haagsche schilders beoordeeld', *Oud Holland* 4 (1886), pp. 41-46 and 278-280

BREDIUS 1889
A. Bredius, 'Kunstkritiek der XVIIe eeuw', *Oud Holland* 7 (1889), pp. 41-44

BREDIUS 1891
A. Bredius, 'De kunsthandel te Amsterdam in de XVIIe eeuw', *Amsterdamsch Jaarboekje* 1891, pp. 54-71

BREDIUS 1899
A. Bredius, 'Nieuwe Rembrandtiana', *Oud Holland* 17 (1899), pp. 1-5

BREDIUS 1906
A. Bredius, 'Eenige taxaties van schilderijen in de XVIIe en in het begin der XVIIIe eeuw', *Oud Holland* 24 (1906), pp. 236-241

BREDIUS 1908
A. Bredius, 'Michiel Jansz van Mierevelt. Eene nalezing', *Oud Holland* 26 (1908), pp. 1-17

BREDIUS 1909
A. Bredius, 'Uit Rembrandt's laatste levensjaar', *Oud Holland* 27 (1909), pp. 238-240

BREDIUS 1910A
A. Bredius, 'Rembrandtiana', *Oud Holland* 28 (1910), pp. 1-18

BREDIUS 1910B
A. Bredius, 'Rembrandtiana', *Oud Holland* 28 (1910), pp. 193-204

BREDIUS 1915-1922
A. Bredius, *Künstler-Inventare. Urkunden zur Geschichte der holländischen Kunst des XVIten, XVIIten und XVIIIten Jahrhunderts*, 7 vols. with separate index, The Hague 1915-1922

BREDIUS 1916
A. Bredius, 'Italiaansche schilderijen in 1672 door Haagsche en Delftsche schilders beoordeeld', *Oud Holland* 34 (1916), pp. 88-93

BREDIUS 1930
A. Bredius, 'Archiefsprokkelingen', *Oud Holland* 47 (1930), p. 157

BREDIUS 1934
A. Bredius, 'Een Schilderscontract', *Oud Holland* 51 (1934), pp. 188-190

BREDIUS/DE ROEVER 1885
A. Bredius and N. de Roever, 'Rembrandt: nieuwe bijdragen tot zijne levensgeschiedenis', *Oud Holland* 3 (1885), pp. 85-107

BREDIUS/DE ROEVER 1887
A. Bredius and N. de Roever, 'Rembrandt: nieuwe bijdragen tot zijne levensgeschiedenis', *Oud Holland* 5 (1887), pp. 210-239

BREEN 1909A
J.C. Breen, 'Huis Keizersgracht 567', *Jaarboek Amstelodamum* 7 (1909), pp. 75-80

BREEN 1909B
J.C. Breen, 'Topographische geschiedenis van den Dam te Amsterdam', *Jaarboek Amstelodamum* 7 (1909), pp. 99-196

BREJON DE LAVERGNÉE 1987
A. Brejon de Lavergnée, *L'inventaire Le Brun de 1683. La collection des tableaux de Louis XIV*, Paris 1987

BRIELS 1997
J. Briels, *Vlaamse schilders en de dageraad van Hollands Gouden Eeuw 1585-1630*, Antwerp 1997

VAN DEN BRINK 1997
P.B.R. van den Brink, 'David geeft Uria de brief voor Joah: Niet Govert Flinck, maar Jacob Backer', *Oud Holland* 111 (1997), pp. 177-186

BROOD 1977A
H. Brood, *De vroedschap van Weesp*, Weesp 1977 (typoscript)

BROOD 1977B
H. Brood, *Officianten-register van Weesp 1550-1795*, Weesp 1977 (typoscript)

BROOS 1981-1982
B.P.J. Broos, Recensie van Doc., *Simiolus* 12 (1981-1982), pp. 245-262

BROOS 1991
B. Broos, 'Hippocrates bezoekt Democritus door Pynas, Lastman, Moeyaert en Berchem', *De Kroniek van het Rembrandthuis* 1991, no. 2, pp. 16-23

BROOS 2000
B. Broos, 'Rembrandts eerste Amsterdamse periode', *Oud Holland* 114 (2000), pp. 1-6

BROOS 2005
B. Broos, 'Rembrandts Zeeuwse connectie: François Coopal en Titia Uylenburgh', *De Kroniek van het Rembrandthuis* 2005/1-2, pp. 25-33

BROWN 1995
J. Brown, *Kings and connoisseurs. Collecting art in seventeenth-century Europe*, New Haven/London 1995

BRUINVIS 1909
C.W. Bruinvis, 'Nadere Mededeelingen over Kunstenaars en hun werk in betrekking tot Alkmaar', *Oud Holland* 27 (1909), pp. 115-124

BRULLIOT 1832-1834
F. Brulliot, *Dictionnaire des monogrammes, marques figurées, lettres initiales, noms abrégés...*, 3 vols., Munich 1832-1834

DE BRUNE 1624
J. de Brune, *Emblemata of Zinne-werck: voorghestelt, in beelden, ghedichten...*, Amsterdam 1624

BRUYN 1984-1996
J. Bruyn, review of Sum., I: *Oud Holland* 98 (1984), pp. 146-162; II: *Oud Holland* 101 (1987), pp. 222-234; III: *Oud Holland* 102 (1988), pp. 322-333; IV-V: *Oud Holland* 109 (1995), pp. 101-112; VI: *Oud Holland* 110 (1996), pp. 165-173

BRUYN 1986
J. Bruyn, 'Patrons and early owners', in: Corpus I-III, vol. 2, pp. 91-98

BRUYN/MILLAR 1962
J. Bruyn and O. Millar, 'Notes on the Royal Collection – III: The "Dutch Gift" to Charles I', *The Burlington Magazine* 106 (1962), pp. 291-294

BUIJSEN 1998
E. Buijsen (ed), *Haagse schilders in de Gouden Eeuw. Het Hoogsteder Lexicon van alle schilders werkzaam in Den Haag 1600-1700*, The Hague/Zwolle 1998

CALENDAR OF STATE PAPERS. DOMESTIC SERIES 1913
Calendar of State Papers. Domestic Series. March 1st 1678 to December 31st 1678 with Addenda 1674 to 1679, London 1913

CALENDAR OF STATE PAPERS. TREASURY BOOKS 1911
Calendar of State Papers. Treasury Books, volume 5.2, 1676-1679, London 1911

TEN CATE 1988
F. ten Cate, *Dit volckje seer verwoet. Een geschiedenis van de Sint Antoniesbreestraat*, Amsterdam 1988

CHANTELOU 1981
P. Fréart de Chantelou, *Journal de Voyage du Cavalier Bernin en France* (notice de Ludovic Lalanne, notes Jean Paul Guibbert), Paris 1981

CLAUSSEN 1997
N. Claussen, 'Friedrichstadt – Friedrich III. Und seine neue Stadt', in: Spielmann/Drees 1997, pp. 107-109

DE CLERCQ 1998A
D.C. de Clercq, 'Verkennende beschouwingen over de doopsgezinde elite in Amsterdam', *Doopsgezinde Bijdragen, nieuwe reeks* 24 (1998), pp. 249-262

DE CLERCQ 1998B
D.C. de Clercq, 'Een verdwenen en vergeten "mennistenhemel"', in: M. Carasso-Kok and J. Slofstra (eds.), *Het Gein. Levensloop van een rivier*, Abcoude 1998, pp. 111-121

CORPUS I-III
J. Bruyn, B. Haak, S.H. Levie, P.J.J. van Thiel and E. van de Wetering, *A Corpus of Rembrandt paintings*, 3 vols., The Hague/Boston/London 1982-1989

CORPUS IV
E. van de Wetering et al., *A Corpus of Rembrandt paintings*, vol. 4, Dordrecht 2005

COX 1911
M.L. Cox, 'Notes on the collections formed by Thomas Howard', *The Burlington Magazine* 20 (1911), pp. 282-286 and 323-325

CROFT-MURRAY 1962
E. Croft-Murray, *Decorative painting in England 1537-1837*, vol. 1, London 1962

DAVIES
A.I. Davies, *Allart van Everdingen 1621-1675. First painter of Scandinavian landscape*, Doornspijk 2001

THE HAGUE 1997-1998
exh. cat. *Vorstelijk Verzameld. De kunstcollectie van Frederik Hendrik en Amalia* (The Hague: Mauritshuis 1997-1998), Zwolle 1997

DETHLOFF 1992
D. Dethloff, 'Patterns of collecting drawings in late seventeenth and early eighteenth-century England', in: D. Dethloff (ed.), *Drawings: Master and Methods, Raphael to Redon. Papers presented to the Ian Woodner Master Drawings Symposium at the Royal Academy of Arts*, London 1992, pp. 197-207

DETHLOFF 1996
D. Dethloff, 'The executor's account book and the dispersal of Sir Peter Lely's collection', *Journal of the History of Collections* 8 (1996), pp. 15-51

DETHLOFF 2003
D. Dethloff, 'Sir Peter Lely's collection of prints and drawings', in: C. Baker, C. Elam and G. Warwick (eds.), *Collecting prints and drawings in Europe, c. 1500-1750*, Aldershot/Burlington 2003, pp. 123-139

DEZAILLIER D'ARGENVILLE 1745-1752
A.J. Dezaillier d'Argenville, *Abrégé de la vie des plus fameux peintres...*, 3 vols, Paris 1745-1752

DICKEY 2004
S.S. Dickey, *Rembrandt. Portraits in print*, Amsterdam 2004 (Oculi. Studies in the Arts of the Low Countries, 9)

DIRKSE 1984
P. Dirkse, 'Nicolaes Roosendael (1634/35-1686). Historieschilder voor katholiek Amsterdam', *Antiek* 19 (1984), pp. 86-98

DIRKSE 2001
P. Dirkse, *Begijnen, pastoors en predikanten*, Leiden 2001

DOC.
W.L. Strauss and M. van der Meulen, *The Rembrandt documents*, New York 1979

DOHME 1883
R. Dohme, 'Die Ausstellung von Gemälden älterer Meister in Berliner Privatbesitz', *Jahrbuch der Königlich Preussischen Kunstsammlungen* 4 (1883), pp. 119-130

DREES 1997
J. Drees, 'Jürgen Ovens (1623-1678) als höfischer Maler. Beobachtungen zur Portrait- und Historienmalerei am Gottorfer Hof', in: Spielmann/Drees 1997, pp. 245-258

DUDOK VAN HEEL 1975A
S.A.C. Dudok van Heel, 'De kunstverzameling van Lennep met de Arundel-tekeningen', *Jaarboek Amstelodamum* 67 (1975), pp. 137-148

DUDOK VAN HEEL 1975B
S.A.C. Dudok van Heel, 'Honderdvijftig advertenties van kunstverkopingen uit veertig jaargangen van de Amsterdamsche Courant 1672-1711', *Jaarboek Amstelodamum* 67 (1975), pp. 149-173

DUDOK VAN HEEL 1975C
S.A.C. Dudok van Heel, 'Waar woonde en werkte Pieter Lastman (1583-1633)?', *Maandblad Amstelodamum* 62 (1975), pp. 31-36

DUDOK VAN HEEL 1976
S.A.C. Dudok van Heel, 'De schilder Claes Moyaert en zijn familie', *Jaarboek Amstelodamum* 68 (1976), pp. 13-48

DUDOK VAN HEEL 1978
S.A.C. Dudok van Heel, 'Mr. Joannes Wtenbogaert (1608-1680) een man uit remonstrants milieu en Rembrandt van Rijn', *Jaarboek Amstelodamum* 70 (1978), pp. 146-169

DUDOK VAN HEEL 1980
S.A.C. Dudok van Heel, 'Doopsgezinden en schilderkunst in de 17de eeuw. Leerlingen, opdrachtgevers en verzamelaars van Rembrandt', *Doopsgezinde Bijdragen, nieuwe reeks* 6 (1980), pp. 105-123

DUDOK VAN HEEL 1982
S.A.C. Dudok van Heel, 'Het "schilderhuis" van Govert Flinck en de kunsthandel van Uylenburgh aan de Lauriergracht te Amsterdam', *Jaarboek Amstelodamum* 74 (1982), pp. 70-90

DUDOK VAN HEEL 1985
S.A.C. Dudok van Heel, 'De schilder Nicolaes Eliasz. Pickenoy (1588-1650/6) en zijn familie. Een geslacht van wapensteensnijders, goud- en zilversmeden te Amsterdam', in: *Liber amicorum Jhr. Mr. C.C. van Valkenburg*, The Hague 1985, pp. 152-160

DUDOK VAN HEEL 2001A
S.A.C. Dudok van Heel, 'Rembrandt: his life, his wife, the nursemaid and the servant', in: exh. cat. *Rembrandt's Women* (Edinburgh: The National Gallery of Scotland; London: The Royal Academy of Arts), s.l. 2001, pp. 19-27

DUDOK VAN HEEL 2001B
S.A.C. Dudok van Heel, 'Een nieuwe generatie Bicker-de Graeff geportretteerd', *Maandblad Amstelodamum* 88 (2001), pp. 1-16

DUDOK VAN HEEL 2002
S.A.C. Dudok van Heel, 'Toen hingen er burgers als vorsten aan de muur', in: exh. cat. *Kopstukken. Amsterdammers geportretteerd, 1600-1800* (Amsterdam: Amsterdams Historisch Museum), Bussum 2002, pp. 46-63

DULLAERT 1652
J. Dullaert, *Karel Stuart of Rampzalige Majesteit,* Amsterdam 1652

DULLAERT 1653
J. Dullaert, *Alexander de Medicis, of 't Bedrooge betrouwen*, Amsterdam 1653

DULLAERT 1719
H. Dullaert, *H. Dullaerts gedichten*, Amsterdam 1719

DUVERGER 1965
E. Duverger, 'Een betwist schilderij van Paulus Bril bij een Gents Kanunnik', *Revue belge d'Archéologie et d'Histoire de l'Art* 35 (1965), pp. 191-200

DUVERGER 1969
E. Duverger, *Nieuwe gegevens betreffende de kunsthandel van Matthijs Musson en Maria Fourmenois te Antwerp tussen 1633 en 1681*, Ghent 1969

DUVERGER 1984-2004
E. Duverger, *Antwerpse kunstinventarissen uit de zeventiende eeuw*, 12 vols. with separate index, Brussels 1984-2004 (Fontes Historiae Artis Neerlandicae. Bronnen voor de kunstgeschiedenis van de Nederlanden)

DUVERGER 2004
E. Duverger, *Documents concernant le commerce d'art de Francisco-Jacomo van den Berghe et Gillis van der Vennen de Gand avec la Hollande et la France pendant les premières décades du XVIIIe siècle*, Wetteren 2004

EARLE 2001
P. Earle, 'The economy of London, 1660-1730', in: O'Brien 2001, pp. 81-96

VAN EEGHEN 1953
P. van Eeghen, 'Abraham van den Tempel's Familiegroep in het Rijksmuseum', *Oud Holland* 68 (1953), pp. 170-174

VAN EEGHEN 1956
I.H. van Eeghen, 'De familie de la Tombe en Rembrandt', *Oud Holland* 71 (1956), pp. 43-49

VAN EEGHEN 1962
I.H. van Eeghen, 'Het huis Herengracht 468', *Jaarboek Amstelodamum* 44 (1962), pp. 170-192

VAN EEGHEN 1968
I.H. van Eeghen, 'Het geslacht Nijs (Nederlandse cosmopolieten in de 17de eeuw)', *Jaarboek Amstelodamum* 60 (1968), pp. 74-102

VAN EEGHEN 1969A
I.H. van Eeghen, 'Handboogstraat 5', *Maandblad Amstelodamum* 56 (1969), pp. 169-175

VAN EEGHEN 1969B
I.H. van Eeghen, 'Het Amsterdamse Sint Lucasgilde in de 17de eeuw', *Jaarboek Amstelodamum* 61 (1969), pp. 65-102

VAN EEGHEN 1973
I.H. van Eeghen, 'Archivalia betreffende Jan van der Heyden', *Maandblad Amstelodamum* 60 (1973), pp. 128-134

VAN EEGHEN 1984
I.H. van Eeghen, 'Anna Wijmer en Jan Six', *Jaarboek Amstelodamum* 76 (1984), pp. 38-68

VAN EEGHEN 1986
I.H. Eeghen, '"Over Rembrant de schilder"', *Maandblad Amstelodamum* 73 (1986), p. 23

EEKHOFF 1862
W. Eekhoff, 'De vrouw van Rembrand: bijzonderheden omtrent het huwelijk van den schilder Rembrand van Rijn van Leiden met Saske Ulenburgh van Leeuwarden', *Europa. Verzameling van uit- en inlandsche lettervruchten* 1862

EKKART 1991
R.E.O. Ekkart, 'Gerbrand Ban', *Bulletin van het Rijksmuseum* 39 (1991), pp. 426-434

EKKART 1992
R.E.O. Ekkart, 'Gerbrand Ban. Een aanvulling', *Bulletin van het Rijksmuseum* 40 (1992), p. 93

EKKART 2002
R. Ekkart, Amsterdamse portretschilders in de zeventiende en achttiende eeuw, in: exh. cat. *Kopstukken. Amsterdammers geportretteerd 1600-1800* (Amsterdam: Amsterdams Historisch Museum 2002-2003), s.l. 2002, pp. 28-45

ELIAS 1903-1905
J.E. Elias, *De vroedschap van Amsterdam 1578-1795*, 2 vols., Haarlem 1903-1905 (reprint: Amsterdam 1963)

ENKLAAR 2005
M. Enklaar, 'Twee genrestukken van Jan van Vliet', *De Kroniek van het Rembrandthuis* 2005/1-2, pp. 35-45

ENNO VAN GELDER 1918
H.A. Enno van Gelder, *De levensbeschouwing van Cornelis Pieterszoon Hooft, burgemeester van Amsterdam, 1547-1626*, Amsterdam 1918 (reprint: Utrecht 1982)

ERTZ 1979
K. Ertz, *Jan Brueghel del Ältere (1568-1625). Die Gemälde mit kritischem Œuvrekatalog*, Cologne 1979

FÉLIBIEN 1705
A. Félibien, *Entretiens sur les vies et sur les ouvrages des plus excellens peintres anciens et modernes*, London 1705 (ed. princ. 1688)

FENLON 2000
J. Fenlon, 'Episodes of Magnificence: the material worlds of the Dukes of Ormonde', in: Barnard/Fenlon 2000, pp. 137-160

FLOERKE 1901
H. Floerke, *Der niederländische Kunst-handel im 17. und 18. Jahrhundert*, Basel 1901

FLOERKE 1905
H. Floerke, *Die Formen des Kunsthandels, das Atelier und die Sammler in den Niederlanden vom 15.-18. Jahrhundert*, Munich/Leipzig 1905 (reprint: Soest 1972)

FOKKENS 1663
M. Fokkens, *Beschrijvinge der wijdt-vermaarde koop-stadt Amstelredam*, Amsterdam 1663

FOUCART 1988
J. Foucart, *Peintres rembranesques au Louvre*, Paris 1988

FOUCART 1989
J. Foucart, 'Peter Lely, Dutch history painter', *Hoogsteder-Naumann Mercury* 8 (1989), pp. 17-26

FRANKFURT/KYOTO 2002-2003
J. Giltaij, exh. cat. *Rembrandt Rembrandt* (Frankfurt am Main: Städelsches Kunstinstitut und Städtische Galerie; Kyoto: National Museum, 2002-2003), s.l. 2002

FRIJHOFF/SPIES 1999
W. Frijhoff and M. Spies, *1650. Bevochten eendracht*, The Hague 1999 (Netherlands culture in European context, 1)

FRUIN 1922
R. Fruin (compiler), *Brieven aan Johan de Witt, Tweede deel, 1660-1672*, Amsterdam 1922

FÜSSLI/FÜSSLI 1779-1821
J.R. Füssli and H.H. Füssli, *Allgemeines Künstlerlexicon, oder: Kurze Nachricht von dem Leben und den Werken der Mahler, Bildhauer*, 7 vols., Zurich 1779-1821

GAETELA BERTELA 1987
G. Gaeta Bertela, *Cardinal Leopoldo de'Medici. Rapporti con il mercato Veneto (Archivio del collezionismo Mediceo)*, Naples 1987

GALESLOOT 1868
L. Galesloot, 'Un procès pour une vente de tableaux attribués à Antoine van Dyck, 1660-1662', *Annales de l'Académie d'Archéologie de Belgique* 24, second series, vol. 4 (1868), pp. 561-578

GALLAND 1893
G. Galland, *Der Grosse Kurfürst und Moritz von Nassau der Brasilianer*, Frankfurt am Main 1893

GALLAND 1911
G. Galland, *Hohenzollern und Oranien (Studien zur Deutsche Kunstgeschichte)*, Strasbourg 1911

GARBOLI/BACCHESCHI 1971
C. Garboli en E. Baccheschi, *L'opera completa di Guido Reni*, Milaan 1971

GEHLEN 1986
A.Fl. Gehlen, *Notariële akten uit de 17e en 18e eeuw. Handleiding voor gebruikers*, Zutphen 1986

VAN GELDER 1959
J.G. van Gelder, 'Anthonie van Dyck in Holland in de zeventiende eeuw', *Bulletin Koninklijke Musea voor Schone Kunsten* 8 (1959), pp. 43-86

VAN GELDER 1963
J.G. van Gelder, 'Notes on the Royal Collection, IV. The "Dutch Gift" of 1610 to Henry, Prince of "Whalis", and Some Other Presents', *The Burlington Magazine* 105 (1963), pp. 541-544

VAN GELDER 1971
J.G. van Gelder, 'Jan de Bisschop 1628-1671', *Oud Holland* 86 (1971), pp. 201-288

VAN GELDER 1978
J.G. van Gelder, 'Caspar Netschers portret van Abraham van Lennep uit 1672', *Jaarboek Amstelodamum* 70 (1978), pp. 227-238

VAN GELDER 1992
R. van Gelder, 'Liefhebbers en geleerde luiden. Nederlandse kabinetten en hun bezoekers', in: Bergvelt/Kistemaker 1992, pp. 259-292

VAN GELDER/JOST 1976
J.G. van Gelder and I. Jost, 'Two marble statuettes from seventeenth-century Amsterdam collections', in: *Festoen. Opgedragen aan A.N. Zadoks-Josephus Jitta bij haar zeventigste verjaardag*, Groningen/Bussum 1976, pp. 297-304

VAN GELDER/JOST 1985
J.G. van Gelder and I. Jost, *Jan de Bisschop and his Icones and Paradigmata*, Doornspijk 1985

GERSON 1942
H. Gerson, *Ausbreitung und Nachwirkung der holländischen Malerei des 17. Jahrhunderts*, Haarlem 1942

GERSON 1947
H. Gerson, 'De Meester P.N.', *Nederlandsch Kunsthistorisch Jaarboek* 1 (1947), pp. 95-111

GIERSBERG 1988
H-J. Giersberg et al., exh. cat. *Der Grosse Kurfürst 1620-1688: Sammler, Bauherr, Mäzen* (Potsdam-Sanssouci: Neues Palast 1988), s.l. 1988

GILTAIJ 1999
J. Giltaij, *Ruffo & Rembrandt*, Zutphen 1999

GOLDSTEIN 1996
C. Goldstein, *Teaching art. Academies and schools from Vasari to Albers*, Cambridge 1996

GOOL 1750-1751
J. van Gool, *De Nieuwe Schouburg der Nederlantsche kunstschilders en schilderessen*, 2 vols., The Hague 1750-1751

GROSSMANN 1951
F. Grossmann, 'Holbein, Flemish Painting and Everhard Jabach', *The Burlington Magazine* 93 (1951), pp. 16-23

GROUCHY 1894
E.-H. de Grouchy, 'E·verhard Jabach collectionneur parisien (1695)', *Mémoires de la société de l'Histoire de Paris et de l'Ile-de-France* 21 (1894), pp. 217-292

HAES 1740
J. de Haes, *Het leven van Geeraert Brandt*, The Hague 1740

HALEY 1978
K.H.D. Haley, 'Sir Johannes Rothe: English Knight and Dutch Fifth Monarchist', in: D. Pennington en K. Thomas (eds.), *Puritans and revolutionaries. Essays in seventeenth-century history presented to Christopher Hill*, Oxford 1978, pp. 310-332

HARTMANN 1657-1659/PRÜMERS 1899-1900
R. Prümers, 'Tagebuch Adam Samuel Hartmann über seine Kollektenreise im Jahre 1657-1659', *Zeitschrift der Historischen Gesellschaft für die Provinz Posen* 14 (1899), pp. 67-140 and 241-308; II. 15 (1900), pp. 95-160 and 203-246

HEERINGA 1910-1917
K. Heeringa, *Bronnen tot de geschiedenis van den Levantschen handel, eerste deel 1590-1660, tweede deel 1661-1726*, The Hague 1910-1917 (Rijks Geschiedkundige Publicatiën, 10, 11 and 34)

HEIJBROEK 1982-1983
J.F. Heijbroek, D.J. Roorda, M. Schapelhouman and E. de Wilde, exh. cat. *Met Huygens op reis. Tekeningen en dagboeknotities van Constantijn Huygens jr. (1628-1697), secretaris van stadhouder-koning Willem III* (Amsterdam: Rijksmuseum, Rijksprenten-kabinet; Ghent: Museum voor Schone Kunsten 1982-1983), s.l. 1982-1983

HEIMBÜRGER 1988
M. Heimbürger, *Bernardo Keilhau detto Monsú Bernardo*, Rome 1988

HEINRICH 2003
A. Heinrich, *Thomas Willeboirts Bosschaert (1613/14-1654). Ein Flämischer Nachfolger Van Dijcks*, Turnhout 2003

HERES 1977
G. Heres, 'Die Anfänge der Berliner Antiken-Sammlung zur Geschichte des Antikenkabinetts', *Staatliche Museen zu Berlin. Forschungen und Berichte* 18 (1977), pp. 93-130

HERVEY 1921
M.F.S. Hervey, *The life, correspondence & collections of Thomas Howard Earl of Arundel. 'Father of Vertu in England'*, Cambridge 1921

HINTERDING 2001
E. Hinterding, *Rembrandt als etser. Twee studies naar de praktijk van productie en verspreiding*, 2 vols. s.l. 2001

HIOOLEN 1915
C.N. Hioolen, *Het geslacht Hioolen*, s.l. 1915

HIRST 1981
M. Hirst, *Sebastiano del Piombo*, Oxford 1981 (Oxford Studies in the History of Art and Architecture)

HOET/TERWESTEN 1752-1770
G. Hoet and P. Terwesten, *Catalogus of Naamlyst van Schilderijen met derzelver pryzen*, 3 vols., The Hague 1752-1770

OP 'T HOF 1990
W.J. op 't Hof, 'De godsdienstige ligging van De Brune', in: P.J. Verkruijsse (ed.), *Johan de Brune de Oude (1588-1658), een Zeeuws literator en staatsman uit de zeventiende eeuw*, Middelburg 1990 (Werken uitgegeven door het Koninklijk Zeeuwsch Genootschap der Wetenschappen, 6), pp. 26-52

OP 'T HOF 1994
W.J. op 't Hof, 'Gereformeerde piëtisten. Opposanten én geestverwanten van de doopsgezinden', *Doopsgezinde Bijdragen, nieuwe reeks* 20 (1994), pp. 83-128

HOOGEWERFF 1913
G.I. Hoogewerff 'Theodoor Helmbreker schilder van Haarlem (1633-1696)', *Oud Holland* 31 (1913), pp. 27-64

HOOGEWERFF 1947
G.J. Hoogewerff, *De geschiedenis van de St. Lucasgilden in Nederland*, Amsterdam 1947 (Patria. Vaderlandsche cultuurgeschiedenis in monografieën, 41)

HOUBRAKEN 1718-1721
A. Houbraken, *De groote schouburgh der Nederlantsche konstschilders en schilderessen*, 3 vols., Amsterdam 1718-1721

HOURTICQ 1905
L. Hourticq, 'Un amateur de curiosités sous Louis XIV. Louis-Henri de Loménie, comte de Brienne d'après un manuscrit inédit', *Gazette des Beaux-Arts* (1905), pp. 326-340

HOWARTH 1998
D. Howarth, 'The patronage and collecting of Aletheia, Countess of Arundel 1606-54', *Journal of the History of Collections* 10 (1998), pp. 125-137

D'HULST/DE POORTER/VANDENVEN 1993
R.-A. D'Hulst, N. de Poorter and M. Vandenven, exh. cat. *Jacob Jordaens (1593-1678)* (Antwerp: Koninklijk Museum voor Schone Kunsten 1993), Antwerp 1993

HUYGENS 1888-1950
Œuvres complètes de Christiaan Huygens, 22 vols., The Hague 1888-1950

HUYGENS DE JONGE 1876-1888
Journaal van Constantijn Huygens, den zoon (Handschrift van de Koninklijke Akademie van Wetenschappen te Amsterdam), Werken van het Historisch Genootschap, 4 vols., Utrecht 1876-1888

HUYS JANSSEN 1992
P. Huys Janssen, 'Rembrandt's academy', in: exh. cat. *Rembrandt's academy* (The Hague: Hoogsteder & Hoogsteder), Zwolle 1992, pp. 20-35

HUYS JANSSEN 2002
P. Huys Janssen, *Caesar van Everdingen 1616/17-1678. Monograph and Catalogue Raisonné*, Doornspijk 2002

JACOBS 1925
E. Jacobs, 'Das Museo Vendramin und die Sammlung Reynst', *Repertorium für Kunstwissenschaft* 46 (1925), pp. 15-38

JAGER 1990
R. de Jager, 'Meester, leerjongen, leertijd. Een analyse van de 17de-eeuwse leerlingcontracten van kunstschilders, goud- en zilversmeden', *Oud Holland* 104 (1990), pp. 69-111

JELLEMA/PLOMP 1992
R.E. Jellema, M. Plomp, *Episcopius. Jan de Bisschop (1628-1671) advocaat en tekenaar*, Amsterdam 1992

JOHN HOPE 1913
W.H. St. John Hope, *Windsor Castle. An architectural history*, London 1913

DE JONG 1976-1977
K.K. de Jong, 'Joan Dullaert, dichter-koopman', *Spektator. Tijdschrift voor Neerlandistiek* 6 (1976-1977), pp. 552-566

JOUIN 1889
H. Jouin, *Charles Le Brun et les arts sous Louis XIV [d'après le manuscrit de Nivelon]*, Paris 1889

JUDSON/EKKART 1999
J.R. Judson and R.E.O. Ekkart, *Gerrit van Honthorst 1592-1656*, Doornspijk 1999

KAM 1968
J.G. Kam, *Waar was dat huis in de Warmoesstraat*, Amsterdam 1968

KAM 1969
J.G. Kam, 'Mr. van Rhijn betaalt de verponding over het huis in de Breestraat', *Maandblad Amstelodamum* 56 (1969), pp. 157-160

KANDT 2003
K.E. Kandt, 'Netherlandish artists in 17th-century Danzig: new evidence from archival sources', in: M. Kapustki et al. (ed.), *Niderlandyzm na Sląsku i w krajach ościennych*, Wroclaw 2003 (Historia Sztuki, 17), pp. 304-321

KERNKAMP 1906
G.W. Kernkamp, 'Amsterdamsche patriciërs', *Vragen des Tijds* 32 (1906), no. I, pp. 1-41

KETELSEN/STOCKHAUSEN 2002
Th. Ketelsen and T. von Stockhausen, *The index of paintings sold in German-speaking countries before 1800*, 3 vols., Munich 2002

KILIAN 2005
J.M. Kilian, *The paintings of Karel Du Jardin. Catalogue raisonné*, Amsterdam/Philadelphia 2005

KIRBY TALLEY S.A.
M. Kirby Talley, *Portrait painting in England: Studies in the technical literature before 1700* (Published privately by the Paul Mellon Centre for Studies in British Art), s.l.s.a.

KLEMM 1986
Chr. Klemm, *Joachim von Sandrart. Kunst-Werken und Lebens-Lauf*, Berlin 1986

KLESSMANN 1997
R. Klessmann, 'Elsheimers "Verspottung der Ceres" – zur Frage des Originals', *Städel-Jahrbuch. Neue Folge* 16 (1997), pp. 239-248

KLOEK 1998
E. Kloek et al., *Vrouwen en kunst in de Republiek. Een overzicht*, Hilversum 1998

KOLLMANN 2000
S. Kollmann, *Niederländische Künstler und Kunst in London*, Hildesheim/Zurich/New York 2000

KOHIER 1631
J.G. Frederiks and P.J. Frederiks, *Kohier van den tweehonderdsten penning voor Amsterdam en onderhoorige plaatsen over 1631*, Amsterdam 1890

KOLDEWEIJ 1998
E.F. Koldeweij, *Goudleer in de Republiek der Zeven Verenigde Provinciën. Nationale ontwikkelingen en de Europese context*, s.l.1998

KÖLTZSCH 2000
G-W. Költzsch, *Der Maler und sein Modell. Geschichte und Deutung eines Bildthemas*, Cologne 2000

KONING 2001
P. Koning, 'Julius Caesar Scaligers Epidorpides in de Emblemata van Johan de Brune. Een substantiële schakel tussen Neolatijnse en zeventiende-eeuwse Nederlandse literatuur', *Tijdschrift voor Nederlandse Taal- en Letterkunde* 117 (2001), pp. 166-187

VAN KOOLBERGEN 1983
H. van Koolbergen, 'De materiële cultuur van Weesp en Weesperkarspel in de zeventiende en achttiende eeuw', *Volkskundig Bulletin* 9 (1983), pp. 3-52

KOPENHAGEN 2006
exh. cat. *Rembrandt? The master and his workshop* (Copenhagen: Statens Museum for Kunst), s.l. 2006

KROL 1985
H. Krol (ed.), *Adriaen Pauw (1585-1653), staatsman en ambachtheer*, Heemstede 1985

KUIJPERS 2005
E. Kuijpers, *Migrantenstad: immigratie en sociale verhoudingen in 17e-eeuws Amsterdam*, Hilversum 2005 (Amsterdamse Historische Reeks, grote serie, 32)

KUIJPERS/PRAK 2002
E. Kuijpers and M. Prak, 'Burger, ingezetene, vreemdeling: burgerschap in Amsterdam in de 17e en 18e eeuw', in: J. Kloek and K. Tilmans (eds.), *Burger*, Amsterdam 2002 (Nederlandse Begripsgeschiedenis, 4), pp. 113-132

KUTSCH LOJENGA 1982
J.C. Kutsch Lojenga, 'De oudste generaties Ulenburch te Leeuwarden', *Jaarboek van het Centraal Bureau voor Genealogie* 36 (1982), pp. 51-73

VAN LAER 1925
A.J.F. van Laer, 'Familie-aanteekeningen Juyst', *De Nederlandsche Leeuw* 1925, col. 250-251

LAING 1993
A. Laing, 'Sir Peter Lely and Sir Ralph Bankes', in: D. Howarth (ed.), *Art and patronage in the Caroline courts: Essays in honour of Sir Oliver Millar*, Cambridge 1993, pp. 107-133

LAMBOUR 2001
R. Lambour, 'Doopsgezind of niet? Sybrandt Hansz Cardinael, Abraham de Graaf en Gerrit Uylenburgh', *Doopsgezinde Bijdragen, nieuwe reeks* 27 (2001), pp. 177-194

LAMMERTSE 2002
F. Lammertse, 'Van Dyck's Apostles series, Hendrick Uylenburgh and Sigismund III', *The Burlington Magazine* 144 (2002), pp. 140-146

LAMMERTSE 2005
F. Lammertse, 'Fromantiou', in *Saur. Allgemeines Künstler-Lexikon*, dl. 45, Munich/Leipzig 2005, pp. 418-419

LARSEN 1995
E. Larsen, '"Meleager und Atalante" in der Konzeption von Abraham Janssens, Rubens und Jordaens', *Jaarboek van het Koninklijk Museum voor Schone Kunsten Antwerpen* 1995, pp. 177-194

LEESBERG 1993-1994
M. Leesberg, 'Karel van Mander as a painter', *Simiolus* 22 (1993-1994), pp. 5-57

LEIDEN 1976-1977
exh. cat. *Geschildert tot Leyden anno 1626* (Leiden: Stedelijk Museum De Lakenhal 1976-1977), Leiden 1976

LEIDEN 1988
exh. cat. *Leidse fijnschilders. Van Gerrit Dou tot Frans van Mieris de Jonge 1630-1760* (Leiden: Museum 'De Lakenhal'), Zwolle 1988

LEIDEN 2006
exh. cat. *Rembrandts moeder. Mythe en werkelijkheid* (Leiden: Stedelijk Museum De Lakenhal), Zwolle 2006

LEMMENS 1979
G.Th.M. Lemmens, 'Die Schenkung an Ludwig XIV. Und die Auflösung der brasilianischen Sammlung des Johan Moritz 1652-1679', in: exh. cat.. *Soweit der Erdkreis reicht. Johann Moritz von Nassau-Siegen 1604-1679* (Cleves: Städtisches Museum Haus Koekkoek 1979), s.l. 1979, pp. 265-293

LESGER 1986
C. Lesger, *Huur en conjunctuur. De woningmarkt in Amsterdam, 1550-1850*, s.l. 1986 (Amsterdamse Historische Reeks, 10)

LESGER 2001
C. Lesger, *Handel in Amsterdam ten tijde van de Opstand. Kooplieden, commerciële expansie en verandering in de ruimtelijke economie van de Nederlanden ca.1550-ca.1630*, Hilversum 2001 (Amsterdamse Historische Reeks, grote serie, 27)

LEUPE 1876
P.A. Leupe, 'Schilderijen en Satuen voor Karel de Tweede, Koning van Engeland 1660', *De Nederlandsche Spectator* 1876, pp. 184-186; 1878, pp. 82-83

LEVEY 1991
M. Levey, *The later Italian pictures in the collection of Her Majesty the Queen*, Cambridge 1991

LIEDTKE 1989
W. Liedtke, 'Reconstructing Rembrandt. Portraits from the early years in Amsterdam (1631-1634)', *Apollo* 129 (1989), pp. 321-331

LIEDTKE 1997
W. Liedtke, 'Reconstructing Rembrandt and his circle. More on the Workshop Hypothesis', in: R.E. Fleischer and S.C. Scott (eds.)., *Rembrandt, Rubens and the art of their time. Recent perspectives*, s.l. 1997 (Papers in Art History from the Pennsylvania State University, 11), pp. 37-48

LIEDTKE 2004
W. Liedtke, 'Rembrandt's "Workshop" revisited', *Oud Holland* 117 (2004), pp. 48-69

LOGAN 1979
A-M.S. Logan, *The 'cabinet' of the brothers Gerard and Jan Reynst*, Amsterdam/Oxford/New York 1979

LOGAN 1991
A-M.S. Logan, 'Kunstenaars, kooplieden en verzamelaars', in: M. de Roever (ed.), *Amsterdam: Venetië van het Noorden*, The Hague/Amsterdam 1991, pp. 137-155

LOHMEIER 1997A
D. Lohmeier, 'Die Gottorfer Bibliothek', in: Spielmann/Drees 1997, pp. 325-348

LOHMEIER 1997B
D. Lohmeier, 'Adam Olearius', in: Spielmann/Drees 1997, pp. 349-353

LONDON 1988-1989
D. Bomford, C. Brown and A. Roy, *Art in the making: Rembrandt* (London: The National Gallery, 1988-1989), s.l. 1988

LOUGHMAN 1997
J. Loughman, 'Salomon Koninck's "St Mark the Evangelist"', *The Burlington Magazine* 139 (1997), pp. 692-695

LUNSINGH SCHEURLEER 1986-1992
Th.H. Lunsingh Scheurleer, C.W. Fock and A.J. van Dissel (compilers), *Het Rapenburg. Geschiedenis van een Leidse gracht*, 6 vols.with separate index, Leiden 1986-1992

MAHON 1949
D. Mahon, 'Notes on the "Dutch Gift" to Charles II: I, II', *The Burlington Magazine* 91 (1949), pp. 303-305 and 349-350

MAHON 1950
D. Mahon, 'Notes on the "Dutch Gift" to Charles II: III', *The Burlington Magazine* 92 (1950), pp. 12-17

MANUTH 2005
V. Manuth, 'Rembrandt's Apostles: pillars of Faith and witnesses of the Word', in: exh. cat. *Rembrandt's late religious portraits* (Washington: National Gallery of Art; Los Angeles: The J. Paul Getty Museum), s.l. 2005, pp. 39-55

VAN DER MEER 1971
D.J. van der Meer, 'Ulenburg', *Genealogysk Jierboekje* 1971, pp. 74-99

MEIJER 1983
B.W. Meijer, *Rembrandt nel Seicento toscano*, Florence 1983

MEIJER 1991
B.W. Meijer, *Amsterdam en Venetië. Een speurtocht tussen IJ en Canal Grande*, The Hague 1991

MEIJER 1999
B.W. Meijer, 'Gerard Uylenburgh's Italian paintings', *Oud Holland* 113 (1999), pp. 75-87

MEIJER 2000
B.W. Meijer, 'Italian paintings in 17th century Holland. Art market, art works and art collections', in: F. Fehrenbach (ed.), *L'Europa e l'arte Italiana*, Venice 2000, pp. 376-417

MEIJER 2003
B.W. Meijer, 'Disegni Italiani in Olanda: collezioni di oggi e di ieri', in: A. Forlani Tempesti and S. Prosperi Valenti Rodino (eds.), *Disegno e disegni. Per un rilevamento delle collezioni dei disegni Italiani*, Florence 2003, pp. 79-107

MEISCHKE 1956
R. Meischke, 'Het Rembrandthuis', *Jaarboek Amstelodamum* 48 (1956), pp. 1-27

MEISCHKE 1975
R. Meischke, *Amsterdam Burgerweeshuis (De Nederlandse Monumenten van Geschiedenis en Kunst)*, The Hague 1975

MELBOURNE/CANBERRA 1997-1998
exh. cat. *Rembrandt, a genius and his impact* (Melbourne, National Gallery of Victoria; Canberra, National Gallery of Australia, 1997-1998), Zwolle 1997

MIEDEMA 1987
H. Miedema, 'Kunstschilders, gilde en academie. Over het probleem van de emancipatie van de kunstschilders in de Noordelijke Nederlanden van de 16de en 17de eeuw', *Oud Holland* 101 (1987), pp. 1-34

MIEDEMA 1980
H. Miedema, *De archiefbescheiden van het St. Lukasgilde te Haarlem*, 2 vols., Alphen aan den Rijn 1980

MIEDEMA 1994-1999
H. Miedema, *Karel van Mander. The Lives of the illustrious Netherlandish and German painters*, 6 vols., Doornspijk 1994-1999

MIELKE 1965
F. Mielke, 'Philipp de Chieze', *Jahrbuch für die Geschichte Mittel- und Ostdeutschlands* 13-14 (1965), pp. 384-392

MILLAR 1970-1972
O. Millar, 'The inventories and valuations of the King's goods 1649-1651', *The Walpole Society* 43 (1970-1972), pp. 1-458

MILLAR 1977
O. Millar, *The Queen's pictures*, London 1977

MILLAR 1978
O. Millar, exh. cat. *Sir Peter Lely* (London: National Portrait Gallery 1978-1979), London 1978

MIRTO/VAN VEEN 1993
A. Mirto and H.Th. van Veen, *Pieter Blaeu: lettere ai fiorentini. Antonio Magliabechi, Leopoldo e Cosimo III de' Medici e altri, 1660-1705*, Florence/Maarssen/Amsterdam 1993

MÖLLER 1984
G. J. Möller, 'Het album Pandora van Jan Six (1618-1700)', *Jaarboek Amstelodamum* 76 (1984), pp. 69-101

MONBEIG GOGUEL 1988
C. Monbeig Goguel, 'Taste and trade: the retouched drawings in the Everard Jabach collection at the Louvre', *The Burlington Magazine* 130 (1988), pp. 821-835

VON MOLTKE 1965
J. W. von Moltke, *Govaert Flinck 1615-1660*, Amsterdam 1965

MONTIAS 1982
J. M. Montias, *Artists and artisans in Delft*, Princeton, N. J. 1982

MONTIAS 1988
J. M. Montias, 'Art dealers in the seventeenth-century Netherlands', *Simiolus* 18 (1988), pp. 244-256

MONTIAS 1989
J. M. Montias, *Vermeer and his milieu. A web of social history*, Princeton, N. J. 1989

MONTIAS 1996
J. M. Montias, *Le marché de l'art aux Pays-Bas (XVe-XVIIe siècles)*, Paris 1996

MONTIAS 2002
J. M. Montias, *Art at auction in 17th century Amsterdam*, Amsterdam 2002

MONTIAS 2004-2005
J. M. Montias, 'Artists named in Amsterdam inventories, 1607-80', *Simiolus* 31 (2004-2005), pp. 322-346

NAGLER 1835-1852
G. K. Nagler, *Neues allgemeines Künstler-Lexicon*, 22 vols., Munich 1835-1852

NAUMANN 1981
O. Naumann, *Frans van Mieris*, 2 vols., Doornspijk 1981

NEW YORK 1995-1996
exh. cat. *Rembrandt/Not Rembrandt in The Metropolitan Museum of Art. Aspects of connoisseurship* (New York: The Metropolitan Museum of Art 1995-1996), 2 vols., s.l. 1995

NICOLAI 1786
F. Nicolai, *Nachricht von den Baumeistern, Bildhauern, Kupferstechern, Malern, Stukaturern, und andern Künstlern...*, Berlin/Stettin 1786

NICOLSON 1958
B. Nicolson, *Hendrick Terbrugghen*, The Hague 1958

NNBW
Nieuw Nederlandsch Biografisch Woordenboek, 10 vols., Leiden 1911-1937

O'BRIEN 2001
P. O'Brien et al., *Urban achievement in early modern Europe. Golden Ages in Antwerp, Amsterdam and London*, Cambridge 2003

OGDEN/OGDEN 1944
H. and M. Ogden, 'Sir Peter Lely's Collection: Further Notices', *The Burlington Magazine* 85 (1944), pp. 154-155

OGDEN/OGDEN 1955
H.V.S. Ogden and M.S. Ogden, *English Taste in Landscape in the Seventeenth Century*, Ann Arbor 1955

OGIER 1636/SCHOTTMÜLLER 1910
K. Schottmüller, 'Reiseeindrücke aus Danzig, Lübeck, Hamburg und Holland 1636. Nach dem neuentdeckten II. Teil von Charles Ogiers Gesandt-schaftstagebuch', *Zeitschrift des Westpreussischen Geschichtsvereins* 52 (1910), pp. 199-273

OLDEWELT 1942A
W. F. H. Oldewelt, 'Restauratie van schilderijen in de zeventiende en achttiende eeuw', in: *Amsterdamsche Archiefvondsten*, Amsterdam 1942, pp. 7-11

OLDEWELT 1942B
W. F. H. Oldewelt, 'Jacob Colijns een kunstschilder-genealoog uit de zeventiende eeuw', in: *Amsterdamsche Archiefvondsten*, Amsterdam 1942, pp. 101-106

ORLERS 1641
J. J. Orlers, *Beschrijvinge der stadt Leyden...*, Leiden 1641²

ORMROD 2001
D. Ormrod, 'Cultural production and import substitution: the fine and decorative arts in London, 1660-1730', in: O'Brien 2001, pp. 210-230

VAN OVERBEKE 1991
Aernout van Overbeke, *Anecdota sive historiae jocosae. Een zeventiende-eeuwse verzameling moppen en anek-dotes. Uitgegeven door Rudolf Dekker en Herman Rodenburg met medewerking van Harm Jan van Rees*, Amsterdam 1991

DE PAUW-DE VEEN 1969
L. de Pauw-de Veen, *De begrippen 'schilder', 'schilderij' en 'schilderen' in de zeventiende eeuw*, Brussels 1969

PEPPER 1984
D. Stephen Pepper, *Guido Reni. A complete catalogue of his works with an introductory text*, Oxford 1984

POELMANS 1917
W. J. L. Poelmans, 'Hendrik en David Beck', *Rotter-dams Jaarboekje*, second series 5 (1917), pp. 74-80

POPHAM/POUNCEY 1950
A. E. Popham and P. Pouncey, *Italian drawings in the Department of Prints and Drawings in the British Museum*, 2 vols., London 1950

POPHAM/WILDE 1949
A. E. Popham and J. Wilde, *The Italian drawings of the XV and XVI centuries in the collection of His Majesty the King at Windsor Castle*, London 1949

POSNER 1971
D. Posner, *Annibale Carracci. A study in the reform of Italian painting around 1590*, 2 vols. London 1971

POSTMA 1988
H. J. Postma, 'De Amsterdamse verzamelaar Herman Becker (ca. 1617-1678); nieuwe gegevens over een geldschieter van Rembrandt', *Oud Holland* 102 (1988), pp. 1-18

PRAK 2001
M. Prak, 'Het oude recht der burgeren. De betekenis van burgerschap in het Amsterdam van de zestiende en zeventiende eeuw', in: H. Hendrix and M. Meijer Drees (eds.), *Beschaafde Burgers. Burgerlijkheid in de vroegmoderne tijd*, Amsterdam 2001 (Utrecht Renaissance Studies, 6), pp. 23-42

PRIJST DE LIJST
P. J. J. van Thiel and C. J. de Bruyn Kops, *Prijst de lijst: de Hollandse schilderijlijst in de zeventiende eeuw* (Amsterdam, Rijksmuseum), The Hague 1984

PRINZ 1971
W. Prinz, *Geschichte der Sammlung (Die Sammlung der Selbstbildnisse in den Uffizien, Band 1)*, Berlin 1971

PUGLISI 1999
C. R. Puglisi, *Francesco Albani*, New Haven/London 1999

VAN PUTTE 1978A
P. C. A. van Putte, *Heijmen Dullaert*, Groningen 1978

VAN PUTTE 1978B
P. C. A. van Putte, 'Twee brieven van Joan Dullaert met den aankleve van dien': in P. C. A. van Putte and H. J. Verkuyl (eds.), *Nieuwe tegenstellingen op Nederlands taalgebied*, Utrecht 1978, pp. 108-129

PY 2001
B. Py, *Everhard Jabach collectionneur (1618-1695). Les dessins de l'inventaire de 1695*, Paris 2001 (Notes et Documents des musées de France, 36)

QUIRINI-POPLAWSKA 1977
D. Quirini-Poplawska, 'Die italienischen Ein-wanderer in Kraków und ihr Einfluß auf die polnischen Wirtschaftsbeziehungen zu österrei-chischen und deutschen Städten im 16. Jahrhundert', *Wissenschaftliche Zeitschrift. Veröffentlichung der Friedrich-Schiller-Universität Jena. Gesellschafts- und Sprachwissenschaftliche Reihe* 26 (1977), pp. 337-354

RAIMBAULT 2002
C. Raimbault, 'Evrard Jabach, quelques précisions sur la constitution des collections', *Bulletin de l'Association des Historiens de l'Art Italien* 8 (2002), pp. 35-45

REIDEMEISTER 1932
L. Reidemeister, 'Der Große Kurfürst und Friedrich III als Sammler Ostasiatischer Kunst', *Ostasiatische Zeitschrift* 18 (1932), pp. 175-188

RIDOLFI 1648
C. Ridolfi, *Le Maraviglie dell' Arte*, Venice 1648

RODING 2003
J. Roding et al. (ed.), *Dutch and Flemish artists in Britain 1550-1800*, Leiden 2003 (Leids Kunsthistorisch Jaarboek, 13)

RODING/STOMPÉ 1997
J. Roding and M. Stompé, *Pieter Isaacsz (1569-1625). Een Nederlandse schilder, kunsthandelaar en diplomaat aan het Deense hof*, Hilversum 1997 (Zeven Provinciën Reeks, 4)

DE ROEVER 1885
N. de Roever, 'Drie Amsterdamsche schilders (Pieter Isaaksz, Abraham Vinck, Cornelis van der Voort)', *Oud Holland* 3 (1885), pp. 171-208

ROGEAUX 1999
N. Rogeaux, *Wallerant Vaillant (1623-1677) graveur à la manière noire, dessinateur à la pierre noire et peintre de portraits* (diss. Paris, typescript), Paris 1999

ROORDA 1971
D.J. Roorda, *Het Rampjaar 1672*, Bussum 1971

ROY 1995
A. Roy, *Gérard de Lairesse (1640-1711)*, Paris 1995

RYLANDS 1988
Ph. Rylands, *Palma il Vecchio. L'opera completa*, Milan 1988

SAFARIK 1999
E.A. Safarik, 'Invention and reality in Roman still-life painting of the seventeenth century: Fioravanti and the others', in: S. Walker and F. Hammond (eds.), *Life and the arts in the Baroque palaces of Rome*, New York/New Haven/London 1999, pp. 71-81

SANDERSON 1658
W. Sanderson, *Graphice. The use of the Pen and Pensil...*, London 1658

SANDRART 1675/PELTZER 1925
A.R. Peltzer, *Joachim von Sandrarts Academie der Bau-, Bild- und Mahlrey-Künste von 1675*, Munich 1925

SCHÄFKE 2000
W. Schäfke (ed.), exh. cat. *Coellen eyn Croyn. Renaissance und Barock in Köln. (Der Riss im Himmel. Clemens August und seine Epoche)* (Brühl: Schloß Augustusburg 2000), s.l. 2000

SCHATBORN 1981
P. Schatborn, 'Van Rembrandt tot Crozat. Vroege verzamelingen met tekeningen van Rembrandt', *Nederlands Kunsthistorisch Jaarboek* 32 (1981), pp. 1-54

SCHELTEMA 1853
P. Scheltema, *Rembrand: redevoering over het leven en de verdiensten van Rembrand van Rijn*, Amsterdam 1853

SCHMIDT 1914
H. Schmidt, 'Das Nachlass-Inventar des Malers Jürgen Ovens', *Oud Holland* 32 (1914), pp. 29-49

SCHMIDT 1917
H. Schmidt, 'Niederländer in den Gottorffer Rentekammerbüchern', *Oud Holland* 35 (1917), pp. 79-92

SCHMIDT 1922
H. Schmidt, *Jürgen Ovens. Sein Leben und seine Werke*, Kiel 1922

SCHNAPPER 1994
A. Schnapper, *Curieux du grand siècle. Collections et collectionneurs dans la France du XVIIe siècle, II, Œuvres d'art*, Paris 1994

SCHNEIDER 1990
C.P. Schneider, *Rembrandt's landscapes*, New Haven, Conn./London 1990

SCHNEIDER/EKKART 1973
H. Schneider and R.E.O. Ekkart, *Jan Lievens. Sein Leben und seine Werke*, Amsterdam 1973

SCHOLTEN 2003
F. Scholten, 'Rombout Verhulsts ivoren Madonna met Christus', *Bulletin van het Rijksmuseum* 51 (2003), pp. 102-117

SCHUTTE 1983
O. Schutte, *Repertorium der buitenlandse vertegenwoordigers, residerende in Nederland 1584-1810*, The Hague 1983

SCHWARTZ 1984
G. Schwartz, *Rembrandt, zijn leven, zijn schilderijen*, Maarssen 1984

SEIDEL 1890
P. Seidel, 'Die Beziehungen des Grossen Kurfürsten und König Friedrichs I zur Niederländischen Kunst', *Jahrbuch der Königlich Preussischen Kunstsammlungen* 11(1890), pp. 119-149

SEYFARTH 1995
J. Seyfarth, 'Bildbesitz in Kölner Familien zur Zeit des Gülischen Wirren und ein neues Inventarium des Sammlung Imstenraedt', *Wallraf-Richartz-Jahrbuch* 56 (1995), pp. 225-254

SEYFARTH 2000
J. Seyfarth, 'Ein Schatzhaus des Apelles (Iconophylacium). Beschreibung der Bildersammlung des Kölner Ratsherrn Franz von Imstenraedt, 1667', in: Schäfke 2000, pp. 157-254

SHEARMAN 1983
J. Shearman, *The early Italian pictures in the collection of Her Majesty the Queen*, Cambridge etc. 1983

SIRET 1883
A. Siret, *Dictionnaire historique et raisonné des peintres de toutes les écoles...*, Brussels/Paris/Leipzig/London 1883³

SIX 1925-1926
J. Six, 'La famosa accademia di Eeulenborg', *Jaarboek der Koninklijke Akademie van Wetenschappen te Amsterdam* 1925-1926, pp. 229-241

SLATKES 1992
L.J. Slatkes, *Rembrandt. Catalogo completo dei dipinti*, Florence 1992

SLIVE 1970-1974
S. Slive, *Frans Hals*, 3 vols., London 1970-1974

SLUIJTER 2003
E.J. Sluijter, 'The English Venture: Dutch and Flemish artists in Britain 1550-1800', in: Roding 2003, pp. 11-27

SLUIJTER-SEIJFFERT 1984
N.C. Sluijter-Seijffert, *Cornelis van Poelenburch (ca. 1593-1667)*, Leiden 1984

VAN DER SMAN 1996
M.C. van der Sman, 'Het rampjaar 1672', in: D. Haks and M.C. van der Sman (eds.), *De Hollandse samenleving in de tijd van Vermeer*, The Hague 1996, pp. 136-140

SPIELMANN/DREES 1997
H. Spielmann en J. Drees, exh. cat.. *Gottorf im Glanz des Barock. Kunst und Kultur am Schleswiger Hof 1544-1713* (Sleeswijk: Schleswig-Holsteinisches Landesmuseum 1997), s.l. 1997

SPRUNGER 1992
M. Sprunger, 'Hoe rijke mennisten de hemel verdienden. Een eerste verkenning van de betrokkenheid van aanzienlijke doopsgezinden bij het Amsterdamse zakenleven in de Gouden Eeuw', *Doopsgezinde Bijdragen, nieuwe reeks* 18 (1992), pp. 39-52

SPRUNGER 1993
M.S. Sprunger, *Rich mennonites, poor mennonites. Economics and theology in the Amsterdam Waterlander congregation during the Golden Age*, Ph.D. University of Illinois 1993

SPRUNGER 1995
M. Sprunger, 'Entrepreneurs and ethics. Mennonite merchants in seventeenth-century Amsterdam', in: C. Lesger and L. Noordegraaf (eds.), *Entrepreneurs and entrepreneurship in early modern times. Merchants and industrialists within the orbit of the Dutch staple market*, s.l. 1995, pp. 213-221

STERCK 1927-1940
J.F.M. Sterck et al., *De werken van Vondel*, 10 vols., Amsterdam 1927-1940

STRAAT 1925
H.L. Straat, 'Lambert Jacobsz, schilder', *De Vrije Fries* 28 (1925), pp. 53-76

VAN STRATEN 2005
R. van Straten, *Rembrandts Leidse tijd, 1606-1632*, Leiden 2005

SUM.
W. Sumowski, *Gemälde der Rembrandt-Schüler*, 6 dln, Landau/Pfalz 1983-1990

SZMYDKI 2002
R. Szmydki, *Kontakty artystyczne królewicza Wladyslawa Zygmunta Wazy z Antwerpią / Prince Ladislaus Sigismund Vasa's artistic contacts with Antwerp*, Warsaw 2002

TACKE 1995
A. Tacke, *Die Gemälde des 17. Jarhunderts im Germanischen Nationalmuseum*, Mainz 1995

TH.-B.
U. Thieme en F. Becker (red.), *Allgemeines Lexikon der bildenden Künstler von der Antike bis zur Gegenwart*, 37 vols., Leipzig 1907-1950

THEUNISZ 1927
J. Theunisz, *Het stadhuis te Enkhuizen*, Assen 1927

THIJSSEN 1992
L. Thijssen, *1000 Jaar Polen en Nederland*, Zutphen 1992

THOMAS 2005
B. Thomas, 'The Academy of Baccio Bandinelli', *Print Quarterly* 22 (2005), pp. 3-14

THOMASSEN 1990
K. Thomassen (ed.), *Alba Amicorum, vijf eeuwen vriendschap op papier gezet: het album amicorum en het poëziealbum in de Nederlanden*, Maarssen/The Hague 1990

VAN TIELHOF 2002
M. van Tielhof, *The 'mother of all trades'. The Baltic grain trade in Amsterdam from the late 16th to the early 19th century*, Leiden/Boston/Cologne 2002 (The Northern World. North Europe and the Baltic c. 400-1700 AD. Peoples, Economies and Cultures, 3)

TISSINK/DE WIT 1987
F. Tissink and H.F. de Wit, *Gorcumse schilders in de Gouden Eeuw*, Gorinchem 1987 (Merewade. Facetten van Gorcums verleden, 10)

TOMKOWICZ 1912
S. Tomkowicz, *Przyczynki do historyi kultury Krakowa w pierwszej polowie XVII wieku*, Lvov 1912

VAN TRICHT 1976-1979
H.W. van Tricht, *De briefwisseling van Pieter Corneliszoon Hooft*, 3 vols., Culemborg 1976-1979

TYLICKI 2005
J. Tylicki, *Rysunek gdański ostatniej ćwierci XVI i pierwszej potowy XVII wieku*, Torun 2005

UNGER 1885
J.H.W. Unger, 'Dagboek van Constantijn Huygens', *Oud Holland* 3 (1885), pp. 1-87

URK.
C. Hofstede de Groot, *Die Urkunden über Rembrandt (1575-1721)*, The Hague 1906 (Quellenstudien zur holländischen Kunstgeschichte, 3)

VACCARO 2002
M. Vaccaro, *Parmigianino. The paintings*, Turin/London etc. 2002

VAN DER VEEN 1992
J. van der Veen, 'Liefhebbers, handelaren en kunstenaars. Het verzamelen van schilderijen en papierkunst', in: Bergvelt/Kistemaker 1992, pp. 117-134

VAN DER VEEN 1996
J. van der Veen, 'De Delftse kunstmarkt in de tijd van Vermeer', in: D. Haks and M.C. van der Sman (eds.), *De Hollandse samenleving in de tijd van Vermeer*, Zwolle 1996, pp. 124-135

VAN DER VEEN 1997
J. van der Veen, 'Faces from life. Tronies and portraits in Rembrandt's painted œuvre', in: Melbourne/ Canberra 1997-1998, pp. 69-80

VAN DER VEEN 1998
J. van der Veen, 'Onbekende opdrachtgevers van Rembrandt. Jacomo Borchgraeff en Maria van Uffelen en hun portretten door Rembrandt, Jonson van Ceulen, Van Zijl, Van Mol en Jacob Backer', *De Kroniek van het Rembrandthuis* 1998, no.1/2, pp. 14-31

VAN DER VEEN 2001
J. van der Veen, 'Hendrick en Gerrit Uylenburgh, oud en nieuw', *De Kroniek van het Rembrandthuis* 2001, no.1/2, pp. 44-56

VAN DER VEEN 2003
J. van der Veen, 'Onbekende opdrachtgevers van Rembrandt (3). Portretten van leden van de familie Sijen door Rembrandt, hoogstwaarschijnlijk Pieter Sijen (ca. 1592-1652) en Marretje Cornelisdr. van Grotewal (ca. 1593-1666)', *De Kroniek van het Rembrandthuis* 2003, no.1/2, pp. 47-60

VAN DER VEEN 2005
J. van der Veen, 'By his own hand. The valuation of autograph painting in the 17th century', in: Corpus IV, pp. 3-44

VAN DE VELDE 1975
C. Van de Velde, *Frans Floris (1519/20-1570). Leven en werken*, 2 vols., Brussels 1975

VERHOEK 1726
P. Verhoek, *Pieter Verhoeks Poëzy. Nevens zyn Treurspel van Karel den Stouten, Hertogh van Bourgondie*, Amsterdam 1726

VERTUE NOTE BOOKS I
The eighteenth volume of the Walpole Society, 1929-1930. Vertue Note Books, volume 1

VERWEY 1937
A. Verwey, *Vondel. Volledige dichtwerken en oorspronkelijk proza*, Amsterdam 1937

VEY 1967
H. Vey, 'Die Bildnisse Everhard Jabachs', *Wallraf-Richartz-Jahrbuch. Westdeutsches Jahrbuch für Kunstgeschichte* 29 (1967), pp. 157-187

VEY 2000
H. Vey, 'Eberhard Jabach III. (1567-1636)', in: Schäfke 2000, pp. 101-155

VIER EEUWEN HERENGRACHT 1976
H. de la Fontaine Verwey et al., *Vier eeuwen Herengracht*, Amsterdam 1976

VISSER 1978
D. Visser, 'De Geest buiten spel. Jacob Aertsz. Colom, een onorthodox drukker en uitgever te Amsterdam', in: I.B. Horst et al. (eds.), *De Geest in het geding. Opstellen aangeboden aan J.A. Oosterbaan ter gelegenheid van zijn afscheid als hoogleraar*, Alphen aan den Rijn 1978, pp. 268-282

VISSER 1988
P. Visser, *Broeders in de geest. De doopsgezinde bijdragen van Dierick en Jan Philipsz. Schabaelje tot de Nederlandse stichtelijke literatuur in de zeventiende eeuw*, 2 vols., Deventer 1988 (Deventer Studiën, 7)

VOLPE/LUCCO 1980
C. Volpe en M. Lucco, *L'opera completa di Sebastiano del Piombo*, Milan 1980

DE VRIES 1883
A.D. de Vries, 'Willem Schellinks, schilder-teekenaar-etser-dichter', *Oud Holland* 1 (1883), pp. 150-163

DE VRIES 1886
A.D. de Vries, 'Biografische aanteekeningen betreffende voornamelijk Amsterdamsche schilders, plaatsnijders, en hunne verwanten', *Oud Holland* 4 (1886), pp. 137-144

DE VRIES 1998
L. de Vries, *Gerard de Lairesse. An artist between stage and studio*, Amsterdam 1998

VAN DER WAALS 1988
J. van der Waals, *De prentschat van Michiel Hinloopen*, Amsterdam 1988

WAGENAAR 1760-1802
J. Wagenaar, *Amsterdam in zyne opkomst, aanwas, geschiedenisse*, 4 vols., Amsterdam 1760-1802

WEBER 1996
G. Weber, 'Johannes Vermeer, ormai italiano?', *Daidalos* 60 (1996), p. 154

WEBER 2003
G.J.M. Weber, 'Neues zum Werk von Hendrick Fromantiou, Kunstagent und Hofmaler in Brandenburg', *Dresdener Kunstblätter* 2003, pp. 131-138

WEGNER 1973
W. Wegner, *Die niederländischen Handzeichnungen des 15.-18. Jahrhunderts. Kataloge der staatlichen Graphischen Sammlung München*, Berlin 1973

WEIGERT/HERNMARCK
R.A. Weigert and C. Hernmarck (eds.), *Les relations artistiques entre la France et la Suède 1693-1718. Nicodème Tessin le jeune et Daniel Cronström correspondence (extraits)*, s.l. s.a.

WEISSMAN 1907
A.W. Weissman, 'De Schoorsteenen van het Amsterdamsch Stadhuis', *Oud Holland* 25 (1907), pp. 71-82

VIENNA 2004
exh. cat. *Rembrandt* (Vienna: Albertina), s.l. 2004

VAN DE WETERING 1997
E. van de Wetering, *Rembrandt. The painter at work*, Amsterdam 1997

VAN DE WETERING 2000
E. van de Wetering, 'Remarks on Rembrandt's oil-sketches for etchings', in: exh. cat.. *Rembrandt the printmaker* (Amsterdam: Rijksmuseum; London: The British Museum), s.l. 2000, pp. 36-63

VAN DE WETERING 2002
E. van de Wetering, 'Rembrandts verborgen zelfportretten / Rembrandt's hidden self-portraits', *De Kroniek van het Rembrandthuis* 2002/1-2, pp. 2-15

VAN DE WETERING 2005
E. van de Wetering, 'Rembrandt's self-portraits: problems of authenticity and function', in: Corpus IV, pp. 89-317

WHEELOCK 1995
A.K. Wheelock jr., *Dutch paintings of the seventeenth century. The collections of the National Gallery of Art. Systematic catalogue*, Washington, DC 1995

WHITE 1982
C. White, *The Dutch pictures in the collection of Her Majesty the Queen*, Cambridge/London etc. 1982

WICKEVOORT 1660
A. Wickevoort, *Verhael in forme van journael, van de reys ende 't vertoeven van den seer doorluchtige ende machtige prins Carel II, koning van Groot Britannien &c, welcke hy in Hollandt gedaen heeft zedert den 25 Mey tot den 2 Junij 1660*, The Hague 1660

WIESEMAN 2002
M.E. Wieseman, *Caspar Netscher and late seventeenth-century Dutch painting*, Doornspijk 2002

WIESEMAN 2004
M. Wieseman, 'Paper trails: drawings in the work of Caspar Netscher', in: V. Manuth and A. Rüger (eds.), *Collected opinions. Essays on Netherlandish art in honour of Alfred Bader*, London 2004, pp. 251-257

WIJNMAN 1930A
H.F. Wijnman, 'Nieuwe gegevens omtrent den schilder Lambert Jacobsz. I', *Oud Holland* 47 (1930), pp. 145-157

WIJNMAN 1930B
H.F. Wijnman, 'Vondel en de Anslo's', *Vondel-Kroniek* I (1930), pp. 167-173

WIJNMAN 1934
H.F. Wijnman, 'Nieuwe gegevens omtrent den schilder Lambert Jacobsz. II', *Oud Holland* 51 (1934), pp. 241-255

WIJNMAN 1932
H.F. Wijnman, 'De stamvader van het geslacht Bastert', *De Nederlandsche Leeuw* 50 (1932), cols. 36-40

WIJNMAN 1956
H.F. Wijnman, 'Rembrandt en Hendrick Uylenburgh te Amsterdam', *Maandblad Amstelodamum* 43 (1956), pp. 94-103

WIJNMAN 1959
H.F. Wijnman, 'Rembrandt als huisgenoot van
Hendrick Uylenburgh te Amsterdam (1631-1635)', in:
*Uit de kring van Rembrandt en Vondel. Verzamelde studies
over hun leven en omgeving*, Amsterdam 1959, pp. 1-18,
180-181 and 182

VAN DER WILLIGEN/MEIJER 2003
A. van der Willigen and F.G. Meijer, *A Dictionary
of Dutch and Flemish still-life painters working in oils,
1525-1725*, Leiden 2003

VON WINCKELMAN 1796
L. von Winckelman, *Neues Mahlerlexikon zur nähern
Kenntniss alter und neuer guter Gemählde...*, Augsburg
1796

WITTENAAR 1952
J.A.C.Ab. Wittenaar, 'De geboorteplaats en de naam
van Peter Lely', *Oud Holland* 67 (1952), pp. 122-124

WOOD 2003
J. Wood, 'Nicholas Lanier (1588-1666) and the
origin of drawings collecting in Stuart England', in:
C. Baker, C. Elam and G. Warwick (eds.), *Collecting
prints and drawings in Europe, c. 1500-1750*,
Aldershot/Burlington 2003, pp. 85-121

WORP 1911-1917
J.A Worp, *De Briefwisseling van Constantijn Huygens
(1608-1687)*, 6 vols., The Hague 1911-1917

ZESEN 1664
F. von Zesen, *Beschreibung der Stadt Amsterdam*,
Amsterdam 1664

ZIJLSTRA 2000
S. Zijlstra, *Om de ware gemeente en de oude gronden.
Geschiedenis van de dopersen in de Nederlanden
1531-1675*, Hilversum 2000

ZONDERGELD-HAMER 1990
A.J. Zondergeld-Hamer, *De geschiedenis van Weesp.
Van prehistorie tot de moderne tijd*, Weesp 1990

PHOTO ACKNOWLEDGEMENTS

AMSTERDAM
- Museum Amstelkring, *Ons' Lieve Heer op Solder*: fig. 169
- Fortis Bank: fig. 147
- Gemeentearchief: figs. 3a, 3b, 20, 21, 25, 26, 27, 38, 40, 41, 68, 179, 196
- Stichting Koninklijk Paleis: figs. 62, 154, 155
- The Rembrandt House Museum: figs. 8, 13, 19, 80, 84, 85, 96, 97, 98, 99, 100, 101, 104, 114, 120, 121, 137, 211
- Rijksmuseum (Copyright © Rijksmuseum): figs. 102, 119, 133, 180
- Rijksprentenkabinet (Copyright © Rijksmuseum): figs. 6, 10a, 10b, 22, 43, 53, 59, 92, 106, 145, 170, 171, 175
- Six Collection: fig. 55
- Universiteitsbibliotheek: figs. 1, 9, 12, 24, 29, 30, 39, 44, 118

BASEL
- Kunstmuseum Basel, Photo Martin Bühler: fig. 127

BERLIN
- Staatliche Museen zu Berlin, Antikensammlung: figs. 46, 47, 48, 49
- Das Geheime Staatsarchiv, Stiftung Preußischer Kulturbesitz: fig. 42
- Staatliche Museen zu Berlin, Gemäldegalerie (Copyright Staatliche Museen zu Berlin, Gemäldegalerie): fig. 7; Photo Jörg P Anders, Berlin: figs. 109, 117, 187, 209
- Staatliche Museen zu Berlin, Kupferstichkabinett: figs. 45, 159

BOSTON, MASS.
- The Isabella Stewart Gardner Museum (© Isabella Stewart Gardner Museum, Boston): figs. 115, 122, 124
- Museum of Fine Arts, Boston (Photograph © 2006 Museum of Fine Arts, Boston): figs. 86, 90

BRAUNSCHWEIG
- Herzog Anton Ulrich-Museum Braunschweig, Kunstmuseum des Landes Niedersachsen, Museumsfoto B.P. Keiser: fig. 54; Photo Claus Cordes: figs. 173, 213

BREMEN
- Kunsthalle Bremen: fig. 203

BRUSSELS
- Koninklijke Musea voor Schone Kunsten van België, Brussel, Photo Cussac: fig. 140; Photo RoScan - J. Geleyns: fig. 161

BUDAPEST
- Szépmüvészeti Múzeum, Museum of Fine Arts, Budapest: fig. 146

CAMBRIDGE, MASS.
- Courtesy of the Fogg Art Museum, Harvard University Art Museums (© 2004 President and Fellows of Harvard College), Photo Katya Kallsen: fig. 18; Photographic Services: fig. 136

CINCINNATI, OHIO
- Taft Museum of Art, Cincinnati, Ohio: fig. 93

COLOGNE
- Wallraf-Richartz-Museum, Rheinisches Bildarchiv Köln: fig. 210

COGNAC
- Musées de la Ville de Cognac (© Musées de Cognac): fig. 191

COPENHAGEN
- Statens Museum for Kunst (SMK Foto): figs. 167, 200

CRACOW
- Muzeum Czartoryskich: figs. 4a, 4b
- Archiwum Państwowe: fig. 5

DAYTON, OHIO
- The Dayton Art Institute: fig. 188

DRESDEN
- Staatliche Kunstsammlungen Dresden, Gemäldegalerie Alte Meister: figs. 15, 16, 17, 185; Kupferstich-kabinett: fig. 176

DUNKIRK
- Musée des Beaux-Arts de Dunkerque: fig. 164

EDINBURGH
- National Galleries of Scotland, Duke of Sutherland Collection, on loan to the National Gallery of Scotland: fig. 52

FRANKFURT AM MAIN
- Städelsches Kunstinstitut Frankfurt: fig. 139

GLASGOW
- Glasgow City Council (Museums), The Burrell Collection: fig. 69
- Hunterian Museum and Art Gallery (Photo © Hunterian Museum and Art Gallery, University of Glasgow): fig. 105

HAARLEM
- Frans Hals Museum, Photo Tom Haartsen: fig. 165; fig. 190

THE HAGUE
- Koninklijke Bibliotheek: figs. 23a, 23b, 23c
- Koninklijk Kabinet van Schilderijen Mauritshuis (© Stichting Vrienden van het Mauritshuis): figs. 35, 74, 192
- Collectie Rijksbureau voor Kunsthistorische Documentatie: figs. 135, 168, 189

HAMBURG
- Hamburger Kunsthalle (© Hamburger Kunsthalle/bpk), Photo Elke Walford: figs. 76, 199; Photo Christoph Irrgang: figs. 201, 202, 215

HEINO/WIJHE
- Museum de Fundatie, Photo Hans Westerink, Zwolle: fig. 186

KARLSRUHE
- Staatliche Kunsthalle Karlsruhe: fig. 193

KASSEL
- Staatliche Museen Kassel, Gemäldegalerie Alte Meister: figs. 91, 108

KINGSTON, CANADA
- Collection of the Agnes Etherington Art Centre, Queen's University, Kingston, Gift of Dr. Alfred and Isabel Bader 1974. Photo Cheryl O'Brien, 2005: fig. 184

LEEUWARDEN
- Fries Museum: fig. 132

LE HAVRE
- Musée des Beaux-Arts André Malraux, Le Havre: fig. 66

LEIDEN
- Regionaal Archief Leiden: fig. 3c, 138
- Rijksmuseum van Oudheden (© fotografie Rijksmuseum van Oudheden): figs. 172, 214